BLACK EXPERIENCE

Analysis and Synthesis

Edited by

Carlene Young

LESWING PRESS

San Rafael, California

For Howard and Loren

Contents

PART II

B: RACISM

PART III

A: DIMENSIONS OF BLACK COMMUNITY LIFE— SOCIOLOGY

PART III

B: DIMENSIONS OF BLACK COMMUNITY LIFE—
PSYCHOLOGY

PART III

C: DIMENSIONS OF BLACK COMMUNITY LIFE—
ECONOMICS

PART III

D: DIMENSIONS OF BLACK COMMUNITY LIFE—
POLITICS

PREFACE

The Black Experience: Analysis and Synthesis has grown out of a need felt for materials that depict the circumstances and forces that played a major role in the development of black communities. The Black Experience in the United States is unique. It can never be duplicated, but it can be understood and relived through the writings of those whom it has most profoundly affected. Oftentimes the uniqueness of the Black Experience manifests itself, most clearly, in the subtleties and nuances of responses and interaction patterns, which elude all but those who have either come out of this experience or have for an extended period of time immersed (figuratively or literally) themselves in the on-going processes of ghetto life.

This book attempts to portray for the reader the varied aspects of the Black Experience, touching all facets of the society in which black people found—and still find—themselves. This is the Black Experience from the point of view of those who have lived it, together with the perceptions of others who have studied and analyzed the situation. Beginning with the historical antecedents of West African societies, this anthology traces the development and dimensions of nearly four hundred years of black community life. These dimensions include the ideological foundations that supported and sustained racism, as well as the particularistic forms of its sociological, psychological, economic, and political development.

Selections in this volume are presented in an attempt to provide a frame of reference for analyzing some of the historical, sociocultural, and legal aspects of this experience. Hopefully, the reader will bring his own insights and expertise to the material so that it can be that much more meaningful. The importance of this work lies not in its being the sole answer or definitive study but in providing an alternative for analysis in a field where much of the information has come from a singular perspective.

In the interests of economization of space, citational references have been omitted in all but original articles; interested readers should consult references listed under Acknowledgments.

CARLENE YOUNG

September 1972
California State University
San Jose, California

– Prologue –

The Black Ethos
– What It Is

Carlene Young

HARLEM

LANGSTON HUGHES

What happens to a dream deferred?

Does it dry up
like a raisin in the sun?

Or fester like a sore—
And then run?
Does it stink like rotten meat?
Or crust and sugar over—
like a syrupy sweet?

Maybe it just sags
like a heavy load.

Or does it explode?

In analyzing the black community, sociologists have generally taken one of two positions, namely, that all peoples in the society internalize the values of the society as a whole, or that there are values peculiar to differing classes in society. In so doing, they have attempted to categorize black people under one or the other generalization and thereby eliminate the contradictions. This procrustian approach has not worked simply because black people are not so easily categorized; equally important is the fact that *there are* these contradictions, which do not allow for neat packaging.

The history of black people in this country is in itself a contradiction—the circumstances under which black people find themselves in a so-called Christian society. The inconsistencies of prejudice and discrimination manifest themselves time and again. For example take the matter of "mammies" and separate accommodations: black females nursed and reared white babies, many times forming some of the closest attachments in their lives, and yet in a public vehicle these same women were not permitted to sit next to whites, even to the children they had reared. Another instance is the hysteria brought about by miscegenation: the "Would you want your daughter to marry one?" syndrome. And yet if the ideology of the subhuman, animallike, depraved black was fully subscribed to, why would there be any danger of the paragon of virtue—the white woman—desiring or actually marrying this beast? Why also does the South, which has been the most vituperative in its denouncements of race-mixing, have disproportionately more racial hybrids than the rest of the country? These are only two of the most glaring contradictions, but the Black Experience has been filled with them, and it as a synthesis of contradictories that uniquely black culture has evolved.

Culture has been defined as a people's total way of life. This includes everything—ideals, religious beliefs, manner of dress, language, folklore, customs, sense of time, humor, secular beliefs, tools and material products, institutions, and leisure pursuits. As Ashley Montagu has stated, "Culture of persons, as of groups, will differ according to the kinds of experiences they have undergone."[1] There are aspects of the American culture that black people subscribe to and have incorporated into their communities. At the same time, there are distinctive characteristics in major aspects of their life that set them apart. They have been excluded from white society and institutions and as a result have developed institutions, such as the church, family, mutual-aid societies, peer relationships, language and customs, that distinguish them from the majority society and serve their specific needs. There is *black ethos*. It is evident in

any ghetto in the music, patterns of dress, language, interrelationships with friends and relatives, and the extended family. The family has often been overlooked as a strong supportive force that serves as a reservoir of strength in the face of a hostile nonrewarding world. It offers, regardless of the members who constitute it and the physical surroundings, a place where one is valued for one's self. In it the yardstick for measuring the moral worth of an individual is not based on material or social success but on whether he is good or bad to his family and friends. Manipulating appearances and environment is often refined to consummate levels of accomplishment. Symbolic behavior, cues, and systems of communication through gestures and kinesthesis play an important role in survival and success in ghetto life. There is a premium on language facility—the ability to verbally manipulate others in order to attain desired ends. Identity becomes recognizable through unique styles, e.g., the descriptive nicknames by which many ghetto inhabitants are known, as opposed to their formal or legal names.

> The rhythms of black music are distinctive, and it is perhaps the only unique American music. The dialect and intonation of black sermons are powerful and enthralling; they capture ... the ethos of their people in a way that it has never been captured by a white American. The patterns of imagery and the astute wit employed in the folk narratives are magnificent. These and other traditional forms of black expression have provided a firm, skillfully crafted base for the works of subsequent black artists.[2]

One of the resultant discontinuities is that behavior that is different is assessed as problematic, subnormal, or abnormal rather than as growing out of life experiences and functional adaptation to environment and circumstances. The truth is that the person who attempted to function in the ghetto setting according to the norms of the majority society could destroy himself, because his immediate environment would not provide the support structure and means for acting out or reinforcing those values of career success, upward mobility, and positive rewards of the "good life."

St. Clair Drake graphically portrays some of what the ghetto is all about:[3]

> The "ghettoization" of the Negro has resulted in the emergence of a ghetto subculture with a distinctive ethos, most pronounced, perhaps, in Harlem, but recognizable in all Negro neighborhoods. For the average Negro who walks the streets of any American Black Ghetto, the smell of barbecued ribs, fried shrimps, and chicken emanating from numerous restaurants gives ol-

factory reinforcement to a feeling of "at-home-ness." The beat of "gut music" spilling into the street from ubiquitous tavern juke boxes and the sound of tambourines and rich harmony behind the crude folk art on the windows of storefront churches give auditory confirmation to the universal belief that "We Negroes have 'soul'." The bedlam of an occasional brawl, the shouted obscenities of street corner "foul mouths," and the whine of police sirens break the monotony of waiting for the number that never "falls," the horses that neither win, place, nor show, and the "good job" that never materializes. The insouciant swagger of teenage dropouts masks the hurt of their aimless existence and contrasts sharply with the ragged clothing and dejected demeanor of "skid-row" types who have long since stopped trying to keep up appearances and who escape it all by becoming "winoes." The cheerful rushing about of adults, free from the occupational pressures of the "white world" in which they work, create an atmosphere of warmth and superficial intimacy which obscures the unpleasant facts of life in the overcrowded rooms behind the doors, the lack of adequate maintenance standards, and the too prevalent vermin and rats.

The essence of the black ethos is survival and soul. Every facet of life in the ghettoes—crowded, active, violent, and filled with the hum of living—can be subsumed under these two categories. The attempt to define soul has been made by many and many have failed. Lerone Bennett, writing in *The Negro Mood*, has come closest to clarifying the concept as it evolved from Negro folk tradition:[4]

Soul . . . [is] a distinct quality of Negro-ness growing out of the Negro's experience and not his genes. Soul is a metaphorical evocation of Negro being as expressed in the Negro tradition. It is, the feeling with which an artist invests his creation, the style with which a man lives his life. It is, above all, the spirit rather than the letter: a certain way of feeling, a certain way of being. . . . a relaxed and noncompetetive approach to being, a complex acceptance of the contradictions of life, a buoyant sadness, a passionate spontaneity, and a gay sorrow.

The colors, sights, sounds, movements, and just plain "doin's" of these communities carry a trademark as vivid and real as though stamped "Made in America," as well they might. In any case, the characteristics of black life from storefront churches to the "mack" man (hustler) on the corner are not to be found anywhere else. There are some manifestations of lower classes that are found in any poor area, but there are

far more that can only be found in the Harlems and Black Bottoms of the United States. Lerone Bennett writing in *The Negro Mood*, describes some of its components:[5]

The Negro folk tradition confronts life in the raw, celebrates the here and now, and takes no thought of tomorrow. The songs of the ethos and its dances affirm that which God made, the body; and they say that that which God made was good. Flowing out of this radical affirmation of the facticity of flesh is a healthy respect for the sacredness of sex as communion and creation. Accepting all that God accepts, the tradition is tolerant of everything except right angles of the spirit. The pretender, the imposter, the striver, the strainer, the "Square" are condemned. Being is recommended instead of seeming, the natural response instead of the contrived one. The tradition urges men to turn themselves up to spontaneity and improvisation.

W.E.B. DuBois, describing some aspects of the black world, says:[6]

. . . it is the spirit that knows Beauty, that has music in its soul and the color of sunsets in its headkerchiefs; that can dance on a flaming world and make the world dance, too. Such is the soul of the Negro. . . . This race has the greatest of the gifts of God, laughter. It dances and sings; it is humble; it longs to learn; it loves men; it loves women. It is frankly, baldly, deliciously human in an artificial and hypocritical land . . . .We are the supermen who sit idly by and laugh and look at civilization. We, who frankly want the bodies of our mates and conjure no blush to our bronze cheeks when we own it. We, who exalt the Lynched above the Lyncher, and the Worker above the Owner, and the Crucified above Imperial Rome.

In attempting to make assessments and statements about the black community, many white social scientists have fallen into the trap of drawing conclusions that come out of a middle-class or white ethnic frame of reference. They have failed to recognize that the lower-class community and the black community are cultural entities in their own right. Behavior, which to all outward appearances is the same as in the white community, does not necessarily have the same meanings in the black community. Generalizations that apply to one are not necessarily transferable to the other. Life styles, value systems, and survival techniques unique to the need system of the people involved constitute important variables in this cultural entity. This need system has grown out of the role relationships prescribed for black members of this society and has not, as some have suggested, become part of the hereditary structure and personality types of descendants of slaves. Black America can justifiably say that it possesses a true culture—a whole way of life that includes its own standards of moral and aesthetic judgment. The black American need not engage in arguments over the superiority or the inferiority of particular attributes; he need not fight pitched battles over different bodies of intellectual and imaginative work and attempt to assess their way of life. And only that same culture can evolve the standards by which its intellectual and imaginative work is to be judged. The malaise of the black psyche has come, in part, from the attempts of white Americans to set both "race" and "culture" in an unreal context.[7]

Black Americans need to be analyzed (if at all) and investigated from the framework of cultural relativity. That is, judged in relation to their own history, with culture seen as a result of the responses to the conditions that history may or may not record. Black Americans are not very many generations away from slavery. They have been formally defined free but have never experienced full social, political, or economic freedom. The isolation in the ghetto pockets of subjugation and exclusion from the mainstream has led to the creation of institutions, language, folklore, beliefs, etc., that are distinctively part of the black heritage in America. Acquiescence to white control or norms has been maintained by violence, legalistic manipulations, and social ostracism. R. P. Cuzzort states:[8] "Violence for all its dramatic simplicity, does not control individuals other than by the most outward manifestations . . . while it produces a minimal outward conformity, this is at the price of generating hatred toward the conformity-inducing agent." There has been a refusal on the part of many social scientists to see other than the broad categories. The effect of this categorization has been to deny the variations in personality, behavior, goals, ideas, aspirations, and belief systems.

The prevailing concept has generally been that there is no such thing as black culture. Increasing criticism and writings, however, that challenge this assumption are invalidating it, yet some of the most highly respected names in the field have reflected this assumption, including the distinguished black sociologist E. Franklin Frazier. Thomas F. Pettigrew, a frequently quoted authority says:[9] "Being a Negro in America is less of a racial identity than a necessity to adopt a subordinate social role." "The Negro is only an American and nothing else. He has no values and culture to guard and protect," state Nathan Glazer and Daniel Moynihan.[10] Edward Byron Reuter, a former president of the American Sociological Association had this to say about the matter:[11]

> The American Negroes are without such a background [history and culture]. . . . in freedom they have been a culturally backward and excluded group. . . . Recently there has been a marked tendency to emphasize early African civilizations and to exploit the part that Negroes have had in the building of other cultures. The fact that the historic structure thus being woven is largely one of myth and fiction in no way lessens its importance; it is adequate for the purposes of nationalistic movement.

This was written in 1927 in *The American Race Problem*, which dealt realistically and sympathetically with conditions and problems facing many Negroes. Oscar Handlin and Philip Hauser view the experiences and problems of the black community as essentially no different from foreign-white immigrant groups.

There are others, however, in the tradition of Hylan Lewis, Lee Rainwater, Erik Erickson, Charles Keil, and G. Franklin Edwards who provide a different perspective. Carmichael and Hamilton in *Black Power*, Harold Cruse in *Crisis of the Negro Intellectual*, Kenneth Clark in *Dark Ghetto*, Robert Blauner writing in *Social Problems* on "Studies in Violence" and even the Kerner Commission Report have all made the case for an analysis of the black community based on colonialization of Afro-Americans within the confines of the mother country. In the words of DuBois:[12] "These black colonies in the United States, separate and isolated from the ongoing activities of mainstream America, have created institutions and evolved patterns of behavior which operate to give him a social world and mental peace." Blauner makes the distinction between colonialism as a social, economic, and political system and as a process:[13] "The common features [internal colonialism and classical colonialism] ultimately relate to the fact that the classical colonialism of the imperialist era and American racism developed out of the same historical situation and reflected a common world economic and power stratification." Blauner states further:[14] "A final fundament of colonization is racism. Racism is a principle of social domination by which a group seen as inferior or different in terms of alleged biological characteristics is exploited, controlled, and oppressed socially and psychologically by a superordinate group. . . . Thus racism has generally accompanied colonialism." In order for anticolonial movements or revolutions to occur, Blauner maintains that cultural revitalization movements (or cultural nationalism as envisioned, for example, by Imamu Baraka (LeRoi Jones)) must play a key role:[15]

> In the U.S., an Afro-American culture has been developing since slavery out of the ingredients

of African world-views, the experience of bondage, southern values and customs, migration and the northern lower-class ghettoes, and most importantly, the political history of the Black population in its struggles against racism. Researchers on lower-class family life in the Caribbean and South America have generally concluded that middle-class values coexist with unique lower-class values: "A moral system within a moral system" is Raymond T. Smith's assessment; Braithwaite concludes there is "a duality of allegiance to values." [16]

Hyman Rodman has developed the concept of "value stretch," which he describes as follows: [17]

The lower-class person, without abandoning the general values of the society, develops alternative sets of values. Without abandoning the values placed upon success, such as high income and high educational and occupational attainment, he stretches the values so that lesser degrees of success also become desirable. Without abandoning the values of marriage and legitimate childbirth he stretches these values so that a non-legal union and legally illegitimate children are also desirable. The result is that the members of the lower class, in many areas, have a wider range of values than others within the society. They share the general values of the society with members of other classes, but in addition they have stretched these values, or developed alternative values, which help them to adjust to their deprived circumstances.

Words are elusive and attempts to relate many of the feeling tones, the psychological nuances, and the subtlety of *what it is* lose something in the telling; for those who have lived amidst a people who have survived so many tragedies, too many words may lessen the vitality of the experience. However, some of the tangible and common experiences of black people in America are the following.

1. The black youth raised in the North and socialized and educated into the white value structure experiences an urgent need at some point to immerse himself in blackness, either by going South or by hibernating in the black ghetto without white contacts for a period of time.

2. The upwardly mobile black family, which can afford to move from the ghetto but whose choice is restricted to a suburban or predominantly white area and the ghetto, chooses the ghetto with all of its debilitating aspects.

3. The rituals of "down home" meals ema-

nating a fragrance and warmth that has never been recaptured in the most highly praised restaurants or in white homes boasting the most outstanding cooks can make one homesick for a time and place that has no reality in the broader community.

4. Laughing, jostling, exchange of information and news, the latest dances, hip phrases, and fashions are part of any streetcorner gathering and unavailable in the antiseptic world beyond the confines of the ghetto. This camaraderie involves an interaction that is natural, spontaneous, and therapeutic and that certainly makes the idea of encounter groups and T-sessions for black people as ludicrous as many other of the practices and solutions foisted on society in general by the all-knowing white expert.

5. The gathering of friends, neighbors, and passers-by on the porch or stoop to pass the time of day and watch the events in the neighborhood.

6. The realization that although you don't have much by way of material goods, in case of illness or death, someone from next door or on the block will help out with the children, the wash, the food, and the chores and that you will not be left alone to suffer or die without the comfort of the presence of others.

Streetcorner society is one of the major socializing agencies in the black community, particularly for the male. These peer groups form at an early age and can be viewed as age-graded phenomena since they form along these lines.

The male models may not be the ones middle-class society defines as appropriate, but they are there in vast numbers: preachers, con men, day laborers, pimps, hustlers, singers, factory workers, city workers, and drifters. Lawrence Levine notes: [18]

There have been equally superficial and incomplete discussions of the available peer group models upon which Negro youth could pattern their lives and aspirations. On the whole, such discussions have ignored the evidence of black folklore, black music, and black humor with their array of such heroes and models as tricksters, bad men, and signifiers, and the evidence of lower-class black culture in which entertainers, preachers, and underworld hustlers often occupy central positions.

Few investigators have bothered to examine the importance of these groups in serving as models for roles and patterns of behavior. As Charles Keil has observed:[19]

> If we are ever to understand what urban Negro culture is all about, we had best view entertainers and hustlers as culture heroes — integral parts of the whole — rather than as deviants or shadow figures.

Common meanings and emotionalized responses to situations are part of the shared heritage of a people, and their language reflects this. Language is an index of culture, the labeling of concepts, and symbolic behavior. Kinesis, or body language, is a highly developed part of daily communication "on the block." Language not only transmits social heritage or culture but also typifies culture. Investigations of language systems and structure have revealed that perceptions of reality and man's interpretations of this reality are influenced and in some instances controlled by the particular language that he uses. Members of a particular society share common meanings and expressions that have grown out of shared experiences and interpretations of these. Idiomatic expressions are one of the primary indicators of the "understood quality" of language.

The argot, or slang, of black life has served a vital need in the ghetto and has also expanded the English language itself, e.g., "up tight," "rap," "rip off," etc. Standard English is filled with expressions that have their roots in the shared experiences of a people subjugated and ruled from without. They had a need to develop means of communication that would not be easily distinguishable to those under whom they lived, worked, and often feared for their safety and very lives. Common meanings and emotionalized responses to situations are part of the shared heritage of a people, and their language reflects this.

In every society there is the ideal culture and the real culture. The ideal culture is used to assess behavior. The real culture is the behavior actually exhibited in everyday life, as contrasted with the ideal culture, which is expressed in terms of abstract sentiment and which members think they possess. No idealized norms are ever completely fulfilled in overt behavior. An example may be seen in the idealized concepts of marriage in Western society in terms of romantic love and fidelity as contrasted with the extramarital behavior as documented by Kinsey and others. Nonetheless, the behavior, achievements, and life styles of blacks who have always been excluded from citizenship and community are assessed and evaluated by the idealized norms and in most cases

have thereby been found wanting. This is one of the realities of power—being in a position to define what is and what ought to be. Take for example the question of illegitimacy. How much meaning can it have to a group whose forefathers were legally prohibited from marriage and whose births were not recorded officially in many areas until the mid-1900s? How can a people who view the moment of conception as the beginning of life for the child and believe that abortion is murder, plain and simple—people who feel that this child has as much right to his chance at life as anyone else—do anything else but accept the child no matter how society defines the situation? How can the agencies of this society, which in many instances have been the initiators of pain and humiliation for so many of their brethren, expect that the word and concept—*illegitimate*—with its implications for white society could have the same meaning for black people? It is again an irrevelancy that does not deal with the reality, the issue at hand. A child is conceived. What do we do about taking care of it? Who can best help? Who has the most to offer? These are the questions; not, What will the neighbors think? How will the family be embarrassed? How can we make the situation respectable? The questions, alternatives, and responses are different in the two communities. The black poor have their illegitimacy, and the white affluent have homes for unwed mothers, trips to Europe, relatives in another state, adoptions, and abortions. The statistics do not reflect this, but the question has to be put: Who is the more moral? The answer depends on the operative value system and who is in the position of defining morality. Higher incidences of disease, poor health, infant mortality rates 58 percent higher than for whites, complications and death during pregnancy six times greater than for whites, a life expectancy rate seven years less than whites, and homicide rates nine times that of the white community force the reality of life and death into the consciousness and everyday affairs of ghetto life. With poverty, frustration, and violence ever at hand, the imminence of the death of one's friends or loved ones leads to both a reverence for life in the humanistic sense and often a seemingly devil-may-care attitude.

It is unreasonable to expect that these islands of poverty and frustration—the ghettoes—should look outside to the dominant society asking to be judged and approved when they have to look to each other for survival. The less contact ghetto dwellers have with others, the less meaning any of the norms of the dominant group have for them. It is not a matter of rebuffing or rejecting white values, but a matter of relevancy to the situation in which they find themselves. Upon investigation of the Black Ex-

7

perience it should become readily apparent that parallel comparisons from white to black are in a majority of instances invalid.

The experiences of black people have primarily grown out of adaptation to and for survival strategy. The need to deal with present exigencies of life creates a life style of its own. Lee Rainwater, an observer of lower-class families and value systems, points out:[20] "Negroes creatively adapt to the system in ways that keep them alive and extract what gratification they can find, but in the process of adaptation they are constrained to behave in ways that inflict a great deal of suffering on those with whom they make their lives, and on themselves." Rainwater also notes:[21] "The subculture that Negroes have created may be imperfect but it has been viable for centuries; it behooves both white and Negro leaders and intellectuals to seek to understand it even as they hope to change it."

A group consciousness grows out of these enclaves, a sense of being in this all together and in some cases a fostering of the rejection of white standards. As Peter I. Rose has observed:[22]

Minority status has been found to intensify already existing group identity or to create it when it has not existed prior to discrimination. Forced to live in particular areas and to associate with one another, members of minority groups frequently come to view *themselves* as a community and it feel a keen sense of responsibility for one another.

The spatial isolation and non-assimilation into the larger society has, in many instances, provided the framework for developments and life styles unique to the Afro-American. The negative and pathological aspects of ghetto life have captured the interests of white social scientists for decades. Seldom have these researchers attempted to investigate the strengths and positive adaptations necessary to function in an essentially hostile and racially prohibitive society. As Richard Wright cogently remarks:[23]

But few white Americans have found the stength to cease being victims of their culture to the extent that they can throw off their socially inherited belief in a dehumanized image of the Negro. Indeed, the whole inner landscape of American Negro life, born of repression, is so little known that when whites see it they brand it "emotionally running amuck" or "psychopathic manifestations."

The guise of professionalism, objectivity, value-free research is not sufficient to hide the fact that social scientists, too, are products of the society in which they invest parts of themselves and incorporate the value system and beliefs into their own personalities.

The mere fact of selecting one topic over another or of choosing to focus on this particular facet for investigation over that is in itself indicative of a priority and thereby a value statement. Interpretation also lends itself to variability: "One social scientist looking at the delinquency statistics in Harlem could rejoice in the facts that show that the vast majority of young people in the ghetto—nearly 90 percent—do not come in conflict with the law. Another social scientist might concentrate on the fact of the 10 percent who do become delinquent."[24] Studies on black family life have been most noted for this kind of social fact reporting and interpreting. One often hears about the 20 percent of the families headed by females in the black community, but seldom about the 75 percent with both parents present (5 percent are headed by males).

A word of caution may perhaps be uttered here for those who may tend to overstate the peculiarity of the Black Experience. It is wise to keep in mind that there is no such being as the all-pervasive Negro or black man. The *Negro* or *Black Man* does not exist. There are as many black people as there are personality types. Assessments and interpretations of experiences will vary depending upon individual experiences—negative and positive—the amount and tenor of contact with whites, temperament, family background, and perceptions. Marcus Garvey, Richard Wright, and W.E.B. DuBois are notable cases in point. But at the same time commonalities of interest and experience, racial identity and caste-like status, and isolation serve to bridge the other differences. Diversity is characteristic of any people, and to deny black people their differences is to deny them their peoplehood. Has there ever been a people, a nation, or even a tribe where there was no diversity—where all thoughts were the same? Even in Huxley's *Brave New World* and Orwell's *1984* special thought monitors, technological and human, had to be employed to assure conformity to a pattern. And even then, there were those who escaped their scrutiny and dared to think. This categorical way of thinking about black people, lumping all of them together as a single unit, has been the undoing of many of our most promising blacks in their bid for leadership roles and has undergirded the stereotypic thinking that is characteristic of most white Americans. St. Clair Drake has made the sociological distinction by pointing out that the life styles that differentiate inhabitants of the black ghetto into social classes are "based more upon differences in education and basic values (crystallized, in part, around occupational differences) than in meaningful differences in income."[25] He goes on to point out:[26]

Some families live a "middle-class style of

life," placing heavy emphasis upon decorous public behavior and general respectability, insisting that their children "get an education" and "make something out of themselves" ....Within the same income range, and not always at the lower margin of it, other families live a "lower-class life style" being part of the "organized" lower class, while at the lowest income levels an "unorganized" lower class exists whose members tend always to become *dis*organized—functioning in an anomic situation where gambling, excessive drinking, the use of narcotics, and sexual promiscuity are prevalent forms of behavior, and violent interpersonal relations reflect an ethos of suspicion and resentment which suffuses this deviant subculture. It is within this milieu that criminal and semi-criminal activities burgeon.

DuBois in *Dusk of Dawn* makes the clear distinction between *what is* and what is commonly believed to be the case:[27]

In no place nor at any time do they form a homogeneous group. Even in the country districts of the lower South, Allison Davis likens the group to a steeple with wide base tapering to a high pinnacle. This means that while the poor, ignorant, sick and anti-social form a vast foundation, that upward from the base stretch classes whose highest members, although few in number, reach above the average not only of the Negroes but of the whites, and may justly be compared to the better-class white culture. ... The Negro group is spoken of continually as one undifferentiated low-class mass. The culture of the higher whites is often considered as typical of all the whites.

Black culture has on the whole been ignored by students of social behavior as either nonexistent or perceived as some pathological manifestation of white values. Walter B. Miller makes some assessment of their position of "expert":[28]

Some analysts of lower-class culture— Havighurst, Davis, Cohen, Loeb—have taken as their analytic and perceptual starting point a set of practices and standards identified as "middle class" and have considered lower-class culture primarily in reference to this baseline. Using such concepts as "the middle-class measuring rod" or "the Core Culture" as key terms in treating lower-class culture leads to a conceptualization of that culture as a defective variant or imperfect reflection of middle-class culture.

Miller goes on to state a significant point that has too often been the exception rather than the rule:[29]

A starting point of equal validity for some purposes and greater validity for others is the concept of lower-class culture as a cultural system *in its own right* with an integrity of its own, a characteristic set of practices, focal concerns, and ways of behaving that are meaningfully and systematically related to *one another*, rather than to corresponding features of middle-class culture. The lower-class community is frequently characterized as "disorganized," but this probably reflects a middle-class conception of what organization is.

Erik Erikson, in a classic article on the concept of identity among black people, attests to the fact that "the 'disorganization' of the Negro family must not be measured solely by its distance from the white or Negro middle-class family with its one-family housing and legal and religious legitimizations. Disintegration must be measured and understood also as a distortion of the *traditional* if often unofficial *Negro family pattern.*"[30] "How can one respect," says James Baldwin, "let alone adopt, the values of a people who do not, on any level whatever, live the way they say they do, or the way they say they should?"[31] The fact that this kind of critical assessment is expressed to the larger society does not mean that the thought is new. Generations of domestics, chauffers, and other servants have known and shared the secrets of their "betters" for too long to stand much in awe of them or their standards of behavior. They have witnessed behind-the-scenes manipulations, bending of the law to suit the needs of friends and associates, moral deviations, emptiness of wealth and power without the attendant humanistic values, and, most of all, the loneliness and frustrations of being on top and successful. As Baldwin observes:[32]

There is certainly little enough in the white man's public or private life that one should desire to imitate. ... Therefore, a vast amount of the energy that goes into what we call the Negro problem is produced by the white man's profound desire not to be judged by those who are not white, not to be seen as he is, and at the same time a vast amount of the white anguish is rooted in the white man's equally profound need to be seen as he is, to be released from the tyranny of his mirror.

The questions raised by respectable citizens— generally those farthest removed from the ghetto— both white and black, about the behavior of "those people" are best answered in the words of Ralph Ellison's protagonist in *Invisible Man:*[33]

I can hear you say, "What a horrible irresponsible bastard!" And you're right. I leap to agree with you. I am one of the most irresponsible beings that ever lived. Irresponsibility is part of my invisibility; any way you face it, it is a denial. But to whom can I be responsible, and why should I be, when you refuse to see me? And wait until I reveal how truly irresponsible I am. Responsibility rests upon recognition, and recognition is a form of agreement.

The interrelationships of community require some reciprocity and communication. There is little of either between whites and blacks. Power has always rested in the hands of the white Anglo-Saxon Protestants, so they have never had the need to probe the depths of the ghetto. As Rose so accurately observes:[34]

Because of limited interaction with selected members of minorities—outstanding figures, workers, or servants—individuals in the dominant group tend to have distorted images of life in the minority community. The pattern is asymmetrical, however, for minorities are continually exposed to the values and norms of the dominant group through public schooling, mass media, employment, advertising, and just "living." They must learn the ways of the dominant group.

Ghetto communities have created little interest other than serving as the focal points of the prurient interests of those who seek excitement, mystery, the exotic, and a chance to let their hair down on Saturday night and return to respectability on Monday, with their peers being none the wiser. As long as these self-contained enclaves remain just that, even violence and destructiveness are tolerated, since in most cases they involve only other members of devalued groups.

Kenneth Clark, writing in *Dark Ghetto*, has superbly delineated the terrible toll that many ghetto residents have to pay for living among their brethren —the ones who have succumbed to the destruction and degradation that are forever looming in the shadows of rejection and hatred. His chapters on the psychology and pathology of the ghetto deal with what Clark calls institutionalized pathology — "the chronic, self-perpetuating. . .symptoms of social disorganization and disease as high rates of juvenile delinquence, venereal disease, narcotic addiction, illegitimacy, homicide and suicide."[35] These are persistent and urgent problems, but as Clark, together with Drake and others, notes:[36] "There is considerable psychological safety in the ghetto where one lives among one's own and does not risk rejection among strangers." Drake makes a similar assessment, when he says:[37] "But for the masses of the ghetto dwellers this is a warm and familiar milieu, preferable to the sanitary coldness of middle-class neighborhoods and a counterpart of the communities of the foreign-born, each of which has its own distinctive subcultural

flavor." It has not been within the province of this present essay to delve into the debilitating features of ghetto life, although they are as real and urgent an influence as any other aspect of the black ethos. Suffice it to say that the causes and not the symptoms have to be extricated from the black society in particular and the white society in general.

NOTES

1. Ashley Montagu, *Man's Most Dangerous Myth: The Fallacy of Race* (New York: The World Publishing Co., 1967), p.39.

2. Houston A. Baker, "Completely Well: One View of Black American Culture," in Nathan I. Huggins, Martin Kilson, and Daniel M. Fox, eds., *Key Issues in the Afro-American Experience* (New York: Harcourt, Brace, Jovanovich, Inc., 1971), vol. 1, p. 30.

3. St. Clair Drake, "Social and Economic Status," in Talcott Parsons and Kenneth B. Clark, eds., *The Negro American* (Boston: Beacon Press, 1969), p. 9-10.

4. Lerone Bennett, *The Negro Mood* (New York: Ballantine Books, Inc., 1965), p. 89.

5. Ibid., p. 88.

6. W. E. B. DuBois, *Dusk of Dawn* (New York: Schocken Books, 1968), pp. 147-148.

7. *See* Baker, op. cit., p. 24.

8. R. P. Cuzzort, *Humanity and Modern Sociological Thought* (New York: Holt, Rinehart and Winston, Inc., 1969), p. 198.

9. Thomas F. Pettigrew, *A Profile of the American Negro* (New York: Van Nostrand, 1964), p. 25.

10. Nathan Glazer and Daniel Moynihan, *Beyond the Melting Pot* (Cambridge, Mass.: MIT Press, 1963), p. 53.

11. Edward Byron Reuter, *The American Race Problem* (New York: Thomas Y. Crowell Co., Apollo ed., 1970), p. 371.

12. DuBois, op. cit., p. 173.

13. Robert Blauner, "Internal Colonialism and Ghetto Revolt," in Michael Wertheimer, ed., *Confrontation* (Glenview, Ill.: Scott, Foresman and Co., 1970), p. 122.

14. Ibid.

15. Ibid., p. 127.

16. Raymond T. Smith, *The Negro Family in British Guiana* (London: Routledge and Kegan Paul, 1956), p. 149; Lloyd Braithwaite, "Sociology and Demographic Research in the British Caribbean," *Social and Economic Studies,* 6 (March 1957), p. 534.

17. Hyman Rodman, "The Lower-Class Value Stretch," in Raymond W. Mack, ed., *Race, Class and Power* (New York: American Book Co., 1968), p. 301.

18. Lawrence Levine, "The Concept of the New Negro and the Realities of Black Culture," in Nathan I. Huggins, Martin Kilson, and Daniel M. Fox, op. cit., vol. 2, p. 134.

19. Charles Keil, *Urban Blues* (Chicago: University of Chicago Press, 1969), p. 20.

20. Lee Rainwater, "Crucible of Identity: The Negro Lower-Class Family," in Talcott Parsons and Kenneth B. Clark, eds., op. cit., p. 125.

21. Ibid., p. 166.

22. Peter I. Rose, *They and We* (New York: Random House, 1968), p. 25.

23. Richard Wright, "Introduction," in St. Clair Drake and Horace R. Cayton, *Black Metropolis: A Study of Negro Life in a Northern City* (New York: Harcourt, Brace and World, Inc., rev. ed., 1970), vol. 1, p. xxxi.

24. Kenneth B. Clark, *Dark Ghetto* (New York: Harper & Row, 1967), p. xxiv.

25. Drake, "Social and Economic Status," p. 11.

26. Ibid.

27. DuBois, *Dusk of Dawn,* p. 183.

28. Walter B. Miller, "Cultural Features of an Urban Lower-Class Community" (unpublished manuscript; Wayne State University, Detroit, Mich., 1965), p. 5.

29. Ibid., p. 12.

30. Erik H. Erikson, "The Concept of Identity in Race Relations," in Talcott Parsons and Kenneth B. Clark, op. cit., p. 244.

31. James Baldwin, *The Fire Next Time* (New York: Dell Publishing Co., 1963), p. 129.

32. Ibid., p. 128.

33. Ralph Ellison, *Invisible Man* (New York: New American Library, Signet Books ed., 1952), p. 16.

34. Rose, op. cit., p. 127.

35. Clark, op. cit., p. 81.

36. Ibid., p. 19.

37. Drake, op. cit., p. 10.

PART I:

ORIGINAL NARRATIVES

Editor's Note:

The words of the following hymn, set to music by the author's brother, Rosamond Johnson, have stirred the hearts of generations of black Americans. They have claimed it as their national anthem. This anthem belongs to those black people who have worked long hours for little or no pay; who have never had a single thought of rebellion or desire to leave this country; and yet whose subliminal awareness and perception attest the fact that "The Star-Spangled Banner" is not theirs.

LIFT EVERY VOICE AND SING

JAMES WELDON JOHNSON

Lift every voice and sing
Till earth and heaven ring,
Ring with the harmonies of Liberty;
Let our rejoicing rise
High as the listening skies,
Let it resound loud as the rolling sea.
Sing a song full of faith that the dark past has
    taught us,
Sing a song full of the hope that the present has
    brought us,
Facing the rising sun of our new day begun
Let us march on till victory is won.

Stony the road we trod,
Bitter the chastening rod,
Felt in the days when hope unborn had died;
Yet with a steady beat,
Have not our weary feet
Come to the place for which our fathers sighed?
We have come over a way that with tears has
    been watered,
We have come, treading our path through the
    blood of the slaughtered,
Out from the gloomy past,
Till now we stand at last
Where the white gleam of our bright star is cast.

God of our weary years,
God of our silent tears,
Thou who has brought us thus far on the way;
Thou who has by Thy might
Let us into the light,
Keep up forever in the path, we pray.
Lest our feet stray from the places, our God,
    where we met Thee,
Lest, our hearts drunk with the wine of the
    world, we forget Thee;
Shadowed beneath Thy hand,
May we forever stand.
True to our God,
True to our native land.

Spirituals or "sorrow songs" as W.E.B. DuBois calls them are one of the rare artifacts of Americana. It is an irony of circumstances that this contribution to American culture came from a people who have never been accepted as full members of the society. To hear them sung is to know the pain and agony of a people who have suffered much and yet can raise their voices in the faith that someone hears. The words are simple and many of the authors unknown. The chorus response pattern is reminiscent of the African chant. Two are presented here, but there are hundreds more and they should not become part of the lost heritage.

NOBODY KNOWS
THE TROUBLE I'VE SEEN

Nobody knows the trouble I've seen,
Nobody knows but Jesus.
Nobody knows the trouble I've seen,
Glory, Hallelujah!

Sometimes I'm up, sometimes I'm down
Oh, yes, Lord!
Sometimes I'm almost to the ground,
Oh, yes, Lord!
Although you see me going along, so,
Oh, yes, Lord!
I have my troubles here below,
Oh, yes, Lord!

Nobody knows the trouble I've seen,
Nobody knows my sorrow.
Nobody knows the trouble I've seen,
Glory, Hallelujah!

One day when I was walking along,
Oh, yes, Lord!
The elements opened and His love came down,
Oh, yes, Lord!
I never shall forget that day,
Oh, yes, Lord!
When Jesus washed my sins away,
Oh, yes, Lord!

Oh, nobody knows the trouble I've seen,
Nobody knows my sorrow.
Nobody knows the trouble I've seen,
Glory, Hallelujah!

MOTHERLESS CHILD

Sometimes I feel like a motherless child,
Sometimes I feel like a motherless child,
Sometimes I feel like a motherless child,
A long ways from home,
A long ways from home.

Sometimes I feel like I'm almost gone,
Sometimes I feel like I'm almost gone,
Sometimes I feel like I'm almost gone,
A long ways from home,
A long ways from home.

Sometimes I feel like a feather in the air,
Sometimes I feel like a feather in the air,
Sometimes I feel like a feather in the air,
And I spread my wings and I fly,
I spread my wings and I fly.

Twelve Years a Slave (1853) by Solomon Northup is an account of slavery by a free black citizen of New York. Northup was kidnapped in Washington, D.C., in 1841, and was enslaved on a cotton plantation near the Red River in Louisiana. He was freed in 1853 and proceeded to recount his experiences. This description of a slave auction is taken from that account.

A SLAVE AUCTION

SOLOMON NORTHUP

In the first place we were required to wash thoroughly, and those with beards to shave. We were then furnished with a new suit each, cheap, but clean. The men had hat, coat, shirt, pants and shoes; the women frocks of calico, and handkerchief to bind about their heads. We were now conducted into a large room in the front part of the building to which the yard was attached, in order to be properly trained, before the admission of customers. The men were arranged on one side of the room, the women at the other. The tallest was placed at the head of the row, then the next tallest, and so on in the order of their respective heights. Emily was at the foot of the line of women. Freeman [the slave auctioneer] charged us to remember our places; exhorted us to appear smart and lively,—sometimes threatening, and again, holding out various inducements. During the day he exercised us in the art of "looking smart," and of moving to our places with exact precision.

After being fed, in the afternoon, we were again paraded and made to dance. Bob, a colored boy, who had some time belonged to Freeman, played on the violin. Standing near him, I made bold to inquire if he could play the "Virginia Reel." He answered he could not, and asked me if I could play. Replying in the affirmative, he handed me the violin. I struck up a tune, and finished it. Freeman ordered me to continue playing, and seemed well pleased, telling Bob that I far excelled him—a remark that seemed to grieve my musical companion very much.

Next day many customers called to examine Freeman's "new lot." The latter gentleman was very loquacious, dwelling at much length upon our several good points and qualities. He would make us hold up our heads, walk briskly back and forth, while customers would feel of our hands and arms and bodies, turn us about, ask us what we could do, make us open our mouths and show our teeth, precisely as a jockey examines a horse which he is about to barter for or purchase. Sometimes a man or woman was taken back to the small house in the yard, stripped, and inspected more minutely. Scars upon a slave's back were considered evidence of a rebellious or unruly spirit, and hurt his sale.

An old gentleman, who said he wanted a coachman, appeared to take a fancy to me. . . . I learned he was a resident in the city. I very much desired that he would buy me, because I conceived it would not be difficult to make my escape from New Orleans on some northern vessel. Freeman asked him fifteen hundred dollars for me. The old gentleman insisted it was too much as times were very hard. Freeman, however, declared that I was sound of health, of a good constitution, and intelligent. He made it a point to enlarge upon my musical attainments. The old gentleman argued quite adroitly that there was nothing extraordinary about the Negro, and finally, to my regret, went out, saying he would call again.

During the day, however, a number of sales were made. David and Caroline were purchased together by a Natchez planter. They left us, grinning broadly, and in a most happy state of mind, caused by the fact of their not being separated. Sethe was sold to a planter of Baton Rouge, her eyes flashing with anger as she was led away.

The same man also purchased Randall. The little fellow was made to jump, and run across the floor, and perform many other feats, exhibiting his activity and condition. All the time the trade was going on, Eliza was crying aloud, and wringing her hands. She besought the man not to buy him, unless he also bought herself and Emily. She promised, in that case, to be the most faithful slave that ever lived. The man answered that he could not afford it, and then Eliza burst into a paroxysm of grief, weeping plaintively. Freeman turned round to her, savagely, with his whip in his uplifted hand, ordering her to stop her noise, or he would flog her. He would not have such work—such snivelling; and unless she ceased that minute, he would take her to the yard and give her a hundred lashes. Yes, he would take the nonsense out of her pretty quick—if he didn't might he be d_____d. Eliza shrunk before him, and tried to wipe away her tears, but it was all in vain. She wanted to be with her children, she said, the little time she had to live.

All the frowns and threats of Freeman could not wholly silence the afflicted mother. She kept on begging and beseeching them, most piteously, not to separate the three. Over and over again she told them how she loved her boy. A great many times she repeated her former promises—how very faithful and obedient she would be; how hard she would labor day and night, to the last moment of her life; if he would only buy them all together. But it was of no avail; the man could not afford it. The bargain was agreed upon, and Randall must go alone. Then Eliza ran to him; embraced him passionately; kissed him again and again; told him to remember her—all the while her tears falling in the boy's face like rain.

Freeman damned her, calling her a blubbering, bawling wench, and ordered her to go to her place, and behave herself, and be somebody. He swore he wouldn't stand such stuff but a little longer. He would soon give her something to cry about, if she was not mighty careful, and that she might depend upon.

The planter from Baton Rouge, with his new purchase, was ready to depart.

"Don't cry, mama. I will be a good boy. Don't cry," said Randall, looking back, as they passed out of the door.

What has become of the lad, God knows. It was a mournful scene indeed. I would have cried myself if I had dared.

_____

Editor's Note:

Frederick Douglass began life as a slave. Escaping in 1838, he became an abolitionist, world traveler, orator, newspaper publisher, and minister and consul general in Haiti. Douglass wrote a powerful autobiography, *My Bondage and My Freedom*. The following excerpts tell of his longing to be free, of his passion for liberty, and of his determination to act on behalf of gaining his freedom. The section devoted to hymns clearly indicates the role of the spiritual as a means of communication between slaves. Both as an eyewitness and as a victim, Douglass experienced unequivocated acts of brutality. The last excerpt from Douglass' autobiography, a brief description of the type of treatment meted out by some slaveowners on their property, typifies the institution of slavery.

MY BONDAGE AND MY FREEDOM

FREDERICK DOUGLASS

Longing to be free

"Notwithstanding," thought I, "the many resolutions and prayers I have made, in behalf of freedom, I am, this first day of the year 1836, still a slave, still wandering in the depths of spirit-devouring thralldom. My faculties and powers of body and soul are not my own, but are the property of a fellow mortal, in no sense superior to me, except that he has the physical power to compel me to be owned and controlled by him. By the combined physical force of the community, I am his slave,—a slave for life." With thoughts like these, I was perplexed and chafed; they rendered me gloomy and disconsolate. The anguish of my mind may not be written.

At the close of the year 1835, Mr. Freeland, my temporary master, had bought me of Capt. Thomas Auld, for the year 1836. His promptness in securing my services, would have been flattering to my vanity, had I been ambitious to win the reputation of being a valuable slave. Even as it was, I felt a slight degree of complacency at the circumstance. It showed he was as well pleased with me as a slave, as I was with him as a master. I have already intimated my regard for Mr. Freeland, and I may say here, in addressing northern readers—where there is no selfish motive for speaking in praise of a slaveholder—that Mr. Freeland was a man of many excellent qualities, and to me quite preferable to any master I ever had.

But the kindness of the slavemaster only gilds the chain of slavery, and detracts nothing from its weight or power. The thought that men are made for other and better uses than slavery, thrives best under the gentle treatment of a kind master. But the grim visage of slavery can assume no smiles which can fascinate the partially enlightened slave, into a forgetfulness of his bondage, nor of the desirableness of liberty.

I was not through the first month of this, my second year with the kind and gentlemanly Mr. Freeland, before I was earnestly considering and devising plans for gaining that freedom, which, when I was but a mere child, I had ascertained to be the natural and inborn right of every member of the human family. The desire for this freedom had been benumbed, while I was under the brutalizing dominion of Covey; and it had been postponed, and rendered inoperative, by my truly pleasant Sunday school engagements with my friends, during the year 1835, at Mr. Freeland's. It had, however, never entirely subsided. I hated slavery, always, and the desire for freedom only needed a favorable breeze, to fan it into a blaze, at any moment. The thought of only being a creature of the *present* and the *past,* troubled me, and I longed to have a *future*—a future with hope in it. To be shut up entirely to the past and present, is abhorrent to the human mind; it is to the soul—whose life and happiness is unceasing progress—what the prison is to the body; a blight and mildew, a hell of horrors. The dawning of this, another year, awakened me from my temporary slumber, and roused into life my latent, but long cherished aspirations for freedom. I was now not only ashamed to be contented in slavery, but ashamed to *seem* to be contented, and in my present favorable condition, under the mild rule of Mr. F., I am not sure that some kind reader will not condemn me for being over ambitious, and greatly wanting in proper humility, when I say the truth, that I now drove from me all thoughts of making the best of my lot, and welcomed only such thoughts as led me away from the house of bondage. The intense desire, now felt, *to be free,* quickened by my present favorable circumstances, brought me to the determination to *act* as well as to think and speak. Accordingly, at the beginning of this year 1836, I took upon me a solemn vow, that the year which had now dawned upon me should not close, without witnessing an earnest attempt, on my part, to gain my liberty. This vow only bound me to make my escape individually; but the year spent with Mr. Freeland had attached me, as with "hooks of steel," to my brother slaves. The most affectionate and confiding friendship existed between us; and I felt it my duty to give them an opportunity to share in my virtuous determination, by frankly disclosing to them my plans and purposes. Toward Henry and John Harris, I felt a friendship as strong as one man can feel for another; for I could have died with and for them. To them, therefore, with a suitable degree of caution, I began to disclose my sentiments and plans; sounding them the while, on the subject of running away, provided a good chance should offer. I scarcely need tell the reader, that I did my *very best* to imbue the minds of my dear friends with my own views and feelings. Thoroughly awakened, now, and with a definite vow upon me, all my little reading, which had any bearing on the subject of human rights, was rendered available in my communications with my friends. That (to me) gem of a book, the Columbian Orator, with its eloquent orations and spicy dialogues, denouncing oppression and slavery—telling of what had been dared, done and suffered by men, to obtain the inestimable boon of liberty—was still fresh in my memory, and whirled into the ranks of my speech with the aptitude of well trained soldiers, going through the drill. The fact is, I here began my public speaking. I canvassed, with Henry and John, the subject of slavery, and dashed against the condemning brand of God's eternal justice, which it every hour violates. My fellow servants were neither indifferent, dull, nor inapt. Our feelings were more alike than our opinions. All, however, were ready to act, when a feasible plan should be proposed. "Show us *how* the thing is to be done," said they, "and all else is clear."

Religion and the slave

We were all, except Sandy, quite free from slaveholding priestcraft. It was in vain that we had been taught from the pulpit at St. Michael's, the duty of obedience to our masters; to recognize God as the author of our enslavement; to regard running away an offense, alike against God and man; to deem our enslavement a merciful and beneficial arrangement; to esteem our condition, in this country, a paradise to that from which we had been snatched in Africa; to consider our hard hands and dark color as God's mark of displeasure, and as pointing us out as the proper subjects of slavery; that the relation of master and slave was one of reciprocal benefits; that our work was not more serviceable to our masters, than our master's thinking was serviceable to us. I say, it was in vain that the pulpit of St. Michael's had constantly inculcated these plausible doctrines. Nature laughed them to scorn. For my own part, I had now become altogether too big for my chains. Father Lawson's solemn words, of what I ought to be, and might be, in the providence of God, had not fallen dead on my soul. I was fast verging toward manhood, and the prophecies of my childhood were still unfulfilled. The thought, that year after year had passed away, and my best resolutions to run away had failed and faded —that I was *still a slave*, and a slave, too, with chances for gaining my freedom diminished and still dimi-

nishing—was not a matter to be slept over easily; nor did I easily sleep over it.

To know the mind and heart of a slave

But here came a new trouble. Thoughts and purposes so incendiary as those I now cherished, could not agitate the mind long, without danger of making themselves manifest to scrutinizing and unfriendly beholders. I had reason to fear that my sable face might prove altogether too transparent for the safe concealment of my hazardous enterprise. Plans of greater moment have leaked through stone walls, and revealed their projectors. But, here was no stone wall to hide my purpose. I would have given my poor, tell tale face for the immovable countenance of an Indian, for it was far from being proof against the daily, searching glances of those with whom I met.

It is the interest and business of slaveholders to study human nature, with a view to practical results, and many of them attain astonishing proficiency in discerning the thoughts and emotions of slaves. They have to deal not with earth, wood, or stone, but with *men*; and, by every regard they have for their safety and prosperity, they must study to know the material on which they are at work. So much intellect as the slaveholder has around him, requires watching. Their safety depends upon their vigilance. Conscious of the injustice and wrong they are every hour perpetrating, and knowing what they themselves would do if made the victims of such wrongs, they are looking out for the first signs of the dread retribution of justice. They watch, therefore, with skilled and practiced eyes, and have learned to read, with great accuracy, the state of mind and heart of the slave, through his sable face. These uneasy sinners are quick to inquire into the matter, where the slave is concerned. Unusual sobriety, apparent abstraction, sullenness and indifference—indeed, any mood out of the common way —afford ground for suspicion and inquiry. Often relying on their superior position and wisdom, they hector and torture the slave into a confession, by affecting to know the truth of their accusations. "You have got the devil in you," say they, "and we will whip him out of you." I have often been put thus to the torture, on bare suspicion. This system has its disadvantages as well as their opposite. The slave is sometimes whipped into the confession of offenses which he never committed. The reader will see that the good old rule—"a man is to be held innocent until proved to be guilty"—does not hold good on the slave plantation. Suspicion and torture are the approved methods of getting at the truth,

17

here. It was necessary for me, therefore, to keep a watch over my deportment, lest the enemy should get the better of me.

But with all our caution and studied reserve, I am not sure that Mr. Freeland did not suspect that all was not right with us. It *did* seem that he watched us more narrowly, after the plan of escape had been conceived and discussed amongst us. Men seldom see themselves as others see them; and while, to ourselves, everything connected with our contemplated escape appeared concealed, Mr. Freeland may have, with the peculiar prescience of a slaveholder, mastered the huge thought which was disturbing our peace in slavery.

Hymns with a double meaning

I am the more inclined to think that he suspected us, because, prudent as we were, as I now look back, I can see that we did many silly things, very well calculated to awaken suspicion. We were, at times, remarkably buoyant, singing hymns and making joyous exclamations, almost as triumphant in their tone as if we had reached a land of freedom and safety. A keen observer might have detected in our repeated singing of

"O Canaan, sweet Canaan,
I am bound for the land of Canaan,"

something more than a hope of reaching heaven. We meant to reach the *north*—and the north was our Canaan.

"I thought I heard them say,
There were lions in the way,
I don't expect to stay
Much longer here.

Run to Jesus—shun the danger—
I don't expect to stay
Much longer here,"

was a favorite air, and had a double meaning. In the lips of some, it meant the expectation of a speedy summons to a world of spirits; but, in the lips of *our* company, it simply meant, a speedy pilgrimage toward a free state, and deliverance from all the evils and dangers of slavery.

I had succeeded in winning to my (what slaveholders would call wicked) scheme, a company of five young men, the very flower of the neighborhood, each one of whom would have commanded one thousand dollars in the home market. At New Orleans, they would have brought fifteen hundred dollars a piece, and, perhaps, more. The names of our party were as follows: Henry Harris; John Harris, brother to Henry; Sandy Jenkins, of root memory; Charles Roberts, and Henry Bailey. I was the youngest, but one,

of the party. I had, however, the advantage of them all, in experience, and in a knowledge of letters. This gave me great influence over them. Perhaps not one of them, left to himself, would have dreamed of escape as a possible thing. Not one of them was self-moved in the matter. They all wanted to be free; but the serious thought of running away, had not entered into their minds, until I won them to the undertaking. They all were tolerably well off—for slaves—and had dim hopes of being set free, some day, by their masters. If any one is to blame for disturbing the quiet of the slaves and slave-masters of the neighborhood of St. Michael's, *I am the man.* I claim to be the instigator of the high crime, (as the slaveholders regard it,) and I kept life in it, until life could be kept in it no longer.

Pending the time of our contemplated departure out of our Egypt, we met often by night, and on every Sunday. At these meetings we talked the matter over; told our hopes and fears, and the difficulties discovered or imagined; and, like men of sense, we counted the cost of the enterprise to which we were committing ourselves.

These meetings must have resembled, on a small scale, the meetings of revolutionary conspirators, in their primary condition. We were plotting against our (so called) lawful rulers; with this difference—that we sought our own good, and not the harm of our enemies. We did not seek to overthrow them, but to escape from them. As for Mr. Freeland, we all liked him, and would have gladly remained with him, *as freemen.* LIBERTY was our aim; and we had now come to think that we had a right to liberty, against every obstacle—even against the lives of our enslavers.

We had several words, expressive of things, important to us, which we understood, but which, even if distinctly heard by an outsider, would convey no certain meaning. I have reasons for suppressing these *pass-words*, which the reader will easily divine. I hated the secrecy; but where slavery is powerful, and liberty is weak, the latter is driven to concealment or to destruction.

The prospect was not always a bright one. At times, we were almost tempted to abandon the enterprise, and to get back to that comparative peace of mind, which even a man under the gallows might feel, when all hope of escape had vanished. Quiet bondage was felt to be better than doubts, fears and uncertainties, which now so sadly perplexed and disturbed us.

The infirmities of humanity, generally, were represented in our little band. We were confident, bold and determined, at times; and, again, doubting, timid and wavering; whistling, like the boy in the graveyard, to keep away the spirits.

Ignorance of geography

To look at the map, and observe the proximity of Eastern Shore, Maryland, to Delaware and Pennsylvania, it may seem to the reader quite absurd, to regard the proposed escape as a formidable undertaking. But to *understand,* some one has said a man must *stand under.* The real distance was great enough, but the imagined distance. was, to our ignorance, even greater. Every slaveholder seeks to impress his slave with a belief in the boundlessness of slave territory, and of his own almost illimitable power. We all had vague and indistinct notions of the geography of the country.

The distance, however, is not the chief trouble. The nearer are the lines of a slave state and the borders of a free one, the greater the peril. Hired kidnappers infest these borders. Then, too, we knew that merely reaching a free state did not free us; that, wherever caught, we could be returned to slavery. We could see no spot on this side of the ocean, where we could be free. We had heard of Canada, the real Canaan of the American bondmen, simply as a country to which the wild goose and the swan repaired at the end of winter, to escape the heat of summer, but not as the home of man. I knew something of theology, but nothing of geography. I really did not, at that time, know that there was a state of New York, or a state of Massachusetts. I had heard of Pennsylvania, Delaware and New Jersey, and all the southern states, but was ignorant of the free states, generally. New York city was our northern limit, and to go there, and to be forever harassed with the liability of being hunted down and returned to slavery—with the certainty of being treated ten times worse than we had evern been treated before—was a prospect far from delightful, and it might well cause some hesitation about engaging in the enterprise. The case, sometimes, to our excited visions, stood thus: At every gate through which we had to pass, we saw a watchman; at every ferry, a guard; on every bridge, a sentinel; and in every wood, a patrol or slave-hunter. We were hemmed in on every side. The good to be sought, and the evil to be shunned, were flung in the balance, and weighed against each other. On the one hand, there stood slavery; a stern reality, glaring frightfully upon us, with the blood of millions in his polluted skirts—terrible to behold—greedily devouring our hard earnings and feeding himself upon our flesh. Here was the evil from which to escape. On the other hand, far away, back in the hazy distance, where all forms seemed but shadows, under the flickering light of the north star—behind some craggy hill or snow-covered mountain—stood a doubtful freedom, half frozen, beckoning us to her icy domain. This was, the good to be sought. The inequality was as great as that between certainty and uncertainty. This, in itself, was enough to stagger us; but when we came to survey the untrodden road, and conjecture the many possible difficulties, we were appalled, and at times, as I have said, were upon the point of giving over the struggle altogether.

Imaginary difficulties

The reader can have little idea of the phantoms of trouble which flit, in such circumstances, before the uneducated mind of the slave. Upon either side, we saw grim death assuming a variety of horrid shapes. Now, it was starvation, causing us, in a strange and friendless land, to eat our own flesh. Now, we were contending with the waves, (for our journey was in part by water,) and were drowned. Now, we were hunted by dogs, and overtaken and torn to pieces by their merciless fangs. We were stung by scorpions —chased by wild beasts—bitten by snakes; and, worst of all, after having succeeded in swimming rivers— encountering wild beasts—sleeping in the woods— suffering hunger, cold, heat and nakedness—we supposed ourselves to be overtaken by hired kidnappers, who, in the name of the law, and for their thrice accursed reward, would, perchance, fire upon us—kill some, wound others, and capture all. This dark picture, drawn by ignorance and fear, at times greatly shook our determination, and not unfrequently caused us to

"Rather bear those ills we had
Than fly to others which we knew not of."

I am not disposed to magnify this circumstance in my experience, and yet I think I shall seem to be so disposed, to the reader. No man can tell the intense agony which is felt by the slave, when wavering on the point of making his escape. All that he has is at stake; and even that which has not, is at stake, also. The life which he has, may be lost, and the liberty which he seeks, may not be gained.

Patrick Henry, to a listening senate, thrilled by his magic eloquence, and ready to stand by him in his boldest flights, could say, "GIVE ME LIBERTY OR GIVE ME DEATH," and this saying was a sublime one, even for a freeman; but, incomparably more sublime, is the same sentiment, when *practically* asserted by men accustomed to the lash and chain— men whose sensibilities must have become more or less deadened by their bondage. With us it was a *doubtful* liberty, at best, that we sought; and a certain, lingering death in the rice swamps and sugar fields, if we failed. Life is not lightly regarded by men of sane minds. It is precious, alike to the pauper and to the prince—to the slave, and to his master; and yet, I believe there was not one among us, who would not rather have been shot down, than pass away life in hopeless bondage.

Arrest and resistance

Mr. Freeland came inside the kitchen door, and with an agitated voice, called me by name, and told me to come forward; that there were some gentlemen who wished to see me. I stepped toward them, at the door, and asked what they wanted, when the constables grabbed me, and told me that I had better not resist; that I had been in a scrape, or was said to have been in one; that they were merely going to take me where I could be examined; that they were going to carry me to St. Michael's, to have me brought before my master. They further said, that, in case the evidence against me was not true, I should be acquitted. I was now firmly tied, and completely at the mercy of my captors. Resistance was idle. They were five in number, armed to the very teeth. When they had secured me, they next turned to John Harris, and, in a few moments, succeeded in tying him as firmly as they had already tied me. They next turned toward Henry Harris, who had now returned from the barn. "Cross your hands," said the constables, to Henry. "I won't" said Henry, in a voice so firm and clear, and in a manner so determined, as for a moment to arrest all proceedings. "Won't you cross your hands?" said Tom Graham, the constable. "No I won't," said Henry, with increasing emphasis. Mr. Hamilton, Mr. Freeland, and the officers, now came near to Henry. Two of the constables drew out their shining pistols, and swore by the name of God, that he should cross his hands, or they would shoot him down. Each of these hired ruffians now cocked their pistols, and with fingers apparently on the triggers, presented their deadly weapons to the breast of the unarmed slave, saying, at the same time, if he did not cross his hands, they would "blow his d—d heart out of him."

"Shoot! shoot me!" said Henry. "You can't kill me but once. Shoot!—shoot! and be d—d. I won't be tied." This, the brave fellow said in a voice as defiant and heroic in its tone, as was the language itself; and, at the moment of saying this, with the pistols at his very breast, he quickly raised his arms, and dashed them from the puny hands of his assassins, the weapons flying in opposite directions. Now came the struggle. All hands now rushed upon the brave fellow, and, after beating him for some time, they succeeded in overpowering and tying him. Henry put me to shame; he fought, and fought bravely. John and I had made no resistance. The fact is, I never see much use

in fighting, unless there is a reasonable probability of whipping somebody. Yet there was something almost providential in the resistance made by the gallant Henry. But for that resistance, every soul of us would have been hurried off to the far south. Just a moment previous to the trouble with Henry, Mr. Hamilton *mildly* said—and this gave me the unmistakable clue to the cause of our arrest—"Perhaps we had now better make a search for those protections, which we understand Frederick has written for himself and the rest." Had these passes been found, they would have been point black proof against us, and would have confirmed all the statements of our betrayer. Thanks to the resistance of Henry, the excitement produced by the scuffle drew all attention in that direction, and I succeeded in flinging my pass, unobserved, into the fire. The confusion attendant upon the scuffle, and the apprehension of further trouble, perhaps, led our captors to forego, for the present, any search for *"those protections"* which Frederick was said to have written for his companion; so we were not yet convicted of the purpose to run away; and it was evident that there was some doubt, on the part of all, whether we had been guilty of such a purpose.

Guilt or innocence?

Could the kind reader have been quietly riding along the main road to or from Easton, that morning, his eye would have met a painful sight. He would have seen five young men, guilty of no crime, save that of preferring *liberty* to a life of *bondage*, drawn along the public highway—firmly bound together—tramping through dust and heat, bare-footed and bareheaded—fastened to three strong horses, whose riders were armed to the teeth, with pistols and daggers—on their way to prison, like felons, and suffering every possible insult from the crowds of idle, vulgar people, who clustered around, and heartlessly made their failure the occasion for all manner of ribaldry and sport. As I looked upon this crowd of vile persons, and saw myself and friends thus assailed and persecuted, I could not help seeing the fulfillment of Sandy's dream. I was in the hands of moral vultures, and firmly held in their sharp talons, and was being hurried away toward Easton, in a southeasterly direction, amid the jeers of new birds of the same feather, through every neighborhood we passed. It seemed to me, (and this shows the good understanding between the slaveholders and their allies,) that every body we met knew the cause of our arrest, and were out, awaiting our passing by, to feast their vindictive eyes on our misery and to gloat over our ruin. Some said, *I ought to be hanged,* and others, *I ought to be burnt;* others, I ought to have the *"hide"* taken from my back; while no one gave us a kind word or sympathizing look, except the poor slaves, who were lifting their heavy hoes, and who cautiously glanced at us through the post-and-rail fences, behind which they were at work. Our sufferings, that morning, can be more easily imagined than described. Our hopes were all blasted, at a blow. The cruel injustice, the victorious crime, and the helplessness of innocence, led me to ask, in my ignorance and weakness—"Where now is the God of justice and mercy? and why have these wicked men the power thus to trample upon our rights, and to insult our feelings?" And yet, in the next moment, came the consoling thought, *the day of the oppressor will come at last.* Of one thing I could be glad—not one of my dear friends, upon whom I had brought this great calamity, either by word or look, reproached me for having led them into it. We were a band of brothers, and never dearer to each other than now. The thought which gave us the most pain, was the probable separation which would now take place, in case we were sold off to the far south, as we were likely to be. While the constables were looking forward, Henry and I, being fastened together, could occasionally exchange a word, without being observed by the kidnappes who had us in charge. "What shall I do with my pass?" said Henry. "Eat it with your biscuit," said I; "it won't do to tear it up." We were now near St. Michael's. The direction concerning the passes was passed around, and executed. "*Own nothing!*" said I. "*Own nothing!*" was passed around and enjoined, and assented to. Our confidence in each other was unshaken; and we were quite resolved to succeed or fail together—as much after the calamity which had befallen us, as before.

On reaching St. Michael's, we underwent a sort of examination at my master's store, and it was evident to my mind, that Master Thomas suspected the truthfulness of the evidence upon which they had acted in arresting us; and that he only affected, to some extent, the positiveness with which he asserted our guilt. There was nothing said by any of our company, which could, in any manner, prejudice our cause; and there was hope, yet, that we should be able to return to our homes—if for nothing else, at least to find out the guilty man or woman who had betrayed us.

To this end, we all denied that we had been guilty of intended flight. Master Thomas said that the evidence he had of our intention to run away, was strong enough to hang us, in a case of murder. "But," said I, "the cases are not equal. If murder were committed, some one must have committed it—the thing is done! In our case, nothing has been done! We have not run away. Where is the evidence against us?

We were quietly at our work." I talked thus, with unusual freedom, to bring out the evidence against us, for we all wanted, above all things, to know the guilty wretch who had betrayed us, that we might have something tangible upon which to pour our execrations. From something which dropped, in the course of the talk, it appeared that there was but one witness against us—and that that witness could not be produced. Master Thomas would not tell us *who* his informant was; but we suspected, and suspected *one* person *only.* Several circumstances seemed to point SANDY out, as our betrayer. His entire knowledge of our plans—his participation in them—his withdrawal from us—his dream, and his simultaneous presentiment that we were betrayed—the taking us, and the leaving him—were calculated to turn suspicion toward him; and yet, we could not suspect him. We all loved him too well to think it *possible* that he could have betrayed us. So we rolled the guilt on other shoulders.

Disregard of human life

I speak advisedly when I say this,—that killing a slave, or any colored person, in Talbot county, Maryland, is not treated as a crime, either by the courts or the community. Mr. Thomas Lanman, ship carpenter, of St. Michael's, killed two slaves, one of whom he butchered with a hatchet, by knocking his brains out. He used to boast of the commission of the awful and bloody deed. I have heard him do so, laughingly, saying, among other things, that he was the only benefactor of his country in the company, and that when "others would do as much as he had done, we should be relieved of the d—d niggers."

As an evidence of the reckless disregard of human life—where the life is that of a slave—I may state the notorious fact, that the wife of Mr. Giles Hicks, who lived but a short distance from Col. Lloyd's, with her own hands murdered my wife's cousin, a young girl between fifteen and sixteen years of age—mutilating her person in a most shocking manner. The atrocious woman, in the paroxysm of her wrath, not content with murdering her victim, literally mangled her face, and broke her breast bone. Wild, however, and infuriated as she was, she took the precaution to cause the slave-girl to be buried; but the facts of the case coming abroad, very speedily led to the disinterment of the remains of the murdered slave-girl. A coroner's jury was assembled, who decided that the girl had come to her death by severe beating. It was ascertained that the offense for which this girl was thus hurried out of the world, was this: she had been set that night, and several preceding nights, to mind Mrs. Hicks's baby, and having fallen into a sound sleep, the baby cried, waking Mrs. Hicks, but not the slave-girl. Mrs. Hicks, becoming infuriated at the girl's tardiness, after calling her several times, jumped from her bed and seized a piece of fire-wood from the fireplace; and then, as she lay fast asleep, she deliberately pounded in her skull and breast-bone, and thus ended her life. I will not say that this most horrid murder produced no sensation in the community. It *did* produce a sensation; but, incredible to tell, the moral sense of the community was blunted too entirely by the ordinary nature of slavery horrors, to bring the murderess to punishment. A warrant was issued for her arrest, but, for some reason or other, that warrant was never served. Thus did Mrs. Hicks not only escape condign punishment, but even the pain and mortification of being arraigned before a court of justice.

Whilst I am detailing the bloody deeds that took place during my stay on Col. Lloyd's plantation, I will briefly narrate another dark transaction, which occurred about the same time as the murder of Denby by Mr. Gore.

On the side of the river Wye, opposite from Col. Lloyd's, there lived a Mr. Beal Bondley, a wealthy slaveholder. In the direction of his land, and near the shore, there was an excellent oyster fishing ground, and to this, some of the slaves of Col. Lloyd occasionally resorted in their little canoes, at night, with a view to make up the deficiency of their scanty allowance of food, by the oysters that they could easily get there. This, Mr. Bondley took it into his head to regard as a tresspass, and while an old man belonging to Col. Lloyd was engaged in catching a few of the many millions of oysters that lined the bottom of that creek, to satisfy his hunger, the villainous Mr. Bondley, lying in ambush, without the slightest ceremony, discharged the contents of his musket into the back and shoulders of the poor old man. As good fortune would have it, the shot did not prove mortal, and Mr. Bondley came over, the next day, to see Col. Lloyd—whether to pay him for his property, or to justify himself for what he had done, I know not; but this I *can* say, the cruel and dastardly transaction was speedily hushed up; there was very little said about it at all, and nothing was publicly done which looked like the application of the principle of justice to the man whom *chance*, only, saved from being an actual murderer. One of the commonest sayings to which my ears early became accustomed, on Col. Lloyd's plantation and elsewhere in Maryland, was, that it was *"worth but half a cent to kill a nigger, and a half a cent to bury him;"* and the facts of my experience go far to justify the practical truth of this strange proverb. Laws for the protection of the lives of the slaves, are, as they must

needs be, utterly incapable of being enforced, where the very parties who are nominally protected, are not permitted to give evidence, in courts of law, against the only class of persons from whom abuse, outrage and murder might be reasonably apprehended. While I heard of numerous murders committed by slave-holders on the Eastern Shore of Maryland, I never knew a solitary instance in which a slaveholder was either hung or imprisoned for having murdered a slave. The usual pretext for killing a slave is, that the slave has offered resistance. Should a slave, when assaulted, but raise his hand in self-defense, the white assaulting party is fully justified by southern, or Maryland, public opinion, in shooting the slave down. Sometimes this is done, simply because it is alleged that the slave has been saucy. But here I leave this phase of the society of my early childhood, and will relieve the kind reader of these heart-sickening details.

Editor's Note:

Holidays in the United States have traditionally excluded the contributions of any people other than Anglo-Americans. In the final selection, Douglass poignantly expresses the feelings of countless black voices that have long been silent but who share with him this feeling of exclusion from so much that white America takes for granted.

WHAT TO THE SLAVE IS THE FOURTH OF JULY?

FREDERICK DOUGLASS

Fellow citizens:

Pardon me, and allow me to ask, why am I called upon to speak here today? What have I or those I represent to do with your national independence? Are the great principles of political freedom and of natural justice, embodied in that Declaration of Independence, extended to us? And am I, therefore, called upon to bring our humble offering to the national altar, and to confess the benefits, and express devout gratitude for the blessings resulting from your independence to us?

Would to God, both for your sakes and ours, that an affirmative answer could be truthfully returned to these questions. Then would my task be light, and my burden easy and delightful. For who is there so cold that a nation's sympathy could not warm him? Who so obdurate and dead to the claims of gratitude, that would not thankfully acknowledge such priceless benefits? Who so stolid and selfish that would not give his voice to swell the hallelujahs of a nation's jubilee, when the chains of servitude had been torn from his limbs? I am not that man.

...I say it with a sad sense of disparity between us. I am not included within the pale of this glorious anniversary! Your high independence only reveals the immeasurable distance between us. The blessings in which you this day rejoice are not enjoyed in common. The rich inheritance of justice, liberty, prosperity, and independence bequeathed by your fathers is shared by you, not by me. The sunlight that brought life and healing to you has brought stripes and death to me. This Fourth of July is *yours*, not *mine. You* may rejoice, *I* must mourn. To drag a man in fetters into the grand illuminated temple of liberty, and call upon him to join you in joyous anthems, were inhuman mockery and sacrilegious irony. Do you mean, citizens, to mock me, by asking me to speak today? If so, there is a parallel to your conduct. And let me warn you, that it is dangerous to copy the example of a nation whose crimes, towering up to heaven, were thrown down by the breath of the Almighty, burying that nation in irrecoverable ruin. I can today take up the lament of a peeled and woe-smitten people.

"By the rivers of Babylon, there we sat down. Yes! We wept when we remembered Zion. We hanged our harps upon the willows in the midst thereof. For there they that carried us away captive, required of us a song; and they who wasted us, required of us mirth, saying, Sing us one of the songs of Zion. How can we sing the Lord's song in a strange land? If I forget thee, O Jerusalem, let my right hand forget her cunning. If I do not remember thee, let my tongue cleave to the roof of my mouth."

Fellow citizens, above your national, tumultuous joy, I hear the mournful wail of millions, whose chains, heavy and grievous yesterday, are today rendered more intolerable by the jubilant shouts that reach them. If I do forget, if I do not remember those bleeding children of sorrow this day, "may my right hand forget her cunning, and may my tongue cleave to the roof of my mouth!" To forget them, to pass lightly over their wrongs, and to chime in with the popular theme, would be treason most scandalous and shocking, and would make me a reproach before God and the world. My subject, then, fellow citizens, is "American Slavery." I shall see this day and its popular characteristics from the slave's point of view. Standing here, identified with the American bondman, making his wrongs mine, I do not hesitate to declare, with all my soul, that the character and conduct of this nation never looked blacker to me than on this Fourth of July. Whether we turn to the declarations of the past, or to the professions of the present, the conduct of the nation seems equally hideous and revolting. America is false to the past, false to the present, and solemnly binds herself to be false to the future. Standing with God and the crushed and bleeding slave on this occasion, I will, in the name of humanity, which is outraged, in the name of liberty, which is fettered, in the name of the Constitution and the Bible, which are disregarded and trampled upon, dare to call in question and to denounce, with all the emphasis I can command, everything that serves to perpetuate slavery—the great sin and shame of America! "I will not equivocate; I will not excuse"; I will use the severest language I can command, and yet not one word shall escape me that any man, whose judgment is not blinded by prejudice, or who is not at heart a slave-holder, shall not confess to be right and just.

But I fancy I hear some of my audience say it is just in this circumstance that you and your brother Abolitionists fail to make a favorable impression on the public mind. Would you argue more and denounce less, would you persuade more and rebuke less, your cause would be much more likely to succeed. But, I submit, where all is plain there is nothing to be argued. What point in the anti-slavery creed would you have me argue? On what branch of the subject do the people of this country need light? Must I undertake to prove that the slave is a man? That point is conceded already. Nobody doubts it. The slave-holders themselves acknowledge it in the enactment of laws for their government. They acknowledge it when they punish disobedience on the part of the slave. There are seventy-two crimes in the State of Virginia, which, if committed by a black man (no matter how ignorant he be), subject him to the punishment of death; while only two of these same crimes will subject a white man to like punishment. What is this but the acknowledgement that the slave is a moral, intellectual, and responsible being? The manhood of the slave is conceded. It is admitted in the fact that Southern statute-books are covered with enactments, forbidding, under severe fines and penalties, the teaching of the slave to read and write. When you can point to any such laws in reference to the beasts of the field, then I may consent to argue the manhood of the slave. When the dogs in your streets, when the fowls of the air, when the cattle on your hills, when the fish of the sea, and the reptiles that crawl, shall be unable to distinguish the slave from a brute, then I will argue with you that the slave is a man!

For the present it is enough to affirm the equal manhood of the Negro race. Is it not astonishing that, while we are plowing, planting, and reaping, using all kinds of mechanical tools, erecting houses, constructing bridges, building ships, working in metals of brass, iron, copper, silver, and gold; that while we are reading, writing and cyphering, acting as clerks, merchants, and secretaries, having among us lawyers, doctors, ministers, poets, authors, editors, orators, and teachers; that while we are engaged in all the enterprises common to other men—digging gold in California, capturing the whale in the Pacific, feeding sheep and cattle on the hillside, living, moving, acting, thinking, planning, living in families as husbands, wives, and children, and above all, confessing and worshipping the Christian God, and looking hopefully for life and immortality beyond the grave—we are called upon to prove that we are men?

Would you have me argue that man is entitled to liberty? That he is the rightful owner of his own body? You have already declared it. Must I argue the wrongfulness of slavery? Is that a question for republicans? Is it to be settled by the rules of logic and argumentation, as a matter beset with great difficulty, involving a doubtful application of the principle of justice, hard to understand? How should I look today in the presence of Americans, dividing and subdividing a discourse, to show that men have a natural right to freedom, speaking of it relatively and positively, negatively and affirmatively? To do so would be to make myself ridiculous, and to offer an insult to your understanding. There is not a man beneath the canopy of heaven who does not know that slavery is wrong *for him.*

What! Am I to argue that it is wrong to make men brutes, to rob them of their liberty, to work them without wages, to keep them ignorant of their relations to their fellow men, to beat them with sticks, to flay their flesh with the lash, to load their limbs with irons, to hunt them with dogs, to sell them at auction, to sunder their families, to knock out their teeth, to burn their flesh, to starve them into obedience and submission to their masters? Must I argue that a system thus marked with blood and stained with pollution is wrong? No; I will not. I have better employment for my time and strength than such arguments would imply.

What, then, remains to be argued? Is it that slavery is not divine; that God did not establish it; that our doctors of divinity are mistaken? There is blasphemy in the thought. That which is inhuman cannot be divine. Who can reason on such a proposition? They that can, may; I cannot. The time for such argument is past.

At a time like this, scorching irony, not convincing argument, is needed. Oh! had I the ability, and could I reach the nation's ear, I would today pour out a fiery stream of biting ridicule, blasting reproach, withering sarcasm, and stern rebuke. For it is not light that is needed, but fire; it is not the gentle shower, but thunder. We need the storm, the whirlwind, and the earthquake. The feeling of the nation must be quickened; the conscience of the nation must be roused; the propriety of the nation must be startled; the hypocrisy of the nation must be exposed; and its crimes against God and man must be denounced.

What to the American slave is your Fourth of July? I answer, a day that reveals to him more than all other days of the year, the gross injustice and cruelty to which he is the constant victim. To him your celebration is a sham; your boasted liberty an unholy license; your national greatness, swelling vanity; your sounds of rejoicing are empty and heartless; your denunciation of tyrants, brass-fronted impudence; your shouts of liberty and equality, hollow mockery; your prayers and hymns, your sermons and thanksgivings, with all your religious parade and solemnity, are to him mere bombast, fraud, deception, impiety, and hypocrisy—a thin veil to cover up crimes which would disgrace a nation of savages . . . .

Editor's Note:

Interviews with former slaves were conducted by the Federal Writers Project from 1936 to 1938. In 1941 the Library of Congress WPA Project for the District of Columbia arranged these typewritten records by state. These slave narratives are an excellent primary source for reconstruction of daily events in the slave community. The following selections exhibit a range of experience from humor to tragedy.

SLAVE NARRATIVES

A bit of humor

I remember Mammy told me about one master who almost starved his slaves. Mighty stingy, I reckon he was.

Some of them slaves was so poorly thin they ribs would kinda rustle against each other like corn stalks a-drying in the hot winds. But they gets even one hog-killing time, and it was funny, too, Mammy said.

They was seven hogs, fat and ready for fall hog-killing time. Just the day before Old Master told off they was to be killed, something happened to all them porkers. One of the field boys found them and come a-telling the master: "The hogs is all died, now they won't be any meats for the winter."

When the master gets to where at the hogs is laying, they's a lot of Negroes standing round looking sorrow-eyed at the wasted meat. The master asks: "What's the illness with 'em?"

"Malitis," they tells him, and they acts like they don't want to touch the hogs. Master says to dress them anyway for they ain't no more meat on the place.

He says to keep all the meat for the slave families, but that's because he's afraid to eat it hisself account of the hogs' got malitis.

"Don't you all know what is malitis?" Mammy would ask the children when she was telling of the seven fat hogs and seventy lean slaves. And she would laugh, remembering how they fooled Old Master so's to get all them good meats.

"One of the strongest Negroes got up early in the morning," Mammy would explain, "long 'fore the rising horn called the slaves from their cabins. He skitted to the hog pen with a heavy mallet in his hand. When he tapped Mister Hog 'tween the eyes with that mallet, 'malitis' set in mighty quick, but it was a uncommon 'disease,' even with hungry Negroes around all the time."

Patrols — "Padderollers"*

They had what you call patrollers who would catch you from home and wear you out and send you back to your master. If a master had slaves he just could not rule (some of 'em was hard and just would not mind the boss), he would ask him if he wanted to go to another plantation and if he said he did, then he would give him a pass, and that pass would read: "Give this nigger hell." Of course, when the patrollers or other plantation boss would read the pass, he would beat him nearly to death and send him back. Of course, the nigger could not read and did not know what the pass said. You see, they did not 'low no nigger to have a book or piece of paper of any

kind, and you know they was not going to teach any of 'em to read.

●　　●　　●

There was one woman owns some slaves and one of 'em asks her for a pass, and she give him the piece of paper supposed to be the pass, but she writes on it:

His shirt am rough and his back am tough,
Do, pray, Mr. Paddleroller, give him enough.

The paddlerollers beat him nearly to death, 'cause that's what's wrote on the paper he give 'em.

Superstitions

Ef a dog turns on his back and howls, 'tis a sign of death.

●　　●　　●

Ef yer drops a dish rag on de floor and it spreads out, 'tis de sign dat a hungry woman is gwine ter come to yer house. Ef de rag don't spread out den a hungry man is coming.

●　　●　　●

Ef a black cat crosses yer path going to de right, 'tis good luck. Ef de cat goes to de left, 'tis bad luck.

●　　●　　●

Ef a girl walks aroung wif one shoe off and one on, she'll stay single many years as de number of steps she taken.

Wasn't scared of nothing

I was scared of Marse Jordan, and all of the grown niggers was too, 'cept Leonard and Burrus Allen. Them niggers wasn't scared of nothing. If the devil hisself had come and shook a stick at them, they'd hit him back. Leonard was a big black buck nigger; he was the biggest nigger I ever seed. And Burrus was near 'bout as big. And they 'spised Marse Jordan worse'n pizen.

I was sort of scared of Miss Sally too. When Marse Jordan wasn't round she was sweet and kind, but when he was round she was a yes-sir, yes-sir woman. Everything he told her to do she done. He made her slap Mammy one time 'cause when she

---

*Every slave state had a system of patrols to monitor unlawful assemblies, arrest slaves visiting other plantations, and runaways. All eligible males had to serve in this role for a specified number of nights during the month. (Ed.)

passed his coffee she spilled some in the saucer. Miss Sally hit Mammy easy, but Marse Jordan say: "Hit her, Sally, hit the black bitch like she 'zerve to be hit. Then Miss Sally draw back her hand and hit Mammy in the face, pow! then she went back to her place at the table and play like she eating her breakfast. Then when Marse Jordan leave, she come in the kitchen and put her arms round Mammy and cry, and Mammy pat her on the back, and she cry too. I loved Miss Sally when Marse Jordan wasn't round.

Marse Jordan's two sons went to the war; they went all dressed up in they fighting clothes. Young Marse Jordan was just like Miss Sally, but Marse Gregory was like Marse Jordan, even to the bully way he walk. Young Marse Jordan never come back from the war, but 'twould take more than a bullet to kill Marse Gregory. He too mean to die anyhow 'cause the devil didn't want him and the Lord wouldn't have him.

One day Marse Gregory come home on a furlough. He think he look pretty with his sword clanking and his boots shining. He was a colonel, lieutenant, or something. He was strutting round the yard showing off, when Leonard Allen say under his breath, "Look at that goddam soldier. He fighting to keep us niggers from being free."

'Bout that time Marse Jordan come up. He look at Leonard and say, "What you mumbling 'bout?"

That big Leonard wasn't scared. He say, "I say, 'Look at that goddam soldier. He fighting to keep us niggers from being free.'"

Marse Jordan's face begun to swell. It turned so red that the blood near 'bout bust out. He turned to Pappy and told him to go and bring him his shotgun. When Pappy come back, Miss Sally come with him. The tears was streaming down her face. She run up to Marse Jordan and caught his arm. Old Marse flung her off and took the gun from Pappy. He leveled it on Leonard and told him to pull his shirt open. Leonard opened his shirt and stood there big as a black giant, sneering at Old Marse.

Then Miss Sally run up again and stood 'tween that gun and Leonard.

Old Marse yell to Pappy and told him to take that woman out of the way, but nobody ain't moved to touch Miss Sally, and she didn't move neither; she just stood there facing Old Marse. Then Old Marse let down the gun. He reached over and slapped Miss Sally down, then picked up the gun and shot a hole in Leonard's chest big as your fist. Then he took up Miss Sally and toted her in the house. But I was so scared that I run and hid in the stable loft, and even with my eyes shut I could see Leonard laying on the ground with that bloody hole in his chest and that sneer on his black mouth.

Past a hundred and four years old

My name is Tines Kendricks. I was borned in Crawford County, Georgia. You see, boss, I is a little nigger, and I really is more smaller now than I used to be when I was young 'cause I so old and stooped over. I mighty nigh wore out from all these hard years of work and serving the Lord. My actual name what was give to me by my white folks, the Kendricks, was "Tiny." They called me that 'cause I never was no size much. After us all sot free I just changed my name to "Tines," and that's what I been going by for nigh on to ninety years.

'Cording to what I 'member 'bout it, boss, I is now past a hundred and four year old this past July the fourth, two hours before day. What I means is what I 'member 'bout what the old marse told me that time I comed back to the home place after the war quit, and he say that I past thirty then. My mammy, she said I born two hours before day on the Fourth of July. That what they told me, boss. I is been in good health all my days. I ain't never been sick any in my life 'scusing these last years when I git so old and feeble and stiff in the joints, and my teeth 'gin to cave, and my old bones, they 'gin to ache. But I just keep on living and trusting in the Lord 'cause the Good Book say, "Wherefore the evil days come and the darkness of the night draw nigh, your strength, it shall not perish. I will lift you up 'mongst them what 'bides with me." That is the Gospel, boss.

My old marse, he was named Arch Kendricks, and us lived on the plantation what the Kendricks had not far from Macon in Crawford County, Georgia. You can see, boss, that I is a little bright and got some white blood in me. That is 'counted for on my mammy's side of the family. Her pappy, he was a white man. He wasn't no Kendrick though. He was a overseer. That what my mammy she say, and then I know that wasn't no Kendrick mixed up in nothing like that. They didn't believe in that kind of business. My old marse, Arch Kendricks, I will say this, he certainly was a good fair man. Old Miss and the young marse, Sam, they was strictly tough and, boss, I is telling you the truth, they was cruel. The young marse, Sam, he never taken at all after he pa. He got all he meanness from Old Miss, and he sure got plenty of it, too. Old Miss, she cuss and rare worse'n a man. 'Way 'fore day she be up hollering loud enough for to be heared two miles, 'rousing the niggers out for to git in the fields ever 'fore light. Marse Sam, he stand by the pots handing out the grub and giving out the bread, and he cuss loud and say: "Take a sop of that grease on your hoecake and move along fast 'fore I lashes you." Marse Sam, he was a big man too, that he was. He was nigh on to six and a half feet tall. Boss, he certainly was a child of the devil. All the cooking in them days was done in pots hanging on the pot racks. They never had no stoves enduring the times what I is telling you 'bout. At times they would give us enough to eat. At times they wouldn't—just 'cording to how they feeling when they dishing out the grub. The biggest what they would give the field hands to eat would be the truck what us had on the place, like greens, turnips, peas, side meat, and they sure would cut the side meat awful thin too, boss. Us always had a heap of corn-meal dumplings and hoecakes. Old Miss, her and Marse Sam, they real stingy. You better not leave no grub on your plate for to throw away. You sure better eat it all iffen you like it or no. Old Miss and Marse Sam, they the real bosses, and they was wicked. I's telling you the truth, they was. Old Marse, he didn't have much to say 'bout the running of the place or the handling of the niggers. You know, all the property and all the niggers belonged to Old Miss. She got all that from her peoples. That what they left to her on their death. She the real owner of everything.

Just to show you, boss, how 'twas with Marse Sam and how contrary and fractious and wicked that young white man was, I wants to tell you 'bout the time that Aunt Hannah's little boy Mose died. Mose, he sick 'bout a week. Aunt Hannah, she try to doctor on him and git him well, and she tell Old Miss that she think Mose bad off and ought to have the doctor. Old Miss she wouldn't git the doctor. She say Mose ain't sick much, and, bless my soul, Aunt Hannah she right. In a few days from then Mose is dead. Marse Sam, he come cussing and told Gabe to get some planks and make the coffin and sont some of them to dig the grave over there on the far side of the place where they had a burying-ground for the niggers. Us toted the coffin over to where the grave was dug and gwine bury little Mose there, and Uncle Billy Jordan, he was there and begun to sing and pray and have a kind of funeral at the burying. Everyone was moaning and singing and praying, and Marse Sam heard 'em and come sailing over there on he hoss and lit right in to cussing and raring and say that if they don't hurry and bury that nigger and shut up that singing and carrying on, he gwine lash every one of them, and then he went to cussing worser and 'busing Uncle Billy Jordan. He say iffen he ever hear of him doing any more preaching or praying round 'mongst the niggers at the graveyard or anywheres else, he gwine lash him to death. No, sir, boss, Marse Sam wouldn't even 'low no preaching or singing or nothing like that. He was wicked. I tell you he was.

Old Miss, she generally looked after the niggers when they sick and give them the medicine. And, too, she would get the doctor iffen she think they real bad off 'cause like I said, Old Miss, she mighty stingy, and she never want to lose no nigger by them dying. Howsomever, it was hard sometime to get her to believe you sick when you tell her that you was, and she would think you just playing off from work. I have seen niggers what would be mighty near dead before Old Miss would believe them sick at all.

Before the war broke out, I can 'member there was some few of the white folks what said that niggers ought to be sot free, but there was just one now and then that took that stand. One of them that I 'member was the Rev. Dickey what was the parson for a big crowd of the white peoples in that part of the county. Rev. Dickey, he preached freedom for the niggers and say that they all should be sot free and gived a home and a mule. That preaching the Rev. Dickey done sure did rile up the folks—that is, the most of them, like the Kendricks and Mr. Eldredge and Dr. Murcheson and Nat Walker and such as them what was the biggest of the slaveowners. Right away after Rev. Dickey done such preaching, they fired him from the church and 'bused him, and some of them say they gwine hang him to a limb or either gwine ride him on a rail out of the country. Sure enough, they made it so hot on that man he have to leave clean out of the state, so I heared. No, sir, boss, they say they ain't gwine divide up no land with the niggers or give them no home or mule or their freedom or nothing. They say they will wade knee deep in blood and die first.

•   •   •

It was this way, boss, how come me to be in the war. You see, they 'quired all of the slaveowners to send so many niggers to the army to work digging the trenches and throwing up the breastworks and repairing the railroads what the Yankees done 'stroyed. Every marse was 'quired to send one nigger for every ten that he had. Iffen you had a hundred niggers, you had to send ten of them to the army. I was one of them that my marse 'quired to send. That was the worst times that this here nigger ever seen, and the way them white men drive us niggers, it was something awful. The strap, it was going from 'fore day till 'way after night. The niggers, heaps of 'em, just fall in they tracks—give out—and them white men laying the strap on they backs without ceasting. That was 'zackly way it was with them niggers like me what was in the army work. I had to stand it, boss, till the war was over.

That sure was a bad war that went on in Georgia. That it was. Did you ever hear 'bout the Andersonville prison in Georgia? I tell you, boss, that was 'bout the worstest place that ever I seen. That was where they keep all the Yankees that they capture, and they had so many there they couldn't nigh take care of them. They had them fenced up with a tall wire fence and never had enough houseroom for all them Yankees. They would just throw the grub to 'em. The mostest that they had for 'em to eat was peas, and the filth, it was terrible. The sickness, it broke out 'mongst 'em all the while, and they just die like rats what been pizened. The first thing that the Yankees do when they take the state 'way from the Confederates was to free all them what in the prison at Andersonville.

Slavery time was tough, boss. You just don't know how tough it was. I can't 'splain to you just how bad all the niggers want to get they freedom. With the free niggers it was just the same as it was with them that was in bondage. You know there was some few free niggers in that time even 'fore the slaves taken outen bondage. It was really worse on them than it was with them what wasn't free. The slaveowners, they just despised them free niggers and make it just as hard on them as they can. They couldn't get no work from nobody. Wouldn't ary man hire 'em or give 'em any work at all. So because they was up against it and never had any money or nothing, the white folks make these free niggers 'sess the taxes. And 'cause they never had no money for to pay the tax with, they was put up on the block by the court man or the sheriff and sold out to somebody for enough to pay the tax what they say they owe. So they keep these free niggers hired out all the time 'most, working for to pay the taxes. I 'member one of them free niggers mighty well. He was called Free Sol. He had him a little home and a old woman and some boys. They was kept bounded out nigh 'bout all the time working for to pay they tax. Yes, sir, boss, it was heap more better to be a slave nigger than a free one. And it was really a heavenly day when the freedom come for the race.

In the time of slavery another thing what make it tough on the niggers was them times when a man and he wife and their children had to be taken 'way from one another. This separation might be brung 'bout 'most any time for one thing or another, such as one or t'other, the man or the wife, be sold off or taken 'way to some other state like Louisiana or Mississippi. Then when a marse die what had a heap of slaves, these slave niggers be divided up 'mongst the marse's children or sold off for to pay the marse's debts. Then at times when a man married to a woman that don't belong to the same marse what he do, then they is liable to git divided up and separated 'most any day. They was heaps of nigger families that I

know what was separated in the time of bondage that tried to find they folkses what was gone. But the mostest of 'em never git together again even after they sot free 'cause they don't know where one or the other is.

After the war over and the slaves taken out of they bondage, some of the very few white folks give them niggers what they liked the best a small piece of land for to work. But the mostest of them never give 'em nothing, and they sure despise them niggers what left 'em. Us old marse say he want to 'range with all his niggers to stay on with him, that he gwine give 'em a mule and a piece-a ground. But us know that Old Miss ain't gwine agree to that. And sure enough she wouldn't. I's telling you the truth, every nigger on that place left. They sure done that; and Old Marse and Old Miss, they never had a hand left there on that great big place, and all that ground laying out.

The government seen to it that all of the white folks had to make contracts with the niggers that stuck with 'em, and they was sure strict 'bout that too. The white folks at first didn't want to make the contracts and say they wasn't gwine to. So the government filled the jail with 'em, and after that everyone make the contract.

When my race first got they freedom and begin to leave they marses, a heap of the marses got raging mad and just tore up truck. They say they gwine kill every nigger they find. Some of them did do that very thing, boss, sure enough. I's telling you the truth. They shot niggers down by the hundreds. They just wasn't gwine let 'em enjoy their freedom. That is the truth, boss.

After I come back to the old home place from working for the army, it wasn't long 'fore I left there and git me a job with a sawmill and worked for the sawmill peoples for 'bout five years. One day I heared some niggers telling 'bout a white man what done come in there gitting up a big lot of niggers to take to Arkansas. They was telling 'bout what a fine place it was in Arkansas and how rich the land is and that the crops grow without working, and that the 'taters grow big as a watermelon and you never have to plant 'em but the one time, and all such as that. Well, I 'cided to come. I joined up with the man and come to Phillips County in 1875. A heap-a niggers come from Georgia at the same time that me and Callie come. You know Callie, that's my old woman what's in the shack there right now. Us first lived on Mr. Jim Bush's place over close to Barton. Us ain't been far off from there ever since us first landed in this county. Fact is, boss, us ain't been outen the county since us first come here, and us gwine be here now, I know, till the Lord call for us to come on home.

A hard time

Boss, I's born in Georgia, in Norcross, and I's ninety years old. My father's name was Roger Stielszen, and my mother's name was Betty. Massa Earl Stielszen captures them in Africa and brung them to Georgia. He got kilt, and my sister and me went to his son. His son was a killer. He got in trouble there in Georgia and got him two good-stepping hosses and the covered wagon. Then he chains all he slaves round the necks and fastens the chains to the hosses and makes them walk all the way to Texas. My mother and my sister had to walk. Emma was my sister. Somewhere on the road it went to snowing, and Massa wouldn't let us wrap anything around our feet. We had to sleep on the ground, too, in all that snow.

Massa have a great, long whip platted out of rawhide, and when one the niggers fall behind or give out, he hit him with that whip. It take the hide every time he hit a nigger. Mother, she give out on the way, 'bout the line of Texas. Her feet got raw and bleeding, and her legs swoll plumb out of shape. Then Massa, he just take out he gun and shot her, and whilst she lay dying he kicks her two-three times and say, "Damn a nigger what can't stand nothing." Boss, you know that man, he wouldn't bury mother, just leave her laying where he shot her at. You know, then there wasn't no law 'gainst killing nigger slaves.

He come plumb to Austin through that snow. He taken up farming and changes he name to Alex Simpson and changes our names, too. He cut logs and builded he home on the side of them mountains. We never had no quarters. When nighttime come, he locks the chain round our necks and then locks it round a tree. Boss, our bed were the ground. All he feed us was raw meat and green corn. Boss, I et many a green weed. I was hungry. He never let us eat at noon, he worked us all day without stopping. We went naked, that the way he worked us. We never had any clothes.

He brands us. He brand my mother before us left Georgia. Boss, that nearly kilt her. He brand her in the breast, then between the shoulders. He brand all us.

My sister, Emma, was the only woman he have till he marries. Emma was wife of all seven Negro slaves. He sold her when she's 'bout fifteen, just before her baby was born. I never seen her since.

Boss, Massa was a outlaw. He come to Texas and deal in stolen hosses. Just before he's hung for stealing hosses, he marries a young Spanish gal. He sure mean to her. Whips her 'cause she want him to leave he slaves alone and live right. Bless her heart, she's the best gal in the world. She was the best thing God ever put life in, in the world. She cry and cry every time Massa go off. She let us a-loose, and she feed us good one time while he's gone. Missy Selena, she turn us a-loose, and we wash in the creek clost by. She just fasten the chain on us and give us great big pot cooked meat and corn, and up he rides. Never says a word but come to see what us eating. He pick up he whip and whip her till she falls. If I could have got a-loose I'd kilt him. I swore if I ever got a-loose I'd kill him. But before long after that he fails to come home, and some people finds him hanging to a tree. Boss, that long after war time he got hung. He didn't let us free. We wore chains all the time. When we work, we drug them chains with us. At night he lock us to a tree to keep us from running off. He didn't have to do that. We were 'fraid to run. We knew he'd kill us. Besides, he brands us, and they no way to git it off. It's put there with a hot iron. You can't git it off.

If a slave die, Massa made the rest of us tie a rope round he feet and drag him off. Never buried one, it was too much trouble.

Massa always say he be rich after the war. He stealing all the time. He have a whole mountainside where he keep he stock. Missy Selena tell us one day we s'posed to be free, but he didn't turn us a-loose. It was 'bout three years after the war they hung him. Missy turned us a-loose.

I had a hard time then. All I had to eat was what I could find and steal. I was 'fraid of everybody. I just went wild and to the woods, but, thank God, a bunch of men taken they dogs and run me down. They carry me to they place. General Houston had some niggers, and he made them feed me. He made them keep me till I git well and able to work. Then he give me a job. I marry one the gals before I leaves them. I'm plumb out of place there at my own wedding. Yes, sir, boss, it wasn't one year before that I'm the wild nigger. We had thirteen children.

I farms all my life after that. I didn't know nothing else to do.

The Klan

I never will forgit when they hung Cy Guy. They hung him for a scandalous insult to a white woman, and they comed after him a hundred strong.

They tries him there in the woods, and they scratches Cy's arm to git some blood, and with that blood they writes that he shall hang 'tween the heavens and the earth till he am dead, dead, dead, and that any nigger what takes down the body shall be hunged too.

29

Well, sir, the next morning there he hung, right over the road, and the sentence hanging over his head. Nobody'd bother with that body for four days, and there it hung, swinging in the wind, but the fourth day the sheriff comes and takes it down.

There was Ed and Cindy, who 'fore the war belonged to Mr. Lynch, and after the war he told 'em to move. He gives 'em a month, and they ain't gone, so the Ku Kluxes gits 'em.

It was on a cold night when they comed and drugged the niggers outen bed. They carried 'em down in the woods and whup them, then they throws 'em in the pond, their bodies breaking the ice. Ed come out and come to our house, but Cindy ain't been seed since.

Sam Allen in Caswell County was told to move, and after a month the hundred Ku Klux come a-toting his casket, and they tells him that his time has come and iffen he want to tell his wife goodbye and say his prayers hurry up.

They set the coffin on two chairs, and Sam kisses his old woman who am a-crying, then he kneels down side of his bed with his head on the pillow and his arms throwed out front of him.

He sets there for a minute and when he riz he had a long knife in his hand. 'Fore he could be grabbed he done kill two of the Ku Kluxes with the knife, and he done gone outen the door. They ain't catch him neither, and the next night when they comed back, 'termined to git him, they shot another nigger by accident.

I know one time Miss Hendon inherits a thousand dollars from her pappy's 'state, and that night she goes with her sweetheart to the gate, and on her way back to the house she gits knocked in the head with a axe. She screams, and her two nigger servants, Jim and Sam, runs and saves her, but she am robbed.

Then she tells the folkses that Jim and Sam am the guilty parties, but her little sister swears that they ain't, so they gits out of it.

After that they finds that it am five mens—Atwater, Edwards, Andrews, Davis, and Markham. The preacher comes down to where they am hanging to preach their funeral, and he stands there while lightning plays round the dead men's heads and the wind blows the trees, and he preaches such a sermon as I ain't never heard before.

Bob Boylan falls in love with another woman, so he burns his wife and four young-uns up in their house.

The Ku Kluxes gits him, of course, and they hangs him high on the old red oak on the Hillsboro road. After they hunged him, his lawyer says to us boys, "Bury him good, boys, just as good as you'd bury me iffen I was dead."

I shook hands with Bob 'fore they hunged him, and I helped to bury him too, and we bury him nice, and we all hopes that he done gone to glory.

• • •

After us colored folks was 'sidered free and turned loose, the Klu Klux broke out. Some colored people started to farming, like I told you, and gathered the old stock. If they got so they made good money and had a good farm, the Klu Klux would come and murder 'em. The government builded schoolhouses, and the Klu Klux went to work and burned 'em down. They'd go to the jails and take the colored men out and knock their brains out and break their necks and throw 'em in the river.

There was a colored man they taken, his name was Jim Freeman. They taken him and destroyed his stuff and him 'cause he was making some money. Hung him on a tree in his front yard, right in front of his cabin.

There was some colored young men went to the schools they'd opened by the government. Some white woman said someone had stole something of hers, so they put them young men in jail. The Klu Klux went to the jail and took 'em out and killed 'em. That happened the second year after the war.

After the Klu Kluxes got so strong, the colored men got together and made the complaint before the law. The governor told the law to give 'em the old guns in the commissary, what the Southern soldiers had used, so they issued the colored men old muskets and said protect themselves. They got together and organized the militia and had leaders like regular soldiers. They didn't meet 'cept when they heared the Klu Kluxes was coming to get some colored folks. Then they was ready for 'em. They'd hide in the cabins, and then's when they found out who a lot of them Klu Kluxes was, 'cause a lot of 'em was kilt. They wore long sheets and covered the hosses with sheets so you couldn't recognize 'em. Men you thought was your friend was Klu Kluxes, and you'd deal with 'em in stores in the daytime, and at night they'd come out to your house and kill you. I never took part in none of the fights, but I heared the others talk 'bout them, but not where them Klu Klux could hear 'em.

One time they had twelve men in jail, 'cused of robbing white folks. All was white in jail but one, and he was colored. The Klu Kluxes went to the jailor's house and got the jail key and got them men out and carried 'em to the river bridge, in the middle. Then they knocked their brains out and threw 'em in the river.

•   •   •

The Ku Klux got after Uncle Will once. He was a brave man. He had a little mare that was a race horse. Will rode right through the bunch before they ever realized that it was him. He got on the other side of them. She was gone! They kept on after him. They went down to his house one night. He wouldn't run for nothing. He shot two of them, and they went away. Then he was out of ammunition. People urged him to leave, for they knew he didn't have no more bullets; but he wouldn't, and they came back and killed him.

They came down to Hancock County one night, and the boys hid on both sides of the bridge. When they got in the middle of the bridge, the boys commenced to fire on them from both sides, and they jumped into the river. The darkies went on home when they got through shooting at them; but there wasn't no more Ku Klux in Hancock County. The better-thinking white folks got together and stopped it.

The Ku Klux kept the niggers scared. They cowed them down so that they wouldn't go to the polls. I stood there one night when they were counting ballots. I belonged to the County Central Committee. I went in and stood and looked. Our ballot was long; theirs was short. I stood and seen Clait Turner calling their names from our ballots. I went out and got Rube Turner, and then we both went back. They couldn't call the votes that they had put down they had. Rube saw it.

Then they said, "Are you going to contest this?"

Rube said, "Yes." But he didn't because it would have cost too much money. Rube was chairman of the committee.

The Ku Klux did a whole lot to keep the niggers away from the polls in Washington and Baldwin counties. They killed a many a nigger down there.

They hanged a Ku Klux for killing his wife, and he said he didn't mind being hung, but he didn't want a damn nigger to see him die.

But they couldn't keep the niggers in Hancock County away from the polls. There was too many of them.

•   •   •

Does I 'member anything 'bout the Ku Kluxes? Jesus, yes! My old master, the doctor, in going round, say out loud to people that Ku Kluxes was doing some things they ought not to do, by 'storting money out of niggers just 'cause they could.

When he was gone to Union one day, a low-down pair of white men come, with false faces, to the house and ask where Dick Bell was. Miss Nancy say her don't know. They go hunt for him. Dick made a beeline for the house. They pull out hoss pistols, first time, pow! Dick run on, second time, pow! Dick run on, third time, pow! and as Dick reach the front yard the ball from the third shot keel him over like a hit rabbit. Old Miss run out, but they git him. Her say: "I give you five dollars to let him 'lone." They say: "Not 'nough." Her say: "I give you ten dollars." They say: "Not 'nough." Her say: "I give you fifteen dollars." They say: "Not 'nough." Her say: "I give you twenty-five dollars." They take the money and say: "Us'll be back tomorrow for the other Dick." They mean Dick James.

Next day, us see them a-coming again. Dick James done load up the shotgun with buckshot. When they was coming up the front steps, Uncle Dick say to us all in the big house: "Git out the way!" The names of the men us find out afterwards was Bishop and Fitzgerald. They come up the steps, with Bishop in front. Uncle Dick open the door, slap that gun to his shoulder, and pull the trigger. That man Bishop hollers: "Oh, Lordy." He drop dead and lay there till the coroner come. Fitzgerald leap 'way. They bring Dick to jail, try him right in that courthouse over yonder. What did they do with him? Well, when Marse Bill Stanton, Marse Elisha Ragsdale, and Miss Nancy tell 'bout it all from the beginning to the end, the judge tell the jurymen that Dick had a right to protect his home and hisself and to kill that white man, and to turn him loose. That was the end of the Ku Kluxes in Fairfield.

•   •   •

I was pretty good when I was a boy. So I never had any trouble then. I was right smart size when I saw the Ku Klux. They would whip men and women that weren't married and were living together. On the first day of January, they would whip men and boys that didn't have a job. They kept the Negroes from voting. They would whip them. They put up notices: "No niggers to come out to the polls tomorrow." They would run them off of government land which they had homesteaded. Sometimes they would just persuade them not to vote. A Negro like my father, they would say to him, "Now, Brown, you are too good to get messed up. Them other niggers round here ain't worth nothing, but you are, and we don't want to see you get hurt. So you stay 'way from the polls tomorrow." And tomorrow my father would stay away, under the circumstances. They had to depend on the white people for counsel. They didn't know what to do themselves. The other niggers they would threaten them and tell them if they came out they would kill them.

Voting

The darkies and the white folks in Union County had an insurrection over the polls about the year 1888. In them days, when you wanted to put a Republican man in, you didn't have to do much campaigning. They just went to the polls and put him in. Everybody that could vote was Republican. In the fall of 1888 they had a great trouble down there, and some of them got killed. They went around and commanded the Negroes not to go to the polls the next day. Some of the Negroes would tell them, "Well, I am going to the polls tomorrow if I have to crawl." And then some of them would say, "I'd like to know how you going to vote." The nigger would ask right back, "How you going to vote?" The white man would say, "I'm going to vote as I damn please." The nigger would say, "I'm going to do the same thing." That started the trouble.

On Sunday before the election on Monday, they went around through that county in gangs. They shot some few of the Negroes. As the Negroes didn't have no weapons to protect theirselves, they didn't have no chance. In that way, quite a few of the Negroes disbanded their homes and went into different counties and different portions of the state and different states. Henry Goodman, my grandfather, came into Hot Spring County in this way.

Editor's Note:

Slaveholders alleged that slavery was a natural and happy state for the enslaved, but there is limitless evidence that this was not so. The correspondence that follows is an exchange of letters between a slave owner, Mrs. Sarah Logue of Tennessee, and her escaped slave, Rev. J. W. Logue, of Syracuse, New York. The reply from the fugitive clearly indicates his aversion to being chattel.

SLAVE AND MASTER: AN EPISTOLARY EXCHANGE

Master

To Jarm:—I now take my pen to write you a few lines, to let you know how we all are. I am a cripple, but I am still able to get about. The rest of the family are all well. Cherry is as well as common. I write you these lines to let you know the situation we are in,—partly in consequence of your running away and stealing Old Rock, our fine mare. Though we got the mare back, she never was worth much after you took her;—and, as I now stand in need of some funds, I have determined to sell you, and I have had an offer for you, but did not see fit to take it. If you will send me one thousand dollars, and pay for the old mare, I will give up all claim I have to you. Write to me as soon as you get these lines, and let me know if you will accept my proposition. In consequence of your running away, we had to sell Abe and Ann and twelve acres of land; and I want you to send me the money, that I may be able to redeem the land that you was the cause of our selling, and on receipt of the above-named sum of money, I will send you your bill of sale. If you do not comply with my request, I will sell you to some one else, and you may rest assured that the time is not far distant when things will be changed with you. Write to me as soon as you get these lines. Direct your letter to Bigbyville, Maury County, Tennessee. You had better comply with my request.

I understand that you are a preacher. As the Southern people are so bad you had better come and preach to your old acquaintances. I would like to know if you read your Bible. If so, can you tell what will become of the thief if he does not repent? and, if the blind lead the blind, what will the consequence be? I deem it unnecessary to say much more at present. A word to the wise is sufficient. You know where the liar has his part. You know that we reared you as we reared our own children; that you was never-abused, and that shortly before you ran away, when your master asked if you would like to be sold, you said you would not leave him to go with anybody.

Slave

Mrs. Sarah Logue: Yours of the 20th of February [1860] is duly received, and I thank you for it. It is a long time since I heard from my poor old mother, and I am glad to know that she is yet alive, and, as you say, "as well as common." What that means, I don't know. I wish you had said more about her.

You are a woman; but, had you a woman's heart, you never could have insulted a brother by telling him you sold his only remaining brother and sister, because he put himself beyond your power to convert him into money.

You sold my brother and sister, Abe and Ann, and twelve acres of land, you say, because I ran away. Now you have the unutterable meanness to ask me to return and be your miserable chattel, or in lieu thereof, send you $1000 to enable you to redeem the *land*, but not to redeem my poor brother and sister! If I were to send you money, it would be to get my brother and sister, and not that you should get land. You say you are a *cripple*, and doubtless you say it to stir my pity, for you knew I was susceptible in that direction. I do pity you from the bottom of my heart. Nevertheless, I am indignant beyond the power of words to express, that you should be so sunken and cruel as to tear the hearts I love so much all in pieces; that you should be willing to impale and crucify us all, out of compassion for your poor *foot* or *leg*. Wretched woman! Be it known to you that I value my freedom, to say nothing of my mother, brothers and sisters, more than your whole body; more, indeed, than my own life; more than all the lives of all the slaveholders and tyrants under heaven.

You say you have offers to buy me, and that you shall sell me if I do not send you $1000, and in the same breath and almost in the same sentence, you say, "You know we raised you as we did our own children." Woman, did you raise your *own children* for the market? Did you raise them for the whipping-post? Did you raise them to be driven off, bound to a coffle in chains? Where are my poor bleeding brothers and sisters? Can you tell? Who was it that sent them off into sugar and cotton fields, to be kicked and cuffed, and whipped, and to groan and die; and where no kin can hear their groans, or attend and sympathize at their dying bed, or follow in their funeral? Wretched woman! Do you say *you* did not do it? Then I reply, your husband did, and *you* approved the deed—and the very letter you sent me shows that your heart approves it all. Shame on you!

But, by the way, where is your husband? You don't speak of him. I infer, therefore, that he is dead; that he has gone to his great account, with all his sins against my poor family upon his head. Poor man! gone to meet the spirits of my poor, outraged and murdered people, in a world where Liberty and Justice are *Masters*.

But you say I am a thief, because I took the old mare along with me. Have you got to learn that I had a better right to the old mare, as you call her, than Mannasseth Logue had to me? Is it a greater sin for me to steal his horse, than it was for him to rob my mother's cradle, and steal me? If he and you infer that I forfeit all my rights to you, shall not I infer that you forfeit all your rights to me? Have you got to learn that human rights are mutual and reciprocal, and if you take my liberty and life, you forfeit your own liberty and life? Before God and high heaven, is there a law for one man which is not a law for every other man?

If you or any other speculator on my body and rights, wish to know how I regard my rights, they need but come here, and lay their hands on me to enslave me. Did you think to terrify me by presenting the alternative to give my money to you, or give my body to slavery? Then let me say to you, that I meet the proposition with unutterable scorn and contempt. The proposition is an outrage and an insult. I will not budge one hair's breadth. I will not breathe a shorter breath, even to save me from your persecutions. I stand among a free people, who, I thank God, sympathize with my rights, and the rights of mankind; and if your emissaries and venders come here to re-enslave me, and escape the unshrinking vigor of my own right arm, I trust my strong and brave friends, in this city and State, will be my rescuers and avengers.

Editor's Note:

Henry Highland Garnet, a free black whose father had been a slave and whose grandfather had been a Congolese, was a Presbyterian minister and abolitionist. His address to a convention of free blacks, held in Buffalo, New York, in 1843 was a vociferous appeal to his enslaved brethren to revolt. The convention was asked to endorse his sentiments, but the resolution lost by a single vote. Garnet's "call to arms" was not positively received by his fellow abolitionists.

AN ADDRESS TO THE SLAVES OF THE UNITED STATES OF AMERICA

HENRY HIGHLAND GARNET

Your brethren of the North, East, and West have been accustomed to meet together in National Conventions, to sympathize with each other, and to weep over your unhappy condition. In these meetings we have addressed all classes of the free, but we have never, until this time, sent a word of consolation and advice to you. We have been contented in sitting still and mourning over your sorrows, earnestly hoping that before this day your sacred liberty would have been restored. But, we have hoped in vain. Years have rolled on, and tens of thousands have been borne on streams of blood and tears, to the shores of eternity. While you have been oppressed, we have also been partakers with you; nor can we be free while you are enslaved. We, therefore, write to you as being bound with you.

Many of you are bound to us, not only by the ties of a common humanity, but we are connected by the more tender relations of parents, wives, husbands, children, brothers, and sisters, and friends. As such we most affectionately address you.

Slavery has fixed a deep gulf between you and us, and while it shuts out from you the relief and consolation which your friends would willingly render, it affects and persecutes you with a fierceness which we might not expect to see in the fiends of hell. But still the Almighty Father of mercies has left to us a glimmering ray of hope, which shines out like a lone star in a cloudy sky. Mankind are becoming wiser, and better—the oppressor's power is fading, and you, every day, are becoming better informed, and more numerous. Your grievances, brethren, are many. We shall not attempt, in this short address, to present to the world all the dark catalogue of this nation's sins, which have been committed upon an innocent people. Nor is it indeed necessary, for you feel them from day to day, and all the civilized world look upon them with amazement.

Two hundred and twenty-seven years ago, the first of our injured race were brought to the shores of America. They came not with glad spirits to select their homes in the New World. They came not with their own consent, to find an unmolested enjoyment of the blessings of this fruitful soil. The first dealings they had with men calling themselves Christians, exhibited to them the worst features of corrupt and sordid hearts; and convinced them that no cruelty is too great, no villainy and no robbery too abhorrent for even enlightened men to perform, when influenced by avarice and lust. Neither did they come flying upon the wings of Liberty, to a land of freedom. But they came with broken hearts, from their beloved native land, and were doomed to unrequited toil and deep degradation. Nor did the evil of their bondage end at their emancipation by death. Succeeding generations inherited their chains, and millions have come from eternity into time, and have returned again to the world of spirits, cursed and ruined by American slavery.

The propagators of the system, or their immediate ancestors, very soon discovered its growing evil, and its tremendous wickedness, and secret promises were made to destroy it. The gross inconsistency of a people holding slaves, who had themselves "ferried o'er the wave" for freedom's sake, was too apparent to be entirely overlooked. The voice of Freedom cried, "Emancipate yourselves." Humanity supplicated with tears for the deliverance of the children of Africa. Wisdom urged her solemn plea. The bleeding captive plead his innocence, and pointed to Christianity who stood weeping at the cross. Jehovah frowned upon the nefarious institution, and thunderbolts, red with vengeance, struggled to leap forth to blast the guilty wretches who maintained it. But all was in vain. Slavery had stretched its dark wings of death over the land, the Church stood silently by—the priests prophesied falsely, and the people loved to have it so. Its throne is established, and now it reigns triumphant.

Nearly three millions of your fellow-citizens are prohibited by law and public opinion, (which in this country is stronger than law,) from reading the Book of Life. Your intellect has been destroyed as much as possible, and every ray of light they have attempted to shut out from your minds. The oppressors themselves have become involved in the ruin. They have become weak, sensual, and rapacious—they have cursed you—they have cursed themselves—they have cursed the earth which they have trod.

The colonists threw the blame upon England. They said that the mother country entailed the evil upon them, and that they would rid themselves of it if they could. The world thought they were sincere, and the philanthropic pitied them. But time soon tested their sincerity.

In a few years the colonists grew strong, and severed themselves from the British Government. Their independence was declared, and they took their station among the sovereign powers of the earth. The declaration was a glorious document. Sages admired it, and the patriotic of every nation reverenced the God-like sentiments which it contained. When the power of Government returned to their hands, did they emancipate the slaves? No; they rather added new links to our chains. Were they ignorant of the principles of Liberty? Certainly they were not. The sentiments of their revolutionary orators fell in burning eloquence upon their hearts, and with one voice they cried, Liberty or Death. Oh what a sentence was that! It ran from soul to soul like electric fire, and nerved the arm of thousands to fight in the holy cause of Freedom. Among the diversity of opinions that are entertained in regard to physical resistance, there are but a few found to gainsay that stern declaration. We are among those who do not. Slavery! How much misery is comprehended in that single word. What mind is there that does not shrink from its direful effects? Unless the image of God be obliterated from the soul, all men cherish the love of Liberty. The nice discerning political economist does not regard the sacred right more than the untutored African who roams in the wilds of Congo. Nor has the one more right to the full enjoyment of his freedom than the other. In every man's mind the good seeds of liberty are planted, and he who brings his fellow down so low, as to make him contented with a condition of slavery, commits the highest crime against God and man. Brethren, your oppressors aim to do this. They endeavor to make you as much like brutes as possible. When they have blinded the eyes of your mind—when they have embittered the sweet waters of life—then, and not till then, has American slavery done its perfect work.

To such degradation it is sinful in the extreme for you to make voluntary submission. The divine commandments you are in duty bound to reverence and obey. If you do not obey them, you will surely meet with the displeasure of the Almighty. He requires you to love him supremely, and your neighbor as yourself—to keep the Sabbath day holy—to search the Scriptures—and bring up your children with respect for his laws, and to worship no other God but him. But slavery sets all these at nought, and hurls defiance in the face of Jehovah. The forlorn condition in which you are placed, does not destroy your moral obligation to God. You are not certain of heaven, because you suffer yourselves to remain in a state of slavery, where you cannot obey the commandments of the Sovereign of the universe. If the ignorance of slavery is a passport to heaven, then it is a blessing, and no curse, and you should rather desire its perpetuity than its abolition. God will not receive slavery, nor ignorance, nor any other state of mind, for love and obedience to him. Your condition does not absolve you from your moral obligation. The diabolical injustice by which your liberties are cloven down, *neither God, nor angels, or just men, command you to suffer for a single moment. Therefore it is your solemn and imperative duty to use every means, both moral, intellectual, and physical that promises success.* If a band of heathen men should attempt to enslave a race of Christians, and to place their children under the influence of some false religion, surely Heaven would frown upon the men who would not resist such aggression, even to death. If, on the other hand, a band of Christians should attempt to enslave a race of heathen men, and to entail slavery upon them, and to keep them in heathenism in the midst of Christianity, the God of

heaven would smile upon every effort which the injured might make to disenthral themselves.

Brethren, it is as wrong for your lordly oppressors to keep you in slavery, as it was for the man thief to steal our ancestors from the coast of Africa. You should therefore now use the same manner of resistance, as would have been just in our ancestors when the bloody foot-prints of the first remorseless soul-thief was placed upon the shores of our fatherland. The humblest peasant is as free in the sight of God as the proudest monarch that ever swayed a sceptre. Liberty is a spirit sent out from God, and like its great Author, is no respecter of persons.

Brethren, the time has come when you must act for yourselves. It is an old and true saying that, "if hereditary bondmen would be free, they must themselves strike the blow." You can plead your own cause, and do the work of emancipation better than any others. The nations of the world are moving in the great cause of universal freedom, and some of them at least will, ere long, do you justice. The combined powers of Europe have placed their broad seal of disapprobation upon the African slave-trade. But in the slave-holding parts of the United States, the trade is as brisk as ever. They buy and sell you as though you were brute beasts. The North has done much—her opinion of slavery in the abstract is known. But in regard to the South, we adopt the opinion of the *New York Evangelist*—We have advanced so far, that the cause apparently waits for a more effectual door to be thrown open than has been yet. We are about to point out that more effectual door. Look around you, and behold the bosoms of your loving wives heaving with untold agonies! Hear the cries of your poor children! Remember the stripes your fathers bore. Think of the torture and disgrace of your noble mothers. Think of your wretched sisters, loving virtue and purity, as they are driven into concubinage and are exposed to the unbridled lusts of incarnate devils. Think of the undying glory that hangs around the ancient name of Africa—and forget not that you are native born American citizens, and as such, you are justly entitled to all the rights that are granted to the freest. Think how many tears you have poured out upon the soil which you have cultivated with unrequited toil and enriched with your blood; and then go to your lordly enslavers and tell them plainly, that you *are determined to be free.* Appeal to their sense of justice, and tell them that they have no more right to oppress you, than you have to enslave them. Entreat them to remove the grievous burdens which they have imposed upon you, and to remunerate you for your labor. Promise them renewed diligence in the cultivation of the soil, if they will render to you an equivalent for your services. Point them to the increase of happiness and prosperity in the British West Indies since the Act of Emancipation.

Tell them in language which they cannot misunderstand, of the exceeding sinfulness of slavery, and of a future judgment, and of the righteous retributions of an indignant God. Inform them that all you desire is *freedom*, and that nothing else will suffice. Do this, and for ever after cease to toil for the heartless tyrants, who give you no other reward but stripes and abuse. If they then commence the work of death, they, and not you, will be responsible for the consequences. You had better all die—*die immediately*, than live slaves and entail your wretchedness upon your posterity. If you would be free in this generation, here is your only hope. However much you and all of us may desire it, there is not much hope of redemption without the shedding of blood. If you must bleed, let it all come at once—rather *die freemen, than live to be slaves*. It is impossible like the children of Israel, to make a grand exodus from the land of bondage. The Pharaohs are on both sides of the blood-red waters! You cannot move *en masse*, to the dominions of the British Queen—nor can you pass through Florida and overrun Texas, and at last find peace in Mexico. The propagators of American slavery are spending their blood and treasure, that they may plant the black flag in the heart of Mexico and riot in the halls of the Montezumas. In the language of the Rev. Robert Hall, when addressing the volunteers of Bristol, who were rushing forth to repel the invasion of Napoleon, who threatened to lay waste the fair homes of England, "Religion is too much interested in your behalf, not to shed over you her most gracious influences."

You will not be compelled to spend much time in order to become inured to hardships. From the first moment that you breathed the air of heaven, you have been accustomed to nothing else but hardships. The heroes of the American Revolution were never put upon harder fare than a peck of corn and a few herrings per week. You have not become enervated by the luxuries of life. Your sternest energies have been beaten out upon the anvil of severe trial. Slavery has done this, to make you subservient, to its own purposes; but it has done more than this, it has prepared you for any emergency. If you receive good treatment, it is what you could hardly expect; if you meet with pain, sorrow, and even death, these are the common lot of slaves.

Fellow men! Patient sufferers! behold your dearest rights crushed to the earth! See your sons murdered, and your wives, mothers and sisters doomed to prostitution. In the name of the merciful God, and by all that life is worth, let it no longer be a debatable question whether it is better to choose *Liberty or death.*

In 1822, Denmark Vesey, of South Carolina, formed a plan for the liberation of his fellow men. In the whole history of human efforts to overthrow slavery, a more complicated and tremendous plan was never formed. He was betrayed by the treachery of his own people, and died a martyr to freedom. Many a brave hero fell, but history, faithful to her high trust, will transcribe his name on the same monument with Moses, Hampden, Tell, Bruce and Wallace, Toussaint L'Ouverture, Lafayette and Washington. That tremendous movement shook the whole empire of slavery. The guilty soul-thieves were overwhelmed with fear. It is a matter of fact, that at that time, and in consequence of the threatened revolution, the slave States talked strongly of emancipation. But they blew but one blast of the trumpet of freedom and then laid it aside. As these men became quiet, the slaveholders ceased to talk about emancipation; and now behold your condition today! Angels sigh over it, and humanity has long since exhausted her tears in weeping on your account!

The patriotic Nathaniel Turner followed Denmark Vesey. He was goaded to desperation by wrong and injustice. By despotism, his name has been recorded on the list of infamy, and future generations will remember him among the noble and brave.

Next arose the immortal Joseph Cinque, the hero of the *Amistad*. He was a native African, and by the help of God he emancipated a whole ship-load of his fellow men on the high seas. And he now sings of liberty on the sunny hills of Africa and beneath his native palm-trees, where he hears the lion roar and feels himself as free as that king of the forest.

Next arose Madison Washington, that bright star of freedom, and took his station in the constellation of true heroism. He was a slave on board the brig *Creole*, of Richmond, bound to New Orleans, that great slave mart, with a hundred and four others. Nineteen struck for liberty or death. But one life was taken, and the whole were emancipated, and the vessel was carried into Nassau, New Providence.

Noble men! Those who have fallen in freedom's conflict, their memories will be cherished by the true-hearted and the God-fearing in all future generations; those who are living, their names are surrounded by a halo of glory.

Brethren, arise, arise! Strike for your lives and liberties. Now is the day and the hour. Let every slave throughout the land do this, and the days of slavery are numbered. You cannot be more oppressed than you have been—you cannot suffer greater cruelties than you have already. *Rather die freemen than live to be slaves.* Remember that you are *four millions!*

It is in your power so to torment the God-cursed slaveholders that they will be glad to let you go free. If the scale was turned, and black men were the masters and white men the slaves, every destructive agent and element would be employed to lay the oppressor low. Danger and death would hang over their heads day and night. Yes, the tyrants would meet with plagues more terrible than those of Pharaoh. But you are a patient people. You act as though, you were made for the special use of these devils. You act as though your daughters were born to pamper the lusts of your masters and overseers. And worse than all, you tamely submit while your lords tear your wives from your embraces and defile them before your eyes. In the name of God, we ask, are you men? Where is the blood of your fathers? Has it all run out of your veins? Awake, awake; millions of voices are calling you! Your dead fathers speak to you from their graves. Heaven, as with a voice of thunder, calls on you to arise from the dust.

Let your motto be resistance! *resistance!* RE-SISTANCE! No oppressed people have ever secured their liberty without resistance. What kind of resistance you had better make, you must decide by the circumstances that surround you, and according to the suggestion of expedience. Brethren, adieu! Trust in the living God. Labor for the peace of the human race, and remember that you are *four millions.*

Editor's Note:

In 1858, John S. Rock, an ardent abolitionist, physician, and first black attorney to plead cases before the United States Supreme Court addressed a meeting held to commemorate the Boston Massacre and death of Crispus Attucks in 1770. The illustrious oratory presented here demonstrates Rock's keen insight into some of the rationalizations for the racism practiced in this country and his own pride in being black.

AN ADDRESS TO A MEETING IN BOSTON, 1858

JOHN S. ROCK

You will not expect a lengthened speech from me to-night. My health is too poor to allow me to indulge much in speech-making. But I have not been able to resist the temptation to unite with you in this demonstration of respect for some of my noble but misguided ancestors.

White Americans have taken great pains to try to prove that we are cowards. We are often insulted with the assertion, that if we had had the courage of the Indians or the white man, we would never have submitted to be slaves. I ask if Indians and white men have never been slaves? The white man tested the Indian's courage here when he had his organized armies, his battle-grounds, his places of retreat, with everything to hope for and everything to lose. The position of the African slave has been very different. Seized a prisoner of war, unarmed, bound hand and foot, and conveyed to a distant country among what to him were worse than cannibals; brutally beaten, half-starved, closely watched by armed men, with no means of knowing their own strength or the strength of their enemies, with no weapons, and without a probability of success. But if the white man will take the trouble to fight the black man in Africa or in Haiti, and fight him as fair as the black man will fight him there—if the black man does not come off victor, I am deceived in his prowess. But, take a man, armed or unarmed, from his home, his country, or his friends, and place him among savages, and who is he that would not make good his retreat? 'Discretion is the better part of valor,' but for a man to resist where he knows it will destroy him, shows more fool-hardiness than courage. There have been many Anglo-Saxons and Anglo-Americans enslaved in Africa, but I have never heard that they successfully resisted any government. They always resort to running indispensables.

The courage of the Anglo-Saxon is best illustrated in his treatment of the Negro. A score or two of them can pounce upon a poor Negro, tie and beat him, and then call him a coward because he submits. Many of their most brilliant victories have been achieved in the same manner. But the greatest battles which they have fought have been upon paper. We can easily account for this; their trumpeter is dead. He died when they used to be exposed for sale in the Roman market, about the time that Cicero cautioned his friend Atticus not to buy them, on account of their stupidity. A little more than half a century ago, this race, in connection with their Celtic neighbors, who have long been considered (by themselves, of course,) the bravest soldiers in the world, so far forgot themselves, as to attack a few cowardly, stupid Negro slaves, who, according to their accounts, had not sense enough to go to bed. And what was the result? Why, sir, the negroes drove them out from the island like so many sheep, and they have never dared to show their faces, except with hat in hand.

Our true and tried friend, Rev. Theodore

Parker, said, in his speech at the State House, a few weeks since, that 'the stroke of the axe would have settled the question long ago, but the black man would not strike.' Mr. Parker makes a very low estimate of the courage of his race, if he means that one, two or three millions of these ignorant and cowardly black slaves could, without means, have brought to their knees five, ten, or twenty millions of intelligent, brave white men, backed up by a rich oligarchy. But I know of no one who is more familiar with the true character of the Anglo-Saxon race than Mr. Parker. I will not dispute this point with him, but I will thank him or any one else to tell us how it could have been done. His remark calls to my mind the day which is to come, when one shall chase a thousand, and two put ten thousand to flight. But when he says that 'the black man *would not* strike,' I am prepared to say that he does us great injustice. The black man is not a coward. The history of the bloody struggles for freedom in Haiti, in which the blacks whipped the French and the English, and gained their independence, in spite of the perfidy of that villainous First Consul, will be a lasting refutation of the malicious aspersions of our enemies. The history of the struggles for the liberty of the U.S. ought to silence every American calumniator. I have learned that even so late as the Texan war, a number of black men were silly enough to offer themselves as living sacrifices for our country's shame. A gentleman who delivered a lecture before the New York Legislature, a few years since, whose name I do not now remember, but whose language I give with some precision, said, 'In the Revolution, colored soldiers fought side by side with you in your struggles for liberty, and there is not a battle-field from Maine to Georgia that has not been crimsoned with their blood, and whitened with their bones.' In 1814, a bill passed the Legislature of New York, accepting the services of 2,000 colored volunteers. Many black men served under Com. McDonough when he conquered on Lake Champlain. Many were in the battles of Plattsburgh and Sackett's Harbor, and General Jackson called out colored troops from Louisiana and Alabama, and in a solemn proclamation attested to their fidelity and courage.

The white man contradicts himself who says, that if he were in our situation, he would throw off the yoke. Thirty millions of white men of this proud Caucasian race are at this moment held as slaves, and bought and sold with horses and cattle. The iron heel of oppression grinds the masses of all European races to the dust. They suffer every kind of oppression, and no one dares to open his mouth to protest against it. Even in the Southern portion of this boasted land of liberty, no white man dares advocate so much of the Declaration of Independence as declares that 'all men are created free and equal, and have an inalienable right to life, liberty,' &c.

White men have no room to taunt us with tamely submitting. If they were black men, they would work wonders; but, as white men, they can do nothing. 'O, Consistency, thou art a jewel!'

Now, it would not be surprising if the brutal treatment which we have received for the past two centuries should have crushed our spirits. But this is not the case. Nothing but a superior force keeps us down. And when I see the slaves rising up by hundreds annually, in the majesty of human nature, bidding defiance to every slave code and its penalties, making the issue Canada or death, and that too while they are closely watched by paid men armed with pistols, clubs and bowie-knives, with the army and navy of this great Model Republic arrayed against them, I am disposed to ask if the charge of cowardice does not come with ill-grace.

But some men are so steeped in folly and imbecility; so lost to all feelings of their own littleness; so destitute of principle, and so regardless of humanity, that they dare attempt to destroy everything which exists in opposition to their interests or opinions which their narrow comprehensions cannot grasp.

We ought not to come here simply to honor those brave men who shed their blood for freedom, or to protest against the Dred Scott decision, but to take counsel of each other, and to enter into new vows of duty. Our fathers fought nobly for freedom, but they were not victorious. They fought for liberty, but they got slavery. The white man was benefitted, but the black man was injured. I do not envy the white American the little liberty which he enjoys. It is his right, and he ought to have it. I wish him success, though I do not think he deserves it. But I would have all men free. We have had much sad experience in this country, and it would be strange indeed if we do not profit by some of the lessons which we have so dearly paid for. Sooner or later, the clashing of arms will be heard in this country, and the black man's services will be needed: 150,000 freemen capable of bearing arms, and not all cowards and fools, and three quarters of a million slaves, wild with the enthusiasm caused by the dawn of the glorious opportunity of being able to strike a genuine blow for freedom, will be a power which white men will be "bound to respect." Will the blacks fight? Of course they will. The black man will never be neutral. He could not if he would, and he would not if he could. Will he fight for this country, right or wrong? This the common sense of every one answers; and when the time comes, and come it will, the black man will give an intelligent answer. Judge Taney may outlaw us; Caleb Cushing may show the depravity of his heart by abusing us; and this wicked government may oppress us; but the black man will live when Judge Taney, Caleb Cushing and this wicked government are no more. White man may despise, ridicule, slander and abuse us; they may seek as they always have done to divide us, and make us feel degraded; but no man shall cause me to turn my back upon my race. With it I will sink or swim.

The prejudice which some white men have, or affected to have, against my color gives me no pain. If any man does not fancy my color, that is his business, and I shall not meddle with it. I shall give myself no trouble because he lacks good taste. If he judges my intellectual capacity by my color, he certainly cannot expect much profundity, for it is only skin deep, and is really of no very great importance to any one but myself. I will not deny that I admire the talents and noble characters of many white men. But I cannot say that I am particularly pleased with their physical appearance. If old mother nature had held out as well as she commenced, we should, probably, have had fewer varieties in the races. When I contrast the fine tough muscular system, the beautiful, rich color, the full broad features, and the gracefully frizzled hair of the Negro, with the delicate physical organization, wan color, sharp features and lank hair of the Caucasian, I am inclined to believe that when the white man was created, nature was pretty well exhausted—but determined to keep up appearances, she pinched up his features, and did the best she could under the circumstances. (Great laughter.)

I would have you understand, that I not only love my race, but am pleased with my color; and while many colored persons may feel degraded by being called Negroes, and wish to be classed among other races more favored, I shall feel it my duty, my pleasure and my pride, to concentrate my feeble efforts in elevating to a fair position a race to which I am especially identified by feelings and by blood.

My friends, we can never become elevated until we are true to ourselves. We can come here and make brilliant speeches, but our field of duty is elsewhere. Let us go to work—each man in his place, determined to do what he can for himself and his race. Let us try to carry out some of the resolutions which we have made, and are so fond of making. If we do this, friends will spring up in every quarter, and where we least expect them. But we must not rely on them. They cannot elevate us. Whenever the colored man is elevated, it will be by his own exertions. Our friends can do what many of them are nobly doing, assist us to remove the obstacles which prevent our elevation, and stimulate the worthy to persevere. The colored man who, by dint of perseverance and industry, educates and elevates himself, prepares the way for others, gives character to the race, and hastens the day of general emancipation. While the Negro who hangs around the corners of the streets, or lives in the grog-shops or by gambling, or who has no higher ambition than to serve, is by his vocation forging fetters for the slave, and is 'to all intents and purposes' a curse to his race. It is true, considering the circumstances under which we have been placed by our white neighbors, we have a right to ask them not only to cease to oppress us, but to give us that encouragement which our talents and industry may merit. When this is done, they will see our minds expand, and our pockets filled with rocks. How very few colored men are encouraged in their trades or business! Our young men see this, and become disheartened. In this country, where money is the great sympathetic nerve which ramifies society, and has a ganglia in every man's pocket, a man is respected in proportion to his success in business. When the avenues to wealth are opened to us, we will then become educated and wealthy, and then the roughest looking colored man that you ever saw, or ever will see, will be pleasanter than the harmonies of Orpheus, and black will be a very pretty color. It will make our jargon, wit—our words, oracles; flattery will then take the place of slander, and you will find no prejudice in the Yankee whatever. We do not expect to occupy a much better position than we now do, until we shall have our educated and wealthy men, who can wield a power that cannot be misunderstood. Then, and not till then, will the tongue of slander be silenced, and the lip of prejudice sealed. Then, and not till then, will we be able to enjoy true equality, which can exist only among peers.

Editor's Note:

Freedom for many former slaves meant no more than a substitution of owners. Sharecropping and migration were often the only alternatives available for ekeing out a meager existence. Sharecropping is very much a part of the southern scene today. It is a way of life for thousands of nameless and faceless victims who find themselves at the mercy of planters free to exploit them with impunity. The planter supplies the materials and keeps the accounts. The inevitable result is often peonage or compulsory servitude for the debtor. The convict-lease system is a further extension of this process. One of the victims of this process relates his entrapment, brutalization, and subsequent release.

THE LIFE STORY OF A NEGRO PEON

I am a Negro and was born sometime during the war in Elbert County, Ga., and I reckon by this time I must be a little over forty years old. My mother was not married when I was born, and I never knew who my father was or anything about him. Shortly after the war my mother died, and I was left to the care of my uncle. All this happened before I was eight years old, and so I can't remember very much about it. When I was about ten years old my uncle hired me out to Captain ——. I had already learned how to plow, and was also a good hand at picking cotton. I was told that the Captain wanted me for his houseboy, and that later on he was going to train me to be his coachman. To be a coachman in those days was considered a post of honor, and young as I was, I was glad of the chance.

But I had not been at the Captain's a month before I was put to work on the farm, with some twenty or thirty other Negroes—men, women and children. From the beginning the boys had the same tasks as the men and women. There was no difference. We all worked hard during the week, and would frolic on Saturday nights and often on Sundays. And everybody was happy. The men got $3 a week and the women $2. I don't know what the children got. Every week my uncle collected my money for me, but it was very little of it that I ever saw. My uncle fed and clothed me, gave me a place to sleep, and allowed me ten or fifteen cents a week for "spending change," as he called it.

I must have been seventeen or eighteen years old before I got tired of that arrangement, and felt that I was man enough to be working for myself and handling my own wages. The other boys about my age and size were "drawing" their own pay, and they used to laugh at me and call me "Baby," because my old uncle was always on hand to "draw" my pay. Worked up by these things, I made a break for liberty. Unknown to my uncle or the Captain I went off to a neighboring plantation and hired myself out to another man. The new landlord agreed to give me forty cents a day and furnish me one meal. I thought that was doing fine. Bright and early one Monday morning I started for work, still not letting the others know anything about it. But they found it out before sundown. The Captain came over to the new place and brought some kind of officer of the law. The officer pulled out a long piece of paper from his pocket and read it to my employer. When this was done I heard my new boss say:

"I beg your pardon, Captain. I didn't know this Negro was bound out to you, or I wouldn't have hired him."

"He certainly is bound out to me," said the Captain. "He belongs to me until he is twenty-one, and I'm going to make him know his place."

So I was carried back to the Captain's. That night he made me strip off my clothing down to my waist, ordered his foreman to give me thirty lashes with a buggy whip across my bare back, and stood by until it was done. After that experience the Captain made me stay on his place night and day—but my uncle still continued to "draw" my money.

I was a man nearly grown before I knew how to count from one to one hundred. I was a man nearly grown before I ever saw a colored teacher. I never went to school a day in my life. Today I can't write my own name, though I can read a little. I was a man nearly grown before I ever rode on a railroad train, and then I went on an excursion from Elberton to Athens. What was true of me was true of hundreds of other Negroes around me—'way off there in the country, fifteen or twenty miles from the nearest town.

When I reached twenty-one the Captain told me I was a free man, but he urged me to stay with him. He said he would treat me right, and pay me as much as anybody else would. The Captain's son and I were about the same age, and the Captain said that, as he had owned my mother and uncle during slavery, and as his son didn't want me to leave them (since I had been with them so long), he wanted me to stay with the old family. And I stayed. I signed a contract—that is, I made my mark—for one year. The Captain was to give me $3.50 a week, and furnish me a little house on the plantation—a one-room log cabin similar to those used by his other laborers.

During that year I married Mandy. For several years Mandy had been the house-servant for the Captain, his wife, his son and his three daughters, and they all seemed to think a good deal of her. As an evidence of their regard they gave us a suit of furniture, which cost about $25, and we set up housekeeping in one of the Captain's two-room shanties. I thought I was the biggest man in Georgia. Mandy still kept her place in the "Big House" after our marriage. We did so well for the first year that I renewed my contract for the second year, and for the third, fourth and fifth year I did the same thing. Before the end of the fifth year the Captain had died, and his son, who had married some two or three years before, took charge of the plantation. Also, for two or three years, this son had been serving at Atlanta in some big office to which he had been elected. I think it was in the Legislature or something of that sort—anyhow, all the people called him Senator. At the end of the fifth year the Senator suggested that I sign up a contract for ten years; then, he said, we wouldn't have to fix up papers every year. I asked my wife about it; she consented; and so I made a ten-year contract.

Not long afterward the Senator had a long, low shanty built on his place. A great big chimney, with a wide, open fireplace, was built on one end of it and on each side of the house, running lengthwise, there was a row of frames or stalls just large enough to hold a single mattress. The places for these mattresses were fixed one above the other; so that there was a double row of these stalls or pens on each side. They looked for all the world like stalls for horses. Since then I have seen cabooses similarly arranged as sleeping quarters for railroad laborers.

Nobody seemed to know what the Senator was fixing for. All doubts were put aside one bright day in April when about forty able-bodied Negroes, bound in iron chains, and some of them handcuffed, were brought out to the Senator's farm in three big wagons. They were quartered in the long, low shanty, and it was afterward called the stockade. This was the beginning of the Senator's convict camp. These men were prisoners who had been leased by the Senator from the State of Georgia at about $200 each per year, the State agreeing to pay for guards and physicians, for necessary inspection, for inquests, all rewards for escaped convicts, the cost of litigation and all other incidental expenses.

When I saw these men in shackles, and the guards with their guns, I was scared nearly to death. I felt like running away, but I didn't know where to go. And if there had been any place to go to, I would have had to leave my wife and child behind. We free laborers held a meeting. We all wanted to quit. We sent a man to tell the Senator about it. Word came back that we were all under contract for ten years and that the Senator would hold us to the letter of the contract, or put us in chains and lock us up—the same as the other prisoners. It was made plain to us by some white people we talked to that in the contracts we had signed we had all agreed to be locked up in a stockade at night or at any other time that our employer saw fit; further, we learned that we could not lawfully break our contract for any reason and go and hire ourselves to somebody else without the consent of our employer; and, more than that, if we got mad and ran away, we could be run down by bloodhounds, arrested without process of law, and be returned to our employer, who, according to the contract, might beat us brutally or administer any kind of punishment that he thought proper. In other words, we had sold ourselves into slavery—and what could we do about it? The white folks had all the courts, all the guns, all the hounds, all the railroads, all the telegraph wires, all the newspapers, all the

money, and nearly all the land—and we had only our ignorance, our poverty and our empty hands. We decided that the best thing to do was to shut our mouths, say nothing, and go back to work. And most of us worked side by side with those convicts during the remainder of the ten years.

But this first batch of convicts was only the beginning. Within six months another stockade was built, and twenty or thirty other convicts were brought to the plantation, among them six or eight women! The Senator had bought an additional thousand acres of land, and to his already large cotton plantation he added two great big sawmills and went into the lumber business. Within two years the Senator had in all 200 Negroes working on his plantation—about half of them free laborers, so called, and about half of them convicts. The only difference between the free laborers and the others was that the free laborers could come and go as they pleased, at night—that is, they were not locked up at night, and were not, as a general thing, whipped for slight offenses.

The troubles of the free laborers began at the close of the ten-year period. To a man they all refused to sign new contracts—even for one year, not to say anything of ten years. And just when we thought that our bondage was at an end we found that it had really just begun. Two or three years before, or about a year and a half after the Senator had started his camp, he had established a large store, which was called the commissary. All of us free laborers were compelled to buy our supplies—food, clothing, etc.—from that store. We never used any money in our dealings with the commissary, only tickets or orders, and we had a general settlement once each year, in October. In this store we were charged all sorts of high prices for goods, because every year we would come out in debt to our employer. If not that, we seldom had more than $5 or $10 coming to us—and that for a whole year's work. Well, at the close of the tenth year, when we kicked and meant to leave the Senator, he said to some of us with a smile (and I never will forget that smile—I can see it now):

"Boys, I'm sorry you're going to leave me. I hope you will do well in your new places—so well that you will be able to pay me the little balances which most of you owe me."

Word was sent out for all of us to meet him at the commissary at 2 o'clock. There he told us that, after we had signed what he called a written acknowledgement of our debts, we might go and look for new places. The storekeeper took us one by one and read to us statements of our accounts. According to the books there was no man of us who owed the

41

Senator less than $100; some of us were put down for as much as $200. I owed $165, according to the bookkeeper. These debts were not accumulated during one year, but ran back for three and four years, so we were told—in spite of the fact that we understood that we had had a full settlement at the end of each year. But no one of us would have dared to dispute a white man's word—oh, no; not in those days. Besides, we fellows didn't care anything about the amounts—we were after getting away; and we had been told that we might too, if we signed the acknowledgement. We would have signed anything, just to get away. So we stepped up, we did, and made our marks. That same night we were rounded up by a constable and ten or twelve white men, who aided him, and we were locked up, every one of us, in one of the Senator's stockades. The next morning it was explained to us by the two guards appointed to watch us that, in the papers we had signed the day before, we had not only made acknowledgement of our indebtedness, but that we had also agreed to work for the Senator until the debts were paid by hard labor. And from that day forward we were treated just like convicts. Really we had made ourselves lifetime slaves, or peons, as the laws called us. But call it slavery, peonage, or what not, the truth is we lived in a hell on earth what time we spent in the Senator's peon camp.

I lived in that camp, as a peon, for nearly three years. My wife fared better than I did, as did the wives of some of the other Negroes, because the white men about the camp used these unfortunate creatures as their mistresses. When I was first put in the stockade my wife was still kept for a while in the "Big House," but my little boy, who was only nine years old, was given away to a Negro family across the river in South Carolina, and I never saw or heard of him after that. When I left the camp my wife had had two children by some one of the white bosses, and she was living in a fairly good shape in a little house off to herself. But the poor Negro women who were not in the class with my wife fared about as bad as the helpless Negro men. Most of the time the women who were peons or convicts were compelled to wear men's clothes. Sometimes, when I have seen them dressed like men, and plowing or hoeing or hauling logs or working at the blacksmith's trade, just the same as men, my heart would bleed and my blood would boil, but I was powerless to raise a hand. It would have meant death on the spot to have said a word. Of the first six women brought to the camp, two of them gave birth to children after they had been there more than twelve months—and the babies had white men for their fathers!

The stockades in which we slept, were, I believe, the filthiest places in the world. They were cesspools of nastiness. During the thirteen years that I was there I am willing to swear that a mattress was never moved after it had been brought there, except to turn it over once or twice a month. No sheets were used, only dark-colored blankets. Most of the men slept every night in the clothing that they had worked in all day. Some of the worst characters were made to sleep in chairs. The doors were locked and barred, each night, and tallow-candles were the only lights allowed. Really the stockades were but little more than cow sheds, horse stables, or hog pens. Strange to say, not a great number of these people died while I was there, though a great many came away maimed and bruised and, in some cases, disabled for life. As far as I can remember only about ten died during the last ten years that I was there, two of these being killed outright by the guards for trivial offenses.

It was a hard school that peon camp was, but I learned more there in a few short months by contact with those poor fellows from the outside world than ever I had known before. Most of what I learned was evil, and I now know that I should have been better off without the knowledge, but much of what I learned was helpful to me. Barring two or three severe and brutal whippings which I received, I got along very well, all things considered; but the system is damnable. A favorite way of whipping a man was to strap him down to a log, flat on his back, and spank him fifty or sixty times on his bare feet with a shingle or a huge piece of plank. When the man would get up with sore and blistered feet and an aching body, if he could not then keep up with the other men at work he would be strapped to the log again, this time face downward, and would be lashed with a buggy trace on his bare back. When a woman had to be whipped it was usually done in private, though they would be compelled to fall down across a barrel or something of the kind and receive the licks on their backsides.

The working day on a peon farm begins with sunrise and ends when the sun goes down; or, in other words, the average peon works from ten to twelve hours each day, with one hour (from 12 o'clock to 1 o'clock) for dinner. Hot or cold, sun or rain, this is the rule. As to their meals, the laborers are divided up into squads or companies, just the same as soldiers in a great military camp would be. Two or three men in each stockade are appointed as cooks. From thirty to forty men report to each cook. In the warm months (or eight or nine months out of the year) the cooking is done on the outside, just behind the stockades; in the cold months the cooking is done inside the stockades. Each peon is provided with a great big tin cup, a flat tin pan and two big tin spoons. No knives or forks are ever seen, except those used by the cooks. At meal time the peons pass in single file before the cooks, and hold out their pans and cups to receive their allowances. Cow peas (red or white, which when boiled turn black), fat bacon and old-fashioned Georgia cornbread, baked in pones from one to two and three inches thick, made up the chief articles of food. Black coffee, black molasses and brown sugar are also used abundantly. Once in a great while, on Sundays, biscuits would be made, but they would always be made from the kind of flour called "shorts." As a rule, breakfast consisted of coffee, fried bacon, cornbread, and sometimes molasses—and one "helping" of each was all that was allowed. Peas, boiled with huge hunks of fat bacon, and a hoe-cake, as big as a man's hand, usually answered for dinner. Sometimes this dinner bill of fare gave place to bacon and greens (collard or turnip) and pot liquor. Though we raised corn, potatoes and other vegetables, we never got a chance at such things unless we could steal them and cook them secretly. Supper consisted of coffee, fried bacon and molasses. But, although the food was limited to certain things, I am sure we all got a plenty of the things allowed. As coarse as these things were, we kept, as a rule, fat and sleek and as strong as mules. And that, too, in spite of the fact that we had no special arrangements for taking regular baths, and no very great effort was made to keep us regularly in clean clothes. No tables were used or allowed. In summer we would sit down on the ground and eat our meals, and in winter we would sit around inside the filthy stockades. Each man was his own dishwasher—that is to say, each man was responsible for the care of his pan and cup and spoons. My dishes got washed about once a week!

Today, I am told, there are six or seven of these private camps in Georgia—that is to say, camps where most of the convicts are leased from the State of Georgia. But there are hundreds and hundreds of farms all over the State where Negroes, and in some cases poor white folks, are held in bondage on the ground that they are working out debts, or where the contracts which they have made hold them in a kind of perpetual bondage, because, under those contracts they may not quit one employer and hire out to another except by and with the knowledge and consent of the former employer.

One of the usual ways to secure laborers for a large peonage camp is for the proprietor to send out an agent to the little courts in the towns and villages, and where a man charged with some petty offense has no friends or money the agent will urge him to plead guilty, with the understanding that the agent will pay his fine, and in that way save him from the disgrace of being sent to jail or the chain-gang! For this high favor the man must sign beforehand a paper signify-ing his willingness to go to the farm and work out the amount of the fine imposed. When he reaches the farm he has to be fed and clothed, to be sure, and these things are charged up to his account. By the time he has worked out his first debt another is hanging over his head, and so on and so on, by a sort of endless chain, for an indefinite period, as in every case the indebtedness is arbitrarily arranged by the employer. In many cases it is very evident that the court officials are in collusion with the proprietors or agents, and that they divide the "graft" among themselves. As an example of this dickering among the whites, every year many convicts were brought to the Senator's camp from a certain county in South Georgia, 'way down in the turpentine district. The majority of these men were charged with adultery, which is an offense against the laws of the great and sovereign State of Georgia! Upon inquiry I learned that down in that county a number of Negro lewd women were employed by certain white men to entice Negro men into their houses; and then, on a certain night, at a given signal, when all was in readiness, raids would be made by the officers upon these houses, and the men would be arrested and charged with living in adultery. Nine out of ten of these men, so arrested and so charged, would find their way ultimately to some convict camp, and, as I said, many of them found their way every year to the Senator's camp while I was there. The low-down women were never punished in any way. On the contrary, I was told that they always seemed to stand in high favor with the sheriffs, constables and other officers. There can be no room to doubt that they assisted very materially in furnishing laborers for the prison pens of Georgia, and the belief was general among the men that they were regularly paid for their work. I could tell more, but I've said enough to make anybody's heart sick. This great and terrible iniquity is, I know, widespread throughout Georgia and many other Southern States.

But I didn't tell you how I got out. I didn't get out—they put me out. When I had served as a peon for nearly three years—and you remember that they claimed I owed them only $165—when I had served for nearly three years one of the bosses came to me and said that my time was up. He happened to be the one who was said to be living with my wife. He gave me a new suit of overalls, which cost about seventy-five cents, took me in a buggy and carried me across the Broad River into South Carolina, set me down and told me to "git." I didn't have a cent of money, and I wasn't feeling well, but somehow I managed to get a move on me. I begged my way to Columbia. In two or three days I ran across a man looking for laborers to carry to Birmingham, and I joined his gang. I have been here in the Birmingham district since they released me, and I reckon I'll die either in a coal mine or an iron furnace. It don't make much difference which. Either is better than a Georgia peon camp. And a Georgia peon camp is hell itself!

Editor's Note:

The pimp has long been a model for youngsters in the recesses of the ghetto. He projects a false image of glamor, ease of living, and success. The behind-the-scenes struggle for perpetuation of this image is often lost on those who see only the "front." Robert Beck ("Iceberg Slim") has stated that in this age of revolutionary consciousness and thrust of black people to build communities, the pimp has become an anachronism. Beck's position is that there is no place in the black community for one who would exploit and destroy his people, particularly his woman. "Iceberg Slim" had been a successful pimp for over thirty years. The following excerpt from his autobiography, *Pimp*, describes the turning point in his life, the combination of forces and circumstances that led to his decision to become a "square."

PIMP: THE STORY OF MY LIFE

ROBERT BECK ("ICEBERG SLIM")

Mama came from California to visit me. She was sick and old. In fact she was dying. She had heart trouble and diabetes. I don't see how she made the trip. It was an old scene. I was in a barred cage. She was crying on the outside of it.

She sobbed, "Son, this is the last time we are going to see each other. Your Mama's so tired. God gave me the strength to make the long trip to see my poor baby before I go to sleep in Jesus' arms. Son, it's too bad you don't love me as much as I love you."

I was crying. I was squeezing her thin, pale hands in mine between the bars.

I said, "Now look Mama, you know we all got Indian blood in us. Mama, you ain't gonna die. Mama, you'll live to get a hundred like Papa Joe, your father. Come on now, Mama, stop it. Ain't I got enough worry? Mama, I love you. Honest, Mama. Forgive me for not writing regular and stuff like that. I love you, Mama, I love you. Please don't die. I couldn't take it while I'm locked up. I'll take care of you when I get out. I swear it, Mama. Just don't die. Please!"

The screw came up. The visit was over. His hard face softened in pity as he looked at her. He knew she was critically sick. I watched her move slowly away from me down the jail corridor. She got to the elevator. She turned and looked at me. She had a sad, pitiful look on her face. It reminded me of that stormy morning long ago she had stood in the rain and watched the van taking me to my first prison bit. I get a terrible lump in my throat even now when I relive that moment.

A week passed after Mama visited me and went back to California.

I went into court for the third and last time. The judge ordered me into the custody of the joint's captain of screws. Stacy was released.

The captain and his aide were grimly silent. Their prison sedan sliced through the sparkling April day. I was on the rear seat. I gazed at the scurrying, lucky citizens on the street. I wondered what they'd use on me at the joint, rubber hoses or blackjacks? I felt so low. I wouldn't have cared if I'd dropped dead right on the car seat.

We went through the big gate into the joint. The warm April sun shone down on the ancient grimy buildings.

The yard cons leaned on their brooms. They stared through the car window at me. The sedan came to a stop. We got out. They took off my handcuffs. I was taken into the same cell house from which I'd made the escape thirteen years before. I was locked in a cell on the flag.

In the early afternoon a screw marched me to the office of the chief of the joint's security. He looked like a pure Aryan storm trooper sitting behind his desk. He didn't have a blackjack or a rubber hose in his hand. He was grinning like maybe Herr Schickelgruber at that railroad coach in France. His voice was a lethal whisper.

He said, "Well, well, so you're that slick blackbird who flew the coop. Cheer up, you only owe us eleven months. You're lucky you escaped before the new law. There's one on the books now. It penalizes escapees with up to an extra year.

"Ah, what a shame it isn't retroactive. I am going to put you into a punishment cell for a few days. Nothing personal mind you. Hell, you didn't hurt me with your escape. Tell me confidentially, how did you do it?"

I said, "Sir, I wish I knew. I am subject to states of fugue. I came to that night and I was walking down the highway a free man. Sir, I certainly wish I could tell you how I did it."

His pale cold eyes hardened into blue agates.

His grin widened.

He said, "Oh, it's all right my boy. Tell you what, you're a cinch to get a clear memory of just how you did it before long. Put in a request to the cell-house officer to see me when you regain the memory. Well good luck, my boy, 'til we meet again."

A screw took me to the bath house. I took a shower and changed into a tattered con uniform. A croaker examined me, then back to the cell house. The screw took me to a row of tiny filthy cells on the flag. My first detention cell was on the other side of the cell house. The screw stopped in front of a cell. He unlocked it. He prodded me into it. It was near the front of the cell house. I looked around my new home.

It was a tight box designed to crush and torture the human spirit. I raised my arms above me. My fingertips touched the cold steel ceiling. I stretched them out to the side. I touched the steel walls. I walked seven feet or so from the barred door to the rear of the cell. I passed a steel cot.

The mattress cover was stained and stinking from old puke and crap. The toilet and wash bowls were encrusted with greenish-brown crud. It could be a steel casket for a weak skull after a week or two. I wondered how long they'd punish me in the box.

I turned and walked to the cell door. I stood grasping the bars, looking out at the blank cell-house wall in front of me.

I thought, "The Nazi figures after a week or so in this dungeon, I'll be crying and begging to tell him how I escaped. I'm not going to pussy-out. Hell, I got a strong skull. I could do a month in here."

I heard a slapping noise against the steel space between the cells. I saw a thin white hand holding a square of paper. I stuck my arm through the bars of my cell door. I took the paper. It was a kite with two cigarettes and three matches folded inside.

It read, "Welcome to Happiness Lane. My name is 'Coppola.' The vine said you're Lancaster, the guy who took a powder thirteen years ago. I was clerking in an office up front. I took my powder a year and a half ago.

"They brought me back six months ago. I've started to cash in my chips a dozen times. You'll find out what I mean. I've been right in this cell ever since. I got another year to go with the new time stacked on top for the escape. I got a detainer warrant from Maine for forgery up front.

"We're in big trouble, buddy. The prick up front has cracked up four or five cons in these cells since I came back. . . . There's six of us on the row now. Only three are escapees. The rest are doing short punishment time like two days to a week. I'll give you background on other things later. I know what screws will get anything you want for a price."

I lit a cigarette and sat on the cot. I thought, "Coppola" is a helluva stud to keep his skull straight

for six months on Happiness Lane. He doesn't know I'm just here for a few days.

That night we had a supper of sour Spanish rice. I heard the shuffling feet of cons filing into the cell house. They were going into their cells on the tiers overhead. The blaring radio loudspeakers and the lights went off at nine. Over the flushing of toilets and epidemic farting, I heard my name mentioned. The speaker was on the tier just above my cell.

He said, "Jim, how about old 'Iceberg,' the mack man? Jim, a deuce will get you a sawbuck the whitefolks will croak him down there. A pimp ain't got the heart to do a slat down there."

Jim said, "Jack, I hope the pimp bastard croaks tonight. One of them pimps put my baby sister on stuff."

I dozed off. After midnight I woke up. Somebody was screaming. He was pleading with someone not to kill him. I heard thudding sounds. I got up and went to the cell door. I heard "Coppola" flush his john.

I stage whispered, "Coppola," what's happening, man?"

He whispered, "Don't let it bug you, Lancaster. It's just the night screws having their nightly fun and exercise. They pull their punching bags from the cells on the other side. It's where drunks and old men are held for court in the morning.

"Buddy, you ain't seen nothing yet. Don't give them any lip if they ever come by and needle you. They'll beat hell out of you. Then take all your clothes off and put you in a stripped cell. That's one with nothing in it, just the cold concrete floor. Buddy, there are at least a dozen ways to die in here."

All the rest of the night I lay staring at the blank dirty wall in front of me. I wondered what Rachel and Stacy were doing. I had to make contact with a screw to mail some letters on the outside for me. The joint censors would never let whore instructions pass through. Every few minutes a screw would pass and flash his light on me.

That morning I watched the cell-house cons file past my cell on the way to breakfast and then to their work. All new arrivals the day before were also in this line.

That afternoon, I got letters from Stacy and Rachel. They had also sent money orders. They missed their strong right arm. They were working bars downtown. "Bet" was handling any falls they might take.

"Coppola" within the first week hipped me to the angles of survival. I had a screw who would take letters directly to the girls. He would get his pay-off from them. He would bring me cash from them.

I got a letter from Mama. I could hardly read the shaky writing. She sent me religious tracts inside it. I was really worried about her. The tight cell and the fear of a year in it was getting to me. The little sleep I got was crowded with nightmares. I was eating good at high prices. I still lost weight.

The first month I lost thirty pounds. Then I got bad news twice within the fifth week. I got a letter from Stacy. "Bet" had been found dead on his toilet stool at home. It really shook me. He had been a real friend. I got a very short note from Rachel. She was in Cleveland.

It said, "I ran into an old doctor friend of yours the other night. He was looped. He bought me a drink. Lucky for me the bartender asked how you were doing. The doctor spilled his guts. He told me about a dead patient of his who came back to life. My worst wishes. P.S. Please drop dead. I'll keep the 'Hog.' "

The joint waived the balance of "Coppola's" time to face the rap in Maine. The skull pressure was getting larger. The cell was getting tighter. With "Coppola" gone I was in real trouble the third month. It was like a deadly hex was at work to crack me up.

None of the screws would cop heavy drugs for me. I settled for whiskey. I stopped using the safety razor. I didn't want to see the gaunt ugly stranger in my sliver of mirror. It wasn't just the cell. It was the sights and sounds of the misery and torment on the row and in the nightmares.

Mama was bed-ridden. She was too sick to write. I got telegrams and letters from her friends. They were all praying that I'd get out before Mama passed. I got a pass to the visitors cage. A screw took me and stood behind me the whole time. It was Stacy. She was pregnant and living with an old hustler. Her eyes told me how bad I looked. Her letters dropped off to one a month with no scratch.

At the end of the fourth month my skull was shaking on my shoulders like I had palsy. A con on the row blew his top one night around midnight. He woke up the whole cell house. At first he was cursing God and his mother. The screws brought him past my cell.

In my state the sight of him almost took me into madness. He was buck naked and jabbering a weird madman's language through a foamy jib. It was like the talking in tongues Holy Rollers do. . . . I gnawed into my pillow like the runt to keep from screaming.

The next day I put in a request to see the Nazi. Nothing happened. A week later I was sitting on the john with my head between my knees. I heard the morning line moving to breakfast. The line had stalled for a moment right outside my cell door.

I looked up into a pair of strange almost orange eyes sunk into an old horribly scarred face. It was Leroy. I had stolen Chris from him many years ago. He still remembered me. He stared at me and smiled crookedly as the line moved out.

I got my screw to check his rap sheet. The screw gave me the whole rundown. Since nineteen-forty Leroy had been arrested more than a hundred times for common drunk. He had also been committed to mental hospitals twice. I was forty-two. I was twenty when I stole Chris from him. I asked the screw to pull strings to send him to another cell house. I gave him a rundown on the Chris steal and how weak Leroy had been for her. The screw told me he couldn't cut it.

Leroy was doing only five days for drunk. Leroy had to stay in the cell house. I wondered how Leroy would try for revenge. I had to be careful in the morning for the next five days. I had to keep my feet and legs away from the cell door. Leroy might score for a shiv and try to hack something off when he passed my cell. I worried all day about what he would do. Could he somehow get gasoline and torch me?

That night I heard the voice for the first time. The lights were out. The cell house was quiet. The voice seemed to be coming through a tiny grille at the head of the cot.

A light always burned in the breezeway behind the grille. The pipes for all the plumbing for the cells were there. I got down on my hands and knees and looked through the grille's tiny holes. I couldn't see anybody.

I got back on the cot. The voice was louder and clearer. It sounded friendly and sweet like a woman consoling a friend. I wondered if cons on one of the tiers above me were clowning with each other.

I heard my name in the flow of chatter. I got back down and listened at the grille. A light flooded the corner. It was the screw. I spun around on my knees facing him. The light was in my eyes.

He said, "What the hell are you doing?"

I said, "Officer, I heard a voice. I thought some one was working back there."

He said, "Oh, Oh, you poor bastard. You won't pull this bit. You're going nuts 'Slim.' Now stop that nonsense and get in that cot and stay there."

The cell-house lights woke me up. My first thought was Leroy. I got up and sat on the cot. Then I thought about the voice. I wasn't sure now. Maybe it had been a dream.

I wondered whether I should ask the screw about it. One thing for sure, dream or not, I didn't want to go nuts. My mind hooked on to what I'd heard the old con philosopher say about the screen in the skull. I remembered what the books at Federal prison said about voices and even people that only existed inside a joker's skull.

I thought, "After this when I git the first sign of a sneaky worry thought, or idea, I'll fight it out of my skull."

Maybe I wasn't dreaming when I heard that voice. If I hear it again I'll have some protection. I'll keep a strong sane voice inside to fight off anything screwy from going on.

Every moment I'll stand guard over my thoughts until I get out of here. I can do it. I just have to train that guard. He's got to be slick enough not to let trouble by him. I'll make him shout down the phony voices. He'll know they're not real right away.

I got up and went to the face bowl. I heard the rumbling feet of the cons coming off the tiers. I was washing my face. I heard a series of sliding bumps on the floor behind me. It was like maybe several newsboys all throwing your paper on the porch in rotation. Then I smelled it. I turned toward the door. I squinted through the soap on my eyelids. I had been bombed with crap.

It was oozing off the wall. The solid stuff had rolled to my feet. Pieces of loosely rolled newspaper were the casings. Cons were passing my door snickering. I felt dizzy. A big lead ballon started inflating inside my chest. I remembered the inside guard. He was new and late on the job. I puked.

I shouted over and over, "Watch out now, it's only crap, it's only crap. It's just crap. Watch out, it can't hurt you. It's only stinking crap."

A screw stood at the cell door twitching his nose. He was screaming, "Shut Up!"

He opened the cell. I got a bucket of hot water and a scrub brush. I cleaned the cell. The screw asked me who fouled my nest. I told him I didn't know.

My screw came to see me at noon. He told me how Leroy had enlisted the crap-bombers. Leroy told them I had put the finger on him years ago when he got the bit for the Papa Tony beating. My screw dropped the truth around the cell house. All the bombers were down on Leroy. They dared him to bother me again. I was safe from Leroy.

I didn't mourn when Leroy finished his five-day bit.

It was the end of my sixth months. I beat down worry, voices, and countless thoughts of suicide with the skull-guard plan.

A friend of Mama's sent me a telegram. Mama had been stricken. The hospital doctors had given her up. Then she bounced back. She was very sick now, but still alive. The telegram gave my skull gimmick a tough test.

I had a very sad day around the middle of the seventh month. A booster from New York busted on his second day in town was on the tier above me. A con on my row several cells down called me one night to borrow a book. A moment later I heard my name called from up above. He came down next morning and rapped to me. His job was in the cell house.

The booster asked me if I were the "Iceberg" who was a friend of "Party Time." I told him yes. He didn't say anything for awhile. Finally he told me "Party" had often spoken of me as the kid he once hustled with who grew up to be "Iceberg" the pimp.

He told me "Party" had copped the beautiful girlfriend of a dope dealer when he got a bit. "Party" turned her out. The dope dealer did his bit. The broad tried to cut "Party" loose to go back to a life of ease.

"Party" went gorilla on her. He broke her arm. Two months later "Party" copped some "H." He didn't know his connection was a pal of the dealer who got the bit. It was "H" all right mixed with flakes of battery acid. I didn't sleep that night.

I had come to a decision in that awful cell. I was through with pimping and drugs. I got insight that perhaps I could never have hoped to get outside. I couldn't have awakened if I had been serving a normal bit. After I got the mental game down pat I could see the terrible pattern of my life.

Mama's condition and my guilty conscience had a lot to do with my decision. Perhaps my age and loss of youth played their parts. I had found out that pimping is for young men, the stupid kind.

I had spent more than half a lifetime in a worthless, dangerous profession. If I had stayed in school in eight years of study I could have been a M.D. or lawyer. Now here I was, slick but not smart, in a cell. I was past forty with counterfeit glory in my past, and no marketable training, no future. I had been a bigger sucker than a square mark. All he loses is scratch. I had joined a club that suckered me behind bars five times.

A good pimp has to use great pressure. It's always in the cards that one day that pressure will backfire. Then he will be the victim. I was weary of clutching quicksilver whores and the joints.

I was at the end of the ninth month of the bit. I got a front office interview. I was contesting my discharge date. I was still down for an eleven month bit.

An agent of the joint had been in the arresting group. I spent thirty days in County Jail before the transfer to the joint to finish out the year. I knew little or nothing about law. I was told at the interview

I had to do eleven months. I wasn't afraid I'd crack up serving the extra month. By this time I had perfect control of my skull.

Mama might die in California at any time. I had to get to her before she died. I had to convince her I loved her, that I appreciated her as a mother. That she and not whore-catching was more important to me. I had to get there as much for myself as for her.

I lay in that cell for two weeks. I wrote a paper based on what I believed were the legal grounds for my release at the expiration of ten months. It had subtle muscle in it too. I memorized the paper. I rehearsed it in the cell. Finally I felt I had the necessary dramatic inflection and fluid delivery. I was called in two weeks after I had requested the second interview.

I must have looked like a scarecrow as I stood before him. I was bearded, filthy, and ragged. He was immaculate seated behind his gleaming desk. He had a contemptuous look on his face.

I said, "Sir, I realize that the urgent press of your duties has perhaps contributed to your neglect of my urgent request for an interview. I have come here today to discuss the vital issue of my legal discharge date.

"Wild rumors are circulating to the effect that you are not a fair man, that you are a bigot, who hates Negroes. I discounted them immediately that I heard them. I am almost dogmatic in my belief that a man of your civic stature and intellect could ill afford or embrace base prejudice.

"In the spirit of fair play, I'm going to be brutally frank. If I am not released the day after tomorrow, a certain agent of mine here in the city is going to set in motion a process that will not only free me, but will possibly in addition throw a revealing spotlight on certain not too legal, not too pleasant activities carried on daily behind these walls.

"I have been caged here like an animal for almost ten months. Like an animal, my sensitivity of seeing and hearing has been enhanced. I only want what is legally mine. My contention is that if your Captain of guards, who is legally your agent, had arrested me and confined me on such an unlikely place as the moon for thirty days, technically and legally I would be in the custody of this institution. Sir, the point is unassailable. Frankly I don't doubt that my release will occur on legal schedule. Thank you, Sir, for the interview."

The contempt had drained out of his face. I convinced him I wasn't running a bluff. His eyes told me he couldn't risk it. After all, surely he knew how easy it was to get contraband in and out of the rotten joint. Getting a kite to an agent would be child's play. I didn't sleep that night. The next day I got a discharge notice. I would be released on legal schedule!

Editor's Note:

Clarence Harris, writing while an inmate at Indiana State Prison, provides a brief glimpse into the life of a young black male who ultimately becomes the personification of the "Bigger Thomases."

TESTAMENT

CLARENCE HARRIS

I was born in Mississippi, but my father and mother, being young and the parents of two children, a girl and boy, decided to escape to the promised land. They heard that there were golden opportunities in Memphis, Tennessee, and so they went there. My father acquired a skill as a house painter. His salary was $12 a week. My mother became a housekeeper at $6 a week. We lived in a clapboard shack with an outside toilet. The house set upon four tiers of bricks; inside we had oil lamps, coal stove, and no running water. I spent my time wandering the unpaved streets or playing in our packed-clay yard. I had an old dog, and together we played games of Caucasian heroes and villains. Funny now, as I look back, the villains were always darker than the heroes, with thick mustaches like my father wore, and almost always they were dressed in black clothes. I never realized that I was playing the villain in a much larger and serious game: that of emulation which had been passed on to me in my parents' ignorance and fear.

In the beginning I had very little contact with the white man. However, one particular incident sticks out in my mind even now. A white man, speeding through our street, ran over my dog. I screamed and the man stopped. My dad came out of the house to calm me down and to talk to the man, and that's when I discovered that men were different because of their skin color. The white man told my father: "Nigger, it should have been that little nigger there instead of the dog. You should've kept them both out of the street. And don't you ask me nothing about that dog!" My father shivered, and retreated with me into the house. We never mentioned the incident again. But from that time on I was taught that the white man was king and was to be treated as such; I learned that they were to be idolized, feared, catered to, and also to be emulated as much as possible without stepping out of your place.

Not long after that we prepared to move to another promised land, further North, where we would really be saved. The new state that we were moving to had been a dream, but soon after we arrived there, the bubble burst. The Northern promised land was only a larger plantation with buildings instead of fields. There were more white overseers and exploiters, and even though you didn't come under the domination of one man, you came under the rule of all white men; though they wouldn't physically hold you or punish you, the police were still their legal fist to hold you in line. Still, there were more subtle boundary lines, and the cruelest thing of all was their paternalism.

So I became a part of the black environment in the North that had a smattering of white middle-class bourgeois values, but I couldn't handle the unreality of trying to be white. And I took to the streets. There, we had our own thing, our own language, our own special walks, our hipness and our soul, which we attributed to heart and toughness, and the ability to survive. We wanted to be kings, too, but not kings of rats. By now, I had quit school, and I knew what was happening with whitey.

My father, and others like him, was told to vote for whoever the power structure wanted him to, or no jobs could be had. And those who had jobs were paying taxes for inferior schools, no garbage pickups, no police protection, and on and on and on. So I gave up and withdrew from the whole scene. Why should I follow the rules and conduct of such a hypocritical society? Naturally I ran head on into white power: the police. And eventually I came to prison.

In prison I began to think. I saw myself for what I was, which is completely different from what I am. I saw myself as what whitey had made me, which is completely different from what I am, and I saw society as it really is for making me what I was. And knowing all this, how can I be expected to accept this society that has tried to kill me, or its religion that makes a fool out of any black man.

And prison here is nothing but a smaller version of what's happening outside. There is just as much racism here, both openly and under cover, and just like on the outside, nothing is ever done about it but talk. I've been thinking. All this talking and protesting is just another one of whitey's trick bags, because when you protest and demonstrate and all the rest, it is understood that you believe that the people you're protesting to are really fair and honest and that once you make them see, then they'll apologize and take their feet off your neck. But once that belief fades

and protesting ends, then revolution begins. And the belief is fading fast.

Editor's Note:

Athletics has been one of the primary avenues for the limited success allowed black people in this country. Bill Russell, former NBA superstar and player-coach for the Boston Celtics, relates some of the experiences that he encountered simply because he was black.

GO UP FOR GLORY*

BILL RUSSELL

One major incident during my years with the Celtics came during a non-Celtic NBA All Star exhibition tour after the 1958 playoffs. We were being paid in good, cold cash per game so don't think that I only do this when I'm already on a seasonal payroll.

Dallas was on the schedule and we were told Negro members of the team would be treated as much like Americans as anyone else.

We flew from Louisville to Dallas in a DC-3 on a particularly bad day. The plane almost crashed. We were late getting in. When we arrived, the promoter still said everything was all right, although I wanted to call the hotel from the airport. But we went and played because we were late.

When we finally got to the hotel, the promoter and his local aide said: "You're going to stay at . . . ."

No thanks, baby. Money never meant that much to me.

They protested it wasn't their fault. The man put out his hand for me to shake. I spat at it. I went back to the airport and flew home. It cost me several thousand dollars. About one quarter of what I was earning that year. I was broke. But I was a man. I would do it again. It is the people who say they're not responsible who are just as responsible as anyone else.

The only thing you can do is make the cost of being a bigot just that—costly. I try. It cost them on the tour. Regrettably, it cost me, too. But it was worth it. Success in having all Americans just that—all

---

*Written in collaboration with William McSweeney.

49

Americans—will only come when the cost of being a bigot becomes too high to pay.

Another time, I was going to Miami for an exhibition. They told me the hotel was all right. I called up and the guy said: "Yes."

I didn't believe it. I stayed on him. Finally, he said, "Oh, yes. You can stay here. You may use the dining room and the swimming pool. We ask only one thing. Be inconspicuous."

I broke up in laughter and in anger.

Six-ten. A Negro. Wearing a beard. Can you just see me using the swimming pool and being inconspicuous?

I checked into a Negro hotel, instead. It wasn't like the one in North Carolina. I had a ball.

And got a suntan.

The other time "it" happened with the Celtics was in Lexington, Kentucky.

Ramsay was an All-American graduate of the University of Kentucky and it was a Homecoming Day Exhibition with St. Louis for Rams and his Kentucky teammate (then with the Hawks) Cliff Hagan.

We flew all day from Wichita to Lexington and had no breakfast or lunch. We checked into the hotel.

I was just leaving my room to eat when Sam Jones and Tom Sanders came down the hall and met K.C. and me.

"Where are you going?" they asked.

"To get something to eat in the coffee-shop," K.C. said.

"Not down there you're not," said Sam.

They had gone in to eat and the waitress refused to serve them.

I just went back in the room and called the airport. "I would like a plane," I said.

"To where?" asked the girl.

"Whichever is the next plane going to Washington, New York or Chicago," I said.

I told "you guys" that I was leaving. They could guide themselves accordingly.

They all wanted to leave.

Al Butler, another teammate, was absent from the hotel and we couldn't find him. We did see Woody Sauldsberry and Cleo Hill of St. Louis and informed them of the circumstances of our "residence" in this palatial hostelry for Americans and they left as well.

Next, we called Auerbach who tried to convince us that it was better for our race, better for all Negroes, if we stayed. I was sick and tired of that argument. I believe, most sincerely, that for decades a proud race—the American Negro—has attempted to make it better "for your people" by playing the game of life with bigots by maintaining the status quo. It

never worked. The only way to gain rights is to fight for them. Regardless of whether I was suspended, fined, or whatever, I was going to fight.

"I speak for no one but myself, Red," I said. "I'm leaving. I've gone through all the arguments. I am simply no longer satisfied to go along with the status quo."

The others agreed. Auerbach took us to the airport.

Later, Ramsay sided with us and there were many apologies. We were not condemning one waitress, one person, but rather the climate which makes such a thing possible.

The people of Lexington, who had a double standard at that time, were not offended at the game that evening. They got just what they apparently wanted—a lily-white basketball game.

A St. Louis sportswriter, Bob Burns, insisted in his column that I should be suspended and fined for insulting two such fine gentlemen as Ramsay and Hagan.

I wondered then and I wonder now—what about me being insulted? Or am I a person?

Success rode easily with the Celtics. I do not believe we ever became swell-headed. God knows, we had to fight for everything. More often than not crucial series went to the final, gasping minute. Sometimes into overtime.

But, black, white, religious, irreligious, we somehow put together a rather unique example of Americans—a mixed team of men who in forty-eight tumultuous minutes of play could survive it all to go on and win championship after championship.

There were Jews, Catholics, Protestants, agnostics, white men, black men. The one thing we had in common was an Irish name. The Celtics.

Believe me. We did the Irish name proud. Through it all—though I tell truths which may nip occasionally at the heels and the hearts of some members—we never had a clique, we never had a quarrel. A man might be a black super star or a white super star. It made no difference. You might see me, the bombthrower, out one night with whites, another night with Negroes, a third night with whites and Negroes. We never considered it unusual. We simply considered ourselves a proud group of men who bore the distinction of being something no one else could be in our sport—the champions of the world.

Felton X

When you become a so-called "name" athlete, you get involved in many State Department trips overseas.

Mine started before the Olympics when we went to South America. After the 1959 season, I went to Africa alone.

My first stop was Tripoli where a large press conference had been arranged. I was warned to be careful. Communist writers were present. They would try to embarrass the United States.

The first question was: "Why are you really here?"

I said: "I am here to play basketball and to show the people of Tripoli something about a sport which I love because I believe they will love it, too."

The Communist writer now threw his bomb and I saw our State people flinch: "What's the name of the King?"

What do you do now, baby?

No one had thought to brief me on the political aspects of Triploi and I didn't have the vaguest idea of the name of the King, or even if there was one.

I figured truth was a better answer than a stutter, so I said:

"I don't know the name of the King. I am not a politician. I am not interested in politics. I'm interested only in teaching basketball. Were I a spy then I would be very well informed. I have come here only to work with kids."

Suddenly all the press corps were on their feet and giving me a cheer and they were even throwing a few barbed chuckles at the Communist. No one bothered me any more in press conferences.

From Tripoli, I flew to Ethiopia.

The State Department has been labelled "Ugly" in some countries. In Ethiopia, they did not make a strong impression on me.

I was met at the airport by the cultural attaché. I knew he was there by the yell:

"Hey, Bill. . .Hey, Bill. . .Hey, Boy. . ."

Along came this charging American."You're a big boy, aren't you? Yeah, Bill Boy, you're a big one."

How to make friends.

No Negro man likes to be called "Boy."

We are men . . . not boys. Not some dumb backwoods slave . . . the connotation of "boy" to the Negro is of servitude . . . of being less than a man.

Then he told me: "You'd better apply for your exit visa two weeks in advance. Their system is so bad it will take that long."

Later, when the time came, I got my exit visa in five minutes.

Then they pulled the really classic boner. In the province of Harra, old tribalism is still very much existent. There were two schools and they were separate entities. One tribe, one school, would not talk to the other.

So, the State Department invited them both to a clinic I was conducting.

Talk about a rumble. You should have been there. Stones. Clubs. Fists.

Where was Russell? Where do you think. I was running as fast as anyone else. The only guy who passed me was the charging American from State. Cultural advisor.

There was one memorable experience. I was giving a clinic one day when an escorted limousine drove up. In it was the Lion himself, Haile Selassie. I was invited to join him in the back seat of the car.

The tiny little giant of a man appologized to me for requiring the conference in the automobile, but explained that it simply would not do to have the Emperor looking up at someone six-ten.

Giant? I felt like a pygmy beside him.

We talked on and on for about ten minutes. He spoke impeccable English. Our State people had told me he did not understand the language. Years later, I watched him being interviewed on television. All the questions went through an interpreter and it was explained that he did not speak English.

Yeah.

It was on this first trip to Africa that I was confronted with the deep emotional feeling of returning to a homeland. I was overwhelmed with the beauty and the depth of the land.

I finally found the most beautiful of all in Liberia.

It crystallized in a schoolroom far upcountry. A question and answer period was held and a child asked me: "Why are you here?"

Without even thinking, I answered: "I came here because I believe that somewhere in Africa is my ancestral home. I came here because I am drawn here, like any man, drawn to seek the land of my ancestors."

The kids stood up and cheered. The demonstration touched me so deeply I began to cry and was unable to continue. In that one short statement I had expressed, poured forth a deep, inner feeling I had never previously recognized.

It welled up from deep inside me like something clean and beautiful and new and it is a feeling I have had ever since. America is my native land. To it I owe my fidelity, my trust, my loyalty. Yet, like any man, I am moved to great emotion by the memory of my ancestors and of their triumphs and their despairs.

Perhaps that was one major reason why I invested in Liberia. Mr. Buchanan, the Commissioner of the Department of Public Works, took me on a tour of the countryside and showed me the excellent economic opportunities in Liberia. Indeed, many U.S.

firms have deep investments. Later I found some acreage and I thought, "This is it. This is the place." I obtained it. We started with investments in rubber. Since then the plantation has grown considerably and after six years of worrying and pouring in money and frustrations, and learning about business and rubber, we now appear to be on the verge of making a success of it.

Believe me, however. It wasn't a present. And it didn't come easy.

Things didn't come easy when I returned to the United States either. There was speculation about my investments in Liberia and my statements about my ancestral home. Was I planning to reject the United States and live in Liberia? Being the usual grouchy guy I can be when pestered with questions which are patently ridiculous—and being deeply frustrated by the continuing unequal (at that time, 1959) struggle for equality—I answered: "Yeah. Maybe I will. I'll get away from you, anyway."

The reporter left out the last sentence. The story just read that I was planning to move to Liberia.

No one could understand that a man can be caught between two worlds. West Africa is my ancestral home. The United States is my native land.

But because of what I said, the avalanche began. From there, it went on and at one point I was being labeled a Black Muslim.

"Felton X" they called me.

For the record—I am not a Black Muslim.

For the record, I am a proud, reasonably happy man, who was blessed by God in being born a Negro. I am happy to be a Negro. I am happy to share in the problems of the Negro here in America. I hope to do more about it. I understand that the Irish are proud of Ireland, the Italians are proud of Italy and the Jews are proud of Israel. Just like them, I am proud of my ancestral home—West Africa.

And as far as being a Black Muslim goes, let me phrase it this way:

Someone asked me if I was in favor of Muslimism. I answered: "I don't know, because I don't know enough about it."

They wrote: Felton X.

A man should not be against something until he has studied it. I was not against Communism until I thoroughly studied it and recognized that the whole theory was not for me.

I am not a Muslim because I cannot intellectually follow their line of reasoning, although I agree with some of the points they make and honor their right to their philosophy.

But a man cannot be against a name. He cannot just be "anti-Muslim." Or "anti-Communist." He must be against the philosophy, having understood it.

Because I am what I am, it was easy for some persons to fail to accept the true answer and instead dismiss it with: "He's a Muslim."

That is their prerogative but, in turn, any thoughtful person must agree that the basic problems of our society which have created an organization such as Muslimism cannot be answered if people react with "He's a Muslim" when confronted with the naked facts of the human rights issue here in the United States.

And if people don't really realize what Black Muslimism was caused by.

If nothing else, it served a unique purpose. It was so far out—so desperately far out—that it caused more people to move towards the center, to move towards a rational way of thought about civil rights.

Yet, for some, Black Muslimism was an answer. It served as a focal point for the torments of men who needed a far out proposal to shock them from their depravity. Men who were dope addicts, drunks, wife beaters, jailbirds, who had fought all their lives against a society they could not comprehend in a manner they could not comprehend, were attracted to Black Muslimism and embraced it.

They didn't realize it, but they were seeking their manhood . . . the manhood so many Negroes have been deprived of.

But for the record . . . Bill Russell already had his manhood. The name is Felton, yes.

But not Felton X.

The Battleground

It was July 1963, and the phone rang at my home in Reading, Massachusetts.

Charlie Evers was on the phone from Jackson, Mississippi.

He said: "When Medgar was shot you told me you'd do anything you could to help. I can use some help right now. But you may get killed."

He wanted me in Mississippi two days later to give basketball clinics. The City of Jackson was torn with violence. Other towns came later. Selma . . . Birmingham . . . Bogalusa . . . Oxford . . . the roll-call of the battles of our generation in the 1960s.

I didn't want to go to Mississippi. I was like anyone else. I was afraid to get killed.

My wife asked me not to go. Some friends said the same thing. A man must do what he thinks is right. I called Eastern Airlines and ordered my ticket.

Thirty-six hours later I was playing for a different kind of championship in Jackson, Mississippi. The baggage agent at Eastern couldn't find my suitcase. "You sure you had one, boy?"

I had one, baby.

I had been forewarned. I knew what I was getting into. Jackson was another skirmish in a long battle. The red-necks were out to fight one more delaying action, one more last stand.

Men like Medgar Evers were dead and other men had taken up his flag. Charlie Evers was a man marked for death, who slept with a pistol in his hand. The first night in Jackson I had no pistol, but I stayed with a friend with the door bolted. It would be rattled once in a while. There were noises in the alley. My friend couldn't sleep. "They're coming for us, they're after us," he said.

The kind of men who come after you in the darkness do not frighten me. I went to sleep.

The next day I started giving my basketball clinics. They were the first integrated clinics ever held in the Jackson Auditorium.

There was no trouble in the Auditorium. The Mayor was even pleased, proud, that Jackson could hold such an event.

I was not proud or pleased. It was a century in coming. I could hold clinics anywhere in the world — except in certain places in the United States.

But I was in Jackson to stay for three days. No one was going to drive me out. And no papers were going to print big stories about Bill Russell. It was just something I had to do. Not for credit. Just because I was a man.

At night, darkness came down on the no-man's land which is the Negro segment on the world south of Washington, D.C. Cars followed us down the road. Full of drunken red-necks. Later, they would shoot a soldier, a lady, a kid. They would shoot the unarmed ones. They would lose their taste for it when they came abreast of our car. They would see guns and they would pull back and fall away, the headlights fading into the background.

A coward will never fight a man who is equal. The sadness is that in the darkness of Jackson it had to be men who were equal only with guns.

I was having dinner in Jackson with two priests. Four red-necks came in. Paunchy, sick, loudmouth men who were drinking. They showed their guns as they took the table next to us. They began talking about the priests. I am not overly religious, but they were good men. I said: "I know how you are at praying, but can you fight?" I laughed. They laughed back. The red-necks kept on our backs.

I stood up and went to their table. My knees were shaking. Was it anger? Was it fear?

I stood beside the big one. "Baby," I said, "I am a peaceful man. But to me life is a jungle. When people threaten me or mine, then I go back to the law of the jungle. Now I tell you—which law are we living by here? Because if this is the jungle then I am going to start killing."

They jumped up and left. The priests and I went back to our supper.

Was it hatred?

Was it bitter anger?

Who am I?

Why should I go through this?

I am, in the final sense, just a man. I am neither all right nor all wrong. I was born in this nation, in this century. I was born to be a member of the nation, a member of the century, a member of the world.

A man, nothing more.

Neither right nor wrong.

Maybe I've soured on life, or maybe I'm a cynic, but I wasn't born that way. Maybe, I am an idealist—a frustrated idealist—but I wasn't born that way either. Things that I have experienced have made me what I am.

All I have finally asked is for everybody to succeed or fail on their own merits. I have tried to have a difference in values as values are computed in our modern society. I have worked hard for money. But I have not worshiped it.

I have never worked to be well-liked or well-loved, but only to be respected. I have fought a problem the only way I know how. Maybe it was right or wrong in the approach, but a man can only ultimately be counted if he thinks he is doing right. Then, at least, he is a man.

In this book, I think that some of the problems of being a man, being a super star, being a Negro in the United States today have been pointed out.

I have my own ideas for the future.

I have my own hopes and my own dreams.

I believe that I can contribute something far more important than mere basketball.

I said before three emotions have always been very real to me—fear, prejudice and bitterness.

It is the reactions to these emotions that make a man.

In the end, I live with the hopes that when I die, it will be inscribed for me:

Bill Russell.

He was a man.

PART II. A:

HISTORICAL GENESIS AND AFRICAN HERITAGE

OUTCAST

CLAUDE McKAY

For the dim regions whence my fathers came
My spirit, bondaged by the body, longs.
Words felt, but never heard, my lips would frame;
My soul would sing forgotten jungle songs.
I would go back to darkness and to peace,
But the great western world holds me in fee,
And I may never hope for full release
While to its alien gods I bend my knee.
Something in me is lost, forever lost,
Some vital thing has gone out of my heart,
And I must walk the way of life a ghost
Among the sons of earth, a thing apart.

For I was born, far from my native clime,
Under the white man's menace, out of time.

Editor's Note:

Ghana, Mali, and Songhai were powerful, highly developed kingdoms of Western Africa. Records of Arab travelers describing Ghana date from 734, but it is believed that this nation-state had been a power since the fourth century. The Arab geographer, al-Bakri, writing in the eleventh century, can be credited with providing much of the important data on the Sudan. The *Masalik al-Absar* of al-Umari provides a vivid account of the Hajj, or pilgrimage to Mecca, by Mansa Musa, a ruler of Mali whose fame had spread throughout Europe and the Middle East. Al-Umari visited Cairo twelve years after Mansa Musa's sojourn and found the townspeople still singing his praises. The money market in Egypt had not yet recovered from the vast amount of gold suddenly put into circulation during the pilgrimage.

Ibn Batuta, the great traveler of North Africa, reported in great detail on his mid-fourteenth century visit to the Muslim country of Mali. Leo Africanus, a highly educated and intelligent Moor captured on an Arab galley by Christian pirates, was presented to Pope Leo X instead of the slave markets of Italy. His talents were immediately recognized; he gained his freedom, a pension, and his name. His extensive knowledge of the world beyond the Muslim barriers in North Africa soon earned him many honors. *The History and Description of Africa and the Notable Things Therein Contained* vividly described the extremely active trans-Saharan trade and the countries he had visited. In addition to the oral tradition passed on from generation to generation, Muslim scholars in Africa also compiled many valuable works that are still studied today. One of these was a history of the Songhai empire, *The Tarikh al-Fattash*, written between 1520 and 1660.

Ghana, Mali, and Songhai were not the only kingdoms in Africa, and they differed in many ways from the modern nation-states of the same names. They are, however, representative of West Africa, which supplied the vast numbers of Africans enslaved in North and South America, and in intellectual and material culture they were the equal of any country of the time. Slavery in the United States, which was justified and rationalized on the basis of alleged black savagery, heathenism, defective mental abilities, and sub-human development, can be nowhere substantiated in the reality of the situation. The "dark continent" was a darkness that existed only in the minds of those who had a need to exploit and subjugate.

TIME CHART OF AFRICAN HISTORY

BASIL DAVIDSON

West Africa	*Central and South Africa*	*East Africa*
		1,750,000 BC First hominid at Olduvai Gorge
		60,000-40,000 BC *Homo sapiens* enters Africa and begins to replace earlier hominid forms; fire and microlithic tools appear about this time
5000 BC Modern races of Africa have developed; beginnings of Saharan rock paintings		**5000-4500 BC** Agriculture in Nile Valley
3500 BC Sahara area still fertile; pastoralists and agriculturalists are established		**3100 BC** First Egyptian Dynasty
2500 BC Sahara begins to dry; Caucasoid peoples tend to move north; Negroid peoples south	**2500 BC** Bantu-speaking peoples begin to move south from their homeland in the Nigeria-Cameroun area; they expand at the expense of Pygmies and the Khoisan peoples	**2500 BC and after** Egyptian contacts with the south; trading voyages to Punt (coast of modern Somalia); conquests of Nubia; trading caravans to the "land of Yam" for ivory, leopard skins, and a "dancing dwarf"
1000 BC Evidence for animal-drawn vehicles in trans-Saharan trade; traces of iron-working in northern Ghana		**950 BC** Kush independent of Egypt
		8th-7th centuries BC Kushitic dynasty rules Egypt; beaten in 666 BC by the iron-using Assyrians; the Kushitic dynasty retires southward along the Nile, masters iron-working, and remains independent for 1000 years as the kingdom of Meroë
500 BC Agriculture begins to spread from savannah to forest		**600-595 BC** Phoenician sailors said by Herodotus to have circumnavigated Africa from east to west

West Africa	Central and South Africa	East Africa

300 BC
Nok culture of Nigeria distinguished by iron-working and realistic terra-cotta sculpture

100 AD
Iron-working reaches Zambia; this probably suggests colonization by Bantu agriculturalists

200 AD
Periplus of the Erythraean Sea gives the first account of trade on the East African coast, but does not mention black people among the local inhabitants

330 AD
Axum wipes out declining Meroë

333 AD
Conversion of King of Axum to Christianity; birth of the Ethiopian church

300-500(?) AD
Indonesian contacts with East Africa and colonization of Madagascar

710 AD
Muslims complete conquest of North Africa

8th-9th centuries AD
Kisale culture in the southern Congo; Katanga copper mined and worked

c. 710 AD
Axum ravaged by Muslims; the kingdom's center moves southward and evolves into the Ethiopian state; Christian states are already flourishing in the Nilotic Sudan

8th century AD
Bantu-speaking peoples have reached the coast; black slaves in Iraq, Indonesia, India, and China

800 AD
Ghana a powerful trading state; first penetration of Islamic traders south of the desert

9th century AD
Foundation of Kilwa

850 AD
Origin of Kanem

1000 AD
Ghana prosperous; Gao and Jenne exist as the early forerunners of Mali; Hausa and Yoruba states begin to form

1000 AD
Bigo earthworks suggest centralized state in Uganda

1000-1200 AD
Zagwe rulers of Ethiopia build the rock churches of Lalibela

West Africa	Central and South Africa	East Africa
1050 AD Bedouin Arabs from Egypt invade North Africa		
1076 AD Almoravid Berbers defeat Ghana		
1088 AD Ruler of Kanem becomes Muslim		
1230 AD Sundiata founds the Mali Empire as the successor state to Ghana		**1200-1500 AD** Height of the Indian Ocean trade and the heyday of the Swahili city states
1300 AD Ife leads the Yoruba states; Benin well established		**1270 AD** Restoration of the Solomonic Dynasty, the present ruling house of Ethiopia
1312-1337 AD Reign of Mansa Musa in Mali		
1400 AD Songhai people of Gao begin to weaken Mali	**1400 AD** Foundation of the Kongo state	
1456 AD Islam reaches Zaria in Hausaland	**1400-1450 AD** Monomotapa rulers have built Zimbabwe, set up a large state, and are continuing the ancient trade of Rhodesian gold for luxury goods from the coast (the Rozwi completed Zimbabwe c. 1700, after the decline of the Monomotapa state)	**1452 AD** Ethiopian embassy visits Lisbon
1400-1480 AD Kanem defeated by Bulala; state moves to southwest of Lake Chad and reconstitutes itself as the Empire of Bornu		
1461 AD Sunni Ali begins to create Songhai Empire		
1472 AD Portuguese build fort of El Mina on the Gold Coast	**1482 AD** Diogo Cao, Portuguese navigator, reaches Kongo	
c. 1490 AD Al-Maghili visits sub-Saharan Africa		**1498 AD** Vasco da Gama rounds the Cape of Good Hope, reaches East Africa, and sails to India
1493-1528 AD Reign of Askia Mohammed in Songhai		**15th-16th centuries** Arabs destroy the Christian states of the Nilotic Sudan

West Africa	Central and South Africa	East Africa
	c. 1500 AD and after Buganda and the other interlacustrine states are being formed; they have no contact with the coast until late 18th century	16th century AD Portuguese disrupt the old Indian Ocean trading network; coastal cities now under Portuguese influence or control; a period of decline in African power
	Rise of the Luba-Lunda states in southern Congo, Zambia, and eastern Angola	
1580-1617 AD Kanem-Bornu at the height of its power under Mai Idris Alooma	1575 AD Portugal begins the long conquest of Angola	
1591 AD Moroccan invaders crush Songhai at the battle of Tondibi		17th century AD Omani Arabs aid local peoples in driving the Portuguese away from most of the coast; by 1700, Portuguese influence remains only in Mozambique
1650 AD Oyo dominates Yoruba states	1652 AD Dutch set up a provision station at the Cape of Good Hope; the indigenous Hottentots and Bushmen are caught between the Europeans and the Bantu, who already occupy Natal and the Transvaal and are still moving south; by 1800 the indigenous peoples are destroyed, disorganized, or driven into desert and mountain areas	17th-18th centuries AD Ethiopia, exhausted after long wars against Muslims and troubled by migrating Galla, is fragmented by powerful lords at the expense of a series of weak kings
1700 AD Formation of the Ashanti state by Osei Tutu and Okomfo Anokye		
1725 AD Fon state of Dahomey reaches to coast	1700 AD Kongo in full decline; Portugal victorious in Angola	
Islamic revolution (*jihad*) in Futa Jallon		
1750-1807 AD Niger Delta city states thrive on coastal trade	1775 AD First war in South Africa between the Boers and the Bantu, both of whom are expanding into new territory	
1764-1824 AD Bureaucratization of Ashanti state; process begins during reign of Osei Kwadwo (1764-1777)		
1791 AD British establish Freetown (Sierra Leone) as a haven for freed slaves		

West Africa	Central and South Africa	East Africa

West Africa

1804-1811 AD
Teachings of Uthman Dan Fodio
lead to Islamic revolution *(jihad)*
in Northern Nigeria and the conquest of the Hausa states by the
Fulani

1807 AD
Britain outlaws the slave trade

1817 AD
Bowditch visits Ashanti capital,
Kumasi

1821 AD
Foundation of Liberia

Dahomey revolts against Oyo;
Oyo Empire is in decline

1823-1825 AD
Denham and Clapperton travel in
Northern Nigeria

1827 AD
Ashanti beat British and Fante
force

1851-1855 AD
Barth's travels in the western Sudan

1874 AD
Britain defeats Ashanti and sacks
Kumasi

1892-1894 AD
France conquers Dahomey

Central and South Africa

1816 AD
Shaka ruler of the Zulus; his wars
establish a powerful Zulu state;
fugitives form the Basuto and
Swazi states (both now independent), and Nguni-speaking peoples
migrate north and set up states as
far away as Lake Tanganyika

19th century AD
Extension of East Coast slave
trade and more peaceful commerce into the interior

1890 AD
European settlers enter Rhodesia

East Africa

19th century AD
Egypt invades the Sudan (1822);
ousted; 1881-1885 Sudanese religious revolt led by the Mahdi

1850-1900 AD
Ethiopian rulers begin process of
centralization and subjugation of
powerful lords; Menelik II crushes
invading Italians at Adowa (1896)
and lays the foundations for a
modern state

KINGDOMS OF THE WESTERN SUDAN

THOMAS HODGKIN

The Sudan, meaning "the country of the Black People," is the name the Arabs gave to the great belt of savannah stretching across Africa from the Atlantic to the Red Sea. North of it lies the Sahara desert; south of it is tropical forest. In the west the river Niger flows through the Sudan for most of its course, providing a natural link for the peoples who live along it. It was in this region that large, well-organized, predominantly Negro states—which at the height of their power could reasonably be called empires—were established during the period known to Europeans as the Middle Ages. Three of these states stand out in history: Ghana, Mali, and Gao.

Why were these states important? Principally because they played the part of middlemen. They were middlemen in the commercial sense: their towns were the great markets—for gold and slaves from the forest countries to the south; for salt from the Sahara mines; for horses, cloth, swords, books, and haberdashery from North Africa and Europe. But they were also intermediaries as regards ideas: from the eleventh century onwards the towns of the western Sudan were the main centres from which the teachings of Islam, carried across the desert from North Africa, began to be spread among West Africans. The spread of Islam meant a great deal to West Africa. Among other things, it meant much closer contact across the Sahara between the Arab and Negro worlds, and the growth of Muslim learning and scientific interests. Indeed, what we know about these kingdoms comes mainly from the works of Arab geographers, who were interested in describing this frontier Muslim region, or of Negro scholars writing in Arabic.

One way of looking at these Sudanese kingdoms is to take certain familiar dates in English history, and ask: 'What was the state of affairs in the western Sudan at this particular point in time?' This may help us to fit the rise, development, and decline of Ghana, Mali, and Gao into some kind of historical framework.

Let us begin with that well-known date, 1066. When William of Normandy invaded England, what was happening in West Africa? The most powerful state at this time was certainly Ghana, ruled over by a still surviving people called the Sarakole, which since the eighth century or earlier dominated the region north of the Senegal and Niger rivers. We need to remember, of course, that this ancient Ghana, on the edge of the Sahara, lay several hundred miles north of modern Ghana—the Gold Coast, as it used to be called. The main link between the two is that the people of modern Ghana, the first West African colony to become an independent state, look back to this ancient kingdom of Ghana as their cultural ancestor, rather in the way that modern Europeans look back to Greece and Rome. Much the best account of eleventh-century Ghana comes from the excellent Arab geographer al-Bakri, who completed his *Description of North Africa* in 1067. Though al-Bakri lived all his life at Cordova, in Spain, he must have collected information from merchants who knew Ghana at first-hand, as well as drawing on the Cordova archives. Here are a few sentences from his account:

'Ghana consists of two towns situated in a plain. The one inhabited by Muslims is very big and includes twelve mosques .... The town the king lives in is six miles away and is called *al-Ghaba*, which means "the forest." The territory between the two towns is covered with dwellings. The houses are built of stone and wood.... The king's interpreters, the controller of his treasury, and the majority of his vizirs are chosen from among the Muslims. ...

The religion of these Negroes is paganism and the worship of idols.... All the gold nuggets found in the mines belong to the king; but he leaves to his people the gold dust, with which everybody is familiar.... The king of Ghana can raise 200,000 warriors, 40,000 of them being armed with bows and arrows. ...'

Al-Bakri speaks here of the capital of Ghana as consisting of two towns—one Muslim, the other predominantly pagan. The site of the Muslim town is almost certainly the modern Koumbi Saleh, in the extreme south of what is now Mauretania, where recent excavations have revealed a number of well-built stone houses, with triangular niches in the walls and Koranic inscriptions on the plaster; a mosque; and several large tombs outside the city. Al-Bakri also makes clear that in his day the ruling dynasty was pagan. But ten years after our reference date, in 1076-77, the situation changed. The Berber Almoravids, puritan Muslim reformers from the western Sahara, who had already established their power in Morocco, attacked and captured Ghana, and converted the dynasty to Islam. This clearly was the time when Islam was beginning to spread throughout the western Sudan, as much as a result of the peaceful penetration of North African merchants and scholars as of the shock of the Almoravids' holy war.

Let us now jump nearly three centuries and consider the state of the western Sudan in 1346, the year of the battle of Crecy. How did things stand then? The Empire of Ghana had totally disappeared. Its power was finally broken by its southern neighbours, the Sosso, probably in the year 1203. Most of the Ghana merchants and scholars fled north to a new caravan city on the extreme edge of the Sahara, Walata—though there may have been some southward migration of the Ghana people too. By 1346 Walata, and Jenne on the upper Niger, were handling most of the trans-Saharan trade that had formerly flowed through Ghana. And Timbuktu, on the Niger bend to the east, was already at the beginning of its period of commercial greatness.

Politically the larger part of the western Sudan —from Senegal in the west to the Hausa states (in what is now Northern Nigeria) in the east—was included in, or dependent upon, the widespread Mali Empire. Mali, the kingdom of the Mandingo people, began to be a powerful force in the thirteenth century. But it was the great fourteenth-century emperor, Mansa Musa (*mansa* in Mamde means simply 'emperor') who succeeded in pushing forward the frontiers of the Mali Empire to their furthest extent; and who, by his magnificently equipped state pilgrimage to Mecca, by way of Cairo, literally put Mali on to the fourteenth-century European map. (A picture of *Rex Melli*, "the king of the gold mines," first appeared on a Majorca map of 1339.) The lavish presents of gold which Mansa Musa distributed in Cairo, and their inflationary effect upon the currency, were remembered in Egypt long after the event.

The best first-hand account of the Empire of Mali in the mid-fourteenth century is by Ibn Battuta of Tangier, the most enterprising of the medieval Arab travellers, who had already visited India and China, Indonesia and Turkestan. Ibn Battuta arrived at Niani, the Mali capital, in June, 1353, and stayed there eight months. His first impressions of the reigning Emperor, Mansa Sulayman, Mansa Musa's brother, were not at all favourable. 'He is a miserly king,' wrote Ibn Battuta; 'not a man from whom one might hope for a rich present.' However, relations improved when Ibn Battuta obtained free board and lodging during his longish stay; and he gives a vivid description of the elaborate court ritual:

The Sultan's usual dress is a velvety red tunic. . . . He is preceded by his musicians, who carry gold and silver guitars, and behind him come three hundred armed slaves. He walks in a leisurely fashion, affecting a very slow movement, and even stops from time to time. On reaching the dais he stops and looks round the assembly, then ascends it in the sedate manner of a preacher ascending a mosque-pulpit. As he takes his seat the drums, trumpets, and bugles are sounded.

Eventually Ibn Battuta came round to a very favourable view of the Mali political system:

'The Negroes possess some admirable qualities. They are seldom unjust, and have a greater abhorrence of injustice than any other people. Their sultan shows no mercy to anyone who is guilty of the least act of it. There is complete security in their country. Neither traveller, nor inhabitant in it, has anything to fear from robbers or men of violence. They do not confiscate the property of any white man who dies in their country, even if it be uncounted wealth.'

Such a judgement could hardly have been passed on contemporary France or England.

Let us take as our last point of reference the year 1513—the year of the Battle of Flodden, when Henry VIII was the young king of England. What was the situation in the western Sudan at this time?

The kingdom of the Songhai people, with its capital at Gao on the middle Niger, which had been expanding during the previous century, was now at the height of its power. Its ruler was one of the ablest of the West African sovereigns, Muhammad Askia, generally known as Askia the Great; a former general in the Songhai army, who in 1493 had overthrown the last ineffective representative of the dynasty that had governed for eight centuries, and taken over power in Gao. Under the Askia dynasty, which ruled Gao through the sixteenth century—coinciding roughly with the period of Tudor power in England—the greater part of the western Sudan was again united under a single government. Indeed, the Empire of Gao at this time stretched a long way farther north into the Sahara, including the vitally important salt mines on the frontiers of modern Algeria, than ever Mali had done. In the east, Askia the Great occupied the powerful caravan city of Agades, which controlled the main trade routes to Tunis, Tripoli and Egypt; and in this actual year, 1513, he invaded the Hausa States—including Kano, today the commercial centre of northern Nigeria—bringing them, for a time, within the Gao Empire. But it was not so much in his military achievements that Askia's genius showed itself as in the efficient system of administration which he developed, with the support of the Muslim religious leaders and the merchants, as a means of unifying this extensive empire. A system of provincial governors was introduced, and a number of central ministries created—for finance, justice, home affairs, agriculture, and forests, as well as a distinct ministry for 'White People' (i.e., for the Moors and Tuareg, living on the Saharan frontiers of the empire).

It was a little after this date, 1513, that a young Arab—his full name was al-Hasan ibn Muhammad al-Wazzān al-Zayyāti—who had been brought up at Fez in Morocco, visited the western Sudan in the company of his uncle, on a diplomatic mission from the Sultan of Morocco to Askia the Great. Later, while still only in his early twenties, he was captured by Sicilian pirates and handed over to Pope Leo X, who encouraged him to write about Africa and baptized him, giving him his own Christian names—John Leo. Thus al-Hasan ibn Muhammad came to be known to the European world as Leo Africanus. One of the points about the Gao Empire at this time which particularly impressed Leo Africanus was the influence of its merchants and intellectuals:

'The inhabitants of Timbuktu are very rich, especially the foreigners who have settled in the country; so much so that the king gave two of his daughters in marriage to two merchants who were brothers, on account of their great wealth. . . .

There are numerous judges, doctors, and clerics in Timbuktu, all receiving good salaries from the king. He pays great respect to men of learning. There is a big demand for books in manuscript, imported from Barbary. More profit is made from the book trade than from any other line of business. . . . '

Timbuktu was the acknowledged intellectual centre of Askia's empire. Its university provided courses in theology, Muslim law, rhetoric, grammar, and literature, given by visiting lecturers from Cairo and Fez as well as by local scholars, and attended by students—'young men eager for knowledge and virtue,' as a writer of the day described them—from the surrounding West African region.

Ghana, Mali, Gao: what—one inevitably asks—were the causes of the break-up of these large, relatively centralized Negro empires, and the flourishing civilizations associated with them, after about the year 1600? Lack of natural frontiers—meaning exposure to attack from desert and forest? Poor communications? Excessive dependence on the trade in gold and slaves? The sharp contrast (which struck Leo Africanus) between the splendour of the royal courts and the poverty of the masses? To try to answer this question at all adquately would take us too far. But in the case of Gao one point is clear: the invasion of the empire in 1590 by Moroccan forces, armed with harquebus and cannon, which had succeeded in solving the problems of trans-Saharan transport, was the beginning of a time of troubles. The old equilibrium—between Negro and Arab, pagan and Muslim, settled and nomad, city and countryside—was destroyed. As a seventeenth-century Timbuktu historian, who himself lived through the troubles he described, expressed it:

'From that moment everything changed. Danger took the place of security; poverty of wealth. Peace gave way to distress, disasters, and violence. . . . '

Seventeenth-century African writers, preoccupied with the political upheavals of their day, naturally looked back to the period of the Askias as a golden age. For the present generation of West Africans, involved in the building of new independent states, these Sudanese kingdoms of the past have acquired a new kind of importance, as a stimulus to future achievement.

THE EMPIRE OF GHANA

BASIL DAVIDSON

Traditions of origin

Our three main sources of knowledge about the past—archaeology, oral history, and the books of North Africans—speak repeatedly enough about Ancient Ghana, but tell tantalisingly little about the tone and texture of its life.

We can be sure of some of the things they tell us; others must be left in doubt. What we can be sure of is that early West Africans who lived to the north of the upper waters of the Niger river formed themselves into a strong trading state before the ninth century, and spread their power into an early empire. This empire exercised domain over many neighbouring peoples. It commanded a large region of trade, security, and strong government, and lasted for several hundred years. It was deeply respected by travellers who came within its borders, and by others, living far beyond those borders, who heard or read of it.

We can be fairly sure, too, that the peoples who formed this state and empire spoke one of the languages of the Mande group, languages that are spoken today by many of the peoples of the western region (and also by some of the central region). These founders of Ghana, who were probably Soninke, had good trading relations with the Berber chiefs and traders who lived to the north of them, in oasis towns in the Sahara; and it was through these that they conducted trade across the desert.

Their empire was called Aoukar. The word *ghana* was a title, which meant "war chief," and was borne by the king of the country. The king was also known as *kaya maghan*, "king of the gold," evidently because he controlled the export of that precious metal. Late in the eighth century A D, if not earlier, North Africans began to call this empire Ghana* after the title of its ruler.

How long did Ancient Ghana endure as a state? If we accept that its beginnings were in the fourth or fifth century AD—a date that is far from sure, but seems to be supported by traditions as well as by the evidence relating to gold imports in Roman North Africa—then we can say that Ghana survived for nearly a thousand years. Not until about AD 1240 did this great structure finally crumble and disappear. Useful and detailed information about the latter years of Ghana is available in books written by North African and Spanish Arab authors in the eleventh and twelfth centuries AD. One of these books—the *Kitab al-Masalik wa'l Mamalik* of al-Bakri—offers a brilliant-

---

* There are two reasons why the modern state of Ghana, though situated far away from Ancient Ghana, has the same name. One is that the old traditions speak of a movement of some of the people of Ancient Ghana southward into the region of Asante. Another reason is that the modern leaders of Ghana wished to celebrate the independence of their country—formerly the Gold Coast—by linking their new freedom to the glorious traditions of the past.

ly clear picture of the court of the emperor of Ghana in about AD 1065, and of the way in which that emperor, whose name was Tenkaminen, organised his power and wealth.* One may perhaps note, to situate it in a wider history, that it was completed in 1067, just a few months after the Norman-French invasion of a north European island, then little known, called England.

Growth of Ghana

From this account of al-Bakri's one can guess a good deal of what had happened during earlier times. It appears that many of the North African and Berber traders of the Sahara accepted Islam after the Arab conquest of the eighth century. They abandoned their old religions and became Muslims. They were made welcome at the capital of the emperor of Ghana, who was not a Muslim but a believer in Ghana's own religion, probably the religion of the Soninke, and were allowed to build a town of their own.

The "town of the Muslim traders" was six miles away from the emperor's own town with its surrounding settlements. While the latter were built in the traditional materials of West Africa—hardened clay, thatch, and wooden beams—the more successful Muslim traders preferred to build their houses in stone, according to their own customs in North Africa. It is not exactly known where the capital was when al-Bakri wrote his book. In the course of Ghana's long history, the king's capital was undoubtedly moved from one place to another. But we can add a good deal to al-Bakri's picture by studying the remains of Ghana's last capital, which lay at Kumbi Saleh about two hundred miles north of modern Bamako. Here too there was a town where the king of Ghana lived, and another nearby town where the Muslim traders had their houses and stables. At the height of its prosperity, before AD 1240, this city of Kumbi was evidently the biggest West African city of its day, and may have had as many as fifteen thousand inhabitants or even more.

So long as they observed the laws of Ghana and paid their taxes, the traders from the north were assured of safety and hospitality. This was a partnership in long-distance trade that endured for a very long time. Its safety depended on the strength of the emperor and his system of government. al-Bakri has left us a masterly description of all that. King Tenkaminen, he wrote, "is the master of a large

empire and of a formidable power." So powerful was this king, indeed, that he could put "two hundred thousand warriors in the field, more than forty thousand of them being armed with bow and arrow." But the real strength of the Ghana armies, as we know from other North African sources, came from their power in iron-pointed spears. Their weapons, like their organisation, were stronger than those of their neighbouring peoples; and this was the strength which underpinned their political supremacy.

Working from eye-witness accounts received from Muslim travellers, al-Bakri describes the pomp and majesty of this powerful ruler in these words:

'When the king gives audience to his people, to listen to their complaints and to set them to rights, he sits in a pavillion around which stand ten pages holding shields and gold-mounted swords. On his right hand are the sons of the princes of his empire, splendidly clad and with gold plaited in their hair. The governor of the city is seated on the ground in front of the king, and all around him are his counsellors in the same position. The gate of the chamber is guarded by dogs of an excellent breed. These dogs never leave their place of duty. They wear collars of gold and silver, ornamented with metals. The beginning of a royal audience is announced by the beating of a kind of drum they call *deba*. This drum is made of a long piece of hollowed wood. The people gather when they hear its sound . . . .'

The brilliance of these old glories was long remembered among the peoples of the western Sudan. Five hundred years later, a writer of Timbuktu called Mahmud Kati entertained his readers with the legends of those ancient days. In a book of outstanding historical value, the *Tarikh al-Fattash*, the "Chronicle of the Seeker," he tells how a certain king of Ghana of the seventh century, called Kanissa'ai, possessed one thousand horses, and how each of these horses "slept only on a carpet, with a silken rope for halter," and had three personal attendants, and was looked after as though it were itself a king. These old legends, magnified and embroidered with the passing of the years, also tell how the early kings of Ghana used to give great banquets to their subjects, feeding ten thousand at a time, and dispensing gifts and justice to all who came. Such legends show something of the grandeur of Ghana's reputation in its years of power and magnificence.

• • •

The ruler of Ghana, al-Bakri tells us, had two main sources of revenue. These were taxes of two kinds. The first of these was what today we should

---

*Al-Bakri did not visit Ghana himself, but collected information from many travellers who did.

call an import and export tax. This tax consisted of sums of money (or more probably their equal in goods) which traders had to pay for the right to bring goods into Ghana, or to take other goods out of the empire. "The king of Ghana," wrote al-Bakri, "places a tax of one dinar of gold on each donkey-load of salt that comes into his country." But he also "places a tax of two dinars of gold on each load of salt that goes out." Similar taxes, higher or lower in value as the case might be, were applied to loads of copper and other goods.

The second kind of tax was a form of production tax. It was applied to gold, the most valuable of all the products of the country.

"All pieces of gold that are found in the empire," says al-Bakri on this point, "belong to the emperor." But this regulation was more than a means of collecting royal wealth. It also appears to have been a way of keeping up the price of gold. If the emperor had not insisted on taking possession of all pieces of gold, al-Bakri explains, then "gold would become so abundant as practically to lose its value."

Ancient Ghana, in short, adopted the monopoly system that is employed in our own times for another precious commodity, diamonds. Most diamonds are mined by a handful of big companies, which work hand-in-hand with each other and have agreed among themselves not to put all the diamonds they mine upon the market, for if they did, they would drive down the price. Instead, the diamond companies sell their diamonds in dribbles and trickles, according to the demand for them. And their price accordingly stays high. The old emperors of Ghana acted not too differently with regard to gold.

They were able to do this because of Ghana's strong trading position. West African gold was important to Europe as well as to North Africa and the Near East. In earlier times the Europeans had obtained the gold they needed, whether for money, ornaments, or the display of personal wealth, from mines in Europe or in western Asia, but these were becoming worked out at about the time of the rise of Ghana.

And so it came about that the gold used in North Africa and Europe was largely supplied, century after century, by the producers of West Africa. Even kings in distant England had to buy West African gold before they could order their craftsmen to make coins in this prince of metals. It was on this steady demand for gold that the states and empires of the western Sudan founded their prosperity. West Africa's miners and prospectors, ore-crushers, goldsmiths and traders: these, first and foremost, were the men who made that prosperity possible.

Ghana began the trade in gold. As time went by, other peoples envied Ghana's success. When Ghana disappeared in the thirteenth century, its place was eventually taken by another great empire built on the same foundations and by much the same methods. This was the empire of Mali, even larger and more powerful than Ghana had ever been. Mali carried the organisational progress made under Ghana to a new level of development.

MANSA MUSA

BASIL DAVIDSON

The great political problem in the western region of the western Sudan was how to bring peace and order into the confusion which had followed on the collapse of Ghana. The problem was tackled, and largely solved, by a Mali emperor whose name became more famous even than that of Sundiata. This was Mansa Kankan Musa, who carried Mali to the height of its power and thrust its fame far across the world.

Mansa Musa came to power in about 1312. By the time of his death, in 1337, Mali had grown into one of the largest empires in the world.* What Mansa Musa did was to repeat the success of Ghana on a still more ambitious scale. He already had firm control of the trading routes to the gold lands of the south, as well as some authority within those lands. Now he brought the lands of the middle Niger under his control, and enclosed the key trading cities Timbuktu and Gao within his empire. He imposed his rule on southern Saharan trading cities like Walata, and pushed his armies northward until their influence was felt as far as the salt deposits of Taghaza on the other side of the desert. He sent them eastward beyond Gao to the very frontiers of Hausaland, westward into Tekrur and the lands of the Fulani and Tucolor, and brought those countries, too, under his dominion.

Through twenty-five successful years Mansa Musa progressively enclosed a large part of the central and western regions of the western Sudan within a single system of law and order. He did this so well that Ibn Batuta, travelling through Mali some twelve years after the great emperor's death, could find "complete and general safety in the land." It was a

---

*The year of Musa's death is often given as 1332. But the great North African historian, Ibn Khaldun, whose writings remain the best source of information on the dates of the rulers of Mali, has recorded that Musa was still alive in 1337.

grand political success, and it made Mansa Musa into one of the greatest statesman of his time.

The Dyula or Wangara traders of Kangaba grew in strength with the widening power of Mali. Their trading groups began to spread into many parts of West Africa, pushing their enterprises far down into the forest lands as well as across the plains of the north.

This was also a period of large Islamic expansion in the western Sudan. Unlike the rulers of Ghana, Mansa Musa had accepted the new religion. Many lesser rulers followed him. So did some of their peoples. Other rulers and peoples remained loyal to their own religions, but Islam steadily widened its influence. More and more West Africans went on pilgrimage to Mecca. More and more Arabs and Egyptians came to visit Mali. Trade and Islam grew together, and both prospered.

Mansa Musa himself made a famous pilgrimage to Mecca in 1324. His magnificent journey through the Egyptian capital of Cairo was long remembered with admiration and surprise throughout Egypt and Arabia, for Musa took with him so much gold, and gave away so many golden gifts, that "the people of Cairo earned incalculable sums" thanks to his visit. So lavish was Musa with his gifts, indeed, that he upset the value of goods on the Cairo market. Gold became more plentiful and therefore less valued, and prices accordingly rose. The North African scholar Al-Omari, who lived in Cairo a few years after Mansa Musa's visit and wrote the words just quoted, declared that of all the Muslim rulers of West Africa Musa was "the most powerful, the richest, the most fortunate, the most feared by his enemies and the most able to do good to those around him." Behind these words of praise one may glimpse the power and reputation that Mali drew from its control of a very wide region of trade in precious goods such as gold, salt, ivory, and kola nuts.

Mali was now a world power, and recognized as such. Under Mansa Musa, Mali ambassadors and royal agents were established in Morocco, Egypt, and elsewhere. Mali's capital was visited by North African and Egyptian scholars. On returning from pilgrimage, Mansa Musa brought back with him a number of learned men from Egypt. These settled in Mali and Timbuktu. One of them, called As-Saheli, is said to have designed new mosques at Gao and Timbuktu, and built a palace for the emperor. The fashion of building houses in brick now began to be popular among wealthy people in the cities of the western Sudan.

Niani, the capital of all this empire, has long since disappeared. Yet as late as the sixteenth century, the Moroccan traveller Leo Africanus could still describe it as a place of "six thousand hearths," and its inhabitants as "the most civilised, intelligent, and respected" of all the peoples of the Western Sudan.

Decline of Mali

But the very success of this far-reaching empire was also a reason for its decline. The onward movement of civilisation, the spread of metal-working and of trade, the growth of the ideas of kingship and of strong central government, the pressures of wealth and commercial rivalry—all these and similar influences stirred many peoples in West Africa. Some of these saw that there were new advantages in being free to run their own affairs. The ruler and people of the city of Gao, for example, who had to pay taxes to the emperor of Mali, became determined to be rid of these taxes. They believed they could do better on their own, and others thought the same.

The truth seems to have been that Mali had outgrown its political and military strength. Only supremely skilful leadership at the centre could now hold these far-flung provinces together. Mansa Musa had possessed that skill. His successors, generally, did not.

Yet, Mali remained a powerful empire until soon after 1400.

THE RISE OF THE AKAN

ADU BOAHEM

According to the 1960 census of Ghana, the Akan constitute 44.7 percent of the entire population of the modern state. They include the Asante (Ashanti), the Akyem, the Kwahu, the Fante, the Wassa, the Assin and the Akuapem. All these people speak the same language, namely Twi or Akan. And they also share identical social and political institutions. For instance they all follow the Forty Day Calendar; they all have the same marriage and naming rites; they all have matrilineal system of inheritance, that is one based on the idea that it is through the mother that the birthright of each family passes from generation to generation; and they all share a traditional law which rules that it is forbidden to choose a marriage partner from within your maternal or your paternal clan. Very closely related to the Akan, ethnically, culturally and linguistically, are the Guan, the Bono, the Sefwi and the Nzima of Ghana and the Baule and the Anyi of Ivory Coast.

Our knowledge of the history of this dominant section of the population of Ghana has greatly increased over the last ten years. Until about ten years ago we had to rely mainly on oral traditions and the published sources in English which were used by earlier historians such as Ward and Claridge. But recently new work on published and unpublished sources in Portuguese, Danish, Dutch and Arabic has added considerably to our store of knowledge of Akan history. We have also been helped by new archaeological discoveries and detailed study of the Akan language.

Many historians were once of the opinion that these Akan peoples, as well as the two other principal peoples of southern Ghana, the Ewe and the Ga-Adangbe, migrated from the east and north into Ghana only in the fifteenth and sixteenth centuries. It now appears from linguistic and archaeological evidence that all these peoples have been living in Ghana for well over a thousand years, and that it was in Ghana that their languages and cultural and social institutions finally crystallized.

The evolution of the Akan cluster of peoples probably occurred in the area round the confluence of the Pra and Ofin rivers, just south of modern Kumasi. This area was and still is very rich in gold and kola nuts. Both these commodities were in great demand in the western Sudan and northern Africa, and by the thirteenth century commercial relations were established by the Akan with the Mande peoples of the upper Niger and with the Hausa people to the north of the lower Niger. Through the Mande and the Hausa, the Akan participated in the trans-Saharan trade with North Africa, Europe and the Middle East. The Akan also traded with the Guan and Ga peoples to the south of them, principally in cloth and beads imported from Benin, but also in salt and fish. The Akan increased in wealth, mainly as a result of these early commercial activities before the arrival of the Europeans. They therefore began to disperse northwards and southwards in clan or lineage groups to carve out kingdoms for themselves. These groups of Akan are known today by the kingdoms they formed. For example the Asante are those Akan who moved north and founded the Asante state, which as we shall see they transformed into an empire, and the Akyem are those who moved eastwards across the Pra River.

All the kingdoms and empires founded by the Akan had the monarchical system of government. The kings and queens were, and still are, elected from a single royal family, usually the founding family, which belongs to one of the eight matrilineal clans into which all the Akan are divided.

It is clear from Portuguese records that when they arrived on the coast of Ghana in the 1470s a number of states were already in existence, not only along the coast but also in the interior. The arrival of the Europeans and the opening up of the Atlantic added a new dimension to the commerce of the Akan. A steady increase in population and wealth followed, and this led to a rapid multiplication of their states. There is a most revealing map of what is now southern Ghana as it was in 1629, on which a great number of states are shown. Thirty-four of these states are named and twenty-eight of them are Akan.

It is clear from oral traditions, as well from the records of the Dutch, Danish and English trading companies, that the seventeenth century saw a bitter competition among the Akan states both for political supremacy and for the domination of the trade routes, especially to the coast. Some states were able to grow at the expense of others. During the next one hundred years one state after another was to emerge supreme in the western region. First Twifo, then Adansi, then Assin and finally Denkyira. In the eastern region Akyem and Akwamu, founded by clan groups which emigrated from the states of Adansi and Twifo across the Pra, gained an early lead over the Guan and Akan states by the beginning of the seventeenth century. By the turn of that century Akwamu had established her sway not only over Akyem and Kwahu but also over the coastal kingdoms of Accra and even across the Volta, over the Ewe states. A map of Ghana drawn in 1750 shows that by that date all these competing states had been absorbed by two main ones; the sprawling empire of Asante and the relatively much smaller kingdom of Fante extending about one hundred and fifty miles along the coast and twenty miles inland.

The Asante empire was the product of an intelligent blend of shrewd diplomacy and naked force. The nucleus of the empire was five kingdoms founded within a radius of some thirty miles from Kumasi by families who all belonged to the same line of the Oyoko matrilineal clan. Probably these Oyoko clan groups entered the area during the second half of the seventeenth century. They came from the region around the confluence of the Ofin and the Pra. The five kingdoms which formed the basis of the Asante empire were Kumasi, Dwaben, Bekwai, Kokofu and Nsuta. To this day the kings of the first four of these regard themselves as 'brothers' and they look on the king of the fifth as their 'uncle.' So, instead of competing among themselves as earlier Akan states had done, they co-operated together very closely. The leader of this group of Oyoko states was Osei Tutu, the king of Kumasi, who is referred to in the early eighteenth-century European records as 'the great Asante Caboceer Zaay.' In an attempt to increase the area of influence of the Oyoko states this king of Kumasi attempted to bring in the neighbouring non-Oyoko states. His attempt was made much easier by the common hatred of all these states for Denkyira. Oral traditions are unanimous on the oppressive nature of the Denkyira yoke and this is corroborated from documentary sources. For instance, Bosman, a contemporary Dutch observer of the 1680s, describes Denkyira as 'elevated by its great riches and power,' and 'so arrogant that it looked on all negroes with a comtemptible eye, esteeming them no more than slaves.'

So that he might endow his new union of states with a soul and a sacred and everlasting symbol of power, unity and stability, the king of Kumasi, Osei Tutu, and his 'chief priest' created the Golden Stool. Or, as oral traditions persistently and vociferously maintain, he brought the Golden Stool down from the sky. This stool soon became the rallying point of the Asante and even today is regarded by them with the utmost veneration. Osei Tutu went on to devise a constitution, a national army organized into four wings, a supreme court of appeal and the national Odwira or harvest festival. These nation-building devices of Osei Tutu proved so effective that members of the Union soon developed a sense of identity and national consciousness which grew in intensity with the years.

Having constructed this hard and sacred core of an empire Osei Tutu and his successor Opoku Ware, who ruled from 1720 until 1750, together with their confederate kings, embarked on a course of conquest. Their main aim was to gain control of the trade routes radiating northwards and southwards from the region of Kumasi, and to defeat the domineering people of Denkyira. They conquered Denkyira and her tributary states of Wassa, Sefwi, Aowin, Assin and Twifo between 1699 and 1701; between 1722 and 1745 Takyiman, Gyaman, Gonja and Dagomba to the north and north-west were vanquished; and between 1742 and 1744 so were Akyem, Accra and Akwamu to the south-east. In other words, by 1750 virtually all the Akan states of modern Ghana and Gyaman in the Ivory Coast had been incorporated into the Asante empire.

The only kingdom in southern Ghana which was able to resist the Asante imperial drive was the old kingdom of Fante. Indeed the Fante reacted to Asante expansionism by streamlining their political organization. And at the beginning of the eighteenth century they conquered and annexed the ancient coastal principalities of Kommenda, Asebu and Fetu to the west of them and Agona to the east.

So by the middle of the eighteenth century the area of modern Ghana, and parts of Ivory Coast and Togo, had been partitioned among these two Akan people, the Asante and the Fante, with the lion's share going to the Asante, thanks to the nationalist spirit, martial ardour and political genius of their leaders. As the Fante persistently refused to allow the Asante direct access to European forts on the coast, relations between the two powers remained strained throughout the eighteenth century and it was mainly the energetic support of the British which enabled them to maintain their independence. However during the first two decades of the nineteenth century, by exploiting the weakness of the British on the coast, the Asante finally accomplished the reduction and annexation of the Fante kingdom; thereby they achieved the first political unification of the states and peoples of modern Ghana, Ivory Coast and Togo.

How did the Asante govern their huge empire? It used to be generally accepted that, in the words of the historian Claridge, 'though the Ashantees could conquer, they could not govern, in fact they never made any serious attempt to do so.' It is now clear from the records of the eighteenth and nineteenth centuries that this view is wholly erroneous. As Bowdich learnt in Kumasi in 1816, Osei Tutu and Opoku Ware placed each subject ruler 'under the immediate care of some Ashantee chief, generally resident in the capital,' and imposed on him an annual tribute. However, since these chiefs hardly ever visited their client states, this system of administration proved ineffective. Later rulers, particularly Osei Kwadwo, who reigned from 1765 to 1777, and Osei Bonsu, whose dates were 1801 to 1824, therefore revolutionized the old system. Cruickshank has described these changes most graphically: 'The King was not content to leave the government entirely in the hands of the native chiefs, who might possibly, in the course of time, rally the prostrate energies of the country, and combine to throw off his yoke. In consequence of this suspicion . . . he appointed pro-consuls of the Ashantee race, men of trust and confidence, to reside with the fallen chiefs, to notify to them the royal will, to exercise a general superintendence over them, and especially to guard against and to spy out any conspiracies that might be formed to recover their independence.' And Cruickshank's writing is not the only evidence we have of the Asante system of government. For instance there are records which provide us with the names of the three Asante resident officials posted to Accra in the 1700s, and also those for Abora, Cape Coast and Elmina in the 1810s and 1820s. So we can see that the Asante did certainly make serious attempts to govern, and the fact that their empire lasted so long was due partly to the improved system of their provincial administration. But it was also due, and this was probably the most important factor, to the bravery of their army which enabled them to crush all the insurrections that periodically broke out in the eighteenth and the early part of the nineteenth century.

The political experiment of the Asante was the last and the most successful of the experiments conducted by the Akan. At the turn of the eighteenth century the Asante empire was at the height of its fame and glory. It was easily the greatest and most powerful empire on the west coast of Africa; and it was at the courts of the Asante kings that the culture of the Akan—their language, music, dancing and art—had a chance to flower and develop.

THE RISE OF THE BENIN KINGDOM

ALAN RYDER

By name, at least, Benin is probably the best known of all the old West African states. To the European it has been, since the sixteenth century, a symbol of everything which popular imagination and prejudice associated with the equatorial regions of Africa. During the era of partition it won fame by its resistance to the British advance into the interior. More recently, Benin art has had a fruitful influence on western art. In its own African setting, Benin was for many centuries one of the greatest states in the western equatorial region, ruling over a considerable territory to the west of the River Niger.

This kingdom was in many respects an anomaly among the small, unstable chiefdoms of the West African coast. It was the only large centralized state and its capital was the only great city within easy reach of the sea. Yet the basic social structure and customs of Benin were very similar in essentials to those found in the neighboring, small-scale societies. The Benin people themselves belong to a larger linguistic group known as the Edo-speaking peoples, which is characterized by the same highly localized forms of social and political grouping.

Why then did Benin depart from a political pattern seemingly in harmony with its social structure and suited to its physical environment, where the tropical forest hindered the communications that were essential to large-scale organization? Why did Benin set out on a path of conquest and expansion? Or, to look at the problem from a different point of view, what were the origins of this exceptional state?

Some new light has been thrown on these questions in the past few years by a research project which set out to investigate the history of Benin by studying its language, its social and political institutions, its religion and its art, as well as the rather more obvious historical evidence provided by local oral traditions and European written sources. No final answers can yet be given, because it is clear that they depend on knowing much more than we do at present about other peoples and states of West Africa. But from the evidence we do have it would seem that Benin owed its extraordinary development to three factors: its monarchical traditions, the creation of a complex political and social hierarchy and, arising from these two, the growth of an imperial tradition.

I put the monarchy first, because it was both the mainspring in the functioning of the state and the chief creator of the apparatus of government. The Benin monarchy arose more than six centuries ago, and it had its origins outside Benin. There is a tradition which says that the founder of the dynasty, which still rules today, was Oranmiyan, son of Odudua. He is believed to have come to Benin from Ile-Ife, the original home of the Yoruba people, and to have founded the Oyo dynasty in Yorubaland as well as the royal line of Benin. Similarities between the political institutions of Benin and those of Yoruba kingdoms lend some weight to the belief that they had a common origin. And more support for the tradition comes when we look at the words for political ideas in the Benin and the Yoruba languages. We find that the political vocabularies of the two languages are much more similar than the range of more general words. Yet in spite of this evidence there are still many difficulties in accepting the tradition at its face value; it does not fit in with what we know of the chronology of events in the area. In particular, the Benin dynasty seems to be older than its Yoruba counterparts.

What the stories may represent is the establishment among both peoples of an alien group or dynasty endowed with a reputation for supernatural abilities in the mysteries of government. Dynasties and empires have arisen elsewhere in Africa on such a basis, as among the Mossi, to take an example near at hand. It may be significant that Benin tradition insists that Oranmiyan did not come as a conqueror, but at the invitation of the people who had asked Oduda to send a member of his family to rule them because they were unable to agree among themselves on a system of government. But more must be known about the vanished states on the middle course of the Niger before we can advance beyond speculation on this question.

Wherever its place of origin may have been, the

dynastic tie with a foreign overlord for long remained of great importance to the Benin monarchy. Portuguese reports tell us that in the fifteenth century rulers of Benin were still receiving their insignia of office from a spiritual overlord ruling a country farther inland. 'Without these emblems,' wrote the Portuguese chronicler DeBarros, 'the people would consider that they did not reign lawfully, nor could they call themselves true kings.' Such was the situation some two centuries after the establishment of the dynasty. The link between the kings of Benin and their overlords weakened in the sixteenth century, possibly because something happened to destroy the power or prestige of the latter; but some form of relationship with the senior branch of the dynasty persisted, and we know for certain that in the nineteenth century the ruler of the Yoruba city of Ife was looked upon as a kind of spiritual suzerain by the rulers of Benin. When they died, parts of their bodies were buried in a special cemetery at Ife which is still known in that town as the burial place of the kings of Benin. Excavations have confirmed the existence of the cemetery, but the mean character of the objects found in the graves suggests that the ceremonial attached to them was a perfunctory kind.

Their relationship to a far-off potentate was one factor which won for the kings of Benin the reverence of their subjects. Another, of still greater importance, was the aura of supernatural power with which they surrounded themselves. The creation of this mystique began with Oranmiyan, who is said to have been accompanied from Ife by a famous practitioner of magic arts. Ewedo,.the best known of the early rulers, is remembered as a 'great idolater', who introduced 'various gods' into Benin and instituted numerous ceremonies concerned with worship of the earth spirits and the king's good luck or fortune. The technique of brass-casting by the cire-perdue process also came to Benin from the dynasty's ancestral home, and served to enhance the spiritual authority of the king; for it was by this method— which must have seemed magical to the uninitiated— that the symbols of royal authority and the heads and plaques commemorating the feats of the dynasty were produced.

In course of time, the kings came to lay still greater stress on their supernatural attributes by further elaborating the ritual which surrounded them. This development became most marked from the seventeenth century, when rulers abandoned their function as active military commanders and confined themselves within the palace. In seclusion they devoted much of their time to an increasingly complex routine of religious ceremonial. Human sacrifice grew to the proportions which earned Benin

notoriety in the nineteenth century, largely as a result of this emphasis upon the priestly, mystical function of kingship.

But the kingdom of Benin owed its existence over five centuries to something more than the authority and trappings of a semi-divine monarchy. The functioning of the state depended as much, and probably more, upon an elaborate and finely balanced political organizaton which channelled ambition and ability into its service, while it neutralized conflicts by institutionalizing them. Its essential feature was the association or group of title-holders and aspirants to titles. There were several of these associations, each with a corporate existence and special function within the state. They evolved piecemeal and experimentally over a long period of time; for in Benin there was no sudden transformation of the political structure coinciding with the advent of the dynasty. On the contrary, the successors of Oranmiyan for some time held a precarious position, being obliged to share power with the existing chiefs before they managed to reduce them to the status of one, albeit the senior, titled order. The ruler who thus freed himself from the trammels of the old political system also took the first major step towards the creation of the new by building himself a palace and organizing a hierarchy of household servants and advisers. In so doing, the king, who is said to have been the fourth of his line, was almost certainly following the pattern of government familiar to his dynasty in its ancestral home. Later developments may also have been influenced by the same foreign tradition, but the palace inevitably began to unfold its own needs and potentialities in relation to the new environment, so we must look mainly to the situation within Benin in order to explain the subsequent elaboration of the political system.

According to the traditional reckoning, seven reigns elapsed between the revolution just described and the second major series of political innovations. A new ruler, who had overthrown and murdered his predecessor, consolidated his hold upon Benin by thoroughly remodelling its institutions. His most significant move was the establishment of a new association of titled chiefs sufficiently numerous and influential to balance the powerful palace associations. The circumstances in which he had gained the throne partly explain this seemingly paradoxical action; and one must remember that in Benin as elsewhere organizations, such as the royal household, tended to develop their own vested interests and become the master of those they were created to serve. This ruler found his counter-weight in the men who were prominent in that part of the capital known as the 'town'—that is, those quarters not occupied by the palace, from which they were separated by a broad belt of open land. Many offices and functions of government were assigned to the new order: its senior member, for example, was for long the regular commander of the Benin armies, and its titled chiefs participated with those of the palace in the councils of state which advised the ruler.

In all essentials this was the political structure that governed Benin during the remainder of its independent existence. It endured because it was flexible. With few exceptions, the titles were non-hereditary and in the gift of the ruler, who could also create new ones at his pleasure. In addition the hierarchy was open, at least in theory, to all freeborn men from any part of the kingdom. Thus an able ruler could manipulate the system in such a way as to check over-mighty subjects, balance factions and reward those who served him well.

The close-knit association of monarch and titled orders generated the force which enabled the small city-state of Benin to impose its rule on a great diversity of other peoples, some Edo, some Yoruba and some Ibo. Many submitted in awe of the magical or divine character of the ruler. Others, loosely integrated communities as Benin itself had once been, were overcome by the concentrated power of the autocratic state. A tendency among the subject peoples to copy the political institutions of Benin, especially the title system, and the settlement in some areas of colonists from Benin, introduced an appearance of administrative uniformity in many parts of the Benin dominions. But there was little real unity, and the state remained to the end a heterogeneous empire only held together at the centre by the prestige of the ruler, the watchfulness of the palace and the title-holders, and by the armed might which they could muster against any rebellious town or province.

Thus Benin grew from a small forest town to become the hub of one of the most powerful political systems in West Africa. By the time Europeans first visited Benin at the end of the fifteenth century the structure was already complete, and so well-founded that it survived essentially unchanged through many upheavals for another five hundred years.

AFRICAN FAMILIES

PAUL BOHANNAN

Family life

It has often and correctly been said that the family image is at the foundation of the images of all social relationships. Whether we make the statements from a psychic or a social, a historical or an evolutionary point of view, it is incontrovertible.

Kinship is, actually, a simple business. It springs out of the fact that a man marries a woman and they beget and bear children. These are " the facts of life." On such facts, all sorts of changes can be rung; and only a few of the possible changes are not found institutionalized and valued somewhere. Therefore, it behooves us to look at African kinship practices in order to understand Africa and better understand ourselves.

There are two kinds of kinship. One is a relationship of descent; the other is a relationship of sexuality. Each may occur in two modes: the direct mode and the shared mode.

"Male" assumes the existence of female. "Child" assumes the existence of parent. Such are the direct mode relationships. But co-wives assume a common and shared husband, with no direct "organic" relationship. Just so, siblings assume a common shared parent (perhaps more than one), with no direct "organic" relationship no matter how many genes they may have in common. These are indirect modes of kinship.

Out of these differences, and the relationships which exhibit them, all kinship groups have to be built. The only building blocks there are are those of sexuality and descent, which English-speaking Westerners see as the relationships of husband-wife, mother-son, mother-daughter, father-son, father-daughter, brother-brother, sister-sister, brother-sister, and co-spouse relationships. The blocks can be compounded into great edifices; nevertheless, the blocks themselves are of a very precise nature and number.

American families contain all the relationships except those of shared sexuality. African families, being polygynous, contain all the relationships familiar to Americans, plus that of co-wife to co-wife, and the ramified relationships of half-siblings and of "father's wife-husband's child."

In all cultures, such kinship relationships must be given a more or less restricted content. It is necessary to know what husbands are supposed to do, as husbands; and what wives are supposed to do, as wives; what fathers are supposed to do, and what daughters are supposed to do. Then, on the basis of these understandings, human beings can act more or less comfortably as they make their compromises between reality and the ideal.

The content of the mother-child relationship bears greater similarity from one society to the next than does the father-child relationship. The brother-brother relationship can go all the way from the minimal content which Americans give it today, to the maximal content that some African patrilineal societies give it, where it is fundamental. The husband-wife relationship, and the kind of content that it involves, can vary just as widely: from the maximal content that Americans give it to the minimal content that some African societies give to it.

What, then, is polygyny? A married man marries a second or third woman, and they produce children. The content of each husband-wife relationship will be altered; the relationships of the co-wives and half-siblings have been added. The difference between monogamy and polygyny is contained in this: it is possible, even if it is not usual, to create a deeply intense relationship between husband and wife that probably most men cannot enter into with two women at once. If the intense and unique quality in that relationship is what is most highly valued, then polygyny must be opposed. But if something else— say security of position and the road to children—is most highly valued, polygyny is not a contradiction. Indeed, the added relationship among co-wives may provide some of the very cultural content and psychic satisfaction among adults which modern Americans try to cram solely into the husband-wife relationship. And it is no more fair to say that a rewarding husband-wife relationship cannot develop in polygyny than it is to say that intense community of interest among women cannot develop alongside monogamy.

The birth rate in a polygynous situation is never higher than the birth rate in a monogamous situation. It is usually lower. A man may beget many more children in polygyny than in monogamy. A woman does not bear any more. We can cease to worry about the birth rate in polygyny, because the moment that enforced monogamy comes into the African situation, the birth rate always soars (although monogamy is not the only factor—enforced monogamy is always accompanied by many other factors which change the way people live). African women do not, in their indigenous cultures, bear more than one child every two and a half or three years. They achieve this spacing by the only sure means—continence during the time they are nursing a child. When the situation changes so as to favor monogamy, their inclination and opportunity to shun their husbands for such a

long period of time is usually reduced. In the indigenous culture, polygyny gives security to both husbands and wives during the time when a mother withdraws from cohabitation with her husband during a nursing period. The number of men in any society who can undergo such a long period of celibacy is small. If you are a wife in a polygynous society, would you rather have your husband at home with your co-wife or gallivanting around the countryside?

Americans think that the impossible thing to share is the husband. If American women would really look into their souls, they know that it is really the kitchen that they would refuse to share. And the wives of African polygynists do not try. There are separate houses for each wife or for each group of wives; there is also usually a separate sphere for the husband.

Obviously, to make polygyny work it is necessary constantly to re-create a situation in which the rewards and obligations among co-wives are as neatly and precisely stated as are the obligations and rules among parents and children, husbands and wives. There are some things that a co-wife must do to be a good co-wife. There are others that she must not do if she is to be a good co-wife. If she does the one cheerfully and well and refrains from the other, she is by definition a good co-wife, whatever her husband's other wives may do.

If one examines divorces in Africa, he will find that some women leave their husbands not because they do not like their husbands but because they do not like their co-wives. Living in an impossible situation, whether that impossibility is created by husband or co-wife, leads in some societies and under some conditions to divorce. There are African women who divorce their husbands because they can't stand their co-wives; there are others who stay with impossible husbands because the co-wives are congenial. A good senior wife or mother-in-law may be as important in providing security, pleasant surroundings, and a rewarding place for a woman to bring up her children as is her husband.

If they have separate quarters and a pronounced code of behavior known to everybody, it is possible for co-wives not only to live next door, but to share their husband and even to become quite fond of one another. They have a great deal in common. The ideals of polygyny always are such that harmony among co-wives is possible. At the same time, in many African languages, the word for co-wife springs from the same root as the word for jealousy. The situation is fraught with difficulty—but are not all family relationships fraught with difficulty: the husband-wife relationship in monogamy? The parent-child relationship everywhere? The polygynous family is more complex than the monogamous family, and there are certain difficulties built into it. But the rewards involved may be great: it is possible, in a polygynous family, to spread your regard, your love, and your dependence over a wider range of people. You don't put all your emotional eggs in one basket. For this reason alone it can be seen to have great rewards. A large group of people has the welfare of each member at heart. And in the worst of all possible situations, the very number may dilute the hate pointed at each one.

Women in polygyny have grave trouble only when the interests of their children are involved and when real or supposed slights from the father toward one set of children or the other affect the smooth running of the whole. A woman, as a co-wife, can learn to accept all sorts of real or fancied slights. The same woman, as a mother, will have difficulty in accepting either real or fancied slights to her children. Here is the source of the difficulty: tension between my mother and the mothers of my half-siblings.

Polygyny has nothing to do with the position of women in society. African women, by and large, have a high social position: legal rights, religious and political responsibility, economic independence. Where there are kings in sub-Saharan Africa, there are queen-mothers. At the basis of every secret cult of men, there are women: the innermost secret of every religious club barred to women is the male's ultimate dependence on women. Women are often excluded from rituals, but there are two things that initiation into religion and society involve: initiation into society is a ritualized teaching to the novitiates that they embody, in themselves personally and in their relationships collectively, the moral force of society —they are themselves the gods (not God) and the sanctions. Initiation is also a ritualized teaching to the initiates that women must stand behind and support men. In the Ivory Coast, for example, initiation has two denouements: one when the boys find that the masked dancers who have represented the gods and the social forces suddenly take the masks off and put them on the boys themselves; the other when the innermost hidden secret of the men's religious societies is exposed to them—and turns out to be a woman.

Women in Africa are not, in short, a deprived group as they were in the nineteenth-century Western world. African men ritualize rather than deny their basic dependence on women.

The next myth that must be banished is that polygyny has anything to do with the concupiscence of the male. Polygyny is a state into which most African men enter with certain trepidation. If you think that one wife can henpeck a husband, you should see what three in league can do. If co-wives live up to the ideals of the roles, even just barely, no man exists but is under greater strain and control than he would be if there were only one woman involved. The man who has a strong senior wife is a fortunate individual, because she will run the household and will straighten out the fusses among the co-wives. He will not have to bother. If he does not have such a wife, two-thirds of his energy goes into administration.

Men must treat their wives in accordance with the station of the wives—not necessarily with absolute equality, unless the society dictates that their stations are those of absolute equals. The greater number of societies lay down quite precise obligations on the part of the husband, but others insist that the obligation is to make the personal adjustments necessary to keep all the parties contented.

It is all but inevitable, in all probability, that polygynists have favorite wives. It should never, however, show up in the way the husband carries out his obligations: clothing them, feeding them, giving them children. Occasionally romantic love enters into this situation. I have seen an old Tiv chief with seventeen wives who loved them all, but loved one of them in the sense given that term by the troubadours and adapted by latter-day American marriage counselors. The senior ones had given him families and comforted his years. But unfortunately—and even he considered it unfortunate—he "fell in love" with one of the younger ones. It kept him from being a good family man; it kept him from being a good chief. I judge that romantic love occurs in an African familial situation about as commonly as it does in a European or American one. The difference is that Westerners have a series of myths which make them simulate romantic love to see them over the time between initial attraction and the regard that sensitive and sensible living together, breeding, and growing together can foster. The myth makes it possible for Westerners to select their spouses on something besides random choice—indeed, under it they can arrange their own marriages.

Old-fashioned Africans select their spouses by "giving in to their parents' wishes." But in most cases in which the parents' wishes do not correspond with their own, they elope. Seldom do Africans make their children marry someone they do not like.

The other aspect of African family life that is most likely to be misunderstood is the institution of bridewealth. Initially, the European observers who went to Africa said that Africans bought their wives. In a sense, that is true. It is *not* true that wives enter the market place or that they are commercialized or anything of the sort. It is easiest to explain by noting that part of the marriage contract in any society is that the wife gets certain rights in the husband and he gets certain rights in her. The rights of each are the obligations of the other.

Initially the husband has to make a bridewealth payment that is tantamount to posting a bond that he will carry out his obligations, thus guarding his new wife's rights. The analogy can be carried too far, because the nature of the bond and the purpose of the bridewealth changes, and ultimately its nature is in the sphere of legitimizing the children. But, in return for his "bond" and his obligations, the husband gets certain rights.

To sum them up quickly, a man may get in his wife, domestic rights—the right to establish a domestic unit with her and to her domestic work and time and care. He may get rights to her extradomestic economic substance or labor; such was the case in the late nineteenth-century West, but is seldom so in Africa. He gets sexual rights in her and obligations toward her. Finally, he may or may not get the right to filiate that woman's children to his kinship group. In most African societies, traditionally, a man acquired such rights in exchange for cattle or ceremonial currency such as spears or pieces of iron, or else for service of the sort Jacob performed for his two wives, in the Book of Genesis. The difference between matriliny and patriliny can be summed up by determining whether it is common to transfer the rights to filiate the children.

It is these rights that the bridewealth purchases, these obligations that it symbolizes. If a woman "has cows on her back," as the East African idiom has it, then her children belong to the man and to the social group that paid the cows. This is a matter of legitimizaion. It is, indeed, a symbol of legitimization.

If the marriage breaks up, the bridewealth must be returned, totally or in part.

Polygyny does not necessarily mean that some men do not have wives, but only that men marry later than women. Polygyny must also be distinguished from concubinage. Concubines are not wives, for all that in some places they have legal rights. In many societies there are, besides concubinage, several "degrees" of marriage, and in some there is allowable sexual and other relationships which may not be granted the status of full marriage. Indeed, in the Roman Republic there were two forms of marriage—heiresses would not marry by the ritual that gave their husbands control of their property, but rather formed a recognized, common-law union in which this economic right was not transferred. There were, thus, two "types" of "marriage": one involved the acquisition by the husband of all the rights; the other

of only part of them. Many—probably most—African societies exhibit just such variation in the possible marriage arrangements.

Rights in women are considered, in most African societies, to be heritable. If my father or my older brother dies, leaving a couple of wives, I may inherit his rights in those not my mother. Since all rights involve obligations, it would be more accurate to say that I inherit my father's obligations to his wives. If the widow has several children and her children are members of her late husband's kinship group, she has an important position within that kinship group, even though she is not a member of it. Her position in life, indeed, may depend upon her children—thus underscoring the hard fate of a barren woman. Her natal group has little obligation to her after her initial marriage—ultimately none. As some Africans put it, "your wife of long-standing becomes your sister." A woman's status derives from her being a mother of lineage members. Therefore, it is only sensible for her to remarry into that group. And most widows are women of maturity (which may, of course, begin at twenty); they do not expect from a second marriage what they expect from a first—sometimes the second may be happier for that reason.

The result is the institution of inheritance of rights in widows. In one situation the widow is inherited as a wife; there is another, quite different, situation in which (to use the Old Testament term) the brother of the dead husband raises up seed, which is to say that the widow moves in as his "wife," but that the dead husband remains the legal father of any children that she bears. Such an arrangement is called the true levirate. The new husband acquires domestic and sexual rights in the widow; he does not acquire rights to filiate her children, which are thought to be part of the "spiritual property" of the dead husband.

It is possible, in most African societies, for a widow to decide not to remain with her deceased husband's people. She therefore probably marries someone else and the bridewealth is adjusted.

American and Western European society does not cope very well with widows. They are an anomaly. They occupy an insecure position, are to be pitied, particularly if they have children; they are not quite to be trusted, although the divorcee has in the twentieth century taken over the role assigned to the widow in the nineteenth. African societies cope well with both divorcees and widows—getting them back into families quickly and simply. Loneliness is not an indigenous African peoblem.

Nonfamilial Kinship Groups

In addition to families, there are other sorts of kinship groups in Africa based on a more limited range of relationships than are families. Extended families can have only a certain size—after that, the members cannot know all their kinsmen, or respond equally to them all. Since the functions of the family are usually associated largely with households, the household limit—certainly the neighborhood limit—is, in most cases, the effective limit of the family. But certain types of limiting kinship groups can gear their purposes to other ends and still use kinship amity as the sanction for carrying out the cooperation of the group and the achievement of its ends. The descent groups contain fewer relationships, but can control much larger numbers of people.

There are two sorts of descent groups: patrilineal descent groups, which includes the father-son and father-daughter relationships and the three sibling relationships. The matrilineal descent group includes the mother-son and mother-daughter and the three sibling relationships. Each of these, being limited in the way that they are and specifically not being able to take care of the basic functions of bearing and rearing children, can be brilliantly adapted to political and economic ends.

Descent groups may contain several million people and use the sanction of kinship obligations—"blood is thicker than water"—to reward their members and bind them to "right" courses of action. These groups can be called lineages; some types are called "clans." The word "clan" in the anthropological literature is used broadly—it may cover any kinship group that is not a family, and even some extended families (the Chinese *tsu* usually called a "clan" in English, in in fact a type of extended family).

Unilineal descent groups are very widespread in Africa and were—indeed, still are—the basis for most of the extrafamilial social organization. They form political groups, religious congregations, and even production and landowning units. They are still strong. They are strong among the educated as well as among the "bush" people. They will continue to be strong.

There is a favorite myth among anthropologists that the African family and the other kinship groups are breaking down. The unilineal descent groups—the uses to which they are put—can be truly undermined by only one thing: that is a police system so effective that contractual obligations can be maintained with as great security and less responsibility than by kinship groups. In the absence of such a police system, there must be *something* else. And the African answer is the efflorescence of the descent group. The economic and legal sanction is to be found in kinship obligations.

There are some societies in Africa in which unilineal descent groups are not found, but such groups are overwhelmingly present in many more. It is loyalty to the descent group, as well as to the family, that is under discussion when Africans talk about their obligations to "their" people.

In addition to the economic and political purposes that such groups can be made to serve, they are often central to religious ritual and belief. They are, moreover, often associated with the history and the view of the cosmography. They are, in short, one way in which the small world of the faily can be tied to the greater world and ultimately to the supernatural.

African children grow up in an intense situation of kinship and family. They continue throughout their lives to learn their family obligations and family histories. And, perhaps most importantly, they learn from a very early age to spread their regard, their rewards, and their concern.

Among the Tiv of eastern central Nigeria, for example, a child when he is about six months old is assigned to an older sister or brother, preferably the same sex as the child; the older becomes the nurse of the younger. For the next three or four years—almost until the younger child is ready to become a nurse, they accompany their nurses everywhere. When they cry, the nurses take them to their mothers. When the nurses go out to play, the babies go with them. The bond between a child and his nurse becomes an enduring bond. I have been many times introduced by old men to men just older who had been their nurses. Children learn a great deal about the culture from one another and especially from their nurses. In our society, children more and more learn from adults.

Tiv children, as an example, are allowed to go any place, so long as they keep quiet. They can go into the most solemn court proceedings and sit down and listen. The moment one of them makes a noise, out they all go. Older children of eight or nine often get interested in court cases or political meetings. When their younger charges will not behave, they have to go away; therefore they are very adept in silencing the babies. There is nothing from which children are excluded, unless they misbehave and intrude. As a result, they tend to be well-behaved children, aware from an early age what goes on in adult culture. The abrupt break such as Westerners know, between children's culture and adult culture, is not to be found.

African children get into their cultures early, and there are no abrupt shifts. After they are twelve or thirteen, and sometimes earlier, boys form groups that range the countryside, hunt, and (where there are cattle and goats) tend the herds. Girls by this time are more closely kept at home and are on the brink of marriage.

At marriage, the vast majority of girls shift homesteads. They leave the households in which they are daughters and join those in which they are wives and in which they will become mothers. Men do not undergo this kind of change, but continue to live imbedded in a group of their own kinsmen.

It is probably impossible for anyone who has never lived in a kinship-dominated society to realize the combination of security and bondedness that it implies. In discussion, Africans always emphasize the positive factors: a group of their own, on which they can depend totally and to which they owe allegiance, a group which transcends them and gives them position in society and in history—importance and status as well as physical necessities or even wealth. Nevertheless, they do, to some extent, chafe under the demands of their kinsmen. Until the present century, there was no "way out" of the kinship situation. There was no place to go if one was exiled. The kinship sanction was sufficient to control all of one's behavior. Modern Westerners would see such a fate in terms of the lack of individuality and freedom. Africans do not. Although today many of them do leave when faced with choices in which they consider they must give more than they get, few intend to stay away for good.

Africans who felt it necessary to maintain their relationships within their kinship groups have discovered ways and means that have made them all but geniuses in personal relationships—at least it is so at a kinship level. The story is told of a South African chief whose murder was attempted by his brother. The brother got out of prison several years later. The chief met him and welcomed him back to the fold of the kinship group. The balance between individuality and security is solved quite differently in a kinship-dominated society from the way it is solved in a contract-dominated society.

Parenthood is important everywhere. It is trebly so in a society in which rights to the most important parts of all aspects of life are dependent upon kinship, and when most of one's status derives from kinship factors. Only on the birth of a child does a woman become truly a kinsman in her husband's group. Only on the birth of a child is a man assured of the "immortality" of a position in the genealogy of his lineage, or even of security of esteem among the important people of his community. Only on the birth of a grandchild is a man in a position to be truly sure that his name and spirit will live in the history and genealogy of his people. This factor, combined with that other factor that is so true

everywhere—that grandparenthood allows a perfect and rewarding position for summing up the meaning of the life cycle—makes grandparenthood enviable, and elderhood the finest estate.

Many Africans express concern lest the kinship groups to which they are bound will wither and perish in the course of industrialization and mechanization of the new Africa. They are determined that, if possible, no such fate will befall them. It will be an interesting experiment. From it we may learn whether or not it is truly modern technology and the development of contract which destroys the ramified kinship system, or whether Western reasons for abandoning it were quite different from those they themselves use to explain their distrust of all kinship groups save the nuclear family.

HOW PEOPLE LIVED

BASIL DAVIDSON

West Africa has about eighty-five million people today. In the sixteenth century there were certainly far fewer. There were also fewer kinds of food. But more were now added. Valuable plants and fruits such as maize and pineapples were brought from Central and South America in the ships of Portugal. These new crops were eagerly accepted, and spread rapidly. Though without any knowledge of modern science, West Africans had already solved many of the essential problems of living in their vast and difficult region. They had developed a degree of immunity against dangerous fevers. They had learnt the secret of many medicinal herbs and how to use them to cure sickness. They had discovered how to look after cattle in conditions of great heat. They had become experts at growing food in the forest. They had found out how to recognise minerals in rocks, how to sink mines, how to get the ore and smelt and work it. They had developed a wide range of hand-manufacture in many materials. They had worked out religions of their own. They had evolved effective methods of government, though mostly without the use of writing.

These skills understandably impressed foreign visitors. A Portuguese report of 1506, that of Duarte Pacheco Pereira, tells how high-quality cotton goods could be purchased at many points along the Guinea coast. An English captain called William Towerson wrote in 1556 of the "fine iron goods" that were hand-made in Guinea: "spears, fish-hooks, farming tools, and swords that are exceedingly sharp on both edges."

Of all their material skills, tropical farming and mining deserve a leading place in the record. In both these fields, West Africans were far advanced among the peoples of the sixteenth century—so far advanced, indeed, that it was Africans, even though working as slaves, who later pioneered the development of tropical farming and mining in the Americas.

But these advances were made within the framework of a subsistence economy, and this subsistence production, as distinct from production for exchange in money, placed clear economic and social barriers around further development. A farmer, then, would see little or no point in producing more food than was needed for his family. A blacksmith would make enough hoes or spears to be sure of getting the food his family needed, but he would not sell them for money, since money had little or no part in his economy; he would take them to market and barter them for what he needed.

Of course the detailed picture was not quite so simple. There was a growing quantity of internal and external trade; and this trade was carried on in foods that were grown, and goods that were manufactured, with the idea of exchanging them for other goods or for various kinds of money. The beginnings of a money economy did indeed develop wherever traders gathered in markets and began to deal in goods for sale. This development will need some further discussion.

The fact remains that nearly all West Africans still lived outside the centres of this small though steadily expanding money economy of the towns and big markets. Even inside these centres, the idea of employing men and women in exchange for wages or salaries was still in the future. The only form of regular employment that was known was a kind of servitude, domestic or household slavery, in which wages played no part. Employment outside the towns and market-centres was likewise in the same form of slavery, or else, as in the forest areas, in work provided by customary duties and age-grade organisations. Once again money and wages played no part.

This is not the place to speculate on the full effects of this absence of money and of the habit of working for money. One main effect, though, was to keep the production of goods at the same general level as before. People were content to live as they had always lived. They felt no need for the invention or adoption of machinery that would enable them to produce more goods, as well as more kinds of goods. In short, all the goods that were required for a subsistence way of life could be well enough grown on made by the simple tools that were already known.

Within the limits of their subsistence way of life, West Africans in the sixteenth century worked in many skills and produced many different kinds of goods. But these limits made it hard, even impossible, for West Africans to move towards a scientific view of life, or to invent and use machines. For it has always been the need for new methods of production that has led to the invention and use of such methods; and here the need was scarcely felt. In this respect West Africa now fell rapidly behind Europe.

These points go some way to explain many of the setbacks, as well as many of the achievements, of the populations of the sixteenth century.

PRODUCTION, TRADE, AND MONEY

BASIL DAVIDSON

Yet even within the limits of a largely subsistence economy, forms of production and trade were already many and valuable.

West Africa exported a wide range of goods to the outside world. These included gold, ivory, cotton stuffs, animal hides and leather, kola, peppercorn, and mutton. Some of these goods, such as mutton, went only as far as the oasis peoples of the Sahara. Others, such as gold, went as far as northern Europe and Asia.

How large was this production? It was often surprisingly great. So far as cotton goods are concerned,* some idea of its size may be had from the writings of the outstanding nineteenth-century German traveller Heinrich Barth. He wrote about cotton production in the busy Hausa city of Kano during the 1850s, but what he said of Kano then will have been largely true of other cotton-weaving towns in earlier times.

"The great advantage of Kano," Barth wrote, "is that commerce and manufactures go hand in hand, and that almost every family has its share in them. There is really something grand in this kind of industry, which spreads to the north as far as Murzuk, Ghat, and even Tripoli; to the west, not only to Timbuktu, but in some degree even as far as the

---

*First brought to West Africa across the Sahara, long before the sixteenth century, cotton was grown in many West African countries, and was much used for clothing.

shores of the Atlantic, the very inhabitants of Arguin [on the coast of Mauretania] dressing in the cloth woven and dyed in Kano; to the east, all over Bornu, although there it comes in contact with the native industry of the country; and to the south it maintains a rivalry with the native industry of the Igbira and Igbo, while towards the south-east it invades the whole of Adamawa, and is only limited by the nakedness of pagan peoples who wear no clothing."

The hand-manufacture of cotton stuffs, in short, was valuable to many West African peoples.

And what about gold? It is no exaggeration to say that the prosperity of many states and empires was founded on the mining and export of gold from very early times.

There are many thousands of old mine-workings in West Africa, especially in the regions of Asante and upper Guinea. Nobody will ever know exactly how much they produced in pre-colonial times, but it was certainly a great deal. Professor Raymond Mauny, who has made the most careful estimates so far available, believes that West African gold production during the sixteenth century amounted to about nine tons a year. He also considers that about the same amount of gold was produced for a long time both before and after that time.

Of these nine tons of gold produced every year, about four probably came from the goldfields of central Guinea (Asante and its neighbourhood), and about four from western Guinea (the Buré region of the modern Republic of Guinea). "The total amount of gold extracted in West Africa from ancient times until 1500," Mauny estimates, "may be placed at several thousand tons; with an amount of about the same size, perhaps 3,500 tons, for the period between 1500 and 1900."

These large figures speak eloquently of the skill and determination of West Africa's miners. They were obliged to find and mine the gold-bearing ore, crush it, and extract the gold by primitive hand-methods. Yet they produced every year a total that was nearly half as much as the amount produced by modern methods in the colonial period. As late as 1938, for example, the production of West African gold stood at only twenty-one and a half tons.

Growing production led to more trade, more markets, and more trading routes. The trans-Saharan trade had first set in motion this process of expansion. People had come south across the Sahara and bargained for gold and other goods. They brought their own goods in exchange—fine metalware, silks and woolens, beads and horses—and West Africans were glad to have them. New appetites were created.

New trading systems were opened, and new sources of production were tapped.

All this expansion, in trade and production for trade, was well advanced by the beginning of the sixteenth century. It still affected only a minority of West Africans; but this minority was much larger than in earlier times. Nearly all main regions were now linked together by well-established trading routes. These ran between the south and the north: between southern Nigeria and Hausaland or Bornu, between Asante and the middle Niger, and between upper Guinea and the upper Niger. They also ran between east and west: between Asante and Hausaland, for example, and between Asante and upper Guinea.

All these centres of production and markets were linked to the great northern cities which had conducted the trans-Saharan trade since very early times: with Jenne, Timbuktu, Gao, and their sister-cities to west and east. These cities, just like their vanished forerunners, Kumbi and Tekrur, Audaghost and others, were the biggest and most prosperous markets in all West Africa. Along the coast of Guinea, meanwhile, a new system of trade with sea merchants was beginning to grow in size and value. Small as yet, this now rapidly expanded.

With the growth of trade, there came increasing modifications of the subsistence economy by the spreading use of a wide variety of forms of money. These forms were seldom or never coins. The main types of money were cowrie shells, various weights of brass, various sizes of iron bars, various lengths of cotton cloth. Europeans discovered in this century something that North African traders had found out much earlier: West Africans were careful traders. "These people," reported an English captain, John Lok, after a voyage to Guinea in 1553, "are very clever in their bargaining. They will not overlook a single bit of the gold they offer for sale. They use their own weights and measures, and they are very careful how they use them. Anyone who wants to deal with them must do so decently, for they will not trade if they are badly treated."

Who were the merchants? Along the trade routes they were mostly Hausa and Mandinka, often established in small towns they had founded or enlarged along these routes. In the big cities of the north they were also Kanuri and Songhay, Soninke, Fulani, Woloff, and many others. Along the coast they were Ibo, Ga, Akan, Nzima, and their neighbours. In many markets the biggest merchants were the most important men of the country: chiefs and kings, elders and counsellors. These were all men who needed wealth to pay for government and soldiers, to maintain their courts, to make gifts to visitors.

Long before, King Tenkaminen of Ancient Ghana had monopolised the gold and salt trade. Many of the sixteenth-century kings and chiefs now did the same with new items of production and new means of trade. When European ships sailed up the Benin river, for example, and dropped their anchors off Gwato, the river-port of Benin, they entered into trade not with anyone they might meet but only with agents and merchants selected by the king. "Nobody is allowed to buy anything from Europeans on this coast," observed a Dutch report of the seventeenth century,* "except the agents and merchants whom the king has named for this purpose. As soon as one of our ships drops anchor, the people inform the king, and the king appoints two or three agents and twenty or thirty merchants whom he empowers to deal with the Europeans."

It was much the same in the western Sudan. Passing through Bornu at the beginning of the sixteenth century, Leo Africanus reported that the king of that empire was especially interested in buying horses from North Africa and Egypt. He paid for these horses in various ways, but notably in war-captives who were used as slaves in North Africa and the Mediterranean countries. Yet the merchants who brought the horses, and took away the slaves, were allowed to deal only with the agents of the king himself. If the king happened to be away when they arrived at his capital, custom obliged them to sit and wait until he came back again.

In return for its exports, West Africa bought a wide range of goods from many parts of the world: cheap cottons and expensive silks from Asia, swords and knives and kitchenware from the dark little workshops of early industrial Europe, hand-written books and thoroughbred horses from the Muslim north, jewellery and trinkets, early types of firearms, gunpowder and shot, bars of iron and rings of copper in great quantity, and much else besides. All these had their accumulating influence on West African ways of life.

When considering what these kings and merchants did with their wealth one has again to bear in mind that this was not yet an economy of investment. Wealth brought a new measure of personal comfort to those who could obtain it: luxury tableware and clothing were often high on the list of African imports. The power to trade for firearms, gunpowder and ammunition often became of critical military and political importance at least in the eighteenth century, though scarcely in the sixteenth. Wealth also supported royal prestige. But above all it supported royal expenses, not indeed by allowing the payment of wages, for the concept of wage-labour still lay ahead, but in making possible the feeding and equipment of dependents and the bestowing of gifts by means' of which the political system was largely motored and made to work. Taking their wealth with one hand, and giving it away with the other, the kings and chiefs were able to keep it circulating among a large number of their subjects.

CITIES

BASIL DAVIDSON

A Dutchman has described the city of Benin as he saw it in 1602. It greatly impressed him. "When you go into it," he wrote, "you enter a great broad street, which is not paved, and seems to be seven or eight times broader than the Warmoes street in Amsterdam. This street is straight, and does not bend at any point. It is thought to be four miles long.

"At the gate where I went in on horseback, I saw a very big wall, very thick and made of earth, with a very deep and broad ditch outside it. . . . And outside this gate there is also a big suburb. Inside the gate, and along the great street just mentioned, you see many other great streets on either side, and these also are straight and do not bend. . . .

"The houses in this town stand in good order, one close and evenly placed with its neighbour, just as the houses in Holland stand. . . . They have square rooms, sheltered by a roof that is open in the middle, where the rain, wind, and light come in. The people sleep and eat in these rooms, but they have other rooms for cooking and different purposes. . . .

"The king's court is very great. It is built around many square-shaped yards. These yards have surrounding galleries where sentries are always placed. I myself went into the court far enough to pass through four great yards like this, and yet wherever I looked I could still see gate after gate which opened into other yards. . . ."*

---

*Recorded in O. Dapper's *Description of Africa*, first published in Amsterdam in 1668. Dapper did not himself visit Africa but collected reports from other Dutchmen who did. Most of these reports, at any rate as regards West Africa, referred to the early decades of the seventeenth century; and Dapper's book was in some respects out of date by the time he published it.

---

*The same had certainly been true here in earlier times.

80

Little or no stone was used in building these cities, for it was easier and cheaper to build in wood and clay, one reason why the archaeologists have found West Africa so exasperatingly short of satisfactory ruins. The wealthy market centre of Jenne, for example, was built entirely of short-lived materials. Leo Africanus tells us that "the king, the men of religion, the doctors of learning, the merchants and those of wealth and authority" lived in "houses made like huts, of clay and thatched straw." Yet absence of stone was not a sign of absence of civilisation. This same traveller found that the people of Jenne were "very well dressed." They had reason to be. They enjoyed a lucrative trade with the Akan peoples in the south and those of the western Sudan in the north. "It is because of this blessed city of Jenne," wrote the author of the *Tarikh al-Sudan*, Abd al-Rahman as-Sadi, in the seventeenth century, "that caravans come to Timbuktu from every side," for Jenne, standing where it did, had become "one of the great markets of the Muslim world."

The architecture of Timbuktu was much the same, though it had a few buildings in brick as well. Leo Africanus found "many handicraft workers, merchants and cotton-weavers" there. European goods were much in use. There was also an abundance of grain and other foods, while milk and butter were in good supply. The king possessed a huge treasure in gold. "The royal court," Leo wrote, "is very well organised and splendid. When the king goes from one town to another with his train of courtiers, he rides a camel; but horses are walked behind him by his servants. Should there by any need for fighting, the servants take charge of the camels and all the soldiers mount horses." He estimated that the king had about 3,000 horsemen and a much larger number of infantry. The best of these horses were brought across the Sahara from North Africa.

Gao, capital on the rising Songhay empire, was described by the same observer as "a very large town without any defensive wall." He thought that most of its houses were poor and ugly, but reported that there were "several fine ones where the king and his courtiers live." Gao's inhabitants were mostly rich traders who spent their time in travelling on business. "Bread and meat are very abundant, but they have no wine or fruit. Yet their melons and cucumbers are excellent, and they have enormous quantities of rice. Fresh-water wells are numerous there."

Leo considered that the revenues of Songhay were great, but so were its expenses. Luxury goods brought across the Sahara for the king, nobility, and rich merchants were very dear. Imported horses, woolens, swords, cavalry harness, medicines, and jewellery all cost far more than in the countries where they were made.

Yet the cities grew. They too were a fruitful part of West African civilisation.

Methods of government

Government through a highly trained and educated civil service is a modern development. But the states and empires of the sixteenth century had civil services of a less complicated sort. Their rules governed through a system of governors and sub-governors; and each of these had his own bureaucracy. These office-holders or officials operated early forms of civil service.

This was a process which had begun long before, and certainly in the days of Ancient Ghana. Little is known of the ways in which the lords of Ghana organised their government, but they must clearly have had some form of civil service, rudimentary though it doubtless was, since they were able to secure law and order over wide regions and draw tribute from many peoples.

With the passing of the years, we learn more about these methods of government. A writer of the early fourteenth century, Al-Omari of Cairo, has described how Mansa Kankan Musa of Mali (1312-37) carried on his rule. It was one of this emperor's customs, we are told by Al-Omari, "that whenever someone who had been charged with a certain task or important affair reports to the king, the latter questions him on everything that has happened from the time of his departure to the time of his return, and in great detail. Legal cases and appeals also go up to the king who examines them himself. Generally, he writes nothing himself, but gives his orders by word of mouth. For this, he has secretaries and offices." Already, in fourteenth-century Mali, there were the beginnings of a regular administration.

Yet early forms of civil service such as these tended to be easy-going and unreliable. The officials might be prompt and obedient when the king or governor was present, but when he was not they might also stop bothering about his orders. Or they might simply go on doing things as they had always done them, irrespective of what the king or governor might say. The governments of these early states, in short, were very loosely organized.

The sixteenth century brought developments in government, and not only in those areas where Islam had become important. The rulers of Benin, by no means Muslim, introduced a number of reforms that were aimed at tighter organisation and stronger central control. These were especially the work of

Oba Esigie, who came to power at the beginning of the century and ruled for nearly fifty years. Esigie emerged as victor in an old power-struggle, which had been fought by many Benin kings before him, against Benin's most influential group of nobles, the Uzama. These Uzama nobles had previously enjoyed the right to choose, by election among themselves, who was going to be the king of Benin. Now they lost this right, and royal succession from this time onwards became inheritance by primogeniture.

Law and order

Some peoples had many laws, many social rules and regulations, and went to great trouble to enforce them. Other peoples got along with far fewer laws, and bothered far less about applying them. It depended on where they lived and how they lived. The sixteenth century also saw changes in this field.

There was a growth in the means of *enforcing* law, whether by specially appointed officials, by special associations elected or recognised for the purpose, or by the formation of soldier groups who took their orders from judges or kings (though judges and kings were often the same men). But there was also a growth in the means of *making* law. This development of African law, of what is sometimes called customary law because it was not written down, formed an important aspect of the social scene.

It is an aspect that has been little studied; and we cannot follow it here. But an exceptional problem in the development of law does call for special comment. This was the clash between Muslim law and traditional African law. (Later on, a similar though more limited clash would occur between African law and European or Christian law.)

Muslim law rested on the *sharia*, a code of beliefs, observances, and rules laid down long ago, based on the teachings of the Koran. In its pure form, the *sharia* not only preaches that there is only one God, but frowns severely on all forms of sorcery and witchcraft. From its first introduction, accordingly, Islam clashed repeatedly with West African beliefs in many gods and in many forms of magic.

It clashed, of course, for various practical as well as religious reasons. . . . One reason for this opposition of interests lay in the very different rules which govern the inheritance of wealth among Muslims and non-Muslims. Another practical reason, especially important when it came to deciding on the choice of kings and chiefs, lay in the contrast between systems of primogeniture increasingly promoted by Islamic influence, and traditional systems of election from a more or less large number of possible candidates.

THE STRATIFICATION OF SOCIETY

BASIL DAVIDSON

But wherever the process of centralisation went on, and people formed themselves into states under elders, chiefs, or kings, something very important happened to society. Its old natural equality began to disappear. It became stratified, as social position became determined by one's degree of power and authority. Some men had the right to become chiefs. Others could not become chiefs, but had the right to elect them. Others again could not elect chiefs, but only had the right to say how chiefs ought to behave. Still others were pushed down into a lowly position where they had to obey their masters without question.

Together with these horizontal divisions there remained, however, older divisions of another kind, vertical divisions which separated all the people of one clan from the people of other clans, all the inhabitants of one village from their neighbours, all the descendants of one set of ancestors from the descendants of other ancestors. These vertical divisions were in some ways even more important than the horizontal divisions, and they were already very ancient by the sixteenth century.

There also took place a third kind of stratification of society, caused by changing and expanding methods by which people worked and produced wealth. Craftsmen formed themselves into different groups, according to their skills: metalworkers, boat-builders, fishermen, farmers, diviners, priests, singers of song, and many others. Some of these groups of craftsmen and specialists possessed much social power; others possessed little. How much social power each group possessed also varied from place to place. Among some peoples, for example, metalworkers were greatly honoured; among others, they were not.

Now these community divisions had already gone very far in West Africa by the early years of the sixteenth century, especially where the political consequences of Islam had taken their effect. Society had built, in other words, a ladder of social power.

This marked an important if often painful stage in social growth; and it happened, as we know, in nearly every part of Africa as in nearly every part of the world.

Needless to say, men were seldom able or content to go on standing for long on the same rung of the ladder of social power. Slaves pushed upward into freedom. Kings were pulled downward. Poor men climbed to wealth, and rich men became poor. There was constant movement up and down. And this movement greatly influenced the events of political history, setting one people or state against another, and promoting wars and conquests. The progress of one people, as elsewhere in the world at this stage of society, had to be at the expense of some other people.

One further point. We have said that the dividing-up of society occurred nearly everywhere in the world. But it needs to be remembered that it went much further, and became much more painful, in many of the countries of Europe and Asia. There, because of much greater development in production and exchange of goods and wealth, society became divided into a class stratification of masters and servants, with a few people having great social power, and most people having little or none. There, too, movement up and down the ladder of social power became difficult or rare, at least until after the French Revolution.

This far stiffer stratification had not happened in West Africa. Indeed, it has still not happened. The horizontal divisions have often remained of less influence than the vertical divisions into different clans, descent-lines, and communities. This is one reason why many of the old equalities of life, much of the old democracy of the clan and kinship system, are still alive and vivid in the West African country-side today. This is also why most West African governments during the sixteenth and seventeenth centuries were much more democratic, much more respectful of the rights of individual men, than were most of the governments of Europe.

By the sixteenth century, for example, much of the land of Europe was in the private possession of a landowning class. In West Africa, even today, most of the land is not so divided. Yet the horizontal divisions in West African society were, as we shall see, of growing importance.

There was, it should be emphasized, much movement up and down the ladder of power. Free men were taken prisoner in wartime, and were thrust down to the bottom rung; they could be used or sold as slaves. The Muslim rulers of the western Sudan often raided their non-Muslim neighbours so as to secure supplies of free labour; and their non-Muslim

neighbours did the same in reverse. Lawbreakers of some kinds were also reduced to slavery. Regular slave markets were held. In the city of Gao, for example, Leo Africanus observed "a market where many slaves, men and women, are sold every day. A girl of fifteen is worth about six ducats.* Little children are sold for about half the price of grown-ups." Many such slaves were sent northward across the Sahara.

At the same time we should remember, if only for the purposes of political and social analysis, that slavery in West Africa was seldom the harsh and pitiless bondage reserved for those who were taken across the Atlantic to the mines and plantations of the Americas. Rarely did this become chattel slavery. Traditional slavery in Africa—the term itself can be misleading—was usually a different institution, and a much milder one. Often it scarcely deserved the name of slavery in the sense that we have come to use it, being only a form of service which carried special duties and obligations. In strong contrast to trans-Atlantic customs and attitudes, slaves could easily work themselves into freedom. The very structures of society imposed upon owners the need to fit their slaves or bonded workers into the framework of family life. A slave could marry his master's daughters, become a trader on his own account, acquire ranks of authority over free men, and, as several well-known cases prove, even rise to the eminence of kingship itself.

---

*A ducat was a coin in use among North African traders.

SLAVERY AND THE SLAVE TRADE

PAUL BOHANNON

The nature of slavery is not always understood by modern Westerners. Both the Europeans and the Africans at the time the trade developed had a tradition of slavery, but the two traditions were of very different sorts. African slavery (usually called benign, domestic, or household slavery) was a domestic institution—there were only a few exceptions on the continent. Domestic slaves are interesting because their economic value was not the most important thing about them (although they may, like house-wives, be of economic value). It was rather their value as political followers and as indicators of prestige that was dominant.

It is necessary to do *something* with war captives, with criminals, and with the generally bad lots that are found in small numbers in all societies. The African answer was to turn them into slaves, which meant giving them a special (and humble) status in which they—either rejected by or removed from kinsmen—could be carefully watched at the same time that they were given security and position. The word "slave" in this sense refers to people who are attached to domestic groups by non-kinship links of a sort that contain elements of servility. Many slaves could occupy high positions within households—such was also the case with some slaves in classical societies—and to this day, an African will take up arms, joining his slave, if the slave is "insulted" in public by being addressed as such.

A slave was, thus, a kind of kinsman—with different rights from other kinsmen, different positions in the family and household from other kinsmen, but nevertheless a kind of kinsman. Slaves had either to be captured or they had to be acquired from their kinsmen who were "selling them into slavery." This means that, as a form of banishment, some groups took their criminal or generally unsatisfactory kinsmen and performed a ritual which "broke the kinship" and then sold him. The people who bought such men brought them into their own domestic groups and attached them by non-kinship, but kin-like, links to various "huts" within the household. Such slaves did work—often the hardest work—but they married, brought their families into the social group, and formed a thorough going part of the extended household.

Indigenous African slavery was benign in another sense—there were not very many people involved in it. The wars that Africans fought, until they met Europeans or until the Zulu and Ngoni began their progress through South Africa in the eighteenth century, did not produce very many captives. And very few people are totally unsatisfactory to their kinsmen.

Throughout Africa, slaves were no more than otherwise kinless persons who were attached by non-kinship links into households. The few exceptions are those in which they were attached to kings and courts, and in one or two places such as Dahomey, where there were plantation slaves working for the king (probably a feedback from New World institutions).*

One of the most important distinguishing characteristics of the American Negro slaves is that they too were kinless people. We who live in such a loose kinship system as that of middle-class America forget the tremendous importance of kin. But even in works of Harriet Beecher Stowe, one finds the classical distinction between the good master and the bad master: the bad master "broke up families." Every slaveowner in the New World has the right, obviously, to break up families. To this day, in lower-class Negro families, the matricentric family, consisting of a woman and her children with the link to the husband-father weak and ephemeral, is commonly found. When Negroes move into middle- or upper-class culture, this trait disappears. However, in the lower-class culture and through much of the Caribbean area, such is the standard family pattern, left over from the days of slavery. Slaves, even in our own society in the nineteenth century, were kinless people. In the African situation, this is about all that slavery amounted to.

In Europe slavery was a very different institution. It arose on a different basis, had a different history, and led to totally different conditions. European slavery was, from the beginning, primarily economic—perhaps it would be better to say that domestic slavery was the exception, for all that it existed side by side with economic slavery both in the classical world and in the American South. Even in Aristotle's time there were economic slaves being worked to death in salt mines—that expression has been with us for a long time.

Particularly in the medieval world, the form of subservience or servility was scarcely "slavery" in the African sense at all, because it consisted of the institution that European history knows as the "bond servant." Bond service was of an almost purely economic character. For reasons of debt, or some other, it was possible for me to bond myself, or a member of my family, to work until the debt was paid. The whole notion of bond service developed out of a feudal ethic and carried over into the subsequent period.

What happened in the slave trade is that the economically dominated feudal version of servility from the European area met the basically benign, family-dominated slavery from Africa. Like many other aspects of culture, they met first in the market

---

*On the contrary, Herskovits points out in *The Myth of the Negro Past* that "Slavery has long existed in the entire region, and in at least one of its kingdoms, Dahomey, a kind of plantation system was found under which an absentee ownership, with the ruler as principal, demanded the utmost return from the estates, and thus created conditions of labor resembling the regimes the slaves were to encounter in the New World." (Ed.)

place. Africans saw nothing wrong in selling slaves. Europeans found nothing wrong in buying them—indeed, many of the Negroes in the earliest importations were treated as bond slaves, their bondage limited by contract to a period of years. But the idea that each had about the role of the slave in the world's work was totally different from that of the other. Supply of slaves became expensive, and the "bond" became permanent. From the meeting of the two and the establishment of new nations and new economies, a new institution—New World slavery—emerged.

Given this particular impetus in the form of a labor force, Portugal got a tremendous shot in the arm. Spain was not far behind. And as Portugal went down the coast of Africa, with sea captains under contract to the princes, working on a commission basis, they found themselves by 1460-70 in the Bight of Benin. They built fortresses along the coast at a slightly later date.

The Dutch were not far behind the Portuguese. The Brandenburgers, the Danes, the English by 1540—all got into the trade.

When the Portuguese came down the coast, they found large African kingdoms on the Guinea coast and at the mouth of the Congo. The sources of slaves extended from Cape Verde down the coast deep into Angola. Slaves going into Latin America and Brazil tended, after the first few years, to come from the coast south of the Cameroons; those into the West Indies and North America from the Guinea coast. Portuguese slavers eventually even exported slaves from the east coast, particularly from what is today Mozambique, into Brazil.

RESISTANCE TO THE SLAVE TRADE

BASIL DAVIDSON

We have seen how the lords of old West Africa indulged in the buying and selling of men and women—sending many across the Sahara both before and during the ocean slave trade—in the same way as did the lords of Europe and Asia. We have discussed how the massive export of millions of Africans to the Americas was founded on customs such as these.

One might have expected, though, that there would be African efforts to cut down the ocean slave trade, or even to stop it altogether, when the

damaging effects of this trade became clear. And such efforts were indeed made. They failed, because the pressure of European and American demand was too great for them, but they are none the less worth remembering. Here are three examples.

The first occurred as early as the sixteenth century. In 1526 a famous king of the Bakongo state of Congo, near the mouth of the river of that name, wrote an angry letter of protest to the king of Portugal. King Nzinga Mbemba, whose Christian name was Affonso, complained to the Portuguese king, his ally and partner in trade, that the slave trade was doing great harm to his country. Together with certain Bakongo "thieves and men of evil conscience," he wrote, Portuguese traders were "grabbing and selling" his people, even including members of his own family. He wanted nothing from Portugal, he went on, except "priests and people to teach in our schools, and no other goods but wine and flour for the holy sacrament." Above all, he demanded that the Portuguese king, who was himself deep in the business of the slave trade, should recall his traders from the Congo, "because it is our will that in these kingdoms of Congo there should not be any trade in slaves nor any market for slaves." But the advantages and temptations offered by European-made goods, for which the sea merchants increasingly demanded slaves, were too much for many of King Affonso's chiefs and sub-chiefs. They went on with the trade.

Another example occurred on the Dahomey coast of West Africa, the stretch of seaboard which the Europeans knew as the Slave Coast. When King Agaja sent his armies to capture the city-states of Ardrah and its slave-dealing neighbours, in 1724, he seems to have had it in mind to bring the slave trade to a halt. He sent a message to the British government, by the hand of an Englishman whom his generals had found in one of the coastal towns, telling it that he wanted to stop the export of people from his country. The Fon of Dahomey, after all, had every reason to know the damage that was done by the trade, for they had greatly suffered from it. King Agaja was no more successful in ending the trade than King Affonso two centuries earlier, though he certainly checked it for a time.

A third and similar example was noted in 1789 by a Swedish traveller who visited the imamate of Futa Toro in northern Senegal. A year before his visit, wrote this traveller, the almamy of Futa Toro had passed a law, "very much to his honour," which declared that no slaves were to be taken through Futa Toro for sale abroad. But the almamy was up against a powerful trading system which yielded great profits; and this system defeated his good intentions. Waiting in the Senegal river, as usual, were several French slave ships. Their captains, seeing they could not now hope to buy any slaves in Futa Toro, complained to the almamy, asking him to change his mind and do away with the law.

The almamy refused to do so, and followed this refusal by sending back to the agents of the French slave-trading company a number of presents they had given him, adding that "all the riches of that company would not make him change his mind." Faced with this refusal, the French captains discussed among themselves what they should do next. Then they found that the inland slave-dealers, also damaged by the almamy's new law, had worked out another route for taking slaves to the coast. So the French captains weighed anchor and sailed down the coast to this new market; and there they supplied themselves with the captives whom the almamy had prevented them from buying in the Senegal river.

There were other such acts of resistance, or attempted resistance, at Benin and elsewhere. They all failed. And they failed because the slave trade, until the early years of the nineteenth century, was a central part of the commercial system of the western world, the system to which large regions of Africa increasingly belonged. Only a change in this system could stop the trade in slaves. The beginnings of this change occurred in the closing years of the eighteenth century and led, among other things, to the foundation of Sierra Leone and Liberia. Before considering these events, however, another main consequence of the Atlantic trade needs at least to be touched upon. This happened outside Africa, and yet it is in many ways a large and inseparable part of African history. Great populations of African origin were implanted in the lands beyond the Atlantic. Their toil, skills, and achievements played a large and even essential role in building the civilisations of the Americas. Without Africa's contribution, those civilisations could not have become what they are today.

PART II. B:

RACISM

SOUTHERN COP

STERLING A. BROWN

Let us forgive Ty Kendricks
The place was Darktown. He was young.
His nerves were jittery. The day was hot.
The Negro ran out of the alley.
And so Ty shot.

Let us understand Ty Kendricks
The Negro must have been dangerous,
Because he ran;
And here was a rookie with a chance
To prove himself man.

Let us condone Ty Kendricks
If we cannot decorate.
When he found what the Negro was running for,
It was all too late;
And all we can say for the Negro is
It was unfortunate.

Let us pity Ty Kendricks
He has been through enough,
Standing there, his big gun smoking,
Rabbit-scared, alone,
Having to hear the wenches wail
And the dying Negro moan.

Editor's Note:

Social Darwinism, Manifest Destiny, and the White Man's Burden are three of the prevailing ideologies that have greatly influenced the institutions and practices of American life both domestically and internationally. Expansionism, imperialism, and racial subjugation were direct by-products of the implicit understandings which had developed between North and South by the turn of the century. The *Boston Evening Transcript* of January 14, 1899, admitted that Southern race policy was "now the policy of the Administration of the very party which carried the country into and through a civil war to free the slave," a sentiment echoed in a nearly contemporary *Atlantic Monthly* assessment: "If the stronger and cleverer race is free to impose its will upon newcaught, sullen peoples on the other side of the globe [Philippines, Hawaii, Cuba], why not in South Carolina and Mississippi?"

THE IDEOLOGICAL ROOTS OF RACISM

LOUIS L. KNOWLES and KENNETH PREWITT

It has, of course, been the white man's relationship with the black man which has led to the most powerful expressions of institutional racism in the society. This is a history which hardly needs retelling, although it might be instructive to consider how closely related was the justification of Indian extermination to that of black slavery. It was the heathenism or savagery, so-called, of the African, just as of the Indian, which became the early rationale for enslavement. A particularly ingenious version of the retionale is best known under the popular label "Social Darwinism."

The Social Darwinian theory of evolution greatly influenced social thought, hence social institutions, in nineteenth-century America. Social Darwinists extended the concept of biological evolution in the development of man to a concept of evolution in development of societies and civilizations. The nature of a society or nation or race was presumed to be the product of natural evolutionary forces. The evolutionary process was characterized by struggle and conflict in which the "stronger, more advanced, and more civilized" would naturally triumph over the "inferior, weaker, backward, and uncivilized" peoples.

The idea of natural selection was translated to a struggle between individual members of a society; between members of classes of society, between different nations, and between different races. This conflict, far from being an evil thing, was nature's indispensable method of producing superior men, superior nations, and superior races.

Such phrases as "the struggle for existence" and "the survival of the fittest" became *lingua franca,* and white Americans had a full-blown ideology to explain their treatment of the "inferior race."

The contemporary expression of Social Darwinian thinking is less blatant but essentially the same as the arguments used in the nineteenth century. The poverty and degradation of the non-white races in the United States are thought to be the result of an innate lack of ability rather than anything white society has done. Thus a long line of argument reaches its most recent expression in the now famous "Moynihan Report": the focal point of the race problem is to be found in the pathology of black society.

Social Darwinism was buttressed with two other ideas widely accepted in nineteenth-century America: manifest destiny and white man's burden. Briefly stated, manifest destiny was simply the idea that white Americans were destined, either by natural forces or by Divine Right, to control at least the North American continent and, in many versions of the theory, a much greater share of the earth's surface. Many churchmen supported the idea that such expansion was the will of God. The impact of this belief with respect to the Indians has already been noted. Let it suffice to say that manifest destiny helped provide the moral and theological justification for genocide. The belief that American expansion was a natural process was rooted in Social Darwinism. Expansionism was simply the natural growth process of a superior nation. This deterministic argument enjoyed wide popularity. Even those who were not comfortable with the overt racism of the expansionist argument were able to cooperate in policies of "liberation" in Cuba and the Philippines by emphasizing the evils of Spanish control. Many, however, felt no need to camouflage their racism. Albert J. Beveridge, Senator from Indiana, stated his position clearly:

> The American Republic is a part of the movement of a race—the most masterful race of history—and race movements are not to be stayed by the hand of man. They are mighty answers to Divine commands. Their leaders are not only statesmen of peoples—they are prophets of God. The inherent tendencies of a race are its highest law. They precede and survive all statutes, all constitutions.... The sovereign tendencies of our race are organization and government.

In any case, if racism was not invoked as a justification for imperialist expansion in the first place, it subsequently became a justification for continued American control of the newly "acquired" territories.

90

This was particularly true in the Philippines. "The control of one country by another and the denial of rights or citizenship to the Filipinos were difficult ideas to reconcile with the Declaration of Independence and with American institutions. In order to make these opposing ideas of government compatible at all, the proponents of the acquisition of the Philippines were forced to rely heavily on race theories."

An argument commonly expressed was that the Filipinos were simply incapable of self-government. "The Declaration of Independence,' stated Beveridge, 'applies only to peoples capable of self-government. Otherwise, how dared we administer the affairs of the Indians? How dare we continue to govern them today?' " The decision, therefore, as to who was capable of self-government and who was not so capable was left to the United States Government. The criteria were usually explicitly racist, as it was simply assumed that whites, at least Anglo-Saxons, had the "gift" of being able to govern themselves while the inferior nonwhite peoples were not so endowed.

The ideology of imperialist expansion had an easily foreseeable impact on the domestic race situation. As Ronald Segal points out in *The Race War,*

Both North and South saw and accepted the implications. What was sauce for the Philippines, for Hawaii and Cuba, was sauce for the Southern Negro. If the stronger and cleverer race is free to impose its will upon "new-caught sullen peoples" on the other side of the globe, why not in South Carolina and Mississippi? asked the *Atlantic Monthly.* "No Republican leader," proclaimed Senator Tillman of South Carolina, "... will now dare to wave the bloody shirt and preach a crusade against the South's treatment of the Negro. The North has a bloody shirt of its own. Many thousands of them have been made into shrouds for murdered Filipinos, done to death because they were fighting for liberty." Throughout the United States doctrines of racial superiority received the assent of influential politicians and noted academics. The very rationalizations that had eased the conscience of the slave trade now provided the sanction for imperial expansion.

Another component of the ideology which has nurtured racist policies is that of "the white man's burden." This phrase comes from the title of a poem by Rudyard Kipling, which appeared in the United States in 1899. Whatever Kipling himself may have wished to convey, Americans soon popularized and adopted the concept as an encouragement for accepting the responsibility of looking after the affairs of the darker races. This notion of the "white man's burden" was that the white race, particularly Anglo-Saxons of Britain and America, should accept the (Christian) responsibility for helping the poor colored masses to find a better way of life.

It should be clear that this notion is no less racist than others previously mentioned. Behind the attitude lies the assumption of white supremacy. In exhorting Americans to follow British policy in this regard, the philosopher Josiah Royce stated the assumption clearly:

... The Englishman, in his official and governmental dealings with backward peoples, has a great way of being superior without very often publicly saying that he is superior. You well know that in dealing, as an individual, with other individuals, trouble is seldom made by the fact that you are actually superior to another man in any respect. The trouble comes when you tell the other man, too stridently, that you are his superior. Be my superior, quietly, simply showing your superiority in your deeds, and very likely I shall love you for the very fact of your superiority. For we all love our leaders. But tell me I am your inferior, and then perhaps I may grow boyish, and may throw stones. Well, it is so with the races. Grant then that yours is the superior race. Then you can say little about the subject in your public dealings with the backward race. Superiority is best shown by good deeds and by few boasts.

Both manifest destiny and the idea of a white man's burden, in disguised forms, continue to shape white America's values and policies. Manifest destiny has done much to stimulate the modern-day myth that colored peoples are generally incapable of self-government. There are whites who continue to believe that black Afro-Americans are not ready to govern themselves. At best, blacks must first be "properly trained." Of course, this belief influences our relations with nonwhites in other areas of the world as well.

The authors have found the concept of manifest destiny helpful in analyzing white response to "black power." Black power is based on the belief that black people in America are capable of governing and controlling their own communities. White rejection of black power reflects, in part, the widely accepted white myth that blacks are incapable of self-government and must be controlled and governed by whites. Many whites apparently still share with Albert Beveridge the belief that "organization and government" are among the "sovereign tendencies of our race."

The belief in a "white man's burden" also has

91

its modern-day counterpart, particularly in the attitudes and practices of so-called "white liberals" busily trying to solve "the Negro problem." The liberal often bears a strong sense of responsibility for helping the Negro find a better life. He generally characterizes the Negro as "disadvantaged," "unfortunate," or "culturally deprived." The liberal generally feels superior to the black man, although he is less likely to publicly state his sense of superiority. He may not even recognize his own racist sentiments. In any case, much like Josiah Royce, he senses that "superiority is best shown by good deeds and by few boasts." Liberal paternalism is reflected not only in individual attitudes but in the procedures and policies of institutions such as the welfare system and most "war on poverty" efforts.

It is obvious that recent reports and action plans carry on a traditional, if diversionary, view that has long been acceptable to most white Americans: that it is not white institutions but a few bigots plus the deprived status of Negroes that cause racial tension. Such a view is mythical....We are not content with "explanations" of white-black relations that are apolitical, that would reduce the causes of racial tension to the level of psychological and personal factors. Three hundred years of American history cannot be encapsulated so easily. To ignore the network of institutional controls through which social benefits are allocated may be reassuring, but it is also bad social history. America is and has long been a racist nation, because it has and has long had a racist policy. This policy is not to be understood by listening to the proclamations of intent by leading citizens and government officials; nor is it to be understood by reading off a list of compensatory programs in business, education, and welfare. The policy can be understood only when we are willing to take a hard look at the continuing and irrefutable racist consequences of the major institutions in American life. The policy will be changed when we are willing to start the difficult task of remaking our institutions.

Editor's Note:

Thomas Jefferson, one of the principal authors of the Declaration of Independence, at one time held the same beliefs about blacks that were prevalent among advocates of slavery. These ideas were presented in *Notes on the State of*

Virginia (1787), which was a response to series of questions put to Jefferson by the Marquis de Barbé-Marbois while Jefferson was governor of Virginia. Jefferson believed that slaves were human and should be free, but that they suffered from inferior mental abilities and were incapable of functioning as full members in a democracy that required an intelligent and educated electorate. His proposal was emancipation, with training, assistance, and subsequent colonization outside the United States. Jefferson's views are by no means moribund. Contemporary writers such as William Shockley and Arthur R. Jensen maintain that there is real genetic inferiority among blacks and propose eugenics and sterilization as solutions to the race problem in the United States.

NOTES ON THE STATE OF VIRGINIA

THOMAS JEFFERSON

What is to be done with the blacks?

It will probably be asked, Why not retain and incorporate the blacks into the State, and thus save the expense of supplying by importation of white settlers, the vacancies they will leave? Deep-rooted prejudices entertained by the whites; ten thousand recollections, by the blacks, of the injuries they have sustained; new provocations; the real distinctions which nature has made; and many other circumstances, will divide us into parties, and produce convulsions, which will probably never end but in the extermination of the one or the other race. To these objections, which are political, may be added others, which are physical and moral. The first difference which strikes us is that of color. Whether the black of the negro resides in the reticular membrane between the skin and scarf-skin, or in the scarf-skin itself; whether it proceeds from the color of the blood, the color of the bile, or from that of some other secretion, the difference is fixed in nature, and is as real as if its seat and cause were better known to us. And is this difference of no importance? Is it not the foundation of a greater or less share of beauty in the two races? Are not the fine mixtures of red and white, the expressions of every passion by greater or less suffusions of color in the one, preferable to that eternal monotony, which reigns in the countenances, that immovable veil of black which covers the emotions of the other race? Add to these, flowing hair, a more elegant symmetry of form, their own judgment in favor of the whites, declared by their preference of them, as uniformly as is the preference of the Oranootan for the black woman over those of his own species. The circumstance of superior beauty, is thought worthy attention in the propagation of our horses, dogs, and other domestic animals; why not in that of man? Besides those of color, figure, and hair, there are other physical distinctions proving a difference of race. They have less hair on the face and body. They secrete less by the kidneys, and more by the glands of the skin, which gives them a very strong and disagreeable odor. This greater degree of transpiration, renders them more tolerant of heat, and less so of cold than the whites. Perhaps, too, a difference of structure in the pulmonary apparatus, which a late ingenious experimentalist has discovered to be the principal regulator of animal heat, may have disabled them from extricating, in the act of inspiration, so much of that fluid from the outer air, or obliged them in expiration, to part with more of it. They seem to require less sleep. A black after hard labor through the day, will be induced by the slightest amusements to sit up till midnight, or later, though knowing he must be out with the first dawn of the morning. They are at least as brave, and more adventuresome. But this may perhaps proceed from a want of forethought, which prevents their seeing a danger till it be present. When present, they do not go through it with more coolness or steadiness than the whites. They are more ardent after their female; but love seems with them to be more an eager desire, than a tender delicate mixture of sentiment and sensation. Their griefs are transient. Those numberless afflictions, which render it doubtful whether heaven has given life to us in mercy or in wrath, are less felt, and sooner forgotten with them. In general, their existence appears to participate more of sensation than reflection. To this must be ascribed their disposition to sleep when abstracted from their diversions, and unemployed in labor. An animal whose body is at rest, and who does not reflect, must be disposed to sleep of course. Comparing them by their faculties of memory, reason, and imagination, it appears to me that in memory they are equal to the whites; in reason much inferior, as I think one could scarcely by found capable of tracing and comprehending the investigations of Euclid; and that in imagination they are dull, tasteless, and anomalous. It would be unfair to follow them to Africa for this investigation. We will consider them here, on the same stage with the whites, and where the facts are not apocryphal on which a judgment is to be formed. It will be right to make great allowances for the difference of condition, of education, of conversation, of the sphere in which they move. Many millions of them have been brought to, and born in America. Most of them, indeed, have been confined to tillage, to their own homes, and their own society; yet many have been so situated, that they might have availed themselves of the conversation of their masters; many have been brought up to the handicraft

arts, and from that circumstance have always been associated with the whites. Some have been liberally educated, and all have lived in countries where the arts and sciences are cultivated to a considerable degree, and all have had before their eyes samples of the best works from abroad. The Indians, with no advantages of this kind, will often carve figures on their pipes not destitute of design and merit. They will crayon out an animal, a plant, or a country, so as to prove the existence of a germ in their minds which only wants cultivation. They astonish you with strokes of the most sublime oratory; such as prove their reason and sentiment strong, their imagination glowing and elevated. But never yet could I find that a black had uttered a thought above the level of plain narration; never saw even an elementary trait of painting or sculpture. In music they are more generally gifted than the whites with accurate ears for tune and time, and they have been found capable of imagining a small catch. Whether they will be equal to the composition of a more extensive run of melody, or of complicated harmony, is yet to be proved. Misery is often the parent of the most affecting touches in poetry. Among the blacks is misery enough, God knows, but no poetry. Love is the peculiar oestrum of the poet. Their love is ardent, but it kindles the senses only, not the imagination. Religion, indeed, has produced a Phyllis Wheatley; but it could not produce a poet. The compositions published under her name are below the dignity of criticism. The heroes of the Dunciad are to her, as Hercules to the author of that poem. Ignatius Sancho has approached nearer to merit in composition; yet his letters do more honor to the heart than the head. They breathe the purest effusions of friendship and general philanthropy, and show how great a degree of the latter may be compounded with strong religious zeal. He is often happy in the turn of his compliments, and his style is easy and familiar, except when he affects a Shandean fabrication of words. But his imagination is wild and extravagant, escapes incessantly from every restraint of reason and taste, and, in the course of its vagaries, leaves a tract of thought as incoherent and eccentric, as is the course of a meteor through the sky. His subjects should often have led him to a process of sober reasoning; yet we find him always substituting sentiment for demonstration. Upon the whole, though we admit him to the first place among those of his own color who have presented themselves to the public judgment, yet when we compare him with the writers of the race among whom he lived and particularly with the epistolary class in which he has taken his own stand, we are compelled to enrol him at the bottom of the column. This criticism supposes the letters published under his name to be genuine, and to have received amendment from no other hand; points which would not be of easy investigation. The improvement of the blacks in body and mind, in the first instance of their mixture with the whites, has been observed by every one, and proves that their inferiority is not the effect merely of their condition of life.

Editor's Note:

Dr. John H. Van Evrie, a northern physician and part owner of *The Old Guard*, a journal that defended slavery and the South, was as vitriolic and derisive in attacks on Negroes as the most impassioned Southerner. According to Van Evrie, education, if it were possible at all, would irrevocably damage the brain of the Negro, since it would develop the forward position of the cranium and give the Negro a broad forehead and small cerebellum similar to that of the white man. The relationship of the cranium to the body would thus be seriously altered, the Negro's center of gravity would be disturbed, and he would find it impossible to stand erect or to walk! This brief selection from *Negroes and Negro Slavery: The First, an Inferior Race—the Latter, Its Normal Condition* postulates the plurality theory, affirming separate creations for the various species of man.

A DIFFERENT AND INFERIOR SPECIES

JOHN H. VAN EVRIE

The Negro is a man, but a different and inferior *species* of man, who could no more originate from the same source as ourselves, than the owl could from the eagle, or the shad from the salmon, or the cat from the tiger; and who can no more be forced by *human power* to manifest the faculties, or perform the purposes assigned by the Almighty Creator to the Caucasian man, than can either of these forms of life be made to manifest faculties other than those inherent, *specific*, and eternally impressed upon their organization.

We are no defender of "materialism," and utterly reject the impious doctrine, that the human soul is the *result* of organization, and therefore, perishes with it; but the identity of organism and functions, of structure and faculties, of form and capabilities, in short of *specific* organization and a *specific* nature, is a *fact* universal, invariable and indestructible.

The Caucasian brain measures 92 cubic inches —with the cerebrum, the centre of the intellectual functions, relatively predominating over the cerebellum, the centre of the animal instincts; thus, it is capable of indefinite progression, and transmits the knowledge or experience acquired by one generation to subsequent generations—the record of which is history.

The Negro brain measures from 65 to 70 cubic inches—with the cerebellum, the centre of the animal instincts relatively predominating over the cerebrum, the centre of the intellectual powers; thus, its acquisition of knowledge is limited to a single generation, and incapable of transmitting this to subsequent generations, *it can have no history*. A single glance at eternal and immutable *facts*, which perpetually separate these forms of human existence will be sufficient to cover the whole ground—thus, could the deluded people who propose to improve on the works of the Creator, and *elevate* the Negro to the standard of the white, actually perform an act of omnipotence, and add 25 or 30 per cent to the totality of the Negro brain, they would still be at as great a distance as ever from their final object, while the relations of the anterior and posterior portions of the brain remained as at present.

And were they capable of performing a second act of creative power, to diminish the posterior portion, and add to the anterior portion of the Negro brain, to make it in form, as well as size, correspond to that of the Caucasian man, they would even then, after all this effort, and all this display of omnipotent force, come back again to the starting point, for such a brain could no more be born of a negress, than can an elephant pass through the eye of a needle. Historical fact is in perfect accordance with these physiological facts, thus, while there are portions, nationalities or branches of the Caucasian race that have relapsed, become effete, decayed, lost—the *race* has steadily progressed, and from the banks of the Nile, to those of the Mississippi, civilization, progress, intellectual development, the *specific* characteristics of the Caucasian have alone changed locations. The Negro on the contrary is at this moment just where the race was four thousand years ago, when sculptured on Egyptian monuments. Portions of it in contact with the superior race have been temporarily advanced, but invariably, without exception, they have returned to the African standard as soon as this contact has ceased, or as soon as the results of amalgamation between them have disappeared.

The Abyssinians originally pure Caucasian, the Lybians, the Numidians of Roman history, and Ethiopeans, the two latter, and possibly the Lybians also of mixed Caucasian blood are often confounded with the Negro or the typical wooly haired, and thus it has been claimed that the latter were capable of progress; but it is a historical truth beyond contradiction or doubt even that the typical African, *the race now in our midst,* has never of its own volition passed beyond the hunter condition, that condition which it now occupies in Africa, when isolated from all other races.

The Creator has beneficently as wisely permitted amalgamation to a certain extent between the extremes of "humanity," the Caucasian and Negro—otherwise there would be slavery, oppression, brutality, death, but this is limited within fixed boundaries; thus, the Mulatto or Hybrid of the fourth generation, is as sterile as the mule or most *animal* hybrids are in the first generation.

Editor's Note:

Hinton R. Helper, a North Carolinian, saw the Negro as belonging to "a lower and inferior order of beings." He presents an argument for exclusion based on the "defective characteristics" of black people described in this selection from *The Negroes in Negroland* . . . (1868). Helper maintains that only a white person whose reason and honor had been perverted would disagree with his position. Helper also wrote *The Impending Crisis*, which further develops his premise about the detrimental effects of slavery on the economic growth of North and South, and *Nojoque*, in which he clarified his opposition to slavery and his violent hatred of Negroes, with the ultimate proposal of extermination as a solution.

THE NEGROES IN NEGROLAND

HINTON R. HELPER

There are now in the United States of America thirty millions of white people, who are (or ought to be) bound together by the ties of a kindred origin, by the affinities of a sameness of noble purpose, by the links of a common nationality, and by the cords of an inseparable destiny. We have here also, unfortunately for us all, four millions of black people, whose ancestors, like themselves, were never known (except in very rare instances, which form the exceptions to a general rule) to aspire to any other condition than that of base and beastlike slavery. These black people are, by nature, of an exceedingly low and groveling disposition. They have no trait of character that is lovely or admirable. They are not high-minded, enterprising, nor prudent. In no age, in no part of the world, have they, of themselves, ever projected or advanced any public or private interest, nor given expression to any thought or sentiment that could worthily elicit the praise, or even the favorable mention, of the better portion of mankind. Seeing, then, that the negro does, indeed, belong to a lower and inferior order of beings, why, in the name of Heaven, why should we forever degrade and disgrace both ourselves and our posterity by entering, of our own volition, into more intimate relations with him? May God, in his restraining mercy, forbid that we should ever do this most foul and wicked thing!

Acting under the influence of that vile spirit of deception and chicanery which is always familiar with every false pretence, the members of a Radical Congress, the editors of a venal press, and other peddlers of perverted knowledge, are now loudly proclaiming that nowhere in our country, henceforth, must there be any distinction, any discrimination, on account of color; thereby covertly inculcating the gross error of inferring or supposing that color is the only difference—and that a very trivial difference—between the whites and the blacks! Now, once and for all, in conscientious deference to truth, let it be distinctly made known and acknowledged, that, in addition to the black and baneful color of the negro, there are numerous other defects, physical, mental, and moral, which clearly mark him, when compared with the white man, as a very different and inferior creature. While, therefore, with an involuntary repugnance which we cannot control, and with a wholesome antipathy which it would be both unnatural and unavailing in us to attempt to destroy, we behold the crime-stained blackness of the negro, let us, also, at the same time, take cognizance of

His low and compressed Forehead;
His hard, thick Skull;
His small, backward-thrown Brain;
His short, crisp Hair;
His flat Nose;
His thick Lips;
His projecting, snout-like Mouth;
His strange, Eunuch-toned Voice;
The scantiness of Beard on his Face;
The Toughness and Unsensitiveness of his Skin;
The Thinness and Shrunkenness of his Thighs;
His curved Knees;
His calfless Legs;
His low, short Ankles;
His long, flat Heels;
His glut-shaped Feet;
The general Angularity and Oddity of his Frame;
The Malodorous Exhalations from his Person;
His Puerility of Mind;

His Inertia and Sleepy-headedness;

His proverbial Dishonesty;

His predisposition to fabricate Falsehoods; and

His Apathetic Indifference to all Propositions and
    Enterprises of Solid Merit.

Many other differences might be mentioned; but the
score and more of obvious and undeniable ones here
enumerated ought to suffice for the utter confusion
and shame of all those disingenuous politicians and
others, who, knowing better, and who are thus guilty
of the crime of defeating the legitimate ends of their
own knowledge, would, for mere selfish and partisan
purposes, convey the delusive impression that there is
no other difference than that of color. There are
many points of general dissatisfaction and dispute,
which should not, on any account, be overlooked in
the discussion of the subjects here presented. One of
these is, that white people, whose reason and honor
have not been vitiated, object to close relationship
with negroes, not wishing to live with them in the
same house; not wishing to fellowship with them in
the same society, assembly, or congregation; not
wishing to ride with them in the same omnibus, car,
or carriage; and not wishing to mess with them at the
same table, whether at a hotel, in a restaurant, on a
steamer, or elsewhere. Now, any and every white
person who does not think and act in strict accordance with the just and pure promptings here indicated, is, in reality, a most unworthy and despicable
representative of his race. Even the lower animals, the
creatures of mere instinct—the beasts, the birds, and
the fishes—many distinct species of which are apparently quite similar, set us daily and hourly examples
of the eminent propriety of each kind forming and
maintaining separate communities of their own; and
so we always find them—in herds, in flocks, and in
shoals. How can the negro be a fit person to occupy,
in any capacity, our houses or our hotels, our theatres
or our churches, our schools or our colleges, our
steamers or our vehicles, or any other place or places
of uncommon comfort and convenience, which owe
their creation, their proper uses, and their perpetuity,
to the whites alone—places and improvements about
which the negro, of himself, is, and always has been,
absolutely ignorant and indifferent? Neither in his
own country nor elsewhere has the negro ever built a
house or a theatre; he has never erected a church nor
a college; he has never constructed a steamer nor a
railroad, nor a railroad-car—nor, except when under
the special direction and control of superior intelligence, has he ever invented or manufactured even the
minutest appendage of any one of the distinctive
elements or realities of human progress. Yet, let this
not, by any means, be understood as an argument,
nor even as a hint, in behalf of slavery. It is to the
great and lasting honor of the Republic that slavery in
the United States is abolished forever. In losing her
slaves, the South lost nothing that was worth the
keeping. Had slavery only been abolished by law
many years ago, our whole country would be
infinitely better off today.

Never will it be possible for the compiler to
erase from his memory the feelings of weighty
sadness and disgust which overcame him, a few
months since, when, while sojourning in the city of
Washington, he walked, one day, into the Capitol,
and, leisurely passing into the galleries of the two
houses of Congress, beheld there, uncouthly lounging
and dozing upon the seats, a horde of vile, ignorant,
and foul-scented negroes. He was perplexed, shocked,
humiliated, and indignant—and could not sit down.
With merited emotions of bitterness and contempt
for those narrow-minded white men, through whose
detestable folly and selfishness so great an outrage
against public propriety and decency had been
perpetrated, he turned away—indeed, it was not in his
power to contemplate with calmness that motley and
monstrous manifestation of national incongruity,
ugliness, and disgrace. Then it was that, for the first
time in his life, he wished himself a Hercules, in order
that he might be able to clean, thoroughly and at
once, those Augean stables of the black ordure and
Radical filth which, therein and elsewhere, had
already accumulated to an almost insufferable excess.
It was the powerful and long-lingering momentum of
the impressions received on that occasion, more than
any other circumstance, that gave definite form and
resolution to the purpose (although the idea had been
previously entertained) of preparing this compilation.
The object of the compiler will have been well
attained if the work aids materially in more fully
convincing his countrymen, North, South, East and
West, that negro equality, negro supremacy, and
negro domination, as now tyrannically enforced at
the point of the bayonet, are cruel and atrocious
innovations, which ought to be speedily terminated.

Editor's Note:

Racism in the South subsequent to the Civil War raised
a variety of everyday problems, some almost ludicrous,
others of a deadly—to blacks, often fatal—significance.
Several of these problems are dissected in the following
excerpts from George Brown Tindall's *South Carolina
Negroes.*

ETIQUETTE AND MISCEGENATION

GEORGE BROWN TINDALL

Forms of address

In the subtle forms of personal address racial distinctions found frequent expression. Negroes were expected to address whites as Massa, Master, Boss, Miss. or Missis. The use of Mr. or Mrs. in addressing a white was by many considered an impertinence. Whites generally addressed Negroes by their first names, except the elderly ones, who were addressed as uncle, daddy, aunty, or mama. It was extremely rare for whites to use Mr. before the name of a Negro except where they needed his vote in the legislature or had some other favor to seek. In formal relationships, however, Negro leaders or officeholders were given the courtesy title and newspapers occasionally referred to the leaders of the race as "Mr.," although they usually tried to avoid it by using some other title, as "Senator," "Sheriff," "Colonel," or "Professor." As late as 1900 the practice had not faded, and the *News and Courier* referred to Booker T. Washington as "Mr. Washington." Capitalization of the proper noun "Negro," a minor point of grammar that has since assumed major proportions as a symbol of attitudes, never became an issue during the period. Whites and Negroes alike wrote the word with an uncapitalized "n." Only one white paper, the Yorkville *Enquirer,* adopted the practice of capitalization, stating that it did so out of deference to the decision of a group of Negroes who had met in Memphis, Tennessee, in the early nineties, and after canvassing various terms for the race, as "nigger," "Afro-American," "colored man," and "freedman," had finally settled on the term "Negro."

Mixing of the races

The question of miscegenation always created the most tense issue of race relations where the intimacy involved a Negro man and a white woman. Under the system of slavery there had sometimes been a degree of intimacy between the plantation owner, his sons, and the overseers and the female slaves. It was through relationships of this kind that the greater portion of the mulatto population came into existence. After freedom such relationships continued, but in a less favorable atmosphere for their perpetuation. Nevertheless, relationships of this kind had never come into conflict with the widespread white fear of "amalgamation," since the children of such relationships followed the race of the mother and became Negroes.

The intimacies of white women with Negro men seem to have been rare, but some such cases, because they were unusual and because they attracted almost unanimous white disapproval, were more forcefully brought to the public eye. When legislation was introduced in the Democratic legislature of 1879 to outlaw interracial marriage, one of the most telling arguments in its favor was the statement by a member from York County that in Fort Mill township, where he resided, there were at least twenty-five or thirty white women living with colored men as husbands, most of them having come from North Carolina which already had a law against interracial marriage. There was, on the other hand, a surprising amount of opposition to the measure. One white Democrat held it to be "impolitic, unnecessary, unwise and unconstitutional both under the Federal and State constitution"; another argued that because of religious scruples he deemed it "preferable that our people should enter the marriage relation rather than live in concupiscence." Negro members adopted the argument that the measure interfered with individual liberty, and a Negro Democrat from Charleston argued,

> The prevention of the intermarriage of the races is not a political issue. This is a social question, which is regulated by the parties themselves. I object to this bill only on the ground that it is striking at the liberty of the colored man, while it is an indirect assault upon the white man's rights. Each individual has the right to choose his own companion. Efforts have been made to show that intermarriages injuriously affect the white race. You have so effectually held yourselves together in the past, that there seems but little prospect of our race affecting the white race now. This legislation is wholly unnecessary.

The legislature, however, passed the bill making it "unlawful for any white man to intermarry with any woman of either the Indian or negro races, or any mulatto, mestizoe or half breed, or for any white woman to intermarry with any person other than a white man, or for any mulatto, half breed, negro, Indian or mestizoe to intermarry with a white woman." Persons who violated the act were guilty of a misdemeanor and subject to a fine of not less than $500 or imprisonment for not less than twelve months. The person who performed a marriage ceremony in violation of the act was subject to a like penalty.

A Northern reporter who observed the action of the legislature could not see the objective as anything other than political, "as legitimate miscegenation has never been a habit in South Carolina." It would seem that his interpretation of the measure as chiefly political in motivation was correct; certainly, only few cases can be found of its application. A white woman charged with marrying a Negro in Kershaw County pleaded guilty in 1881 and was sentenced to twelve months in the county jail. In York the same year a white woman and Negro man were convicted of living unlawfully in wedlock. The woman insisted that her family was generally regarded as being of mixed blood, but the presiding judge in the case charged the jury to decide all doubt as to her white ancestry "in her favor." It was so decided, and she was found guilty. A white man of Union County was sentenced in 1882, although he pleaded in palliation of his case that he had married the Negro woman in question while drunk and had deserted her as soon as he became sober.

Despite the law against interracial marriage there seems to have been no action taken against the illegitimate relationships of white men and Negro women. The Columbia *Daily Register* in 1879 complained of the "white male adulterers who more or less infest every community in our State," and urged that "White men living unlawfully with negro women must be taught that virtuous society will not endure the evil which the law has especially condemned and provided punishment for." A Negro girl who worked during the nineties in a hotel patronized by travelling salesmen and construction workers building Clemson College complained that her job "meant constant battle against unwanted advances, a studied ignoring of impudent glances, insulting questions." The informal relationships of white men and Negro women, however, received practically no mention in the press, and there seems to have been little will to bring the power of the law to bear against those who participated in such liaisons.

When it was sought in 1895 to write the law against interracial marriage into the new state constitution, Robert Smalls sought to back the white delegates into a corner by introducing an amendment providing that any white person guilty of cohabiting with a Negro should be barred from holding office, and further that the child of such a relationship should bear the name of its father and inherit property the same as if legitimate. James Wigg, sharp-tongued delegate from Beaufort, noting the consternation that Smalls had thrown into the white delegates, commented that the "coons" had the dogs up the tree for a change and intended to keep them there until they admitted that they must accept such a provision. The Columbia *State* felt that the white delegates had no choice but to swallow the dose concocted by Smalls with the best grace they could muster. Ben Tillman, not entirely unsympathetic with

Smalls' proposal, introduced a substitute amendment to punish miscegenation as a crime in order to "protect negro women against the debauchery of white men degrading themselves to the level of black women," but the convention refused to accept either his substitute or Smalls' original motion. It contented itself with a simple provision against intermarriage, leaving the punishment to the discretion of the legislature.

The issue of miscegenation also posed for the convention the delicate question of defining "Negro." The legislative committee's report spoke of "one eighth or more" Negro ancestry. One delegate proposed that this be changed to read "any" Negro ancestry. George Tillman, with rare realism, opposed reducing the quota below one-eighth, pointing out that he was acquainted with several families in his Congressional District which had a small degree of Negro ancestry, yet had furnished able soldiers to the Confederacy and were now accepted in white society. He did not want to see such families needlessly embarrassed. In addition he made the astounding claim that there was not one pure-blooded Caucasian on the floor of the convention. He maintained that all had ancestors from at least one of the colored races, though not necessarily the Negro race. Therefore he called for a provision that would define "Negro" as a person with one-fourth or more Negro ancestry. But as finally included in the constitution the provision was allowed to stand as reported by the committee, with the limitation set at one-eighth.

Segregation

The issue of segregation in public carriers was not early raised by Democratic politicians. Robert Smalls in 1884 found cause for pride in the fact that the state of South Carolina had a statute providing that Negroes should get equal accommodations for equal fares on the railroads of the state. T. McCants Stewart in the following year reported that "a colored lady or gentleman with a first-class ticket rides with Senator Hampton, and neither is hurt; nor, so far as I know, is amalgamation encouraged in my native State because Negroes dine with whites in a railroad saloon and ride with them in the same car." As late as 1895 Ben Tillman rode from a station near Augusta to Columbia, side by side with a Negro reporter, while he explained to him his plans for the disfranchisement of Negroes. Arguing against Jim Crow, the Charleston *News and Courier* found the *reductio ad absurdum* in the argument that if segregation were required on the railway cars it would have to be provided also in separate waiting rooms and separate eating facilities in the stations, a prohibitive item of expense. Nevertheless, the absence of any formal provision for segregation did not prevent its occasional application. A Negro passenger complained in 1887 that he was unable to get a cup of coffee in the station at Florence because he was unable to produce his own cup from which to drink it.

The repeal of the state civil rights law in 1889, removing the statutory prohibition against segregation was the signal for the introduction of legislation to give segregation the sanction of law. In the legislative session of 1889 the first bill was introduced providing for segregation on railways of the state. Thereafter it became a perennial issue until passed in 1898. The inertia of white public opinion was one reason for the hesitation of the legislature to pass such a measure, but the strong opposition of the railway companies, made effective through conservative Low Country senators, was the greatest factor in preventing its passage. The *News and Courier*, sympathetic to the railroad viewpoint, held in 1897 that the measure would increase "the burdens and troubles of the already over-burdened railroads without due cause," and expressed the opinion "that we have no more need for a Jim Crow car system this year than we had last year, and a great deal less need than we had twenty and thirty years ago."

Jim Crow bills naturally found opposition among Negroes. The first measures provided for segregation only in first-class cars, and James Wigg pointed out that a poor man would have to seat his wife in a second-class car along with the Negroes. "If it is degrading to the rich," he asked, "why is it not degrading to the poor?" In states that had already adopted similar Jim Crow provisions it had become customary for white men who wished to smoke, drink, or otherwise disport themselves to retire to the second-class cars. The members of the Claflin faculty, in an address to the legislature asked:

Why should you, who treasure the honor of your weaker sex more highly than life wish to subject our helpless children, our wives, our mothers, our daughters to the insults and vile actions of drunken and vulgar men and more vulgar women. . . .
Think, gentlemen, that while we have no rights, we have at least feelings. Spare us this injustice. Follow the golden rule. Legislate, we pray you, for the whole people. Give greater police power, if you please, to the train officers; but save our mothers, our wives, our daughters from further humiliation and insults.

In 1898 a bill finally got through the senate by one vote despite an unfavorable report by the senate's railroad committee. The measure became effective on September 1, 1898. It provided that separate first-class coaches or apartments, "separated by a substantial partition," should be provided for passengers on all railroads more than forty miles in length. It also provided that equal accommodations should be supplied to both races. Shortly after its effective date one conductor noticed that Negroes generally preferred second-class accommodation to those in the Jim Crow apartments or cars. He suggested that the eventual solution would be elimination of the second-class cars and the provision of separate cars for white and colored. In 1900 the law was amended to require separate coaches for the two races except on trains that did not require more than one coach. The law did not apply to extraordinary emergencies, nurses attending the children or sick of the other race, prisoners and guards, or to freight and through-vestibuled trains.

Segregation rapidly became an established and unquestioned fact in all the institutions and relationships of the two races. Judge Christie Benet, presiding over a session of court at Beaufort in 1899, called attention to the fact that whites and Negroes were sitting together on the courtroom benches and directed that one side of the room be allotted to whites and the other side to Negroes. "God Almighty never intended," he said, "that the two races should be mixed. . . . " Thus, by the end of the century a new social arrangement had been established by statute, by custom, by direction of the dominant whites, and by the institutional segregation of schools, churches, and private organizations. Slavery was replaced as an instrument of maintaining the subordination of the Negro by a caste system based on race under which white and black seldom came into personal contact except in the relationship of employer and laborer.

Editor's Note:

Chief Justice Taney's remark in the Dred Scott case (1857) that "the Negro was regarded as having no rights which a white man was bound to respect" typified the situation wherein slavery was supplanted by the Jim Crow system. The fixed social position of the slave was changed by his emancipation. The resultant hysteria on the part of white society asserted itself through the notorious Black Codes adopted in 1865 by President Johnson, the Compromise of 1877, the *Plessy v. Ferguson* decision of 1896, and increasing rigidification of codes of discrimination and segregation, legally and extralegally. The description of Jim Crow which follows is taken from the excellent documentation of Professor Woodward in *The Strange Career of Jim Crow*. A common misconception about Jim Crow is clarified in this statement: "One of the strangest things about the career of Jim Crow was that the system was born in the North and reached an advanced age before moving South in force."*

JIM CROW

C. VANN WOODWARD

The mushroom growth of discriminatory and segregation laws during the first two decades of this century piled up a huge bulk of legislation. Much of the code was contributed by city ordinances or by local regulations and rules enforced without the formality of laws. Only a sampling is possible here. For up and down the avenues and byways of Southern life appeared with increasing profusion the little signs: 'Whites Only' or 'Colored.' Sometimes the law prescribed their dimensions in inches, and in one case the kind and color of paint. Many appeared without requirement by law—over entrances and exits, at theaters and boarding houses, toilets and water fountains, waiting rooms and ticket windows.

A large body of law grew up concerned with the segregation of employees and their working conditions. The South Carolina code of 1915, with subsequent elaborations, prohibited textile factories from permitting laborers of different races from working together in the same room, or using the same entrances, pay windows, exits, doorways, stairways, 'or windows [*sic*]' at the same time, or the same 'lavatories, toilets, drinking water buckets, pails, cups, dippers or glasses' at any time. Exceptions were made of firemen, floor scrubbers, and repair men, who were permitted association with the white proletarian elite on an emergency basis. In most instances segregation in employment was established without the aid of statute. And in many crafts and trades the written or unwritten policies of Jim Crow unionism made segregation superfluous by excluding Negroes from employment.

State institutions for the care of the dependent or incapacitated were naturally the subject of more legislation than private institutions of the same sort, but ordinarily the latter followed pretty closely the segregation practices of the public institutions. Both types had usually made it a practice all along. The fact that only Mississippi and South Carolina speci-

fically provided by law for general segregation in hospitals does not indicate that non-segregation was the rule in the hospitals of other states. The two states named also required Negro nurses for Negro patients, and Alabama prohibited white female nurses from attending Negro male patients. Thirteen Southern and border states required the separation of patients by races in mental hospitals, and ten states specified segregation of inmates in penal institutions. Some of the latter went into detail regarding the chaining, transportation, feeding, and working of the prisoners on a segregated basis. Segregation of the races in homes for the aged, the indigent, the orphans, the blind, the deaf, and the dumb was the subject of numerous state laws.

Much ingenuity and effort went into the separation of the races in their amusements, diversions, recreations, and sports. The Separate Park Law of Georgia, adopted in 1905, appears to have been the first venture of a state legislature into this field, though city ordinances and local custom were quite active in pushing the Negro out of the public parks. Circuses and tent shows, including side shows, fell under a law adopted by Louisiana in 1914, which required separate entrances, exits, ticket windows, and ticket sellers that would be kept at least twenty-five feet apart. The city of Birmingham applied the principle to 'any room, hall, theatre, picture house, auditorium, yard, court, ball park, or other indoor or outdoor place' and specified that the races be 'distinctly separated ... by well defined physical barriers.' North Carolina and Virginia interdicted all fraternal orders or societies that permitted members of both races to address each other as brother.

Residential segregation in cities, still rare in the older seaboard towns, developed along five different patterns in the second decade of the century. The type originating in Baltimore in 1910 designated all-white and all-Negro blocks in areas occupied by both races. This experiment was imitated in Atlanta and Greenville. Virginia sought to legalize segregation by a state law that authorized city councils to divide territories into segregated districts and to prohibit either race from living in the other's district, a method adopted by Roanoke and Portsmouth, Virginia. The third method, invented by Richmond, designated blocks throughout the city black or white according to the majority of the residents and forbade any person to live in any block 'where the majority of residents on such streets are occupied by those with whom said person is forbidden to intermarry.' This one was later copied by Ashland, Virginia, and Winston-Salem, North Carolina. A still more complicated law originated in Norfolk, which

*See Woodward, p. 17.

applied to both mixed and unmixed blocks and fixed the color status by ownership as well as occupancy. And finally New Orleans developed a law requiring a person of either race to secure consent of the majority of persons living in an area before establishing a residence therein. After these devices were frustrated by a Supreme Court decision in 1917, attempts continued to be made to circumvent the decision. Probably the most effective of these was the restrictive covenant, a private contract limiting the sale of property in an area to purchasers of the favored race.

The most prevalent and widespread segregation of living areas was accomplished without need for legal sanction. The black ghettos of the 'Darktown' slums in every Southern city were the consequence mainly of the Negro's economic status, his relegation to the lowest rung of the ladder. Smaller towns sometimes excluded Negro residents completely simply by letting it be known in forceful ways that their presence would not be tolerated. In 1914 there were six such towns in Texas, five in Oklahoma, and two in Alabama. On the other hand there were by that time some thirty towns in the South, besides a number of unincorporated settlements, inhabited exclusively by Negroes. In August 1913, Clarence Poe, editor of the *Progressive Farmer,* secured the unanimous endorsement of a convention of the North Carolina Farmer's Union for a movement to segregate the races in rural districts.

The extremes to which caste penalties and separation were carried in parts of the South could hardly find a counterpart short of the latitudes of India and South Africa. In 1909 Mobile passed a curfew law applying exclusively to Negroes and requiring them to be off the streets by 10 p.m. The Oklahoma legislature in 1915 authorized its Corporation Commission to require telephone companies 'to maintain separate booths for white and colored patrons.' North Carolina and Florida required that textbooks used by the public-school children of one race be kept separate from those used by the other, and the Florida law specified separation even while the books were in storage. South Carolina for a time segregated a third caste by establishing separate schools for mulatto as well as for white and Negro children. A New Orleans ordinance segregated white and Negro prostitutes in separate districts. Ray Stannard Baker found Jim Crow Bibles for Negro witnesses in Atlanta courts and Jim Crow elevators for Negro passengers in Atlanta buildings.

A search of the statute books fails to disclose any state law or city ordinance specifying separate Bibles and separate elevators. Right here it is well to admit, and even to emphasize, that *laws are not an adequate index of the extent and prevalence of segregation and discriminatory practices in the South.* The practices often anticipated and sometimes exceeded the laws. It may be confidently assumed—and it could be verified by present observation—that there is more Jim Crowism practiced in the South than there are Jim Crow laws on the books.

To say that, however, is not to concede the position so often taken by Southern as well as Northern writers that the laws were of little consequence anyway. This view consciously or unconsciously voices a laissez-faire bias and often leans for support upon the authority of William Graham Sumner. It was the contention of Sumner's classic *Folkways,* published in 1907, that 'legislation cannot make mores' and that 'stateways cannot change folkways.' Sumner described these 'folkways' as 'uniform, universal in the group, imperative, and invariable.' Perhaps it was not his intention, but Sumner's teachings lent credence to the existence of a primeval rock of human nature upon which the waves of legislation beat in vain. This concept as it was applied to Southern race practices and caste penalties was further buttressed by an American apostle of Herbert Spencer, the sociologist Franklin Henry Giddings. His emphasis upon 'consciousness of kind' in works appearing in 1896 and the decade following gave aid and comfort the the followers of Sumner. So did the racist interpretations of the psychologist William McDougall, whose *Introduction to Social Psychology* appeared in 1908.

Since the works mentioned represented the dominant American social theory of the early twentieth century, and since they appeared in the years when the wave of Southern and American racism was reaching its crest, it was natural that they should have influenced thinking upon the South's major social preoccupation. Their influence was to encourage the notion that there was something inevitable and rigidly inflexible about the existing patterns of segregation and race relations in the South; that these patterns had not been and could not be altered by conscious effort; and that it was, indeed, folly to attempt to meddle with them by means of legislation. These early twentieth-century theories have been characterized by a present-day psychologist, Kenneth B. Clark, as 'the modern attempt at acceptable restatement of the medieval doctrine of *innate ideas.'* Conceived of as biological or social imperatives, these modern 'innate ideas' were presented as 'folkways' or 'mores' which explained and, by inference, justified the existing structure of society, the privileges and policies of the dominant race, and the subordination of the minority race.

This body of social theory, though outmoded

by later discovery and disproved by recent experience, continued to be pressed into use for various purposes down to quite recent times. Thus David L. Cohn of Mississippi wrote in the *Atlantic Monthly* of January 1944, 'It is William Graham Sumner's dictum that you cannot change the mores of a people by law, and since the social segregation of the races is the most deep-seated and pervasive of the Southern mores, it is evident that he who attempts to change it by law runs risks of incalculable gravity.' Among such risks he cited 'civil war' as one.

There was a curious contradiction or inconsistency implicit in the theory of this school in so far as it was applied to the history of race relations in the South. When William Graham Sumner wrote that 'The whites [in the South] have never been converted from the old mores' and that 'Vain attempts have been made to control the new order by legislation,' he was thinking of the legislative efforts of radical Reconstruction. Those were the laws he had in mind when he said that 'The only result is the proof that legislation cannot make mores.' It was the same experiment that the historian William H. Dunning, Giddings's colleague at Columbia, referred to in saying, 'The enfranchisement of the freedman was as reckless a species of statecraft, as that which marked "the blind hysterics of the Celt" in 1789-95.' And yet Southerners cited these authorities upon the utter futility of legislation in the alteration of relations between races to justify and support an elaborate program of legislation to change the relations between races in a different direction. The inference would seem to be that while sound scientific theory proved that folkways and mores could not be changed for some purposes, it proved at the same time that they could be changed for other purposes.

At any rate, the findings of the present investigation tend to bear out the testimony of Negroes from various parts of the South, as reported by the Swedish writer Gunnar Myrdal, to the effect that 'the Jim Crow statutes were effective means of tightening and freezing—in many cases instigating—segregation and discrimination.' The evidence has indicated that under conditions prevailing in the earlier part of the period reviewed the Negro could and did do many things in the South that in the latter part of the period, under different conditions he was prevented from doing.

We have seen that in the 'seventies, 'eighties, and 'nineties the Negroes voted in large numbers. White leaders of opposing parties encouraged them to vote and earnestly solicited their votes. Qualified and acknowledged leaders of Southern white opinion were on record as saying that it was proper, inevitable, and desirable that they should vote. Yet after the disfranchisement measures were passed around 1900 the Negroes ceased to vote. And at that time qualified and acknowledged leaders of white opinion said that it was unthinkable that they should ever be permitted to vote. In the earlier decades Negroes still took an active, if modest, part in public life. They held offices, served on the jury, sat on the bench, and were represented in local councils, state legislatures, and the national Congress. Later on these things were simply not so, and the last of the Negroes disappeared from these forums.

It has also been seen that their presence on trains upon equal terms with white men as once regarded in some states as normal, acceptable, and unobjectionable. Whether railways qualify as folkways or stateways, black man and white man once rode them together and without a partition between them. Later on the stateways apparently changed the folkways—or at any rate the railways—for the partitions and Jim Crow cars became universal. And the new seating arrangement came to seem as normal, unchangeable, and inevitable as the old ways. And so it was with the soda fountains, bars, waiting rooms, street cars, and circuses. And so it probably was with the parks in Atlanta, and with cemeteries in Mississippi. There must even have been a time in Oklahoma when a colored man could walk into any old telephone booth he took a notion to and pick up the receiver.

Editor's Note:

Benjamin R. ("Pitchfork Ben") Tillman (Governor of South Carolina, 1890-94; U.S. Senator, 1895-1918) has long been recognized as one of the most vocal and vituperative spokesman for the racist ideology so proudly espoused by civic leaders of his time. He once threatened to stab President Grover Cleveland with a pitchfork, thereby, earning the nickname "Pitchfork Ben." He was equally as forceful in carrying out and presenting his ideas on the bestiality of Negroes. He was an active promoter of the bloody Hamburg, S.C., riot in 1876; an effective organizer of the vigilante Red Shirts, whose successful goal was preventing Negroes from voting; and an advocate of lynching. This excerpt from a speech seemingly addressed to Sen. Spooner of Wisconsin, on the floor of the Senate, is in fact a verbalization of, and appeal to the phobic and obsessive fears about sex and race that underlie much of the hostility and fear prevalent among majority group members.

SEX AND RACE

BENJAMIN R. TILLMAN

Tacitus tells us that the "Germanic people were ever jealous of the virtue of their women." Germans, Saxons, Englishmen, they are practically one, springing from the same great root. That trinity of words, the noblest and holiest in our language, womanhood, wifehood, motherhood, have Saxon origin. I believe with Wordsworth—it is my religion—"A mother is a mother still, the noblest thing alive."

And a man who speaks with lightness or flippancy or discusses cold-bloodedly a matter so vital as the purity and chastity of womanhood is a disgrace to his own mother and unworthy of the love of a good wife.

Look at our environment in the South, surrounded, and in a very large number of counties and in two States outnumbered, by the negroes—engulfed, as it were, in a black flood of semi-barbarians. Our farmers, living in segregated farmhouses, more or less thinly scattered through the country, have negroes on every hand. For forty years these have been taught the damnable heresy of equality with the white man, made the puppet of scheming politicians, the instrument for the furtherance of political ambitions. Some of them have just enough education to be able to read, but not always to understand what they read. Their minds are those of children, while they have the passions and strength of men. Taught that they are oppressed, and with breasts pulsating with hatred of the whites, the younger generation of negro men are roaming over the land, passing back and forth without hindrance, and with no possibility of adequate police protection to the communities in which they are residing.

Now let me suppose a case. Let us take any Senator on this floor—I will not particularize—take him from some great and well-ordered State in the North, where there are possibly twenty thousand negroes, as there are in Wisconsin, with over two million whites. Let us carry this Senator to the backwoods in South Carolina, put him on a farm miles from a town or railroad, and environed with negroes. We will suppose he has a fair young daughter just budding into womanhood; and recollect this, the white women of the South are in a state of siege; the greatest care is exercised that they shall at all times where it is possible not be left alone or unprotected, but that can not always and in every instance be the case. That Senator's daughter undertakes to visit a neighbor or is left home alone for a brief while. Some lurking demon who has watched for the opportunity seizes her; she is choked or beaten into insensibility and ravished, her body prostituted, her purity destroyed, her chastity taken from her, and a memory branded on her brain as with a red-hot iron to haunt her night and day as long as she lives. Moore has drawn us the picture in most graphic language:

One fatal remembrance, one sorrow that throws
Its bleak shade alike o'er our joys and our woes,
To which life nothing darker or brighter can bring.
For which joy hath no balm and affliction no sting.

In other words, a death in life. This young girl thus blighted and brutalized drags herself to her father and tells him what has happened. Is there a man here with red blood in his veins who doubts what impulses the father would feel? Is it any wonder that the whole countryside rises as one man and with set, stern faces seek the brute who has wrought this infamy? Brute, did I say? Why, Mr. President, this crime is a slander on the brutes. No beast of the field forces his female. He waits invitation. It has been left for something in the shape of a man to do this terrible thing. And shall such a creature, because he has the semblance of a man, appeal to the law? Shall men coldbloodedly stand up and demand for him the right to have a fair trial and be punished in the regular course of justice? So far as I am concerned he has put himself outside the pale of the law, human and divine. He has sinned against the Holy Ghost. He has invaded the holy of holies. He has struck civilization a blow, the most deadly and cruel that the imagination can conceive. It is idle to reason about it; it is idle to preach about it. Our brains reel under the staggering blow and hot blood surges to the heart. Civilization peels off us, any and all of us who are men, and we revert to the original savage type whose impulses under any and all such circumstances has always been to "kill! kill! kill!"

I do not know what the Senator from Wisconsin would do under these circumstances; neither do I care. I have three daughters, but, so help me God, I had rather find either one of them killed by a tiger or a bear and gather up her bones and bury them, conscious that she had died in the purity of her maidenhood, than have her crawl to me and tell me the horrid story that she had been robbed of the jewel of her womanhood by a black fiend. The wild beast would only obey the instinct of nature, and we would hunt him down and kill him just as soon as possible. What shall we do with a man who has outbruted the brute and committed an act which is more cruel than death? Try him? Drag the victim into court, for she alone can furnish legal evidence, and make her testify to the fearful ordeal through which she has passed, undergoing a second crucifixion?

Never in the history of the world has a high-spirited and chivalrous people been called on to face a more difficult and dangerous situation. That a crisis is approaching every thoughtful man must confess. That there is a promise of a safe or happy solution is doubted by all. The Senator from Wisconsin dismisses the question with a wave of the hand and with an admonition to me and others who think like me to keep quiet and be good, urging that he had originally advocated the force bill, but confessed that he was wrong, and that it is better it did not pass. He contends the southern people, black and white, must live together and that the rest of the nation have for the time being left the matter alone; that there has been no discussion among the Republicans in this Chamber such as marked his earlier service in the Senate upon the subject. He says he knows of no better way to precipitate a race conflict than to be always talking about one. And he holds me up as the greatest sinner in that regard. You can not pick up a paper any day but that you will find an appeal from some negro in the North, some convention, some resolution of some kind somewhere denouncing the wrongs done the negroes in the South and demanding justice for them. Those papers circulate in the South. They go everywhere. Our schools, supported by the taxes paid by the white people, are educating these negroes to read such appeals.

I realize that there are millions of good negroes, if they are let alone and not taught heresies and criminal thoughts and feelings and actions. I should like to see this good, easy, good for nothing people given a chance to live. Give them justice; give them equal rights before the law; enable them to get property and keep it, and be protected in its enjoyment; give them life, liberty, and the pursuit of happiness, provided their happiness does not destroy mine.

The Senator from Wisconsin read the other day, with great pathos and effect, the eloquent speech of Henry Grady. There is not a line or a sentence in that noble deliverance to which I do not subscribe. The negroes whom Grady described were the negroes of the old slave days—the negroes with whom he played in childhood, the negroes with whom I played in childhood, the negroes who knew they were inferior and who never presumed to assert equality. For these negroes there is throughout the South a universal feeling of respect and love. I have not got it here, but I have at my home in the city a photograph of one of these. I might term him "Old Black Joe," for he is a full-blooded negro, about 60 years old. He has been living with me thirty-five years. He now has the keys to my home in South Carolina. He has full charge and control over my stock, my plantation. He is in every way a shining example of what the negro can be and how he can get along with the white man peacefully

and pleasantly and honorably, enjoying all of his liberties and rights. But he has never meddled with voting. He occupies the same attitude as the white man and the negro do in this District. They do not meddle with voting. I do not hesitate to say, however, that a more loyal friend no man ever had. Every child that I have would share his last crust with that negro to-morrow.

Grady spoke of the loyalty of the slaves during the war, and the Senator from Wisconsin amplified the picture in eloquent phrase. I myself, as a schoolboy of 13, saw the Confederate soldiers as they took their departure for the front to battle for home and liberty. I saw the parting between the husband and his family, kissing one after another of his children, saving the last kiss for the wife and mother, and then turning to the group of faithful slaves and shaking them by the hand, give the parting injunction, "Take care of your mistress and the children." How did the slaves redeem the promise? They all said "Yes, master." How they lived up to the promise history tells. There were in the South at that time 4,000,000 negroes, 800,000 males of adult age. The women and children of the white men who were in the Confederate army were left there, entirely helpless for support and protection, with these negroes. With 800,000 negro men, there is not of record a solitary instance of one white woman having been wronged until near the close of the war, when some of the negro soldiers who had been poisoned by contact with northern ideas came along and perpetrated some outrages.

The negro slave was true to the faith. When Sherman's army marched through South Carolina, leaving behind it a 40-mile breadth of burned houses, the chimneys marking where the habitations of the Confederate soldiers had been, every house that had a plank on it gone, the women and children turned out in the rain and sleet of February to find shelter in the negro cabins, everything to eat burned or having been seized and carried off by the army, I knew some of these slaves to go behind in the track of the army and rake up the corn off the ground where the horses had been fed, wash it and dry it and carry it to the starving wives and children of the white men of the South.

Talk to me about hating these people! I do not do it. We took them as barbarians, fresh from Africa, the first generation we will say, or some of them twice removed, some of them once removed, some of them thrice removed, some of them a fourth removed from barbarism, but the bulk of them only twice. We taught them that there was a God. We gave them what little knowledge of civilization they have to-day. We taught them to tell the truth. We taught them not to steal. We gave them those characteristics which differentiate the barbarian and savage from the civilized man.

In 1865 the South, prostrate and bleeding and helpless, a very Niobe of nations, had the dead carcass of slavery chained to it by the fourteenth and fifteenth amendments. For eight years two States labored under it. One after another the others had thrown off for a little while the incubus—not getting loose, but simply getting relief, being able to stand up, to move, to breathe, and to make some progress. But there the carcass hangs, riveted to our civilization. The putrefaction is going on. A return to barbarism is evident in every day of our contact with these people in the South. Relieved from police control, they are no longer compelled, as the Indians have been by the troops, to stay on their reservations. These negroes move where they please. They have a little smattering of education. Some of them have white blood in their veins and taught that they are as good as the white man, they ask, Why not as good as a white woman? And when caste feeling and race pride and every instinct that influences and controls the white women makes them spurn the thought, rape follows. Murder and rape become a monomania. The negro becomes a fiend in human form.

We can not police those people to-day under the fourteenth amendment without taking from the whites their own liberties. In my desperation to seek some remedy to prevent rape and not have the necessity of avenging rape, I have gone so far as to plead with the people of the South to inaugurate a passport system, by which we should keep in control and under supervision all of the wandering classes, white and black.

Race hatred grows day by day. There is no man who is honest, going through the South and conversing with the white people and blacks, but will return and tell you this is true.

Some of the negroes have a good excuse. I will not dispute it. If I were negro I would do probably as they do, but being a white man, I do just as I am doing, and I expect to do so, so help me God, as long as I have breath in my body.

Then I say to you of the North, who are the rulers of the land, who can change this or do something to relieve conditions, what are you going to do about it? Are you going to sit quiet? If nothing else will cause you to think, I notify you, what you already know, that there are a billion dollars or more of northern capital invested in the South in railroads, in mines, in forests, in farm lands, and self-interest, if nothing else, ought to make you set about hunting some remedy for this terrible situation.

Editor's Note:

The exponents of genetic inferiority represent an ever-constant but one-sided view in the community of researchers. Just as there have always been proponents of white intellectual supremacy, there have always been those who have refuted these assertions. Their voices were often drowned out in a milieu that was supportive of racist claims and beliefs. Conclusions on the inherent inferiority of blacks could be challenged by the very same data that had been used to make the point. The following selection depicts the circumstances and attitudes that were prevalent when intelligence tests became a part of the American ranking and classification system, and also points out some of the distortions of data which occur. The arguments of the small but vocal minority represented by Garrett, McGurk, Shuey, Tanser, Jensen, and Shockley have been and are presently used to support segregation, discrimination, and violence.

INTELLIGENCE AND RACE

THOMAS F. GOSSETT

When mental tests were introduced into this country in the 1890s, one of the first experiments undertaken was an attempt to determine race differences. R. M. Bache, using tests which had been developed in Germany to measure quickness of sensory perception, compared twelve whites, eleven Indians, and eleven Negroes. The Indians had the quickest reactions, the Negroes were second, and the whites were third. But Bache calmly explained that the results proved the whites were the superior group. Their reactions were slower because they belonged to a more deliberate and reflective race than did the members of the other two groups.

In 1897, B.R. Stetson compared five hundred white children with an equal number of Negro children in a test which evaluated memory. The Negro children made slightly higher scores, but this result was explained on the basis that they were older than the white children. This study was frequently quoted by later writers who saw in its result that Negroes may sometimes excel whites in "mechanical" intellectual processes requiring no extensive "cerebration." E.L. Thorndike, one of the pioneers of mental testing, explained that "the apparent mental attainments of children of inferior races may be due to lack of inhibition and so witness precisely to a deficiency in mental growth."

In France, Alfred Binet, together with Théodore Simon, developed in 1905 a series of tests which were designed to measure degrees of intelligence. The original purpose of these tests was to recognize various degrees of feeblemindedness, but standards were set up for different age groups and the concept of mental age was introduced to indicate how a child might compare with other children of his age. The second Binet-Simon scale, which appeared in 1908, defined mental age more precisely by measuring it in terms of the ability of a child to answer a group of questions which 75 per cent of the children of his age could answer. Binet and Simon still regarded the chief value of mental tests as their ability to detect degrees of feeblemindedness in children. They admitted that environment and educational opportunity would inevitably affect the achievement scores and, therefore, they concluded that the tests would indicate the approximate intelligence only of those children who had closely similar environments.

In spite of early warnings against interpreting tests as measuring hereditary intelligence without relation to environment, the temptation to do so was so strong that a great many psychologists succumbed to it. In 1912, William Stern introduced the idea of the intelligence quotient—the I.Q.—which was to be obtained by comparing one's mental age with his actual, or chronological, age. For example, if a ten-year-old child scored 100 on an examination, his mental age might correspond with his actual age. If he scored 80, his mental age was said to be eight years, and if he scored 120 his mental age was said to be twelve years. After the death of Binet, the center of intelligence testing shifted from France to the United States. By 1916, Lewis Terman and his associates published the Stanford-Binet scale of intelligence, a revision of the second Binet scale. The idea that the intelligence of a person could be expressed in terms of a number began to intrigue not only psychologists but the public at large.

It requires an effort of the imagination to perceive the almost limitless horizon which seemed to stretch out before the psychologists. They hoped for tests that would make irrevelant the old question of which characteristics are the result of heredity and which of environment. In 1903, E.L. Thorndike observed that with "sufficient knowledge" we could "analyze any man's original mental nature into elements." In addition, we could determine what innate differences, if any, existed in the intelligence of different races. We could even discover whether they were innate differences in the mental processes "of the European stocks, of the Anglo-Saxon breed." If differences in innate intelligence could be measured, then a racial scale could eventually be worked out with considerable exactitude.

One result of the intelligence tests was to show that the children of bank presidents and lawyers and college professors generally did much better than did the children of laboring men, a fact which was often interpreted to prove, not the fortunate effects of a good environment, but the supreme importance of a good heredity in the struggle for success. This conclusion had racial as well as class implications, since members of races were unevenly distributed among the social classes. In 1915, Lewis Terman observed that his tests showed that a low level of intelligence "is very, very common among Spanish-Indian and Mexican families of the Southwest, and also among negroes. Their dullness seems to be racial, or at least inherent in the family stocks from which they come." He admitted that the question had not been sufficiently studied, but he thought he knew what future studies would disclose. "The whole question of racial differences in mental traits will have to be taken up anew and by experimental methods," he said. "The writer predicts that when this is done there will be discovered enormously significant racial differences in general intelligence, differences which cannot be wiped out by any scheme of mental culture." Such tests would probably demonstrate that many children "are uneducable beyond the merest rudiments of training. No amount of school instruction will ever make them intelligent voters or capable citizens in the true sense of the word." Such children were the future "hewers of wood and drawers of water."

An opportunity to employ intelligence tests on a mass scale occurred in 1917 after the United States entered the war. The military services were interested in finding out which men would be the most effective in particular categories, especially as officers. A committee of psychologists—with Dr. Robert M. Yerkes as chairman—was asked to draw up a series of tests which would determine the intelligence and aptitudes of the great numbers of men then coming into the armed services. In all, more than 1,700,000 men were tested. So many extravagant claims and outright misinterpretations of these tests followed the publication of their results that it is necessary to examine them in some detail.

There were two tests—the "army alpha" which was the test generally used, and the "army beta" which was a nonlanguage test taken by immigrants unfamiliar with English and by illiterates. The tests were designed to measure not mental age but general intelligence without respect to age. They were first tried out at selected camps to discover at what point about 5 per cent of the men would fall into the A category, the superior group from which officers would generally be chosen. It was hardly surprising, then, that when the tests were applied on a mass scale, 4.5 per cent of the men attained an A rating. Yet it was sometimes assumed that the tests had proved that only one man in twenty in the army was intelligent.

Although the men were rated not by mental age

but by the letters A–for superior–down through B, C, D, and E, an attempt was made to translate the scores of the army tests into mental age groups. The published report of the army psychologists lists mental ages according to the Stanford-Binet scale–without explaining how the scores had been transposed. Now, the mental tests given in the armed services could be interpreted to show the average intelligence of the men tested. Even this was not the full extent of the misinterpretation. The tests were used to "prove" what percentage of the American people were intelligent and what the average I.Q. was. There was still one more inconsistency in all this. The Stanford-Binet scale was based upon a few hundred tests and the army test on 1,700,000, but the Stanford-Binet scale was used in order to measure the intelligence of the men in the army. Walter Lippmann pointed out the inconsistency of assuming that the average intelligence of men in the army was that of an immature child. "The average adult intelligence . . . cannot be less than the average adult intelligence." To assume that it could be was like saying that an "average mile was three quarters of a mile long." Lewis Terman, who was a member of the committee of psychologists, replied to Lippmann's criticism by saying that the army tests were established "independently of any other tests." Since Terman does not explain how this was done, it is no satisfactory explanation of the question of average mental age. The average adult mental age would have to be the average mental age and vice versa.

The fact that the tests were constructed and administered, as the army report declared, "to minimize the handicap of men who because of foreign birth or lack of education are little skilled in the use of English," made it easy to exploit them for purposes of class and racial prejudice. Large claims were made for the effectiveness of the tests in measuring innate ability. The examinations "were originally intended, and are now definitely known, to measure native intellectual ability. They are to some extent influenced by educational acquirement, but in the main the soldier's inborn intelligence and not the accidents of environment determine his mental rating or grade in the Army."

It is easy to see what a powerful tool was thus placed in the hands of the racists. The great lesson which many of the psychologists drew from the army tests was that intelligence is influenced relatively little by environment. The conclusion readily reached was that great numbers of people–in fact, the majority–were not capable of benefiting from improved education. The Negroes were the farthest removed from any possible hope. The tests, said Dr. Yerkes, "Brought into clear relief . . . the intellectual inferiority of the Negro. Quite apart from educational status, which is utterly unsatisfactory, the negro soldier is of relatively low grade intelligence." This discovery was "in the nature of a lesson, for it suggests that education alone will not place the negro race on a par with its Caucasian competitors."

From all this, it can readily be seen how the army intelligence tests would provide a field day for racists who would argue that racial superiority and inferiority are simple facts which must be recognized. The end of the war would have brought difficult problems of adjustment even if this seemingly irrefutable scientific evidence for differences of intelligence among races had not been developed at this particular time. With the dislocations of the war and with the new status given to the importance of hereditary and racial differences, the early 1920s became the time when racist theories achieved an importance and respectability which they had not had in this country since before the Civil War.

•   •   •

The psychologists followed the initial success of the army mental tests with a veritable avalanche of testing. In many of these studies, the racist implications were not far below the surface. E.L. Thorndike declared that "race directly and indirectly produces differences so great that government, business, industry, marriage, friendship, and almost every other feature of human instinctive and civilized life have to take account of a man's race." The original uncertainties about the effect of environment upon test scores all but disappeared. As late as 1940, Thorndike was willing to express the relative importance of heredity and environment in terms of percentages. Intelligence could be allocated "roughly" 80 per cent to the genes, 17 per cent to training, and 3 per cent to "accident."

Dr. Carl C. Brigham, an assistant professor of psychology at Princeton, wrote one of the most bizarre of the studies of mental tests as applied to race. In *A Study of American Intelligence*, he accepted the division of Europeans into the three races of Nordic, Alpine, and Mediterranean and interpreted the army intelligence tests of 1917 and 1918 in such a way as to prove the superiority of the Nordic. The army had not attempted this sort of classification of the soldiers taking the test, but it had listed the national origin or descent of the soldiers. Brigham attempted to estimate the amount of Nordic, Alpine, and Mediterranean in each of the European nations. Sweden had 100 per cent Nordic blood, Norway had 90 per cent; Denmark, Holland, and Scotland followed with 85 per cent; England, 80 per cent; Wales and Germany, 40 per cent;

France and Ireland, 30 per cent; Poland and Spain, 10 per cent; Italy, Russia, and Portugal, 5 per cent. The nations with the highest Nordic blood contributed the largest number of soldiers with A and B ratings, so Brigham concluded the Nordics must be the most intelligent. "In a very definite way, the results which we obtain by interpreting the army data by means of the race hypothesis support Mr. Madison Grant's thesis of the superiority of the Nordic type."

Looking back upon this test, one hardly knows which is its more curious aspect—Brigham's conviction that it was possible to express Nordic, Alpine, and Mediterranean "races" in terms of percentages for whole nations, or his conviction that intelligence was almost wholly unrelated to the quality of the education which different ethnic groups had received. How far he was willing to carry the argument that environmental differences were negligible in determining mental ability may be judged by the conclusion he drew from the fact that more recent immigrants from a given country did not do as well on these tests as those who had been here a considerable time. He discovered that immigrants who had been here twenty years did better on the tests than those who had been here fifteen; those who had been here ten years did better than those who had been here five. These facts did not lead him to conclude that perhaps environment might be a considerable factor; instead, he interpreted the figures as conclusive proof that the innate quality of the more recent immigrants was lower and was steadily declining. From the point of view of the racists among the advocates of immigration restriction, Brigham's study was a real triumph. Even Jewish immigrants did badly on the tests. "Our figures, then, Brigham concluded, "would rather tend to disprove the popular belief that the Jew is highly intelligent."

A critic of Brigham's pointed out that not merely did northern Negroes do better than southern Negroes on the army tests, but the Negroes of some northern states did better than the whites of some southern states. The literate Negroes from Illinois had higher median scores than the literate whites from nine southern states; the literate Negroes from New York surpassed the literate whites from five southern states; the literate Negroes from Pennsylvania surpassed the literate whites from two southern states. None of this convinced Dr. Brigham that education and environment might radically change the intelligence scores. The superiority of the northern Negroes over southern Negroes was to be explained on the basis of their greater admixture of white blood and the fact that better opportunities in the North prompted the more intelligent Negroes of the South to migrate there. Dr. Robert M. Yerkes, who had

been in charge of the army tests, agreed with Brigham's thesis that the higher scores of northern Negroes did not constitute an argument for the power of education and environment. He wrote a foreword to Brigham's book in which he endorsed the thesis that the tests proved that the Negroes were inferior in intelligence and that immigrants could be generally rated intellectually by the amount of Nordic blood in their veins.

It was probably inevitable that the psychologists should devise scales for testing the "personalities" of race, now that the matter of racial intelligence medians had apparently been established. A study of the "will-temperament" of Negroes appeared in 1922. An elaborate racial personality study was made on Japanese schoolchildren and another on Chinese, Japanese, and Hawaiians; there was a study of the personalities of Indian children with the implication that the innate character of the race was thus disclosed. Psychologists attempted to measure such "racial" characters as "integrity," "kindliness," "courage," "unselfishness," "reasonableness," "refinement," "cheerfulness and optimism," "motor inhibition," "noncompliance," and "finality of judgment." As one might have predicted, the tests generally showed that Negroes, Indians, Mexicans, and other nonwhite races were ordinarily inferior in their personality traits to the whites. The difficulty common to all the studies was that the researchers had discovered no means of determining the differences between traits caused by heredity and those caused by environment.

Toward critics who doubted that scores in the tests were influenced only slightly by education and environment, a number of the psychologists were patronizing or even contemptuous. Lewis Terman placed such critics on a par with those "many excellent people who do not 'believe in' vaccination against typhoid and small pox, operations for appendicitis, etc." When Walter Lippmann questioned some of the conclusions which psychologists had drawn from the army tests, Lewis Terman brushed his objections aside. The fact was, said Terman, that "a majority of the psychologists of America, England and Germany are now enrolled in the ranks of the 'intelligence tests,' and all but a handful of the rest use their results." Further in the same article Terman argued that the racial implications of intelligence tests were undeniable: The "average Portuguese child carries through school and into life an IQ of about 80" as compared with 100 for the child of Nordic descent. Dr. William MacDougall, professor of psychology at Harvard, admitted that it could not be proved that intelligence was wholly or largely a matter of heredity, but he contended that all the evidence pointed in that direction. If Lippmann chose to argue that mental ability is not largely a matter of inheritance, he was "denying also the theory of organic evolution, and he should come out openly on the side of Mr. Bryan. For the theory of the heredity of mental qualities is a corollary of the theory of organic evolution." Terman also relegated Lippmann to the camp of William Jennings Bryan.

MacDougall was perhaps the most indefatigable of the race theorizers among the psychologists of the time. He was a very different man from the intelligence testers, who stressed exact methods of experimental psychology. An Englishman who came to this country in 1920, he had a strongly teleological or purposive view of life and mind and a conviction that psychology ought to be useful to the historian, the sociologist, the anthropologist, the economist, and especially the intelligent political leader. He was a champion of the instincts theory of psychology and the great opponent of the behaviorists. MacDougall's *Introduction to Social Psychology* (1908) went through more impressions and editions than any other psychological work of its time, about twenty-five in all.

When MacDougall directed his attention to the importance of race, his great theme was the superiority of the Nordics. In 1921, he published a series of his lectures at the Lowell Institute under the title *Is America Safe for Democracy?*, a warning to the nation on the perils of racial intermixture. The book is a kind of compendium on racial psychology. We learn that the art of northern Europe is essentially "subjective" and "individualist" and that of southern Europe is "public," "formal," "ritualistic," and "conventional" because northern Europe is inhabited by Nordics whereas southern Europe is composed largely of Mediterraneans. The "herd instinct is relatively weak in the Nordic, strong in the Mediterranean peoples." Thus, Nordics are usually Protestants rather than Catholics because they are more fearlessly self-reliant than other races. They are also endowed preeminently with curiosity, a characteristic which makes them scientists and inventors par excellence. It is their Nordic blood which explains the fact that the Greeks were important innovators in science and philosophy, whereas the Mediterranean blood of the Romans explains their lack of talent in these fields. But curiosity has its price. We are told that the Swedes have a high rate of suicide because in that country the trait of curiosity is so strongly developed among the relatively pure Nordics that the people desire "to penetrate by their own act the impenetrable veil. . . ." Thus, a seeming defect is rationalized into a virtue.

The racists could take comfort from many prominent biologists as well as from the psychologists. Some of the biologists regarded it as axiomatic that race mixture, at least among peoples widely different from one another, would lead to "disharmonies." These disharmonies were not necessarily produced by any defects of either race, but simply resulted from the fact that each of them was so unlike the other that to mix them led to physical, mental, and emotional deformities. Even biologists who recognized that the proof for this contention was lacking often thought that race mixture was bad because certain races were poor biological material, and therefore intermarriage with them would have "dysgenic" effects.

Editor's Note:

A mutual point of agreement for the legal and extra-legal agencies and the formal and informal groups in American society following the abolition of slavery was the "place" the newly created black citizen was to occupy. Discussion centered primarily around utilization of the most effective means of assuring his subjugation. Gossett provides a discerning view of measures taken on both the national and local level to ensure continued subordination of black people.

RACISM AT THE TURN OF THE CENTURY

THOMAS F. GOSSETT

As might have been forseen, the South after the Civil War was strongly opposed to the enfranchisement of Negroes. As soon as they were able, several southern states passed laws, the so-called "Black Codes," which were designed to limit drastically the rights of the newly liberated slaves. When the Black Codes of South Carolina were published in 1866, H. Melville Myers, the editor, explained in the preface why such laws were necessary. The Negro race, he declared, at all times had "been excluded, as a separate class, from all civilized governments and the family of nations," since it was "doomed by a mysterious and Divine ordination. . . ." The war had settled the matter of the abolition of slavery, but this did not mean that Negroes were to be considered as citizens. They were to be "equal before the law in the possession and enjoyment of all their rights of person—of liberty and of property," but they were not to be voters and jurymen. "To institute . . . between the Anglo Saxon, the high-minded, virtuous, intelligent, patriotic Southerner and the *freedman* a

109

social or political approximation more intimate—to mingle the social or political existence of the two classes more closely," said Myers, "would surely be one of the highest exhibitions of treason to the race." Both whites and Negroes were "distinctly marked by the impress of nature. They are races separate and distinct, the one the highest and noblest type of humanity, the other the lowest and most degraded." Benjamin G. Humphreys, the new governor of Mississippi and still an unpardoned ex-Confederate brigadier general, put the matter succinctly. "The Negro is free, whether we like it or not .... To be free, however, does not make him a citizen or entitle him to social or political equality with the white man. But the constitution and justice do entitle him to protection and security in his person and property."

The Black Codes varied in their provisions, but generally they forbade the Negroes the rights of holding office or of voting. Negroes were not eligible for military service; they could not serve on juries nor could they testify in court except against other Negroes. They were required to have passes in moving from place to place and they were forbidden to assemble without proper permit by representatives of the law. If they refused to work, they could be fined and hired out to work by labor contractors. Young Negroes were bound out as "apprentices" until they attained the age of legal majority. The rights of Negroes were generally restricted to ownership and inheritance of property, suing and being sued in court, and marriage.

The Black Codes led Congress to institute the drastic Reconstruction Act of 1867 in which the South was divided into five military districts and southern states were to be readmitted to the Union only after they had ratified the Fourteenth Amendment, which, among other things, decreed that

> no state shall make or enforce any law which shall abridge the privileges or immunities of citizens of the United States; nor shall any state deprive any person of life, liberty, or property, without due process of law; nor deny to any person within its jurisdiction the equal protection of the laws.

The suffrage of those whites who had supported the Confederacy was drastically curtailed, and thus the South for a time was under the control of a Republican party made up of Negroes, whites loyal to the Union (the so-called scalawags), and northerners (the so-called carpetbaggers) who had come South as latter-day frontiersmen looking for business and political opportunities or as missionaries of northern altruism and philanthropy.

• • •

The phrase "separate and equal," comments Arthur Raper, "symbolizes the whole system, fair words to gain unfair ends." Only a year after the *Plessy vs. Ferguson* decision of 1896 we find James K. Vardaman in a campaign against Negro education in Mississippi. The state, he complained, was spending half a million dollars a year to prepare the Negro for "the higher duties of citizenship." Everybody knew that the Negro would not be allowed to be a citizen. His vote would either be "cast aside or Sambo will vote as directed by the white folks." Money spent on education of the Negro was a "positive unkindness to him." It rendered him "unfit for the work which the white man has prescribed, and which he will be forced to perform." Vardaman objected just as much to money sent by northern philanthropists for private Negro colleges in the South. "What the North is sending South is not money but dynamite," he exclaimed. "This education is ruining our Negroes. They're demanding equality." When he became governor in 1900, he drastically reduced the amount of state money spent for Negro schools. The only kind of education he thought suitable for the Negroes was vocational education and not much of that. The state colleges for Negroes in Mississippi were closed.

The possibilities of segregation as a tool in the denial of rights to Negroes were almost unlimited. Public services which existed for whites were sometimes wholly nonexistent for Negroes. In many communities library facilities, for example, were and are supported by public funds but wholly limited to white patrons. Usually, separate facilities were available for Negroes but they were vastly unequal. As late as 1936, the state of Mississippi was paying its white elementary public school teachers an average of three times as much as it paid its Negro teachers. The rest of the South was not this bad, but white teachers in the region were paid an average of over 60 per cent more than Negro teachers. White schools offered courses which Negro schools did not. White schools were frequently of sound construction, whereas Negro schools were frequently ramshackle affairs. John Dollard tells how a southern community as late as the 1930s built only the shell of a building for a Negro high school, and then the Negro members of the community were obliged to donate their time and money to build the interior of the building and to pay for the coal to heat it.

In the South, segregation laws were also a means of denying Negroes the right to certain types of occupation. There were scores of ordinances like that of Atlanta which forbade barbers to shave or cut the hair of both whites and Negroes—they were obliged to choose one race or the other. This was a method of preventing Negro barbers from competing with whites for the white trade. In 1915, South Carolina passed a law forbidding factories and other places of business to employ Negroes to work alongside whites except as janitors or scrubwomen or in other menial positions. The law was aimed at preventing the state's industries, the growth of which was partly the result of the war in Europe, from taking advantage of Negroes' willingness to work at wages lower than those of whites—but wages which still meant economic betterment and wider opportunities for the Negroes.

Where could the Negro turn at this time to have the injustices against him redressed? Not to the courts. Just as the Supreme Court refused to pass on the constitutionality of the "grandfather clause" which prevented Negroes from voting in the South for many years, so it was also unwilling to examine the question of whether segregated facilities for Negroes actually were equal. In the 1890s a town in Georgia closed its Negro high school but nots its white high school. The Negroes of the community in their suit did not challenge the segregation law, but only asserted their right to a Negro high school if there was a white one. The Supreme Court in 1899 denied the appeal of the Negro plaintiffs and, in effect, left the matter of how much education the Negroes were to receive wholly up to the states. In 1908, the Court had before it a case in which there was at issue a Kentucky law aimed at Berea College's practice of educating Negroes along with whites. The Court refused to pass on the constitutionality of the issue, and, in effect, sanctioned laws against integrated education even in private schools.

The executive department of the federal government was equally deaf to the pleas of Negroes. Grover Cleveland hailed Booker T. Washington's speech of 1895 which had asked the Negroes to accept segregation without protest. William McKinley remained silent as the southern states proceeded one after another to disfranchise Negroes. Theodore Roosevelt outgrew the willingness he had displayed early in his first administration to champion the cause of Negroes. By 1912, he apparently concurred when the Bull Moose convention which nominated him refused to seat most of the Negro delegates, turned down a civil rights plank for Negroes, and selected a "lily white" southerner as his running mate. William Howard Taft began his administration in 1909 by assuring the white South that he would appoint no federal officials in their region who would be offensive to them, and of course the white South knew what he meant.

It was the administration of Woodrow Wilson, however, which took the most drastic action against Negroes. In 1912, Josephus Daniels, who was then a North Carolina supporter of Wilson and was soon to become a member of his cabinet, was convinced that with the election of a southerner as President there was a chance that the South's atittudes and practices with regard to Negroes might be extended indefinitely in the North. It was in Wilson's administration and with his express approval that federal civil service workers were segregated by race in their employment, with separate eating and toilet facilities. When a Negro leader protested this segregation, Wilson all but ordered him out of his office because his language was "insulting." Post Office and Treasury officials in the South were given the freedom to discharge or downgrade Negro employees. In Atlanta, thirty-five Negroes were discharged from their jobs at the post office. "There are no Government positions for Negroes in the South," declared the Collector of Internal Revenue for Georgia in 1913. "A Negro's place is in the cornfield."

The political leaders of the South were well aware that no one of them could survive in office if he were to champion the rights of Negroes. When Pitchfork Ben Tillman of South Carolina would rise in the Senate to engage in one of his coarse and violent diatribes, some other southern senators might silently leave the floor in protest, but no one of them dared directly to challenge him. Tillman gloried in his speeches that the white South had illegally deprived the Negroes of their rights:

We took the government away. We stuffed ballot boxes. We shot them. We are not ashamed of it. The Senator from Wisconsin would have done the same thing. I see it in his eye right now. He would have done it. With that system—force, tissue ballots, *etc.*—we got tired ourselves. So we called a constitutional convention, and we eliminated as I said, all of the colored people whom we could under the fourteenth and fifteenth amendments.

Tillman also claimed the support of large sections of opinion in the North for his statements on Negroes. He said that in his many speeches on the lecture circuit in the North he had met with enthusiastic crowds and wide acclaim for the opinions he expressed there. On the floor of the Senate, he taunted northerners for the race riots in their part of the country and for the hypocrisy of their avowal of the "brotherhood of man":

The brotherhood of man exists no longer because you shoot negroes in Illinois, when they come in competition with your labor, as we shoot them in South Carolina when they come in competition with us in the matter of elections. You do not love them any better than we do. You used to pretend that you did, but you no longer pretend it, except to get their votes.

• • •

Any age can display its fanatics, but what is more disappointing is the racism to be found among thoughtful and reflective men in the latter part of the nineteenth century and the early part of the twentieth. There was, for example, Nathaniel Southgate Shaler, who became dean of the Lawrence Scientific School at Harvard. In 1884 he wrote an essay, "The Negro Problem," published in the *Atlantic*, in which he viewed with sympathy the attempts in the South to disenfranchise the Negro. Shaler had been a pupil of Louis Agassiz; he subscribed to the old theory that a Negro child is just as bright as a white child up to the age of puberty, but beyond this point his "animal nature settled like a cloud over that promise." In addition, the Negro's innate and uncontrollable immorality made him "unfit for an independent place in a civilized state." What progress the Negro had made he owed to the discipline of slavery. As a free man, the Negro showed a strong tendency, which was probably ineradicable, to return to his naturally savage state. Convinced that the Negroes were a dying race, Shaler recommended that they be scattered over the United States to prevent their becoming an overwhelming burden for any one section. Because they were incapable of higher education, their schools should be limited to instruction in the lower trades, since "as a race they are capable of taking pride in handiwork."

A racist work widely read and quoted in the South was Frederick L. Hoffman's *Race Traits and Tendencies of the American Negro*, published by the American Economic Association in 1896. Hoffman was a statistician for the Prudential Life Insurance Company in New York, who was convinced that the high incidence of tuberculosis, syphilis, gonorrhea, scrofula, and other diseases among Negroes would lead to their extinction as a race. He rejected the argument that better conditions would improve the health record of Negroes. For him, the "root of the evil" was the "immense amount of immorality, which is a race trait." "It is not in the *conditions of life*" that we should look for reasons for the poor health record of Negroes,

> but in the *race traits and tendencies* that we find the causes of excessive mortality. So long as these tendencies are persisted in, so long as immorality and vice are a habit of life of the vast majority of the colored population, the effect will be to increase the mortality by hereditary transmission of weak constitutions,

and to lower still further the rate of natural increase, until the births fall below the deaths, and gradual extinction results.

• • •

It is striking how often one finds among intelligent and sensitive people of the period—North as well as South—crude reflections of racism. One thinks of Henry Adams' contemptuous references to "niggers" and of John Fiske's account of a visit in 1877 to Baltimore, where he saw "elegant niggers" promenading on the streets. Rayford W. Logan has studied the files of eminent magazines of the last part of the nineteenth century and found in *Harper's*, *Scribner's*, *Century*, and to a lesser degree the *Atlantic* a fairly constant barrage of epithets applied to Negroes—such terms as nigger, niggah, darkey, coon, pickaninny, mammy, buck, uncle, aunt, high-yaller, yaller hussy, and light-complected yaller man. A standard device of humor was to give the Negro a fancy but revealing name—Colonel, Senator, Sheriff, Apollo Belvedere, George Washington, Abraham Lincum, Napoleon Boneyfidey Waterloo, Lady Adeliza Chimpanzee, Prince Orang Outan, Ananias, Piddlekins, Asmodeus, Bella Donna Mississipp Idaho, with the ultimate in the name Henri Ritter Demi Ritter Emmi Ritter Sweet-potato Cream Tarter Caroline Bostwick. Thomas Nelson Page wrote a humorous article for *Harper's* entitled "All the Geography a Nigger Needs to Know."

Henry James, who explored moral issues in his novels and stories with perception and delicacy, was impervious to moral issues raised by the status of Negroes. On a visit to the South in 1907, he had the following reaction to the Negro porters he encountered in Washington:

> I was waiting, in a cab, at the railway-station, for the delivery of my luggage after my arrival, while a group of tatterdemalion darkies lounged and sunned themselves within range. To take in with any attention two or three of these figures had surely been to feel one's self introduced at a bound to the formidable question, which rose suddenly like some beast that had sprung from the jungle. These were its far outposts; they represented the Southern black as we knew him not, and had not within the memory of man known him, at the North; yet all portentous and in possession of his rights as a man, was to be not a little discomposed. . . . One understood at a glance how he must loom, how he must count in . . . [the South.]

112

Editor's Note:

Lynchings evoke vivid images of brutality, sadism, cruelty, and lawlessness. That, however, was not a universal view. Large sectors of the populace have justified and supported lynching as a disciplinary device against blacks and as a means of maintaining the racial status quo.

Statistics on lynchings were first collected by Tuskegee Institute in 1889. Gossett's excellent summary on lynching depicts a level of functioning that was ubiquitous in a supposedly civilized and Christian society.

LYNCHING

THOMAS F. GOSSETT

A kind of fever chart in the history of American racism may be discovered by examining the annual statistics on lynching. For a long time, the word *lynch* had no connection with the death penalty or with Negroes. The name goes back to Colonel Charles Lynch of Bedford County, Virginia, who in the uncertain times of the American Revolution organized an informal court to deal with Tories and criminals on the Virginia frontier. The "court" limited itself to fines and whippings and did not hand down death penalties. When times became more peaceful, it was indemnified and exonerated by the Virginia legislature. "Lynch-Law" came to mean extralegal administration of punishment, particularly by whipping. In the 1850s, the term usually referred to the executions of horse-thieves and desperadoes by vigilance committees in the West. But during the Civil War and afterward during Reconstruction, the word *lynch* came to have something approaching its modern meaning—the killing of someone by a mob.

It is a curious fact that in the early years of the 1880s —when statistics on lynching began to be kept—considerably more whites were lynched than Negroes. Between 1882 and 1888, 595 whites and 440 Negroes were lynched in the United States. But inexorably the figures changed. In 1889, 76 whites and 94 Negroes were lynched. By 1892, lynching reached its highest recorded point, with 69 whites and 162 Negroes suffering this fate. Thereafter the number declined, though for the next twelve years, from 1893 to 1904, an average of more than a hundred Negroes a year were lynched as compared with an average of 29 whites. In the thirty-three year period from 1883 to 1915, the annual toll of Negroes lynched never fell below 50 but once—in 1914, when the number was 49. In nine of these years the figures rose to more than a hundred. During the same period, the number of whites lynched was rapidly declining. In the years from 1906 through 1915, ten times as many Negroes (620) were lynched as whites (61).

What was supposed to explain and justify the horrors of lynching as an instrument of "justice" was the raging urge of Negro men to rape white women. In 1942, a study of lynching disclosed that of the 3811 Negroes lynched between 1889 and 1941, only 641, or less than 17 per cent, were even accused of rape, either attempted or committed. Negroes were lynched for such "crimes" as threatening to sue a white man, attempting to register to vote, enticing a white man's servant to leave his job, engaging in labor union activities, "being disrespectful to" or "disputing with" a white man, or sometimes for no discoverable reason at all. Mary Turner, in Georgia, was hanged and burned when she was almost at the point of childbirth because she threatened to disclose the names of the men who had killed her husband.

To read the details of lynching is to be reminded of the torture of the Middle Ages. Indeed, the lynchers could sometimes have taught the torturers of the era some lessons. The victims were lucky indeed if they were merely hanged. In Paris, Texas, in 1893 a Negro had his eyes gouged out with a red-hot poker before he was burned to death. In Arkansas in 1921 a crowd of five hundred, including women, watched a Negro slowly burned to death. He was chained to a log and "fairly cooked to death" as small piles of damp leaves were burned under different parts of his body. When the victim would try to hasten his own death by swallowing hot ashes, his tormentors would kick the ashes out of his reach. The victim did not cry out or beg for mercy but answered questions a considerable time after the flesh had fallen away from his bones. A reporter from the *Memphis Press* described the scene in detail and noted how after the victim was dead there was a wild scramble of the mob to secure his bones as souvenirs. W.E.B. DuBois tells of seeing the fingers of a lynched Negro displayed in the windows of a butcher shop in Atlanta. Sometimes victims had their teeth pulled out one by one, their fingers and toes chopped off by axes while they were still alive, and frequently they were castrated or otherwise mutilated. Anyone who is nostalgic for the superior virtue of the past should read a history of lynching in this country.

During this period a generation of flamboyant southern political leaders arose whose major appeal was to the poor white tenant farmers and whose stock in trade was hatred of the Negro. One of these was James Kimble Vardaman of Mississippi, who campaigned for governor in 1900 in an eight-wheeled lumber wagon drawn by eight yokes of oxen. "We would be justified," Vardaman declared, "in slaughtering every Ethiop on the earth to preserve unsullied the honor of one Caucasian home." The Negro was a "lazy, lying, lustful animal which no conceivable amount of training can transform into a tolerable citizen." One didn't inquire into the justice of killing predatory animals. "We do not stop when we see a wolf," he reasoned, "to find if it will kill sheep before disposing of it, but assume that it will." He admitted the cruelty of this logic. But, he said, "I am ... writing ... to present the cold truth however cruel it may be." Pitchfork Ben Tillman of South Carolina declared in 1913 that from "forty to a hundred Southern maidens were annually offered as a sacrifice to the African Minotaur, and no Theseus had arisen to rid the land of this terror." He said he had taken the oath as governor of South Carolina, "to support the law and enforce it," but added that he "would lead a mob to lynch any man, black or white, who ravished a woman, black or white. This is my attitude calmly and deliberately taken, and justified by my conscience in the sight of God." On another occasion, he declared that his opinion was "to hell with the Constitution" when it stood in the way of mob justice to rapists. Tom Watson of Georgia said that the Negro simply has "no comprehension of virtue, honesty, truth, gratitude and principle." The South had "to lynch him occasionally, and flog him, now and then, to keep him from blaspheming the Almighty, by his conduct, on account of his smell and his color." Lynch law was "a good sign"; it showed "that a sense of justice yet lives among the people." Negro-baiting became so profitable political-ly that there is evidence that white politicians sometimes subsidized Negro party activity in order to keep the opposition strong enough to seem to be worth combating.

A literary source of the most sordid kind of racism was to be seen in the novels of Thomas Dixon, Jr. *The Clansman* (1905), a story of Reconstruction days in South Carolina, reflects a violent hatred of Negroes. There is the following description of a Negro rapist:

He had the short, heavy-set neck of the lower order of animals. His skin was coal black, his lips so thick that they curled both ways up and down with crooked blood-marks across them. His nose was flat and its enormous nostrils seemed in perpetual dilation. The sinister bead eyes, with brown splotches in their whites, were set wide apart and gleamed ape-like under his scant brows. His enormous cheekbones and jaws seemed to protrude beyond the ears and almost hide them.

The mulatto mistress of the northern senator in the novel, who is apparently modeled upon Thaddeus Stevens, has "animal" movements and the eyes of a "leopard." Another Negro in the novel has a head which was "small and seemed mashed on the sides until it bulged into a double lobe behind." His "spindle-shanks supported an oblong, protruding stomach, resembling an elderly monkey's which seemed so heavy it swayed his back to carry it."

As the tide of lynchings rose in the 1890s, Walter Hines Page protested against them and correct-ly forecast where they would lead. "The gravest significance of this whole matter," he declared in 1893, "lies not in the first violation of the law, nor in the crime of lynching, but in the danger that Southern public sentiment itself under the stress of this new and horrible phase of the race-problem will lose the true perspective of civilization." In 1907, William Graham Sumner—hardly one to be accused of an excessive sensibility—marveled that the country had apparently come to accept as a matter of course lynchings accompanied by torture. "It might have been believed a few years ago," he wrote, "that torture could not be employed under the jurisdiction of the United States, and that, if it was employed, there would be a unanimous outburst of indignant reprobation against those who had so disgraced us." He confessed that he did not understand why the country had been so little moved to protest against lynchings.

Sometimes lynching was condoned or at least explained on the basis of the sexual nature of the Negro man. "The intelligent Negro may understand what social equality truly means," said Thomas Nelson Page in 1904, "but to the ignorant and brutal young Negro, it signifies but one thing: the oppor-tunity to enjoy, equally with white men, the privilege of cohabiting with white women." The South under-stood the tendency of Negro men, and thus there was among the whites "universal and furious hostili-ty to even the least suggestion of social equality." A number of modern writers have attempted to explain and interpret the relationship between sexual atti-tudes and race prejudice, especially the violent kind exemplified in lynchings. John Dollard has mentioned the conviction of many southerners that Negro men have exceptionally large genitals and thus their raping of a white woman is a peculiarly horrible and brutal offense. Dollard speculates whether sexual jealousy on the part of white men may be a factor in lynchings. One still hears the idea expressed by white men in the Deep South that they wish they could be Negroes, at least on Saturday nights. Lillian Smith and Oscar Handlin have maintained that the puritani-cal code of religion in the South has in the minds of the whites invested Negroes with both the attraction and the horror of being completely free sexually. James Baldwin, the Negro author, is convinced that whites generally are obsessed with the Negro as a symbol of sexuality.

The most open and avowed attacks on the rights of Negroes came from lynchings and from denial to the right to vote. More insidious in the denial of equality were the Jim Crow laws requiring separate facilities for Negroes.

Editor's Note:

James K. Vardaman (Governor of Mississippi, 1904-08; U.S. Senator 1913-19) carried on a program of disfranchising blacks in the state of Mississippi with as much fervor and dedication as Tillman had manifested in South Carolina. This address before the U.S. Senate reflected many of the current scientific theories, the belief in the inevitability of white rule or government, and fond recollections of relations between whites and Negroes before the question of rights and equality became an issue.

WHITE RULE

JAMES K. VARDAMAN

But the door of hope might have remained closed so far as the progress the negro was to make for himself was concerned. He has never created for himself any civilization. He has never risen above the government of a club. He has never written a language. His achievements in architecture are limited to the thatched-roofed hut or a hole in the ground. No monuments have been builded by him to body forth and perpetuate in the memory posterity the virtues of his ancestors.

For countless ages he has looked upon the rolling sea and never dreamed of a sail. In truth, he has never progressed, save and except when under the influence and absolute control of a superior race.

He is living in Africa to-day, in the land where he sprang, indigenous, in substantially the same condition, occupying the same rude hut, governed by the same club, worshiping the same fetish that he did when the Pharaohs ruled in Egypt. He has never had any civilization except that which had been inculcated by a superior race. And it is a lamentable fact that his civilization lasts only so long as he is in the hands of the white man who inculcates it. When left to himself he has universally gone back to the barbarism of the jungle.

Now, I know the negro has made a certain order of progress in the South. He has acquired property. He is acquiring book learning. I am advised that there is a decrease of illiteracy of something like 12 per cent in every decade. There is no doubt about that. But I am going to make a statement which, I dare say, will astonish some of the gentlemen who have shown such honest and sincere interest in the negro's advancement. While he has progressed mentally, he has deteriorated morally and physically. It is a lamentable fact that as a race the negro in America is more criminal to-day than he was in 1861. And certain diseases which were unknown among them before the war are decimating their ranks, filling the hospitals with incurables and the asylums with lunatics. I predict that these diseases will cause a marked falling off in the birth rate in the next decade.

Now, Mr. President and Senators, I do not want to do anything that will arrest the negro's progress. I would not raise my hand against his material advancement. I believe that I am his real friend. I know him; I understand him in all the relations of life. I have lived with him from my infancy. I was nursed by an old black mammy, the recollection of whose tender ministrations to me are among the sweetest assets of my life. A dear old negro woman nursed every one of our babies. A most faithful, trustworthy, devoted servant and friend was this good old woman. I never permit an opportunity to pass to pay the tribute of my love and respect for her memory. As governor of my State I am sure that I exerted myself as much to protect the negro in the enjoyment of his life, his liberty, the pursuit of happiness, and the products of his own toil as any executive in America has ever done. He does not vote much in Mississippi, but I really think that he votes more than he ought to vote, if he votes at all. I do not think it was ever intended by the Creator that the two races should live together upon equal terms—enjoy equal political and social advantages. One or the other must rule. The people of the South tried to share with the negro in the government of the country after the war, but the negro declined to share with the white man. Black heels rested cruelly upon white necks for many years after the close of the war. The white man endured the negro's misrule, his insolence, impudence, and infamy. He suffered his criminal incapacity to govern until the public domain had been well-nigh squandered and the public treasury looted. We saw the civilization reared by the genius of our fathers, glorified and cemented by their sacred blood, vanishing from the earth, and by means, I will not say in this presence, fair, but by means sufficient, we invoked the law of self-preservation; we arose in the might of an outraged race and as the Saviour scourged the money changers from the temple, so the southern white man drove from power the scalawag, the carpetbagger, and the incompetent negro.

God Almighty never intended that the negro should share with the white man in the government of this country; and you can not improve upon the plans of God Almighty or defeat His purposes, either, by legislative enactments. Do not forget that. It matters not what I may say or others may think; it matters not what constitutions may contain or statutes provide, wherever the negro is in sufficient numbers to imperil the white man's civilization or question the white man's supremacy the white man is going to find some way around the difficulty. And that is just as true in the North as it is in the South. You need not deceive yourselves about that. The feeling against the negro in Illinois when he gets in the white man's way is quite as strong, more bitter, less regardful of the negro's feelings and conditions than it is in Mississippi. And that is true of every other Northern State. I have been all over the States of Illinois, Ohio, Iowa, Indiana, some of the Western States, and New England States. I know the temper of the white people on this question. I had the pleasure of speaking in the city of Springfield soon after they had had a lynching fest. A negro was thought to have committed an unmentionable crime. The mob got after him. The sheriff and his friend carried the negro away in his friend's automobile. They returned, and the mob found the negro had made his escape. To wreak their vengeance upon those who undertook to uphold the law they proceeded to destroy the automobile, and they demolished the restaurant belonging to the man who had carried the negro away. A thing of that kind could hardly happen in the South.

The difference between the southern man's conduct in a matter of this character and that of the people of Illinois is this: The southern mob sometimes gets the guilty man and hangs him. In the North, if the mob finds itself unable to punish the beast who committed the outrage, they proceed to destroy property and kill everything of a dark color. Mr. President, I am not the negro's enemy. I know what is best for him. I think I can measure his productive capacity. I know the influences that move him. I am familiar with the currents of passion which sweep through his savage blood. I understand his hates, his jealousies, and his attachments. In a word, I think I know him as he really is. And knowing him, I believe I know what is best for him. You can not measure the negro by the standard you would measure accurately the white man. He is different from the white man physically, morally, and mentally. The pure-blooded negro is without gratitude. He does not harbor revenge. He is not immoral—he is unmoral. I have never known one who ever felt the guilt of sin, the goading of an outraged conscience, or the binding force of a moral obligation. The pure-blooded negro reaches mental maturity soon after he passes the period of puberty. The cranial sutures become ossified by the time he reaches 20 years of age, and it is not uncommon to find one who reads fluently at 15 years of age not to know a letter in the book at the age of 25 or 30.

No; I am not an enemy to the negro; I want to educate him—or rather train him—along proper lines; I want to train him in a way that we may improve his hand and educate his heart; I want to build, if possible, a moral substratum upon which to rear this mental superstructure; but if that is not done, with his ideas of morality, or a Froude, the historian, would put it, his ideas of "unmorality"—when you enhance his mentality without building this moral substratum, upon which it is to rest, you simply increase his capacity for harm. Your education will only serve to make a less desirable citizen.

I want, first, to build the foundation. The white man and the negro of the South are not enemies. They may be made so if you continue to insist on trying to bring them into abnormal relationship. The relations that existed between them before and immediately succeeding the war was akin to that of father and son. My recollections of the black folk on the farm during my boyhood are among the pleasant memories of my life. The negroes in Mississippi know that I am not their enemy. I would not permit them to vote, but I would protect them in the enjoyment of their life, liberty, and the pursuit of happiness and the product of their toil. And if the white people of the South are permitted to proceed along proper rational lines, knowing and recognizing the negro's inferiority, desiring, however, his betterment; if they are permitted to work out, although handicapped, as they are, with laws which were conceived in hatred and brought forth in a spasm of venom and revenge—if they are permitted to do it, Mr. President, in their own proper way, very much more progress will be made for the negro's uplifting, for the negro's improvement than will be made if it shall be directed by men who do not know any more about it personally than I do about the political economy of the planet Mars.

Editor's Note:

Henry E. Garrett, former president of the American Psychological Association and a professor at Columbia University, expresses views held by a number of his colleagues, both past and present. Henry Baxter Adams of the Johns Hopkins University was an active proselytizer for the Teutonic Germ Theory. John Burgess, a political scientist, also of Columbia, applied this theory and influenced his pupil Theodore Roosevelt. William McDougall, a psychologist, attributed the achievements of civilization to Nordic blood and maintained that the prevelant use of Negroes as slaves indicated an instinct for submission. This "instinct psychology" was popularized in the widely used text authored by him, *Introduction to Social Psychology* (1908). Presidents Eliot and Lowell of Harvard and Shaler of MIT all expressed overtly racist opinions. And there were many more whose ideas of racial superiority provided the rationale for discrimination within the confines of the United States and for the imperialistic subjugation of the colored peoples in the Philippines, Hawaii, and Cuba. Interestingly enough, many of the advocates of racism proclaim themselves, as Garrett does here, friends of the people whom they view with such benign contempt. The history of Africa to which he refers is replete with abysmal ignorance and exemplifies the fact that on many issues the educated show as much prejudice as the less educated and on some they show more. Suffice it to say that these statements are replete with errors and distortions. These remarks in opposition to desegregation were made August 9, 1967, before a subcommittee of the Senate Committee on the Judiciary.

A "FRIEND" SPEAKS

HENRY E. GARRETT

Dr. Garrett: I can say all that I know in a very short space. In the first place, I think that the present exacerbation of trouble between black and white has come largely out of misunderstanding of the civil rights issues and the civil rights laws by both the black and the white. Now, the white man has been made over the past 30 or 40 years, particularly 30 years, to feel very guilty. He has been told that he has mistreated the Negro, in spite of the fact that the Negro has made more progress in this country than he has anywhere on the face of the earth, that he is responsible for slavery, and all that. And for a long time the white man who was most often lambasted was the southerner. Now, the northern white people are beginning to take the same point of view, the pendulum has swung quite a bit, and so they are now being lambasted. The only people who seem not to have been converted at all—and I don't think they have read anything for the last 6 or 8 months—is the President's Commission on Civil Rights which made these recommendations the other day here.

Now, white people, then, are full of the idea that they are guilty for something that they have never done. So much for that.

Now, the black people—in whom I am very much interested, and to whom I consider myself a friend—the black people are immature relative to the white. They are more primitive, they are more childlike, their abstract intelligence is on the average considerably lower. All of the evidence, not just a piece of it, but all of it shows that.

The evidence can be drawn from four sources. In the first place, we have the anthropological and the fossil evidence to show that the black race broke away from the tree of evolution about 200,000 years later than the white race did, which means, as I said, that they are not inferior, they are immature.

In the second place, the Negro's brain on the average is somewhat smaller, somewhat lighter, and somewhat less fissured than the white. And some of the more recent developments in the front lobes are smaller, not so thick in the Negro as they are in the white.

I think these differences alone could account for much of the difficulty that we find in the behavior of the two races.

On the psychological side, with which I think I ought to be fairly familiar after 40 years of work in the field, the average intelligence quotient of the white child in the United States is arbitrarily set at 100. That is the way the test was made. The Negro child in the Southeastern States has an average intelligence quotient of 80. They overlap—that is, the number of Negroes who do as well, as the average white child, ranges from 10 to 15 percent, which means that if you put these children into classrooms indiscriminately as they are being forced in by federal judges, they will be, first of all, confused, and then, to use the famous word, "frustrated," and finally they will be disappointed and drop out or quit.

Now, the teachers are afraid to fail them because of reprisals. So what they generally do is to promote them, passing the burden over to the next grade, the the child pushes on up the way he does in New York City, by seniority, until finally he graduates, because he is old enough to, though he might not be able to read. I have known a number of youngsters in New York City who have graduated, or they were ready to graduate, and they couldn't read to save their lives. One of them was the son of a friend of mine. He was a masseur of a track team. And so I got him a special tutor and we brought him up to where he could read his fifth-grade level. I think it was a great accomplishment. His intelligence quotient was 83.

Now, in the Army tests over 50 years—I have just made an analysis of them—the proportion of Negroes who do as well as the average white man has varied from 14 percent in 1917 to 12 percent in 1966. That is, in spite of all the money that has been poured into education of white and black, the comparative standing is the same as it was 50 years ago.

Now, that to me seems to mean that there must be a basis for it other than just experience or teaching or bad schools or something of the sort.

The third source of evidence is history. We do know something about the history of black Africa over the last 5,000 years. And we find that in black Africa south of the Sahara desert there was never a literate civilization. There was no system of measurement. The black African did not discover the principles of a plow, he just used the stick, nor of a wheel. The wheel was discovered in the third century B.C. by the Samarians in Asia Minor. But the black African didn't get it. He never built a terrace or a bridge any more than a stick across a stream. His architectural achievements were a mud hut in a stockade.

Now, all of this means to say that the Negro is necessarily an inferior creature; he isn't. If you take the intelligence on the abstract level, that is, the kind of thing which people in school and in the professions and in business have to use, numbers, and words and diagrams and figures, that is where he falls down. And his history shows it. He doesn't have it.

Now, Dr. Connelly, a well-known British investigator in Kenya, advanced the theory of what he called the lazy frontal lobe. He said that the black African has a lazy frontal lobe, which accounts for the fact that he doesn't think. He had the satisfaction of seeing his book taken off the market; you can't buy it any longer now.

That is one way you can always quiet criticism, you know, is to step on people, either take their books off the market, or fire them. As I have told people, fortunately I am over age where you can be fired, I amount. And I don't give a hoot what anybody says, I am impressed by the evidence, not by people, and not by howling, whining, and yelling.

Well, the history, then, of the black African gives us every reason to think that he falls significantly below the white man in his intelligence.

One has to look only around him to see that in the last 12 or 14 years we have plenty of evidence of what I have just said. The New York City schools have now become what one author called a custodial institution for children who have no future.

The Washington schools, even the Washington Post, which is—well not a conservative paper—says that the Washington schools were sick. Well, they are not only sick, they are moribund. And you people know that as well or better than I do.

The riots and the rest of it that breaks out is not brought about by by any special strange disease.

Here you have got a childish, primitive sort of people, whose thinking is shallow, they start burning, somebody yells to them, "burn, baby, burn," and they began to burn. And everybody loots that can get something. And the cops don't shoot at them, the cops have been ordered not to shoot at them, so the looters take it on out. It is never recovered.

Now, the record of the Negro in crime in this country is literally scandalous. In 1963 the FBI report, which is the last one I have looked at, showed that the Negro, who constitutes about 10 or 11 percent of our population, committed 10 times as many murders, 6 times as many robberies, 7 times as many rapes, and had 10 times as many illegitimate children.

Civil rights laws, then, do what? They make the Negro think that he is going to be suddenly equal and able to do anything he wants.

I heard the story the other day of the Negro boy who walked into a bank and talked to one of the tellers. And the teller said, "What do you want?" thinking he probably wanted to be a porter. And he said, "Well, I want your job."

Now, it didn't occur to him that he had to be trained to get that man's job.

Negro mothers in Washington have told me that they were bitterly disappointed when their children, who had always ranked in the upper 25 percent of the class, were put into the white schools and they began to drop down to the middle and even lower than the middle. If the Civil Service Commission and HEW continue to push and force desegregation of schools in the South, you have only one result, a destruction, ultimately, of the school system; there isn't another thing that you can look forward to than that, a demoralization, a disorganization, the fading out of all the good teachers who can get into the private schools, with the final end in chaos.

Now, we are living in an insane age. But this is insanity raised to the nth power. And sometimes I can't believe that it is possible that things have gone the way they have.

That is all I have to say, sir.

Senator Ervin: Don't you have the impression that those who have advocated and demanded the passage of civil rights bills have in effect assured the minority race that they can be lifted merely by the force of law, and without substantial exertion on their part, to social and economic heavens?

Dr. Garrett: Even if they haven't told them in so many words, Senator, they have certainly given them—that is what they think; they think they suddenly—I know one Negro mother in Charlottesville told me, "I want to put my child in the white schools so he will be as smart as they are."

118

They think by osmosis or something they will absorb and be as bright as the white man.

It is a cruel thing; the whole business has been stupid and cruel.

Senator Ervin: Do you agree with me that no men of any race can be lifted to social economic heavens except by their own exertions and their own sacrifices?

Dr. Garrett: I certainly do.

Senator Ervin: Now, there is an expression in the Bible to this effect. It says, "Hope deferred maketh the heart sick." Does not that Biblical statement contain a profound psychological truth?

Dr. Garrett: Absolutely. That is one of the real reasons for all the rioting, disappointment, and limited ability to comprehend what is going on, which, of course, always makes it worse.

Senator Ervin: Don't you agree with me that the growing promises which politicians have made to the minority race, in advocating the passage of civil rights bills, have brought about a sense of frustration among many people? I admire a man who achieves, regardless of his race; but I disfavor those who plant false hopes in the minds of those who cannot achieve greatness overnight.

Dr. Garrett: That is true.

Mr. Hicks: Mr. Chairman, could I comment right at this point that the colored race is not the only sufferer from the illusion here that is created by the passage of civil rights laws. It is our contention that the passage of civil rights laws has also had a profound effect on the psychology of the white American. It has caused him to believe he has done his duty to his fellow man, simply by the passage of a law which can in the end have little result toward accomplishing the true duty of the white man toward the colored man in America. And it has taken him off the hook, so to speak, and left him in a position so that when the colored man rises up in wrath out of the unfulfilled aspirations that he has, the white man looks at him with abasement and says, "What are you hollering about? We passed a Civil Rights Act, you should be happy," and completely ignores the true duties that he has to the colored man.

Senator Ervin: That statement conforms to what I have said on the Senate floor on a number of occasions. Any man who maintains that men of any race can be lifted to a more abundant life by the passage of laws is either fooling himself or fooling somebody else. Doesn't the psychology which demands the passage of laws of this nature have a tendency to blind not only the supposed beneficiaries of the act, but the proponents of the act to an acceptance of something which is absolutely incompatible with life? No man can advance to a more abundant life except by exertion on his part; is that not true?

Mr. Hicks: Yes, sir. To that extent Liberty Lobby feels that we would be far better off to be concentrating on the true problems, and we feel that this concentration on the passage of civil rights laws is a detriment to that aim.

Senator Ervin: I will call your attention to something I said at the opening of the hearings on this bill. Title IV, that is the open occupancy provision, is unwise because it is irrelevant, even to the demands of its supporters. This legislation will not end the ghetto. It will not provide the jobs, the schools, the environmental changes that civil rights groups list as their goals. It does not provide one new dwelling for one inhabitant of slum housing. If enacted, this bill will only bring false hope, and engender further frustrations in those who are deluded about its effective purpose. Do you have any comments that you could make on that?

Mr. Jaffe: No; except that I certainly agree with them, and think it sums up the results or lack of results about this legislation.

Senator Ervin: Do you agree with me—I will ask this question of all you gentlemen—that the only thing you can do by law is to give all men equality before the law itself?

Dr. Garrett: That is all.

Senator Ervin: And do you agree with me that, in this country, every man of every race has been given equality before the law?

Mr. Hicks: I believe, sir, that we can say, by and large, that is completely true. There are perhaps exceptions. But these exceptions are not confined to the inequalities presented to any one race, or in any one locality.

Senator Ervin: Now, isn't one of the inherent vices in the modern civil rights proposals the fact that those proposals are inconsistent with the theory that all men shall stand equal before the law. According to this bill a certain segment of our own society would be singled out and given rights superior to those that have been granted to any other American in the history of this country.

Mr. Hicks: Yes.

Senator Ervin: I have a comment about the open-occupancy provision of this bill. If A has to sell B his house, at B's insistence, whether A wishes to do so or not, is there any equality between A and B?

Mr. Hicks: No, sir.

Senator Ervin: In that kind of a situation, aren't the rights of A subordinated to the rights of B, and inequality produced instead of equality?

Mr. Hicks: Yes, sir.

Senator Ervin: Doctor Garrett, statistics that are

available to me indicate that people of the poverty level are composed of the white race also. Is that substantially in accordance with your understanding?

Dr. Garrett: That is right.

Senator Ervin: Very few of the politicians, these very sincere people, who advocate the passage of laws of this nature, possess any great overriding concern about the welfare of people at the poverty level who happen to be white, do they?

Dr. Garrett: Well, I suppose they are not quarreling and asking for something.

Senator Ervin: Therefore there has been no promise made to them saying they are going to be lifted by law to a social and economic heaven. For that reason they have been given no reason for the frustration which the minority race possesses?

Dr. Garrett: I would like to say one word about this often used phrase, "equality of opportunity," which I think is a cliché which really doesn't mean anything.

If equality of opportunity means the same opportunity, then it isn't equality. If you give a bright person and a dull person the same tasks, exactly the same tasks, it won't be equal for those two, because the bright one will do it very much faster. And what we should say, rather, is that we give each person, Negro and white, an opportunity to work at the highest level of which he is capable. Now, I am all in favor of that. I think again, too, that the urging of everybody to go to college is stupid—I ought not to use that word—is ill advised, let's say, because only about 15 percent of the students of college age are capable of doing good college work. Now, it would be far better for these others to go to a vocational school or something instead of having it brought up to them that they have got to go to college and pull the standards of those colleges down in order to pass.

Senator Ervin: I would like to know your opinion as to whether or not the task of assigning students in the public schools should be a function of the educator or the function of a federal judge?

Dr. Garrett: Well, we generally go on the principle that the person who is educated for a job is likely to be better at it than the man in the street. And that, I think, is pretty generally agreed upon. And I think it is really very incredible almost to see federal judges, as has happened in my own State, putting children into schools over the heads of the principals and the superintendents and everybody else just willy nilly.

Senator Ervin: The schools in the District of Columbia have been desegregated ever since the decision of May 14, 1954, as far as they can be desegregated under the standards of residential areas. And at the present time somewhere in the neighborhood of 90 percent of the students in the public schools of the District of Columbia are colored. Now, there has been a practice here in the District called the track system under which the students, regardless of what their color may be, have been assigned to classrooms according to what teachers have ascertained about their respective capacities. Recently Judge J. Skelly Wright handed down a decision ordering the schools in the District to abandon the track system and assign the children to a school irrespective of their respective capacities. Do you think that kind of judicial decree is calculated to afford the best opportunity for the children to learn?

Dr. Garrett: I don't see how it could, because the promise is that all children are alike, they all learn equally well, you put them here, you put them there, or you put them anywhere else. The track system, it seems to me, was the best thing that the Washington schools had. And when they threw it out I was appalled. But I have been appalled so often at the Washington schools that it has come to be almost a permanent state.

Editor's Note:

Many people are of the opinion that education, particularly higher education, is an objective endeavor free from the stereotyped thinking and petty misconceptions that plague much of the rest of society. This is one of the myths that has been able to flourish, along with many others, particularly about the role and functions of institutions in American society. The educational system, from primary to postgraduate levels is replete with attitudes, practices, and beliefs that have evolved from the racist posture of the society.

"Racism in Education" by Charles E. Wilson provides an overview of the situation as reflected through teachers, specific practices, and the influence of powerful interest groups.

RACISM IN EDUCATION

CHARLES E. WILSON

Western bourgeois racial prejudice ... is a racism of contempt; it is a racism which minimises what it hates. Bourgeois ideology, however, which is the proclamation of an essential equality between men, manages to appear logical in its own eyes by inviting the sub-men to become human and to take as their prototype, western humanity as incarnated in Western bourgeoisie.—Frantz Fanon

Americans as a people are not given either to ideological speculations, evaluations of theoretical conceptions, or examinations of basic assumptions. They are instead driven to material acquisition and find themselves in a state bordering on panic, unable to understand or to deal with the various problems that now confront them. Crises like Castro, Vietnam, the gold standard, the balance of trade, the collapse of cities only stun and temporarily distract them. As a people they stumble uncertainly through the pages of history.

At this point in time the American people are dismayed when this opulent society of theirs is referred to as "racist." For these people have never been taught to examine their institutions or to determine whether what those institutions do for people is worth what the institutions in fact do to them. Without a point of view these same American people are ill equipped to either recognize or deal with their problems. Leadership that combines commitment, forcefulness, and broad insight is largely absent. Thus all problems are magnified, enemies are multiplied, and a great deal of energy is misdirected into either flight from urban centers or in *quixotic* fights against rights, race, and roadways.

Their white racial problem, for let's face it, it is a white problem, stands like a death's-head at their sumptuous domestic banquet table. The dimensions of this racial problem are largely misunderstood and carefully misinterpreted. Like so many human conflicts this "racial problem" is in part a consequence of unexamined assumptions.

Since education reflects the values, the goals, and the confusions of a society, the same aimlessness, the same malaise found in the general culture is also to be found within this sector. The Educational Establishment, fresh from its failure to educate a significant number of students, criticizes efforts to humanize educational systems. Vested educational interests predict "those" advocating change will fall into their own present habits of sloth, thievery, and bureaucratic featherbedding. Teacher union officials decry the desire of local people to develop healthy human communities. Lower-class whites who feel scorned by other upper-class whites seem to be willing to fight to keep the status quo, that is, to keep the niggers (Blacks, Students, Spicks, Indians, and God knows who else) in their place. Education's response to these signs of reaction and retrogression is to deny the problem, or turn to helpless exhortation.

If Americans are to learn to deal with racism in education they will first need a point of view, then they will need trained sense organs which may faithfully send to their brains experimental data, and finally they will need the courage to act upon that which they have perceived; for racism pervades this society like a living cancer, eroding the humanity and capacity of men. Racism lives as a part of the "educational system" producing foul substance of inhumanity so that the educators mindlessly substitute the defecation of European standard values for civilization and foster the establishment of a *dual standard* of behavior, morals, and morality in place of a *single yardstick* unrelated to skin color.

In the first place

Americans have been taught to equate prejudice and discrimination with racism. For the past twenty years people have been misled into believing that the struggle against racial prejudice was actually making headway. How do they say it?—"making progress." This "no view school of racism" perceived prejudice and discrimination as individual, personal problems. This conception led many down the primrose path—unable and ill-prepared to see the institutional racism which is part and parcel of the societal fabric.

First of all, racism is a direct function of a society's organization, a product of a society with its competition-saturated bloodstream and a psyche dominated by self-seeking individualism activated by the single-minded pursuit of the material. Eric Williams (*Capitalism and Slavery*) has shown that the shortage of labor in the New World gave rise to modern new world slavery which in turn has led to its virulent racism. This virulent racism was in turn reinforced by the competition prevalent during the beginning of the factory system and the New World's modern industralization with its class and occupation differentiation and its specialization of labor.

For its part modern industrialization not only brought together a vast number of people, but industry tended to differentiate between the roles and functions of workers individually, by class, by occupational category. Occupational status and job and ethnic status opportunity were established to correlate with jobs and status. The pattern became a basic part of the modern factory, with the most clear-cut examples of this separation of ethnic groups into job categories found in the backwaters and the colonial enclaves rather than in older established industrial areas. The exploitation of a group under this factory production-industrial shortage system could be measured by the degree to which the individual or group could not move ahead either on his own or his group's own merits, and by the degree to which "the system" indicated that an individual or group just could not be assimilated into the total society. What is important if we are to learn from history is that modern industry and the factory

121

system were organized as an interrelated group of ethnic hierarchies organized to produce goods and services. The entire system based on ethnicity operated and still operates because of the existence of a contented or bought-off segment of plodders and workers who believe the myths and slogans of the dominant group and have been taught to want to make it into the "mainstream."

Stereotypes about groups develop in relation to their place in the social and economic order. Those at the apex of the pyramid ownership managerial level learn to perceive workers in terms of their stereotypes; workers learn to stereotype their own group and try to live up to the acceptable generalizations of others, while fighting to remove themselves from the unacceptable ones. This elaborate system designed to butter up the ups, while putting the downtrodden down further, has taken its place in the passage of time as the "normal order of things." The have-nots learn to accommodate the myths of the haves. Language barriers are removed by economic necessity. The group with purchasing power always can make its wishes known to subordinate groups without learning the language of the subordinate. The servants must learn the language of their masters or their exploitation by their masters will be more brutal and more complete.

With the growth of a number of layers, the system prompted the emergence of intermediate types (supervisors and strawbosses) who were to stand between the owners and the workers of a particular layer.

Intermediate groups in such a system maintain their status by their capacity to assure the delivery of the goods and services of their ethnic brothers. Above all the system insures opportunities for intermediate groups to fill their own pockets and enhance their own personal and intermediate group status. And this racist organization of the industrial world becomes the basic superstructure of an entire colonial system in the political world, a system in which European people maintain dominance over those whom they have conquered, enslaved, and exploited.

Even today, one of the tactical weapons used to maintain this colonial system of dominance is the maintenance of a low emphasis on education and welfare and social services in general, while expending money for roads and transportation. This modern-day colonialism still employs as a rationalization for its existence the notion of "backward peoples" with the corresponding ennobling of the mission of white people to bring civilization and education to those backward people. The American race problem then is merely a special domestic aberration of the age-old colonial problem, and the evidence for this concep-

tion can be found in the conclusions of more than one of the social science experts. Lacking the basis or the zest for analysis, the Americans do not care to recognize the basis on which their society is organized. Nor will they perceive how deeply colonialist are their attitudes and assumptions which comprise the very roots and foundations of the society.

The recent years of struggle against prejudice and discrimination have done little to clarify the basic issue. In reality, these years may have further clouded the issues. As a people who had been taught not to understand the origin and nature of racism, Americans are unable to perceive the forest for the trees. Each group and each segment has become committed to its own profitable part of the system, what the racial militants referred to as "cut of the pie." They are far too committed to the notion of their own group, class, and race position to contemplate the recreation of the social order in more humane terms. Therefore, it is apparent that the American people have been taught not to understand, not to remember, and how to substitute motive drive for material success in place of thought. Racism could have no finer protection.

Public education—a pillar of a racist society

A persistent American belief is that the non-white minorities, for whatever reason, are less intelligent than the children of Europeans (read white people). Coupled with the shibboleth of faith there is a favorite boast that there is a superior free system which rests on a cornerstone of a free public school system. But the school system is not free from a deep bourgeois racism nor are these schools public in the sense of being responsive and accountable to the minority public of communities in which these schools stand. The racism which pervades the public school system is at one and the same time subtle, unintentional, unthinking, as well as brutal and deliberately offensive. And more important, this middle-class racism is disguised in a clever rhetoric. Sometimes the talk is liberal, affirming goodwill and genuine social concern and at other times speaking in a subtle racial code: "neighborhood schools," "jungle," "due process," "professional rights," "cultural deprivation," and, oh yes—"love for the children." But generally, behind the words exists an entire reality which protects the professional educator's self-esteem at the expense of the children; protects the educator's status at the expense of the community's interests; protects whites at the expense of the Blacks; protects the middle class from competition with those who they feel aren't ready, or don't deserve to have the good things of this glutted society.

Understanding the bourgeois character of public education's racism is crucial to understanding the public school's capacity to inflict its poison on some of the student victims, making them sullen and rebellious, while other students become just like their teachers.

First, who are the teachers in the racial and economic backwaters—those people, white and nonwhite, who man the public school sub-system? By and large, both whites and nonwhites currently within the system located in the ghettos are heavily drawn from the sons and daughters of the lower class and the working classes, groups notorious for their upward mobility, conservatism, self-seeking opportunism, and anti-Black sentiment—groups whose own status is uncertain, insecure, and threatened. These are the very groups who desperately clutch the security of civil service and tenure rights, who cannot bear to let any group or person question their authority and their wisdom, and who look for the single uniform right way (white way). Militant teacher-trade-unionism, while satisfied with the job it performs, derives much of its fury and aggressive thrust from these sentiments, which combine a fascinating admixture of status panic and cleverly disguised bourgeois racism.

When local communities question the system, they are lucky if they are only told that the local children are culturally deprived, or unprepared for school by virtue of a lack of motivation or as a consequence of the terrible environment. If the racial and economic minority group children are not so lucky, the children may be subjected to various forms of brutality—overt and/or covert, verbal and/or physical, and "always for the children's good." Not too infrequently the children of these backwaters are used as pawns in political fights for higher salaries, for higher teacher benefits, or for larger school expenditures. All these bribes assist teachers and their unions to climb to greater personal affluence as well as collective power.

Class solidarity sometimes binds white and nonwhite teachers in their bourgeois pursuit of security status and prominence. These persons who are grouped together frequently share a similar view of their charges but for different reasons. For the nonwhite person, guilt and insecurity may be most keenly experienced, while for the white, the negative view of the "powerless" emerges from a quiet conviction of superiority. If a nonwhite person chooses to be an advocate for his people, if not his kind, in the person of the children he becomes blacker and may run the risk of being looked on with

suspicion, fear, and anger, ostracized and transferred, then ignored by his professional colleagues. This assertion of concern for his fellows can be the worst error any person can make. For the nonwhite teacher to make this assertion is to jeopardize his own grasp on professional credentials.

At different periods of history, public education has been the gateway of economically mobile groups. Every group trying for political ascendancy has tended to see education with or without civil service restraints as their domain. Since frequently interest and occupational groups are in fact ethnic groups, every city has an ethnic group that uses the school system as its one-way ticket to economic security. In New York City for instance, public education is the domain of a vast number of Jewish persons, who have slowly come to wrest control over the lower and middle areas of the system from the Protestants and Catholics who formerly dominated the system. In other cities the Italians, Irish, and other groups dominate the system.

The practices of the system, which assist such groups to achieve or maintain their control, are of course sacred and easily become institutionalized.

Whatever their particular ethnic background, many teachers seem committed to their myth of the student's deprivation; teachers seem more doubtful of the capacity of the student to learn than they are of their own ability to teach and the qualifications of the school as a place to learn. Further, teachers seem dominated by a certain educational fatalism which justifies their own willingness to participate in and play along with the status quo.

It is against the human predisposition of those who man the system that the racism of education must be examined. To ignore the human condition leads to failure to understand why change has not occurred and why the system cannot recognize its racism.

Racist practices in education

Racism in education specifically is as much a part of the scarring of the human psyche of the American Black or white child and adult as the three r's: reading, 'riting, 'rithmetic. It is a part of the staffing pattern, part of the practices, part of the mythologies, part of the belief system and assumptional basis of public education, perpetuated as well in the private school system through social class and social standing. Racism comfortably coexists with the words of the liberal rhetoric that affirm social concern on the part of the education establishment. For the words of equality are no real threat to the institutionalization of inequality based on skin color, which is as American as apple pie.

To ask to uncover racism in its gross and subtle forms is to ask to examine not only the bloodstream itself, but all the organs serviced by a defective circulatory system. Institutionally based racism in education can easily be found, for example, in sectors where racial discrimination is practiced overtly:

1. segregation of teachers and students by race
2. gerrymandering of students to avoid desegregation
3. discriminatory hiring practices on all levels of personnel from janitorial to pedagogical
4. discriminatory purchasing of supplies, books, and materials
5. discriminatory budget practices which systematically rob the poor to educate the upper and middle classes
6. test standards and practices which are designed to make professional advancement limited for members of minorities in competition with others
7. discriminatory practices in school building maintenance and repair, which insures that school buildings and school facilities for minorities remain less adequate than those for the powerful or influential
8. purchasing of text materials which present racially biased, whether overt or subtle, treatment of school subjects

This enumeration of the discriminatory practices in education presents a formidable list. Careful examination of this list will show that the leaders of education have had access to sufficient information on which to base a counterattack. But they exhibit a "convenient ignorance" about the nature and existence of such flagrant and long-standing violations of the so-called American democratic creed. Rather than admit their inaction, these "educators" busy themselves with meaningless studies of families, housing, health, income, and attitudes.

Personal racism in education covers a wide range of activities from the overtly callous and openly brutal treatment to covert, clever, and calculated silence. There are, as well, a wide range of actions which are unthinking and unfeeling slights, based on unquestioned assumptions or a reliance on popular mythology. Make no mistake about it, the schools nonwhites attend are indeed places where brutality occurs, for the students' own good, of course, for various reasons: because his family is a contemporary version of the Jukes, or because parents unwittingly or deliberately encourage teachers to take the most direct route to the seat of learning.

Recent works like Kozol's *Death at an Early Age* bear witness to the fact that physical violence against school children is not a thing of the past, nor are the racial epithets and racially based snide remarks. With the emergence of the new social class mythology, "cultural deprivation" has put a new mask on racism's tired old face, so that the believers can be both scientifically justified and morally absolved.

The subtleties of personal racism can be difficult, almost impossible to prove. White's difficulties in proving personal bias are fascinating to observe. One story, illustrative of the character of racism in the "highest" levels of the educational system, goes as follows. Recently in a local college a white and a Black student combined to design, develop, and finish a science project. It was agreed that the typed report of their project, an original and carbon, would be turned in to the professor of an advanced biology course. When the papers were graded and returned the white student was given B, the Black student (the original copy) was given C. The instructor was asked about the assignment of different grades. His response was "Well, you know who did the thinking no matter who did the typing." This expectation of racial scholastic differential is not as uncommon as those in education would have us believe.

In the case of institutional racism, one might list a number of actions which should be recognized for what they are or what they may become. In the case of individual racism, categorizing such a wide range of actions which may or may not be racist in nature, proving intent is difficult.

The most pervasive current assumption that has been incorporated into the arsenal of racist assumptions is the feeling that the nonwhite person has nothing to offer culturally. He has no past other than slavery and exploitation, possesses little in the present, and may have even less in the future, unless the teachers and the other people of noble character make him over into a more acceptable being. This assumption and motivation are little different from a dressed-up version of the old imperialist rationalization of yesteryear. It is even more beguiling to present-day teachers who never accept the existence of racism or colonialism. And certainly these individuals don't perceive themselves in their true light. The motivation hides most effectively behind talk of credentials or certification by some sanctified rite. This motivation countenances any sort of treatment for these ruffians (savages) for the sake of "progress." The imperialist will have someone else endure any indignity or discrimination, for after all, this is what these people deserve. The educational imperialist will emasculate instead of liberate; will prefer legalisms to justice; stern retribution to mercy; pompous folly to courageous humility. Modern educational imperialism will do its duty, but never accomplish its job—for its assumptional base, racism, will not permit that job to be done.

Thus, when we look at the shambles of free public education we see it is not public or free, nor does it accomplish its verbalized goal of education for the rank and file of nonwhites. Racism pervades that system and scars the victims held hostage to the New World's deification of European standards. It is important, however, to recognize that the operation of the system scars everyone, frustrates everyone, and perpetuates the system itself.

Scars from the operation of the educational system

Not all of the scarring of the system is a direct product of racism. Scars of racism provide an easy cover for those scars which are derived from inefficiency, ineptitude, and authoritarianism. Some of the scars arise from factors peculiar to the educational system. The diffuseness of educational goals and the lack of evaluation and feedback tend to confuse members of the educational hierarchy about their own status and their societal function. Out of this confusion emerges a need for certainty and a disdain for ambiguity, closely allied to authoritarianism.

Similarly, the supervisory practices of schools in a host of systems are semimilitaristic in nature, predicated on fear, with a high premium paid for obedience to directives and orders from superiors. Security and, more importantly, promotion is gained from spineless and mindless obedience rather than from professional creativity and sober judgment. Reinforcing this particular tendency is the fact that many teachers have not developed and are not encouraged to develop the necessary habits of scholarship. Therefore, they may wander in search of an educational and life philosophy at the same time that they speak authoritatively to their pupils.

Professional imperialism and the union

The local American school system is vulnerable to a great variety of powerful interests, unions, publishers, equipment manufacturers, parents, community people, power elites, political incumbents, mayors, and state officialdom. The vulnerability prompts the development of a kind of conservatism, a status panic, and a deep-seated resistance to change. The vulnerability also contributes to a classic case of professional imperialism which impels educators to have to fight for the "respect" due them. But more

than just fighting to preserve and improve the status quo for themselves, professional imperialists justify carving out sacred professional domains into which no outsider must venture and none can gain admittance to, except through courses of study, degrees arranged sequentially, or other academic rituals. Some of these academic rituals may be only peripherally related, marginally related, or completely unrelated to the task or job. But what is important is the *entrance card*—the modern sign of the guild. Any attempt to examine the job, explore its true nature, or change its requirements is to be resisted, employing the slogans of bygone eras, with their patriotic, emotional, and historic appeals.

Therefore, racism—a system which from its inception was conceived in inequality, dedicated to the veneration of European standards, and operates in such a way as to protect itself from innovation and change—can be ably protected by institutional practice designed to maintain the status quo. The institutional and organizational scarring mechanism described can be and is easily coopted by racism. The mechanism can be employed as plausible explanation for forms of behavior. So it is that individuals who function within the system can vehemently deny racism or discrimination per se and proceed to act in ways that are unconsciously or inadvertently racist and discriminatory.

The current myth that a racist and racism are distinct obvious forms of opposition to racial democracy is just one more subtle protection for the status quo. While subtle, this same myth is powerful and extremely effective. The myths are significant to the understanding of how the system operates. For myths are merely dynamic ways through which the system rationalizes its current practices.

What this system has tried to suggest is that the very practices and actions of the system, despite the verbalizations about freedom, tend to serve the traditional values of discrimination and racial exclusion. The veneration of those sacred traditions of education of the past often suggests a kind of mindlessness about the realities of America's racial history. For was not this nation carved out of the land of the Indian, employing the labor and brain power of groups without political and social power? It is those very people who now wish to move from the backwaters to the center stage and are blocked.

Racism—a challenge to democratic education

Several years ago Murray Kempton wrote, "There are few Negroes who really know what is being done to them." In an examination of racism in education, institutional as well as personal, the mantle of silence about education's collusion with racism has to a degree been removed. Without stretching the imagination, one can perceive the extent to which whites as well as nonwhites have participated in and even profited by the degradation of their fellowmen.

Removal of the mantle of silence surrounding racism and clarifying our understanding of the phenomena has involved looking again at, and applying our new understanding to, the field of contemporary education. What has emerged is a situation close to that postulated by Frantz Fanon—"a racism of contempt, a racism of bourgeois character"—a racism which seeks to maintain its own reasonableness in the face of its obvious unreasonableness by offering the subhuman a chance for imitation. Imitation, after all, is the most sincere form of flattery. Further, the racism pervades an educational fabric that is slow to innovate and even slower to change, acting as it were like another anchor holding the society to its star-crossed position.

The challenge to American schools, to the system of education and educators, is clear. The challenge to the entire society is clear. "American" society must either take its position on the side of creation of a decent human order without the mythology or practice of racism *or* it must be ever on guard internally as well as externally against men who will no longer be enslaved.

PART III. A:

DIMENSIONS OF BLACK COMMUNITY LIFE – SOCIOLOGY

THE NEGRO MOTHER

LANGSTON HUGHES

Children, I come back today
To tell you a story of the long dark way
That I had to climb, that I had to know
In order that the race might live and grow.
Look at my face—dark as the night—
Yet shining like the sun with love's true light.
I am the child they stole from the sand
Three hundred years ago in Africa's land.
I am the dark girl who crossed the wide sea
Carrying in my body the seed of the free.
I am the woman who worked in the field
Bringing the cotton and the corn to yield.
I am the one who labored as a slave,
Beaten and mistreated for the work that I gave—
Children sold away from me, husband sold, too.
No safety, no love, no respect was I due.
Three hundred years in the deepest South:
But God put a song and a prayer in my mouth.
God put a dream like steel in my soul.
Now, through my children, I'm reaching the goal.
Now, through my children, young and free,
I realize the blessings denied to me.
I couldn't read then. I couldn't write.
I had nothing, back there in the night.
Sometimes, the valley was filled with tears,
But I kept trudging on through the lonely years.
Sometimes, the road was hot with sun,
But I had to keep on till my work was done:
I *had* to keep on! No stopping for me—
I was the seed of the coming Free.

Editor's Note:

One of the ironies of American life is that much of the folk culture or contributions to the arts that are uniquely American and not vestiges of European culture have grown out of the Black Experience. Spirituals and blues have been begrudgingly acknowledged as such, but jazz, which is the logical extension of these musical forms, has always been viewed by the majority as some aloof, esoteric expression. A.B. Spellman writing in *Four Lives in the BeBop Business* sagaciously notes the gross indifference with which America receives those aspects of Afro-American culture that are not "entertaining." He observes that "Jazz's entertainment value has decreased as black artists have conscientiously moved out of the realm of folk art and into the realm of high art."

Jazz, which primarily lends itself to a "statement," or direct message between the artist and listener, has reached such a state of refinement that the riffs and techniques of each artist are as individualistic and identifiable as his signature on his check. The soloist brings all the pathos and joy into his music that his skill and experiences permit. Because of this aspect of jazz, a raging debate has centered around the question of whether or not white musicians can be "great" jazz artists. The issue has to do with the nature of the black and white experience and whether the "normal" tribulations and sorrows of a white person can approximate the heritage of suffering, deprivation, and racist subjugation that accompanies the fact of being black in a white-dominated society, whatever personal or situational problems all people are subject to in the course of living.

In this particular article, Thomas J. Porter depicts the role of jazz as a comment and expression on social matters relevant to the conditions of black people as well as the commonly accepted one of the individual's personal statement of his experiences. The author also points out the difficulty these musicians encounter in getting licenses and recording and club dates, and concludes that social consciousness is not welcome in the "entertainment" field.

THE SOCIAL ROOTS OF AFRO-AMERICAN MUSIC: 1950-1970

THOMAS J. PORTER

The systematic and organized attempt by western civilization either to destroy or cool-out all traces of any cultures which challenge the cultural assumptions of the West dates back to the early fourth century, when Constantine I recognized Christianity as the state religion of the Roman Empire. Whereupon the priests and monks immediately set out to destroy all memorials of ancient civilization, in order to preserve the shaky foundation of the Church. This destructiveness reached the height of ugliness in 391 A.D., when a fanatical group of Christians destroyed the cathedral at Serapis, and the library at Alexandria (the greatest library in the ancient world).

This necessity of western civilization to affirm itself through acts of barbarism (witness the shelling and destruction of the ancient city of Hue in Vietnam, and the threatened destruction of Ankor Wat in Cambodia in the present Indo-China War) has changed over historical time only in the sophistication of its tactics and maneuvers; its barbaric nature has remained intact.

A more recent example of this is stated in a quote by Hank Aaron, the Atlanta Braves' player, "I get letters asking me to retire or do anything, but please don't break Babe Ruth's record." Brother Aaron had better be careful. Perhaps the most brutal example in recent years has been the systematic repression of Black music, particularly that music which began in the mid-fifties with Miles Davis, Charlie Mingus, Max Roach, Sonny Rollins, and Jackie McLean and reached its maturity through the music of John Coltrane, Ornette Coleman, Cecil Taylor, and their musical heirs such as Andrew Hill, John Gilmore, Benny Maupin, Albert Ayler, Archie Shepp, Sonny Murray, etc. The relationship between the conditions of one's life and consciousness has been well established. LeRoi Jones has summed it up this way:

> The most expressive music of any given period will be an exact reflection of what the Negro himself is. It will be a portrait of the Negro in America at that time. Who he thinks he is, what he thinks America or the world to be, given the circumstances, prejudices and delights of that particular America.

It is very important to understand that music, like all art regardless of its form, is ideological. That is, it reflects or transmits certain political, class, and national interests. A creative and revolutionary music, however, is more than just reflective, but criticizes the very social substance of the society, and ultimately contributes towards giving direction to the social reconstruction of that society.

There is no abstract Black music. There is Black music reflecting different political positions of Black people. Ramsey Lewis' music is not the same as Cecil Taylor's. So when we talk about Black music, we mean the most advanced, the most socially conscious music which historically has been the music called "jazz."

Because of the critical nature of Black music by 1960, it became increasingly dangerous to the keepers of the nightmare and, quite possibly, has led to spiritual and physical deaths (John Coltrane, Albert Ayler, Eric Dolphy, Booker Little, Booker Ervin) of some of its major forces.

Despite the horrors of the McCarthy period (an attempt to stifle all progressive political and social thought in America), the Robesons and DuBoises had maintained the continuity of the struggle, regardless of the price. As a result, Blacks emerged seemingly more determined than ever to press forward. This determinedness can, perhaps, best be explained by certain fundamental changes in the material conditions of Blacks. By 1956, one out of every three organized workers in the country was Black (a total of two million Black workers). This meant that Black workers were a crystallized force in the production process of the country, which qualitatively changed their social consciousness and intensified the struggle for rights.

This consciousness took many different forms. Politically, there were the bus boycotts at Baton Rouge in 1953, and Montgomery in 1956-57. There was Brown vs. Board of Education in 1954, and Little Rock in 1958. The sit-ins and the freedom rides intensified the struggle which peaked temporarily at the March on Washington in 1963, finally exploding in the open rebellion at Watts, Newark, Washington, D.C., Detroit, Cincinnati and numerous other cities as a material force in the world-wide liberation struggle. Dr. Martin Luther King, Jr., and Malcolm X emerged as the two major ideological leaders with King the more mature, having hooked up the relationship between the class and national character of our opposition.

Culturally, there was a simultaneous motion. While Black music has historically been the most critical and advanced, not only has there, historically, been a dialectical relationship between the various forms of art, but also between the more advanced forms of art and the changing circumstances of Black people. For instance, Charlie Parker did a benefit concert at the request of Paul Robeson for the brothers who were caught in the McCarthy madness: Coltrane did benefits for FREEDOMWAYS, and Black Arts Repertory Theatre. These bits of tangential information are just to disprove the fact that Black artist/musicians are apolitical and that art somehow functions outside the framework of society.

Charlie Parker's *Another Hairdo* ushered out the konk (a backyard process) and all it symbolized. However it was his musical heirs such as Clifford Brown, Miles Davis, Fats Navarro, Horace Silver, Wardell Gray, John Coltrane, etc., through their hard driving, aggressive music who captured the mood of the masses in the mid-fifties. No wonder this music became known as "hard bop."

While the Miles Davis Quintet of the mid-fifties, which included John Coltrane, instinctively reflected the crystallization of a Black proletariat, it was Mingus (*Fables for Faubus, Scenes of the City*), Max Roach (*We Insist: Freedom Now, Garvey's Ghost,*

Mendacity) and Rollins (*Freedom Suite*) in the late fifties who stated it very clearly. Needless to say, neither Mingus nor Max Roach is recorded with any frequency, or is regularly available in clubs. The album which contains *Fables for Faubus* immediately became unavailable for ten years (it was re-released in 1971). Roach's album, *We Insist: Freedom Now*, is still unavailable. Rollins' *Freedom Suite* has since been retitled twice without the original liner notes written by Rollins.

Musicians began to free themselves from the chains of musical orthodoxy, and the limits of worn-out forms. The changes in the form and substance of the music were very similar to the motion in the political and social spheres. The major innovators were Ornette Coleman, John Coltrane, and Cecil Taylor.

Ornette Coleman's music, almost as if he were setting the pace for the cadences counted off by the marchers, the sit-ins, and freedom riders, added a new rhythmic concept which was complex in its simplicity, not unlike the early New Orleans jazz music in its emphasis on freedom and group improvisation. Coltrane's contributions are many, but his major one was in his further development of the harmonic nature of the music. Coltrane's wide-open, go-for-broke solos, played dialectically against a chordal substance, were very similar to the movement's reliance on the religious substance of our historical tradition passed down from the Nat Turners, David Walkers, to Dr. King and Malcolm. Coltrane's uniting of certain elements of music, heretofore considered dissonant, was very reflective of the emergence of a group cohesiveness of the masses. Cecil Taylor was primarily interested with "ordering the music" as he called it. He was concerned with getting beyond tunes to the construction and organization of new sounds. A. B. Spellman best sums up Taylor's contribution in the following statement:

> There is only one musician who has by general agreement, even among those who disliked his music, been able to incorporate all that he wants to take from classical and modern western composition into his own distinctly, individual kind of blues, without in the least compromising those blues, and that is Cecil Taylor, a kind of Bartok in reverse.

Black music through Coltrane, Taylor, Coleman, and the young musicians who followed them such as Archie Shepp, Andrew Hill, Bobby Hutcherson, Benny Maupin, Wayne Shorter, Joe Henderson, Grachan Moncur III, Joe Chamber, Tony Williams, Richard Davis, Cecil McBee, Freddie Hubbard, the late Booker Little, and Eric Dolphy became the Achilles heel, the weak link (and dangerous) in western culture. The music, like the people, was immersed in western culture, yet digested the forms without becoming overwhelmed by them. Thus by 1964, Afro-American music, in its fully developed form, had moved beyond critical realism (criticism of the forms), the high point of western music, to a music which was both critical and analytical of the social substance of the society. By 1964, it became increasingly evident that efforts were being made to formalize or cool-out *both the music and the movement which had produced it.*

These efforts took many forms including political assassinations. Within four years, both King and Malcolm were dead (to say 'nothing of the two Kennedys). Coltrane, Eric Dolphy, Booker Little, and Otis Redding were also dead by 1968. A new motion in the form of nationalism was superimposed on the Movement in the mid-sixties. This reactionary form of nationalism politically disguised itself as the undefinable notion of "Black Power" which has since emerged as "Black capitalism," occultism, and other mysticisms.

One, therefore, should not be surprised that Stokely Carmichael (the sloganeer of "Black Power") when asked on nationwide television if there were a white person whom he admired replied, "Yes, Hitler"; or that Black paramilitary organizations are openly subsidized by the government, the same government of the Pentagon papers.

Culturally, this trend took the form of occultism and mysticism pushed mainly by certain elements which attempted to romanticize the hustler, pimp, and manchild as the substance of our experience. These liberals (Black and white) cop-out musically and politically. Whether it be poetry or music, they merely formalize art for the purpose of monetary gain, always removing the revolutionary essence first. A recent example of this is Frank Kofsky's book *Black Nationalism and the Revolution in Music,* wherein he attempts to manipulate the images of John Coltrane and Malcolm X to support certain erroneous musical and political theses he holds. Kofsky attempts to establish "Black nationalism" as the material basis guiding the music. Neither Coltrane nor Malcolm would support these simple, reactionary notions; both were wider in scope and vision, both understood very clearly the nature of this society which obviously explains their untimely deaths. National consciousness has always been inherent in Black music but the music has always embodied both the *class* and *national* characteristics in its criticism of the society. Or, as Archie Shepp says, as a musician performs his art, he "transmits a class experience." It has been correctly stated that "there is nothing more international than colonial products, there is nothing

more parochial than colonial labor."* It was the Black musicians who went around the world and broke this limited perspective. The music of the Negro people is acclaimed internationally as being very representative among the best in all music. Even Kofsky realizes this when he talks about the use of Black music as a weapon in the cold war. He is perhaps too much of a racist, and is carrying too much historical baggage to accept the reasons behind the State Department's use of the music. The answer is quite simple: progressive people the world over are not as interested in so-called western music as in Afro-American music.

Kofsky misses these points. Black music is not seeking his acceptance, it musically states its superiority to western music, not out of arrogance, but out of struggle. Coltrane's answers in the following interview negate Kofsky's assumptions:

> *Kofsky:* Some musicians have said that there's a relationship between some of Malcolm's ideas and the music, especially the new music. Do you think there's anything in that?
>
> *Coltrane:* Well, I think that music, being an expression of the human heart, or of the human being itself, does express just what *is* happening. I feel it expresses the whole thing—the whole of human experience at the particular time that it is being expressed.
>
> *Kofsky:* What do you think about the phrase, *the new black music,* as a description of some of the newer styles in jazz?
>
> *Coltrane:* Phrases, I don't know. They don't mean much to me, because usually I don't make phrases, so I don't react too much. It makes no difference to me one way or the other what it's called.
>
> *Kofsky:* If you did make the phrases, could you think of one?
>
> *Coltrane:* I don't think there's a phrase for it, that I could make.
>
> *Kofsky:* The people who use *that* phrase argue that jazz is particularly closely related to the black community and it's an expression of what's happening there. That's why I asked you about your reaction to Malcolm X.
>
> *Coltrane:* Well, I think it's up to the individual musician, call it what you may, for any reason you may. Myself I recognize the artist. I recognize an individual when I see his contribution; and when I know a man's sound, well, to me that's him, that's this man. That's

---

*Robert Rhodes, unpublished manuscript on colonialism.

the way I look at it. Labels, I don't bother with.

Kofsky: But it does seem to be a fact that most of the *changes* in the music—the innovations—have come from Black musicians.

Coltrane: Yes, well this is how it is.

Kofsky: Have you ever noticed—since you've played all over the United States and in all kinds of circumstances—have you ever noticed that the reaction of an audience varies or changes if it's a Black audience or a white audience or a mixed audience? Have you ever noticed that the racial composition of the audience seems to determine how the people respond?

Coltrane: Well, sometimes, yes, and sometimes, no.

Kofsky: Any examples? ·

Coltrane: Sometimes it might appear to be one; you might say . . . it's hard to say, man. Sometimes people like or don't like it, no matter what color they are.*

Despite all efforts by Kofsky to conceal the fact, his intentions are very clear: to freeze the music at a point in time, and politically and culturally manipulate it for his own counter-revolutionary objectives.

Another ideological form which is used to cool-out the music is the current blues thrust. I am referring to current efforts to affirm the blues of the 30's and 40's, completely out of historical context, and establish them as the most progressive of all Black music today. Peasant culture is great culture, but must be viewed in a historical context.

One of the goals of the psychology of colonialism is to keep oppressed people culturally frozen in time, preferably in a period where the political and social relationships are to the advantage of the oppressor. The "blues" content of our music *will always be there* whether it is in Cecil Taylor's *Unit Structure* or the Collective Black Artist's rendition of *C. C. Rider;* albeit at a higher level in accordance with the new conditions.

Perhaps the most sophisticated mechanism used is to separate the music psychologically and physically from the masses, the consciousness from the circumstances. Politically, there is the case of Muhammad Ali, whose title was taken from him, at a time when a Black heavyweight champion of the world who refused to be inducted would have serious consequences for the American army, since large numbers of young Blacks are needed in that army. However, Ali was allowed to fight years later and was exonerated by the Supreme Court of draft evasion charges. Another example is the publishing of materials which are progressive in a certain historical context, such as the *Wretched of the Earth* by Fanon, when it had already been superseded by a different political motion.

Culturally this frozen-in-time syndrome is done in several ways. Records such as Mingus's *Fables for Faubus* and Roach's *We Insist: Freedom Now* are held off the market for as long as ten years or released for a short period, only to suddenly become unavailable for all time. We do not yet have all the recordings of Coltrane, Dolphy, Billie Holiday, or Charlie Parker. Clubs are usually located out of the Black community, and are usually priced out of the reach of the average working person.

Socially conscious musicians such as Shepp, Cecil Taylor, Mingus, Max Roach, and the Collective Black Artist, are seldom recorded or featured in clubs or on the festival circuit.

This paper is by no means a history of Black music, but is an attempt to explode certain myths, point out certain dangers, and suggest certain solutions. Simple solutions or narrow-minded subjective analysis not related to concrete reality will only deepen the crisis. Despite its condemnation of western civilization, most art—Black or white—in this country is still rooted in the West. That which purports to relate to the East seems to be stuck in 39 A.D. or B.C., while the Eastern World (Asia, Latin America and Africa) is rapidly embracing the scientific world view, politically and culturally. Those advocates of Negro or Black exceptionalism are protecting their petty, middle-class positions which is why they get so much play.

The Jazz and Peoples' Movement and the Collective Black Artist represent some of the more progressive developments musically, but there are still pockets of occultism, mysticism and reactionary nationalism which are fetters and need to be eliminated. Black music is already international; attempts to nationalize it represent a step backward.

What is desperately needed is a scientific concept of the function of art in society.

---

*Frank Kofsky, *Black Nationalism and the Revolution in Music.* Pathfinder Press, New York, 1970.

Editor's Note:

The church was for many years the only social organization in the United States that Afro-Americans could claim as their own. It was both a refuge, and a training ground for those with leadership potential. The black church was also responsible for the inception of other institutions, such as universities, fraternal orders or lodges, and mutual aid societies. The drudgery of everyday living could be left outside the doors of the church. People who were forced in all other situations to be subservient, abject, and the footstools of society could enter the confines of the church and become their other selves. To be a pastor, choirmaster, head of an auxiliary group, youth leader, deacon, or principal usher was to occupy a position of responsibility and status that was denied black people in any other circumstances. Thus, the role that the church played was a major one.

Outstanding leaders and politicians came from the ranks of the ministry and church community. Nat Turner, Morris Brown, Richard Allen, James Varick, Absalom Jones, Lemuel Hayes, John Chavis, and Lott Cary were some who distinguished themselves. Richard Allen and Absalom Jones, rejecting the segregated gallery and "nigger pews" that white Christians made available for black members, organized the Free African Society of Philadelphia, which evolved into an African Church, with affiliations in the Protestant Episcopal Church. Jones became its first Negro rector and later founded an insurance company and a school for black children in Philadelphia. Allen decided to remain a Methodist and with fifteen other delegates to a convention of Negro Methodists in Philadelphia, April 9, 1816 founded the African Methodist Episcopal Church. James Varick, in 1796 had also withdrawn from the Methodist Episcopal Church and by 1821 had formed the African Methodist Episcopal Zion Church. Andrew Bryan began preaching as a slave and is credited with large conversions to the Baptist religion. Lott Cary also began as a slave, received the license of a Baptist preacher, purchased his freedom and that of his children, organized a missionary society, and then went himself as a missionary to Liberia. John Chavis, a Presbyterian clergyman in Virginia, was sent to Princeton to demonstrate that Negroes could achieve higher learning and was later assigned as master of a school for whites. Lemuel Hayes was a Congregationalist and the first Negro pastor to a white congregation. Prince Hall and fourteen other men were initiated by an army lodge in 1775 into the mysteries of Freemasonary. They applied to the Grand Lodge of England for a warrant in 1784. This warrant was issued to "African Lodge, No. 459," with Prince Hall as master that same year, but it was not received until 1787.

The Negro Church in America by E.F. Frazier is both comprehensive and thorough. The following selections depict the role of the church in fostering and developing educational institutions and the church's adaptation to the urban environment as manifest in the storefront church. The storefront church is found in every community where there are black people, particularly the masses of poor ones. It fills a vital need, provides partial continuity with their roots, and serves as both a refuge and springboard.

THE NEGRO CHURCH IN AMERICA

E. F. FRAZIER

The Church and Economic Co-operation

As DuBois pointed out more than fifty years ago, 'a study of economic co-operation among Negroes must begin with the Church group.' It was in order to establish their own churches that Negroes began to pool their meagre economic resources and buy buildings and the land on which they stood. As an indication of the small beginnings of these churches, we may note that the value of the property of the African Methodist Episcopal Church in 1787 was only $2,500. During the next century the value of the property of this organization increased to nine million dollars. The Negroes in the other Methodist denominations, and especially in the numerous Baptist Churches, were contributing on a similar scale a part of their small earnings for the construction of churches. At the same time, out of the churches grew mutual aid societies. The earliest society of this type was the Free African Society which was organized in Philadelphia in 1787. We have already noted that the Society was organized by Absalom Jones and Richard Allen, the two Negroes who led the secession from the Methodist Church. At the time the Society was organized, Negroes were migrating to Philadelphia in large numbers and the need for some sort of mutual aid was becoming urgent. The Society became a 'curious sort of ethical and beneficial brotherhood' under the direction of Jones and Allen who exercised a 'parental discipline' over its members. The avowed purpose of this organization was to 'support one another in sickness, and for the benefit of their widows and fatherless children.'

In the cities throughout the United States numerous beneficial societies were organized to provide assistance in time of sickness or death. Many of these beneficial societies, like the Free African Society, were connected with churches. These societies continued to be established throughout the nineteenth century. For example, in Atlanta in 1898 there were nine beneficial societies which had been founded from soon after the Civil War up to 1897. Six of these beneficial societies were connected with churches. The names of these beneficial societies are not without significance. At the Wheat Street Baptist Church, for example, there were two beneficial societies—the Rising Star and the Sisters of Love, while at the Bethel (Methodist) Church was the Daughters of Bethel. These associations for mutual aid which were generally known as beneficial societies were often the germ out of which grew the secular insurance companies.

The role of religion and the Negro church in more elementary forms of economic co-operation among Negroes may be seen more clearly in the rural mutual aid societies that sprang up among freedmen after Emancipation. They were formed among the poor, landless Negroes who were thrown upon their own resources. These societies were organized to meet the crises of life—sickness and death; consequently, they were known as 'sickness and burial' societies. The important fact for our study is that these benevolent societies grew out of the Negro church and were inspired by the spirit of Christian charity. They were supported by the pennies which the Negroes could scrape together in order to aid each other in time of sickness but more especially to insure themselves a decent Christian burial. The influence of the simple religious conceptions of the Negro folk and the Bible is revealed in the names of these mutual aid societies which continue to exist in the rural South. They bear such names as 'Love and Charity,' 'Builders of the Walls of Jerusalem,' 'Sons and Daughters of Esther,' 'Brothers and Sisters of Charity,' and 'Brothers and Sisters of Love.'

These 'sickness and burial' societies should be distinguished from the fraternal organizations which played an important role in early economic co-operation among Negroes. Fraternal organizations like the Negro Masonic Lodge and the Odd Fellows came into existence among the free Negroes in the North as the result of the influence of the white fraternal organizations. On the other hand, Negroes began before the outbreak of the Civil War to organize fraternal organizations which reflected their own interests and outlook on life. One such secret society, the Knights of Liberty, was organized by a preacher, Reverend Moses Dickson, who was born in Cincinnati in 1824. This organization was active in the underground railroad and claimed to have nearly 50,000 members in 1856. Dickson joined the Union Army and after the Civil War he disbanded the Knights of Liberty. In 1871 he organized the first Temple and Tabernacle of the Knights and Daughters of Tabor in Independence, Missouri. The object of this secret society was 'to help to spread the Christian religion and education' and its members were advised to 'acquire real estate, avoid intemperance, and cultivate true manhood.' At the end of the nineteenth century this society claimed to have nearly 200,000 members in eighteen jurisdictions scattered from Maine to California and from the Great Lakes to the Gulf of Mexico.

The organization and development of the Grand United Order of True Reformers provides a better example of the manner in which an organiza-tion under the leadership of a preacher fired with religious zeal played an important role in economic co-operation and the accumulation of capital. The founder of the organization was a Reverend Washington Browne who was born a slave in Georgia in 1849. During the Civil War he ran away from a new master and made his way to the North where he received a meagre education. After Emancipation he returned to Alabama where he joined a movement of the Good Templars against the whisky ring. But after observing the various benevolent and burial societies among Negroes, he decided that Negroes should have a separate organization adapted to their special needs. In 1876 he succeeded in bringing together in a single organization, known as the Grand Fountain of True Reformers, twenty-seven Fountains with 2,000 members. Although he was not successful in creating a mutual benefit society, through his paper, *The Reformer*, he attracted the attention of the Organization of True Reformers in Virginia. He was invited to Richmond and became the Grand Worthy Master of the Virginia organization.

The True Reformers organized a variety of enterprises, including a weekly newspaper, a real estate firm, a bank, a hotel, a building and loan association, and a grocery and general merchandising store. The True Reformers took the lead in incorporating an insurance feature in its programme for the benefit of its members, an example of which was followed by the other fraternal organizations among Negroes. The insurance ventures failed because they did not have sound actuarial basis and were not under government supervision. Nevertheless, the Negro gained a certain experience and training which prepared him for his more successful business ventures.

The Church and Education

The educational development of Negroes does not reflect to the same extent as their churches and mutual aid associations the racial experience and peculiar outlook on life of Negroes. Education, that is Western or European education, was something totally foreign to the Negro's way of life. This was because, as Woodson has written, 'The first real educators to take up the work of enlightening American Negroes were clergymen interested in the propagation of the gospel among the heathen in the new world.' In fact, the purpose of education was primarily to transmit to the Negro the religious ideas and practices of an alien culture. In the North the strictly religious content of education was supplemented by other elements, whereas in the South limitations were even placed upon enabling the Negro to read the Bible. By 1850 there were large numbers of Negroes attending schools in northern cities. Then, too, individual Negroes managed to acquire a higher education and most of these were men who were preparing to become ministers.

This does not mean that Negroes took no initiative in setting up schools and acquiring an education. The free Negroes in the cities contributed to the support of schools for Negro children. Generally, the support which the free Negroes provided was greater in southern cities like Baltimore, Washington, and Charleston, South Carolina, than in New York and Philadelphia. As early as 1790, the Brown Fellowship Society in Charleston maintained schools for the free Negro children. An important fact about the schools which the free Negroes maintained was that many of them were Sunday schools. On the eve of the Civil War, 'There were then in Baltimore Sunday schools about 600 Negroes. They had formed themselves into a Bible Association, which had been received into the convention of the Baltimore Bible Society. In 1825 the Negroes there had a day and night school giving courses in Latin and French. Four years later there appeared an "African Free School," with an attendance of from 150 to 175 every Sunday.' Although the Sunday schools represented before the Civil War one of the most important agencies in the education of Negroes, nevertheless the churches through their ministers urged parents to send their children to whatever schools were available.

After Emancipation the initiative on the part of Negroes in providing education for themselves was given a much freer scope. This was because of the great educational crusade which was carried on by northern white missionaries among the freedmen. As the Union armies penetrated the South, the representatives of northern missionary societies and churches sent funds and teachers in the wake of the advancing armies. The majority of the men and women or 'school marms,' as they were called, were inspired by a high idealism and faith in the intellectual capacity of Negroes. They laid the foundation for or established most of the Negro colleges in the South. Working with the Freedmen's Bureau which was created by an Act of Congress in 1865 to aid the freedmen in assuming the responsibilities of citizens, they also laid the foundation for a public school system for the newly emancipated Negro. It was Negroes trained in these schools supported by northern churches and philanthropy who became the educated leaders among Negroes.

The schools—elementary, secondary, and those which provided the beginnings of college education—were permeated with a religious and moral outlook. The graduates of these schools went forth as mission-

aries to raise the moral and religious level of the members of their race. Many of the men were preachers or became preachers. A preacher who was a graduate of a Baptist college founded by white missionaries and who had helped to make the bricks for the buildings of the college, said that when he was graduated, the white president addressed him as follows: 'I want you to go into the worst spot in this State and build a school and a church.' This minister followed the instructions of his white mentor and established the school that provided the primary school and later the only secondary school for Negroes in the county and four Baptist Churches. This is typical of the manner in which the Negro preacher who was often the best educated man in the community took the initiative in establishing schools.

An educated and distinguished bishop in the African Methodist Episcopal Church who was the father of the most distinguished American Negro painter, wrote in his history of the Church in 1867: 'For it is one of the brightest pages in the history of our Church, that while the Army of the Union were forcing their victorious passage through the southern land and striking down treason, the missionaries of our Church in the persons of Brown, Lynch, Cain, Handy, Stanford, Steward, and others, were following in their wake and establishing the Church and the school house. . . .' The work of the Negro preacher in establishing schools was especially important since the southern States provided only a pittance of public funds for the education of Negro children. When the Julius Rosenwald Fund contributed to the building of more than 5,000 schools for Negroes in the South in order to stimulate the public authorities to appropriate money for Negro schools, Negro churches played an important role in making possible the schools aided by the Rosenwald Fund. Negroes contributed 17 per cent of the total cost of the schools which amounted to over $28,000,000. They raised much of their share in this amount through church suppers and programmes under the auspices of their churches.

The impetus among Negroes to build institutions of higher education was due primarily to their need for an educated ministry. But the desire on the part of the masses for an educated ministry was far from universal. The masses of Negroes were still impressed by the ignorant and illiterate minister who often boasted that he had not been corrupted by wicked secular learning. Soon after the 'invisible institution' of the slaves was integrated into the institutional church, it was feared that a schism would occur in the African Methodist Episcopal Church as the result of the conflict between the ignorant and intelligent elements in the church.

136

Nevertheless, the African Methodist Episcopal Church succeeded in establishing a number of so-called colleges and universities. The African Methodist Episcopal Zion Church and the Colored Methodist Episcopal Church also established schools. The Baptists had to depend upon local efforts. In South Carolina the Negro Baptists who became dissatisfied with the white control of the college for Negroes finally established their own school.

The schools and colleges maintained by the Negro church denominations have never attained a high level as educational institutions. They have generally nurtured a narrow religious outlook and have restricted the intellectual development of Negroes even more than the schools established for Negroes by the white missionaries. This has been due only partly to lack of financial resources. It hardly needs to be emphasized that there was no intellectual tradition among Negroes to sustain colleges and universities. The attendance of Negro students at private colleges has reflected the social stratification of the Negro community. The children of the upper class in the Negro community have generally attended the schools established by the Congregational Church and the better type of schools supported by the white Methodists and Baptists for Negroes. Nevertheless, the Negro church has affected the entire intellectual development and outlook of Negroes. This has been due both to the influence of the Negro church which has permeated every phase of social life and to the influence of the Negro preacher whose authoritarian personality and anti-intellectualism has cast a shadow over the intellectual outlook of Negroes.

Religion in the 'Storefront' Church

The inadequacy, from a religious standpoint, of the institutional denominations accounts for the 'storefront' churches which one finds in Negro communities in American cities. In the survey of Negro churches in twelve cities, to which we have referred, out of a total of 2,104 church buildings, 777 were 'storefront' churches or houses and the remainder were conventional church buildings. These 'storefront' churches, as the name suggests, are generally conducted in unrented or abandoned stores, though some may be found in run-down houses. They are located in the poorer and deteriorated areas of Negro communities. They often owe their existence to the initiative on the part of a 'Jack-leg' preacher, that is, a semi-literate or an uneducated preacher, who gathers about him the poorer Negroes who seek a religious leader in the city. Nearly a half of 777 'storefront' churches in the study referred to above were Baptist and a somewhat smaller number were known as

Holiness and Spiritualist churcnes. There were less than ten churches identified with any of the three regularly established Methodist denominations though many of the members of these 'storefront' churches had been in Methodist churches.

The 'storefront' church represents an attempt on the part of the migrants, especially from the rural areas of the South, to re-establish a type of church in the urban environment to which they were accustomed. They want a church, first of all, in which they are known as people. In the large city church they lose their identity completely and, as many of the migrants from the rural South have said, neither the church members nor the pastor know them personally. Sometimes they complain with bitterness that the pastor of the large city church knows them only as the number on the envelope in which they place their dues. In wanting to be treated as human beings, they want status in the church which was the main or only organization in the South in which they had status. Some of the statements concerning their reason for leaving the big denominational churches was that 'back home in the South' they had a seat in the church that everyone recognized as theirs and that if the seat were empty on Sunday the pastor came to their homes to find out the cause of their absence.

The desire for the warm and intimate association of fellow worshippers in church services was not the only reason why the 'storefront' church was more congenial to the recently urbanized Negro than the cold impersonal atmosphere of the large denominational city church. In these small 'storefront' churches the Negro migrant could worship in a manner to which he had been accustomed. The sermon by the pastor is of a type to appeal to traditional ideas concerning hell and heaven and the imagery which the Negro has acquired from the Bible. Much emphasis is placed upon sins of the flesh, especially sexual sins. The preacher leads the singing of the Spirituals and other hymns with which the Negroes with a folk background are acquainted. The singing is accompanied by 'shouting' or holy dancing which permits the maximum of free religious expression on the part of the participants.

In the cities of the North and even in the cities in the South, these 'storefront' churches are constantly being organized by all kinds of so-called preachers in order to attract lower-class Negroes. During the 1920s when southern Negroes were flocking to Harlem in New York City, it was found that only 54 out of 140 churches in Harlem were housed in regular church structures. The remainder were of the 'storefront' type which had been organized by preachers, many of whom were exploiters and charlatans. They based their appeal on the Negro's desire to find salvation in the next world and to escape from sickness and the insecurities of this world. One of these churches advertised:

We Believe that all Manner of Disease Can Be Cured
Jesus is the Doctor
Services on Sunday.

The large number of churches in Negro communities in the North as well as in the South has raised the question as to whether the Negro population is over-churched. There is no way of answering this question and it is irrelevant in a sense when one considers the important role of the Negro church in the organization of the Negro community. The vast majority of Negroes have constituted a lower class, gaining a living as common labourers and in domestic and personal service. Among these people there is little associational life and the churches of all types represent, as we have seen, the main form of organized social life. Even when Negroes have broken away from the traditional churches they have sought in new religious groups a way of life which would conform to their needs.

Afro-American parents have always valued education and desired it as one of the viable means of improving the condition of their children's lives. On the other hand, many parents are alienated from the schools and resent teacher attitudes. Attitudes toward school and education must be considered separately. Hall and Shipman conducted an attitudinal survey asking lower-class black parents (among other questions), What did you miss most in life that you would like your children to have? Over 70 percent responded, Education. The answer was supplied by the respondents, not checked from a list. They could have answered money, happiness, health, or any number of things. These parents recognize that they are second-class citizens and that their children suffer accordingly, hence their anger. The demand for community control or decentralization of school systems will probably continue as long as the system works for the affluent.

"Clash of Cultures in the Classroom" by Kenneth Clark examines some of the euphemistic camouflage that allows practices detrimental to the growth and development of black youngsters to flourish in the schools. One of these subterfuges has been that of equivalence in goals for the poor and the wealthy, which ignores the fact that as the needs in these communities differ, so the goals and techniques should reflect these differences. Clark also points out that much of the damage that has afflicted black youngsters has grown out of fashionable trends and positive-sounding assertions about learning styles and deficiencies of youngsters whom teachers decide are incapable of learning or being taught.

Education has been viewed traditionally as one of the more significant vehicles for achievement and mobility. This view holds true for the white middle class, but does not apply to poor whites, blacks, and other minorities. Hollingshead, Stendler, Abrahamson, and Allison Davis are some of a number of researchers who have found significant relationships between the social class of students and the rewards they receive in education. Havighurst has presented data that typify the schools as sorting and selecting agencies—that is, selecting and training those considered most able (based on IQ) for higher status in society. Vast amounts of data have indicated that inner-city schools have fewer resources and materials than white middle-class schools. Teachers tend to have less experience, transfers are more frequent, and significant numbers of those who are ill or suffering from some serious maladjustment are placed in ghetto schools to pass out their tenure days until retirement. There are excellent, dedicated teachers in ghetto schools, but their numbers are few. Inner-city schools often serve as dumping grounds or punishment centers for teachers and students alike.

CLASH OF CULTURES IN THE CLASSROOM

KENNETH B. CLARK

The clash of cultures in the classroom is not a new problem for American education. In fact, the entire argument that surrounded the development of public education in America was an argument in terms of the role of the government and education in facilitating social mobility. The decision to develop public schools—free public education in America—was essentially a social, economic, and political decision. It represented a major development in the concept of education as an instrument for facilitating movement among classes, rather than as a process that should be restricted to a particular class. I think a very important case could be made that this is a major American contribution to the educational and to the democratic processes; namely, using education as an instrument for socio-economic mobility as distinct from the traditional European approach to education as something that is restricted to more privileged classes.

Role of class

Among social scientists Allison Davis at the University of Chicago has contributed most significantly to our understanding of the educational implications of differences among social classes, and particularly, the difference between the middle-class status or middle-class aspiration of teachers in our public schools, and the fact that the majority of children in the public schools are of working class backgrounds. More recently Patricia Sexton of New York University and Frank Riessman have documented by systematic facts that the quality of education provided in our public schools varied directly according to the socio-economic status and level of the pupils in a given school—that is, the higher the socio-economic status of the average pupil or student of the given school, the higher the educational achievement of these children.

I think Patricia Sexton's book, *Education and Income,* is one of the most devastating documentations of the degree to which social class factors have insidiously permeated the American educational system, that I have (I was going to say "pleasure," but it was certainly not a pleasure) read. Frank Riessman's discussion of the culturally deprived child verifies this, showing unquestionably that public education in America within the last three or four decades is no longer an instrument facilitating social mobility, but has become probably one of the most effective techniques for maintaining class differences and cleavages.

The whole controversy concerning the whole desegregation issue, seems to be basically an issue involving cultural, socio-economic class variables. It is no longer possible for Americans to ignore the fact that public education in America has been contaminated by educationally irrelevant factors such as race and socio-economic status.

One of the most fashionable topics for discussion among educators today is the problem of the education of the culturally deprived child. There have been within the past two or three years countless seminars and symposia organized around this topic. During the summer of 1962, Columbia University Teachers College had what must have been a marathon symposium on cultural deprivation that lasted about six weeks. Out of that symposium, I think, Columbia decided to set up a department on the culturally deprived child. Recently, distinguished educator, diplomat, former president of Harvard University, Mr. James Bryant Conant, popularized the term "social dynamite" in his report on the problems of urban-suburban education. The term social dynamite was used by Mr. Conant in describing the social implications of inadequate education of what he called urban, slum children, another name for the socially deprived. So there is no question that there has been a great deal of concern and discussion, many books and articles dealing with this problem of cultural, socio-economic variables, and the effectiveness of the educational process.

Faulty assumptions

I should like to share with you my view of some of the assumptions which seem to me to underlie these discussions, some of the consequences of these assumptions, and some of my own ideas as to which of these assumptions are worthy of attention and which ones merely make the problem more difficult, if not insoluble. The assumptions concerning the education of culturally deprived children can be divided into two types.

The first group of assumptions, which I will call well-intentioned assumptions, many of them postulated under the guise of social science theory or facts or humanitarian considerations, seem to have dominated educational theory during the last thirty or forty years. Among these well-intentioned or social-science-supported assumptions are:

That each child should be educated in terms of his own needs and his capacities. On the surface this seems like a perfectly logical position and has been offered by individuals whose humanitarian and democratic instincts should certainly not be questioned. I hope to demonstrate, however, that this particular assumption has led to a great deal of confusion, misunderstanding, and injustice in the educational process.

Another assumption which falls under this category is that children from working-class cultures (and this second assumption necessarily follows from the first) need not only a different approach in the educational process, but a different type of education than children from middle-class families. One of the clearest formulations and expressions of this point of view, I think, is found in Conant's book, *Slums and Suburbs.* He categorically makes this distinction in terms of the type and quality of education which are to be provided for children in what he calls the urban slums, as distinct from the quality of education to be provided for children in the more privileged suburban communities. And those of you who read that book, I hope, were as shocked as I in seeing that Mr. Conant took his New England noblesse oblige, snobbish attitude toward the educational process, by categorizing different kinds of education which should be found or provided for children in the suburbs. He had a distinction within the suburbs according to intellectual hierarchy and recognized that even children in the privileged suburbs were not all brilliant and were going to wind up at Harvard, but that some consideration should be made for those children who were not so bright, but whose parents wanted them to go to college anyway, so you send them to junior colleges. But no such distinction is made for the underprivileged youngster in the urban centers, and particularly Negro youngsters. (Mr. Conant reserved most of his praise for what is one of the most shockingly discriminatory segregated school set-ups in the entire United States, namely, the public school system of Chicago, where Negro youngsters are systematically being denied the right to a meaningful and effective education under the leadership of Ben Willis, the darling of the Ford Foundation.) It is to me fantastic that someone with his alleged breadth and depth of educational insights and understandings could have written the kind of book that Mr. Conant wrote under the title *Slum and Suburbs*, asking for class differentiation in the educational process. It was even more fantastic that the educators who reviewed this book did not nail this for the type of moribund, early nineteenth-century, educational snobbery that it actually is.

Further assumptions are as follows: One cannot expect from culturally deprived children adequate educational performance in the classroom because they come from homes in which there is no stimulation for educational achievement. This generalization is usually supported by such specifics as the absence of books and of discussions that would stimulate the intellectual curiosity of children. (It is assumed that in homes in which there are books that these books are read or that these books in any way influence the child.) One finds the assumption stated over and over again that children in the second or third grade cannot be expected to learn to read because their parents do not have books in the home. This assumption seems to me to be in conflict with an earlier educational assumption that parents at home should not attempt to teach their children to read, and certainly not the books that they have on their shelves.

Another of these assumptions would be that children from deprived communities bring into the classroom certain psychological problems which are peculiar to their low socio-economic status and which interfere with the educational process in the classroom.

I repeat, these are assumptions, which for the present I think we can classify as well-intentioned, humanitarian, social-science-theory-based assumptions concerning the difficulty in dealing with the culturally deprived child educationally.

The I.Q. trap

I want to add another of these well-intentioned assumptions; namely, that one can predict the future academic success of the child by knowing his I.Q. score obtained early in the elementary grades. Some educational systems begin to give children I.Q. tests by the first or second grade, and classify them and relegate them to various types of educational procedures on this basis. The test scores will follow them for the rest of their lives. This is considered efficient and economic, so that you don't really waste your time trying to teach children who cannot learn. And this, by the way, is related to the first assumption—that a child should be educated according to his needs, his status in life, and his capacities.

The second group of assumptions are those which I think can be categorically recognized for what they are, namely, class and racial snobbery, and reflecting clear-cut social science ignorance, such as, that it's not really worth putting the time and effort into teaching them because, after all they will only become frustrated. There is no point in their having high academic aspirations if their reality will be restricted to menial jobs. In the 1960's teachers in the New York public school system, whom my white students have interviewed, said that Negro children are inherently inferior in intelligence and therefore cannot be expected to learn as much or as readily as white children; and that all one would do, if one tried to teach them as if they could learn, would be to develop in them serious emotional disturbances—frustrations and anxieties. The humanitarian thing to do, therefore, for these children is to provide schools essentially as custodial institutions rather than educational institutions. I assure you I am not exaggerating. I have in my files many such reports which white students of mine interviewing principals and teachers in the New York City public school system, under the guise that they are interested in the professional teaching, have gotten from a substantial proportion (fifty percent) of the teachers and administrators so interviewed.

It is my contention that each of the above assumptions is essentially an alibi for educational neglect, and in no way is a reflection of the nature of the educational process. Each of these assumptions—the well-intentioned as well as the obvious reflection of prejudice and ignorance—contributes to the perpetuation of inferior education for lower-status children, whether their lower status is socio-economic or racial. Each intensifies racial and class cleavages in our schools and therefore perpetuates and extends such cleavages in our society. Each, when implemented in an educational procedure, makes the public schools and public education not instruments in facilitating social mobility, but very effective instruments in widening socio-economic and racial cleavages in our society, and in imposing class rigidities on our society.

Self-fulfilling prophecy

It is my contention that the most insidious consequence of these assumptions is that they are self-fulfilling prophecies. The fallacy of the assumptions does not mean that they will not be demonstrated to be effective. Once one organizes an educational system wherein children are placed in tracks or that certain judgments about their ability determine what is done for them or how much they are taught or not taught, the horror is that the results tend to justify the assumptions.

The use of intelligence test scores to brand children for life, to determine education based upon tracks and homogeneous groupings of children, are devices which impose on our public school system an intolerable, and I think, undemocratic social hierarchy, and defeats the initial functions of public education. Such devices induce and perpetuate the very pathology which they claim to remedy. Children who are treated as if they are ineducable almost invariably become ineducable. This I would like to call educational atrophy. It is generally known that if an arm or a leg be bound so that it cannot be used, eventually it becomes unusable. This is what we mean by self-fulfilling prophecy in this tautological approach to the discussion of the culturally deprived child.

The consequence of this tremendous wastage in human intellectual potential, based upon fallacious assumptions about the educability of groups of children, is tremendous. The specifics of this wastage, as I see it, are that these children are tool-less early in their school life; are treated as if they are not worthy of respect and are not capable of being taught or educated.

They are not fooled by the various euphemisms that educators use to disguise educational snobbery. From the earliest grades a child knows when he has been relegated to a level that is considered less than adequate. Whether you use letters, numbers, or dog or animal names to describe these groups, within days after these procedures are imposed the children know exactly what they mean. Those children who are relegated to the inferior groups suffer a sense of humiliation, a deep sense of unworthiness, feelings of

inferiority, which stamp their entire attitude toward school and the learning process.

This seems to me to be clearly related to the high drop-out statistics, the hostility, aggression, the seeming unmanageability of these children in such schools. They are in a sense revolting against a deep and pervasive attack upon their dignity and integrity as human beings. Sometimes the results are tragic to observe. This is the essence of what Mr. Conant calls social dynamite. Dynamite that is planted by educators themselves and by a society that seems incapable of understanding its problems of justice; that the dignity and integrity of the human being can not be flagrantly violated in an institution which is called educational. So far our society has not addressed itself to this fundamental while it discusses, in an ostrich-like way, the deprived child—as if he were some special kind of human being, not unlike a leper.

This is my diagnosis. It is obviously the diagnosis of an extremist, a biased individual, who has forfeited his membership in the educators' club—without, I assure you, any regret.

Therapy

What do I suggest as therapy? The first ingredient of my therapeutic prescription is that the so-called culturally deprived child no longer be called a culturally deprived child, because I think the term cultural deprivation is too passive a term. We should be courageous enough to define these children in more accurate descriptive terms, namely, children who are being denied their rights as human beings. These should be called socially denied children or rejected children; children who are rejected by the total conspiracy of a seemingly unconcerned society. I repeat, I think the term cultural deprivation masks the significant aspects of the process, masks the fact that these are human beings who are not in just some God-given state, but are deliberately and chronically victimized by the larger society in general, and by educational institutions, specifically.

Secondly, I think that if we use a term that describes the actual denial and injustice that are imposed upon these children, rather than just their fate, then we might be in a better position to know what to do in order to salvage. And I would suggest that maybe one of the things that we should do is to get rid of our guilt-determined sentimentalism and oversolicitousness in the actual educational process. Let us approach these children in terms of educational requirements, standards, and demands, as if they were human beings and not lepers. Let us not teach these children as if they were different, as if one had to be specially careful how you teach them to read. I submit that there is no psychological or educational evidence, Martin Deutsch to the contrary notwithstanding, that so-called low-socio-economic background children have any greater difficulty in learning to read than any other child will have in learning to read. There is no evidence that there is any cultural factor that is relevant to the complexity of the learning process. To me the irony in this type of discussion and particularly in my perspective of it, is that those very teachers, supervisors, and social scientists who espouse these doctrines of unbridgeable cultural gaps in the educational progress—gaps so wide, say they, that they defy educational effectiveness—are for the most part themselves the product of earlier groups of deprived human beings.

The human memory apparently plays interesting tricks. Allison Davis, I think contributes to obscuring the issue when he insists that teachers, by virtue of their being teachers, are all middle-class. This may be just a temporary phenomenon. Certainly, the majority of teachers in the New York City public school system are first or second or at best third generation products of educationally, culturally, and linguistically handicapped groups. The educational system was sufficiently successful and effective to permit these individuals to move upward in the educational, economic, and social ladder. It is fascinating to hear them—Negro and white—say to me, that the present group of deprived human beings are structurally, organically, or economically incapable of profiting from the educational process.

Children can learn

I submit that either I am wrong, or the very fact that these individuals are espousing this position means that they are examples of the fact that I am right. We need clarity and understanding of the fact that human beings, without regard to their economic, social, cultural, or racial backgrounds are modifiable, that all groups of children have the potential to learn and can be educated.

In the light of the interest of the President of the United States, we are now assured that mentally retarded children can learn. I assure you that the majority of culturally-deprived children are not mentally retarded. If we can demonstrate that it is possible to teach organically defective children certain basic skills we can surely demonstrate that it is possible to teach socially and economically denied children academic skills. The needs and capacities of any given child cannot be determined by any observation of the color or economic group to which he belongs. Human intellectual potentials vary as widely

in one group as they do in all other groups. There is a potential Mozart, Beethoven, Einstein, and Bunche among all groups of children in our society, save those who are clearly organically or intellectually defective. The type of education espoused by Conant, I submit, is arrant nonsense. The cure which he suggests is really the social dynamite. Education of human beings in terms of someone else's assumption of what social and economic level they should belong to can only lead to social stagnation.

I hold that the first eight years of schooling of all American children should be exactly the same, without regard to the gimmick which my colleagues, the psychologists, have imposed upon the unsuspecting American public—the gimmick of the I.Q. There is no better predictor of the future educational potential of the child than the observation of his actual educational performance under optimum, supervised, effective teaching in the first eight years of his school life.

I maintain also that the schools should not and must not assume the responsibility for compensating for all deficits that are relevant to the effectiveness of the educational process which are found in the larger community, including the home. This compensation need concern itself in the educational institution only with those things which are relevant to the educational process. It specifically therefore should concern itself only with such matters as superior teaching, extra stimulation, educational enrichment.

I submit further that educators, parents, and those of us who are really concerned with the human aspects of American public education should dare to look the I.Q. straight in the eye, and reject it or relegate it to the place where it belongs. The I.Q. cannot be considered a sacred or even a relevant factor in making decisions about the future of the child. It should not be used to shackle children, because if the I.Q. is so misused it will contribute to the wastage of human potential. The I.Q. can be a valuable educational tool within the limits of its utility, namely, as an index of what needs to be done for a particular child in the educational situation. The I.Q. as an end product or an end decision for children is criminally neglectful. The I.Q. used as the Russians use it, namely to determine where one must start, to determine what a particular child needs to bring him up to maximum effectiveness, is a valuable education supplement. The I.Q. should not be used as a basis for segregating children and assuming that this is where the child will end up educationally.

A class war

"The clash of cultures in the classroom" is

essentially a class war, a socio-economic and racial warfare being waged on the battleground of our schools, with middle-class and middle-class-aspiring teachers being provided with a powerful arsenal of half truths, prejudices, and rationalizations, arrayed against hopelessly outclassed working-class youngsters. At present this is an uneven balance, particularly since, like most battles, it comes under the guise of righteousness.

The children are being systematically humiliated, categorized, classified, relegated to groups in terms of slow learners, trainables, untrainables, Track A, Track B, the "Pussycats," the "Bunnies," etc. But it all adds up to the fact that they are not being taught; and not being taught, they fail. They have a sense of personal humiliation and unworthiness. They react negatively and hostilely and aggressively to the educational process. They hate teachers, they hate schools, they hate anything that seems to impose upon them this denigration, because they are not being respected as human beings, because they are sacrificed in a machinery of efficiency and expendability, because their dignity and potential as human beings are being obscured and ignored in terms of educationally irrelevant factors—their manners, their initial pattern of speech, their dress, or their apparent disinterest.

I submit and I urgently plead that the battle must shift its emphasis. Let's get off our sentimental, self-righteous basis for rejecting and denying these children and look at them for what they really are—human beings. Human beings who can learn—because there is evidence that their lower-class predecessors of a generation or two ago learned. They can learn if they are respected. They can learn if it is communicated to them that those who are responsible for teaching them believe they can learn. And above all, these children can learn if they are taught, and if they are taught with precisely the same standards and quality of instruction as are given to other, more privileged children; and if they are taught with whatever empirical evidence demonstrates that they need by way of extra attention or increased intensity in skill.

I submit, however, that the extra attention must be framed not in terms of the educational process, but in terms of bridging the gap of suspicion which experience has taught these children may be justified by realities. I think also that these children will learn if those who are required to teach them are held responsible and accountable for an effective job of teaching. I think the day when teachers should be permitted, like psychiatrists, to alibi the results without any standards of judgment of their personal effectiveness must come to an end. Public educational

systems must fill in effective supervision, accountability, and standards for determining effectiveness of teaching, if the discussion of so-called culturally deprived children is going to be moved from the level of words to the level of social action. Teachers can no longer be permitted to get away with crude or sophisticated alibis for their failure to teach children, who like all normal beings are capable of learning.

The viability and the survival of our nation will probably be determined by the ability of our educational system to resolve this clash of cultures in our classrooms, to settle this war, this warfare of class and economic distinctions, in a direction that is consistent with basic assumptions of democracy, and which are, quite fortunately, consistent with the facts of meaningful social and behavioral sciences.

Editor's Note:

We have cited deep hostility between police and ghetto communities as a primary cause of the disorders surveyed by the Commission. —Kerner Commission Report

Patrollers or "paderollers" of slave days established the precedent for relations between law enforcement agencies and the black community. The southern situation after Emancipation saw the policeman as a symbol of civic order and white supremacy. The northern situation differed only in degree. Courts and local police acted as agents of control and punishment for transgressors against caste status and customs. These transgressions were considered aggressive acts against white society and a potential threat to every white individual. Due process was never the practice in dealing with black subjects. Not much has changed.

Police, generally from working–class backgrounds, manifest the same antiblack attitudes that are prevalent in these communities. They tend to perceive the black community as being completely lower-class, primitive, emotional, and criminal. Attitudes range from contempt, to mild hostility, to simple lack of sympathy. Dr. Robert Mendelsohn of Lafayette Clinic, Detroit, found that policemen tend to see blacks as overprivileged, dissatisfied, and ready to use force to gain more material goods. They also believe the goal of black people is domination over whites, not equality. Albert Reiss, Director of Center of Research on Social Organizations, University of Michigan, found that over three-fourths of white policemen in predominantly black precincts expressed prejudice or highly prejudiced attitudes. Another study of police brutality conducted in Boston, Chicago, and Washington, D.C., seven days a week for seven weeks, found that police mistreatment of citizens is a reality; that excessive use of force is acted out on lower-class men of either race; and that police culture legitimatizes these practices although official police codes do not. Studies of personality syndromes have evidenced patterns of authoritarianism.

The police systems in this country have evolved a culture of their own, consisting of particular beliefs, attitudes, interaction and reinforcement patterns. "Cops in the Ghetto" focuses on this closed system and delineates some of the major pitfalls for those who believe that more education and more pay will solve the problem. The socializing and reinforcement patterns of behavior are not affected by those factors. The young officer who enters the force, hoping to bring about some change, usually finds himself faced with two alternatives, either conform to the expected behavior or leave.

The slow but steadily increasing numbers of young black men who join police forces and attempt to create a role for themselves in their communities serve as a wedge between the dissimilar communities. They are important because they know and understand many of the life-styles that appear strange and threatening to their white counterpart. Cultural life-styles of minorities need to become part of educational programs in police training together with community based interaction. Policemen coming from predominantly white communities have had little or no contact with blacks, and their knowledge of the community consists mainly of stereotypes, media images, and criminal statistics. Consequently, much of the behavior which appears suspicious or threatening, if understood in its cultural mileu would be perceived differently. A prime example of this is street-corner society.

COPS IN THE GHETTO—A PROBLEM OF THE POLICE SYSTEM

BURTON LEVY

During the past five years, millions of dollars have been spent by police departments, much of it federally funded, for police-community relations programs (really "police-Negro relations"). The summer of 1967, with the destruction in Newark and Detroit, and the actual and threatened civil disorder in some thirty-five other urban communities, provides good reason to question the premises and assumptions on which these programs are based.

I have been a principal contributor to the notion that the gulf between the black community and the police in urban communities could be breached with lots of money spent for police recruitment and in-service training in human relations; for precinct police-citizen programs; for generally upgrading and professionalizing the police service by raising salaries to retain current employees and to attract college-educated recruits. A short article I wrote two years ago brought requests for thousands of reprints. I suppose I said what everybody wanted to hear; that is, that 96% of the Negro community are completely law-abiding; that 98% of the patrolmen never have complaints of brutality lodged against them; that

whatever negative images now exist on both sides are a result of a history of brutal Southern police and the general stereotypes and prejudices that exist in America today. Therefore, I said, what is needed is a new dialogue based on fact, not myth, and a significant program of training for policemen.

My position is now completely reversed. Two more years of intensive experience with police in all parts of the nation, combined with results of other studies and statements by police officers themselves, have convinced me that the problem of police-Negro relations in the urban centers is one of patterns of values and practice within the *police system*. The new assumption is that the problem is not one of a few "bad eggs" in a police department of 1,000 or 10,000 men, but rather of a police system that recruits a significant number of bigots, reinforces the bigotry through the department's value system and socialization with older officers, and then takes the worst of the officers and puts them on duty in the ghetto, where the opportunity to act out the prejudice is always available.

This paper examines three major questions:

1. What is the present relationship between the urban police and the black community?
2. What, and how effective, are current efforts to improve police-Negro relations?
3. What is the nature of the police system as it relates to police-Negro relations?

Black anger

Every poll and survey of black-white attitudes toward the police produces the same results: Negroes believe that policemen are physically brutal, harsh, discourteous to them because they are black; that police do not respond to calls, enforce the law, or protect people who live in the ghetto because they are black. White people simply do not or are unwilling to believe that such racial discrimination by police officers actually happens. Louis Harris' national survey reported in August, 1967, that Negroes feel "two to one that police brutality is a major cause [of the civil disorder]—a proposition whites reject by eight to one. Only 16% of whites believe that there is any police brutality to Negroes."

These attitudes in the Negro community are neither post-riot excuses to explain the disorder, no new ideas planted by black power advocates Stokely Carmichael or Rap Brown. In 1957, a poll of Detroiters showed that less than one white person in ten rated the police service as "not good"; while over four out of ten Negroes rated the police as "not good" or "definitely bad." Two-thirds of the Negro respondents referred to anti-Negro discrimination and mistreatment by police officers. A 1965 poll in Detroit found 58% of the Negro community believing that law enforcement was not fair and equitable. Similar results occur in other urban areas in the nation, North and South.

Black hostility toward police is not confined to the poor or to those engaged in illicit activity in the Negro community. Black doctors, lawyers, and even police officers share the beliefs. For example, the Guardians, the New York City organization of Negro police officers, endorsed the establishment of a Civilian Review Board in opposition to the organizations of white officers. The Guardian president publicly stated that he had witnessed incidents of police brutality.

Finally, it is factually correct to note that virtually every incident of threatened or actual civil disorder in the urban ghetto began with an encounter between a police officer and a Negro citizen. Whatever the factual reality is—as contrasted to the belief systems—clearly the cops serve as the "flash point" for black anger, mob formation, and civil disorder.

To what extent does police brutality actually exist—i.e., the verbal insults and harassment, the negative selective enforcement and nonenforcement, the physical brutality? The problem here is that systematic evidence outlining patterns of behavior is difficult to obtain. It is equally difficult to gain evidence on individual cases.

The U. S. Civil Rights Commission's 1961 Report *Justice* noted that the U. S. Department of Justice received 1,328 complaints alleging police brutality in the two-and-a-half-year period from January, 1958, to June, 1960. One-third of the complaints were from the South, and somewhat less than one-half of the complainants were Negro. Police officials note that few, if any, of these cases investigated by the F.B.I. have resulted in prosecution and certainly not conviction of any police officer. Still, the Civil Rights Commission concluded that "police brutality in the United States is a serious and continuing problem. . . ."

The Michigan Civil Rights Commission, established by the new State Constitution of 1963, has the legal authority to accept, investigate, and settle complaints of discrimination by police because of race, religion, or national origin. From January 1, 1964, to December, 1965, 103 complaints were filed against the Detroit Police Department. By December 30, 1965, the Commission found probable cause to credit the allegations in 31 cases, and the new Detroit Police Commissioner, in separate investigations by a newly established Citizen Complaint Bureau, had made similar findings. Citizens received apologies and

medical expenses; officers were reprimanded and transferred.

Contrast the 1964-65 results of citizen complaints, when an independent review apparatus was available to Detroit citizens, with the departmental grievance procedure before the establishment of the Civil Rights Commission. The Detroit NAACP filed 51 complaints with the Detroit Police Commissioner from 1957 to 1960, and not one case was upheld. The police "investigated" 121 incidents involving Negro citizens during the first nine months of 1960, and according to the then Police Commissioner's sworn testimony to the U. S. Civil Rights Commission, in only one case was the officer "definitely at fault."

The Detroit statistics cited above, both in terms of charges or findings of police brutality and the polls of attitudes, are not meant to make a special case for or against the Detroit Police Department. Today, Detroit is better in terms of police-Negro relations than some other comparable departments; it is worse than others. What is generally true of Detroit is also true of Boston, New York, Chicago, Los Angeles, and other urban communities. That is, the black community, from top to bottom, is angry about what they call mistreatment by police, from verbal abuse to physical brutality; further, that such mistreatment does occur—perhaps not to the high degree perceived by the Negro community, but certainly to a much greater degree than the police and municipal administrators have been willing to admit or correct. And when this relationship overlies the social and economic despair of the urban ghetto, it is little wonder that the cop on the beat (theoretically, the "foot soldier" of the Constitution) becomes the "flash point" of urban disorder.

Current remedial efforts

Efforts to improve the relationship and increase attitudes of trust between the black community and the urban police move in three major directions: (1) professionalizing police by increasing education, training, and salaries; (2) establishing formal police-community relations programs for police dialogue with the Negro community; and (3) recruiting more Negro police officers.

The first program assumes that education and training—recruit, in-service, and off-duty—will produce policemen better able to cope with the general complexities in law enforcement and also be more understanding of their own conscious and unintended actions toward citizens. Higher salaries will enable departments to recruit more highly educated and talented men.

The following proposal by the Detroit Citizen's Committee for Equal Opportunity reflects the recommendations of most civil rights organizations and professional police societies:

We must support steps to further professionalize the police department. The increasing problems of our society are connected directly to the ever-increasing complexity of life itself. The dignity of the law enforcement profession and the demands we make of the police officers today call for a well-trained, well-educated, adequately staffed and adequately paid police department.

The problem with the education and salary approach to changing police attitudes and behavior is that there is no evidence that these kinds of efforts, while having other effects, do actually change attitudes and behavior. For example, public school teachers in urban communities, all with college degrees, have not shown any particular positive attitudes or actions in their work with Negro children.

The second approach used to improve police-Negro relations is the organization of programs to facilitate communication, education, and understanding between the police and the citizenry. These programs usually involve face-to-face meetings between police and citizens. Some departments organize precinct meetings with adults and youths, or seek out local citizen programs where they may participate. Some police departments have regularly scheduled meetings with civil rights leaders; other departments have tried large and small community forums. Others concentrate on the youths—particularly in the inner-city.

No valid measurement of the precise effectiveness of programs of this sort has been undertaken anywhere in the nation. At best, it would be difficult to measure effectiveness over a short period of time. It is clear that police-community relations efforts in and of themselves are not sufficient to change police behavior. There are usually ten times more citizens than officers present at each meeting. Over the long run, it is difficult to sell a bad product—or to sell the product to people who are severely depressed socially and economically.

The recruitment of Negro officers assumes that the presence of a fairly representative number of Negro officers, at all levels within a police department, will serve to show the Negro community that the police department is not a white "occupation army," and that within the department the Negro officers will affect the attitudes and actions of their white counterparts.

The problem here is that the theory has not been tested because, with one or two minor exceptions, Negroes simply are not employed in any number in any department. Detroit has had between 200-250 Negro officers of a total force of 4,700 for the past decade, and significantly less before that. Officers who entered the Detroit department following World War II openly testify to the difficulties involved in getting a position at that time. Other cities are in similar situations. There are less than 60 Negro officers in all of the State Police departments in the nation.

The police system

My challenge to the traditional programs to improve police-Negro relations is based upon analysis of the police department as a system, not the actions of individual officers—or, as they are sometimes referred to, as the few "bad eggs" in the department.

The systemic approach to the police has been undertaken by few social scientists. However, a recent study by Arthur Niederhoffer provides a record of trained, long-term observation and empirical evidence which strongly supports my own observation and limited research.

Niederhoffer is not an anti-police radical; he retired after 21 years in the New York City Police Department, earned a Ph.D. in Sociology at New York University, and now teaches police at the John Jay College of Criminal Justice. In Niederhoffer's introduction to *Behind The Shield*, he writes: "The great majority of policemen are men of integrity and good will. Yet it is a fact that a 'minority' goes wrong! Why this should occur even to the extent that it does among a body of men so carefully selected, is a mystery, but one that will, I hope, be less of an enigma by the time the reader comes to the last page of this book." In fact, Niederhoffer's conclusions are a devastating indictment of the police system, particularly as it relates to police-Negro relations.

The police system, as described by Niederhoffer, comes out looking something like this: First, the police departments recruit from a population (the working class) whose numbers are more likely than the average population to hold anti-Negro attitudes; second, the recruits are given a basic classroom training program that is unlikely to change the anti-Negro sentiments; third, the recruit goes out on the street as a patrolman and is more likely than not to have his anti-Negro attitudes reinforced and hardened by the older officer; fourth, in the best departments, the most able officers are soon transferred to specialized administrative duties in training, recruitment, juvenile work, etc., or are promoted after three to five years to supervisory positions; fifth, after five years the patrolman on street duty significantly increases in levels of cynicism, authoritarianism, and generalized hostility to the non-police world. Finally, it is highly likely that the worst of the patrolmen will wind up patrolling the ghetto, because that tends to be the least-wanted assignment.

To put it more bluntly, the police system can be seen as one that is a closed society with its own values, mores, and standards. In urban communities, anti-black is likely to be one of a half-dozen primary and important values. The department recruits a sizable number of people with racist attitudes, socializes them into a system with a strong racist element, and takes the officer who cannot advance and puts him in the ghetto where he has day-to-day contact with the black citizens. If this is an accurate description of the urban police system (and my personal observations over the past five years tell me this is so), then the reason is clear why every poll of black citizens shows the same high level of distrust and hostility against policemen.

Another nationally known law enforcement practitioner, now also teaching at John Jay College in New York, Donald J. McNamara, said recently that "the police community is a closed society and it has its own customs, morals and taboos—and those who are not conforming to the police society, to its attitudes, to its customs and traditions, taboos and mores, are ostracized and then excluded . . . whatever prejudices and discrimination, whatever anti-minority attitudes he [the recruit] brought in with him, have been tremendously reinforced because they are part of the community attitudes of this police group of which he becomes a member."

Problems in confrontation

Civil rights organizations and the Negro community have successfully come to a confrontation with almost every other form of institutional racism, save law enforcement (albeit not all confrontations have been successful). Racism in voting, public accommodations, employment, housing, and education have been exposed and well documented, and have either been changed or the march (as in Milwaukee, as this is being written) goes on. Two major problems in confronting the police issue are the information gap and the defensiveness and secrecy of police.

White America's civic, religious, governmental leaders, reporters, and writers, have not dealt with the issue of racism in law enforcement as some have dealt with other civil rights issues. For example, Charles Silberman's best-selling *Crisis in Black and White* lists only two minor and passing references covering four pages to police, but has over twenty references to public schools, covering over one hundred pages. Senator Jacob Javits' excellent *Discrimination, USA,* with separate chapters on housing, education, and employment discrimination, has not one reference to law enforcement. The same is true of other civil rights studies. *The Speeches of John F. Kennedy in the Presidential Campaign of 1960* contains thousands of forthright words on civil rights in housing, employment, education, voting; however, not a mention of police or law enforcement.

Police tend to be secretive and defensive, the good professional advocates as well as the old tough cops. The professional policemen—there are many, and particularly on the highest levels within the departments—seek education, training, and strict standards of professionalism within their departments. The professionals do not decry Supreme Court decisions or believe that local courts, newspapers or citizens are "out to get them," as the old-line tough non-professional "unleash the police" cop believes. The old cop clearly doesn't want interference or review because "only an officer knows how to handle the situation." The good professional doesn't want interference or outside review because the hallmark of a profession, they believe, is the ability to self-regulate the activities of those within the profession, as do doctors, lawyers, etc. Thus, while the professional and the old-line cop will split on most other issues, they do stand together on outside review or criticism.

Government officials and community leaders have another "hang-up" about confronting the harsh reality of the police system and its ability to withstand the minor effects of traditional "remedial" programs. That is, there are good, well-intentioned and intelligent law enforcement officials who recognize a serious problem and themselves are willing to say and often do say the "right" thing. And, in spite of the system, there are good cops actually working in the ghetto.

In November, 1967, a parade of Michigan's top police executives testified before a state legislative committee in opposition to "Stop and Frisk" legislation, an issue bitterly opposed by the organized and general black community, but favored by some politicians looking for a political issue and an anti-crime panacea. At the same hearing, a police chief of a major Michigan city opposed across-the-board pay raises for Michigan officers because "there are thousands [of officers] who don't deserve their present salary."

Other examples include the Michigan Association of Chiefs of Police (MACP), which in 1966 became the first professional police organization to adopt a far-reaching civil rights platform supporting equality not only in law enforcement, but in education, housing, and employment. And the MACP is in 1967 engaged in a joint effort with the State Civil Rights Commission (an incredible and unheard-of combination, say some observers) to recruit hundreds of Negro and Latin American police officers.

The problem, then, for governmental officials (like me) is to retain a working and friendly relationship with the law enforcement professionals who sincerely seek change—and at the same time tell them, and the community, that a basic, long-entrenched part of the police system must be destroyed.

We must say that money alone—whether spent for higher police salaries or more police training—will do little to stop the pattern of police discrimination and brutality against Negroes and other minorities in America's urban ghettoes. Police dialogues with Puerto Ricans in Spanish Harlem, Negroes in Detroit, or Mexican-Americans in Texas, will not significantly reduce the instances of police officers' abuse of their power in those communities. The problem is one of a set of values and attitudes and a pattern of anti-black behavior, socialized within and reinforced by the police system.

Conclusion

This article does not propose specific actions to produce systemic change in police-Negro relations in urban police departments. Systemic change is possible. During the early 1960's, O. W. Wilson, Chicago's Superintendent of Police, significantly destroyed police graft and corruption, attitudes and practices that had become a primary part of Chicago's police system. Secretary of Defense McNamara prevailed over a defense establishment more entrenched and politically powerful than any fraternal order of police officers.

What is required are specific objectives by a mayor and police chief, committed to and strong enough to battle and prevail over the police system in their community—a Wilson or McNamara type. It will also require a political base, a sensitive power structure, and, if the white community is politically dominant, a change in the belief system of a large number of white citizens. The program of change will require internal and external controls over the behavior of cops in the ghetto. A program and process must occur that will restructure the police system to exclude—or at least significantly minimize—the racism of cops in the ghetto.

Editor's Note:

The interaction that takes place on the streetcorner is a significant factor in the socialization of black youth. Here, the young man learns his appropriate role as a male—the acceptable manners of dress, speech, and behavior that ensure membership in the group. These age-graded peer groups provide a forum for developing and refining the latest argot. On display are the newest styles in clothing, new "jams" (records), and dance steps. Rap sessions are an ongoing part of this scene. Discussions cover the conditions of the world, the happenings in the neighborhood, the job or lack of a job, women, parties, likes, dislikes, cops, numbers, immediate and far-reaching plans, the latest news, and life in general. From this vantage point, the men of the ghetto witness the success and failure of those who share the conditions of their lives. Much that goes on in white society's living rooms, family rooms, or structured encounter groups takes place on street corners in the black community.

"Friends and Networks," taken from *Tally's Corner*, provides a glimpse of the world of some of the young men who are a part of this streetcorner scene. The scene is Washington, D.C., but similar patterns are acted out in large urban areas across the country.

FRIENDS AND NETWORKS

ELLIOT LIEBOW

More than most social worlds, perhaps, the streetcorner world takes its shape and color from the structure and character of the face-to-face relationships of the people who live in it. Unlike other areas in our society, where a large portion of the individual's energies, concerns and time are invested in self-improvement, career and job development, family and community activities, religious and cultural pursuits, or even in broad, impersonal social and political issues, these resources in the streetcorner world are almost entirely given over to the construction and maintenance of personal relationships.

On the streetcorner, each man has his own network of these personal relationships and each man's network defines for him the members of his personal community. His personal community, then, is not a bounded area but rather a weblike arrangement of man-man and man-woman relationships in which he is selectively attached in a particular way to a definite number of discrete persons. In like fashion, each of these persons has his own personal network.

At the edges of this network are those persons with whom his relationship is affectively neutral, such as area residents whom he has "seen around" but does not know except to nod or say "hi" to as they pass on the street. These relationships are limited to simple recognition. Also at the edges are those men and women, including former friends and acquaintances, whom he dislikes or fears or who dislike or

148

fear him. These relationships are frequently characterized by avoidance but the incumbents remain highly visible and relevant to one another.

In toward the center are those persons he knows and likes best, those with whom he is "up tight": his "walking buddies," "good" or "best" friends, girl friends, and sometimes real or putative kinsmen: These are the people with whom he is in more or less daily, face-to-face contact, and whom he turns to for emergency aid, comfort or support in time of need or crisis. He gives them and receives from them goods and services in the name of friendship, ostensibly keeping no reckoning. Routinely, he seeks them out and is sought out by them. They serve his need to be with others of his kind, and to be recognized as a discrete, distinctive personality, and he, in turn, serves them the same way. They are both his audience and his fellow actors.

It is with these men and women that he spends his waking, nonworking hours, drinking, dancing, engaging in sex, playing the fool or the wise man, passing the time at the Carry-out or on the streetcorner, talking about nothing and everything, about epistemology or Cassius Clay, about the nature of numbers or how he would "have it made" if he could have a steady job that paid him $60 a week with no layoffs.

So important a part of daily life are these relationships that it seems like no life at all without them. Old Mr. Jenkins climbed out of his sickbed to take up a seat on the Coca-Cola case at the Carry-out for a couple of hours. "I can't stay home and play dead," he explained, "I got to get out and see my friends."

Friendship is sometimes anchored in kinship, sometimes in long-term associations which may reach back into childhood. Other close friendships are born locally, in the streetcorner world itself, rather than brought in by men from the outside. Such friendships are built on neighbor or co-worker relationships, or on a shared experience or other event or situation which brings two people together in a special way.

In general, close friendships tend to develop out of associations with those who are already in one's network of personal relationships: relatives, men and women who live in the area and spend much of their time on the street or in public places, and co-workers. The result is that the streetcorner man, perhaps more than others in our society, tends to use the same individuals over and over again: he may make a friend, neighbor and co-worker of his kinsman, or a friend, co-worker and kinsman of his neighbor. A look at some of the personal relationships can illustrate the many-stranded aspects of friendship and

the bi-directional character of friendship on the one hand, and kinship, neighbor, co-worker and other relationships on the other.

When Tonk and Pearl got married and took an apartment near the Carry-out, Pearl's brother, Boley, moved in with them. Later, Pearl's nephew, J.R., came up from their hometown in North Carolina and he, too, moved in with them. J.R. joined Tonk and Boley on the streetcorner and when Earl told Tonk of some job openings where he worked, Tonk took J.R. with him. These three, then, were kinsmen, shared the same residence, hung out together on the streetcorner, and two of them—for a time at least—were co-workers.

Preston was Clarence's uncle. They lived within a block of each other and within two blocks of the Carry-out. Clarence worked on a construction job and later got Preston a job at the same place. Tally, Wee Tom and Budder also worked at the same construction site. The five men regularly walked back from the job to the streetcorner together, usually sharing a bottle along the way. On Friday afternoons, they continued drinking together for an hour or so after returning to the streetcorner. Tally referred to the other four men as his "drinking buddies."

Tally had met Wee Tom on the job. Through Tally, Wee Tom joined them on the walk home, began to hang around the Carry-out and finally moved into the neighborhood as well. Budder had been the last to join the group at the construction site. He had known Preston and Clarence all along, but not well. He first knew Tally as a neighbor. They came to be friends through Tally's visits to the girl who lived with Budder, his common-law wife, and his wife's children. When Tally took Budder onto the job with him, Budder became a co-worker and drinking buddy, too. Thus, in Tally's network, Wee Tom began as co-worker, moved up to drinking buddy, neighbor and finally close friend; Budder from neighbor and friend to co-worker. Importantly, and irrespective of the direction in which the relationships developed, the confluence of the co-worker and especially the neighbor relationship with friendship deepened the friend relationship.

One of the most striking aspects of these overlapping relationships is the use of kinship as a model for the friend relationship. Most of the men and women on the streetcorner are unrelated to one another and only a few have kinsmen in the immediate area. Nevertheless, kinship ties are frequently manufactured to explain, account for, or even to validate friend relationships. In this manner, one could move from friendship to kinship in either direction. One could start with kinship, say, as did Preston and Clarence or Boley and Tonk and build on this, or conversely, one could start with friendship and build a kin relationship.

The most common form of the pseudo-kin relationship between two men is known as "going for brothers." This means, simply, that two men agree to present themselves as brothers to the outside world and to deal with one another on the same basis. Going for brothers appears as a special case of friendship in which the usual claims, obligations, expectations, and loyalties of the friend relationship are publicly declared to be at their maximum.

Sea Cat and Arthur went for brothers. Sea Cat's room was Arthur's home so far as he had one anywhere. It was there that he kept his few clothes and other belongings, and it was on Sea Cat's dresser that he placed the pictures of his girl friends (sent "with love" or "love and kisses"). Sea Cat and Arthur wore one another's clothes and, whenever possible or practical, were in one another's company. Even when not together, each usually had a good idea of where the other was or had been or when he would return. Generally, they seemed to prefer going with women who were themselves friends; for a period of a month or so, they went out with two sisters.

Sea Cat worked regularly; Arthur only sporadically or for long periods not at all. His own credit of little value, Arthur sometimes tried to borrow money from the men on the corner, saying that the lender could look to his "brother" for payment. And when Sea Cat found a "good thing" in Gloria, who set him up with a car and his own apartment, Arthur shared in his friend's good fortune. On the street-corner or in Sea Cat's room, they laughed and horsed around together, obviously enjoying one another's company. They cursed each other and called each other names in mock anger or battle, taking liberties that were reserved for and tolerated in close friends alone.

A few of the men on the corner knew that Sea Cat and Arthur were, in fact, unrelated. A few knew they were not brothers but thought they were probably related in some way. Others took their claim to kinship at face value. Even those who knew they were merely going for brothers, however, accepted this as evidence of the special character of their friend relationship. In general, only those who are among the most important in one's personal network can distinguish between real and pseudo-kin relationships, partly because the question as to whether two men are really brothers or are simply going for brothers is not especially relevant. The important thing for people to know in their interaction with the two men is that they say they are brothers, not whether they are or not.

The social reality of the pseudo-kinship tie between those who are "going for brothers" is clearly evident in the case of Richard and Leroy. Richard and Leroy had been going for brothers for three months or so when Leroy got in a fight with a group of teenagers and young adults. Leroy suffered serious internal injuries and was hospitalized for more than a month. One week after the fight, Richard and one of the teenagers who had beaten up Leroy, and with whom both he and Leroy had been on friendly terms, got into a fight over a private matter having nothing to do with Leroy, and Richard killed the teenager. Richard was immediately arrested and the police, acting on information from the dead boy's friends, relatives, and others in the community, charged him with first degree murder for the premeditated revenge killing of one who had beaten up "his brother." But when it was established that Leroy and Richard were not related in any way the charge was dropped to murder in the second degree. The dead boy's friends and relatives were outraged and bewildered. To them, and even to some of Richard and Leroy's friends, it was clearly a premeditated, deliberate killing. Hadn't Richard and Leroy been going for brothers? And hadn't Leroy been badly beaten by this same boy just eight days earlier?

Pseudo-kinship ties are also invoked in certain man-woman relationships. Stoopy first met Lucille in the kitchen of an officers' club in Virginia where they both worked. They became friends and later, when Lucille and her teen age son were looking for a place to live, Stoopy told her of a place in the Carry-out area and Lucille moved in. As neighbors as well as co-workers, Stoopy and Lucille's friendship deepened and they "went for cousins." Stoopy and Lucille saw a lot of one another. They frequently went back and forth to work together. They borrowed money from each other and freely visited each other in their homes. Lucille came to know Stoopy's wife through her Saturday morning visits with the children, and Stoopy's relationship with Lucille's son was conspicuously warm and avuncular.

At no time in their relationship was there ever the slightest suggestion of any romantic or sexual connection between them. Indeed, this seems to be the primary purpose behind "going for cousins." It is a way of saying, "This woman [man] and I are good friends but we are not lovers." Given the taboo against cousin marriage, going for cousins permits an unrelated man and woman to enter into a close-friend relationship without compromising their romantic or sexual status in any way. It is a public disclaimer of any romantic or sexual content in a cross-sex, close-friend relationship.

The social utility of going for cousins is evident when one compares Stoopy and Lucille with Tally and Velma. Tally and Velma were good friends, but unlike Stoopy and Lucille, they were not going for cousins. On several occasions Tally and Velma attended parties as part of a foursome, each bringing his own partner. On such occasions, Tally often spoke of his friendship with Velma, noting that he had several times slept in her home but had "never laid a hand on her." Skeptical or even uninterested listeners were dragged before Velma who verified Tally's description of their relationship.

In contrast, Stoopy and Lucille were under no such pressure to validate the asexual nature of their relationship. The question never came up. They were going for cousins. That was enough.

Sometimes pseudo-kinship is invoked in more casual terms, apparently to sharpen and lend formal structure to a relationship which is generally vague. Occasionally, one hears that "he just call her his sister," or that "they just call it brother and sister" or even "they just go for brother and sister." Such was the case with Stanton. His young daughter was living with a married woman whom most people, including Stanton, referred to as his sister. But Stanton, "he just call her his sister." In caring for his child, the woman was, of course, doing what sisters sometimes do. The assignment of the label "sister" to one already performing a function which frequently appears in association with that label was an easy step to take. A vague relationship was rendered specific; it was simplified, and the need for explanations was reduced. This may also have served to discourage public suspicion about the nature of this relationship. In these respects, perhaps going for cousins would have served them equally well. And as in the case of going for brothers, whether Stanton and this woman were in fact brother and sister was less important than the fact that they "called" themselves so. The woman's husband, we must assume, knew they were not related. But since Stanton and the man's wife called themselves brother and sister, the husband's vested interests and public status were not jeopardized, not even by Stanton's visits to his home when he himself was not present.

Most friendships are thus born in propinquity, in relationships or situations in which individuals confront one another day by day and face to face. These friendships are nurtured and supported by an exchange of money, goods, services and emotional support. Small loans, ranging from a few pennies up to two or three dollars, are constantly being asked for and extended. Leroy watches Malvina's children while she goes out to have a few drinks with a friend. Tonk and Stanton help Budder move the old refrigerator he just bought into his apartment. Robert spends an evening giving Richard a home process. Preston lends Stoopy forty cents for bus fare to go to work. Pearl and Tonk throw a party, supplying all of the food and much of the liquor themselves. When Bernice leaves Stanton, Leroy consoles him telling him of how Charlene is always doing this too, but always coming back. Leroy borrows a bottle of milk for the baby from Richard and Shirley. Sara gives Earl three dollars to get his clothes out of the cleaners. Sea Cat and Stoopy find Sweets knocked unconscious on the sidewalk, carry him home and put him to bed. Tonk and Richard go down to the police station to put up five dollars toward Tally's collateral. Clarence returns from his father's funeral where Tally and Preston hung onto him throughout, restraining him physically where necessary and comforting him in his shock as best they could. Back at Nancy's place, Clarence nurses his grief in silence and nonparticipation. Tally urges him again and again to "Come on, Baby, show me you're a man," but Clarence shakes his head no. Tally keeps trying. Finally, taking the glass of whiskey offered him, Clarence sloughs off his mourner's status by dancing with Nancy. Tally laughs with pleasure at his own handiwork. "O.K. now?" he asks, and Clarence smiles back that yes, everything's O.K. now.

In ways such as these, each person plays an important part in helping and being helped by those in his personal network. Since much of the cooperation between friends centers around the basic prerequisites of daily living, friends are of special importance to one's sense of physical and emotional security. The more friends one has or believes himself to have, and the deeper he holds these friendships to be, the greater his self-esteem and the greater the esteem for himself he thinks he sees in the eyes of others.

Editor's Note:

The ongoing struggle for justice and opportunity to achieve one's full potential in a society essentially racist has brought to the fore the question of what are the appropriate roles for black males and for black females. Jean Bond and Pat Perry explore the ramifications of this role relationship and the difficulties that have arisen from the recriminations and accusations evolved from this situation. One of the more pernicious myths they identify is black male emasculation by a black female matriarchy. Great danger lies in the fact that countless blacks subscribe to these ideas like this, act on them, and thereby are effectively neutralized by "divide and rule" tactics.

HAS THE BLACK MAN BEEN CASTRATED?

JEAN CAREY BOND and PAT PEERY

In Black communities all over the country, today, intelligent and imaginative people are discussing the political, economic and cultural aspects of the Black liberation struggle. Viable approaches for changing the Afro-American's condition in America are beginning to emerge. Almost without notice, an issue slipped in the back door of these discussions and then assumed controversial proportions as soon as its presence was acknowledged. We refer to what has become a burning question in our community, and rightly so: What should be the role of women in the movement? Subdivisions of this lead question are: What have been the traditional relations between Black men and women? What are the factors that have defined or determined those relations?

Despite the obvious interest of both men and women in this issue, and despite the inclination of both to comment at length and take rigid positions, we are appalled at a reigning lack of seriousness and sobriety in the debate. Black publications are full of, on the one hand, hysterical and bitter indictments of the past and present conduct of Black men from the bruised and now twisted consciousnesses of sisters who have been driven to irrational extremes by the conditions of a world they never made. On the other hand, we find the equally neurotic but voguish creed that women must abandon their "matriarchal" behavior, learn to speak only when they are spoken to and take up positions three paces (or is it ten?) behind their men.* As far as we know, the question as to whether her place is not properly beside, rather than in front of or behind, the Black man, has yet to be raised.

For their part, many Black men berate Black women for their faults—faults so numerous and so pronounced that one is hard-put to discern in their tirades any ground, short of invisibility, on which Black womanhood might redeem itself. They do this, blind to the age-old implications of such a vociferous rejection of a part of themselves. Others run on about the necessity of subordinating women to their superior and manly will in the planning and execution of revolution with a monumental indisposition to examine their motives for advancing this precept.

We view these superficial and unbalanced attitudes as being predicated on a popular and dangerous fiction: the myth of Black male emasculation, and its descendent concept, the myth of the Black female matriarchy. These companion myths are not recent in their origin; however, they have most recently been popularized through the highly publicized and highly touted work, *The Negro Family: The Case for National Action* by Daniel Patrick Moynihan—so successfully popularized that even Blacks have swallowed his assumptions and conclusions hook, line and sinker. It is ironic that, at a time when Blacks are newly perceiving and denouncing the shallowness of white analyses of the Black experience, many members of the avant-garde are still capable of being mesmerized by racist social scientific thought which has utterly failed to produce in-depth studies of the Afro-American social structure.

The emasculation theory, as interpreted by Blacks, is two-pronged, one version being primarily followed by women, the other commanding the allegiance of both men and women. Version Number One alleges that Black men have failed throughout our history to shield their women and families from the scourge of American racism and have failed to produce a foolproof strategy for liberating Black people. It is therefore concluded that Black men are weak, despicable "niggers" who must be brushed aside and overcome by women in the big push toward freedom. Version Number Two also arrives at the point that Black men are weak via the route that Black women castrated them by, among other things, playing their economic ace-in-the-hole. (Moynihan's Black matriarchy proposition is based, incredibly, on the statistic that one quarter—only one quarter—of all Black families are headed by women.) Also linked to this thesis is the woefully misbegotten notion that Black women complied with their rapists and used their bodies to rise on the socio-economic ladder, leaving Black men behind.

What this all adds up to is that Black men and women are placing ultimate blame for their subjugation on each other, a propensity which fairly reeks of self-hatred. In other words, Blacks are still crippled by self-doubt and, even in 1969, lean painfully towards the view that Europeans could never have

---

*It seems to us that many Black women who give lip service to the latter, male-inspired philosophy have played an interesting psychological trick on themselves. Feeling both guilty and resentful in their relations with Black men, they merely alter the mode of attack to fit the new Black party line. Their aggression now takes the form of patronizing, "understanding" pronouncements about the Black male's so-called inadequacies. Dripping with self-admonition and promises to act right in the by-and-by, they neatly assuage the guilt but not the resentment, which to be sure will rear its ugly head in the near future, as troublesome as ever, never having been honestly confronted by either women or men. In the case of some unmarried sisters, we suspect that sheer opportunism motivates their public approval of this idea. What better way to get a man, they reason, than to proclaim your willingness to be his slave?

kept us in this bind for so long were it not for our own weakness, i.e., inferiority. It is not difficult to understand why we are unable to see the forest for the trees. After all, the cat who sponges off of you, knocks you around every now and then and maybe leaves you, is Black not white. And by the same token, the chick who tells you this is her money, she made it, and you can just get-the-hell-out, is Black not white. But we are, in fact, focusing only on the trees when we expend time and energy in this senseless and debilitating family squabble while the real culprits stand laughing in the wings.

What is emasculation? In the broad sense, an emasculated people (cultural group) are a broken people, a people whose spirit, strength and vigor have been destroyed, who have been reduced to a state of almost total ineffectuality. Specifically applied to a male, emasculation connotes the absence of virility and can mean, though not necessarily, effeminacy. Notwithstanding the colossal suffering which has befallen Black people here and abroad as a result of their colonization by Europeans, with its numerous deleterious effects on the Black psyche, do our people truly fit the description given above? And notwithstanding the often literal, but more often, symbolic castration of hundreds of thousands of Black individuals throughout our sojourn in the wilderness, have Black men really been stripped of their virility? We contend that as a whole people Afro-Americans lack neither spirit nor strength nor vigor, for it is they who have given to this nation the only culture it has, the only humanity it has.

As for Black men, we must ask the question: If the Black male's castration is a *fait accompli* of long standing, why the frantic need on the part of whites to replay the ritual of castration over and over again in a hundred different ways? The answer is simple: The enduring manhood/humanity of Blacks, burning bright despite all efforts to extinguish it, is the nemesis of Western civilization. Nowhere do we find this point more beautifully made than in Ron Milner's brilliant play, *Who's Got His Own*. The memorable character of S—house Tim embodies the compelling thesis that no matter what level of degradation a Black man might be reduced to, within the solitary confinement of his soul his manhood crackles white hot, so potent that even from its grotesque cocoon it sends out vibrations to the next generation. From whence comes the militant fury of Tim Jr., which explodes in a near-fatal assault on his white "buddy," if not from the heart and mind of that tomming, wife-beating, evil-tongued, indomitable S—house Tim?

Moynihan and his gang postulate that Black society is matriarchal, and that Black women have been the primary castrating force in the demise of Black manhood. The casting of this image of the Black female in sociological bold relief is both consistent and logical in racist terms, for the so-called Black matriarch is a kind of folk character, *largely fashioned by whites* out of half-truths and lies about the involuntary condition of Black women. The matriarchal fairy tale is part of a perennial tendency among whites to employ every available device in *their* on-going effort to demasculinize the Black male. Movies and radio shows of the 1930's and 1940's invariably peddled the Sapphire image of the Black woman: She is depicted as iron-willed, effectual, treacherous towards and contemptuous of Black men, the latter being portrayed as simpering, ineffectual whipping boys. Certainly, most of us have encountered domineering Black females (and white ones too). Many of them have been unlucky in life and love and seek a bitter haven from their disappointments in fanatical self-sufficiency. Others, out of a tragic fear, brutalize their sons in the child-rearing process, hoping to destroy in them aggressive tendencies which might eventually erupt in assaults against white men and the white system. But is must be emphasized that the white man's Sapphire caricature does not closely resemble the real domineering Black female, much less the majority of her sisters who do not share that classification.

We submit that in reality Black women, domineering or no, have not had the power in this male-dominated culture to effect a coup against anyone's manhood—in spite of her oft-cited economic "advantage" over the Black man. A matriarchal system is one in which power rests firmly in the hands of women. Whatever economic power may accrue to Black women by way of the few employment escape valves permitted them by the oppressing group for their own insidious reasons, this power is really illusory and should not be taken at face value. American society is patriarchal—white women suffer the slings and arrows of that system, in the first instance. Black women are victimized on two counts: They are women and they are Black, a clear case of double indemnity. For the duration of their lives, many Black women must bear a heavy burden of male frustration and rage through physical abuse, desertions, rejection of their femininity and general appearance. Having a job provides relief for her stomach but not for her soul, for a Black woman's successful coping with the economic problem (and we might throw in the education problem) enhances her rejction by Black men, or else invites acceptance in the form of exploitation. Stymied in his attempt to protect and free the Black woman (and himself), the Black man further degrades her. She, doubly powerless and vengeful, insults his manhood by whatever means at her disposal. Thus are many Black men and women hateful partners in a harrowing dance.

These points have never been lost on white folks, and they continue to bend them to their design of divide and rule. Their past and current success is insured by the persistent adherence of many Blacks—including most would-be revolutionaries—to the basic premises of the American value system, from whence all definitions of masculinity, femininity, right and wrong proceed. It is the transference of values, which work for the oppressor in the capitalist context, to the milieu of the oppressed, where they are dysfunctional, that has pitted Black man against Black woman and vice versa—a situation which, needless to say, is anathema to the pursuit of self-determination.

The salient point, though, in our effort to debunk the castration theory is that although whites falsify the image of Black women and use the distortion as one of several castrating tools, their attempt is ultimately abortive. For while Mr. Charlie does set Black manhood on the run, it always escapes the pursuer's final lurch and turns up, shaken but together, at the wheel of an Eldorado, in a smoke-filled poker den, in a Black woman's bed or on the side of her jaw. More importantly, it has turned up throughout our history in the form of resistance to oppression. Sojourner Truth and Harriet Tubman notwithstanding, Black men hold the majority among our political (and cultural) heroes: Frederick Douglass, W.E.B. DuBois, Marcus Garvey, Malcolm X, etc. Indeed, the Black man always surfaces with his manhood not only intact, but much more intact than that of his oppressor, which brings us to the question: Just who is the emasculated person in this society? Surely it is the white man whose dazzling symbols of power—his goods, his technology—have all but consumed his human essence. Yes, he is effective because his power enables him to rule; but he is emasculated in that he has become a mere extension of the things he produces. The contrary is true of Blacks. Do any of us doubt that Muhammed Ali is the heavyweight champion of the world? What does it matter that whitey took his jewel-encrusted belt away?

If we accept the emasculation theory, we must accept a host of outrageous misrepresentations of the Black personality. We must accept the quaint Southern myth that most slaves were "good niggers" who passively accepted their lot, the companion theory being that slavery was not really so bad. We must accept most of the stereotypes that have been paraded before us down through the ages, as, for example, William Styron's Nat Turner, because any fool knows that eunuchs, figurative or actual, do not lead slave revolts. Eunuchs do not write plays that pulverize the very foundations of American theater. Eunuchs do not refuse to fight in unholy wars, thumbing their noses at such things as trophies and fame, things which some men sell their souls to achieve. Eunuchs only do the bidding of the king. Such acts of defiance as these are wrought by *men* in the name of all Black people.

Editor's Note:

It is commonly known that slave statutes forbade marriage. When liasons of a permanent nature were attempted there was neither recognition nor protection forthcoming from legal or social auspices. And yet, this disorganized mass was able to produce such outstanding figures as Frederick Douglass, who never knew his father and saw his mother infrequently; William Wells Brown, noted novelist and historian, who wrote that his mother had seven children, none of whom had the same father, and that slaves seldom knew their fathers. Harriet Tubman, who was one of eleven children scattered by sales; and Sojourner Truth, who had five children by a "husband" forced on her by her owner who were taken away from her and dispersed before slavery ended. Absalom Jones, Martin R. Delany, Gabriel Prosser, Denmark Vesey, and Nat Turner are but a few additional names in the long list of such notable progeny.

A situation which by definition was destructive and debilitating of personality and ego strength at the same time produced historic figures worthy of emulation, whose deeds by any estimate of probability should never have occurred. At the same time, it is acknowledged that the denial of the stabilizing aspects of marriage was unequivocally destructive. The consequences were so far-reaching that attitudes and perceptions of whites and blacks still suffer some residual effects.

There must have been some other variables operating in the family life of black people providing supports and strengths that have for the most part eluded the majority of social scientists. The black family in countless instances whether matriarchal or mother-centered, nuclear, extended, attenuated, or augmented, as described by Billingsley in the following article, has provided the sustenance and resourcefulness to enable its members to function in an overwhelmingly hostile white world. The positive functions of the black family, whatever its composition, have been overlooked in a great many instances. If one were to accept the Moynihan premise, then one would have to explain persons such as those mentioned above as anomalies. The reality of the situation, however, belies that explanation. Each generation has witnessed blacks who distinguished themselves under the most adverse circumstances, in every field of endeavor available to them. The unsung heroes are those black families—by far the majority—that must confront survival on a day to day basis. While the question of survival is common to all people, the distinguishing feature in the black community is the intensity of the day-in day-out recurring quest for enough to eat, protection against the elements, jobs, clothing, medical care for children who are ill and malnourished, etc.

It is axiomatic that if the alternatives available to one group are different from those available to a different group, then the end product should also be different. So it is with the black family. There are needs generated in a racist society for the subordinate group that may never manifest themselves in the superordinate group. To make assessments and draw conclusions without taking these factors into consideration is to demonstrate a lack of sensitivity that borders on vacuousness. Some of the structural variations apparent in black family life are delineated by Billingsley in the article excerpted here.

BLACK FAMILIES IN PERSPECTIVE

ANDREW BILLINGSLEY

It is very common to observe that there are two types of family structure in America: male-headed families and female-headed families. Such characterization is almost always followed by the assertion or assumption that male-headed families are stable whereas female-headed families are unstable, and that the latter are more than twice as common among Negroes as among whites.

This manner of characterizing the structure of Negro family life has a number of inadequacies. First, it underestimates the variations among Negro families living under different basic conditions.

On the basis of such conditions, three general categories of families may be identified: primary families, extended families, and augmented families. A family is commonly defined as a group of persons related by marriage or ancestry, who live together in the same household. Nuclear families are confined to husband and wife and their own children, with no other members present. Extended families include other relatives or in-laws of the family head, sharing the same household with the nuclear family members. Augmented families include members not related to the family head who share the same household living arrangements with the nuclear family. Each of these three categories of families will be considered in some detail. Roughly two-thirds of all Negro families are nuclear families, a quarter are extended families and a tenth are augmented families.

Further, within the framework of these three categories, twelve different types of family structure may be specified. In addition, this typology allows for the elaboration of subtypes within several of these twelve types of family structure.

Nuclear families

Among nuclear families, three specific types of family structure may be observed. Type I, the *incipient nuclear family*, is composed of husband and wife living together in their own household with no children. Nearly a fifth of all Negro families, or roughly a million families, are of this type. They are young married couples who have not yet had time or economic security to start their family, older couples who have not been able or willing either to have their own children or to adopt others, and still older couples whose children have grown up and left the home. This type also includes a few families whose minor children have been placed in foster homes or institutions because of illness or other incapacity of one or both parents. The largest single subgroup in this category consists of those husbands and wives who do not have children of their own for a variety of reasons. These families are generally economically viable because both partners work, except during illness, old age, or widespread unemployment. Incipient nuclear families, then, are a large, important and complex aspect of the structure of Negro family life. Yet they are almost completely ignored in studies of Negro families. They offer an important potential for the care of children in the Negro community, though there is some indication that among many Negro families those with some children already may be more willing to take in other children than those without children of their own.

A second type of family is the *simple nuclear family*. This family type consists of husband and wife and their own or adopted children living together in their own household with no other members present. This is the traditional type of family structure in America and Europe. Among students of the family, it is considered the ideal and most universal family form.

It might be instructive to note, however, that while this nuclear family arrangement is the ideal and the model against which all other families, particularly Negro families, are compared, it does not encompass the majority—even among white families. A study by Paul C. Glick found that in 1953 only 28.6 per cent of household units consisted of a husband and wife and their own minor children. And a study in 1965 in Richmond, California, by Alan Wilson found that 45 per cent of white families and 49 per cent of Negro families consisted of husband, wife, and their own children. Thus the "ideal" family pattern, the simple nuclear family, may not be any more common among whites than it is among Negroes. Nationally, about 36 per cent of all Negro families, or more than 1½ million families, are of the simple nuclear type.

A third type of family structure is the *attenuated nuclear family*. This type of family structure has either a father or a mother—but not both—living together with minor children in the parent's own household with no other persons present. Commonly referred to as a broken family, this is an important type of family structure in the United States. Its most frequent form is mother and children living together.

Of the more than 2½ million attenuated nuclear families in the United States in 1965, 733,000 were Negro families, constituting about 6 per cent of all Negro families. The vast majority of these families (689,000) were headed by females, while 44,000 were headed by males who were not married and not living with other relatives. A wide variety of families are encompassed within this type. Ten specific subtypes may be derived, depending on whether the single parent is male or female and whether he or she is (a) single, (b) married with an absent spouse, (c) legally separated, (d) divorced, or (e) widowed.

When we speak of attenuated families, then, and when others speak of one-parent families or broken families, we are not referring to a unified entity, for the attenuated family encompasses a wide variety of subtypes, with different meanings, different causes, and different consequences for its members. The concept of attenuated families is designed to minimize some of the invidiousness associated with other terms and to be simply descriptive, suggesting as it does, that somebody important to the family constellation is missing.

Extended families

In all three types of nuclear families described above, the members live together in their own house, every member being related to the head of the household either by marriage or by birth. In the second major category of family structures, other relatives are introduced into this nuclear household, making of it an extended family.

The types of extended families include: (a) the *incipient extended family*, consisting of a married couple with no children of their own who take in other relatives; (b) the *simple extended family*, consisting of a married couple with their own children, who take in other relatives; and (c) the *attenuated extended family*, consisting of a single, abandoned, legally separated, divorced, or widowed mother or father living with his or her own children, who takes into the household other relatives. Each of these patterns exist in appreciable numbers among Negro families. To know which of the subtypes of extended family is under consideration would help to clarify the generalizations which can be made, for these subtypes differ greatly in their causes and their consequences for their members and for society.

It is also possible to distinguish extended families by examining who is being taken into the primary family. Thus it may make a great deal of difference whether the relative coming to live with a nuclear family is a six-year-old nephew, or an 87-year-old aunt.

There are, then, four classes of relatives who can and often do come to live with Negro families. These are (a) minor relatives, including grandchildren, nieces, nephews, cousins, and young siblings under eighteen; (b) peers of the primary parents, including, particularly, siblings, cousins, and other adult relatives; (c) elders of the primary parents, including, particularly, aunts and uncles; and finally, (d) parents of the primary family heads. The structure of authority, to mention only one aspect of family life, may shift considerably, depending on the status of the relative coming to live in the family.

In 1965 nearly 15 per cent of all Negro families had one or more minor relatives living with them who was not their own child, and better than a quarter of all Negro families had a relative living with them who was eighteen or over. Many of these families had more than one relative living with them, and some had more than one level or status of relative living with them. Among the husband and wife families with children of their own, for example, fully 26.7 per cent had one or more additional relatives living with them in their house. A majority of the female-headed attenuated families and a third of the male-headed attenuated families also had another relative living in the home.

There is a further basis for differentiating subtypes of extended families. Some relatives who come to live with a family come alone. They become, then, *secondary members* of the family. Other relatives come with their spouse or their children. These become *subfamilies*. There are, then, *incipient subfamilies*, or husband and wife pairs who come to live in the household of their relatives; *simple nuclear subfamilies*, consisting of husband, wife, and their small children, who live with another family; and *attenuated subfamilies*, consisting of one parent and his or her children, living in a relative's household. Furthermore, it is very common for two families of siblings or other relatives to share the same household.

Among the 4.4 million Negro families in 1965, there lived a total of 248,000 subfamilies. Altogether, 210,000 of these subfamilies had their own children under eighteen. (The average number of children in each subfamily was 2.6.) The heads of these subfamilies were relatively young, with 34.7 per cent under twenty-five years of age and 67.3 per cent being under thirty-five. But many were obviously peers, elders, and parents. Fully 22.6 per cent were thirty-five to forty-four years old and 10.1 per cent were forty-five years old or over.

The subfamilies seem to consist mostly of young families living with relatives before they are able to make it on their own. The median age of heads of these subfamilies was 29.2, compared with a median age of 43.3 for primary family heads. Altogether, among the 248,000 subfamilies in 1965, 43 per cent were married couples—the majority with children of their own; roughly 15 per cent were incipient subfamilies with no children of their own; 30 per cent were simple nuclear subfamilies; and another 57 per cent were attenuated subfamilies, the majority headed by females.

Augmented families

It would not be appropriate to conclude this discussion of structures and substructures in Negro family life without adding a third major category of families. These are families which have unrelated individuals living with them as roomers, boarders, lodgers, or other relatively long-term guests. Since these unrelated persons often exert major influence in the organization of Negro families, this group of families is referred to as "augmented families." While the number of augmented families is unknown, it is obviously substantial. In 1965 there were nearly a half million Negro persons living with family groups with whom they were not related by marriage, ancestry, or adoption. Of these, 326,000 were men and 173,000 were women. They were mostly adults; 80 per cent of the men and 70 per cent of the women were eighteen years of age and over, and nearly a third were fifty-five years of age and over.

In every Negro neighborhood of any size in the country, a wide variety of family structures will be represented. This range and variety does not suggest, as some commentaries hold, that the Negro family is falling apart, but rather that these families are fully capable of surviving by adapting to the historical and contemporary social and economic conditions facing the Negro people. How does a people survive in the face of oppression and sharply restricted economic and social support? There are, of course, numerous ways. But surely one of them is to adapt the most basic of its institutions, the family, to meet the often conflicting demands placed on it. In this context, then, the Negro family has proved to be an amazingly resilient institution.

•   •   •

We have urged that the Negro family be viewed as a social system, deeply imbedded within and highly interdependent with a variety of other systems, both smaller than and larger than itself. According to this theoretical and philosophical perspective, the Negro family is a creature of the Negro community, which surrounds it, defines it, and gives it its identity and mission. Both the family and the community are creatures of the wider society, which provides or withholds the resources for its creation, survival, and development. The Negro family cannot be understood, appreciated, or enhanced in isolation, but only in relation to its place in the Negro community and the wider society. In this regard, we have taken exception to students of the family who view the Negro family as an independent unit which serves as the causal nexus for the difficulties Negroes often have in the wider society. We have argued that while the family and the society are interdependent, the greater force for defining, enhancing, or obstructing, comes from the wider society to the family, and not the other way round. The far-reaching implications of this point of view suggest not only where one might look in an effort to get a comprehensive understanding of the Negro family, but also at what levels of society one might intervene in order to enhance the functioning of Negro family life.

The second point we have made is that Negro families can best be understood by putting them into historical perspective. We have, then, examined some of the major historical transitions or crises in the life of the Negro people moving from their African origins to contemporary social forces, including a kind of caste system which has plagued the Negro people from their first introduction to America in 1619 until the present time. It is within the context of these historical experiences, both negative and positive, that the Negro people have nurtured a sense of historical identification, which we have labeled black peoplehood.

Third, we have argued that the Negro people have developed over the years a highly differentiated set of social structures which help to define certain ethnic subsocieties. Thus, being Negro is not a uniform experience, but is conditioned by such factors as geographic residence and social class. Again, it is not possible, in our view, to understand or enhance Negro family functioning without regard to these important types of differentiation.

Fourth, we have urged that Negro family structure be viewed in its complexity as adaptation to conditions in the wider social environment of the family. In addition, we have argued that the relationship between the structure and the function of Negro family life is not a simple straightforward one, similar in all respects to the relationship which exists in the white subsociety. The variety of structures are often means of trying to meet the demands of society and the needs of family members. We have sought to distinguish instrumental functions—those required for physical survival—from expressive functions—those associated with the social and psychological requirements of life. Both are highly interrelated and highly dependent on the resources available to the family from the wider society. We have used the concept "screens of opportunity" to describe the limited opportunities available to some Negro families which have enabled them to survive and prosper. In addition, we have described several levels of achievement among Negro families. We have argued against the overwhelming concentration, in the literature and in social reform circles, on the lowest income, most troubled and troubling Negro families as an index of Negro family life, or as the exclusive point of entry for efforts to enhance Negro family life. Throughout, we have laid as much stress on the phenomenon of social caste as on social class, and we have sought to depict the Negro community as a mixture of strengths and weaknesses, conformity and deviance, achievement and failure, with the more positive virtues predominating despite historical oppression.

Editor's Note:

I have rarely talked to anyone about my mother, for I believe that I am capable of killing a person, without hesitation, who happened. to make the wrong kind of remark about my mother. So I purposely don't make any opening for some fool to step into. —Malcolm X

Reading Malcolm X's statement would hardly lead one to conjure up the image of an all dominating, male-emasculating female, but Mrs. Little was one of the statistics on which this mythical black matriarchy is drawn. The fact that she succumbed to the pressures and was unable to continue in her role of "matriarch" did not relieve her of the statistical burden. The black female-head of the household, breadwinner, and only parent—provides the raw data for statistical quantification. The quality or circumstances of her life—whether widowed, divorced, deserted, living with relatives in an extended family, or common-law—are not matters for consideration. And neither the fact that a majority (75 percent) of the minority live in two-parent families nor the fact that there is no empirical data signifying a direct correlation between single-parent families and pathology overshadows the propaganda value of projecting the idea of some inherent disorganization in black families.

Some academicians like Dollard (1939), Abrahams (1962), Hammond (1965), Hannerz (1969), and Schulz

(1969) have even taken the "dozens"* and, in attempting to interpret them, have attributed underlying meanings and explanations that have no basis in reality. A sampling of these are: "ritualized exorcism to break away from the family dominated by the mother; defense against rejection by the mother; masculine struggle against feminine domination." The opposite of these interpretations is actually true, that is, the mother is generally considered *the* person to be given respect, consideration, allegiance, and love. Malcolm X's statement is far more typical of the feeling held about the mother in the black community than the image projected by writers or researchers of a person who has to be rejected in order to save one's manhood. The fact that "my mama" is off limits for jokes, the dozens, or negative remarks is expressed and understood by all. A typical remark is "You don't talk about my mama and get away with it," or when someone skirts the issue, "I laugh and joke, but I don't play." Much of the fighting in these communities stems from perceived insults directed to or about one's mother. The writers previously mentioned also overlook the fact that girls are as actively engaged in the dozens as boys, and further that youth from two-parent families, father-dominated families, or families with other structural variations also play the dozens. It is part of the experience of all black youngsters growing up in the ghetto; there is no corollary in the white community. The tragedy is that while the white audiences to whom these writings are directed have no experiences in the black community and thereby accept these explanations as valid and quote them further, black people who know why and how the dozens are used do not read socio-psychological journals and cannot counteract this misinformation. Increasingly, black researchers who have insights and understandings into phenomena that are really inexplicable to "outsiders" are writing and publishing data that challenge or refute much of the material that is inaccurate. This is one of the serendipitous aspects of the black movement and black awareness. Robert Staples is one such scholar. We are indeed fortunate to have the benefit of his more than ten years devotion to the

*Playing the dozens consists of spontaneous, verbal repartee. Each participant "caps" on the other or attempts to top the last remark. It generally begins with some insouciant remark like "The mailman must have made a few extra stops at your house"—to which might be retorted, "Yeah, well, some chimp must have stopped by *your* pad"—and may drop off soon after or continue, escalating to as vile a statement about the *other* person's mother as all their experiences can bring to bear. The goal is to have the last word and to subjugate the other without resort to physical violence. The ultimate insult is reached when one party directly and vehemently levels a supreme insult against the other's mother. It is considered a point of honor to defend the reputation of one's mother. Friends are careful either to avoid the dozens with each other or not to go too far, because there is a point of no return, a boundary not to be crossed; some statements between friends are unforgivable. Involvement in this process reaches a peak around fifth or sixth grade (ten and eleven year olds) and then tends to dissipate. Occasional remarks heard in adult life may get a laughing response of "trying to play the dozens, huh?" Children are never taught this; it simply happens, a part of the cultural heritage. (Ed.)

study of black family life. "The Myth of the Black Matriarchy" deals with some of the more prevalent misconceptions and manipulative techniques that have flourished under the emotion-laden concept of the matriarchy.

THE MYTH OF THE BLACK MATRIARCHY

ROBERT STAPLES

In dealing with the question of the role of the black woman in the black struggle one must ultimately encounter the assertion that the black community is organized along matriarchal lines, that the domineering black female has been placed in a superordinate position in the family by the historical vicissitudes of slavery, and that her ascendency to power has resulted in the psychological castration of the black male and produced a host of other negative results that include low educational achievement, personality disorders, juvenile delinquency, etc. One of the solutions to the "Negro" question we hear is that black males divest themselves of this female control of black society and reorganize it along patriarchal lines which will eventually solve the problem created by black female dominance.

And one can easily understand how the typical black female would react when told that the problem of black liberation lies on her shoulders, that by renouncing her control over the black male, their other common problems such as inadequate education, chronic unemployment and other pathologies will dissipate into a dim memory.

The myth of a black matriarchy is a cruel hoax.

It is adding insult to injury to black liberation. For the black female, her objective reality is a society where she is economically exploited because she is both female and black; she must face the inevitable situation of a shortage of black males because they have been taken out of circulation by America's neo-colonialist wars, railroaded into prisons, or killed off early by the effects of ghetto living conditions. To label her a matriarch is a classical example of what Malcolm X called making the victim the criminal.

To explode this myth of a black female matriarchy, one must understand the historical role of the black woman and the development of that role as it was influenced by the political and economic organization of American society. Like most myths, the one of a black matriarchy contains some elements of truth. Black women have not been passive objects who were satisfied with watching their menfolk make history. If they had been contented to accept the passive role ascribed to the female gender, then the travail of the past four centuries might have found the black race just as extinct as the dinosaur. It is a poor tribute to their historical deeds to characterize them as "sapphires," an opprobrious term that belies their real contribution to the black struggle.

Referring to black women as matriarchs is not only in contradistinction to the empirical reality of their status but also is replete with historical and semantic inaccuracies. It was in the study by J.J. Bachofen that the term matriarchy was first employed. He was attempting to present a case for the high position of women in ancient society. His conclusion was that since free sexual relations had prevailed during that time and the fathers of the children were unknown, this gave women their leading status in the period he called "mother-right."

A matriarchy is a society in which some, if not all, of the legal powers relating to the ordering and governing of the family-power over property, over inheritance, over marriage, over the house—are lodged in women rather than men. If one accepts this formal definition, the consensus of most historians is that "men reign dominant in all societies; no matriarchy (i.e., a society ruled by women) is known to exist."

From a historical perspective, the black woman has always occupied a highly esteemed place in black culture. The African woman who first reached the shores of the American continent was already part and parcel of the fabric of history. She was descended from women who had birthed some of the great militarists of antiquity and from whose number had come some of the most famous queens to sit upon the thrones of ancient Egypt and Ethiopia. Her exploits and beauty were remembered by Semitic writers and fused into Greek mythology.

Despite her important historical role, there is little doubt about the respective authority patterns in the black family of the pre-slave period of African civilization. There, the family organization was patriarchal in character and was a stable and secure institution. E. Franklin Frazier described the African patriarchal family this way:

His wife and children gathered around him, and served him with as much respect as the best drilled domestics serve their masters; and if it was a fete day or Sunday, his sons-in-law and daughters did not fail to be present, and bring him some small gifts. They formed a circle about him, and conversed with him while he was eating. When he had finished, his pipe was brought to him, and then he bade them eat. They paid him their reverences, and passed into another room, where they all ate together with their mother.

The ordeal of slavery wrought many changes in the family life of Afro-Americans, including the male and female roles. Family life of the African model was an impossibility when the slave's existence had to be devoted primarily to the cultivation and manufacture of tobacco and cotton. The buying and selling of slaves involved the splitting up of families, while the maintenance of discipline on the plantation prevented the husband and father from protecting his wife and children against his white masters and other more favored slaves. The financial value set on slave children and the rewards given to successful motherhood in cash, kind, and promotion from field slave to house slave gave an especially high status to the mother, a status which the father could only enjoy if placed in a position akin to that of a stud animal, this leading to a breaking of family ties and the degradation of family life still further.

Under the conditions of slavery, the American black father was forcefully deprived of the responsibilities and privileges of fatherhood. The black family's desire to remain together was subordinated to the economic interests of the slave-owning class. Only the mother-child bond continually resisted the disruptive effect of economic interests that dictated the sale of fathers away from their families. Not only did the practice of selling away fathers leave the black mother as the prime authority in the household but whenever the black male was present, he was not allowed to play the normal masculine role in American culture. Davie reports that:

> In the plantation domestic establishment, the woman's role was more important than that of her husband. The cabin was hers and rations of corn and salt pork were issued to her. She cooked the meals, tended the vegetable patch, and often raised chickens to supplement the rations. If there was a surplus to sell, the money was hers. She made the clothes and reared the children. If the family received any special favors it was generally through her efforts.

Just as in the society at large, power relationships in the family are aligned along economic lines. The power base of the patriarchal family is, in large part, based on the economic dependence of the female member. In the black slave family, the black woman was independent of the black male for support and assumed a type of leadership in her family life not found in the patriarchal family. At the same time, white society continued to deny black males the opportunity to obtain the economic wherewithal to assume leadership in the family constellation.

The reasons for this suppression of the black male are found in both the economic imperatives of slavery and the sexual value system of white America. In the early period of colonial America, the white family was strongly patriarchal and many of the income and property rights enjoyed by women and children were those 'given' to them by the husband or father. White women had primarily a chattel status, particularly in the Southern part of the country. They were expected to remain chaste until marriage while white Southern males were permitted, or often encouraged, to sow their wild oats before, during and after marriage.

A double standard of sexual behavior allowing premarital sex for men while denying it to women, always poses the problem of what females will provide the source of sexual gratification for bachelor males. There is adequate historical evidence that black slave women were forced into various sexual associations with white males because of their captive status. That physical compulsion was necessary to secure compliance on the part of black women is documented by Frazier, in relating this young man's story:

> Approximately a century and a quarter ago, a group of slaves were picking cotton on a plantation near where Troy, Alabama, is now located. Among them was a Negro woman, who despite her position, carried herself like a queen and was tall and stately. The overseer (who was the plantation owner's son) sent her to the house on some errand. It was necessary to pass through a wooded pasture to reach the house and the overseer intercepted her in the woods and forced her to put her head between the rails in an old stake and rider fence, and there in that position my great-great-grandfather was conceived.

Thus, the double-standard of premarital sexual behavior allowed the Southern white woman to remain "pure" and the bodies of the captive female slaves became the objects of their ruler's sexual passion. Consequently, black males had to be suppressed to prevent them from daring to defend the black woman's honor. For those black males who would not accept their suppression passively, the consequences were severe. As one person reports the story of his father's defense of his mother:

> His right ear had been cut off close to his head, and he had received a hundred lashes on his back. He had beaten the overseer for a brutal assault on my mother, and this was his punishment. Furious at such treatment, my father became a different man, and was so morose, disobedient, and intractable, that Mr. N. decided to sell him. He accordingly parted with him, not long after, to his son, who lived in Alabama; and neither mother nor I ever heard from him again.

During the period of slavery, the physical

resistance of black males to the rape of their women was met with all the brutal punishment white society could muster. That they were not totally successful in their efforts to crush the black man is evidenced in the heroic deeds of Denmark Vesey, Nat Turner, Frederick Douglass, David Walker and others. The acts of these black males are sometimes played down in favor of the efforts of Harriet Tubman, Sojourner Truth and other black females in securing the slave's freedom. Such favoritism can be expected of a racist society bent on perpetuating the myth of a black female matriarchy, with males pictured as ineffective husbands and fathers who are mere caricatures of real men. The literary castration of the black male is illustrated by the best selling novel, *The Confessions of Nat Turner,* which generated much heat and little light, in terms of understanding one of the most important black revolutionists of his time.

The cultural stereotype of the domineering black woman belies the existence of the masses of black women who constituted a defenseless group against the onslaught of white racism in its most virulent sexual and economic manifestations. That black women are still involuntarily subjected to the white male's lust is reflected in the revelations of a white employer to John Howard Griffin, as reported in his book, *Black Like Me:*

> He told me how all of the white men in the region crave colored girls. He said he hired a lot of them both for housework and in his business. "And I guarantee you, I've had it in every one of them before they ever get on the payroll."
> "Surely some refuse," I suggested cautiously.
> "Not if they want to eat—or feed their kids," he snorted. "If they don't put out, they don't get the job."

Black women have frequently been slandered by the cultural folklore that the only free people in the South were the white man and the black woman. While there have been a few black women who have gained material rewards and status through the dispensation of their sexual favors to white men, the massive indictment of all black women for the acts of a few only creates unnecessary intra-group antagonisms and impedes the struggle for black self-determination.

Many proponents of the black matriarchy philosophy assert that the black female gained ascendency in black society through her economic support of the family. Although the unemployment rate of black males is disproportionately higher than that of white males, only a very small minority of black families with both parents present are de-

pendent on the mother for their maintenance. It is a rather curious use of logic to assume that black females, who in 1960 earned an annual wage of $2,372 a year as compared to the annual wage of $3,410 for white women and $3,789 for black men, have an economic advantage over any group in this society.

However, what semblance of black female dominance that is found in our society can be traced to the persistent rate of high unemployment among black males which prevents them from becoming the major economic support of their family. The economic causes of female dominance are manifest. For instance, the percentage of black women in the labor market declines as the percentage of black males employed in manufacturing and mechanical industries is increasing. The effect of higher black male employment is the male's added responsibility for his family's support; the authority of the wife declines and that of the husband increases.

Many black men have not been permitted to become the kings of their castles. If black women wanted to work, there was always employment for them—even during depressions. Sometimes it was even a higher kind of work than that available to black men. Historically, black males have suffered from irregularity of employment more than any other segment of the American proletariat. Thus, they have been placed in a weak economic position which prevents them from becoming steady providers for their families. Any inordinate power that black women possess, they owe to white America's racist employment barriers. The net effect of this phenomenon is, in reality, not black female dominance but greater economic deprivation for families deprived of the father's income.

The myth of a black matriarchy was strengthened by the Moynihan Report released in 1965. Moynihan's central thesis was that the black family was crumbling and that a major part of the blame lay with the black matriarchy extant in the black community. Some of the evidence cited would lack credibility to all but a group bent on making the victim responsible for the crimes of the criminal. Such sources of proof as the higher educational level of black females vis-à-vis black males conveniently overlook the alternative possibility—that many black males are forced to terminate their formal education early in order to help support their family. Instead, they cite the wholly unsupported statement by a "Negro" expert that, "Historically, in the matriarchal society, mothers made sure that if one of their children had a chance for higher education the daughter was the one to pursue it." In a society where men are expected to have a greater amount of

161

education and earn a higher income, it is difficult to imagine black women celebrating the fact that over 60 percent of the college degrees awarded American blacks are received by women. The end result of this disparity, according to one study, is that almost 50 percent of black female college graduates are married to men employed at a lower socio-economic level than their wives.

Moreover, according to Moynihan and his co-horts, the black matriarchy is responsible for the low educational achievement of black males. In marshalling this arsenal of evidence, Moynihan was apparently unable to find any likelihood that the racist educational system, with its concomitant racist teachers, bore any responsibility for the failure of black males to reach acceptable educational levels by white standards. In the criminalization of the victim, countervailing evidence is dismissed out of hand. The fact that black schools are more likely to be housed. in inadequate buildings, with inferior facilities, staffed by inexperienced and racist teachers and overcrowded, only confuses the issue, especially when there is a matriarchal structure that is more handily blamed.

According to the "experts" on the black family, the black male is harshly exploited by the black matriarchy. Many black mothers, they report, express an open preference for girls. This charge is confirmed by a white psychologist, described by a major magazine as devoid of any racism, who states that black males have an inordinate hatred for their mothers. Although there are research studies that reveal no sex-role preference on the part of black mothers, it appears that the practitioners of white social science have not been content with pitting husband against wife but also wish to turn sons against mothers, brothers against sisters. The evidence for these assumptions is not only flimsy, but in some cases also non-existent. If the research is similar to other psychological studies, they have probably used a sample of ten blacks, who, on the verge of a psychotic breakup, wandered into their mental clinic.

These charges of black men hating their mothers must be very puzzling to the black mothers aware of them. They would be puzzled because they realize that if a preference is shown for any sex-role in the black family, it would more likely be expressed in favor of the male child. The problems of raising a black male child in a racist society have been great. Many black mothers out of fear—real or fancied— repressed the aggressive tendencies of their sons in order to save them from the white man's chopping block. For to act as a man in a society which feared his masculinity, the black male was subject to the force of brutal white retaliation. The black mother had to constantly live with the realization that her son might be killed for exercising the prerogatives of manhood. For those black mothers who exorcised their sons' aggressive drives out of concern for their safety, hatred seems to be an inappropriate, and most improbable, response.

In addition to the host of pathologies putatively generated by the black matriarchy, the familiar theory of a relationship between fatherless homes and juvenile delinquency is brought up again. While there is nothing inherently wrong with a woman heading a family, the problem arises when she tries to compete in a society which promotes, expects and rewards male leadership. Consequently, she is unable to bring to her family the share of the social and economic rewards received by father-headed households. It is this very factor that probably accounts for any discernible correlation between mother-headed households and juvenile delinquency. The children in a fatherless home are frequently relegated to the lowest living standards in our society. The problems facing husbandless women with children are compounded by the inequities in American society based on sex role ascriptions.

It is impossible to state that the black woman is just like the women of other races. Her history is different from that of the prototypical white woman and her present-day behavioral patterns have evolved out of her historical experiences. In general, she is more aggressive and independent than white women. There are studies that show that black females are more non-conforming than white females as early as age ten. The reason for her greater self-reliance is that it has been a necessary trait in order for her and her children to survive in a racist and hostile society. Moreover, the society has permitted her more self-assertion than the white female.

Among male chauvinists, aggressiveness per se may be considered an undesirable trait in women and should be restricted to the male species. But this is all part of the age-old myth about the inherent nature of woman as a passive creature. More often than not, it has served as a subterfuge for the exploitation of women for the psychological and material gain of the male species. Black women lose nothing by their greater tenacity. That tenacity has, historically, been a source of strength in the black community. While white women have entered the history books for making flags and engaging in social work, black women have participated in the total black liberation struggle.

While recognizing these differences, the question before us now is how much power do black women really have and how is it exercised? Power is commonly defined as the ability to dominate men, to compel their action even against their wishes.

The black woman has often been characterized as a more powerful figure in the family because she participates more in making decisions about what kind of car to buy, where to go on a vacation, etc. In certain cases, she is the only one to make major decisions. A closer inspection of her decision-making powers often reveals that she does not make decisions counter to her husband's wishes, but renders them because he fails to do so. The reason he defers to her in certain decisions is simply because she is better equipped to make them. Usually, she has more formal education than her mate and in matters relating to the white society, she knows her way around better. She is more familiar with the machinations of white bureaucracies since contacts with the white world have been more available to black women than to black men.

Making decisions that black men cannot, or will not, make is a poor measure of the power a black woman has in the family. The chances are good that no decisions are made which he actively opposes. The power of black women is much like American democracy—it is more apparent than real. Power alignments are frequently based on the alternatives an individual has in a situation where there is a conflict of interests. It is here where the black male achieves the upper level of the power dimension.

Whenever a black man and black woman find themselves in objective and irremediable conflict, the best solution is to find another mate. The objective reality of black women is that black men are scarcer than hen's teeth. For a variety of reasons, there is an extremely low sex ratio in the black community, especially during the marriageable years—18 to 45 years. This means that black women must compete for a relatively scarce commodity when they look forward to marriage. They are buyers in a seller's market. Black women, like all women, have their affectional and sexual needs. Many a black male's shortcomings must be tolerated for the sake of affection and companionship. In a sense, many black women have to take love on male terms.

The low sex ratio hardly allows black women to exercise any meaningful control over black men. In fact, as one black woman states:

As long as she is confined to an area in which she must compete fiercely for a mate, she remains the object of sexual exploitation and the victim of all the social evils which such exploitation involves.

---

*In New York City, for instance, there are only 75 black men for every 100 black women in about this same age range.

In the Negro population, the excess of girls is greatest in the fifteen-to-forty-four age group which covers the college years and the age when most marriages occur ... the explosive social implications of an excess of more than half a million Negro girls and women over fourteen years of age are obvious.... How much of the tensions and conflicts traditionally associated with the matriarchal framework of Negro society are in reality due to this imbalance and the pressures it generates.

Another index of the matriarchy is simply the percentage of female-headed households in the black community. The Moynihan theory of the black matriarchy derives from his findings that 25 percent of all black families have a female head. This "proof" of a matriarchal family structure brings up many interesting questions, not excluding the important one: over whom do these women have control? Logically, the only power they have is to face a super-exploitation by the system of white racism that bi-parental black families do not encounter to the same degree.

The matriarchal myth is not always applied to only black families. A number of social scientists claim that suburban white families are matriarchal. They point out that the commuting father's disappearance during the day leaves the mother in charge of the home and children. As a result, the father's power is reduced in these areas, and he is relegated to enacting the "feminine" role of handyman. This observation has prompted one person to suggest that exhorting black slum dwellers to emulate the presumably more stable white middle class, restore father to his rightful place, and build a more durable family life will subsequently expose them to the threat of the suburban matriarchy.

Any profound analysis of the black matriarchy proposition should reveal its fallacious underpinnings. Recognition of this fact raises the crucial question as to why white society continues to impose this myth on the consciousness of black people. This writer submits that it has been functional for the white ruling class, through its ideological apparatus, to create internal antagonisms in the black community between black men and black women to divide them and to ward off effective attacks on the external system of white racism. It is a mere manifestation of the divide-and-conquer strategy, used by most ruling classes through the annals of man, to continue the exploitation of an oppressed group.

In the colonial period of Algeria, the same situation existed wherein the colonists attempted to use the female population to continue their colonial rule. Fanon reports that the colonial administration

163

devised a political doctrine for destroying the structure of Algerian society. By encouraging Algerian women to break the bonds of male domination in their society—setting male against female—the colonialists hoped to dilute the Algerian capacity for resistance. According to Fanon, it was:

> the woman who was given the historic mission of shaking up the Algerian man. Converting the woman, winning her over to the foreign values, wrenching her free from her status, was at the same time achieving a real power over the man and attaining a practical, effective means of destroying Algerian culture.

In contemporary America, a female liberation movement is beginning to gain impetus. This movement is presently dominated by white women seeking to break out of the centuries-old bondage imposed upon them by the male chauvinists of the ruling class. Whether black women should participate in such a movement is questionable. Hatred of a social curse which is part and parcel of an exploitative society that discriminates not only against blacks but also women should not be confused with hatred of men. The adversary is not one sex or the other—it is the racist, capitalist system which needs, breeds and preys upon oppressions of all types.

Any movement that augments the sex-role antagonisms extant in the black community will only sow the seed of disunity and hinder the liberation struggle. Whether black women will participate in a female liberation movement is, of course, up to them. One, however, must be cognizant of the need to avoid a diffusion of energy devoted to the liberation struggle lest it dilute the over-all effectiveness of the movement. Black women cannot be free *qua* women until all blacks attain their liberation.

The role of the black woman in the black liberation struggle is an important one and cannot be forgotten. From her womb have come the revolutionary warriors of our time.* The revolutionary vanguard has a male leadership but the black woman has stepped beside her man engaged in struggle and given him her total faith and commitment. She has thrust herself into the life or death struggle to destroy the last vestige of racism and exploitation in the American social structure. In the process of continuing her life-long fight against racist oppression, the myth of her matriarchal nature will soon join the death agony of America's racist empire. Until that time arrives, the black woman should be revered and celebrated—not only for her historical deeds in the building of African civilization, in the struggle to maintain the black peoples of America as a viable entity—but for her contemporary role in enabling black people to forge ahead in their efforts to achieve a black nationhood.

Editor's Note:

Describing the death of his father, his mother's breakdown, and his feeling about his family, Malcolm X wrote: "Separated though we were, all of us maintained fairly close touch. . . . Despite the artificially created separation and distance between us, we still remained very close in our feelings toward each other." James Weldon Johnson, Richard Wright, James Baldwin, Claude Brown, and Chester Himes also express similar feelings about strong attachments to their family. Others share the feeling but have no recorded statements that can be referred to by those who come after them. This portrayal of the family in positive terms, albeit different from white middle-class models, is far too often the exception rather than the rule in journal reports of white social scientists.

"Culture, Class, and Family Life Among Low-Income Urban Negroes" by Hylan Lewis is one of the exceptions. This article uses field material from a child-rearing study conducted in Washington, D.C. The accumulated data, including interviews with low-income black urban parents, present a picture of variations, complexities, and aspirations for their children that range from deep concern to disinterest. The greater portion of these parents employ positive means within their limited conditions and exhibit a willingness to sacrifice for their children's interests. The fact that two-thirds of all black college graduates come from families earning below $5000 a year is *prima facie* evidence of this willingness to sacrifice.

CULTURE, CLASS, AND FAMILY LIFE AMONG LOW-INCOME URBAN NEGROES

HYLAN LEWIS

Family organization and child rearing among Negroes in the United States are not, to use a phrase of Ralph Ellison's, "a hermetic expression of Negro sensibility." They are, rather, parts of the same forces that have shaped contemporary society and culture in the United States. E. Franklin Frazier demonstrated brilliantly how the family among Negroes, rooted as it is in human nature, "may take protean forms as it

---

*It is interesting to note that, despite unfounded rumors about the emasculation of the black male, the thrust of the black liberation struggle has been provided almost exclusively by a black male leadership. In selecting leaders of black organizations, black females inevitably defer to some competent black male, an act which shows how much they really prefer the dominating position they supposedly have in black society.

survives or is reborn in times of cataclysmic social change."

In a paper written for the 1960 White House Conference on Children and Youth, I suggested that not enough is known about the dynamics of present family forms and functions and about the behavior patterns which are distinctly urban products.... The forms, as in the case of the family headed by the female, may be the same but the context in which they fit and function has probably changed in important details. Knowledge of [the historical] background is necessary but not sufficient to explain and understand the Negro family... in the changing cities of today.

This study has two purposes: first, to illustrate some of the faulty ways in which the terms "culture" and "class" are used to describe and explain family behavior of low-income urban Negroes; and, second, to present some findings and illustrative materials from a study of low-income families in the District of Columbia. These findings and materials accent further the belief that family forms and functions among Negroes in today's cities are understood best, and dealt with best, as products of contemporary urban life.

I

The term "culture" is now widely applied to numerous dimensions and components of the behavior of aggregates, groups, and persons. Like "class," with which it is frequently used in combination—and often interchangeably, it seems— "culture" is sometimes used in an actuarial fashion to describe and predict the life chances of individual, aggregates, and groups. At other times it is used to describe and explain social and physical conditions; and at still other times it is used to describe and to explain the objective and subjective characteristics, the conscious and unconscious behavior, and the character of individuals and groups associated with these life chances and conditions.

"Culture" is used variously to refer to the living conditions, the chances of improving socioeconomic status, and the personality attributed to members of low-income families and to residents in low-income areas. Too frequently some of these things are described, and even defined, in terms of one another. That they are related would hardly be disputed; however, the precise nature of the relationships and their implications for family life among Negroes, for example, are not made clear.

The linkage of culture and class in itself makes for problems: "culture differences and social strati-fication vary independently. They can neither be reduced, nor can they be equated." And David Riesman aptly suggests that "cultural differences, no matter how forcefully they may strike the ear, the eye, or the nose, are not necessarily connected with character differences of equal significance." For example, some of the things frequently referred to as cultural and class differences in the child-rearing behavior of low-income Negroes, and that are seen as significant differences, are probably better seen as temporary gaucheries, or perhaps gaffes, in acting out valued aspects of the culture of the wider society.

A possibly serious consequence of starting with the assumption that the low-income Negro family is a cultural type, particularly when deviant behavior is involved, is indicated in Potter's comments about studies of national character:

This inclination to take culture as a given factor and to explain character in terms of the culture without very much consideration of the forces which determined the culture... is a limiting factor which in the last analysis could interfere with the deepest and fullest understanding of society. The determinants of the culture must themselves be introduced fully and carefully into the analysis.

The constant and basic danger is that the loose use of the term "culture" in explanations of family life among Negroes can easily encourage situations where "pseudofacts have a way of inducing pseudo-problems, which cannot be solved because matters are not as they purport to be." An illustration is taken from a prominent sociologist's address on urbanization problems:

In the case of the Negro, now, it is not a problem of Americanization, because the Negro has been an American citizen, on the average, considerably longer than the white person in the United States. It is a problem of acculturation, however, because the movement represents essentially a movement of people with a primitive folk culture from the rural slum south, to the urban north and west, or to urban areas within the south.

The process of acculturation is one of the most difficult a human being can experience.... It requires time—time measured in human generations rather than years....

Let us illustrate a few of the problems. A Negro in the Mississippi Delta tosses his empty whisky bottle or beer can in a cotton patch, and what difference does it make: But on the asphalt pavements of a city it can make a difference aesthetically and with respect to safety.

None of the key assertions made above about the relationship between culture and the behavior of urban Negroes is an unqualified fact. One ignore the considerable extent to which urban Negroes of the first, second, and third generations are represented in the statistical indications of the problem behavior unevenly distributed among low-income persons that is categorized frequently as lower-class behavior. Social disorganization in some major urban centers is by no means limited to the recently arrived representatives of "a primitive folk culture from the rural slum south."

Social science knowledge and experience indicate that the process of acculturation—assuming that this is the key problem—may or may not be difficult; and that it may or may not require "time measured in human generations rather than years." The degree of difficulty and the amount of time involved vary, and the rate at which differing aspects of differing cultures is taken over varies, even when the two cultures involved are disparate and alien, as is not the case here. It makes a difference in what we seek to know, and to change, about the lives and the life chances of low-income urban Negroes if we assume that their behavior primarily reflects either the lack of acculturation of the migrant or the imperatives of a Negro lower-class culture.

The last illustration suggests important questions that need to be answered: In the search for cultural differences that *make* a difference in family living and child rearing, how is the salience of tossed whisky bottles figured? How really significant is this trait in comparison with church attendance, latch-key children, illegitimacy rates, and housing availability and costs, for example? Do lower-class persons toss the empty whisky bottles or beer cans on the streets because of a significant difference in shared norms, because they do not know any better, or because they know better and do not care? And what distinguishes their behavior from that of other American litterbugs? Assuming they do not know any better, how long would it take them to learn not to? And what would be needed to properly cue and reinforce the preferred custom—or is it a habit?

Among the unplanned effects of the linkage of the term "class" with the term "culture," as seen in the popular circulation of the term "lower-class culture," are the tendency to select the more colorful, dramatic, "different"—but not necessarily significant—traits and to encourage invidious and double standards of judgment. The inclinations to condemn or to condone, to denigrate or to romanticize, get in the way of accurate description and interpretation of family and neighborhood life among contemporary low-income urban Negroes.

Some students of persons who are termed lower class frequently insist on having it both ways: On the one hand, there is the frequent assertion that such people are characteristically inarticulate, noncommunicative, which can be taken to mean either that they have little to say or that they do not have the native or "cultural" equipment to do so. On the other hand, when representatives from this category do talk, there is a disposition to raise serious questions about what they say, particularly when it is inconsistent with their behavior or with assumptions about the mainsprings of their behavior. Of course, either or both of these allegations may be objectively true. The point is that neither low or inadquate communication nor a gap between professions and behavior is a class trait.

First, there is a question as to how much the differences in behavior reported and perceived are reflections of the methods used and how much they are due to the class and culture of the subjects.

Second, "pretend rules"—reflections of what A. L. Kroeber called "the trick of professing one thing and doing another"—are probably common to all individuals and groups, regardless of class and cultural placement: "They [societies] vary chiefly in what they are inconsistent about." According to Kroeber, we should not feel too harshly about some of the gaps themselves: "Professions after all mean standards and ideals; and it may be better . . . to have standards and fall short of them than not to have them." Whether or not this is a sound position, there is still the key question: Are the things that Negro parents are inconsistent about, for example in their child-rearing behavior, reflective of class and cultural differences? And if they are, why?

A summing up of some of our concerns about the ways in which culture and class are sometimes used to describe and to explain the child-rearing behavior of low-income people would stress dangers arising from:

1. Confusions about the meanings and uses of culture and class, and about the kinds of dimensions of behavior to which they might be appropriately and usefully applied;

2. Questionable extensions of assumptions and of limited data; and what is probably more serious, the partial and garbled versions that filter into other fields and into popular thinking;

3. Tendencies toward perception of culture and class as fixed and "determinative"—as the inflexible arbiters of life chances as well as behavior;

4. Preoccupations with culture and class that divert not only the consideration of the forces that affect them, but also divert consideration of the probabilities, the pace, and the direction of changes in them;

5. The urge to order, under one general rubric, varying and frequently disparate behaviors, or aspects of them. In at least some instances these behaviors might best be understood and dealt with as lacking in the coherence and consistency of cultural systems and all that this conception connotes;

6. Tendencies to impute to a total category, such as the lower class, the depreciated, and probably more dramatic and threatening, characteristics of a segment of that category;

7. Underestimation or exclusion from attention of the range in behavior: "for some problems the range rather than the mode may be the crucial datum";

8. Tendencies to oversimplify complex behavior, frequently obscuring the fact that people today, in Aldous Huxley's words, tend to be "multiple amphibians living in a number of worlds at once";

9. Misplaced emphasis on differences, to the exclusion and underemphasis of basic similarities that derive from the same general culture. Some of these differences are of questionable significance and tenacity, while the similarities might be the keys to understanding behavior, and to programing change. Best results might come from leading to the child-rearing strengths of individuals and groups, rather than to their perceived weaknesses.

II

In the discussion that follows, some of the data and propositions that accent these concerns will be presented.

Family and community field reports and family ratings of the families studied in the District of Columbia yield indications of underestimated diversity and range in the child-rearing behavior of low-income families. There is variability in the degree and quality of parental concern about children's health, education, and welfare demonstrated among the low-income families studied. Evidences of positive concern and a willingness to sacrifice for children, despite deprivation and trouble, are found in a good proportion of the families. Mrs. R., a low-income parent with a limited education, provides one illustration of a combination of these elements.

Mr. and Mrs. R. are the parents of eleven children, nine of whom are living at home. They have lived in Washington less than three years. Recently Mrs. R. remained in jail for two weeks while awaiting trial for assaulting her husband. Her minor children were placed in Junior Village when she was taken to jail. Excerpts from the mother's account of the experience and of the manner in which she weighed personal and family alternatives follow:

You know, I didn't have to stay in jail those two weeks. I could have paid forty dollars for bail and gotten out, but I just kind of felt that I'd stay there for a while. I just though I'd be better off.

I had seventy-three dollars on me because I had the rent money. One mind told me to pay the bail and the other mind said no. So when they told me I could make one telephone call and asked me who I wanted to call, I told them to just call the rent man and tell him to come and get the rent and I would stay in jail.

The rent man came and got it that Tuesday. I was glad I paid the rent, as we had to have a place to stay when I got out. The only thing that worried me while I was in jail was the children. I worried about them, as they have never been separated from me before. When I got out of jail my husband came for me and asked me if I didn't want to come home and fix something to eat for the children. I told him, "No, I just want to get the children," and I kept right on from the jail out to Junior Village to get them. They had been taken good care of there, but there won't be no more separations. The next separation will just have to be a death separation because I know I won't do anything like that again. . . .

I have always treated my husband nice and tried to help him. I also tried to share. When I have worked I have given him money when he needs it. I don't drink and I told him that if he can't control his drinking then he shouldn't drink. I didn't like him out there in the yard acting ugly in front of all the neighbors. . . .

Before I go back to jail I'll leave. This is the first and last time I'll go to a place like that. Not to jail. Not to be locked up. But I did get some relief in that place. Somehow you don't mind it when you've been listening to cursing day and night. It worried me to be away from the children so long but I did get some rest. I got tired of sitting around there and asked for some work to do and they put me in the laundry. The matron was sorry to see me go because I was such a good worker.

Our materials and analysis indicate that parents who show a high degree of concern as well as parents who show a low degree of concern are found both among families receiving public assistance and those which are not, among one-parent and two-parent families, among recently arrived families, and among those either native to Washington or long-time residents in the city. Distinguishable are parents with high concern who demonstrate it in their behavior, parents with considerable verbal concern who exhibit inconsistent or contradictory behavior, and parents who express little or no concern and are extremely neglectful.

Field reports have documented the impression that regardless of the quality of active concern about their children, parents, with few exceptions, do not prefer or approve the circumstances in which they now live and in which their children are being brought up. Even in the case of the most neglectful parents, the evidence points to the fact that they ascribe no virtue to neglectful behavior in themselves or in others or to neighborhood disorganization and poor housing. If there is any suggestion of approval, it smacks of perverseness, defiance, bravado, or desperation of the I-don't-care type.

The field materials of the Child Rearing Study lend support to the proposition that these low-income urban parents tend to show greater conformity to, and convergence with, middle-class standards in their verbalizations of values—in what they say they want (or would like to want)—than in their actual behavior.

It was suggested earlier that some things that are statistically true about child-rearing forms, circumstances, and activities may be quite misleading clues to the complex child-rearing behavior of low-income urban Negroes.

III

Gross statistics and descriptions of family social structure among low-income urban Negroes provide at best partial and limited indications of the dynamics of child rearing. Following are some propositions that are pertinent to this assertion, and that have come out of our study on child-rearing practices among low-income families in the District of Columbia.

1. The amount and the implications of the diversity among Negroes in low-income urban families are too frequently overlooked or underrated in popular and scientific thinking.

2. Negro family behavior, and especially those with low-income, is marked by a shifting back and forth between, and a compartmentalizing of, selected aspects of poverty and deprivation and of adequacy and affluence.

3. Much low-income family behavior has a strongly pragmatic cast, essentially nonclass, noncultural (or transcending class and culture, as currently used) in its derivations.

4. The answer to the problem of family disorganization is not one of inculcating marriage and family values in young couples; there is ample

evidence that they exist. The critical test is to find ways and means for the young adult male to meet the economic maintenance demands of marriage and family life.

Since the job is a crucial determinant of where and how the family fits in the society and of the effectiveness of its claims on many of the society's rewards, probably the most important single clue to the quality of change in the Negro family and on the community [in which Negroes live in any numbers] is ... in the job picture . . . for the male.

The evidence suggests that Negro mothers from the low-income category, as much as any mothers in any category of our population, want and prefer their men to be strong and supportive in marriage, family, and community relationships. There is no need to invoke a mystique of the matriarchy to explain low-income, female-headed child-rearing units when we take into consideration the economic pressures of late twentieth-century urban living upon the young adult Negro male, and especially the ways in which these alter the choices open to low-income women and men.

Related to these key propositions about child rearing among contemporary urban Negroes are several factors, the most important of which are:

1. The contrast found in many low-income urban Negro families between the parents' verbalizations about their own childhood and life values and the actual behavior of these parents;

2. The crucial nature of the family cycle—the age of parents in relation to years married and the number and ages of children;

3. The relationship between the lack of child-rearing options and the early and differential effects of extra-family influences on low-income families;

4. Indications of pressures toward early social weaning (independence training) among many low-income Negro families, particularly those with large numbers of minor children;

5. Indications of pressures both inside and outside the family that operate on some parents to diminish confidence in their ability to control children who are not yet adolescent, sometimes as young as five and six;

6. Some of the presumed freedom of lower-class children to move outside the household and freedom from parental control reflecting the results of either early independence training (early social weaning) in large families or the urban child's success in wresting this freedom from overburdened, confused, and sometimes inadequate parents.

Presented next are some materials that suggest the complex nature of the relationships between behavior and conditions, and professions and preferences, among low-income urban Negro parents, drawn from field notes of two field workers, Camille Jeffers and Elliot Liebow, who did participant observation, the first as a resident in a public housing project and the second with "street corner" young male adults. In the first set of illustrations, two Negro male adults indicate something of their slants on themselves, their families, and life.

Although the present condition and outlook of each of the men is different, their expressions share the marks of human inconsistency and voice strong preferences for recognizable goals of the greater society. In the first set of excerpts from field documents, a semiliterate thirty-year-old construction worker expresses himself on a variety of subjects, including himself.

Sonny has been in Washington nine years. During this period he has been married and separated and fathered eight children, three on his wife and, by his account, five others on five different women.

On education and "being somebody":
[Sonny is talking about a man the field worker (FW) and he had met]

SONNY: That's what I ought to be doing. I ought to be in his place ... dressed nice, going to school, got a good job.

FW: You make more than he does.

SONNY: It's not the money.... It's position, I guess. He's got a position. When he finish school he gonna be a supervisor. People respect him.... Just thinking about people with an education and position gives me a feeling right here [touching his stomach].

FW: You're educated too, Sonny.... You have a skill, a trade. You're a cement finisher. You can make a building, pour a sidewalk.

SONNY: That's different. Look, can anybody do what you're doing? Can anybody just come up and do your job?

FW: I don't think so.

SONNY: Well, in one week I can teach you cement finishing. You won't be as good as me because you won't have the experience but you'll be a cement finisher. That's what I mean. Anybody can do what I'm doing and that's what gives me this feeling....

Suppose I like this girl. I go to her house and I meet her father. He starts talking about what he done today. He talks about operating on somebody and sewing them up and about surgery. I know he's a doctor cause of the way he talks. Then she starts talking about what she did. Maybe she's a boss or a supervisor. Maybe she's a lawyer and her father say to me, "and what do you do, Mr. Washington?"...

You remember, at the court house, Lonnie's trial? You and Jim Marshall was talking in the hall? ... You remember, I just stood there listening. I didn't say a word ... because I didn't even know what you were talking about. That's happened to me a lot.

FW: Hell, you're nothing special. That happens to everybody. Nobody knows everything. One man is a doctor, so he talks about surgery.... But doctors and teachers don't know nothing about concrete. You're a cement finisher and that's your specialty.

SONNY: Maybe so, but when was the last time you saw anybody standing around talking about concrete?

*

Sonny turned away from a TV drama involving a young Mexican boy and his father to say that if he had a million dollars he would travel all over the world and learn a lot of things "like you and those people at the museum." [The field worker asked why this was important to him. (Sonny had earlier accompanied the field worker to visit a museum that he had worked on as a construction worker but had never been inside after it was finished.)]

SONNY: Well, I think about my oldest boy [about nine] a lot. I want to be a big man in his eyes. If he's out on the street playing with some kids and one boy say, "My daddy's a lawyer," I want my boy to be able to say that his daddy is a big man too. It's too late for that now. I can't hardly read or write but I still want to learn things.

On being a parent, in wedlock and out of wedlock:

We were sitting in Dickie's Grill and Sonny was recalling the circumstances in which Hattie had told him he was the father of her unborn child. "When a woman says it's your baby, you just got to go along with her."

169

Later, we talked about Linda, the mother of his youngest child. He said that when Linda told his she was pregnant, she said she knew an old woman who would get rid of it for fifty dollars: "You're a married man, you can't help me."

"You have the baby," Sonny told her, "I'll do what I can."

I [the field worker] asked whether the fifty dollars had anything to do with it. He said the money had nothing to do with it. "Everybody should have a chance. My mother didn't get rid of me like that, so why should I do that to somebody else? That wouldn't be right. . . . When he grows up, maybe he be a doctor or lawyer. He come to me when I'm old. He say, 'You help me when I was little, now you old and I help you.'"

Shirley, the white waitress and co-owner of Dickie's Grill, joined us for a beer. Shirley, who lived alone and was five months pregnant, said she was making arrangements to put her baby up for adoption because she wouldn't be able to give the baby the care, time, and attention he had a right to. "It wouldn't be fair for me to keep it," she said. "I know I'm doing the right thing." When she left I asked Sonny if he thought Shirley was doing the right thing.

"No. If you got a baby and you got to scuffle, you scuffle. You don't give him away. Suppose it's a boy. A boy always likes a older head. Suppose he starts going out with this woman. He say he an orphan—is that what you call it?—and she say that she had a baby once but she give him away. Then they find out that she's his mother." ["Do you know anyone that's happened to?"] "No, but I've heard about it."

*

Sonny had just confessed to me that he had been lying about his wife and children living with him. He said his wife had left him in November, 1960. "It was all a lie, Ralph, but I love my wife. When I go to bed at night she's with me and my kids are too and deep down in my heart I believe she's coming back. I really believe it. And if she do, I'm going to throw out all these other women and I'm going to change my whole life."

*

Presented next are the roughly parallel comments of a twenty-eight-year-old man who has been in Washington six years. He is married and the father of two children.

On being somebody:

I believe in religion. I live by the Book. . . . I don't drink; it just never appealed to me. I don't gamble and I don't stay out late or run around. I work hard. . . . I always save some pennies from every dollar.

*

I live for wants. I don't fool around. I see something I want, I get it. When I go to the Safeway, if I see a steak marked five dollars and I want a steak, I turn it over, look at both sides, and if I like it I buy it.

*

I live for today. . .but I keep an eye on tomorrow, too. When I go to bed, my wife knows that if I don't live till morning she got ten thousand dollars for herself and the kids.

If I die, flowers won't do no good. . . . All I want is a plain box. Let someone say, "He was a good man," then put me in the hole, cover me with dirt, and let me go.

My wife's check goes straight to the bank. We don't even look trice at it. And we save something from my check too if we can.

When I get paid, we sit down together with pencil and paper and we write down how we're going to spend the money. Everything gets written down, everything. We even write down the sixty or seventy cents I'm going to put in that pinball machine right there. I don't drink, I don't gamble, and I don't stay out late or run around. I work hard and that's relaxation for me.

*

Next year, or the year after that, we're going to buy a house with a piece of ground, maybe out in Virginia. I don't like being next to somebody else and neither does my wife. . . . We want to be by ourselves.

On marriage and the family:

I want my boy to have everything I didn't have. I want him to have everything he wants, within reason. . . .

You can't give a kid too much. You can't give a kid too much loving or anything. There's no such thing as too much for a kid.

*

Sometimes it's good to take a switch to a kid until he's ten or eleven years old. I ain't taken a switch to either one of mine in a year and a half, but I'll do it if I thinks they needs it. But not after they're ten or eleven. When a boy gets that old, it starts getting hard for him to cry. If you take a switch to him and he don't cry, he starts thinking he's tough, and taking a switch to him just makes him hard.

*

You got to talk to children, to explain things to them.

*

When my little girl gets up in the morning, the first thing she wants to do is eat. I tell her no, that she got to take a bath and then she can eat. I don't make her get dressed all the way. I tell her she can set at the table in her underwear if she takes her bath, and while she's doing that I put on the water for oatmeal or something.

*

You gotta know when to see what they're [children] doing too. Sometimes my boy gets to tearing up the Sunday papers. He knows he ain't supposed to do that, and sometimes I don't let on I see him doing it. Then I looks surprised and I say, "Somebody tore up the Sunday paper. Why don't you put it in the trash," and that's all there is to it. A kid needs that sometimes.

*

[Children] got to know when you're just fooling around and when you mean business Most of the time my kids know just from my tone of voice or the way I look whether I'm playing around. They know they gotta listen to me when I ain't playing around.

*

When Dick's eight-year-old son came home from school crying and explained that he had been beaten up by some bigger boys, Dick told him he didn't want him to come home crying from school. He was to return to school the next day, and if the boys bothered him again, he was to stay and fight hard as he could and do as much damage to them as he could. And if he was beaten, he was to do the same thing the next day and the next.

•   •   •

Our Washington family and community materials indicate that the behaviors observed in the varying low-income families were not generated by or guided by an urban lower-class "cultural system in its own right—with an integrity of its own." This is not meant to suggest that there are no differences other than income between this category and the adequate-income category of the population, or that there are no modalities in the characteristics and in the behaviors of this segment. On the contrary, we reconfirm that there are several modes or styles of family living and child rearing rather than a single or basic mode or style among urban Negroes. We are especially impressed by the range of behavior within the low-income category of Negro families.

The behavior of the bulk of the poor Negro families appears as pragmatic adjustments to external and internal stresses and deprivations experienced in the quest for essentially common values. A seeming paradox is that affirmation of, if not demonstration of, some of America's traditional virtues and values in their purest form is found to be strong and recurrent among even the most deprived of Negro families. Our view is that is it probably more fruitful to think of different types of low-income Negro families reacting in various ways to the facts of their position and to relative isolation rather than to the imperatives of a lower-class or significantly different ethnic culture. It is important that we do not confuse the basic life chances and actual behavior of the contemporary Negro parent with his basic cultural values and preferences.

Our experience suggests further that the further that the focus of efforts to change should be on background conditions and on precipitants of deviant behavior rather than on the presumably different class or cultural values operative in child-rearing behavior among Negroes, and particularly low-income Negroes. The way to remove the threat of the problem behavior of low-income Negro families is not likely to be found in a kind of functionalism or cultural relativism, or in sealing off persons who are presumed to be most inclined to exhibit such behavior; nor is it to be found in getting low-income urban Negro families in general, or a segment of them, to revamp what is presumed to be their culture.

PART III. B:

DIMENSIONS OF BLACK COMMUNITY LIFE – PSYCHOLOGY

WE WEAR THE MASK

PAUL L. DUNBAR

We wear the mask that grins and lies,
It hides our cheeks and shades our eyes,—
This debt we pay to human guile;
With torn and bleeding hearts we smile,
And mouth with myriad subtleties.

Why should the world be overwise,
In counting all our tears and sighs?
Nay, let them only see us, while
   We wear the mask.

We smile, but O great Christ, our cries
To Thee from tortured souls arise.
We sing, but oh, the clay is vile
Beneath our feet and long the mile;
But let the world dream otherwise,
   We wear the mask.

Editor's Note:

Studies on mental illness have suggested that a greater proportion of lower-class persons suffer from schizophrenia and other psychoses than higher-status individuals. The methodology generally used by researchers in this area has been epidemiological, with hospitalization the most frequently used approximation or index of severe mental illness. There is a good deal of evidence that many factors other than degree of illness influence whether or not one is hospitalized. Proximity to mental hospitals, labeling processes in the community, attitudes toward mental illness, public vs. private resources and agencies, alternatives available to upper stratum individuals, and outpatient services are some of the variables operative. Recent researchers investigating the incidence and prevalence of mental illness among the social classes found that "once the lower classes came to hospitals for treatment or care, they were more likely to remain there, but the frequence with which they initially became ill was only slightly greater than that of higher status patients." Using, for the first time, evidence of persons receiving treatment either in clinics or from private psychiatrists, this study found the highest rates of hospitalization among the upper social strata. John A. Clausen points out another factor that is frequently overlooked: "Persons whose social backgrounds are grossly divergent from that of the psychiatrist (e.g., lower-class persons) tend to be seen by him as sicker than those whose attitudes and behaviors are closer to his own outlook. Unless and until there are valid tests for the diagnosis of schizophrenia and other mental illnesses, studies of so-called true prevalence must deal with biases in clinical classification due to subcultural perspective, just as studies of treated prevalence must deal with biases in community and professional response."

The article by Benjamin Passamanick, M.D., currently Associate Commissioner, New York State Department of Mental Hygiene, presents data that serves to elaborate on the information presented above and contrasts sharply with that generally found on the prevalence of mental disorders. Dr. Passamanick did not limit himself to the epidemiological approach but utilized additional sources of important data.

A SURVEY OF MENTAL DISEASE IN AN URBAN POPULATION VII: AN APPROACH TO TOTAL PREVALENCE BY RACE

BENJAMIN PASSAMANICK

This paper attempts to deal with the problem of the prevalence of mental diseases among an urban population of nonwhites and to compare, as dispassionately and objectively as possible, these rates with those for whites.

To my knowledge the earliest census which contained data on white and nonwhite rates for mental institutionalization was the 1840 census. The rates contained therein indicated that Northern nonwhites had substantially higher rates than Southern nonwhites. Pro-slavery protagonists found this disparity grist for their mill. They concluded that this discrepancy indicated two things. First, that the innately inferior Negro could not withstand the stress of competition in a comparatively freer society. Second, that nonwhites were better understood and treated in the South and hence, the lower insanity rate. The fact of the matter was that gross inaccuracies had occurred in the census data. For example, Negro rates in some communities were so high that they actually exceeded the total Negro population in the community. The physician who had originally published a paper based on these rates eventually voluntarily retracted his published statements. Despite these inaccuracies, and the obvious biases inherent in using first admissions for incidence rates, these and similar data continued to be used.

By 1880, the issue of white versus nonwhite rates and regional variations in the latter was broadened to include foreign versus native-born rates. The stimulus for the latter, of course, was the increasing entry into this country of Irish and Catholic population and the hostility this immigration aroused. The 1880 census stated, for example, that, "the extraordinary ratio of insanity among the foreign-born has attracted wide attention." The report continued by asserting that "the question of age has a bearing upon the comparative number of the insane who are of native and of foreign birth" and that "the difference disappears, in large measure, when, instead of comparing the number of insane with the total population, we compare it with the population above the age at which insanity ordinarily occurs, that is to say above the age of 15 years."

In time the immigration question, because of increasingly severe restrictions on the number who could enter, became academic. The question of the existence of a racial disparity in rates remains, and if anything, is as heated as ever. As late as 1957 Wilson and Lantz published a paper on this subject which received a great deal of publicity. They contended in this paper that there has been a tremendous increase in the nonwhite mental hospital admission rate in the past 40 years and attempted to interpret this increase in terms of the "uncertainties of the Negro race as they cross from one culture to another." Wilson and Lantz state that, "Cultural changes which are forced on people against their will, by fiat or by authority from outside or above, have been found by the experts of the U.N. to produce major disturbances of mental health." They also quote Margaret Mead to the effect that "the change must be made slowly" and that in the recent past little has been done "to protect the Negro or the white man as this change in relationship is brought about," that is, as the process of integration proceeds.

These conclusions imply a culture shock or cultural breakdown theory and are therefore largely inapplicable to the Negro who shares the same cultural heritage as other Americans. The fact of the matter is that there is almost no vestige of African culture left among the American Negroes. Rarely ever such complete deculturation and reculturation ever occurred in world history. To implicitly liken the primitive African tribesman to the American Negro in a culture shock context is about as realistic as comparing a middle-class, urban dweller undergoing analysis to his preliterate ancestors.

Wilson and Lantz also take other undue liberties in interpreting their data. For example, they cite the higher rate of jail commitments for Negroes in Virginia to show "that the Negro community exhibits the other characteristic of a frustrated community, namely crimes of aggression." Not a word is said about the legal and enforcement problems of majority-implemented laws or any of the many other factors which sociologists and criminologists have painstakingly documented over the years. Finally, Wilson and Lantz cite the high rate of nonwhite admissions to state hospitals in the North to imply that it is the unstable nonwhites who are likely to migrate north. The fact that nonwhites in the North are overwhelmingly urban while those in the South remain predominately rural or small-town dwellers and the implications of this seem to them of no concern. Nor, by way of illustration does the relative availability and adequacy of hospitals in the two regions seem to mean much to them.

Any number of such items can be extracted, discussed and questioned. These, and the other less questionable findings all depend on the use of first admission data. This paper hopes to overcome some of these difficulties by examining prevalence rates by race using methods described below.

Origins of Data

The data to be presented on the prevalence of mental disorders in Baltimore were derived from four sources. These sources constitute a relatively complete assessment of the reported, unreported, and publicly institutionalized cases of mental disorder.

Data on the prevalence of the chronic disorders among noninstitutionalized persons were in part derived from the Commission on Chronic Illness which conducted a questionnaire investigation sup-

ported by clinical evaluations of a large number of carefully selected persons in the community.

1. The Commission on Chronic Illness Report. The Commission on Chronic Illness, an independent agency founded jointly by the American Medical Association, the American Hospital Association, the American Public Health Association, and the American Public Welfare Association in 1952-1955, conducted a survey of the prevalence of chronic disorders in Baltimore. The research design and references to the various phases of the study, the sample characteristics, and the biases and limitations are detailed in the fourth volume of *Chronic Illness in the United States.* The data included in this report are based on a stratified sample of approximately 1,200 individuals, of whom 809 responded and were given thorough clinical and laboratory evaluations at the Johns Hopkins Hospital, as well as consultations with the relevant specialties when necessary. By the proper application of weights, the 809 evaluees were found to be distributed almost identically by age, color, and sex with the Baltimore population, so that the rates to be described within certain limitations may be deemed representative of the noninstitutionalized Baltimore population. A miscellaneous group of childhood behavior disorders, mild mental defect, alcoholism and other minor personality or behavior difficulties which had an adjusted rate of 15.2 per thousand is excluded from this report because it was deemed that the judgments of both examining physicians and psychiatrists were probably not very reliable, and better sources of data exist in other studies.

2. Study of Prematures. In another study there were 500 prematurely born infants and an almost similar number of full-term controls born in Baltimore in 1953 and examined at approximately 40 weeks of age at the Johns Hopkins School of Hygiene. This sample was adjusted to the Baltimore infant population by controlling for the rates of prematurity, race, sex, and socioeconomic status. On this basis, a total rate of 15 per thousand mentally defective infants was derived. These are the organically impaired mental defectives and do not contain among them the socioculturally and educationally retarded children. Inclusion of the latter would result in the estimates of 4% to 14% found in the school-age population.*

---

*Since these sociocultural retardates are not mentally ill or primarily medical problems, it was deemed inadvisable to include them in any total prevalence picture. Infancy is thus the ideal age during which organic impairment can be differentiated from the psychologic effects of an impoverished and deprived environment.

It might be added that re-examination of the children at 3 years of age confirmed these rates and also indicated the high reliability of the infant examination procedures. While the prevalence rate of 15 per thousand is for a pre-school age population, because little or no improvement in intellectual functioning can be anticipated for this population, it is not too unsafe to use it for the total population. Since a number of these cases may be expected to be removed by death, clinical judgment leads us to believe that the rate constancy of this diagnostic category will result from the addition of brain-damaged individuals who at later ages will be pushed down into the definitely defective and severely impaired group by the interaction of sociocultural and organic factors.

3. *Institutional Rates.* A third source of data on mental disorders were those Baltimore residents hospitalized as of June 1, 1954, and consisting of all of the individuals in the 3 state mental institutions admitting patients from Baltimore and from private hospitals. It was unfortunate that hospital census recording did not include city of residence, so the data had to be secured laboriously by hand from the hospital records.

4. *Veterans Administration Facility Rates.* A frequently ignored source of data, particularly when institutionalized cases are considered, are the Veterans Administration facilities. This is a common source of bias, particularly when sex and age differences are considered. We were fortunate in being able to use the data of a 50% systematic sample of the Baltimore residents of the Veterans Hospital serving the Baltimore area.

Findings

Psychoses. The white and nonwhite rates for the psychoses which are presented in Table 1 would appear to refute the Wilson and Lantz hypothesis. These rates indicate that the nonwhite state hospital rates are indeed higher than those for whites. For the Baltimore population the nonwhite rate is 75 percent greater than the white rate. However, this is not by any means the whole of the story. White rates exceed nonwhite rates in both private and V.A. hospitals. The biggest discrepancy of all occurs in the non-institutional rate. At this level, the white rate is over ten times as great as the Negro rate. Assuming the equal reliability of the data obtained from all of these sources—and clearly this is the most parsimonious assumption—the overall rate for whites in Baltimore is 9.46 per thousand while the Negro rate is substantially lower at 7.04 cases per thousand. On the face of

it, therefore, the lower Negro rate clearly vitiates the labored explanations of Wilson and Lantz.

Even when the rates for psychoses are adjusted for age as they should be because as Wilson and Lantz point out, "Negroes die younger," the total prevalence rate is still higher for the white Baltimore population. Finally, it should be noted that the psychoses are among the easiest to diagnose of the mental disorders. This being the case it is most unlikely that noninstitutional Negroes went unrecognized by the team of evaluators in the community. On the contrary, clinicians have stated that because of the inability of white psychiatrists to comprehend the nuances in the Negro subculture and the behavior of individuals socialized in this subculture, there is the tendency to over-diagnose psychoses among Negroes.

From all of this it follows that the discrepancy in prevalence rates is probably small; if there is a disparity at all, it is as likely to favor the nonwhites as the whites. The higher noninstitutional white rates are offset by the higher nonwhite state hospital rates. Two questions follow from this. How may the higher nonwhite institutional rates be explained and conversely, what accounts for the greater white noninstitutional rates? In effect, these questions suggest the answers.

The lower-class population—Negro and white—living under adverse economic and social conditions and with less stable family ties, is simply in no position to maintain, care for and tolerate, a disturbed and disturbingly ill individual. Such individuals consequently are institutionalized. This applies as already noted to lower-class persons in general. Since the Negro population, relative to the white, is overwhelmingly lower class, it follows that nonwhites will be proportionately overinstitutionalized. By the same token, the ability and willingness and wherewithal to maintain a sick person in the community under medical supervision or to send him to a private institution is positively related to class. The white population is therefore likely to send relatively fewer cases to state hospitals. This would appear to be a simpler, more logical and more realistic explanation. In the same vein, it would be easier to tolerate a disturbed person in a rural setting than in an urban and highly complex one. Would not then the higher Northern institutional rates for nonwhites be a function of the urban setting including the greater likelihood of being diagnosed as psychotic?

Psychoneuroses. Racial differences in rates for the psychoneuroses are almost wholly dependent upon an examination of noninstitutional cases. Few psychoneurotics are sent to state hospitals. From

TABLE 1. Prevalence of Mental Disorder in Baltimore as a Rate per 1000 Persons by Diagnosis, Race, and Source of Data. (Reproduced by permission from The American Journal of Orthopsychiatry, 1963, 43, 81, ©American Orthopsychiatric Association, Inc.)

Diagnosis	Noninstitutional				State Hospitals‡			Private Hospitals‡			V.A. Hospitals§			Total Rate	
	Total Rate	No. of Cases Unweighted	Rate White	Rate Nonwhite	No. of Cases Unweighted	Rate White	Rate Nonwhite	No. of Cases Unweighted	Rate White	Rate Nonwhite	No. of Cases Unweighted	Rate White	Rate Nonwhite	White	Nonwhite
Psychoses	8.81	17*	5.20	0.50	3705	3.48	6.10	170	0.24	–	239	0.54	0.44	9.46	7.04
Psychoneuroses	52.69	51*	62.20	27.50	45	0.05	0.04	14	0.02	–	7	0.02	0.01	62.29	27.55
Psychophysiologic Autonomic and Visceral Disorders	36.50	18*	43.70	17.70	–	–	–	–	–	–	–	–	–	43.70	17.70
Acute Brain Syndromes	0.14	–	–	–	124	.04	0.36	4	0.01	–	–	–	–	0.05	0.36
Mental Deficiency	15.00	26†	13.20	21.30	–	–	–	–	–	–	–	–	–	13.20	21.30
Total	113.14	112	124.30	66.80	3874	3.57	6.50	188	0.27	–	246	0.56	0.45	128.70	73.95

* Based on clinical examination of a stratified sample of 809 individuals in the survey by the Commission on Chronic Illness in Baltimore in 1952-1955, and adjusted to the Baltimore population.
† Based on clinical examination of a stratified sample of 992 infants born in Baltimore in 1953, and adjusted to the Baltimore population.
‡ All Baltimore residents in the Maryland state and private hospitals as of June 1, 1954, taken from the hospital records.
§ Based on a 50 per cent systematic sample of the Baltimore residents in the Veterans' Administration Facility serving the Baltimore area.

177

Table 1 it is readily apparent that the psychoneuroses rate is over twice as high for whites as for nonwhites. The exact rates per thousand are 62.29 and 27.55 respectively. This rate discrepancy occasions little surprise. The class explanation invoked above would explain part of the disparity. Higher-class persons are more likely to be diagnosed as psychoneurotics and lower-class persons as psychotics or personality trait disturbances. Again, and as noted earlier, white, middle-class examiners are for cultural reasons and those involving familiarity with symptoms more likely to be aware of psychoneurotic manifestations in whites. There is also the problem of the channeling and content of neurotic manifestations and subcultural variations therein. Certain behaviors—anxiety, hostility and the like may take different subcultural forms and thereby go underdetected in groups removed from one's own. The different meanings which attach to the same gestures, words, and symbols on a subcultural basis may also play some role in this discrepancy.

Psychophysiologic-Autonomic-Visceral Disorders. As in the instance of the psychoneuroses, psychophysiologic, autonomic, and visceral disorders are over twice as frequently encountered in whites as in nonwhites. From Table 1, the rates per thousand population are 43.70 and 17.70. Institutional rates for these disorders are negligible.

In interpreting this finding, the same basic *post hoc* explanations as for the psychoneuroses are suggested. In addition, it is very probable, based on sociological evidence, that nonwhites as lower-class persons are less likely to report symptoms which enter into this diagnosis. The lower-class emphasis on toughness and its lesser awareness of an emphasis on the significance of psychophysiologic disturbances undoubtedly accounts for some of the difference in rates. This should apply even more strongly to white and nonwhite females.

Acute Brain Syndromes. This category of disease is almost wholly confined to the consequences of alcoholism. Institutional rates are nine times greater for nonwhites as is shown in Table 1. Whether this reflects true prevalence rates is again questionable. The extent to which these rates are influenced by the ability of the white population to receive private treatment and the lesser ability of nonwhites to do so is unknown. The opposite results would be obtained, it should be stressed, if membership in Alcoholics Anonymous was sampled. To restate and reemphasize the problem, all of these rate disparities may represent nothing more profound than differential access to private versus public treatment.

Mental Deficiency. Referring again to Table 1, it will be seen that nonwhites have a 60 percent higher rate than whites for mental deficiency in Baltimore. The figures are 21.30 per 1000 nonwhites and 13.20 per 1000 for whites. This higher nonwhite expectancy has been reported in almost every comprehensive study on the subject. The lower rates for Negroes found in Virginia institutions reflect either a lack of facilities for nonwhite mental defectives or the higher percentage of rural nonwhites since mental defectives like mental patients are much more readily cared for in rural areas, or some combination of both of these factors.

In previous investigations we have attempted to ascertain the probable causes for higher mental deficiency rates among Negroes. We have demonstrated that mental deficiency is associated with prematurity and complications of pregnancy. The latter, in turn, are largely determined by socioeconomic variables so that brain damage and neuropsychiatric disorders stemming from a continuum of reproductive casualty should more likely be encountered in the lower socioeconomic groups.

Summary

This paper reported the results of a series of concurrent investigations in Baltimore dealing with the prevalence rates for various psychiatric disorders in the white and nonwhite population. The findings based on a community survey, and state, private and V. A. hospital rates indicate that the white population has the higher rates for the psychoses, psychoneuroses, and the psychophysiologic-autonomic-visceral disorders. Nonwhite rates are higher for the acute brain syndromes and for mental deficiency.

An attempt is made to explain these variations and to refute the conclusions of a previous study by Wilson and Lantz in Virginia.

Editor's Note:

The debate over intelligence—as a fixed quantity vs a mutable quality—has engaged American psychologists ever since the discipline was founded. The question of heredity versus environment has never been resolved. Social conditions and the status of race relations have primarily determined the receptivity of one point of view over the other. The greatest influence on the educational system and institutions of society, however, has been exerted by the hereditarians. Emphasis has been on psychometry and quantification. This approach reflects the influence of Francis Galton, founder of the "eugenics" movement, and coiner of that word and the now famous phrase "nature vs nurture." Galton was one of original developers of intelligence tests in Great Britain, inventor of statistical measurement of individual differences, and formulator of the index known as the coefficient of correlation. Galton, a cousin of Charles Darwin, applied the latter's concept of selective adaptation to the evolution of the races and expressed his convictions that the average intellectual standard of black people was two grades below whites and that of all races the Anglo-Saxon was superior. Louis Terman, E.L. Thorndike, Florence Goodenough, and G. Stanley Hall were directly influenced by these theories. Each of these psychologists subscribed to the idea of intelligence as a static, fixed quality and proceeded to develop and interpret intelligence tests on this basis. Their names and theories are still attached to tests being administered today. Psychologists like George Stoddard and Beth Wellman, who were more influenced by the philosophies of Locke, Mills, and Priestly, which expressed belief that intelligence could be improved through social intervention, were vehemently attacked by the others. Stoddard emphasized the interaction that occurs between inherited brain structure (even cytoplasm and genes) with experiences of the organism, plus its physical and social surroundings. But these voices have been muted. A look at the history of intelligence testing shows that measurement of intelligence has had little to do with theoretical definitions of intelligence.

Jean Piaget, the outstanding Swiss psychologist, has spent more than forty years studying intellectual development in children. Although a significant influence on European thinking, he has been all but ignored in the United States. Piaget has determined sequential stages of development in cognition, explaining a child's intellectual life as it unfolds. Working with children in the laboratory, Piaget has studied the evolution of thought and language as well as the process of mastering concepts like space, mass, weight, volume, numbers (seriation, reversibility), time, morality, abstract thinking, and conceptualization. He stresses the role of social experience. Voyat's article "IQ: God-Given or Man-Made?" contrasts the findings of Piaget with the recent writings of Jensen, Shockley, and Herrnstein and places the present controversy in its proper perspective.

IQ: GOD-GIVEN OR MAN-MADE?

GILBERT VOYAT

Who would have believed that in the declining decades of the twentieth century the antique psychological argument between environment and heredity would garner headlines and rub academic tempers raw? The older, progressive educators scolded each other about the primacy of nurture over nature. The practicing pragmatists insisted that, "You are what you grow up as, not merely what you are born with." The environmentalists declared that slums produce children with more limited intelligence than generous suburbs do. Not so, asserted the genetically per-

suaded; poor performance in intellectual matters is the result of a shallow gene-pool.

And so the argument continues. In this past winter's issue of the *Harvard Educational Review*, Dr. Arthur R. Jensen, professor of educational psychology at the University of California at Berkeley, suggests that intelligence is a trait not unlike eye color and hardly more susceptible to change. This study presents an interesting renewal of the genetic argument. Although many of the ideas defended have the aura of statistical, scientific work, they are neither new, self-evident, nor irrefutable. The fact that Dr. Jensen's findings are corroborated by statistical evidence does not make them true. It makes them misleading.

His central thesis is simple: Intelligence is a natural trait, inscribed in the genetic pool and unequally distributed among individuals. Theoretically, genius can be found anywhere, regardless of race or social milieu. In practice, however, Jensen insists that in terms of the average IQ, whites are more intelligent than blacks. The average IQ for blacks is, according to his calculation, approximately 15 points below the average for whites. Furthermore, only 15 per cent of the Negro population exceeds the white average. This has been shown, for instance, in a study (cited by Jensen) by Dr. A. M. Shuey, author of *The Testing of Negro Intelligence*, who reviewed 382 previous studies of IQ. Here we have a typical case of validation by quantification. It is impressive, precise, and wrongheaded. The difference is intelligence between whites and blacks is also noticeable among privileged children; upper-status Negro children average 2.6 IQ points below the low-status whites. Jensen makes the further assertion that Indians, who are even more disadvantaged than Negroes, are nevertheless more intelligent. Jensen is very cautious about this differential intelligence. Negro infants, he claims, are more precocious in sensory-motor development in their first year or two than are Caucasian infants. The same holds for motor skills. But, he believes, what is crucially missing among Negroes is what constitutes genuine formal intelligence: conceptual learning and problem-solving ability.

Jensen offers a description of the respective roles of genetic and environmental factors as he defines intelligence. His strategy in demonstrating the roles of inheritance and environment is to utilize exclusively statistical evidence. He discusses extensively the notion of "heritability," which for him is a statistical mean allowing him to state the extent to which individual differences in a trait such as intelligence can be accounted for by genetic factors. He comes to the conclusion that this heritability is quite high in the human species, which means that genetic factors are much more important than environmental factors in producing IQ differences. And *this* relationship is almost entirely displayed in achievement on IQ tests which Jensen sees as related to genetic differences.

These analyses lead Jensen to the further conclusion that genetic factors are strongly implicated in the average Negro-white intelligence differences. Given these conclusions, Jensen ascribes the failure of compensatory education and other educational enrichment programs to genetic differences, because any attempt to raise intelligence per se probably lies more in the province of the biological sciences than in that of psychology and education. For example, the magnitude of IQ and scholastic achievement gains resulting from enrichment and cognitive stimulation programs range between 5 and 20 IQ points. But Jensen is inclined to doubt "that IQ gains up to 8 to 10 points in young disadvantaged children have much of anything to do with changes in ability. They are largely the result of getting a more accurate IQ by testing under more optimal conditions."

Nevertheless, Jensen has some positive recommendations. He distinguishes between two genotypically distinct processes underlying a continuum ranging from "simple" associative learning which he calls Level I, to complex conceptual learning which he calls Level II. Level I involves a relatively high correspondence between the stimulus input and the form of the stimulus output. For example, a child will be able to recite, and perhaps remember, a succession of numbers. Object memory, serial rote learning, and selective trial and error learning are other good examples of Level I. In Level II, a child will be able to classify objects according to their similarities. Thus, Level II involves transforming a stimulus before it becomes an overt response. Concept learning and problem solving in a whole range of experiences are good examples of Level II. Jensen believes that schooling maximizes the importance of Level II. But schools must also be able to find ways of utilizing other strengths in children whose abilities are not of the conceptual variety. In other words, the ideal educational world of Dr. Jensen would provide two types of education: one directed toward the acquisition of basic skills and simple associative learning, which is training rather than education. Given such training, children with only Level I skills will "perfectly" adapt to any society.

Such is Jensen's thesis. It is based mainly upon the validity of IQ tests. What, in fact, do they measure? The crucial question which must be asked concerns the value of IQ tests themselves. Not that Jensen does not discuss their value. He defines intelligence too narrowly as what IQ tests measure: "a capacity for abstract reasoning and problem solving." How should we define intelligence? Is it useful to define it at all? In short, the very basis of Jensen's findings must be questioned in the light of what experimental psychology can tell us today about the nature of cognitive development and operations.

For example, fifty years ago any textbook of biology would begin by giving a definition of the word "life." Today, such a procedure is not possible because a definition of life is never adequate. The reason probably lies in the dynamic aspects of the concept, which is incompatible with a static and fixed definition. In a like manner, IQ tests essentially quantify static definitions. Therefore, as in biology it is no longer possible to define life statically, so, too, in psychology a static definition of intelligence is impossible. To understand the limitations of Jensen's basic assumptions, it is helpful to consider the point of view of the Swiss psychologist, Dr. Jean Piaget. A brief summary of the Piagetian approach allows us to differentiate between what is measured by standard intelligence tests and what is discovered through the Piagetian technique.

During more than forty years of experimentation, Dr. Piaget has arrived at a formal description of cognitive development and has divided it into four stages. The first one, before the development of language (symbolic function) in the child, deals with the construction of the logic of actions. This has been called "the period of sensory-motor intelligence." Primarily, the process involves the organization of actions into operational patterns, or "schemata of actions," whose main characteristics are to allow the child to differentiate in his actions, between means and goals. Some conditions are necessary in order to achieve this: Space must become organized as a general container; objects must remain permanent; and, in order to anticipate goals, one must assume some acquisition of practical causal processes.

The main consequence of the appearance of the symbolic function is the reorganization of sensory-motor intelligence. This enables the child to integrate symbols, allowing him to expand the range of his operations. This next stage is called "pre-operational," or "the period of egocentric thinking." Thus, from a response to an event, intelligence is mediated through language, but the child is not yet able to maintain in his mind symbols (abstractions) that lead to ideas whose meanings are constant. Those constancies have to do with those aspects of the "real world," such as measure, mass, motion, and logical categories. In this pre-operational world everything appears to be related to an egocentric point of view. This is a limitation as much as a source of enrichment during this level of intellectual functioning.

The following stage is characterized by the development of concrete operations. From what is essentially a subjective orientation, intellectual functioning moves toward more objectivity in elaborating mental constancies. The child no longer thinks only in terms of himself, but also takes into account the limitations that the external, physical world places upon him. For example, the child no longer believes that the moon follows him down the street. For Piaget, this type of intelligence is called "concrete," because essentially the child is only able to deal with tangible, manipulatable objects. That is, his world is concerned with *necessary* relations among objects.

The final stage of intellectual development deals with the development of formal thinking which permits the formation not only of necessary relations but also *possible* and *impossible* ones. In short, he can "play" with his mind. The child, now an adolescent, can dream things that never were and ask "Why not?" The adolescent is able to make exact deductions, to extract all combinations from a potential or a real situation. He is no longer directed only by concrete relations. He can make hypotheses and elaborate theories. He is able to dissociate the form of his thinking from its content.

Piaget's approach strongly contrasts with Jensen's point of view. In particular, Piagetian "tests" clearly differ from typical IQ tests. Among the major differences, IQ tests are essentially an additive progression of acquired skills. They give a state, a global or overall result for a specific population; their quantitative aspect allows one to place a child among children of his age and development. Piagetian tests, on the other hand, are hierarchial; they describe a progressive organization and individual potentialities. They provide a detailed analysis of the functioning of thinking. In short, they qualify thinking; they do not quantify it. They always respect the intelligence of a specific child.

These differences are important because, given Piaget's theory, we can describe intelligence functionally; we can formalize its structural development. We cannot assign to intelligence a specific, static definition, in terms of properties, for this directly contradicts the idea of development itself. Any static definition reduces intelligence either to exclusively environmental factors or to almost exclusively genetic factors without implying the necessary *equilibrated* interaction between them.

Consider the distinction between Level I and Level II as proposed by Jensen. At first glance, this argument is appealing; transformations are not in-

volved in the process of decoding and understanding information at Level I, whereas transformations are a necessity at Level II.

But what is a transformation? In a fundamental sense, the understanding of *any* transformation is a necessity at both levels of learning. Without distinguishing a transformation in the real world, we would be unable to differentiate one state from another. For instance, we can present to a child glass A of particular width and height and glass B thinner but taller than A. We call the state in which A is filled up and B is empty S-1, and the state in which B is filled and A is empty S-2. We call transformations (T) the pathway from one state to another, that is, in this particular case, the pouring from A to B, as well as the change of level in S-2 since the level of the liquid is higher than in S-1. For the child to understand these two aspects of the transformation, he must be able to understand the operation of conservation because it is this operation which has produced the transformation from one state to another. In other words, the child "makes the discovery" that the amount of water in the short, fat glass is exactly the same when it is poured into the tall, thin glass. Knowledge of the states themselves, however, is only a description of the observable. This point is fundamental. The fact that conservation is achieved by a child around the age of six or seven clearly implies the necessity of mastering invariances even in order to understand Level I. But, to grasp any invariancy requires the ability to think, even at a very low level, in operational terms.

Thus, the two levels proposed by Jensen are inadequate to provide a clear idea of the development of intelligence itself.

Piaget, on the other hand, never gives a static definition of intelligence; essentially, he gives a functional one. The two functions of intelligence are to understand the external world and to build or discover new structures within it. Therefore, Piaget's experiments would always be culture-fair, because they are involved with a description of a progressive organization directed by logic and not greatly influenced by culture. For example, a whole set of Piagetian experiments have been carried out in Africa, Algeria, Iran, and elsewhere.

The main result is that sequential development, in comparable terms, is observed irrespective of the culture or the race. In other words, the stages are respected in their succession and do not permit, even in a theoretical continuum, division into the type of level differences that Jensen describes, and they most strongly suggest the irrelevance of these genotypically distinct basic processes.

In contrast, IQ tests have been designed by

whites for Western culture. Thus, their value is limited to the culture within which they were designed. They can never be culture-fair. Therefore, in any testing procedure of intelligence, relativity, not absolutism, should be the criterion, and even the correction of IQ tests for other populations is not valid. Furthermore, IQ tests are simply not adequate to measure processes of thinking. They provide results, they do not lead to an understanding of how intelligence functions. Piaget's approach not only allows an understanding of intellectual funcioning but describes it. Furthermore, Piaget's tests allow one to make reliable, individual prognostications. Since their interests lie in a description of the mechanism of thinking, they permit an individual, personalized appraisal of further potentialities independent of the culture. This point is important primarily because it is neglected in IQ tests where the global population is assessed rather than individual potentialities estimated.

If one accepts the premises on which IQ tests are based, then Jensen's point of view could be valid for what concerns the differences in Negro-white performances, and nevertheless remain questionable for ethnic differences based on genetic facts. His approach produces logical fallacies: First, he criticizes and compares the results of IQ tests; next, given differences, he sorts out the environmental and genetic factors; then he minimizes the influence of the milieu, analyzes the remainder in terms of biological implications, and finally compares two ethnic groups and ascribes their differences to genetic factors.

Although Jensen's methodology may have its merits, the problem is that the point of departure is wrong. To decide whether compensatory and other educational programs are failures is an important and responsible act. But, to base a judgment on IQ gains or lacks of gains is questionable. Of course, one must have a way to judge such programs. But to decide that the IQ gains are so small that they do not justify the amount of money poured into such educational enterprises, can give people the impression that psychologists and educators know what they are talking about concerning processes of learning. In reality, many factors make it difficult to assess success and failure in educational programs. Of course, any program must be globally appraised and must work for a reasonably large number of children. But one of the problems of education is that very little is known about the underlying processes of learning. *Furthermore, pedagogy provides generalized techniques for what must be individualized teaching.* Not much is known about how the child grasps and achieves important notions such as conservation,

seriation, number, movement, mass, motion, measure, speed, time, and logical categories. This is ture regardless of race, color, or creed. Judging educational programs in terms of IQ does not settle the learning problem. On the contrary, psychologists who place their confidence in IQ tests tend to forget the real issue, which is the critical problem of how the child learns.

The tragedy of education lies in the fact that we are still lacking knowledge about learning processes. This situation should make us modest, and we should accept the fact that the nature of cognitive learning remains an open question for experimental and developmental psychology.

One of the major aims in education is to create openness to cognitive contradictions. One does not learn without confusion. One does not learn without feeling some discrepancy between the actual outlook and an imaginable one. One of the major conditions for cognitive development is the resolution of conflicts which leads to adaptation. Therefore, when Jensen states that we should let those who cannot attain his second level of intellectual functioning develop their capabilities within the limitations of his Level I, his position is a dangerous one strictly on cognitive grounds. It prescribes a limitation on experience for the four- or five-year-old who already has an egocentric view of his world. If learning is to take place in the often confusing circumstances of childhood, then the purpose of teaching is precisely to exploit such circumstances, not to limit them.

Briefly stated, the process of cognitive development in logico-mathematical knowledge is a gradual structuring from inside the child rather than a generalization from repeated external events. Dr. C. Kamii from the Ypsilanti Public Schools makes the point relative to her experience in teaching, following Piaget's model, that if we really want children to learn it is the *process* of interacting with the environment which must be emphasized rather than a specific response already decided upon by the teacher. This idea of process is never considered in Jensen's approach to the problem, either in his theoretical position or in his pedagogical evaluation. In Piaget's conception of process, the idea of emphasizing logical conflicts is naturally involved. Jensen's view of process excludes it.

A primary role of the teacher is to be able to follow the process and to provide creative conflicts at appropriate moments. In the long run, the imposition of rules is a less efficient way to teach than influencing the development of underlying cognitive processes that will eventually enable the child to construct his own rules, which will square with physical reality. Thus, teaching must provide methods whereby the child can make his own discoveries. As stated by the Harvard psychologist, Dr. Lawrence Kohlberg, the cognitive developmental view of teaching aims at building broad, irreversible structures rather than the achievement of immediate gains which may be short-term. Immediate gains, and very specific abilities, measured through IQ increments seem to be the only concern of Jensen. But as Piaget states: "The goal in education is not to increase the amount of knowledge, but to create possibilities for a child to invent and discover. . . . When we teach too fast, we keep the child from inventing and discovering himself. Teaching means creating situations where structures can be discovered; it does not mean transmitting structures which may be assimilated at nothing other than a verbal level."

The whole creative aspect of learning and teaching is completely lost in Jensen's point of view. The child is reduced to a ratio. The teaching act becomes a mechanical adjustment of narrowly identified capacities to severely limited learning goals. Education must be more generous than this.

Editor's Note:

An interesting approach is used by Martin D. Jenkins in this study of "extreme deviants," or Afro-Americans found at the highest levels of psychometric intelligence (IQ's 130 to 200). He provides data that indicate that where the total environment of the black child compares favorable with that of the average white American, there is found a normal proportion of very superior cases whose upper limits of ability coincide with that of the white population. His hypothesis demonstrates, from a negative aspect, that if race or genetic endowments were the crucial variables alone in contradistinction to the influence that environment and culture has on an individual, there would be no incidences of superior performance by Afro-Americans. It is extremely important to keep in mind that no matter how closely the environment of the black American approximates that of his white counterpart, it is impossible ever to consider them equal. The point at which the stigma of race and status inconsistency, which accrues to all members of the black community regardless of their accomplishments, becomes a detriment to the psyche and personality has never been determined.

THE UPPER LIMIT OF ABILITY AMONG AMERICAN NEGROES

MARTIN D. JENKINS

More than three decades of psychometric investigation among American Negroes has yielded a rich fund of information concerning this population group. Perhaps the most generally known finding, and certainly the most emphasized, is that when "comparable" groups of whites and Negroes are tested, the Negro group is almost invariably inferior to the white in psychometric intelligence (intelligence as measured by psychological tests). Preoccupation with the significance of the low *average* performance of Negro groups has served to divert attention from an equally important phenomenon—the variability of the group, and especially the upper limit reached by its really superior members.

The question of the upper limit of ability among Negroes has both theoretical and practical significance. Psychologists generally attribute the low average performance of Negro groups on intelligence tests to cultural factors. It is well known that Negroes generally experience an inferior environment; and there is certainly no question but that an inferior environment tends to depress the psychometric intelligence. There are, however, many Negro children who are nurtured in an environment that is equal or superior to that of the average white child. Thus, we may hypothesize that *if race in itself is not a limiting factor in intelligence, then, among Negroes whose total environment compares favorably with that of the average American white, there should be found a "normal" proportion of very superior cases, and the upper limit of ability should coincide with that of the white population.* This hypothesis is especially attractive from a negative aspect; thus, if very superior individuals are not to be found in the Negro population, the environmental explanation would clearly be inadequate to account for the phenomenon. The existence of such individuals, on the other hand, would afford additional evidence, but not absolute proof, of course, of the validity of the environmental explanation of "racial differences" in psychometric intelligence.

The practical significance of the question is apparent. If Negroes are to be found at the highest levels of psychometric intelligence, then we may anticipate that members of this racial group have the ability to participate in the culture at the highest level. In these days of reconsideration of the role of the dark races throughout the world, this question has more than mere national significance.

Analysis of the literature relating to the intelligence-test performance of Negro children reveals that a considerable number of these children have been found within the range that reaches the best 1 per cent of white children (I.Q. 130 and above) and at the level of "gifted" children (I.Q. 140 and above). There are at least sixteen published studies that give an account of Negro children possessing I.Q.s above 130; twelve of these report cases above I.Q. 140.

These investigations were made by different psychologists in various localities and under varying conditions; moreover, the I.Q.s were derived by a number of different tests. Further, the populations studied were located almost exclusively in Northern urban communities. Consequently, one may not justifiably generalize, from a composite of these studies, concerning the incidence of Negro deviates. It is of significance, however, that of the 22,301 subjects included in the thirteen studies for which N's are reported, 0.3 per cent scored at 140 and above, and fully 1 per cent scored at I.Q. 130 and above. These percentages are similar to those obtained from a "normal" I.Q. distribution of American school children.

Of especial significance are the cases of very bright children of Binet I.Q. 160 and above. It may be estimated that fewer than 0.1 per cent of school children are to be found at or above this level. As the I.Q. rises about 160 the frequency of occurrence, of course, decreases. Statistically, cases at or about I.Q. 180 should occur about once in a million times, although they actually occur with somewhat greater frequency. In his classic California study of the gifted, Terman found only 15 children testing as high as I.Q. 180; and Hollingworth reports: "In twenty-three years seeking in New York City and the local metropolitan area I have found only twelve children who test at or above 180 I.Q. (S-B)." It is apparent then, that children who test upwards of Binet I.Q. 160 are extreme deviates in psychometric intelligence and representative of the very brightest children in America.

I have assembled from various sources the case records of 18 Negro children who test above I.Q. 160 on the Stanford-Binet examination. Seven of these cases test above I.Q. 170, 4 above I.Q. 180, and 1 at I.Q. 200. Two of these cases were tested initially by me; the other 16 were reported by psychologists in university centers and public school systems. Analysis of the case records indicates that these children during the early years of their development, at least, manifest the same characteristics as do other very high I.Q. children: originality of expression, creative ability, and surpassing performance in school subjects. Some of these children, but not all, are greatly accelerated in school progress. Two, for example, had completed their high-school course and were regularly enrolled university students at age thirteen; both of these subjects were elected to Phi Beta Kappa and earned the baccalaureate degree at age sixteen.

It is of some significance that all these children were found in Northern or border state cities (New York, Chicago, Washington, and Cincinnati). No Southern Negro child, so far as I have been able to

ascertain, has been identified as testing at or above Binet I.Q. 160. It is certain that among the 80 per cent of the total Negro population that lives in the Southern states, children with potentiality for such development exist. Whether the fact that no children with this development have been discovered is due to lack of environmental opportunity and stimulation, or merely to lack of identification, is not surely known.

I am not attempting here to show that approximately as many Negro children as white are to be found at the higher levels of psychometric intelligence. There appears little doubt that the number of very bright Negro children is relatively smaller than the number of bright white children in the total American population. Nevertheless, it is apparent that children of very superior psychometric intelligence may be found in many Negro populations, and that the upper limit of the range attained by the extreme deviates is higher than is generally believed.

The performance of extreme deviates at the college and adult levels has not yet been extensively studied. Such evidence as is available, however, indicates that at maturity, as in childhood, some Negroes are to be found at the highest level of psychometric intelligence. In a recent unpublished study conducted at Howard University, it was found that of approximately 3,500 Negro freshmen entering the College of Liberal Arts over a period of seven years, 101 scored in the upper decile, and 8 in the upper centile (national norms) on the American Council on Education Psychological Examination. In a more extensive study, the National Survey of Higher Education of Negroes, there were, among 3,684 students in twenty-seven Negro institutions of higher education located chiefly in the Southern states, 23 cases in the upper decile and 4 in the upper centile on the A.C.E. Psychological Examination. It is of some significance that in the same study 12 upper decile cases were reported among the 105 Negro students in two Northern universities (almost half as many as were found altogether among the 3,684 students in the twenty-seven Negro colleges). This contrast is in accord with the general but undocumented opinion that among Negro college students there are proportionately fewer extreme deviates in psychometric intelligence in the Southern segregated colleges than in the Northern nonsegregated institutions.

The Army General Classification Test data assembled during World War II have not yet become fully available. One may predict with a fair degree of confidence, however, that these data will reveal some Negro cases at the very highest levels of performance. In view of the fact, however, that the Negro selectees were predominantly from communities that provide inadequate provision for the educational and cultural development of Negroes, we may expect that a very small proportion of the total population will be found at the higher levels of performance. Subgroups which have had a normal cultural opportunity should, in accordance with our hypothesis, yield an appreciable proportion of superior deviates.

The findings of the studies cited in this article support the hypothesis formulated at the outset. In some population groups there is to be found a "normal" proportion of Negro subjects of very superior psychometric intelligence, and the extreme deviates reach the upper limits attained by white subjects. Although the incidence of superior cases is much lower among Negroes than whites, a phenomenon which might well be accounted for by differential environmental factors, we may conclude that race per se (at least as it is represented in the American Negro) is not a limiting factor in psychometric intelligence.

The abstract mental tests that contribute to psychometric intelligence do not measure the factors of personality and motivation that largely determine success in life. The findings of studies of gifted children, especially those of Terman, Hollingworth, and Witty, indicate that the highly gifted child usually fulfills his early promise. But not always. Failure among the gifted is also frequent.

The data of this article bring into sharp focus the limitations that our society places on the development of the highly gifted Negro. These superior deviates are nurtured in a culture in which racial inferiority of the Negro is a basic assumption. Consequently, they will typically experience throughout their lives educational, social, and occupational restrictions that must inevitably affect motivation and achievement. The unanswered question relative to the influence of this factor on the adult achievement of superior Negroes is a problem for future investigators to solve.

Editor's Note:

"The Concept of Identity" by Erik H. Erikson raises some pertinent questions about concepts of personality and the spectrum of negative and positive elements within the black community as commonly presented in the literature. One of the significant contributions made by Erikson in this article is the recognition of cultural components in the black community that contribute to positive identity but are in direct contrast with white identity. The matter assumes greater importance when one realizes that interpretations of identity, self-concept and self-esteem in black people are based on instruments developed by and for the white majority. The fact that instruments (MMPI, Thurstone, etc.) used are "objective" lends unwarranted validity to the data drawn from them, since the role patterns used for categorizing these personality traits are drawn from white experiences and the majority frame of reference. Even when it is acknowledged by the researcher that experiences and cultural perceptions differ in black and white communities, conclusions are drawn that indicate no awareness of this reality. As a result, black manners of dress, walking, and socializing, black aspirations, black leisure-time activities, etc., are assessed as latent manifestations of some abnormality instead of functional adaptations to the cultural milieu that has evolved from the circumstances and opportunities available to ghetto dwellers.

THE CONCEPT OF IDENTITY

ERIK H. ERIKSON

Positive and negative

I remember a remark made recently by a warm-hearted and influential American Jew: "Some instinctive sense tells every Jewish mother that she must make her child study, that his intelligence is his pass to the future. Why does a Negro mother not care? Why does she not have the same instinctive sense?" This was a rhetorical question, of course; he wanted to know which of many possible answers I would give first. I suggested that, given American Negro history, the equivalent "instinctive sense" may have told the majority of Negro mothers to keep their children, and especially the gifted and the questioning ones, away from futile and dangerous competition, that is, for survival's sake to keep them in their place even if that place is defined by an indifferent and hateful "compact majority."

That the man said "mothers" immediately marks one of the problems we face in approaching Negro identity. The Jewish mothers he had in mind would expect to be backed up by their husbands or, in fact, to act in their behalf; the Negro mothers would not. Negro mothers are apt to cultivate the "surrendered identity" forced on Negro men for generations. This, so the literature would suggest, has reduced the Negro to a reflection of the "negative" recognition which surrounded him like an endless recess of distorting mirrors. How his positive identity has been undermined systematically—first under the unspeakable system of slavery in North America and then by the system of enslavement perpetuated in the rural South and the urban North—has been extensively, carefully, and devastatingly documented.

Here the concept of a negative identity may help to clarify three related complications:

1. Every person's psychosocial identity contains a hierarchy of positive *and* negative elements, the latter resulting from the fact that the growing human being, throughout his childhood, is presented with evil prototypes as well as with ideal ones (by reward and punishment, by parental example, and by the community's typology as revealed in wit and gossip, in tale and story). These are, of course, culturally related: in the background which gives prominence to intellectual achievement, some such negative roles as the Schlemihl will not be wanting. The human being, in fact, is warned *not* to become what he often had no intention of becoming so that he can learn to anticipate what he must avoid. Thus, the positive identity (far from being a static constellation of traits or roles) is always in conflict with that past which is to be lived down and by that potential future which is to be prevented.

2. The individual belonging to an oppressed and exploited minority, which is aware of the dominant cultural ideals but prevented from emulating them, is apt to fuse the negative images held up to him by the dominant majority with his own negative identity. The reasons for this exploitability (and temptation to exploit) lie in man's very evolution and development as pseudospecies. There is ample evidence of "inferiority" feelings and of morbid self-hate in all minority groups; and, no doubt the righteously and fiendishly efficient way in which the Negro slave in America was forced into and kept in conditions preventing in most the incentive for independent ambition now continues to exert itself as a widespread and deep-seated inhibition to utilize equality even where it is "granted." Again, the literature abounds in descriptions of how the Negro, instead, found escape into musical or spiritual worlds or expressed his rebellion in compromises of behavior now viewed as mocking caricatures, such as obstinate meekness, exaggerated childlikeness, or superficial submissiveness. And yet, is "the Negro" not often all too summarily and all too exclusively discussed in such a way that his negative identity is defined *only* in terms of his defensive adjustments to the dominant white majority? Do we (and can we) know enough about the relationship of positive and negative elements *within* the Negro personality and *within* the Negro community? This alone would reveal how negative is negative and how positive, positive.

3. As yet least understood, however, is the fact that the oppressor has a vested interest in the negative identity of the oppressed because that negative identity is a projection of his own unconscious negative identity—a projection which, up to a point,

makes him feel superior but also, in a brittle way, whole. The discussion of the pseudospecies may have clarified some of this. But a number of questions remain. One comes to wonder, for example, about the ways in which a majority, suddenly aware of a vital split in itself over the fact that it has caused a near-fatal split in a minority, may, in its sudden zeal to regain its moral position and to face the facts squarely, inadvertently tend to *confirm* the minority's negative image of itself and this in the very act of dwelling exclusively and even self-indulgently upon the majority's sins. A clinician may be forgiven for questioning the curative values of an excessive dose of moral zeal. I find, for example, even the designation "culturally deprived" somewhat ironic (although I admire much of the work done under this banner) because I am especially aware of the fact that the middle-class culture, of which the slum children are deprived, deprives some of the white children of experiences which might prevent much neurotic maladjustment. There is, in fact, an exquisite poetic justice in the historical fact that many white young people who feel deeply deprived *because* of their family's "culture" find an identity and a solidarity in living and working with those who are said to be deprived for lack of such culture. Such confrontation may lead to new mutual insights; and I have not, in my lifetime, heard anything approaching the immediacy of common human experience revealed in stories from today's South (and from yesterday's India).

In this connection we may also ask a question concerning the measurements used in diagnosing the Negro American's condition; and diagnosis, it must be remembered, defines the prognosis, and this not least because it contributes to the patient's self-awareness and attitude toward his suffering.

Our fellow panelist Thomas Pettigrew, in his admirable compilation *A Profile of the Negro American*, employs identity terms only in passing. He offers a wealth of solid and all the more shocking evidence of the disuse of the Negro American's intelligence and of the disorganization of his family life. If I choose from the examples reported by Pettigrew one of the most questionable and even amusing, it is in order to clarify the place of single testable *traits* in the whole *configuration* of an individual's development and of his people's history.

Pettigrew, following Burton and Whiting, discusses the problem that

[Boys] from fatherless homes must painfully achieve a *masculine self-image* late in their childhood after having established an original self-image on the basis of the only parental model they have had—their mother. Several

186

studies point to the applicability of this *sex-identity problem* to lower-class Negro males.

He reports that

> Two objective test assessments of widely different groups—Alabama jail prisoners and Wisconsin working-class veterans with tuberculosis—found that Negro males scored higher than white males on a *measure of femininity*... This measure is a part of the Minnesota Multiphasic Inventory (MMPI), a well-known psychological instrument that requires the respondent to judge the applicability to himself of over five hundred simple statements. Thus, Negroes in these samples generally agreed more often with such "feminine" choices as, *"I would like to be a singer"* and "I think that *I feel more intensely* than most people do."

Pettigrew wisely puts "feminine" in quotation marks. We will assume that the M.M.P.I. is an "objective test assessment for widely different groups" including Alabama jail prisoners and patients on a tubercular ward, and that incidental test blemishes in the end all come-out-in-the-wash of statistics so that the over-all conclusions may point to significant differences between Negroes and whites and between indices of femininity and of masculinity. That such assessment singles out as "feminine" the wish to be a singer and "feeling more intensely than most people do," may be a negligible detail. And yet, this detail suggests that the choice of test items and the generalizations drawn from them may say at least as much about the test and the testers as about the subjects tested. To "want to be a singer" or " to feel intensely" seems to be something only a man with feminine traits would acknowledge in that majority of respondents on whom the test was first developed and standardized. But why, one wonders, should a lower-class Negro locked up in jail or in a tuberculosis ward not admit to a wish to be a man like Paul Robeson or Harry Belafonte, and also that he feels more intensely (if, indeed, he knows what this means) than the chilly business-like whites around him? To be a singer and to feel intensely may be facets of a masculine ideal gladly admitted if you grew up in Alabama (or, for that matter, in Napoli), whereas it would be a blemish to be denied in a majority having adjusted to other masculine ideals. In fact, in Alabama and in Naples an emphasis on artistic self-expression and intense feeling may be close to the core of your positive identity—so close that the loss or devaluation of such emphasis by way of "integration" may make you a drifter on the murky sea of adjustable "roles." In the case of the compact white majority, the denial of

"intense feelings" may, in turn, be part of a white identity problem which contributes to the prejudiced rejection of the Negro's potential or periodical intensity. Tests harboring similar distinctions may be offering "objective evidence of racial differences, but may also be symptomatic of them. If this is totally overlooked, and this is my main point, the test will only emphasize, and the tester will only report, and the reader of the report (white or Negro) will only perceive the distance between the Negro's "disintegrated" self-imagery and what is assumed to be the white's "integrated" one.

As Pettigrew (in another connection) says starkly, putting himself in the shoes of a Negro child to be tested:

> . . .After all, an intelligence test is a middle-class white man's instrument; it is a device whites use to prove their capacities and get ahead in the white world. Achieving a high test score does not have the same meaning for a lower-status Negro child, and it may even carry a definite connotation of personal threat. In this sense, scoring low on intelligence measures may for some talented Negro children be a rational response to perceived danger.

The whole *test-event* thus itself underlies a certain historical and social relativity to be clarified in each case in terms of the actual identity configuration. By the same token, it is by no means certain that the individual undergoing such a procedure will be the same person when he escapes the predicament of the test procedure and joins, say, his peers on the playground or on a street corner. Thus, a "profile" of the Negro American made up of different methods under different conditions may offer decisively different configurations of "traits." This does not make one procedure wrong and the other right, but it makes both (and more) essential in the establishment of criteria for an existing identity configuration. On the other hand, it is all too often taken for granted that the *investigator* (and his identity conflicts) invisibly blends into his method even when he is a representative of a highly (and maybe defensively) verbal sub-group of whites and is perceived as such by subjects who are near-illiterate or come from an illiterate background.

In this connection, I would like to refer to Kenneth Clark's moving characterization of the sexual life of the "marginal young people in the ghetto." As a responsible father-figure, he knows he must not condone what he nevertheless must also defend against deadly stereotypes.

> Illegitimacy in the ghetto cannot be understood or dealt with in terms of punitive

hostility, as in the suggestion that unwed mothers be denied welfare if illegitimacy is repeated. Such approaches obscure, with empty and at times hypocritical moralizing, the desperate yearning of the young for acceptance and identity, the need to be meaningful to someone else even for a moment without implication of a pledge of undying fealty and foreverness....To expose oneself further to the chances of failure in a sustained and faithful relationship is too large to risk. The *intrinsic values* of the relationship is the only value because there can be no other.

This places a legal or moral item into its "actual" context—a context which always also reveals something about those who would judge and stereotype rather than understand: for is not the *intrinsic value of the relationship* exactly that item (hard to define, hard to test, and legally irrelevant) which may be lost in some more fortunate youths who suffer under a bewildering and driving pluralism of values?

Past and future

Turning now to the new young Negroes: "My God," a Negro woman student exclaimed the other day in a small meeting, "what am I supposed to be integrated *out of?* I laugh like my grandmother—and I would rather die than not laugh like that." There was a silence in which you could hear the stereotypes click; for even laughter had now joined those aspects of Negro culture and Negro personality which have become suspect as the marks of submission and fatalism, delusion and escape. But the young girl did not give in with some such mechanical apology as "by which I do not mean, of course..." and the silence was pregnant with that immediacy of joint experience which characterizes moments when an identity conflict becomes palpable. It was followed by laughter—embarrassed, amused, defiant.

To me, the young woman had expressed one of the anxieties attending a rapid reconstitution of identity elements: "supposed to" reflects a sense of losing the active, the choosing role which is of the essence in a sense of identity as a continuity of the living past and the anticipated future. I have indicated that single items of behavior or imagery can change their quality within new identity configurations; and yet these same indices once represented an integration as well as an integrity of Negro life—"such as it was," to be sure, but the only existing inner integration for which the Negro is now "supposed to" exchange an unsure outer integration. Desegregation, compensation, balance, re-conciliation—do they all

sometimes seem to save the Negro at the cost of an absorption which he is not sure will leave much of himself left? Thus the "revolution" poses an "identity crisis" in more than one way; the Negro writer's "complicated assertions and denials of identity" (to use Ellison's words) have simpler antecedents, not less tragic for their simplicity.

For identity development has its time, or rather two kinds of time: a *developmental stage* in the life of the individual, and a *period* in history. There is, then, also a complementarity of life-history and history. Unless provoked prematurely and disastrously (and the biographies of sensitive Negro writers as well as direct observations of Negro children attest to such tragic prematurity) psychosocial identity is not feasible before the beginning, even as it is not dispensable after the end of *adolescence*, when the body, now fully grown, grows together into an individual appearance; when sexuality, matured, seeks partners in sensual play and, sooner or later, in parenthood; when the mind, fully developed, can begin to envisage a career for the individual within a historical perspective—all idiosyncratic developments which must fuse with each other in a new sense of sameness and continuity. But the increasing irreversibility of all choices (whether all too open or foreclosed) leads to what we call the *identity crisis* which here does not mean a *fatal turn* but rather (as in drama and in medicine) an *inescapable turning point* for better *or* for worse. "Better" here means a confluence of the constructive energies of individual and society, which contributed to physical grace, sexual spontaneity, mental alertness, emotional directness, and social "actualness." "Worse" means prolonged *identity confusion* in the young individual. Here it must be emphasized—for this is the point at which the psychosexual theories of psychoanalysis fuse with the psychosocial ones—that identity formation is decisive for the integration of sexuality (whether the cultural trend is toward repression or expression) and for the constructive use of agression. But the crisis of youth is also the crisis of a generation and of the ideological soundness of its society. (There is also a complementarity of identity and ideology.) The crisis is least marked and least "noisy" in that segment of youth which in a given era is able to invest its fidelity in an ideological trend associated with a new technical and economic expansion (such as mercantilism, colonialism, industrialization). For here new types and roles of competence emerge. Today this includes the young people in all countries and in all classes who can fit into and take active charge of technical and scientific development, learning thereby to identify with a lifestyle of testing, inventing, and producing. Youth which is eager for such experience but unable to find access to it will feel estranged from society, upset in its sexuality, and unable to apply its aggression constructively. It may be that today much of Negro Youth as well as an artistic-humanistic section of White Youth feel disadvantaged and, therefore, come to develop a certain solidarity in regard to "the crisis" or "the revolution": for young people in privileged middle-class homes as well as in underprivileged Negro homes may miss that sameness and continuity throughout development which makes a grandmother's warmth and a fervent aspiration part of an identical world. One may go further and say that this whole segment of American youth is attempting to develop its own ideology and its own rites of confirmation by following the official call to the external frontiers of the American way of life (Peace Corps), by going to the internal ones (deep South), or by attempting in colleges (California) to fill an obvious void in the traditional balance of the American way of life—a void caused by a dearth of that realism, solidarity, and ideology which welds together a functioning radical opposition.

We will come back to this point. Here we may suggest that identity also contains a complementarity of past and future both in the individual and in society: it links the actuality of a living past with that of a promising future. This formulation excludes, I hope, any romanticizing of the past or any salesmanship in the creation of future "postures."

In regard to "the revolution" and its gains, one can only postulate that the unblinking realism and ruthless de-masking of much of the present literature supports a new sense of toughness in the "face of reality." It fits this spirit that Pettigrew's "Profile," for example, fails to list such at any rate untestable items as (in alphabetical order) companionability, humor, motherhood, music, sensuality, spirituality, sports, and so forth. They all are suspect, I know, as traits of an accommodation romanticized by whites. But this makes presently available "profiles" really the correction of caricatures, rather than attempts at even a sketch of a portrait. But can a new or renewed identity emerge from corrected caricatures? One thinks of all those who are unable to derive identity gains from the "acceptance of reality" at its worst (as the writers do and the researchers) and to whom a debunking of all older configurations *may* become a further *confirmation* of worthlessness and helplessness.

It is in this context also that I must question the fact that in many an index the Negro father appears *only* under the heading of "absence." Again, the relationship between family disintegration, father-absence, and all kinds of social and psychiatric pathology is overwhelming. "Father absence" does belong in every index and in the agenda of national concern. But as the *only* item related to fatherhood *or* motherhood does it not do grave injustice to the presence of many, many mothers, and at least some of the fathers? Whatever the historical, sociological, or legal interpretation of the Negro mother's (and grandmother's) saving presence in the whole half-circle of plantation culture from Venezuela through the Caribbean into our South, is it an item to be omitted from the agenda of the traditional Negro identity? Can Negro culture afford to have the "strong mother" stereotyped as a liability? For a person's (and a people's) identity begins in the rituals of infancy, when mothers make it clear with many pre-literate means that to be born is good and that a child (let the bad world call it colored or list it as illegitimate) is deserving of warmth. As I pointed out in the *Daedalus* issue on Youth, these mothers have put an indelible mark on "Negro Culture" and what they accomplished should be one of the proudest chapters in cultural history.

The systematic exploitation of the Negro male as a domestic animal and the denial to him of the status of responsible fatherhood are, on the other hand, two of the most shameful chapters in the history of this Christian nation. For an imbalance of mother-and-father presence is never good, and becomes increasingly bad as the child grows older; for then the trust in the world established in infancy may be all the more disappointed. Under urban and industrial conditions it may, indeed, become the gravest factor in personality disorganization. But again the "disorganization" of the Negro family must not be measured solely by its distance from the white or Negro middle-class family with its one-family housing and legal and religious legitimizations. Disintegration must be measured and understood also as a distortion of the *traditional* if often unofficial *Negro family pattern*. The traditional wisdom of the mothers will be needed as will the help of the Negro men who (in spite of such circumstances) actually did become fathers in the full sense.

In the meantime, the problem of the function of both parents, each strong in his or her way, and both benignly present in the home when needed most is a problem facing the family in any industrial society on a universal scale. The whole great society must develop ways to provide equality of opportunity in employment and yet also differential ways of permitting mothers and fathers to attend to their duties toward their children. The maternal-paternal dimension may well also serve to clarify the fact that each stage of development needs its own optimum environment, and that to find a balance between maternal and paternal strength means to assign to each a period of dominance in the children's life. The mother's period is the earliest and, therefore, the most basic. There is a deep relation between the first "identity" experienced in the early sensual and sensory exhanges with the mother(s)—the first recognition—and that final integration in adolescence when all earlier identifications are assembled and the young person meets his society and his historical era.

Editor's Note:

The self-concept or self-esteem of black Americans has been a major item of interest in psychological research for a number of years. The common assumption has focused around the belief that the Afro-American, having been forced to function as an inferior in a society that places little value on him as a person and continually reinforces this negative image, has internalized these concepts of himself to such a degree that a positive self-concept is practically impossible. The one crucial aspect of this process that has been overlooked by many is brought to light in the research and data presented by Baughman in this article on self-esteem. The majority of black youngsters are born into a predominantly black environment, interact with their family and others like themselves, and are accepted on an individual basis, not as part of some racial configuration. The child forms ideas about himself from those around him. The others from whom they develop their sense of self are black, living in a black milieu, and acting out of a black cultural framework. It is generally later, when the child enters school, that he is confronted with negative assessments of his heritage and his behavior. The early years thus provide strengths for personality development and the basis for rejection of definitions of oneself by those external to one's own situation.

NEW PERSPECTIVES ON SELF-ESTEEM

E. EARL BAUGHMAN

Did (does) a minority group internalize the majority group's view?

In reading and thinking about the issue at hand, we also began to realize that many "authorities" may have overestimated the extent to which blacks internalized the white's definition of them as inferior human beings. That some blacks have been so affected, there can be no doubt. On the other hand, the fact that so many blacks learned to *act* subservient or inferior in the presence of whites cannot be taken as conclusive evidence that they actually *felt* this way about themselves. Although the analogy is admittedly an imperfect one, this type of thinking would force us to conclude that the Jews have been similarly affected by how their oppressors have defined them. Perhaps they have been, but we know of no evidence that supports such a conclusion.

We are not asserting here that the self-esteem of the blacks was not sometimes damaged by the treatment he received at the hands of his oppressor who controlled most of the sources of power, but we are raising the possibility that the black resisted the white's definition of him more effectively than most observers have usually estimated. After all, the black was caught in a situation where he could see that most of his problems could be attributed to the repressive power of others; realistically, he did not have to look inward for deficiencies in his own self to explain his multitudinous difficulties. If this analysis is correct, then we should not be surprised to find that when the power structure began to change in the 1950's and 1960's there was a substantial reservoir of positive feelings about being black to draw upon.

The literature on the black has, we believe, given undue emphasis to his subservient behavior and roles. (We frequently forget that countless whites act in a similar fashion.) Too little attention has been devoted to blacks who evidenced pride and competence, even when they were not free. Moreover, we need to reconsider the power of any minority group to resist incorporating the definition of itself offered by an oppressive majority group, and this includes the black American minority.

Is the black-white distinction quantitative?

Most discussions of black self-esteem either state explicitly or imply that the average black has *less* self-esteem than the average white. Research by our students . . . causes us not only to doubt the validity of this conclusion *for contempory black youth*, but leads us to question whether it was ever true. Instead, we suggest than an alternate hypothesis should be given serious consideration; namely, that, in the quantitative sense, the supply of self-esteem is not, and has not been, less for the black than for the white.

It is clear, of course, that the life of the average black American continues to differ markedly from that of the average white American; there simply is no basis for argument about this. The hypothesis that we have advanced above, however, is based upon the belief that this difference in life pattern does not in fact produce a meaningful black-white gap in *level* of self-esteem. Blacks and whites may reach this level by different routes because of their different experiences, but they are not to be distinguished because one has *more* self-esteem than the other.

This hypothesis does not require us to reject the idea that the self-esteem of vast numbers of blacks is damaged, to use Grambs's terminology. Rather, it forces us to consider the possibility that the self-esteem of the average white is also significantly damaged by his experiences in the social structure of which he is a part. In this regard, we suspect that the black often overestimates the degree of self-satisfaction that resides in his white neighbor. Indeed, the very fact that the white man has found it necessary to push the black man down as inferior suggests the operation of a compensatory mechanism, the goal being to reassure the white of his own self-worth. If in fact he felt secure and adequate, such behavior would not be necessary. Furthermore, both blacks and whites seem to forget the material possessions and the possession of power do not automatically convert into feelings of self-esteem for those who hold them. One may have vast wealth and great power yet feel deeply inadequate; conversely, the most humble person may have genuine pride and dignity.

What this analysis suggests, of course, is that most discussions of black self-esteem fail to give adequate consideration to white self-esteem and how it may also be damaged within our social structure. While it undoubtedly is true that black self-esteem is frequently impaired, it does not necessarily follow that the black man is worse off in this regard than the white man. The white man, *for different reasons* and despite appearances to the contrary, may not develop more self-esteem than the black man.

How is self-esteem developed?

We have reached the point now where we must ask ourselves how self-esteem is developed. If the possession of material goods, power, and similar conditions do not automatically convert into feelings of self-worth, what factors are critical? Although we cannot explore this problem deeply here, we do want to touch upon several considerations which may be important as far as the black-white comparison is concerned.

There is general agreement that the antecedents of self-esteem are to be found in the childhood experiences of an individual. Furthermore, the child's family is usually regarded as the single most important determinant of how he comes to value himself, and, within the family, the influence of the parents (or parent substitutes) is viewed as having special significance. Stanley Coopersmith (1967), who has conducted an extensive inquiry into the antecedents of self-esteem, concludes that three components of parental behavior stand out as determinants of self-esteem (1968, p.30):

> The major factors that contribute to the formation of *high* self-esteem can be briefly described in terms of three conditions: *acceptance* of the child by his parents (or surrogates); clearly defined *limits* and values; and *respect* and latitude within the defined limits. In effect the parents are concerned and attentive, offer guidance and direction by structuring the world, and permit considerable freedom and individual expression so that initiative and communication are fostered.

Although Coopersmith's research involved white, middle-class boys and should be repeated with black children, there is no reason to believe that parental behavior is not also a critical determinant of black self-esteem. Furthermore, because, on the average, black family life is more disorganized than white family life . . . we might expect that the types of parental behavior found by Coopersmith to be necessary for the development of positive self-regard would be encountered less frequently by black children. If this is true, shouldn't the level of self-esteem among black children be lower than that among white children? This, of course, is a conclusion that we have been arguing against and shall continue to do so.

We believe that the conclusion does not follow because children respond to parental behavior not in terms of its qualities measured along absolute scales but rather in a comparative or relativistic framework. More explicitly, a child perceives how he is treated in comparison with other children in his family—or to how other children in his circle are treated by their parents—and it is this concrete, comparative process that provides him with cues regarding his worth. If other children seem to be favored, for example, this signals to him that he must be less worthy then they. Compared to "parents in general" a particular set of parents may respond favorably to a child, but they may be even more positive in their behavior toward a second child in the family and thereby lay the basis for feelings of inadequacy in the first child. The child has no basis for evaluating the behavior of his parents against the general average, but he can judge the responses he receives against those secured by his siblings and members of his peer group. In a similar way, he can compare how he is treated by his teachers and other significant persons in his world with how other children are treated by the same individuals. This comparative process, we believe, is central to the concept that a child develops of himself.

It is also important to emphasize another point, namely, that the typical black child—whether urban or rural—spends his formative years in essentially a black world. The black community provides him with his frame of reference, and it is within the black community that the comparative process that we described above functions. Thus, the critical consideration in regard to the generation of self-esteem is that the black child compares himself with other black children, not with white children. His evaluative framework is provided by the black community and not by the larger community in which his group is actually a subculture. The pervasiveness of this orientation of black children was indicated by structured interviews conducted by black interviewers with adolescent blacks in the rural South (see Baughman & Dahlstrom, 1968). In answering questions about themselves, their families, their schools, and so on, it was clear that the black children consistently responded by comparing themselves to other black children, or their families to other black families, or their schools to other black schools. The fact that the community contained white families and white institutions did not seem to enter into establishing the framework within which they evaluated themselves and their institutions. This suggests, of course, that the critical factor for the black child—as far as his self-esteem is concerned—revolves around how he perceives himself treated within the black community compared to how other black children are treated in the same community. As long as his world remains overwhelmingly black, the white child's situation is largely irrelevant as far as the black child's self-concept is concerned.

As the black child grows older, however, it becomes increasingly difficult for him to maintain such a completely black orientation. For the urban child this time usually comes earlier than it does for the rural child, and for black children in general it probably comes sooner now than it did even a few years ago. Nevertheless, it continues to be true that this inevitable confrontation with the white world (in any really meaningful sense) occurs for most black children *after the foundation of their self-esteem has been established by their experiences within the black community.*

When the black child's world begins to enlarge, and especially when he is thrown into interactions with whites, the self-esteem that he has generated in a basically black context can be threatened. In some competitive contexts, however, his experiences with whites give him no basis for revising his self-concept to a more negative form; athletic competition is certainly a prime example of this. In other contexts—the desegregated classroom, for example—he is much

more severely pressed and runs the risk of losing self-esteem. This, incidentally, is one reason why massive school desegregation at all grade levels poses such a difficult problem for the black child (especially the older one) and why it might have been advantageous to him if the Supreme Court in 1954 had ordered the immediate implementation of a grade-a-year plan . . . .

When the black child discovers that he does not measure up well in interactions with whites, two psychological paths are open to him. He can interpret his experiences as evidence that he is less adequate than he had been led to believe (thus suffering a loss in self-esteem), or he can blame the "system" for having discriminated against him by providing him with inferior preparatory experiences (thus protecting his self-esteem). In other words, he has a choice between looking inward and finding the insufficiency there, or looking outward and finding the inadequacy there. Today's black youth, we believe, are much more likely to follow the second path than the first, and, of course, it is not difficult for them to find an ample supply of evidence that the "system" has discriminated against them. Furthermore, they are encouraged and supported in this interpretation by many influential voices, both black and white.

The analysis that we have presented leads to a conclusion that may startle some readers: *for some individuals, being black actually is advantageous as far as self-esteem is concerned.* This is true because the discrimination that blacks have endured enables a black man to point "out there" to explain his frustrations, failures, and so on, rather then to deficiencies in his own self. The white man, clearly, cannot protect his self-esteem in the same manner. This may be why some whites are so upset when they see a black man who, by white standards, has achieved a level of success beyond their own. Seldom can they say, "He's achieved that just because he's black," whereas the unsuccessful black man frequently has at least some basis for reaching a comparable conclusion about many relatively successful white men. He does not have to accept their success as a true measure of his inadequacy.

There is, of course, a real danger in this situation for the black man, especially now that many of the barriers to his progress are beginning to crumble. The danger is that he will fail to see how he may improve himself to take advantage of new opportunities, preferring instead to rather passively accept his "fate" as a product of a discriminating system. Discrimination will continue, of course, but today's scene is also speckled with instances of reverse discrimination, or situations where it is actually advantageous to be black. To mine these opportunities productively, the black man must honestly analyze his inner resources and seek opportunities to develop them; he must resist the temptation to protect his self-esteem from failure experiences by concluding in advance that the "system" dooms him to second-class roles.

EMPIRICAL STUDIES

As we noted earlier, much of the traditional thinking about black self-esteem has been based upon rather casual observations of black behavior, and the validity of the inferences that have been drawn therefrom is certainly questionable. Furthermore, the incidence of comparable behavior in the white population has usually been neglected. It is of particular interest, therefore, to consider the results of . . . recent empirical studies which directly asked groups of black and white children to make self-judgments. What do these investigations tell us about the comparative levels of self-esteem in black and white children?

McDonald and Gynther

In 1965, Robert L. McDonald and Malcolm D. Gynther published the results of a study that bears upon the question just posed. Their data were collected in 1961 and 1962 in a southern urban area; the subjects were 261 black high school seniors (151 female, 110 male) and 211 white high school seniors (114 female, 97 male). The black subjects were graduating seniors of the city's only black high school, while the white subjects were graduating seniors of three of the seven white high schools. (The white schools were selected so as to represent different social classes and cultural settings.) Ages of the subjects ranged from 16 to 19.

School counselors (who were of the same race as their subjects) administered the Interpersonal Check List (ICL) to the above students in special group testing sessions. According the McDonald and Gynther (1965, p.86), the ICL " . . . consists of 128 adjectives and phrases (for example, forceful, usually gives in, considerate, sarcastic) with 16 items for each of eight different kinds of interpersonal behavior." (Although the ICL purports to measure 8 dimensions of behavior, Dominance and Love are the primary dimensions tapped by this test; see below.) Each subject rated each item twice, first to describe his self and second to describe the person that he would ideally like to be (that is, his self-ideal). From these ratings, four scores were computed: Dominance (Self), Dominance (Ideal), Love (Self), and Love (Ideal). The Dominance score " . . . is a measure of

assertive, aggressive, leadership qualities" while the Love score " . . . is a measure of friendly, warm, cooperative characteristics (1965, p. 85)." (The two ideal scores, of course, define how the subjects would like to be with respect to Dominance and Love characteristics.)

Results for the two Dominance scores are plotted in Figure 13, separately for the two races. As shown there, the mean Dominance (Self) score for the black students is higher than that of the white students, but the mean Dominance (Ideal) score of the blacks is comparatively low. The same pattern characterizes the two Love scores (figure not shown). For both characteristics, then, the black students are closer to their ideals than the white students are to theirs.

The discrepancy between self and self-ideal is frequently used in psychological research as a

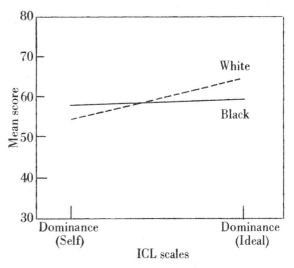

Fig. 13. Mean Dominance scores (Self and Self-Ideal) for black and white high school seniors. (Based upon data from McDonald & Gynther, 1965.)

measure of self-esteem, that is, the greater the discrepancy between self and self-ideal the lower the individual's self-esteem is inferred to be. If this is a justifiable inference, the McDonald–Gynther data lead us to conclude that the self esteem of their black subjects is *higher*, on the average, than that of their white subjects. Although they do not attempt to explain their findings, McDonald and Gynther do point out that " . . . the results involving race would seem contrary to lay expectations . . . . (p. 87)." We would go even further and conclude that the results are contrary to what one would predict based upon much of what has been written about black self-esteem by professionals.

Wendland

A second study of interest to us was conducted by Marilyn M. Wendland in 1967. All of her subjects were in the eighth grade and ranged in age from 13 to 17 (mean age was approximately 14). The total sample of 685 children was composed of 176 white boys, 161 white girls, 151 black boys, and 197 black girls.

Wendland drew her subjects from four different types of residential areas in central North Carolina: one rural area, one village, two small towns (populations approximately 15,000), and one city (population about 90,000). With a few exceptions, all of the children came from either lower or lower-middle class families. The black children were attending all-black schools and the white children were enrolled in essentially all-white schools, although there was token integration in some of the white schools. Data were gathered from these children in small group sessions conducted by a female examiner of the same race as the subjects.

Wendland's primary test instrument was the Tennessee Self Concept Scale (TSCS) which was administered to each of the 685 subjects. According to Wendland (1967, p. 38), this test " . . . consists of 100 short sentences that a subject rates on a five-point continuum from completely true to completely false as they pertain to himself." Examples of the type of statement contained in the TSCS are "I am a decent sort of person" and "I like my looks just the way they are."

Wendland also had her subjects respond to a scale designed to measure feelings of *estrangement* and to a second scale which attempts to determine the degree of one's *cynicism* toward his environment. In addition, each subject filled out a questionnaire to provide personal information about himself and his family. Special precautions were taken (see Wendland, 1967) to ensure that limitations in a child's reading ability did not invalidate his responses to any of the three scales or the questionnaire.

Many scores can be derived from the TSCS (see Fitts, 1965), but our primary interest here is in what is called the Total Positive Score, or, simply, *P*. This score, according to Wendland (1967, p.38), "Reflects the overall level of self-esteem. Persons with high scores tend to like themselves, feel that they are persons of value and worth, and act accordingly. People with low scores are doubtful about their own worth; see themselves as undesirable; often feel

anxious, depressed, and unhappy; and have little confidence in themselves."

The analysis of Wendland's data revealed that the mean self-esteem score (that is, *P* score) of the black children significantly *exceeded* that of the white children. Also, within both races, girls scored higher than boys. Finally,- children living in the country secured, on the average, higher scores than children living in the other three types of residential areas. All of these findings are depicted in Figure 14. (In this figure, the scores of village, town, and city children have been combined to form a "noncountry" group since there were no significant differences in the scores of these children associated with their residential area.)

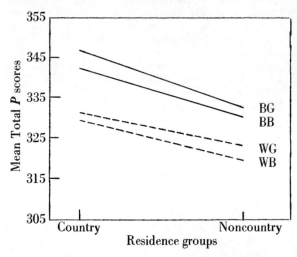

Fig. 14. Mean Total *P* scores for black and white eighth-graders according to sex and residential area. (Based upon data from Wendland, 1967.)

Figure 15 shows the mean Estrangement and Cynicism scores secured by the children of both races. These results are very interesting for they indicate the black children feel more alienated or estranged from others in their environment than the white children, but, simultaneously, as reflected in the Cynicism scores, they are, compared to the white children, much more inclined to find fault with others than with themselves. This suggests, of course, a marked tendency among black children to account for their inner unrest by finding fault with their environment rather than by seeing deficiencies in themselves.

In reflecting upon her findings, Wendland comments as follows (1967, pp. 106--108):

194

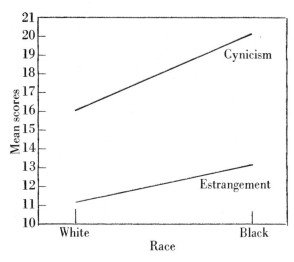

Fig. 15. Mean Cynicism and Estrangement scores for white and black eighth-graders. (Based upon data from Wendland, 1967.)

Contrary to descriptions in much of the literature, the Negro adolescents in this study, regardless of area of residence, do not present a picture of self-devaluation and negative self-esteem in comparison with their white peers. The question remains as to how, in the face of inferior caste status, these adolescents are able to maintain a positive image of themselves. One suggestive possibility emerges from the analysis of the MMPI Cynicism scale scores. While they obtained higher self-concept scores, the Negro group also scored significantly higher on the Cynicism scale, reflecting an orientation of mistrust and unfavorable attitudes toward other people. It is thus suggested that the Negro adolescent may react to the dis-esteem in which he is held by interpreting this as an expression of pathology in the discriminator rather than an inadequacy in himself. . . .

Thus, maintenance of positive self-esteem is coupled with a cynical orientation toward others and, in consequence, a feeling of isolation from others. In part, then, the results of this study suggest that conceptualizations of the Negro found in the older literature may represent unfounded stereotypes and generalizations. It also seems likely, however, that the discrepancy reflects some recent basic changes in Negro self-attitudes. Given the changes in Negro status in the last decade, it is obvious that positive self-feelings have become more possible. Additionally, the adaptive value of

assuming a self-derogatory stance in confrontations with white society is less evident. In Negro sub-groups such as the Black Power movement such self-derogation is, moreover, clearly maladaptive. In reconciling the results of the present study with older literature, it is thus suggested that not only is a basic change in Negro self-evaluation emerging, but also that the instrumental value of *claiming* self-devaluation no longer serves its historical purpose.

Editor's Note:

The self-hatred thesis is challenged in the following article as being of less importance in the psychic development of black people than the "aggression-rage" constellation. This sense of powerlessness in the face of brutality and bigotry and the inability to function in the male role of protector and provider are the seeds of the destructiveness of suppressed rage. The Black Power Movement has been described as a psychological call for manhood. It has provided a positive means of releasing some of the inner rage and hostility-hatred generated in a racist society. The author presents a brief analysis of this phenomenon, as well as the more traditional methods of sublimation.

A NEGRO PSYCHIATRIST EXPLAINS THE NEGRO PSYCHE

ALVIN F. POUSSAINT

In recent years social scientists have come to attribute many of the Negro's social and psychological ills to his self-hatred and resultant self-destructive impulses. Slums, high crime rates, alcoholism, drug addiction, illegitimacy and other social deviations have all been attributed in part to the Negroes' acting out of their feelings of inferiority. Many behavioral scientists have suggested that the recent urban Negro riots are a manifestation of subconscious self-destructive forces in black people stemming from this chronic feeling of self-denigration. Noted psychologist Dr. Kenneth B. Clark has even speculated that these riots are a form of "community suicide" that express the ultimate in self-negation, self-rejection and hopelessness.

Given the self-hatred thesis, it is not surprising that many people, both white and Negro, champion programs intended to generate a positive self-image in the Negro "masses" as a panacea for all black social problems, "Teach Negro history and our African heritage in the schools so those cats won't be ashamed of being black!" A Negro friend says, "Help those boys develop pride in being black and the riots will stop."

The self-hatred thesis appeals on the one hand to racists, who reason that if Negroes develop enough "self-love" they might wish to remain complacently segregated and stop trying to "mongrelize" the white society, and on the other to Negro militants, including the Black Muslims and Black Power advocates, who scream from soapboxes, "We must undo the centuries-old brainwashing by the white man that has made us hate ourselves. We must stop being ashamed of being black and stop wanting to be white!" There is also talk of building a Negro subculture based on "a positive sense of identity." Some militant Negroes seek to boost their self-esteem by legitimizing being black. Last year after a sit-in demonstration in Mississippi, a Negro civil-rights worker said to me, "White racism has made me hate white people and hate myself and my brothers. I ain't about to stop hating white folks, but I'm not gonna let that self-hatred stuff mess me up any more!"

No one denies that many Negroes have feelings of self-hatred. But the limitations of the thesis become apparent when one realizes that a Negro with all the self-love and self-confidence in the world could not express it in a system that is so brutally and unstintingly suppressive of self-assertion. Through systematic oppression aimed at extinguishing his aggressive drive, the black American has been effectively castrated and rendered abjectly compliant by white America. Since appropriate rage at such emasculation could be expressed directly only at great risk, the Negro repressed and suppressed it, but only at great cost to his psychic development. Today this "aggression-rage" constellation, rather than self-hatred, appears to be at the core of the Negro's social and psychological difficulties.

Consider the following. Once last year as I was leaving my office in Jackson, Miss., with my Negro secretary, a white policeman yelled, "Hey, boy! Come here!" Somewhat bothered, I retorted, "I'm no boy!" He then rushed at me, inflamed, and stood towering over me, snorting, "What d'ja say, boy?" Quickly he frisked me and demanded, "What's your name, boy?" Frightened, I replied, "Dr. Poussaint. I'm a physician." He angrily chuckled and hissed, "What's your first name, boy?" When I hesitated he assumed a threatening stance and clenched his fists. As my heart palpitated, I muttered in profound humiliation, "Alvin."

He continued his psychological brutality, bellowing, "Alvin, the next time I call you, you come right away, you hear? You hear?" I hesitated. "You hear me, boy?" My voice trembling with helplessness,

but following my instincts of self-preservation, I murmured, "Yes, sir." Now fully satisfied that I had performed and acquiesced to my "boy status," he dismissed me with, "Now, boy, go on and get out of here or next time we'll take you for a little ride down to the station house!"

No amount of self-love could have salvaged my pride or preserved my integrity. In fact, the slightest show of self-respect or resistance might have cost me my life. For the moment my manhood had been ripped from me—and in the presence of a Negro woman for whom I, a "man," was supposed to be the "protector." In addition, this had occurred on a public street for all the local black people to witness, reminding them that *no* black man was as good as *any* white man. All of us—doctor, lawyer, postman, field hand and shoeshine boy—had been psychologically "put in our place."

The self-hate that I felt at that time was generated by the fact that I and my people were completely helpless and powerless to destroy that white bigot and all that he represented. Suppose I had decided, as a man should, to be forceful? What crippling price would I have paid for a few moments of assertive manhood? What was I to do with my rage?

And if I, a physician in middle-class dress, was vulnerable to this treatment, imagine the brutality to which "ordinary" black people are subjected—not only in the South but also in the North, where the brutality is likely to be more psychological than physical.

Let us briefly look at the genesis and initial consequences of this oppressive behavior and the Negroes' responses to it. The castration of Negroes, and the resulting problems of self-image and inner rage, started more than 350 years ago when black men, women and children were wrenched from their native Africa, stripped bare both psychologically and physically, and placed in an alien white land. They thus came to occupy the most degraded of human conditions: that of a slave, a piece of property, a nonperson. Families were broken up, the Negro male was completely emasculated, and the Negro woman was systematically sexually exploited and vilely degraded.

Whites, to escape the resultant retaliatory rage of black men and women, acted to block its expression. The plantation system implanted a subservience and dependency in the psyche of the Negro that made him dependent upon the goodwill and paternalism of the white man. The more acquiescent he was, the more he was rewarded within the plantation culture. Those who bowed and scraped for the white boss and denied their aggressive feelings were promoted to "house nigger" and "good nigger."

It became a virtue within this system for the black man to be docile and nonassertive. "Uncle Toms" are exemplars of these conditioned virtues. If black people wanted to keep some semblance of a job and a full stomach to survive, they quickly learned "Yassuh, Massa." Passivity for Negroes became necessary for survival both during and after slavery, and holds true even today.

For reinforcement, as if any was needed, white supremacists constructed an entire "racial etiquette" to remind Negroes constantly that they are only castrated humans. In their daily lives, Negroes are called "girl" and "boy"—this in spite of the fact that such "girls" and "boys" as domestics are capable of managing a household with an efficiency and physical endurance that their white middle-class employers seem no longer to possess. Negroes are also addressed by their first names by whites no matter how lowly, but are in turn expected to use courtesy titles when addressing whites. It was sickening for me to hear a Southern white dime-store clerk address a Negro minister with a doctoral degree as "Jimmy," while he obsequiously called her "Miss Joan." If the Negro minister rejected these social mores he would probably be harassed, punished or in some way "disciplined." White racists through the centuries have perpetrated violence on Negroes who demonstrate aggressiveness. To be an "uppity nigger" was considered by white supremacists one of the gravest violations of racial etiquette.

Nonetheless, the passivity to which the black community has been so well conditioned is frequently called apathy and self-hate by those who would lay the burden of white racism on the black man's shoulders. The more reasonable explanation is that Negroes had little choice but to bear the severe psychological burden of suppressing and repressing their rage and aggression.

Nonassertiveness was a learned adaptation to insure survival. For example, the whole system of Southern legal justice has been designed—and still functions—to inflict severe and inequitable penalties on Negroes showing even minor aggression toward whites. In both the North and the South, Negroes who dare show their anger toward whites are usually punished out of proportion. Negroes who are "too outspoken" about racial injustices often lose their jobs or are not promoted to higher positions because they are considered "unreasonable." The recent unseating of Congressman Adam Clayton Powell and the use of guns and bullets by police and National Guardsmen on rioting Negro college students (white

college-age rioters are seldom even tear-gassed) are examples of this inequitable white retaliation.

Black people have learned their lesson well. Both in the North and in the South it is not uncommon to hear young Negro mothers instructing their 2- and 3-year-old children to "behave, and say, 'Yes, sir,' and 'No, sir' when the white man talks to you."

Similarly, various forms of religious worship in the Negro community have fostered passivity in blacks and encouraged them to look to an afterlife for eventual salvation and happiness. Negroes have even been taught that they must love their oppressor and it is "sinful" to hate or show appropriate anger. It is significant that the civil-rights movement had to adopt passive-resistance and nonviolence in order to win the acceptance of white America. But, alas, even in nonviolent demonstrations there was too much "aggression" shown by Negroes. Whites recoiled and accused civil-rights groups of "provoking violence" by peaceful protest.

The lack of self-assertion has had devastating consequences in terms of Negro social behavior and psychic responses. It has been found for instance that Negroes are less likely to go into business than are members of other ethnic groups. The most obvious explanation for this (and one missed by Glazer and Moynihan in their *Beyond the Melting Pot*) is that central to the entrepreneurial spirit is assertiveness, self-confidence and the willingness to risk failure in an innovative venture. A castrated human being is not likely to be inclined in any of these ways.

A trained incapacity to be aggressive would also account in large part for Negroes' below-par achievement in school. Negro girls, who are not as threatening to whites and therefore not as systematically crushed as are Negro boys, have been found to exceed boys in achievement in elementary schools. The pattern of behavior set for the young Negro, especially the male, is directly opposed to that upheld as masculine for the rest of American youth. With our country's emphasis on individualism and the idealization of the self-made man, brutalization into passivity leaves the Negro with a major handicap.

Of course, this is also conveniently protective for the white racist, because Negroes who are nonassertive will be afraid to compete with him for education, jobs and status. Studies have reported that even when Negroes are given objective evidence of their equal intellectual ability they continue to feel inadequate and react submissively. Thus their low aspirations may be due primarily to a learned inability to be normally aggressive and only secondarily to an inferiority complex.

Many psychiatrists feel that self-denigration is

secondary to the more general castration of the black man by white society. Some believe that the self-hatred should be viewed as a rage turned inward rather than as a shame in being black and a desire to be white. Both my white and Negro colleagues agree that central to whatever specific emotional problems their Negro patients exhibit is how they deal with their feelings of hostility and rage. (This problem is particularly relevant to their behavior in the presence of whites.)

Of course, Negroes react and adapt to the stresses of white racism in a myriad of ways depending upon socio-economic level, family life, geographical location, etc. Yet the fact remains that Negroes as individuals must deal with the general effects of racism. Since individual Negroes share the common experiences of Negro castration, rage and self-hatred, group trends can frequently be discerned.

What happens then to the accumulated rage in the depths of each Negro psyche? What does the black man do with his aggression?

The simplest method for dealing with rage is to suppress it and substitute an opposing emotional attitude—compliance, docility or a "loving attitude." A colleague told me about the case of a Negro graduate student he was treating for anxiety. The student was engaged to a white girl and circulated primarily in white social circles. He had a reputation for being very ingratiating and accommodating with his white friends, who described him as a "sweet guy" and a "very loving person." The student took a great deal of pride in this reputation and "acceptance" by whites, although he frequently encountered degrading racial prejudices among them. He attempted to deal with bigoted whites by being "understanding" and hoping that they would begin to see him as "just another human being."

At the beginning of treatment, he painted a rosy picture of his social life and particularly of his engagement to the white girl, although her parents had disowned her. He consistently denied holding any angry feelings toward whites or bitter feelings about being Negro. As therapy progressed and his problems were explored, more and more anger toward whites in general and toward his white friends in particular began to emerge. He became less tolerant of the subtle racial bigotry which he saw in his fiancee and began to quarrel with her frequently. For many weeks he became so overwhelmed by rage that he developed nausea and could not face his white friends for "fear of what I might do." He also became quite guilty about his acquiescence to white racial prejudice and slowly recognized that perhaps he himself had anti-Negro feelings. He began to avoid seeing his fiancee, feeling completely alienated from white people. The

engagement was finally broken. The student left treatment to take a job in another city and shortly thereafter it was reported to his therapist that he had become a "black nationalist."

As this student exemplified, the greater the repressed rage, the more abject the pretense of love and compliance. Thus feet-shuffling, scraping and bowing, obsequiousness and Uncle Tomism may actually indicate inner rage and deep hatred.

Sometimes rage can be denied completely and replaced by a compensatory happy-go-lucky attitude, flippancy or—a mechanism extremely popular among Negroes—"being cool."

Or the aggression may be channeled into competitive sports, music, dance. Witness the numbers of Negroes who flock to these activities, among the few traditionally open to them by white society. Negro males in particular gravitate to sports as a means for sublimating their rage and aggression.

Another legitimate means of channeling rage is to identify with the oppressor and put all one's energy into striving to be like him. The most obvious example of this is the Negro who feels that the most flattering compliment his white friends can pay him is, "You don't act like all the other Negroes," or "You don't seem Negro to me." Such blacks usually harbor strong, angry anti-Negro feelings similar to the white racists. They may project their own self-hatred onto other Negroes. This mechanism is indicated in the high incidence of impulsive violence of Negroes toward each other: assaults and homicides by Negroes are more often against Negroes than against whites.

It is also legitimate and safe for the oppressed to identify with someone like himself who for one reason or another is free to express rage directly at the oppressor. This phenomenon would account for the immense popularity among Negroes of Congressman Adam Clayton Powell and Malcolm X. They were both willing to "tell the white man like it is" and did so, for a while at least, with apparent impunity—something which many of their followers could never do.

Another technique for dealing with rage is to replace it with a type of chronic resentment and stubbornness toward white people—a chip on the shoulder. Trying to control deep anger in this way frequently shows itself in a general irritability and it always has the potential of becoming explosive. Thus the spreading wave of riots in Negro ghettos may be seen as outbursts of rage. Although these riots are contained in the ghetto, the hatred is usually directed at those whom the rioter sees as controlling and oppressing him economically, psychologically and physically—store owners and policemen.

The same hostility which is expressed in a

disorganized way by a collection of people in a riot can be expressed in an organized way in a political movement. In this connection the Black Power movement is relevant.

In the South I observed many civil-rights workers struggling with suppressed rage toward whites until it culminated in the angry, assertive cry of "Black Power!" I remember treating Negro workers after they had been beaten viciously by white toughs or policemen while conducting civil-rights demonstrations. I would frequently comment, "You must feel pretty angry getting beaten up like that by those bigots." Often I received a reply such as, "No, I don't hate those white men, I love them because they must really be suffering with all that hatred in their souls. Dr. King says the only way we can win our freedom is through love. Anger and hatred has never solved anything."

I used to sit there and wonder, "Now, what do they really do with their rage?"

Well, after a period of time it became apparent that they were directing it mostly at each other and the white civil-rights workers. Violent verbal and sometimes physical fights often occurred among the workers on the civil-rights projects throughout the South. While they were talking about being non-violent and "loving" the sheriff that just hit them over the head, they rampaged around the project houses beating up each other. I frequently had to calm Negro civil-rights workers with large doses of tranquilizers for what I can describe clinically only as acute attacks of rage.

As the months progressed and Negro workers became more conscious of their anger, it was more systematically directed toward white Southern racists, the lax Federal Government, token integration and finally the hypocrisy of many white liberals and white civil-rights workers. This rage was at a fever pitch for many months before it became crystallized in the "Black Power" slogan. The workers who shouted it the loudest were those with the oldest battle scars from the terror, demoralization and castration which they experienced through continual direct confrontation with Southern white racism. Furthermore, some of the most bellicose chanters of the slogan had been, just a few years before, exemplars of nonviolent, loving, passive resistance in their struggle against white supremacy. These workers appeared to be seeking a sense of inner psychological emancipation from racism through self-assertion and release of aggressive, angry feelings.

Often the anxiety, fear and tension caused by suppressed emotion will be expressed in psychosomatic symptoms. Tension headaches, diarrhea and low back pain are conditions frequently linked to repressed hostility. Whether these symptoms occur more frequently among Negroes than among whites is an important question that has yet to be explored.

Rage is also directed inward in such deviations as alcoholism, drug addiction and excessive gambling. These escapist expressions are very prevalent among poorer Negroes and often represent an attempt to shut out a hostile world. In psychiatric practice it is generally accepted that a chronic repressed rage will eventually lead to a low self-esteem, depression, emotional dullness and apathy.

It appears that more and more Negroes are freeing themselves of suppressed rage through greater out-spoken release of pent-up emotions. Perhaps this is an indication that self-love is beginning to out-balance self-hate in the black man's soul. A report this June by the Brandeis University Center for the Study of Violence said, "Although most Negroes disliked violence and had mixed feelings about its effect, even moderates were shifting to the opinion that only intense forms of social protest would bring relief from social injustice."

The old passivity is fading and being replaced by a drive to undo centuries of powerlessness, helplessness and dependency under American racism. It is not uncommon now to hear Negro civil rights leaders as well as the teenager in the ghetto say such things as, "White America will have to give us our rights or exterminate us." James Meredith echoed the sentiments of many Negroes after his "march against fear" in Mississippi when he said, "If Negroes ever do overcome fear, the white man has only two choices: to kill them or let them be free."

The implication of all this seems to be that black people can obtain dignity only through continued assertive social and political action against racism until all of their just demands are met. It also appears that old-style attempts to destroy the natural aggression of the black man and to fail to give him his full rights can only provoke further outbreaks of violence and inspire a revolutionary zeal among Negro Americans.

The behavior of young Negroes today implies their recognition that racial pride and self-love alone do not fill the bellies of starving black children in Mississippi. Nor does being proud of one's African heritage alone bring jobs, decent housing or quality education. Perhaps the emphasis by social scientists on self-hatred problems among blacks is just another thesis that is guilt-relieving for whites and misguides the Negro. It's as if many white Americans are saying, "From now on when we oppress you, we don't want you to hate being black, we want you to have racial pride and love each other."

For the fundamental survival problems of black

Americans to be dealt with, a variety of social, economic and political forces controlled primarily by whites must be challenged. "Positive-sense-of-identity" programs are relevant only insofar as they generate greater constructive aggressiveness in Negroes in their struggle for full equality. Since this assertive response appears to be growing more common among Negroes, the implications for American society are clear: stop oppressing the black man or be prepared to meet his expressed rage.

Editor's Note:

William E. Cross, Jr., provides a theoretical framework for analysis and interpretation of the process of discovering what he calls the "black referent," or quest for a black identity. The significance of the fact that the Black Experience is a developmental process—a becoming, as opposed to a fixed or static condition—is vital to an accurate perception of black movements, postures, and ideologies. "The Psychology of Black Liberation" exhibits rare insight into a phenomenon of black life that has seldom been expressed with such forthright perceptiveness and clarity. The author delineates five stages that are necessary for "self-actualization under conditions of oppression." He has thereby equipped us with tools of understanding and the potential for meaningful, substantive change.

TOWARD A PSYCHOLOGY OF BLACK LIBERATION

WILLIAM E. CROSS, JR.

I don't want to think of myself as a Negro and it offends me to be called "Black." If each of us would pay particular attention to self-refinement the degree of racial friction would be significantly decreased.

Yea, it all started when they shot Brother King. Honkies planned that shit and it really shook me up so bad until I began to see what was really happening to Black people. For awhile I could no longer stand to be around White people. I hated all their guts and on some days I swear I wanted to kill the first honky I saw. You know what, I even began to feel that we were better than they were because we had so much soul and love . . . .

To walk around 125th and Lenox Avenue is a powerful thing, can you dig it? When I see all those beautiful Black folks trying to make it,

doing everything just to stay alive, yet still being able to sing and dance with all that soul it just blows my mind and I sometimes want to cry tears of joy. Can you dig it? I'm a part of it all! I see Black, feel Black, oh how wonderful it is to be Black.

Black power must be more than group therapy. To be effective, it must be programmed.

These comments, or similar ones, are being made by Afro-Americans, the educated and uneducated, well-to-do and the poor, the light-skinned or dark-complexioned, as each is transformed from a "Negro" into a *Black American*. Apparently, segments of the Black community have already managed to attain psychological freedom. A crude, unconscious *process* that is generally determined by fortuitous events is operating in our communities busily transforming brainwashed Negroes into men and women of pride, action, and commitment. The "process" has transformed LeRoi Jones, Eldridge Cleaver, the late Malcolm X, and countless other adults and young Black people. The Black rectification process is somewhat chaotic, contradictory, schizophrenic, compassionate, and murderous at the same time; it is a process that no one controls, it is a process of the unconscious, it is a process molded in the discontentment of the Black masses.

Referring again to the four quotations, when each remark was made the person felt, thought, and acted differently; yet each statement reflects the qualities of a particular stage for *one* process. All too frequently analytical articles and commentaries focus on the Black militant, the Black middle class, or the apathetic Black person, creating the impression that each state or condition is unrelated to the other. A closer look suggests that today's Black theoretician *was* a well-programmed conservative three years ago and an impulsive rhetorical revolutionary last year! Obviously, Blackness is a state of mind and as such is explained by dynamic rather than static paradigms. Malcolm X was a Muslim *before* he founded the Organization of Afro-American Unity; Cleaver was immersed in the hatred of White people and his conversion to a humanist camp *required* the rape of White women; LeRoi Jones' struggle for a master's degree in philosophy preceded his quest for a Black identity. In becoming Black or, if you will, in discovering the Black referent the individual *must* pass through a series of well-defined stages; the Black experience is a process. As we analyze and comprehend the process we will be moving toward developing the *psychology of black liberation*. The five stages of this process are: preencounter (prediscovery);

encounter (discovery); immersion-emersion; internalization; and commitment.

Stage One: Preencounter. In the preencounter stage a person is programmed to view and think of the world as being nonBlack, antiBlack, or the opposite of Black. The person's world view is dominated by Euro-American determinants. The sociological, political, cultural, and psychological conditions that result from this world view appear to be the same for both lower- and middle-class Black people. The content of the Black experience within the class system differs but the *context* is similar as both think, act, and behave in a manner that *degrades* Blackness. The person's historical perspective distorts Black history. It is believed that Black people came from a strange, uncivilized, "dark" continent and that the search for Black history begins in 1865—that slavery was a civilizing experience.

Brothers and sisters from the ghetto functioning at the preencounter level assume they are more relevant than Black folks who live "outside" the ghetto; ghetto residents will justify and even romanticize hustling or exploiting other Black people as being "necessary for survival." For preencounter Negroes a White aesthetic transcends class lines. It is dramatized by deifying the White woman, and is also reflected in the content, themes, vehicles of emphasis, colorations, and mode of expressions in numerous cultural and academic preferences. Even in the ghetto where purer forms of Black expressions can be found one discovers the ghetto resident referring to the blues or jazz as something low, bad, or sexy (White cultural value system).

Preencounter Negroes are politically naive and are programmed to believe in the Protestant ethic. There is an extreme dependency on White leadership and the assimilationist-integration paradigm is thought to be the only model for cohesive race relations. The White man is viewed as intellectually superior and technically mystical; Negroes in the preencounter stage tend to become enveloped in the White man's rhetoric, confusing his words for his deeds. Emphasis is on the individual seeking to get "ahead"; the advancement of the race is gauged by how far "I" progress in the system. Preencounter Negroes typically distrust Black-controlled businesses or organizations and prefer to be called Negro, civilized, colored, human being, or American citizen.

Stage Two: Encounter. What experience, information, or event causes a person functioning at the preencounter level to become interested in, or at least receptive to, material that will contest a number of his or her basic assumptions concerning Negroes?

More simply, what motivates a person (in the preencounter world) to encounter or to become Black? A predictable answer is suggested by the word *encounter*: some experience that manages to slip by or even shatters the person's current feeling about himself and his interpretation of the condition of the Negro in America. The encounter is a verbal or visual event, rather than an "in-depth" intellectual experience. For example, the death of Martin Luther King hurled thousands of preencounter Negroes into a search for a deeper understanding of the Black Power movement. Witnessing a friend being assaulted by the police, televised reports of racial incidents, or discussions with a friend or loved one who is further advanced into his or her Blackness may "turn a person on" to his own Blackness.

Encounter entails two steps: first, experiencing the encounter, and, second, beginning to reinterpret the world as a consequence of the encounter. The second part is a testing phase during which the individual cautiously and fearfully tries to validate his new perceptions. On the outside the person is generally very quiet, yet a storm is brewing inside. The person will go to meetings and simply listen as he tries to determine the validity of this ominous thing called Blackness, Black Power, or Black history. "Maybe, just maybe, things are different than I thought them to be and if so, *I want* to find the truth."

Each individual asks himself very personal questions. The Black intellect wonders, "Have I been unaware of the Black experience or was I programmed to be disgusted by it?" A ghetto youth asks, "Is it right to kill another Black person or prostitute my sisters?" And the Black college student says, "Do I date White girls, avoiding Black women?"

The tentative answers are obvious and the person quickly compares the implications of his new insights with the manner in which he had been living (preencounter stance). Previously hostile or at best neutral toward the Black movement, the encounter jolts the person into at least considering a different interpretation of the Black condition. His heart pounding, hands sweating, and eyes filled with tears the person speaks the magic words for the first time in his life, "Black is beautiful." At this point *guilt* becomes a tremendous factor. The middle-class person feels guilty for having "left" the race; the lower-class person feels guilt for degrading his Blackness! At the same time the person becomes increasingly angry as it is realized that he or she has been "programmed or brainwashed" all these years—and the vicious enemy is the White man and all the White world! Black rage and guilt combine to fling the person into a frantic, determined, obsessive, extremely motivated search for Black identity. A "Negro" is dying and a "Black American" is being resurrected. We have reached the immersion-emersion stage.

Stage Three: Immersion–Emersion. In this period the person immerses himself in the world of Blackness. The person attends political meetings, joins the Muslims, goes to rapping sessions, attends seminars and art shows that focus on Blackness. Everything of value must be Black or relevant to Blackness. The experience is an immersion into Blackness and a liberation from Whiteness. Regardless of the opinions of others, the person actually feels that he is being drawn toward qualitatively different experiences as he is being torn from his former orientations. The immersion is a strong, powerful, dominating sensation constantly being energized by Black rage, guilt, and a third and new fuel, a developing sense of pride. As one brother put it, "I was swept along by a sea of Blackness." The White world, White culture, and White person are dehumanized (honky, pig, White devil) and become *biologically* inferior, as the Black person and Black world are *deified*. Superhuman and supernatural expectations are conjured concerning anything Black. Everything that is Black is good and romantic. The person accepts his hair, his brown skin, his very being as now "beautiful." That a person exists and is Black is an inherently wonderful phenomenon. Black literature is passionately consumed; brothers and sisters who *never* had an interest in reading teach themselves to read and write. One spends a great deal of time developing an Afro hairstyle, and it becomes common to wear African-inspired clothing. Persons give themselves African names or drop the "American" name, as in Malcolm X; some babies are named after African heroes. Of course an intense interest in "Mother Africa" develops. The word Negro is dropped and the person becomes an Afro-American, Black, Black-American, or even African.

During the immersion-emersion stage the person has a creative burst, writing poetry, essays, plays, novels, or confessionals; a segment turns to the plastic arts or painting. People who never before sought or experienced creative activity discover they are able to express themselves in a totally new mode; witness the rebirth of LeRoi Jones (Imamu Ameer Baraka). Professional artists speak of profound and fundamental change in the quality of their work. In explaining the change these artists state that although they were born in a Black situation, their training and the pressures from society made them look for substance and content outside the Black experience. For example, some wanted to be "pure" and "free," creating art for art's sake, as others admitted that their eyes, ears, and hands could only perceive Europe and America. With the realization of their Blackness, the professional artist is awakened to a vast and new world full of rich colors, powerful dramas, irony, rage, oppression, survival, and impossible dreams! And it is all there within reach; the artist (and scholar) has simply to look in the mirror.

There is a turning inward and a withdrawal from everything that is perceived as being or representing the White world. Yet, ironically, a need rushes forth to confront the "man" as a means of dramatizing, concretizing, or proving one's Blackness. The confrontation, especially for Black leaders, is a manhood (or womanhood) ritual—a baptismal or purification rite. Carried to its extreme, the impetus is to confront White people, generally the police, on a life-or-death basis. When this impulse is coupled with a revolutionary rhetoric and program, a Black Panther is born. No control or oppressive technique including the threat of death is feared. Fanon's concept of psychological liberation through the violent overthrow of one's oppressor is relevant to the Black American situation, only the circumstances in the United States force the oppressor's death to be thought about or dreamed but not actually carried out. Confrontation, bluntness, directness, and an either/or referent are the primary if not the only basis for communication with other people, Black or White. The much discussed "blacker than thou" syndrome intoxicates the minds of many people at this juncture. Black people are classified into such neat groups or categories as "Uncle Tom," militant, "together," "soulful," middle class, intellectual snob, etc. Labeling others helps the person clarify his own identity, but this name-calling phase can produce disastrous results (California Panther versus "US" murders, or the shooting of Malcolm X). Not only are people stereotyped, but the person's cosmology is greatly simplified and tends to be *racist*. To repeat, the person is concerned that his Blackness be pure or acceptable, and the purification rites are energized by a mixture of guilt, rage, and a sense of pride.

Rhetorically the person shifts preference from individualism to mutualism or collectivism. A constant theme of selflessness, dedication, and commitment is evident and a person feels overwhelming attachment to all Black surroundings. His main focus in life becomes this feeling of "togetherness and soul." The zenith of the immersion-emersion stage is the crystallization of these events.

The first half of the third stage is immersion into Blackness; the second is emergence from the dead-end, either/or, racist, oversimplified aspects of the immersion experience. The person begins to "level off" and control his experiences. In fact, the person cannot continue to handle such an intense and concentrated affect level and must find a plateau. The desire and need to level off is greatly facilitated by the direction of the movement as indicated by national and international Black heroes. Malcom X's trip to Mecca or Cleaver's discussions in *Soul on Ice* swing the person away from a racist ideology. One is able to discard or seriously question the simplistic components of the Black-is-beautiful philosophy, especially the tendency toward reverse racism. Such terms as power, control of one's mind, educational process, economic systems, institutions, programs, and process are considered. The White man is humanized (painfully, White people are recognized as equal to Black people at birth), and synthesizing Black rage with reason becomes the emphasis. The individual is now at least receptive to the critical analysis of the Afro-American condition from a cultural, political, and socioeconomic view. Accepted factors of the Black experience are *incorporated* and the person focuses on, or at least he is highly receptive to, presentations and plans for action for the development (liberation) of the Black community or the necessary transformations of the Black life style. The rage is still evident, however, but guilt sensations are being replaced by feelings of pride. Whereas the immersion period dominated the individual, during the emersion segment of the Black experience the individual begins to gain awareness and control of his behavior. When control, awareness, and incorporation predominate, the person is progressing into the fourth stage.

Stage Four: Internalization. The fourth stage is the most difficult and complex to explain because the events that occur during the immersion-emersion stage may frustrate or inspire an individual. Consequently, the degree of a person's future (or certainly his immediate involvement) in the Black movement may be either negligible or significant. During the immersion-emersion stage the individual develops an idealistic, superhuman level of expectancy toward practically anything "Black," in which case minimal reinforcement may carry the person into continued involvement (evolution into the internalization stage). Yet prolonged or traumatic frustration (and contestment) of these high expectancy levels may produce a Black person more deeply rooted in *nihilistic* expectancies than witnessed in the behavior of individuals functioning at the preencounter level. A surface analysis suggests four options for persons moving beyond the immersion-emersion stage.

Disappointment and Rejection: Some persons have their expectations frustrated and they resort to a nihilistic, hopeless, even antipeople world view, perhaps becoming more believers in the White man's "magic" and the Black man's inferiority.

Continuation and Fixation at Stage Three: Individuals who experience particularly painful perceptions and confrontations will be overwhelmed with hate for White people and fixate at the third stage. An aware brother or sister from the ghetto will be more angry than those who can move in and out of the most oppressive Black conditions (college students, the middle class, or Black researchers).

Internalization: Others internalize and incorporate aspects of the immersion-emersion experience into their self-concept. They achieve a feeling of inner security and are more satisfied with themselves. There is *receptivity* to discussions or plans of action; however receptivenss is as far as it goes. The person is not committed to a plan of action. He or she becomes the "nice" Black person with an Afro hairstyle and an attachment to Black things. Thus, it is possible for a person to progress to a state of psychological Blackness and then stop developing! Furthermore, his world view remains the same—still very American. Cosmologically the person is unchanged, yet psychologically and spiritually the person is significantly different. Frequently the person confuses substantive psychological change for concrete modifications in his world view; this is why such a person will believe himself "more Black" than another. Apparently the self-concept modifications do make the person very receptive to meaningful change in his world view. In fact, Black revolutionary change may only be possible *after* Black people have been exposed to a more positive perspective of themselves.

The Black theorist, planner, or leader must comprehend that a person does not always experience modification of his political views concurrently with changes in his psychological state. Our audience is not automatically enlightened, but it is now captive. The fourth option involves internalization and commitment behavior; this will be discussed in stage five.

Stage Five: Internalization-Commitment. The person functioning at the fifth stage differs from the person in the fourth stage because he is committed to a plan. He is actively involved in trying to change his community. His values also will be decidedly Western. However, he is going beyond rhetoric and into action. He defines change in terms of the masses of Black people, and we might argue that he represents a "relevant" as opposed to a "token" reformer. Should the person develop a comparative referent (nonWestern and Western insights) we have the "ideal" Black person in the political and psychocultural view.

The significance of nonWestern insights is dramatized when considering the problem of liberating Black scholars. The "Negro" scholar hesitates to become involved in the Black experience because his perspective is distorted by the limitations of the philosophy and epistemology of Western science. At least six factors define the constraints that prevent the Black scholar from attaining personal liberation: (1) Western thought relies primarily on *intellectual* factors as it concomitantly suppresses affective inputs; (2) the behavioral sciences, which have evolved from the rational referent, also deify cognitive functions and minimize the value of emotionally energized behavior; (3) the Western science *rhetoric* suggests nonviolent, rational-intellectual solutions and emphatically rejects violent resolutions as irrational and even "immoral"; (4) racism permeates Western thought to the extent that the social sciences have maintained racism rather than produced models for Black liberation; (5) the social sciences have traditionally been content with a statistical, categorical, static, descriptive analysis of the Black community with minimal time and effort spent on prescriptive analysis for rectifying the Black condition; and (6) a Negro trained in a Western university sees the Black experience as a study in gross pathology or cultural deprivation.

In essence the Negro Western scholar seeks continued sophistication of intellect as he prays for emotional impotence. Emphasis is on the negation of affect rather than the eruption, embracement, and living of emotion. It is not surprising, therefore, that so-called Negro scholars have not been capable of presenting models for Afro-American liberation, especially when Black liberation *must* involve two components: first, the discovery, eruption, embracement, and incorporation of affect (Black rage, guilt, and pride); and second, the synthesis of affect with reason. In liberating Black scholars we should add a third requirement: exposure to nonWestern thought.

• • •

The contemporary Black experience is a tribute to the masses of Afro-Americans. *Without* the insight and support of a significant vanguard group, the Black masses have formulated and experimented with methods for liberating themselves! The oppressed Black scholar has been freed by the crude, stumbling, unrefined, global expressions of lowly Black folks. It is the challenge, if not the obligation, of Black scholars to study, amplify, and develop those processes that have created conditions of Black liberation, even if these conditions are not to be ligitimized in the sacred halls of Western scholarship. The implications of the Black experience when viewed as a process are:

1. The process should be viewed as the *Afro-American model for self-actualization under conditions of oppression*. A relevant Black community will be aware that all stages are necessary, including the eruption of Black rage, guilt, and pride.

2. The goals of Black self-actualization will be (a) awareness of the condition of the masses of Black people; (b) development of skills; and (c) preparation for participating in the mass struggle of Black people. Change will be defined as actions that affect the lives of large blocs of people (relevant reform). Achievement, accomplishment, and reward will be correlated with activities related to the collective good of Black people.

3. Black scholars must understand Black rage as genuine human anger that is manifesting itself all over the world. Black rage in combination with guilt and pride is the *fuel* of the Black movement. Our efforts must not mute, distort, or suppress Black rage; rather we must recognize it for what it is: a potentially creative, productive, and unifying force when programmed by the circumstances that are under the conscious control of the Black community.

4. Although he embraces Black rage as a natural and welcome component of the process for discovering the Black referent, the Black scholar must create programs that synthesize affect with ideas that will lead to action.

5. The dynamics of the programs developed to integrate affect and reason must increase the *options* for participation in the Black movement. Either/or, "Blacker-than-thou," or Panther-versus-nationalist arguments must be superseded by paradigms that: (a) teach and define the Black referent (Black condition); (b) allow for the expression of genuine human outrage; (c) synthesize rage, guilt, and pride with ideas that lead to productive, creative action; and (d) allow for participation in the struggle on various levels. Even under conditions of revolutionary warfare, not every "revolutionary" is carrying a gun. Therefore, whether we speak of relevant reform or preparation for revolution the options for participation in the Black struggle must be increased.

The psychology of Black liberation offers insight into the urgent responsibilities of the Black intelligentsia. If the radical aspects of the Black movement are to survive the either/or, alienating programs currently being pressed in our Black communities, the Black vanguard must quickly demonstrate how culture, politics, education, and freedom are in fact components of *one* process: the Black experience.

PART III. C:

DIMENSIONS OF BLACK COMMUNITY LIFE – ECONOMICS

A BLACK MAN TALKS OF REAPING

ARNA BONTEMPS

I have sown beside all waters in my day.
I planted deep, within my heart the fear
that wind or fowl would take the grain away.
I planted safe against this stark, lean year.

I scattered seed enough to plant the land
in rows from Canada to Mexico
but for my reaping only what the hand
can hold at once is all that I can show.

Yet what I sowed and what the orchard yields
my brother's sons are gathering stalk and root;
small wonder then my children glean in fields
they have not sown, and feed on bitter fruit.

Editor's Note:

The Civil War and Emancipation Proclamation freed the slave technically, but economic, political, and social freedom were as elusive after these major events as they had been nonexistent before. The country had prepared neither slave nor master for the dissolution of the "peculiar institution." Even the Abolitionists had dealt with freedom as an abstraction, expressing little concern for the survival needs of the freedman.

Recalling that many of the slaves had been hired out in the cities as craftsmen and possessed considerable skills, one has to reject the notion that the Afro-American was incapable of learning or performing as well as any other man, given the proper training. Rayford W. Logan traces the development of economic inequality from its inception in slavery, through the failure of the federal government to implement a "long-range, comprehensive, and intelligent policy of economic habilitation" to the enactment of the repressive Black Codes, which ensured the former slave an inferior place.

THE ECONOMIC ROOTS OF SECOND-CLASS CITIZENSHIP: AGRICULTURE

RAYFORD W. LOGAN

The economic basis of second-class citizenship for Negroes was rooted deep in slavery. On the eve of the Civil War almost nine out of ten Negroes in the United States were slaves. The vast majority of these 3,953,760 slaves were field hands and domestic servants. A small number were carpenters, coopers, tailors, shoemakers, bootmakers, cabinet makers, plasterers, seamstresses. Others were employed in salt works, iron and lead mines, on railroad construction, on river boats and on docks. Some worked in textile mills, especially in Florida, Mississippi, Alabama, Georgia, South Carolina and Louisiana. The exigencies of the war, which increased the number of Negroes engaged in non-agricultural pursuits, particularly in iron works, coal mines and salt works, clearly demonstrated that "Negro labor, properly directed, was adaptable to diversified agriculture and to a varied industrial program." But, at the end of the war most Southern Negroes were without capital, without the rudiments of education, and without experience in work except as agricultural field hands and as domestic servants.

Contrary to the Marxist interpretations of Reconstruction, there was little sense of solidarity between white and black workers in the South. Prior to the war, most of the non-slaveholding and landless whites held slavery responsible for their own distress. White urban workers particularly resented the hiring of Negro slave artisans. It was, in fact, the plight of the poor whites that had led forward-looking South-erners like William Gregg to favor industrialism. They had accomplished little, however, except perhaps to increase the gulf between free black workers and white workers and to prepare the way for the almost exclusive employment of whites in the post-war industries.

The 488,000 free Negroes encountered many difficulties in their attempts to gain a livelihood. More than forty per cent of them lived in the South where they, like the non-slaveholding and landless whites, had to compete with slave labor. In addition, many Southern states circumscribed the mobility of Negroes even within the state and prohibited them from engaging in certain occupations. Despite all these handicaps, some of them became skilled artisans. They worked in fifty different occupations in Charleston, and in more than seventy in North Carolina. In the slave state of Maryland, some 2,000 free Negroes of Baltimore engaged in nearly one hundred occupations, including paper-hanging, engraving, quarrying, photography and tailoring. New Orleans had colored jewelers, architects and lithographers. Almost every community had its free Negro carpenters, barbers, cabinet makers, and brickmasons; many had shopkeepers, salesmen, and clerks, even where it was a violation of the law.

Free Negroes in the North worked not only as artisans but also in the professions. They were engaged in more than 130 skilled occupations in Philadelphia alone. Many of the urban communities had colored ministers, teachers, lawyers and dentists. But free Negroes in the North were often victims of violence that occasionally flared into riots, especially in cities where there were relatively large numbers of Negroes, such as Cincinnati, Philadelphia and New York. But small towns like Utica and Palmyra, New York, also were the scene of riots. Recent investigation reveals two destructive riots against Negroes in Providence, Rhode Island, in 1824 and 1831. Further research may show that there were others.

A few free Negroes had acquired property in larger amounts than is generally known. In New York City they owned more than $1,000,000 worth of property, in Cincinnati more than $500,000, and comparable amounts in such cities as Philadelphia, Baltimore, Washington and Boston. Negro holdings in Providence were estimated at between $35,000 and $50,000, in 1839. Even more surprising is the amount of property possessed by free Negroes in the South. In Virginia, they owned more than 60,000 acres of farm land, and city real estate valued at $463,000; in North Carolina, more than $1,000,000 in real and personal property. Free Negroes in New Orleans paid taxes on property variously estimated at from $9,000,000 to $15,000,000. A few individual Negroes were wealthy. James Forten, of Philadelphia had accumulated a fortune of more than $100,000 and Thomy Lafon of New Orleans, $500,000. A few Southern Negroes even held slaves.

It is thus inaccurate to assert, as do some orators, that the Negro started from scratch in 1865. Most free Negroes, none the less, in both North and South eked out a precarious existence. Moreover, the war had in many cases increased the bitterness against Negroes. Many Southern poor whites expressed bitter resentment against a "rich man's war and a poor man's fight." In some parts of the North, whites were equally bitter against the "nigger war." The most extreme manifestation of this attitude in the North erupted in the "Draft Riots" in New York City, July, 1863. For four days the city was in the hands of a mob against which the police were powerless. The mob demolished draft headquarters, chased and beat Negroes, hanged them from trees and lampposts. Much of this violence stemmed not only from aversion to fighting a war in which the whites had little interest, but also, perhaps more so, from the competition of Negroes for jobs.

The economic basis for second-class citizenship for Negroes is found also in the failure of the federal government to accept responsibility for a long-range, comprehensive and intelligent policy of economic habilitation of the emancipated Negroes. Some fifty private organizations wrote a memorable chapter in the history of American philanthropy, by providing substantial relief and inaugurating educational programs for the freedmen in the South. But, obviously, the job was too stupendous for private philanthropy. Either private capital or governmental action, therefore, had to provide the freedmen with economic opportunities to undergird their new political and civil rights. Southern capital could not provide the jobs. Northern capital, especially in the years immediately after the war, found more profitable investments in the East and West than in the South. The Black Codes of the Southern states, 1865-1866, showed clearly the determination to deny the freedmen equal economic opportunity. During the critical period immediately after the war, federal action alone could have provided the freedmen with the economic opportunities without which their new political and civil liberties had little foundation.

The nature and extent of the aid that the federal government should give to freedmen, and the South in general, precipitated in 1863 one of the earliest debates in American history of what is today called the "welfare state." Proponents of governmental aid insisted that private charity was insufficient to alleviate the woeful plight of the freedmen, and that the freedmen could not measurably alleviate it through their own efforts. Opponents declared that governmental aid would be "revolutionary," that it would create a large number of bureaucrats and pave the way for corruption in government. They also contended that governmental aid would curtail the freedmen's initiative and self-reliance. After two years of debate, Congress, on March 3, 1865, finally approved a bill, without a record vote, and Lincoln immediately signed it. It was clearly designed as a war measure, for the Bureau of Refugees, Freedmen and Abandoned Lands was placed under the Secretary of War and it was to continue for only one year after the end of the war. The Secretary of War was to issue necessary provisions, clothing and fuel and, under the direction of the President, the commissioner in charge could set aside, for the freedmen and refugees, tracts of land of not more than forty acres to be leased to tenants. The lessees were to be protected in the use of the land for three years at a low rental, and at the end of the term they could purchase the land at an appraised value.

The "Radical" Republicans who dominated the Congress that met in December, 1865, sought to make the Freedmen's Bureau permanent. But President Johnson vetoed the new bill on February 19, 1866, in a message that summarized the views of the opposition expressed during the previous debates. Johnson, a Tennessee Unionist, had frequently revealed, as a member of Congress and as governor of his state, the hostile attitude of many poor whites toward the Negro. He was also determined that he, not Congress, would formulate Reconstruction policies. His conflict with Congress may have prompted in part his veto, but the persistence of his pre-Civil war and Civil War hostility to Negroes was manifest when he wrote:

It [Congress] has never deemed itself authorized to expend the public money for the rent or purchase of homes for the thousands, not to say millions of the white race who are honestly toiling from day to day for their subsistence. A system for the support of indigent persons in the United States was never contemplated by the authors of the Constitution; nor can any good reason be advanced why, as a permanent establishment, it should be founded for one class or color of our people more than another.

He recognized the need that had existed during the war for the freedmen to receive aid from the government, but "it was never intended that they should thenceforth be fed, clothed, educated and sheltered by the United States." The slaves had been assisted to freedom with the idea that, when they became free, "they would be a self-sustaining population. Any legislation that shall imply that they are not expected to attain a self-sustaining condition must have a tendency injurious alike to their character and their prospects." How the freedmen were to lift themselves by their own bootstraps was not indicated in the veto message.

• • •

Until a few years ago, it was popular to make fun of the "naïve" belief encouraged by some agents of the Freedmen's Bureau that the freedmen were going to be given forty acres and a mule by the federal government. The levity decreased somewhat when the Great Depression of the 1930's revealed the plight of white sharecroppers—who outnumbered colored by two to one. Perhaps because federal assistance then included more whites than Negroes, there was less opposition to various agricultural programs, especially after large planters and bankers discovered that they would receive directly and indirectly a great share of the largesse. More recently, the bitter attacks upon these New Deal projects and "socialistic" programs have begun again to influence American historiography. In the meanwhile, however, some historians have stopped sneering and laughing at the "forty acres and a mule" joke. Some of them consider the failure of the federal government to expand and continue the insufficient program of land distribution through the Freedmen's Bureau the greatest blunder of Reconstruction.

The policy of the federal government after the Civil War was all the more fatal to the economic habilitation of the impoverished freedmen because the Southern states had curtailed the right of freedmen to become landowners. The Black Code of Mississippi, for example, stipulated, "Provided, that the provisions of this section shall not be so constructed as to allow any freedman, free negro or mulatto to rent or lease any lands or tenements except in incorporated cities or towns, in which places the corporate authorities shall control the same." As Wharton has remarked, this part of Mississippi's Black Code was the "hardest of the whole group to justify. It stood as a direct discouragement to the most industrious and ambitious of the Negroes, and as an almost insurmountable obstacle to those who hoped to rise from the status of common laborers." In some other states, on the other hand, their holdings were limited to the countryside.

Although the Black Codes were repealed by the Reconstruction legislatures, the freedmen encountered great difficulty in acquiring land for the simple reason that few of them possessed the means of doing so. Some came into possession of land in various ways: through the assistance of the federal government, through a kindly planter who turned over land to them, or an impoverished or indolent planter who allowed them to pay the back taxes and thus acquire title. In Florida, they secured homesteads covering 160,000 acres within a year after emancipation. By 1875, Georgia Negroes owned more than 350,000 acres of land. It is not clear how many had been held by free Negroes prior to the war. Negroes in Virginia acquired perhaps some 80,000 acres of land in the late sixties and early seventies. In 1890, 120,738 Negroes owned farm homes, all of which except 12,253 were unencumbered. By 1900, the number owned had risen to 192,993, but the number of encumbered had risen from 12,253 to 54,017. The vast majority of these farm owners lived in the South. If it may be assumed that those who owned farm homes also owned their farms, they had made commendable progress. But their number was small, for almost 7,000,000 Negroes lived in the South—which included, according to the Census, Delaware, Maryland, West Virginia and the District of Columbia.

These farm owners constituted only one-fourth of Negroes living on farms. The other three-fourths were tenants who were greatly exploited, especially by the crop-lien system. They were compelled to obtain advances from the country merchants for meal, bacon, molasses, cloth and tobacco, as well as for tools, farm implements, fertilizer and work animals. The mark-up for the difference between cash and credit frequently amounted to from 40 per cent to 100 per cent. Since the value of the crops was sometimes less than the advances, the tenant started the new year in debt. Since, moreover, the books were kept by the merchants and many of the debtors could not read, the chances for cheating were usually not allowed to slip. It has been estimated that in some portions of the South, nine-tenths of the farmers fell into debt. Many poor whites found escape in the textile mills. Some Negroes sought escape in flight.

As early as the beginning of the eighteenth century, colonization of Negroes outside the United States had been advocated as a partial solution to slavery and the presence of unwanted free Negroes. In 1816, the American Colonization Society was formed for the purpose of settling Negroes in Africa. But perhaps not more than 25,000 had left the United States for Africa, Haiti and elsewhere by the end of the Civil War. Plans for colonizing in Liberia and other places were revived after the war, but the most important proposals for the migration of Negroes envisaged other parts of the United States. The federal government refused to aid any of the plans for migration. This refusal constitutes the third basis for the second-class citizenship of the Southern black farmers and farm workers who numbered almost one-half of all black workers.

Editor's Note:

Harold Cruse, writing in *Crisis of the Negro Intellectual* (New York: Morrow, 1967) states that Booker T. Washington, W. E. B. DuBois, and Marcus Garvey ". . . are the big three for our century. Anyone who does not understand this cannot talk seriously about Black Power or any other slogan." He goes on to point out the fallacy of attempting to accept one without the others and the danger of underestimating their far-reaching effects on the present black movement. These are important considerations for this generation. These three giants were contemporaries, and, although there were mutual antipathies, there was also mutual respect. The following article provides a précis of their economic programs.

BLACK ECONOMIC PHILOSOPHIES

WILLIAM L. HENDERSON
and LARRY C. LEDEBUR

Booker T. Washington

A prominent characteristic of the contemporary black civil rights movement is the rejection of traditional techniques for achieving social and political integration. Emphasis is now on economic development as a technique of obtaining social and political power. This current focus is not new. Economic independence and economic security was a unique element in Booker T. Washington's theory, which emphasized the economic improvement of the Negro. Washington's emphasis was on keeping the door of economic opportunity open to the Negro and was based on the premise that economic opportunity was more essential than political and social equality to the Negro at that time. This emphasis on economic development was criticized by other Negro leaders who advocated political activities to obtain acceptances into American society.

The radical and conservative tendencies cannot be better described than by comparing, or rather contrasting, the two superlative colored men in whom we find our highest embodiment—Frederick Douglass and Booker T. Washington. The two men are in part products of their times, but are also natural antipodes. Douglass lived in the day of moral giants; Washington in the era of merchant princes. The contemporaries of Douglass emphasized the rights of man; those of Washington his productive capacity. The age of Douglass acknowledged the sanction of the Golden Rule; that of Washington worshiped the rule of gold. The equality of man was constantly dinned into Douglass ears; Washington hears nothing but the inferiority of the Negro and the dominance of the Saxon. Douglass could hardly receive a hearing today; Washington would have been hooted off the stage a generation ago. Thus all truly useful men must become in some measure, time servers; for unless they serve their time, they can scarcely serve at all. . . . Douglass had no limited copyrighted program for his race, but appealed to the Decalog, the Golden Rule, the Declaration of Independence, the Constitution of the United States; Washington, holding these great principles in a shadowy background, presents a practical expedient, applicable to present needs. Douglass was a moralist, insisting upon the application of righteousness to public affairs; Washington is a practical statesman, accepting the best terms which he thinks are possible to secure.

Washington recognized the needs of his time as reflected in the social and economic environment in which he lived. His philosophy was pro-capitalistic. He wanted to bring the Negro into the economy as a productive element. Participant economic power would be the leverage to obtain political and social power. He argued that "the man who has learned to do something better than anyone else, has learned to do a common thing in an uncommon manner, is a man who has a power and influence that no adverse circumstances can take from him."

The individual or race that owns the property, pays the taxes, possesses the intelligence and substantial character, is the one which is going to exercise the greatest control in government whether he lives in the North or whether he lives in the South.

Washington believed that the Negro, because of the indispensable value of his services to the economic sector, could achieve equality of status and win the respect from his neighbors. "Nothing else so soon brings about right relations between the two races in the South as the commercial progress of the Negro."

Washington's program for the economic development of the Negro was directed towards the South. He believed that the opportunities for advancement for the Negro in this region were greater than in the urbanizing North, because of the underdeveloped nature of this region relative to its material resources and potential for further development.

•   •   •

Booker T. Washington's economic philosophy took form at Hampton Institute and was applied in industrial education programs while he was president of Tuskegee Institute. His economic approach received national attention in the now famous Atlanta Exposition Address of July 4, 1881. His remarks contained the essential elements of his philosophy, namely that the Negro in the South would be willing to accept a subordinate position without social equality if given the opportunity to develop economically. Through self-help and self-development the Negro could win respect in the South, then mutual economic progress would break down racial barriers.

• • •

In talking to both blacks and whites Washington commented:

.... In all things that are purely social we can be as separate as the fingers yet one as the hand in all things essential to mutual progress. ... The wisest among my race understand that the agitation of questions of social equality is the extremist folly, and that progress and the enjoyment of all the privileges that will come to us must be the result of severe and constant struggle rather than artificial forcing. No race that has anything to contribute to the markets of the world is long in any degrees ostracized.

This speech brought Washington nationwide attention and acclaim. As a preeminent leader of the Negro in the United States, this approach on the process of social and economic integration prevailed in white attitudes.

Washington thought that the South offered unique opportunity to the Negro because of the relatively underdeveloped agricultural and industrial resources. Thus, education at Tuskegee Institute was oriented towards basic industrial and agricultural vocational training. Despite this rationale for industrial training, Washington did exhibit an agrarian bias. "We are living in a country where, if we are going to succeed at all, we are going to do so largely by what we raise out of the soil."

Washington argued that industrial education would make "an intelligent producer of the Negro who becomes of immediate value to the community rather than one who yields to the temptation to living merely by politics or other parasitical employments." Industrial education was a technique that would secure the cooperation of whites and accomplish the most that is possible for the blacks.

In response to the criticism that industrial education would deprive the Negro of a professional class, Washington argued that the best way for the Negro race to move into professional positions was through the basic occupations.

This will give him a foundation upon which to stand while securing what is called the more exalted positions. The Negro has the right to study law; but success will come to the race sooner if it produces intelligent, thrifty farmers, mechanics, and housekeepers to support the lawyers.

Washington's influence was pervasive, both in the Negro community and in shaping white attitudes towards Negro economic, political, and social development. Because of his dominant position within the Negro community, Washington fell prey to the criticism of other aspiring Negro leaders. W. E. B. DuBois, one of Washington's most vehement critics, criticized both his position and his philosophy:

Mr. Washington represents in the Negro thought the old attitude of adjustment and submission; but adjustment at such a peculiar time as to make his program unique. This is the age of unusual economic development and Mr. Washington's program naturally takes an economic cast, becoming a gospel of work and money to such an extent to almost completely overshadow the higher aims in life. ... Mr. Washington's program practically accepts the alleged inferiority of the Negro races. ... Mr. Washington withdraws many of the high demands of Negroes as men and American citizens. ... Mr. Washington distinctly asks the black people to give up at least for the present three things,—first, political power; second, insistence on civil rights; third, higher education for Negro youths,—and concentrate all their energies on industrial education, the accumulation of wealth, and the conciliation of the south. ... as a result of this tender of the palm branch, what has been returned? In these years there have occurred: one, the disfranchisement of the Negro. Two, the legal creation of a distinct status of civil inferiority for the Negro. Three, the steady withdrawal of aid from institutions for higher training of the Negro.

Both in his philosophical orientation and in the opposition he aroused in other Negroes, Booker T. Washington shaped the philosophy of the Negro in the United States. He was the original advocate of black capitalism. "The businessmen's gospel of free enterprise, competition, and laissez-faire never had a more loyal exponent than the master of Tuskegee."

C. Vann Woodward has criticized Washington's anachronistic economic philosophy because he did not take into account the realities of mass production, industrial integration, financial combinations, and monopoly.

The shortcomings of the Atlanta Compromise, whether in education, labor, or business, were the shortcomings of a philosophy which dealt with the present in terms of the past. Not that a certain realism was lacking in Washington's approach. It is indeed hard to see how he could have preached or his people practice a radically different philosophy in his time and place. The fact remains that Washington's training school, and the many other schools he inspired, taught crafts and attitudes more congenial to the pre-machine age than to the 20th century; that his labor doctrine was a compound of individualism, paternalism, and antiunionism in an age of collective labor action; and that his business philosophy was an anachronism.

W.E.B. DuBois

With the death of Booker T. Washington, William Edward Burghardt DuBois became the spokesman for the American Negro. DuBois' life was spent in preparation for this task. While in college at Fisk University and Harvard, he accepted as duty the leadership role and dedicated himself to the redemption of the Negro. His education was in the social sciences. He believed that these areas were most germane to the study of the Negro in America. At Harvard he studied political economy and history under tutors who emphasized institutions and historical development as a means to achieve an understanding of the present. This orientation was further reinforced by study in Germany under two of the leaders of the historical school of economics, Gustav Schmoller and Adolph Wagner. This education uniquely prepared him to research and interpret the Negroes' relationships to the political, social, and economic institutions.

DuBois' interpretation of the Negro and American society remained in transition throughout most of his lifetime. It is thus difficult to extract a composite picture of his overall economic views. An economic orientation was only a part of his total view of the influences on the future of the Negro. His interpretation of economic possibilities altered with his progressive disillusionment with the prevailing American institutions. Initially, he advocated integration into the industrial system. But later in his life he was critical of capitalism and the profit motive, and espoused a system of industrial democracy and qualified socialism.

DuBois attacked Booker T. Washington's advocacy of industrial education and his accommodation and conciliation to southern racial attitudes. This criticism was most carefully articulated in *The Souls of Black Folk.*

The black men of America have a duty to perform, a duty stern and delicate—a forward movement to oppose a part of the work of their greatest leader. So far as Mr. Washington preaches Thrift, Patience, and Industrial Training for the masses, we must hold up his hands and strive with him, rejoicing in his honors and glorying in the strength of this Joshua called of God and of man to lead the headless host. But so far as Mr. Washington apologizes for injustice, North or South, does not rightly value the privilege and duty of voting, belittles the emasculating effects of caste distinctions, and opposes the higher training and ambition of our brighter minds—so far as he, the South, or the Nation, does this,—we must firmly oppose them.

DuBois refused to accept injustice in order to obtain white support for Negro industrial education. Although not opposed to industrial education per se he was concerned that emphasis on this goal dissipated resources available for liberal arts institutions such as Fisk, Atlanta, and Howard. Liberal arts education would create a vanguard of leaders for the redemption of the Negro race, or the Negro intellectual élite, the "talented tenth." Throughout his lifetime DuBois retained his faith in the ability of an intellectual aristocracy to redeem the masses.

•   •   •

DuBois' program for the economic emancipation of the Negro centered around three complementary concepts: separatism, cooperation, and socialism. Francis Broderick, a biographer of DuBois, relates that over a period of years DuBois realized the dilemma of Negro separatism. The aims of integration, the long-range goal, and security, a short-range goal, were in conflict and pulled in different directions.

•   •   •

Repeated rebuffs in efforts to enlist support of white groups to assist the Negro led DuBois to the conclusion that separation would be necessary to permit the development of the race. The separatism advocated was not physical or geographical, but cultural, social, and economic—that is, a self-sufficient Negro culture exclusive of state and cultural lines.

213

Harold Cruse in *The Crisis of the Negro Intellectual* argues that this rejection of nationalism was the great weakness of DuBois—the only real flaw in the man's intellect. Cruse contends that "It seems not to have occurred to DuBois that any thorough economic reorganization of Negro Existence imposed from above, will not be supported by the popular masses unless an appeal is made to their nationalism." He argued that segregation and discrimination do not necessarily go together. Opposition to segregation should arise only when there is discrimination. Although DuBois believed that, in the long run, the greatest human development would occur in a system permissive of wider contact, the racial barriers confronting the Negro made this wider contact improbable.

> . . . . It is impossible, therefore, to wait for the millennium of free and normal intercourse before we unite, to cooperate among ourselves in groups of like-minded people and in groups of people suffering from the same disadvantages and hatreds.
> . . . . It is the conscious black man cooperating together in his own institutions and movements who will eventually emancipate the colored race. . . .

DuBois accepted an economic segregation when separation resulted in economic benefits for the Negro. In referring to the existence of Negro businesses, he noted that newspapers, barbers, and morticians catering to Negro clientele existed only because of segregated business patterns. In industry Negroes held only unskilled low-income jobs and competed with white labor, creating racial animosities. In small retail stores Negroes were not competing with large chain stores. In the service sector they received insufficient wages to support themselves and their families, and in agriculture blacks faced the general decline of the industry. In 1928, when DuBois argued for "intensive economic organization of the Negro market behind a tariff wall of racial pride," he believed that Negroes must organize on a cooperative basis.

> We see more and more clearly that economic survival for the Negro in America means . . . that he must employ labor, that he must organize industry, that he must enter American industrial development as a group, capable of offensive and defensive action, and not simply as an individual, liable to be made the victim of the white employer and of such of the white labor unions as dare.

Within this cooperative movement a new sense of values would be operative that contrasted with the individualism of the private competitive system.

Under economic cooperation we must strive to spread the idea among colored people that the accumulation of wealth is for social rather than individual ends. We must avoid, in the advancement of the Negro race, the mistakes of ruthless exploitation which have marked modern economic history. To this end we must seek not simple home ownership, small landholding and savings accounts, but also all forms of cooperation, both in production and distribution, profit-sharing, building and loan association, systematic charity for definite, practical ends. . . .

If carefully organized cooperatives would lead to economic prosperity, Negro labor and entrepreneurs would control each successive stage of production. Negro cooperative stores would obtain their goods from Negro producers, which were supplied raw materials from Negro farmers. Intermediate stages of productions, such as extractive industries and transportation, were to be Negro controlled. Final products would be purchased by Negro consumers who patronized only black stores.

The profits derived would remain in the system and benefit everyone who shared in the cooperatives. This economic structure would provide for the Negro's economic independence and eventually lead to cooperation between the American Negro and the West Indies, South America, and Africa.

DuBois was critical of capitalism as an economic system because of its exploitation and constraint of the Negro. The Great Depression revealed the structural weaknesses of capitalism, and he had believed that this disaster would move the United States away from its faith in private capitalism. The system, according to DuBois, was based on the fallacious concept that the pursuit of private profit would produce the best social results with no external interference in the market. His alternative was a system in which distribution was based on social ethics, and where an "industrial democracy" had much greater control of labor and the fruits of the industrial process.

•   •   •

Marcus Garvey

The message that Garvey espoused spoke directly to the needs of the disillusioned urban Negro. He proclaimed that through racial unity and racial cooperation the Negro could achieve respect and dignity. The Negro must be "one race" and have "one God and one destiny." He attempted to mobilize the urban black behind the rallying cry, "Up you mighty race, you can accomplish what you will." The Negro responded to this message. It "brought to the Negro people for the first time a sense of pride in being black. Black pride is the core of Marcus Garvey's philosophy. Around this ideal he centered his life."

The New York *Amsterdam News* stated that ". . . it was because Marcus Garvey made black people proud of their race. In a world where black is despised, he taught them that black is beautiful. He taught them to admire and praise black people and black things. They rallied to him because he heard and responded to the heartbeat of his race."

Garvey's program for the attainment of racial pride contained two complementary dimensions: geographical separatism and economic self-sufficiency. Separation was the only practical manner in which the Negro could obtain release from subjugation. This belief was based on the premise that white cultures could not permit the assimilation of the black because assimilation was a form of racial suicide. He argued for complete separation and particularly against miscegenation.

•   •   •

For Garvey the return-to-Africa or pan-African movement was no visionary or utopian concept. He vigorously sought to implement such a concept throughout his lifetime. A governmental structure was organized, and titles of nobility were established. Garvey was the chief executive. Representatives were sent to Liberia to locate sites for Negro colonies, which were to house Negroes from around the world. Blacks could return to their historical and cultural homeland. Garvey thought that "The other races have countries of their own and it is time for the four hundred million to claim Africa for themselves."

White America, in Garvey's view, had an obligation to assist the Negro to return to Africa. "Let white America help us for 50 years honestly, as we have helped her for 300 years, and before the expiration of many decades there will be no more race problem. Help us to gradually go home, America. Help us as you helped the Jews. Help us as you have helped the Irish. Help us as you have helped the Poles, Russians, Germans, and Armenians."

It is possible that this return-to-Africa program would have become a reality. But Garvey's statements on a united Africa for the Africans induced a strong opposition to his program from the European colonial powers in Africa. Colonial powers brought pressure on the government of Liberia, which resulted in fear within the Liberian government that the rapid influx of American Negroes would be prejudicial to Liberian interests and autonomy.

•   •   •

Garvey's attitude on economic self-sufficiency was attributable to Washington's philosophy that the Negro must become independent of white capital and operate his own business activities.

Garvey recognized that the economic system in the United States was designed to exploit the Negro. The white man's solution for the Negro problem in this country was to utilize the black population to build up the country to the point when black labor was no longer needed and then "throw them off and let them starve economically and die of themselves or emigrate elsewhere, we care not where. Then no one can accuse him of being inhuman to the Negro as we have not massacred him." In addition, Garvey argued that in this country increased wealth of the Negro or the Negro vote could never force the government to recognize Negro needs. The government is dictated by the majority of the people. In the United States when the majority are against something "then the government is impotent to protect that measure, thing or race."

However, the system of capitalism was necessary to the progress of the world. Anyone who opposed this economic system was an enemy of human advancement. Garvey opposed socialism and even labor unionism. In "Capitalism in the State," Garvey argued that there should be strict limitations on the income or wealth that any individual or corporation could hold. The state should use and invest the money above specified limitations. He also argued that warfare was inherent in modern capitalistic systems and was the product of conflicts that arose as a result of the colonialism of capitalists throughout the world.

Garvey intended to use capitalism to supply the means to achieve economic self-sufficiency for the Negro. No race in the world was so just that it would be willing to provide a "square deal in things economic, political and social." The only protection against injustice is physical, financial, and scientific power. It was necessary for the Negro to construct a strong economic base from which to seek his other political and social objectives. Only through material achievement gained by the force of their own effort and initiative would the Negro be recognized. Thus, the Negro must establish an economic organization to achieve effective economic cooperation in the world.

Garvey's goal was to initiate this economic organization within the framework of the Universal

Negro Improvement Association. The purpose of this organization was to construct black-owned and black-operated businesses that would provide sources of incomes for Negroes within the United States. The most prodigious effort to establish black enterprise was the Black Star Steamship Line. Money was raised through contributions and stock subscriptions from Negroes to purchase several steamships to engage in foreign and domestic trade and ostensibly to provide a means of transportation for repatriation to Africa. Several steamships were actually purchased and did make abortive efforts in oceanic trade. The Black Star Steamship Line ultimately failed because Garvey and the Universal Negro Improvement Association were defrauded in the purchase of the ships. There was also evidence of dishonesty and duplicity of some of the Black Star Line executives.

Garvey's unique talent was in his ability to mobilize people and initiate projects. He had little knowledge of financial affairs, however, and lacked the organizational and structural acumen necessary for large ventures. The fact that the Black Star Line failed did not minimize the significance of this venture. It was the first large-scale attempt to establish a black business corporation financed by contributions of the masses of the Negroes, to be managed by black entrepreneurial talent. The Black Star Line was a landmark in Negro history and provides a valuable illustration for contemporary "black-capitalism" programs.

A second type of economic enterprise was organized under the auspices of the Universal Negro Improvement Association. The Negro Factories Corporation was designed to "build and operate factories in the big industrial centers of the United States, Central America, the West Indies and Africa to manufacture every marketable commodity." The corporation was capitalized at one million dollars. Common stock was sold to blacks at $5 a share. Several types of businesses were established by this enterprise: a chain of cooperative grocery stores, a restaurant, a steam laundry, a tailoring-dressmaking shop, a millinery store, and a publishing house. Other related efforts were made to encourage Negro entrepreneurs to start businesses of their own. The Negro Factories Corporation was to supply initial investment capital and organizational, executive, and technical guidance. These enterprises were less than a complete success. However, their significance is not in their economic impact, but as an illustration of Negro operation and entrepreneurship.

Garvey served a prison sentence for supposed malfeasance in the operation of the Black Star Steamship Line. He was deported after his release. Although he attempted to keep his movement alive from Jamaica and from London, his business activities never regained the scope and force they possessed prior to his imprisonment. But the impact of Garvey's enterprise was unique. He was the first to mobilize and hold the allegiance of the masses of urban blacks. He was able to direct Negroes toward the goal of rehabilitation and improvement of the Negro race through black programs of pan-Africanism and economic self-sufficiency. Most of the bases of the potential achievement of economic self-sufficiency and economic separation are found in Garvey's philosophy and work. W.E.B. DuBois, although an enemy of Garvey, provided this assessment of the Garvey enterprises:

It was a grandiose and bombastic scheme, utterly impractical as a whole, but it was sincere and had some practical features; and Garvey proved not only an astonishing popular leader, but a master propagandist. Within a few years, news of his movement, promises and plans, reached Europe and Asia and penetrated every corner of Africa.

Many contemporary economic philosophies and development programs of Negro moderates and militants were contained in the economic philosophies of earlier black leaders such as Booker T. Washington, W.E.B. DuBois, and Marcus Garvey. The black utopian movement and the philosophies of W.E.B. DuBois and Marcus Garvey displayed antecedents of the modern economic separatist movement and the contemporary emphasis on black economic development. Washington and Garvey, in particular, were outspoken advocates of black capitalism and black entrepreneurship. The arguments of DuBois are a nucleus for the concept of black nationalism and cultural separatism, and the modern emphasis on cooperatives as an efficient vehicle for economic development. DuBois' philosophy contained the concept that a black economic system could evolve as a moral system that was more desirable and more ethical than the capitalism of the United States. Marcus Garvey's plan for black capitalism was the most useful contribution to black economic development. Many black militants emulate Garvey's model as the best means for the black to achieve social and economic development. Garvey's ill-fated enterprises represent the essential procedural and conceptual elements of militant nationalism and black capitalism.

Editor's Note:

Economic cooperatives are not new to the Afro-American community. Marcus Garvey was one of the most successful organizers of cooperative enterprises—laundries, groceries, hotels, restaurants, and printing plants. The National Negro Business League, founded by Booker T. Washington in 1929, sponsored a cooperative endeavor, The Colored Merchants Association (CMA) stores. DuBois, in 1918, with twelve other black men from different states established the Negro Cooperative Guild, a national organization for consumers'cooperation. He also proposed a cooperative black industrial system to be "established in midst of and in conjunction with the surrounding national industrial organization."

Today, there are those who view economic cooperatives as a viable means of attaining land and ultimate independence from white society. Many of the black nationalist organizations have either proposed or attempted to implement economic cooperatives. There are others who see them as an anomaly in a capitalistic system that is becoming increasingly one of large conglomerates and corporate monopolies.

This brief excerpt from St. Clair Drake brings us up to date on the current status of cooperatives in the black community.

COOPERATIVES IN
THE BLACK COMMUNITY

ST. CLAIR DRAKE

Some black southerners without any ideological commitment to black nationalism will want to combine to work out their problems using a well-tested institutional form—the cooperative. They find difficulty in trying to do so now, but an extension of Black Power might provide an encouraging environment. The Southwest Alabama Farmers Cooperative, composed of 2,000 poor black farmers, has been in existence since 1967. Governor George Wallace vetoed its OEO grant during its first year, and when his action was overridden in Washington, the Alabama congressmen immediately demanded an audit of SWAF's books. The maneuver failed, but when the cooperative began to truck out its cucumbers and okras to the market, state police held up the vehicles for "inspection" until the produce spoiled. Then, the state called in the FBI to investigate "misuse of federal funds." SWAF received a clean bill of health, but Governor Brewer vetoed the second installment of the OEO demonstration grant. When it came through despite the governor's opposition, he obtained a circuit court injunction, again charging misuse of funds. However, the organization survived all of the harassment, drawing upon over a million dollars in federal and private funds, astute legal assistance by friends, and the courage of its members to see it through the formative state. It did $172,000 worth of business in 1969. Whether SWAF continues to exist and prosper and expand depends upon the speed with which Alabama black voters can win enough influence at the state level to insure protection for it. Eight to ten other cooperatives of this type have sprung up here and there over the South, with three of them leasing land they hope to buy eventually, the others being composed of black landowners. Between forty-five and fifty small cooperatives representing about 15,000 members have organized a Federation of Southern Cooperatives to coordinate production and marketing of handicrafts, candy and bakery products, farm produce and timber, as well as buying clubs and grocery stores, and cooperative wholesales supplying gasoline, clothing, coal, and fish to themselves. The cooperative movement is ideally structured to facilitate racial and ethnic pluralism at the local level with membership of local cooperatives in state and regional bodies that are multiracial and multiethnic, the Central State Cooperative League being an example. In addition to all-black cooperatives, racially mixed units could emerge in local areas where it is feasible and farmers desire it. During the depression, members of the Southern Tenant Farmers Union conducted an interracial cotton producing cooperative in Bolivar County, Mississippi, the same county in which the all-Negro town of Mound Bayou was located. The white plantocracy was hostile to both communities. Black political power could have protected both.

Not all black farmers, of course, are interested in the cooperative movement. Some want assured access to credit and marketing facilities and governmental services so that they can take their chances as individuals or corporations on making profits from the large-scale mechanized capitalistic farming, lumbering, dairying, and ranching operations that will dominate the southern rural future. Many smaller landowners wish to combine some subsistence agriculture with employment in the new rural and semirural factory complexes that are beginning to appear in the South. Some of these will live in all-black rural concentrations. Others will be scattered among white farmers, functioning in the normal county setting, depending upon their own voting strength or upon the influence of regional and national black organizations to protect their interests. The experience of Macon County, Alabama, where Tuskegee is located, indicates how one such group has approached its problems through sharing political power with white residents rather than insisting upon complete black control. Greene County, Alabama, will be the test case of total black political control.

The all-black town that simply grew up naturally or that emerged by deliberate design in an old
phenomenon in the South. The most highly publicized such communities have been Mound Bayou,
Mississippi, and Boley, Oklahoma. In both cases as
well as in the case of some forty-odd other communities that once existed in Oklahoma, lack of supporting political power elsewhere in the state left them
open to intimidation and sometimes terror. They
were also unable to attract the capital needed for
growth. It is likely, however, that the number of
all-black towns will increase in the future due to the
operation of several processes:
(1) Flight of whites from small communities where
    blacks predominate as they assert their political
    strength. Charles Evers attempted to prevent
    this from happening after he was elected mayor
    of Fayette.
(2) Incorporation of present unincorporated black
    settlements. One that has recently been in the
    news is Roosevelt City, a suburb of Birming-
    ham, Alabama. Such communities will need to
    attract both federal and private funds for
    economic and social development.
(3) Planned new towns of which the best known
    case is Soul City, projected as a prototype
    project in rural North Carolina by CORE's
    former director Floyd McKissick as one aspect
    of his scheme for "Black Business Development
    with Social Commitment to Black Communi-
    ties." Federal planning under HUD is likely to
    result in some predominantly black integrated
    new towns.
All such rural and suburban black clusters will,
of course, have growing commercial and associational
ties with a wide range of institutions in urban
communities where the centers of both Black Power
and White Power are located. Insofar as black
financial institutions in cities like Durham, New
Orleans, and Atlanta concern themselves with these
communities they will strengthen the nexus that
binds the black population of the region together as
an ethnic community without any necessary anti-
white or separatist implications.

The proportion of black southerners not living
on farms is approaching two-thirds, and short of a
wholesale reconstruction of rural life that is not likely
to take place, the majority of the black population,
and particularly of the younger segment, will be
concentrated in the cities. The degree of ghettoiza-
tion will continue to vary from city to city, but all
communities will maintain a black institutional structure and social class system that relates them to the
national black community.

Editor's Note:

The crop-lien or cropsharing system was the alternative offered to the former slave by the former master. The
planters leased portions of their land to former slaves or their
descendants on a yearly renewal basis. In return for their
labor, the sharecroppers were to receive up to one-half of the
proceeds. The Freedmen's Bureau had envisioned this system
as a means of aiding both groups; however, with its abolish-
ment the planter class was free to exploit and subjugate.
Many planters operated the stores that advanced supplies on
credit. The owner-planter could withhold up to half the
wages until the end of cotton season, charge whatever he
wished for goods, exercise control by withholding a contract
thereby making the family subject to peonage or the convict-
lease system, and keep the records. It proved to be an excellent method of social and economic control. This brief selection demonstrates how effectively this system operates.

THE ECONOMY
OF RULEVILLE, MISSISSIPPI

CHARLES COBB and CHARLES McLAURIN
(SNCC Field Secretaries)

The cotton picking season in the Mississippi
Delta lasts from the middle of August until the
middle of December. At the end of the season, all of
the debts incurred by the Negro sharecropper during
the year are totaled up by the plantation owner and
deducted from the money that the sharecropper has
made during the cotton picking season. The sharecropper plays no part in the totaling up of debts
which include: cost of raising cotton crop, rent, food,
and miscellaneous bills such as doctor's bills, cost of
buying a car, etc.

The agreement between sharecropper and plantation owner is that the sharecropper will raise a crop
of cotton, and split it 50-50 with the plantation
owner. But the cost of raising the cotton crop is paid
entirely by the sharecropper. All of the cotton is sold
by the plantation owner, who in turn tells the
sharecropper how much the cotton was sold for. The
fact that all finance is handled by the plantation
owner makes the sharecropper subject to all sorts of
financial chicanery from the plantation owner. In
fact, several sharecroppers and day workers have
reported that they had had to pay out Social Security
even though they have no Social Security number.
Mrs. Irene Johnson of Ruleville, who is active in the
voter registration drive there, reports that even her
ten-year-old son has had Social Security taken from
him.

Mrs. Willie Mae Robbinson, who sharecrops on
a plantation near Ruleville, picked twenty (20) bales
of cotton this season; yet she only cleared three

dollars ($3.00) for the entire year. (There are approximately 550 lbs. in a bale of cotton; and the current selling price per pound of picked cotton is $.34. Simple arithmetic shows that before deductions, Mrs. Robbinson should have made $3,740.00.) It is true that she had to split her gross with the plantation owner, and pay for her yearly expenses, but as one man told us in reference to the plight of this lady, "I know that she hasn't eaten what would have come out of ten bales."

We cannot report in much detail on settlements, because most won't be made until after Christmas.

The average amount of money made by sharecroppers for the year is between $300-400. The average amount of money made by day laborers for the year is between $150-160.

The general opinion among the Negro community in Ruleville is that they "won't make anything much" and will need commodities.

Commodities are surplus government foods given out to people on welfare and farming people in need of them. The commodities are usually meal, rice, flour and dry milk. Last year it was announced in Ruleville's paper that butter, peanut butter, and canned meat would be given out; but several people have told us that they never get any.

Before this year, all one had to do in order to receive commodities was to go to City Hall, and sign up. This year, however, there is a registration form to be filled out before anyone becomes eligible. This form has to be signed by the applicant and countersigned by his boss, or a responsible person (which usually means a white person). Due to the voter registration drive that has been and is being carried on in Ruleville, the "responsible people" are not particularly inclined to favors for the Negro.

Mrs. Mary Burris of Ruleville went to City Hall to sign up to receive commodities. As she approached City Hall, she met several Negro citizens coming out. They told her that all persons with their own homes now had to go to the Welfare Department in Indianola (county seat) to sign up for commodities. When she got there, the lady in charge asked her why she hadn't signed up in Ruleville. Mrs. Burris explained that she was told to come to Indianola. She was then told to take a seat. After about two hours, another lady came out and told Mrs. Burris that her papers (registration for commodities) were not filled out properly. Mrs. Burris was told that she would have to go to every person she had picked for, and bring back something showing how much she had earned from each of them. She was given until 9 a.m. the next morning to do this. Mrs. Burris has been receiving commodities for the past three years, and

she says that this is the first time this has happened. She said that this is also the first time that she has had to fill out the papers to get food.

Mrs. Gertrude Rogers of Ruleville went to City Hall to sign up to receive commodities. She was given a card. She heard the Mayor of Ruleville, C.M. Dorrough, say "most of them with cards ain't going to get any food." Mrs. Rogers reports that the Mayor also said that those who went down to register were not going to get anything, "that he was going to mess up all of them."

At this point, I would like to bring to your attention something Mayor Dorrough said a month of two ago in the reference to Negro participation in the voter registration drive in Ruleville, "We gonna see how tight we can make it—gonna make it just as tight as we can—gonna be rougher, rougher than you think it is."

When Mrs. Leona McClendon, a day laborer, went to sign up to receive commodities, she was told that she could not get the food because she had a job, and had earned $15.00 per week. Mrs. McClendon says, "I did not earn $15.00 the whole year."

Mrs. Bessie Lee Greene was told the same thing as Mrs. Mary Burris. In addition, Mrs. Greene was told she would have to bring in what her son-in-law had earned. Both Mrs. Greene and Mrs. Burris have stated that they do not believe that the various bosses they worked for kept records of that sort.

Mrs. Lucy Sadies, a day worker, went to the Ruleville City Hall to apply for receipt of commodities. She was told that she received a check and was not eligible to get the food. When Mrs. Sadies told him that she did not receive a check, she was told to go and talk with the Social Security agent, and that he would apply for her.

Grocers in Ruleville have always objected to commodities being issued there.

Commodities are the only way many Negroes make it from cotton season to cotton season. If this is taken from them, they have nothing at all; and the success of our voter registration program depends on the protection we can offer the individual while he is waiting for his one small vote to become a part of a strong Negro vote. It doesn't take much to tide over the rural Mississippi Negro, but the commodities are *vital*.

The mechanical cotton picker is still imperfect; but it is being used more and more. Essentially what makes the mechanical picker disliked by the plantation owner is that it chops the cotton as it picks, giving a shorter fiber, and thereby lowering the value of the cotton.

Still, Negroes tell us that the machines were used with increasing frequency this year, "Cotton picking machines used all the way this year." Where cotton grew in greatest quantity this year, the machines were used. More cotton was picked by machine than by hand.

Mrs. Anderson runs a small grocery store, and is full of ideas and gossip. She had something to say on where Ruleville stands economically. "People haven't made anything this year.... Folks don't have any money now."

Mrs. Anderson said that the children hadn't been buying their nickel cookies like they used to. "And when the kids aren't buying their cookies, you know things are bad."

Editor's Note:

After its founding in 1881, the American Federation of Labor (AFL) subscribed to a policy of nondiscrimination against Negro workers. This official posture, however, was of no significance, since the AFL has never taken any measures to counteract racial discrimination by its member organizations. Samuel Gompers, organizer and president of the AFL, began with expressions of liberalism but very quickly acquiesced to the forces of Jim Crowism and ended by blaming Negroes for the conditions which he and the society helped to create. This article by Bernard Mandel traces that development and shows to some extent why "liberals" are many times suspect in the black community.

SAMUEL GOMPERS AND THE NEGRO WORKERS, 1886-1914

BERNARD MANDEL

There is no doubt that Gompers, at least in the early years of the Federation, desired the organization of the Negro workers and, if possible, their organization in the same unions with white workers. If that was not possible, he proposed that they should be organized anyhow and harmonious arrangements made between the Negro and white workers as a step toward eventual integration. He explained to his Southern organizer that the unionization of colored workers was not a matter of recognizing social equality, but a question of absolute necessity.

If the colored man is not permitted to organize, if he is not given the opportunity to protect and defend his interests, if a chance is not given him by which he could uplift his condition, the inevitable result must follow, that he will sink down lower and lower in his economic scale and in his conception of his

rights as a worker and finally find himself ... absolutely dependent (worse than chattel slavery) in the hands of unfair and unscrupulous employers.

If our fellow white wage workers will not allow the colored workers to co-operate with him, he will necessarily cling to the other hand (that of the employer) who also smites him, but at least recognizes his right to work. If we do not make friends of the colored men they will of necessity be justified in proving themselves our enemies, and they will be utilized upon every occasion to frustrate our every effort for economic, social and political improvement.
....I wish the slogan would come forth among the toilers of the South, working men organize regardless of color ....

• • •

Of course, there was a great deal of prejudice among many white workers, particularly in the South, against Negroes belonging to their unions. Recognizing this, Gompers was willing to leave the question of integrated unions to local option, but at the same time accepted the obligation of trying to persuade them to take the far-sighted course and eliminate the color line. When he heard that a local teamsters' union was discriminating against Negroes, he informed it that "the American Federation of Labor positively places its stamp of disapproval upon such attempt," and advised it to accept Negroes and accord them every benefit that membership entitled them to. In St. Louis, the hod carriers' union refused to accept Negro workers, and Gompers told them that if they did not admit Negroes, he would issue a charter to them as a separate local, with the requirement that they adopt the same working rules and rate of wages. In another case, the white members of a federal labor union desired to form a separate organization because Negroes were in the majority of the union and held all the offices. Gompers was willing to grant them a charter, but only on condition that the union consent to being divided and that an agreement be reached with regard to cooperation in trade matters. Otherwise, he said, the dissension resulting from dualism and antagonism would be worse than the dissatisfaction existing within the union. In addition, he insisted, no union could be designated as a "white" or "colored" union; if workers desired to form such unions in various localities, the Federation would grant them charters, but it would not give official recognition to the color line in any organization. Gompers hoped and expected that these arrangements would be only temporary, and that they would lead to more satisfactory relations. He wrote to a local union that the organization of both white and Negro workers was the best way to overcome and eliminate prejudice.

Inasmuch, however, as that prejudice still exists, and that many white workmen will not belong to the same local organization with black men, and will not meet with them as members of the same local union, it might be more advantageous to go to work gradually to accomplish the desired end. In other words, have the Union of white men organize, and have the Union of colored men organize also, both unions to work in unison and harmony to accomplish the desired end.

It is useless to be simply trying to ram our heads through stone walls; recognizing conditions which exist is the best way we can secure the organization of all in a way which must ultimately bring about a unity of feeling and action among all toilers. . . .

But Gompers weakened the implementation of his desire to organize the Negro workers by leaving it mainly in the hands of white organizers. The members of the federal labor union in Hot Springs, Arkansas, stated that the organization of Negro workers in that state was being neglected, and urged him to appoint a Negro organizer. Gompers did not reply to their request. As far as can be determined, only two of the Federation's organizers in the 1890s were Negroes, and Gompers found fault with the work of both. One was George L. Norton, organizer of the marine workers in the Mississippi valley. Gompers received complaints from local organizers that Norton was engaged in the organization of white as well as Negro workers. Besides, Norton refused to sanction the formation of separate white locals when mixed unions had already been organized. He insisted that all must join the established and recognized union. Gompers asked Norton to refrain from such activities, which would only intensify prejudices. In view of existing conditions, he said, it would be better to allow separate unions for Negro workers than to leave them unorganized. He authorized Norton to proceed in any union "which is sufficiently advanced in their conception of the identity of the interests of labor regardless of color," but where they were not, he advised him to "be very discreet and allow our agitation and time to work the desired change. . . ." At the same time, he wrote to one of those who had objected to Norton's activities and explained why it was necessary to organize the Negro workers. He urged him to re-examine his attitude, "not with the old prejudices that you may have heard from infancy, but study it in the light of the historical struggles of the people of all nations, and you will find that I am right. . . ."

The other Negro organizer was Joseph Amstead, appointed in 1892 in Austin, Texas. The white organizer for Texas complained to Gompers that Amstead was "encroaching on his authority" and that he was agitating for racial equality. Gompers agreed that Amstead was unwise to discuss such questions, which "lead to no good results." It simply arouses race prejudice, he said, and "practically subordinates the labor movement to the color question." He wrote to Amstead on the necessity of "acting practically in dealing with the organization of the colored wage-workers. Their full recognition," he said, "in social as well as economic equality is a matter of cultivation and development and I doubt that it can be forced to an earlier solution than the natural trend will warrant. All attempts to prematurely bring this about will only result in defeat and disaster to all concerned." Shortly afterward, Gompers revoked Amstead's commission.

An even greater impediment to the organization of Negroes was the craft policy of the A.F. of L. The overwhelming majority of Negro workers were unskilled laborers and factory workers, but the Federation's stubborn refusal to organize these classes of workers, and its opposition to industrial unionism, made the organization of the workers in the mass production industries impossible. The Federation's neglect of the Negroes was part of its opportunistic policy of seeking immediate gains for the skilled workers at the expense of the unskilled workers and consumers. Gompers, viewing the whole labor scene, could see that the competition of the Negro and other unskilled workers could be eliminated only by making common cause with them. But the skilled workers of the well organized trades, regarding only their own narrow domain, proposed to eliminate it by excluding the unskilled workers from their unions and thereby from the labor market. Gompers, albeit reluctantly, yielded to the exclusionist policy of the trade union officialdom.

In 1897 Booker T. Washington, the famous Negro spokesman and educator, stated that the trade unions were hindering the material advancement of the Negroes by failing to organize them. The A.F. of L., at its convention that year, denounced this statement as untrue, and reaffirmed its policy of welcoming all labor, without regard to creed, color, sex, race or nationality, and of encouraging the organization of those most needing its protection. Gompers left the chair to support this resolution, asserting that a union affiliated with the A.F. of L. had no right to bar Negroes from membership. "If we do not give the colored man the opportunity to organize, the capitalist will set him up as a barrier to our progress. Every time we help these men it helps to raise the laborer to a higher plane. . . . It is not a question as to the color of a man's skin, but the power that lies in organization." While some of the Southern delegates were on their feet clamoring for the floor to oppose the resolution, Gompers put it to a vote and declared it adopted.

But resolutions were not actions. In fact, they were often a substitute for action. Most of the A.F. of L. affiliates at that time did actually bar Negroes from membership, and some of their delegates, including O'Connell of the Machinists, were most vociferous in advocating the passage of this resolution. And Gompers and the Federation were already in the process of undermining in practice what they declared in principle. Gompers had often stated that the lack of organization among the Negro workers and their employment as strikebreakers were caused by the prejudice of white workers who refused to make common cause with them in the labor movement. But he had already begun to shift the blame to the Negroes themselves. When asked why there were not more skilled Negro workers, he assigned two reasons for it. First, he said, Negro workers did not possess the required skill, but he did not mention the the fact that most of the trade unions prevented them from acquiring that skill by refusing to accept them as apprentices. The second reason was that in many cases, when white workers were on strike, Negroes took their places and thus helped the employers to tear down labor standards and destroy the unions. While he had previously argued that this was the inevitable result of the white workers' ignoring the organization of the Negroes, he now stated, "If workers will not organize to protect their own interests and the interests of their fellow workers, or if workmen are so lost to their own self respect and interests as to turn the weight of their influence on the side of the capitalists as against that of the workers, these men are the enemies of progress, regardless of whether they be white or black, Caucasian or Mongolian." Ten years later he said, "the Caucasians are not going to let their standard of living be destroyed by negroes, Chinamen, Japs, or any others." In the *American Federationist* he published an article which referred to Negroes who had been brought to Chicago in 1904 to replace the striking stockyard workers as "hordes of ignorant blacks," "possessing but few of those attributes we have learned to revere and love," "huge, strapping fellows, ignorant and vicious, whose predominating trait was animalism."

Just one month after the close of the convention in which the Federation declared for the organization and unity of all workers, Gompers published in the *Federationist* an article by Will Winn, the A.F. of L. organizer in Georgia. Gompers thought that this article, called "The Negro: His Relation to Southern Industry," was a fair presentation of the subject. Winn wrote that even if the Federation threw all its forces into a campaign to unionize Southern Negro workers, little success could be expected for many years, because the Negroes did not possess "those peculiarities of temperament such as patriotism, sympathy, etc., which are peculiar to most of the Caucasian race, and which alone make an organization of the character and complicity of the modern trade union possible. . . ." The Negroes, he continued, were characterized by distrust of each other, prejudice against the whites, ignorance and an "abandoned and reckless disposition." The Negro had a great advantage over the white worker in the South because he would work for anything he could get, as many hours as might be demanded, and was "the happiest and most contented individual imaginable." Since, in his opinion, the Negro workers could not be organized and constituted a growing menace to the status of the white workers, Winn proposed as the best solution to the problem the colonization of the Negroes in Liberia or Cuba. The publication of such white supremacist views reveals the hypocrisy of Gompers' declarations about the organizing Negro workingmen.

•   •   •

Betweem 1899 and 1902, the A.F. of L. abandoned even the formality of equal status for Negro workers. It is significant that it was just in these years that race relations in the South suffered their greatest deterioration, Negro rights reached their lowest ebb, and the movement to disfranchise Negro recrudescence of repressive legislation, white supremacism and extra-legal terrorism against the Negroes was the alarm which was produced among conservatives by the rising tide of Negro-white unity in the Populist movement. When the Southern Populists denounced lynching and called for the defense of the Negroes' political rights; when Tom Watson declared that "the accident of color can make no difference in the interest of farmers, croppers, and laborers. . . . You are kept apart that you may be separately fleeced of your earnings"; when Negroes were seen on leading committees with white Populists—the Southern Bourbons decided that the "time for smooth words has gone by, the extremist limit of forbearance has been reached." Northern Republicans agreed, for they represented the business groups with rapidly increasing investments in the Southern economy, who were just as frightened as the Southern conservatives by the threat of the overthrow of their regime by a united people.

Besides, Northern capital was just assuming the "white man's burden" in the Philippines, Hawaii, Puerto Rico and Cuba, and it was widely observed that the justification for imperialism was equally applicable to the repression of the American Negroes. As the *Atlantic Monthly* commented, "If the stronger and cleverer race is free to impose its will upon 'new-caught, sullen people' on the other side of the globe why not in South Carolina and Mississippi? The advocates of the 'shotgun policy' are quite as sincere. . .as the advocates of 'benevolent assimilation.' The two phrases are, in fact, two names for the same thing." Professor John W. Burgess thought that "the Republican party, in its work of imposing the sovereignty of the United States upon eight millions of Asiatics, has changed its views in regard to the political relations of races and has at last virtually accepted the ideas of the South upon that subject." He assured the South that the leaders of the party would never again "give themselves over to the vain imagination of the political equality of man."

The Southern white supremacists and their Northern business allies instituted a campaign to impose a legal status of inferiority and second-class citizenship on the Negroes, to deprive them of their rights by fraud, force and violence, and to bolster these acts by a modern, "scientific" doctrine of the superiority of the white race. Senator Ben Tillman of South Carolina announced the results of this campaign on the floor of the Senate, "We took the government away. We stuffed the ballot boxes. We shot Negroes! We are not ashamed of it." When Gompers and the A.F. of L. abandoned the effort to organize the Negro workers, established jim-crowism in the labor movement, and contributed to the ideology of white supremacy, they were playing into the hands of the employers who sought to keep the workers divided in order to exploit them more effectively and to prevent their united resistance to big business' domination of the "New South." This was a reflection of the Federation's gradual surrender all along the line to the demands and views of big business.

•　　•　　•

Gompers and the Federation settled into a fixed policy of jim-crowism. In 1901, in response to the demand of the Trades Council of Anniston, Alabama, the Federation decided that even where there were not enough Negro locals to form a separate trades council, the central labor union did

not have to admit their delegates. Gompers no longer viewed the formation of separate locals and central labor unions as a necessary alternative to the preferred policy of unity of organization. He accepted it as the final and best settlement of the problem. He abandoned the earlier requirement that the Negro as well as the white workers should desire separate organization before their formation would be permitted. He did not urge the white unions to accept the Negro workers before yielding to the establishment of separate unions. He even specifically refused to make such a request of a central labor union, deciding in advance that, because of existing prejudice in the South, it was best for both the Negro and white workers that they be segregated to avoid "arousing bitterness." And he reversed his decision to appoint a colored organizer for the South when it was protested by the Alabama Federation of Labor. Finally, he refused to grant charters as federal locals to Negro unions when affiliated unions or the railroad brotherhoods would neither accept them themselves nor surrender jurisdiction over them. In other words, he accepted the policy of those organizations in refusing to allow the organization of Negro workers under any condition. He accepted as permanent the division of the American working force into skilled white and unskilled Negro workers.

The only place Gompers drew the line was in refusing to allow the Federations's directly affiliated locals to prohibit their members from working with Negroes on the same jobs. He stated that such a policy was repugnant to the principles of the A.F. of L. and of justice. Besides, even if it were enforced, the result would be the displacement of white workers by Negroes and the reduction of standards to the level that the unorganized Negro workers were forced to accept. "Is it not better," he asked, "to try and organize men who work and thereby protect the interests of all? Of course, if Negroes are objectionable to membership in your union, they at least should have the right to work and the right to organize in a union of Negro workmen. The attempt to draw the line at nationalities would prove not only injurious but dangerous and in any event is absolutely wrongful. . . .` At the same time Gompers was still arguing with President Carter of the Locomotive Firemen the desirability of organizing Negroes. He did not change his private opinion, but he had completely surrendered his official policy to the local and craft prejudices of the organizations affiliated with the A.F. of L. As in other areas, he sacrificed principle to the "practical" end of making the Federation "work" smoothly and without friction— the typical mark of the bureaucratic administrator.

In 1902, William E. B. DuBois was making a

study at Atlanta University of the Negro in the trade unions. He made a careful tabulation of the status of Negroes in the various unions, showing that forty-three national organizations, including the railroad brotherhoods, had no Negro members, and that in sixteen of them this was due to the discriminatory policies of those organizations. Twenty-seven others had very few Negro members, partly due to the failure of the unions to train Negro apprentices. There were altogether only forty thousand Negroes in the A.F. of L., with a total membership of just over a million. DuBois then prepared a fairly accurate summary of the evolution of the Federation's policy with regard to Negro workers. He added that some broadminded leaders like Gompers had striven to maintain high and just ideals, but because of the narrow prejudices and selfish greed with which they had to contend, the policy of the Federation had retrogressed. He sent this to Gompers before publishing it, with a request that he make any comment on it that he desired. Gompers replied, "... I should say that your statement is neither fair nor accurate. ... You are inclined, not only to be pessimistic upon the subject, but you are even unwilling to give credit where credit is due. Let me say further, that I have more important work to attend to than correct 'copy' for your paper."

The Atlanta Conference on Negro Artisans, for which this report was prepared, recommended that Negroes should support the labor movement where it pursued a fair policy, but denounced the unjust proscription of Negroes practiced by some unions. Negro spokesmen continued to criticize the A.F. of L.'s policy. In 1905, the Niagara movement, one of whose purposes was to bring Negroes and labor unions into mutual understanding, held up to execration the practice of unions "in proscribing and boycotting and oppressing thousands of their fellow-toilers, simply because they are black." The National Association for the Advancement of Colored People, formed in 1909, urged that Negroes make common cause with the working class, but it was pointed out that discrimination by trade unions was crushing and keeping down the Negro competitors of white workers. Gompers took no cognizance of these criticisms, except on one occasion. While in St. Louis in 1910 for the convention of the A.F. of L., he addressed the local trades council. One of the local newspapers the next morning stated that he had "read the negro out of the labor movement." This was reported throughout the country, and resulted in a flood of protests from Negro spokesmen, including Washington. Gompers stated that he had been misquoted and that the alleged remark in now way represented his attitude toward the Negroes. What he did say, he explained, was that it was difficult to organize Negro workers because, being only half a century removed from slavery, they did not have the same conception of their rights and duties as did the white workers and were unprepared for fully exercising and enjoying the possibilities existing in trade unionism. In other words, he did not read the Negroes out of the labor movement, but virtually said that they had read themselves out of it.

Gompers continued to ignore protests, and he continued to ignore the Negro workers. Shortly before he died the convention of the National Associaton for the Advancement of Colored People addressed an open letter to the A.F. of L. It stated that the interests of white and Negro labor were identical, and that the latter had been demanding admission into the unions for many years, but they were still outside the ranks of organized labor because the unions discriminated against them and because "black labor has ceased to beg admission to union ranks." It proposed that the N.A.A.C.P., the A.F. of L., and the railroad brotherhoods form an Interracial Labor Commission. The appeal fell on deaf ears. Gompers had little sympathy with the militant policies of the N.A.A.C.P. Although he had once criticized Washington for recommending that Negroes rely on the good will of their employers to improve their status, he was later reconciled to his conservative policy of achieving freedom "by the slow process of education and development" and by "rendering service to society that would assure their value and independence."

Gompers' attitude toward the Negro question was determined entirely by a narrow trade union point of view. That is, he understood that the protection of the interests of the white workers required the organization of the Negro workers, whom he regarded as competitors in the labor market. But he had little sensitivity for the problems of the Negro people, and shared to a considerable extent the prejudices of which he often complained. In fact, considering the fact that he was an immigrant and a Jew himself, and that he professed a liberal and far-sighted attitude towards social and human problems, he had a remarkably large amount of prejudice against "non-Aryans," and his hatred of Orientals was particularly virulent. Once, when a newspaper reporter fabricated an imaginary interview with him and reported that he was drunk, Gompers said of him, "Beings of his ilk are fit to associate with dagos and Chinese but should not be tolerated among civilized men." He took delight in telling stories in his public addresses which perpetuated some of the unfavorable stereotypes of Negroes, whom he often referred to as "darkies." When a Negro purchased a house about a block from his home in Washington, some of the neighbors instituted legal action to prevent the owner from living in his house. Gompers was asked to join in the effort. He declined, he said, because he did not want the A.F. of L. to be implicated in such an action, but added frankly that he would not want to live in a neighborhood with colored people. Another indication of his attitude was revealed when the meat cutters' union of Stockton, California, gave a picnic for the local unionists. A Negro member of the hod carriers' union attended and was ordered off the dance floor. This man, who was his union's delegate to the local trades council, desired that the council demand an apology from the meat cutters, and his motion was passed. The president of the trades council then asked Gompers if he should enforce the motion. Gompers replied:

> In my judgment you were perfectly right in determining that matters of this character should not be brought before your Central Body. . . . we can not attempt to regulate the social intercourse of the races. It might have been a mistake to have invited or permitted other than members of the caucasian race to attend the picnic, but having acted upon opposite lines, then to deny them equal courtesy would scarcely be in keeping with such a course, but as organized labor it would be most unwise to stir up strife and prejudice rather than peace if we make these questions subject to decision by our organization. It was in equally bad taste for the colored delegate to have brought the matter before your Central Body. . . .

Gompers' opportunistic pandering to the prejudices of the Southern whites was well illustrated by the argument he used to support child labor legislation in the Southern states. He stated that if white children were kept working in the factories, they would become degenerate and illiterate, while the Negroes were advancing in their education. The result would be that more and more whites would be disfranchised by the illiteracy laws, more and more Negroes enfranchised, and the basis would be laid for the decline of the white race and the ascendancy of Negroes.

Gompers never registered any protest against any of the conditions or events which concerned the Negro people. He was silent about the disfranchisement of the Southern Negroes, about lynchings, about exclusion of Negroes from jury service, about inferior and segregated accommodations in the public schools and colleges, railroads, and other public places, about chain gangs, involuntary servitude

through debt peonage, or such injustices as Roosevelt's dishonorable discharge of 160 Negro soldiers for their unproved participation in the so-called "Brownsville riots." Even when the A.F. of L. denounced restrictions on the suffrage and directed the Executive Council to aid, and if necessary take the initiative, in thwarting the disfranchisement movement, Gompers did nothing to carry out the instructions. In an address at Jacksonville, Florida, he stated that he had no desire to interfere with the "internal affairs" of the South. "I regard the race problem as one with which you people of the Southland will have to deal; without the interference, too, of meddlers from the outside." But such scruples did not prevent him from publicly defending the policy of San Francisco in segregating Japanese students in the public schools.

Gompers had begun with a relatively advanced attitude toward Negro workers. But this attitude was based on a narrow trade union desire to keep the Negroes from competing with white labor, and neglected the broader vision of labor solidarity which marked the policy of the Knights of Labor. Furthermore, the positive aspects of his policy were mixed with a considerable amount of racial prejudice and a lack of concern for the special problems of the Negroes. So it was easy for him to retreat to a policy of jim-crowism when his principles were attacked by the trade union leaders who desired to solve the problem by excluding the Negroes from industrial life altogether. In his typically pragmatic way, Gompers could justify this surrender of principle as "theoretically bad but practically necessary," and finally arrive at the conclusion that it was not even theoretically wrong. He kept the Negroes out of the labor movement and then declared that they deserved no better because they had not made common cause with the white workingmen. Thus he sacrificed both his principles and the Negro workingmen, as well as the broader interests of the whole labor movement, to the short-sighted and selfish demands of the aristocratic officialdom of the craft unions, whose spokesman he had agreed to be.

Editor's Note:

Herbert Hill, Labor Director of the NAACP and faculty member of the New School for Social Research, depicts the current status of labor and the racial issue. Not much has changed despite the "rhetorical committment" by the AFL-CIO and some of its affiliates to elimination of racial barriers in hiring, promotion, and equal treatment on the job. A. Philip Randolph, the only black member of the AFL-CIO Executive Council, took the unions publicly to task. He presented detailed charges of "segregation, discriminatory seniority provisions, exclusionist practices, and systematic barring of Negroes from leadership positions even in unions with large Negro memberships." Building trade unions without exception practice discrimination based on race. A variety of state and national commissions on human rights, community relations, and civil rights upon investigation have been forced to draw the same conclusions. And yet, the President's Committee on Equal Employment Opportunity has refused to enforce these findings.

THE RACIAL PRACTICES OF ORGANIZED LABOR

HERBERT HILL

From Gompers to benign William Green to the current era of sophisticated public relations under George Meany, the disparity between the public statements of organized labor on civil rights and the discriminatory practices of many unions continues. Today, lily-white exclusion clauses in union constitutions have been removed, but colored workers remain excluded from many craft unions by tacit consent. Pious resolutions on civil rights are routinely adopted at AFL-CIO conventions but discriminatory provisions in union contracts and segregated locals continue. At best, there is a minimal strategic adjustment, a token reform as a result of direct action by the Negro protest movement and litigation by aggrieved Negro workers.*

When the American Federation of Labor and the Congress of Industrial Organizations united in 1955, resolutions were adopted committing the merged Federation to the rapid elimination of racial discrimination and segregation within unions. These statements were hailed by the NAACP and other civil rights organizations. But more than a decade later the failure to eradicate patterns of discrimination has invalidated the earlier optimism.

During the AFL-CIO convention in September 1959, A. Philip Randolph, President of the Brotherhood of Sleeping Car Porters and the only Negro on the AFL-CIO Executive Council, criticized organized labor's lack of progress. He publicly called upon President George Meany and the Federation to take concrete action against segregated locals, discriminatory seniority provisions in union agreements, exclusionist practices, and the systematic barring of Negroes from leadership positions even in unions with large Negro memberships. Randolph also raised the issue of internal union democracy, so closely related to the question of racial discrimination. After a heated exchange Meany lost his temper and, pounding the rostrum, roared at Randolph, "Who the hell appointed you as guardian of all the Negroes in America?" Later Randolph presented to the Federation's Executive Council detailed charges of anti-Negro practices in affiliated unions together with recommendations on ways to eliminate segregation and discrimination within international and local union organizations.

The Federation sharply rejected the charges. On October 12, 1961, the Executive Council publicly censured Randolph because, as George Meany put it, he was responsible for the "gap that has developed between organized labor and the Negro community" and because he had "gotten close to those militant groups." Instead of taking action against racist practices, The AFL-CIO Executive Council publicly blamed the acknowledged spokesman for Negro workers within the labor movement for the dilemma of labor's own making!*

•   •   •

On October 13, the day after the Federation's censure of Randolph and its rejection of his recommendations, the U.S. Commission on Civil Rights' Report on Employment was issued. The report documented the significant extent of discrimination within organized labor, and concluded that "Existing Federal law has little impact on the discriminatory practices of labor organizations," and that the efforts of the AFL-CIO had proved largely ineffective in curbing discrimination. The impact of union discrimination,-it said, especially in skilled occupations, was a basic factor in contributing to the concentration of

---

*There are a few significant exceptions to this pattern, such as the United Automobile Workers of America (UAW) and the United Packinghouse Workers of America (UPWA). The history of organized labor suggests that discriminatory racial practices were less likely to develop where there was a large early concentration of Negro workers in a given union's jurisdiction, in conjunction with an ideological sensitivity to "the Negro question" on the part of the union leadership. This sensitivity in most instances was rooted in the radical political ideologies of union leadership groups in their formative years, as in the Auto and Packinghouse Workers Unions.

*At the Annual Convention of the Negro American Labor Council, Chicago, Ill., November 10–12, 1961, Richard Parrish, national Treasurer of the Council, voiced the sentiments of the delegates on the Federation's rebuke of Randolph as follows: "Where was David Dubinsky, where was Walter Reuther, where was Joe Curran, where was Jim Carey? Where were all those liberals on the Council when the vote was taken? This was a show of power to demonstrate to Negro union members that they represent nothing when it comes to setting policies in the labor movement even though they pay dues."

Negroes in menial jobs in industry and their virtual exclusion from the construction and machinsts' crafts, and accounted for Negro labor's extreme vulnerability to long-term unemployment. The report urged federal legislation to prohibit discrimination by unions and stressed the inability of the AFL-CIO to take action on its own initiative against the broad pattern of union racist practices.

• • •

[An example] of dubious "progress" is to be found in the Brotherhood of Locomotive Firemen, a union with a history of notorious anti-Negro practices going back to the 1890s. This union is directly responsible for forcing thousands of Negro firemen off the nation's railroads. It was the defendant in several important federal court cases brought on behalf of Negro firemen and did not remove the provision in its constitution that banned Negroes from membership until 1964. But as Arthur M. Ross, Commissioner of Labor Statistics, stated:

> ... the Brotherhood of Locomotive Firemen ... removed a Negro exclusion clause from its constitution in 1964, after the railroad "work rules" arbitration had made it virtually certain that few, if any, additional firemen would ever be hired on American railroads.

Among other industries where unions continued overt discriminatory practices a decade after the merger were paper and pulp manufacturing, chemicals and oil refining, the skilled metal trades, printing, tobacco manufacturing, and Great Lakes shipping— where the Seafarers International Union dispatched Negroes for jobs only in the galley and stewards' departments from SIU hiring halls. In San Francisco the Hotel, Restaurant and Bartenders Union, with the full support of the AFL-CIO Central Labor Council, obtained an arbitrator's ruling invalidating an agreement won by civil rights organizations with the San Francisco Hotel Employers Association that opened new job opportunities for Negro workers.

• • •

The Missouri State Advisory Committee to the United States Commission on Civil Rights reported that in Kansas City Negro membership was "restricted in a number of unions such as plumbers, sheet metal workers, steam fitters, operating engineers, and electricians." Similarly, the Louisiana State Advisory Committee reported that in New Orleans, "In some crafts, notably the electrical workers, plumbers, asbestos workers, boilermakers, pile-drivers, elevator constructors, hoisting engineers, glassworkers, iron-

workers, sheet metal workers and sign painters, Negroes are completely excluded." The report also noted that segregated Negro locals are maintained by the carpenters' and painters' unions and that in Detroit less than 2 per cent of all craft union apprentices were Negroes. These practices are typical of the discriminatory pattern in both North and South. In December 1963 the New York City Commission on Human Rights investigated and found "a pattern of exclusion in a substantial portion of the building and construction industry which bars non-whites from participating in this area of the city's economic life."

• • •

Apprenticeship programs provide from one half to two thirds of all the skilled workers needed to replace older craftsmen and to meet the needs of industry. Unions, however, have the power to fix the number of apprenticeships, and they deliberately maintain an effective shortage of the skilled labor supply on the theory that this enhances their power at the bargaining tables. By restricting to sons and relatives the right to become an apprentice, the construction unions automatically exclude Negroes, since few have ever belonged. Union members view these provisions as a source of job security, and proclaim they do not discriminate against Negroes, but only against nonmembers. Yet this particular form of "security" results in the systematic exclusion of Negroes and Puerto Ricans as a group.

• • •

Local 26 of the International Brotherhood of Electrical Workers in Washington, D.C., is a typical example of how labor union power can be used to exclude Negroes from employment in federal construction projects. For many years Negro workers have been attempting without success to secure admission to Local 26, which controls all hiring for electrical installation work in the nation's capital. Thus, Negro mechanics were not permitted to do electrical work on the construction of the AFL-CIO national headquarters building and other private and public building projects in Washington. The 1961 Employment Report of the United States Commission on Civil Rights stated that "Local 26, like the majority of construction locals in the District of Columbia, has no Negro members. ... Local 26 has a virtual monopoly on electrical jobs in commercial construction work in this area." The report also noted that:

None of the construction unions surveyed have

racially restrictive provisions in their constitutions or bylaws. Most, however, require that an applicant for membership be approved by the local before acceptance. It is clear that the absence of Negro members in the "lily-white" construction locals means that few, if any Negroes will be employed in these highly paid craft jobs on union construction projects. Obviously then to the extent that union membership practices are discriminatory, they deny employment opportunities to Negroes on racial grounds.

The Employment Study of the Commission also stated that some locals:

openly practice racial discrimination in their membership policies. Local union officers have been known to explain the absence of Negro members in the following terms: " 'Nigras' are all afraid of electricity"–"Jews and colored folks don't want to do plumbing work because it is too hard."

After years of avoiding conflict with the politically powerful building trades unions, the Pennsylvania State Fair Employment Practice Commission, beginning on July 9, 1963, held public hearings involving six major unions that had long engaged in anti-Negro practices, and finally issued a series of orders against them. On February 24, 1964, the New York State Commission for Human Rights made its first important step in prohibiting employment discrimination by building trades unions. It found Plumbers Local 373 of Spring Valley guilty of maintaining a pattern of anti-Negro practices.

•   •   •

There is also frequent discrimination against Negroes despite union membership, as in the racially segregated locals of the Carpenters in the North as well as in southern cities. For over a half century the United Brotherhood of Carpenters and Joiners has been among the most important of the unions in the building trades, and, with few exceptions, organizes Negroes and whites into separate locals, when it permits Negroes to join at all. In the South there seem to be no exceptions to this rule and it is often followed in northern cities as well. In Memphis, Negro carpenters in a segregated local union found that members of the white local refused to work on the same job with them. The 1961 Employment Report of the U.S. Commission on Civil Rights refers to similar practices in Atlanta and other cities.

Wherever segregated locals exist in the building trades, the white locals are in control of the union hiring halls and frequently, because of arrangements with municipal and county political machines, all hiring for major public as well as private construction projects is done through these union halls.* In some instances white locals have imported white workers from other cities rather than allow local Negro members to share in attractive work opportunities.

Frequently Negroes are excluded altogether from work in white neighborhoods. This means that Negro mechanics are restricted to marginal repair work within the Negro community or as maintenance electricians and seldom permitted to work on the major public and private new construction projects. The disparity between the wages of construction electricians and maintenance electricians in industry varies between three and four dollars an hour. In New York City construction electrical workers earn $7.70 per hour, for bricklayers the base wage is $7.74 per hour. Wages for the crafts in the building trades unions average about three times the general industrial wage.

The protest against racism in the building trades union goes back to the early twenties. And in the summer of 1963 the Negroes of Philadelphia, New York, and other cities, plagued by rising unemployment, took to the streets to protest the widespread refusal to admit them into union membership and jobs on the many large publicly financed construction projects.**

•   •   •

Racial discrimination in the craft unions has become deeply institutionalized. A form of caste psychology impels many workers to regard their own positions as "white men's jobs" to which no Negro should aspire. These workers and, often, their union leaders regard jobs in their industries as a kind of private privilege to be doled out or denied as they see fit. Often Negroes are not alone in being barred from such unions, which attempt to maintain an artificial labor shortage. In many craft jurisdictions AFL-CIO affiliates do not function as labor unions in an

---

*Daniel P. Moynihan has written, "I would note that 20 years ago the Taft-Hartley Act outlawed the closed shop, and that today the closed shop is probably more completely in effect in our building trade unions than ever in history." "The Politics of Stability," *The New Leader,* October 9, 1967, 8.
**Some 465 thousand man years of employment were produced by programs assisted by the U.S. Department of Housing and Urban Development in 1966. This is only a small part of the jobs created by federal, state and the municipal agencies in public construction. For additional information on employment in public construction, see NAACP Labor Manual, Revised 1968 edition, 124–26.

advanced technological society, but operate as protective associations with much the character of medieval guilds. On the local level the inertia that sustains racial discrimination is to be found among craftsmen in the North almost as commonly as in the South.

The status of Negroes as northern journeymen within the building trades unions of Pittsburgh is significant as it is typical of the pattern in northern urban communities. As of September 1, 1965, the NAACP's investigation revealed: Asbestos Workers—no Negroes; Boilermakers—no Negroes; Bridge and Iron Workers—no Negroes; Carpenters—no Negroes; International Brotherhood of Electrical Workers—no Negroes; Plumbers—no Negroes; Roofers—no Negroes; Sheet Metal Workers—no Negroes; Roofers—no Negroes; Steamfitters—no Negroes; Elevator Constructors—no Negroes; Tile Setters—no Negroes; Terrazzo Helpers—no Negroes. In the Bricklayers Local 2 there were two Negroes; in the Cement Masons Local 526, eighteen Negroes; in the Painters Local 6, three; in the Construction and Common Laborers Local 373, thirty-five; and in the Tile Layers and Helpers Local 20, four.

• • •

A typical example of adamant refusal to admit Negroes into membership and into a union-controlled apprenticeship training program, two and a half years after the enactment of the Civil Rights Act of 1964, is to be found in New Rochelle, New York, where construction unions prevented the employment of Negroes on a four-hundred-million-dollar urban renewal project. The New Rochelle Human Rights Commission, an official agency of the municipal government, found "that seven months of private conferences had failed to induce Local 501 of the Electrical Workers Union, Local 86 of the Plumbers Union, and Local 38 of the Sheet Metal Workers Union to hire Negroes." The Commission asked the Mayor and the City Council "to halt all construction at the Mall which is part of a 68-acre program, until the unions relented," and requested "appropriate action under federal Law." Similar anti-Negro practices by major craft unions continued in many cities with large public construction programs, as in San Francisco and Buffalo, where the Equal Employment Opportunity Commission initiated formal complaints against several construction unions in January 1967.

It is evident that labor unions such as those in the building and construction trades, in the printing industry, among the metal crafts, and elsewhere have become narrow protective associations engaged in a variety of restrictive practices. Given union control of hiring and of apprenticeship programs, it is no longer

possible to regard racial bias by labor unions as simply a private matter involving "voluntary associations" or a "quasi-sovereignty," as Robert M. Hutchins describes American unions today. Such discrimination is a barrier to the welfare of the entire Negro community, no less serious than segregation in the public schools, which the U. S. Supreme Court has declared to be unconstitutional. Clearly, the intervention of the society through the use of enforceable legal sanctions has become necessary to remove discriminatory practices by labor unions as well as by employers.*

Across the country many powerful labor unions are an important part of the "liberal labor" coalitions that are in control of municipal governments. The fundamental failure of this coalition, nationally and locally, is expressed most sharply in the deteriorating condition of the Negro in the cities, and the vast expansion of racial ghettos and urban rot. Furthermore, labor unions with vast treasuries that control banks and real estate, purchase high-yield securities on the stock market, and engage in a variety of enterprises are not using union funds for socially desirable purposes.

Organized labor has not used its political influence and financial power to eliminate segregated slums and to alter the dehumanizing status of Negroes locked in the racial ghettos of the urban North. When the building trades unions directly prevent Negroes from working on highly visible public construction projects or when unions such as the International Ladies Garment Workers Union prevent training opportunities for unemployed Negro workers in their jurisdictions, they are directly contributing to the growing racial crisis of the cities.

In a period of racial upheaval and vast dislocation in the urban centers, labor unions whose base is in the cities have become part of that political coalition attempting to maintain the status quo, a status quo that can no longer be tolerated by the urban Negro. Data released by the U. S. Department of Labor on September 5, 1967, indicate that more white workers were employed than at any previous time in the nation's history, but that during the same period more Negroes were unemployed than ever

---

*On February 7, 1966 the U. S. District Court in St. Louis, Missouri, in response to a lawsuit initiated by the U. S. Department of Justice, issued a temporary restraining order against the AFL-CIO Building and Construction Trades Council and affiliated unions in St. Louis. The court ordered the unions to return to work at the Gateway Arch, a federal construction project at which they had refused to work because three Negroes had been hired in response to previous action by the U.S. government. The NAACP also filed unfair labor practice charges with the NLRB against the unions.

before. At the same time that white workers are earning the highest wages in the nation's history, the economic status of Negro wage earners is deteriorating and the differential between the income of white and Negro workers continues to increase.

Editor's Note:

The exploitative nature of a preindustrialized economy that depended on an almost limitless supply of cheap, unskilled labor has unalterably affected social and race relations in this country. The economics of racism ensured a perpetual class of low-status, unskilled, expendable workers to perform the "dirty-work" of society. This article by Poinsett deals with the current economic status of Afro-Americans and presents the views of outstanding economists like Brimmer of the Federal Reserve Board and McLaurin, author of the Ghetto Economic Development and Industrial Plan (GHEDIPLAN).

THE ECONOMICS OF BLACK LIBERATION

ALEX POINSETT

The white man is perfectly willing to see the black in the role of an employee, and of an efficient, capable and trained worker. He is not willing to view him, however, as his own peer in the area of business and industrial management and control. This unwillingness to allow the black to achieve a role of parity in the management of the industry and economy of this nation has set the two races on a complete collision course. I therefore say that this economic racism on the part of the white power structure is the basic factor with which we have to reckon in our attempts and endeavors to achieve black empowerment . . . .Dr. Dunbar S. McLaurin.

The speaker is a black economist "telling it like it is" before a recent conference of the American Management Assn. in New York. It is yet another of those conferences, endlessly spinning its wheels on the general subject of "what can white America *do for* Black America?" Cool yet intense, Dr. McLaurin bores in on his predominantly white audience, "rapping" to them about a special brand of racism he calles "economic racism," a brand more "subtle, undefined, amorphous, complex and deeply imbedded in the syndromes of whites" than just general racism. He is trying to be precise, even though there is no easy formulation for the elusive sort of racism that

finds a sanctuary, for instance, in the lily-white executive suites of America. Much easier to describe is the racism of the loud-mouth George Wallace or an axe-handle wielding Lester Maddox.

But the picture in Dr. McLaurin's head of American "economic racism" most closely resembles African colonialism. He and other students of the problem contend black America is not only a colony, but also its colonial masters have no intentions of liberating it. The analogy, of course, is not point-for-point perfect. American blacks are not geographically separated from the "Mother Country" as are most African colonials. American blacks do not export anything except human labor. And, for the most part, theoretically at least, they have the same legal rights as other citizens.

Nevertheless, the American black community and the African colony are at least fraternal if not identical twins. Both fight in the wars of their colonizers without receiving equal status. Both are ruled by black puppets manipulated by white masters. Both are victimized by a white political power which aids and abets, sugar-coats and explains away the economic exploitation of black people to insure their economic dependence on the "Mother Country."

Economic racism? Its effect abound. Ghetto economics are such that black income is half, and black unemployment nearly three times the national average. Black dollars buy less, are harder to acquire and are eaten up faster and in larger bits by usurious and fraudulent practices than are "white" dollars. Markups of 100 to 300 per cent are quite common in the ghetto. American colonialism, in short, relegates black people to a subordinate, inferior status, entrapping them in a vicious poverty cycle. Denied good jobs, they are stuck with low incomes and unable to obtain a good education with which to get good jobs, proper housing or adequate medical services. The money that does trickle into the black community only tarries momentarily then returns to the already prosperous white community—a natural consequence of the absentee white ownership of most ghetto businesses.

And so a million blacks live in the New York City ghettos of South Bronx, Harlem and Bedford-Stuyvesant, but operate only 12 registered businesses hiring ten or more people. Or take Newark, N. J.,—about 400,000 people, more than half of them black, but they own only 10 per cent of the city's 12,172 licensed businesses. Or take Los Angeles' 600,000 blacks—its most visible minority owns an almost invisible fraction of its 121,039 licensed businesses. Or take the blacks who are 63 per cent of Washington's 800,000 residents but own less than 13

230

per cent (1,500) of its 11,755 businesses. Take any one of America's 163 black colonies. They are economically underdeveloped, systematically structured to prevent the accumulation of wealth and—like the "abandoned mining communities in Appalachia" —unable to compete in the nation's economic mainstream.

Economic racism, as Rap Brown has said, is as American as apple pie. Not one black firm ranks among the 500 largest U. S. corporations and only two are listed on a major stock exchange. Black-owned businesses are less than one per cent (45,000) of the U. S. total (5 million). They are basically a hodgepodge of restaurants, barbershops, hotels, funeral parlors and similar "Mom and Pop" establishments valued from $5,000 to $50,000. Only the 46 black-owned insurance companies border on business bigness, but all of them lumped together control only a piddling 0.2 per cent of the industry's total assets. Together, they are smaller the the 60th largest white insurance firm. Similarly, the biggest black-owned bank—Harlem's Freedom National with deposits of $28 million—does not even rank as one of the nation's 1,000 largest banks. Clearly, then, black America is an economic calamity and its liberation from white oppression, from white dominance and control—by any means necessary—dominates the black agenda. The task of moving that agenda, of achieving black economic development engages some of the best brains in the black community.

For some strategists, "full employment" in the black community meets the challenge. But as Dr. McLaurin notes, "the Negro had full employment on the plantation. It insured only the economic growth of the white owner." In other words, without black ownership and control of production and distribution, forget it! Mere employment always means helping the man to do his thing, never the black thing. "The black man," argues Dr. McLaurin, "remains a [sieve] for the flow of money through him directly back into the white community."

If jobs, alone, will not bring economic viability, then what will? Negro and white liberals still dream of an integration that will gently float the black ghetto into America's mainstream. Indeed, Dr. Andrew F. Brimmer, a Negro economist securely "integrated" on the Federal Reserve Board, insists the only way blacks can make it in this most economically competitive of societies is through "full participation in an integrated national economy" rather than "in a backwater of separation and segregation." But his judgement flies in the face of a decade of intense integrationist crusading which, if it revealed anything, clearly demonstrated that whites—North and South— were willing least of all to integrate their economic power. In an always-segregated America, the question had never been whether blacks wanted a separate economy, but how they could best exploit the conditions of separateness imposed on them, how, in fact, they could liberate (meaning separate) from white control, black institutions and the black economy.

Since integration has always been more rhetorical than real, some black nationalists dream of securing a patch of American real estate—perhaps five states or so—where black people, at last, can develop their own economy. But they are not powerful enough, either numerically or militarily, to seize nationhood and their white oppressors have not so far indicated a willingness to grant it.

Total integration or total separation? Somewhere between these two extremes move other blacks, bent on improving ghetto social and economic welfare while simultaneously increasing interaction with "outside" communities. Such a modest strategy will not bring blacks major control over their economic destinies, admits black economist Dr. Robert Browne, a thoughtful keynoter for the National Black Economic Development Conference in Detroit last April. But it is worth trying, he believes, simply because it will at least "put additional bread on (black) tables and ease some chronic illnesses."

•   •   •

One method involves locating branches of major firms in black communities. Some black militants dismiss these ghetto plants as "instant concrete plantations," reflecting a new style of economic colonialism. Modest in size, built on investments of $1 million to $2 million, these black-run plants are geared to turn out relatively unsophisticated products. Watts Manufacturing Co., for example, set up by Aerojet-General after the 1966 Watts rebellion in Los Angeles, makes Army tents, wooden shipping containers and other products for the federal government.

Under Nixon's program, black capitalists are also created through partnership arrangements between indigenous ghetto industries and major firms or through such compensatory devices as Small Business Administration loans, or managerial and technical training programs of the Urban Coalition. Early in his administration, the President created an Office of Minority Business Enterprise to co-ordinate and accelerate existing federal programs allegedly designed to help minorities start businesses. Among those was Project OWN, an SBA loan guarantee program launched with much fanfare in the final months of the Johnson administration. Essentially, the program was a national effort whereby banks would supply the capital and financial management assistance and SBA would guarantee up to 90 per cent of the loan (maximum: $350,000). Press releases on Project OWN promised that new ghetto enterprises would be established at a rate of 10,000 a year. Like many other aspects of LBJ's "Great Society," however, the promise was never fulfilled.

"A black man finds it almost impossible to obtain a loan for $250,000, even when the United States government is his co-signer," argues Dr. McLaurin. "The reason is that white banking institutions simply do not conceive of the black man having needs or competence for that amount of money, without white supervision. If you will look at all of the plants which have been spun off, from major corporations, and most of the self-help operations, they are chiefly imbedded with the paternalistic concept that whites must actually hold the ultimate purse-strings and direct the destiny of the corporations."

Nevertheless, supporters of black capitalism sing its praises, claiming it is a way of making the ghetto more productive, of bringing greater tax revenue and reducing welfare rolls, of lessening racial tension, unrest and crime in the cities and expanding the overall labor and management pool for American industry. Most important of all, its supporters believe black capitalism will create the economic institutions and thus the political institutions that can enable blacks to compete on equal terms in white America.

Such notions are vigorously rejected by critics like the Rev. Jesse Jackson of Chicago's Operation Breadbasket who already indict capitalism as a major vehicle of oppression which flourished on slavery and segregation and who see its extension into the black community as, at best, a romantic delusion which can only gild the ghetto without really altering the basic disparity between the affluent white majority and the lagging black minority. Even President Nixon's own National Advisory Council on Economic Opportunity warned him recently that "black capitalism cannot produce large numbers of wealthy black Americans in any short period of time." While such a program is valuable in developing racial pride and confidence, the Council reported, it would not involve enough of the poor and would not reach those most seriously in need in city ghettos.

But an even more telling criticism comes from those who insist a black capitalist is the same as a white capitalist, since regardless of its color, capitalism is a system of exploitation of one set of people by another set of people. These critics cite Atlanta as a classic example of "individual black capitalism." It is one of the few places where blacks have been able

to build their own firms and make them pay. But those Negroes who have made it are part of a power structure and thus no more likely to share their wealth with the poor than are whites.

The ultimate weakness of black capitalism, continue the critics, is that it is a piecemeal approach, attacking only a portion of the problem, narrowly limiting its objectives either to placing a few black men in business or to improving or slightly expanding the businesses of those black persons who already have businesses. What is desperately needed instead, argue the critics, is a comprehensive plan of economic development that will increase the "Ghetto National Product" by increasing the number of ghetto-owned industries that *produce*, as opposed to present businesses that merely *distribute* "foreign" goods and services.

"We are talking about creating and acquiring capital instruments which can maximize our economic interests," explains Roy Innis, bearded and brainy head of CORE. "We are not followers of Marxism or of capitalism. Ours is a pragmatic approach. I doubt that black people can find their answer in either communism or capitalism (since they are economic and political philosophies designed for Europeans and their white American descendants). We must devise our own philosophy. What we will come out with is probably a system which capitalists will call socialism and socialists will call capitalism. What black people need is a broader-based ownership. Sometimes this will be community ownership, sometimes corporate and sometimes individual ownership."

Innis, in other words, proposes not jobs, but the building of economic instruments that themselves create jobs, not the mere substituting of black ownership of a pants-pressing business for white ownership, but the acquiring of capital instruments on a major scale, "to maximize the flow of money in the community and begin a geometric progression toward economic well-being."

But how is that done? What is the most effective approach to black economic development? Now being tested in the marketplace of ideas are three answers: 1) the Community Self-Determination Bill, 2) the GHEDIPLAN and 3) a corporate transfer plan.

The 180-page Community Self-Determination Bill, co-authored by CORE and the Harvard Institute of Politics, was submitted to Congress in July 1968 with the backing of 26 senators. It seeks: 1) to spread business ownership and management among ghetto residents by permitting them to create federally chartered community development corporations (CDC) in which they can buy $5 par value stock and through which they can acquire, create and manage businesses in their areas; 2) to bring financial, managerial and technical resources of established businesses into play (rather than starting from scratch with poverty area resources alone) by permitting "outside" companies to develop ghetto enterprises which they later sell to the CDC as soon as the offshoot firms are self-supporting; 3) to create new sources of funding for community services by channeling profits from the community-owned business (rather than the white power structure) into such community service projects of the people's own choice as day care centers, basic education, legal aid, non-profit housing, health care and the like.

In short, the Community Self-Determination Bill aims at putting the economy of the black community into black hands. Similar in intent is the Ghetto Economic Development and Industrial Plan, "GHEDIPLAN" for short, authored by Dr. McLaurin. Viewing the ghetto panoramically rather than piecemeal as do many other economic development approaches, Dr. McLaurin conceives it as an "underdeveloped nation." His plan seeks to establish machinery with which to restructure the ghetto economy just as economists would revamp an underdeveloped nation. He spells out the underlying logic this way:

When the United States helps underdeveloped nations, it concentrates on extending the free enterprise system. The U.S. wants these nations to have a favorable balance of trade and applies hard and soft money theories in lending money at fair interest rates.

The goal is to create businesses and industries that will use local resources most productively. A central banking system, insurance networks and other instruments of capital accumulation are established. Favorable tariff rates are set so they can trade with us, and production machinery as well as consumer items are sold. The goal, then, is to establish a balanced, diversified and self-supporting economy that will generate capital and support a stable, friendly society. Enlightened and selfish dividends are sought, for only a stable economy can support a society that is free of political upheavals and friendly to us.

. . . as long as ghetto economics are unproductive, unstable and unable to support their inhabitants in dignity, they, too, will breed riots and upheavals.

Like the Community Self-Determination Bill, the GHEDIPLAN seeks to end poverty by creating a strong, locally-owned economy and redressing the adverse balance of payments between the ghetto and the outer white world. Its prime target is not the small service business, since from 80 to 90 per cent of small businesses—black or white—fail within five years (annual failure total: 300,000). Instead the GHEDIPLAN recognizes that in this era of large-scale production and distribution, emphasis should be on establishing large-scale business and industry in the black community. Dr. McLaurin's point is that 10 viable new enterprises, providing substantial employment and capitalized at $1 million each, would do more for ghetto economies than 1,000 additional tiny businesses capitalized at $10,000 each. These economies will be strong enough, he believes, to participate in, compete with, and become a integral part of the national economy, contributing their own part to the gross national product, instead of being mere "colonial" appendages.

Although Dr. McLaurin designed his GHEDIPLAN for a large urban city like New York, he believes it is applicable to almost any large economic entity. The plan provides "foreign aid" for the underdeveloped "ghetto nations" by generating up to $200 million for ghetto economic development, that is, $100 million in new "Guaranteed Financing," and $100 million in new "Guaranteed Markets," at an estimated cost to the city of only one per cent for administrative seed money. A portion of the city's purchasing power will constitute a "Guaranteed Market" for new businesses and industries in the ghetto. This, presumably, will trigger similar "set aside" programs in the private sector and by Federal and State governments.

The GHEDIPLAN has been rejected by New York City and CORE's Community Self-Determination Bill, now floundering in the Senate Finance Committee, may suffer a similar fate. But even if both plans were accepted, infant black-owned businesses probably would not grow fast enough to satisfy the need for significant black economic independence and self-determination in one generation. And so an extremely imaginative alternative comes from a former Stanford Research Institute staffer with the improbable name (for a black man) of Richard F. America, Jr. He proposes a systematic program of transferring portions of larger corporations to black ownership and operation. He would set up an agency for corporate transfer (ACT) in the Commerce Department. ACT would acquire a company wishing to sell to black owners by purchasing 51 per cent of the stock. Then interested groups of black businessmen would be offered a chance to buy control for perhaps 10 per cent of ACT's purchase price. After about eight corporations have been transferred to black control each year for 15 years, the procedure would be discontinued, since by then blacks will have achieved economic parity roughly equivalent to their proportion of the population.

America estimates that at an average purchase price of $100 million each, the total annual cost of his proposed transfer program, including administration and profit supports, should not run above $2 billion. In some years, however, it would exceed $2.5 billion if a giant or two should be transferred.

For all of its boldness, America's corporate transfer plan has not been anywhere near as widely publicized as James Foreman's dramatic demand of $500 million (later upped to $3 billion) in "reparations" from white churches and synagogues or Roy Innis' demand that American bankers come up with $6 billion for a Black Urban Coalition that would 1) strengthen the existing 20 black banks (current assets: $207 million, compared with the $500 billion of the nation's 14,000-plus white banks) 2) create new banking financial institutions to compensate for the inadequacies (to the black community) of existing black and white banks, and 3) create a risk capital pool that would make available funds for economic development programs created by black people who now cannot obtain initial capital or qualify for loans under existing banking criteria.

Innis carefully stresses that his $6 billion demand represents a "recoupment," not a "reparation," in Foreman's sense. For a reparation, he explains, is "a political demand made by a government" or political group to a government. "Reparation will be asked when our people see themselves more and more as totally independent people." And so Innis demands recoupment of earnings black people would have received during the past 400 years were it not for white racism, recoupment of the money white racists made off these potential earnings, recoupment of this long past due debt compounded with interest.

Innis made his demands in June at the Bankers Conference on Urban problems held in Chicago. After a few days hesitation, partially to recover from the shock of the proposal, the conferees overwhelmingly endorsed his concept of compensatory recoupment. But they were only a handful of emissaries, 260 to be exact, from the nation's banking community. The endorsement of that powerful community is still pending.

Similarly, the confidence of white America in the possibilities of black economic development must still be demonstrated. "There is the implication that black America cannot solve its problems and does not have the ability to do so," declares Dr. Dunbar McLaurin. "That these problems must be solved by benevolent white sociologists, economists, and businessmen coming into the ghetto helping and developing it for its underdeveloped children who will never be able to cope with their own problems. Never once is the problem faced that it is white racism which is preventing the black man from solving his own problems. It is because white America simply does not believe that a black man can solve even his own problems."

The economic racism Dr. McLaurin attacks is part of the larger problem of "private affluence and public squalor." Many observors—not necessarily communists and socialists—agree that a redistribution of national wealth is desperately needed. But how? Through modifications of American capitalism? Psychological warfare? Armed revolution? None of these? All of these? The debate mounts in America's black colonies. On its resolution rides the "Mother Country's" future.

PART III. D:

DIMENSIONS OF BLACK COMMUNITY LIFE – POLITICS

IF WE MUST DIE

CLAUDE McKAY

If we must die, let it not be like hogs
Hunted and penned in an inglorious spot,
While round us bark the mad and hungry dogs,
Making their mock at our accursed lot.
If we must die, O let us nobly die,
So that our precious blood may not be shed
In vain; then even the monsters we defy
Shall be constrained to honor us though dead!
O kinsmen! we must meet the common foe!
Though far outnumbered let us show us brave,
And for their thousand blows deal one deathblow!
What though before us lies the open grave?
Like men we'll face the murderous, cowardly pack,
Pressed to the wall, dying, but fighting back!

South Carolina Senator Benjamin R. ("Pitchfork Ben") Tillman's remarks from the floor of the Senate typifies the mood of the country during and after Reconstruction and claimed support from the North as well:

We took the government away. We stuffed ballot boxes. We shot them. We are not ashamed of it. The Senator from Wisconsin would have done the same thing. I see it in his eyes right now. He would have done it. With that system—force, tissue ballots etc.—we got tired ourselves. So we called a constitutional convention, and we eliminated as I said, all of the colored people whom we could under the fourteenth and fifteenth amendments.

Senator Tillman did not exaggerate: every means available *was* used to ensure white supremacy and the concerted efforts to disfranchise black Americans *were* successful. It was not until grass-roots people (like Mrs. Fannie Lou Hamer and others less well known), SNCC, and SCLC, plus the 1965 Voting Rights Act, brought about an upsurge in voting power that increasing numbers of black officials were elected. Alabama now has more black elected officials (105) than any state except Michigan or New York. As recently as April 1972 the Black Panther Party conducted a massive voter registration drive in Oakland, California. The potential for power is in the hands of the urban masses. This potential has to be welded into a force. This fact has always been recognized by those in power and explains why they have so effectively dissipated any moves in this direction. Increasingly, however, members of excluded groups—blacks and other minorities—are coming to the same realization.

THE TRIUMPH OF WHITE SUPREMACY

JOHN H. FRANKLIN

When it became evident that white factions would compete with one another for the Negro vote, and thus frequently give the Negro the balance of power, it was time for the complete disfranchisement of the Negro, the Fifteenth Amendment to the contrary notwithstanding. On this, most Southern whites were agreed. They differed only over the method of disfranchising Negroes. The view prevailed that none but people of property and intelligence were entitled to suffrage. As one writer put it, white Southerners believed that "no person should enjoy the suffrage unless he gives sufficient evidence of his permanent interest in and attachment to the community." And yet there were many who opposed such stringent disfranchisement because it would disqualify numerous whites. The poor whites were especially apprehensive. Some of them had been disfranchised by earlier measures; and when competition grew keen between rival white groups, the Conservatives actually barred radical whites from the polls and permitted their own Negro supporters to vote. More poor whites were bound to be disfranchised by any new measures. The sponsors of a stricter suffrage had to be certain that they did not contravene the Fifteenth Amendment. Despite the fact that the Supreme Court had refused to apply it is the Reese and Cruikshank cases, there was no guarantee that the Court would view so favorably any state action obviously designed to disfranchise a group because of its race.

These were the problems that had to be solved by state constitutional conventions when they undertook to write into their fundamental law a guarantee of White Supremacy. It was in Mississippi, where a majority of the population were Negroes, that the problem was first faced and solved. As early as 1886 sentiment was strong for constitutional revision; a convention met in 1890, for the primary purpose of disfranchising the Negro. A suffrage amendment was written which imposed a poll tax of two dollars, excluded voters convicted of bribery, burglary, theft, arson, perjury, murder, and bigamy, and also barred all who could not read any section of the state constitution, or understand it when read, or give a reasonable interpretation of it. Isaiah T. Montgomery, the only Negro delegate to the convention, said that the poll tax and education requirements would disfranchise 123,000 Negroes and only 11,000 whites. Before the convention Negro delegates from forty counties had met and protested to President Harrison their impending disfranchisement. Doubtless they would have fought ratification, but the Conservatives would run no risk of having their handiwork rejected; after the convention approved the constitution, it was promulgated and declared to be in effect.

South Carolina followed Mississippi by disfranchising the Negro in 1895. Ben Tillman had worked toward this goal after he was elected governor in 1890, but he was unable to obtain sufficient support for a constitutional convention until 1894. Tillman was then in the United States Senate, but he returned to the convention to serve as chairman of the Committee on Rights of Suffrage and thus to be certain that the Negro was effectively disfranchised. The clause, when adopted, called for two years' residence, a poll tax of one dollar, the ability to read and write the constitution or to own property worth $300, and the disqualification of convicts.

Negro delegates bitterly denounced this sweeping disfranchisement. In answer to Tillman's charge that Negroes had done nothing to demonstrate their capacity in government, Thomas E. Miller replied that they were largely responsible for "the laws relative to finance, the building of penal and charitable institutions, and, greatest of all, the establishment of the public school system." He declared that numerous reform laws "touching every department of state, county, municipal and town governments . . . stand as living witnesses (on the statute books of South Carolina) of the Negro's fitness to vote and legislate upon the rights of mankind." James Wigg of Beaufort County said, "The Negro . . . has a right to demand that in accordance with his wealth, his intelligence and his services to the state he be accorded an equal and exact share in its government. . . . You charge that the Negro is too ignorant to be trusted with the suffrage. I answer that you have not, nor dare you, make a purely educational test of the right to vote. You say that he is a figurehead, an encumbrance to the state, that he pays little or no taxes. I answer you, you have not, nor dare you make a purely property test of the right to vote. . . . We submit our cause to the judgment of an enlightened public opinion and to the arbitrament of a Christian civilization." Only two whites joined the six Negroes in voting against the constitution of 1895.

The story was essentially the same in Louisiana in 1898 when a new device, the "grandfather clause," was written into the constitution. This called for an addition to the permanent registration list of the names of all male persons whose fathers and grandfathers were qualified to vote on January 1, 1867. At that time, of course, no Negroes were qualified to vote in Louisiana. If any Negroes were to vote, they would have to comply with educational and property requirements. Booker Washington attempted to prick the conscience of Louisiana Democrats by writing them that he hoped the law would be so clear that "no one clothed with state authority will be tempted to perjure and degrade himself by putting one interpretation upon it for the white man and another for the black man . . . ." Negroes led by T. B. Stamps and D. W. Boatner appeared before the suffrage committee and admitted that a qualified suffrage might remedy demoralized conditions; but they pleaded for an honest test, honestly administered.

By 1898 the pattern for the constitutional disfranchisement of the Negro had been completely drawn. In subsequent years other states followed the lead of Mississippi, South Carolina, and Louisiana. By 1910 the Negro had been effectively disfranchised by constitutional provisions in North Carolina, Alabama, Virginia, Georgia, and Oklahoma. The tension arising from campaigns for white suffrage sometimes flared up into violent race wars. In Wilmington, North Carolina, three white men were wounded, 11 Negroes killed and 25 wounded, in a riot in 1898. In Atlanta, there were four days of rioting after an election in 1906 in which disfranchisement was the main issue. Robbery, murder, and brutality were not uncommon during this period.

For the cause of White Supremacy the effect was most salutary. In 1896 there were 130,344 Negroes registered in Louisiana, constituting a majority in twenty-six parishes. In 1900, two years after the adoption of the new constitution, only 5,320 Negroes were on the registration books; and in no parish did they make up a majority of voters. Of 181,471 Negro males of voting age in Alabama in 1900, only 3,000 registered after the new constitutional provisions went into effect. On the floor of the Virginia convention Carter Glass had said that the delegates were elected "to discriminate to the very extremity of permissible action under the limitations of the Federal Constitution, with a view to the elimination of every Negro voter who can be gotten rid of, legally, without materially impairing the numerical strength of the white electorate." This was accomplished not only in Virginia, but in every state where such means were resorted to.

The South universally hailed the disfranchisement of the Negro as a constructive act of statesmanship. Negroes were viewed as aliens, whose ignorance, poverty, and racial inferiority were incompatible with logical and orderly processes of government. Southern whites said that the Negro had done nothing to warrant suffrage. But as he made progress in many walks of life, it became increasingly difficult to allege that he was natually shiftless and incapable of advancement. The framers of the new suffrage laws, however, were committed to the complete and permanent disfranchisement of the Negro regardless of his progress. Their view was summed up by J. K. Vardaman of Mississippi: "I am just as opposed to Booker Washington as a voter, with all his Anglo-Saxon reenforcements, as I am to the coconut-headed, chocolate-colored, typical little coon, Andy Dotson, who blacks my shoes every morning. Neither is fit to perform the supreme function of citizenship." Southerners would have to depend on the administration of the suffrage laws to keep Negroes disfranchised, for there were many who would gradually meet the most stringent constitutional qualifications. White Supremacy would require an abiding belief in racial inequality, re-enforced, perhaps, by hatred born of bitter memories.

Once the Negro was disfranchised, everything else necessary for White Supremacy could be done. With the emergence of white Democratic primaries, from which all Negroes were excluded by rules of the party, whites planned their strategy in caucuses, and the party itself became the government in the South. Whites solemnly resolved to keep the races completely separate, for there could be no normal relationships between them. Laws for racial segregation had made a brief appearance during Reconstruction, only to disappear in 1868. When the Conservatives resumed power, they revived the segregation of the races. Beginning in Tennessee in 1870, Southerners enacted laws against intermarriage of the races in every Southern state. Five years later, Tennessee adopted the first "Jim Crow" law and the rest of the South rapidly fell in line. Negroes and whites were separated on trains, in depots, and on wharves. Toward the end of the century the Negro was banned from white hotels, barber shops, restaurants, and theatres, after the Supreme Court in 1883 outlawed the Civil Rights Acts of 1875. By 1885 most Southern states had laws requiring separate schools. With the adoption of new constitutions the states firmly established the color line by the most stringent segregation of the races and in 1896 the Supreme Court upheld segregation in its "separate but equal" doctrine set forth in *Plessy v. Ferguson.*

It was a dear price that the whites of the South paid for this color line. Since all other issues were subordinated to the issue of the Negro, it became impossible to have free and open discussion of problems affecting all the people. There could be no two-party system, for the temptation to call upon the Negro to decide between opposing factions would be too great. Interest in politics waned to a point where only professionals, who skillfully deflected the interest from issues to races, were concerned with public life. The expense of maintaining a double system of schools and of other public institutions was high, but not too high for advocates of White Supremacy who kept the races apart in order to maintain things as they were.

Peace had not yet come to the South. The new century opened tragically with 214 lynchings in the first two years. Clashes between the races occurred almost daily, and the atmosphere of tension in which people of both races lived was conducive to little more than a struggle for mere survival, with a feeble groping in the direction of progress. The law, the courts, the schools, and almost every institution in the South favored the white man. This was White Supremacy.

Editor's Note:

The North and West have had the advantage of appearing liberal and enlightened when contrasted with the adamant South. Closer investigation, however, reveals that the differences were more a matter of degree than of substance. The courts, political institutions, employers, and citizenry were for the most part committed to maintaining the privileges of white supremacy and assuring the inferior status of the newly liberated black citizens. A detailed account of these forces in the North is presented by Litwack in *North of Slavery.* This excerpt exemplifies attitudes and practices in the North.

THE POLITICS OF REPRESSION

LEON LITWACK

Legal and extralegal discrimination restricted northern Negroes in virtually every phase of existence. Where laws were lacking or ineffectual, public opinion provided its own remedies. Indeed, few held out any hope for the successful or peaceful integration of the Negro into a white-dominated society. "The policy, and power of the national and state governments, are against them," a Philadelphia Quaker wrote in 1831. "The popular feeling is against them—the interests of our citizens are against them. The small degree of compassion once cherished toward them in the commonwealths which got rid of slavery, or which never were disfigured by it, appears to be exhausted. Their prospects either as free, or bond men, are dreary, and comfortless."

Most northerners, to the extent that they thought about it at all, rebelled at the idea of racial amalgamation or integration. Instead, they favored voluntary colonization, forced expulsion, or legal and social proscription. The young and perceptive French nobleman Alexis de Tocqueville, after an extensive tour of the United States in 1831, concluded that Negroes and whites formed separate communities, that they could never live in the same country on an equal footing, and that the oppressed race—the Negro—consequently faced ultimate extinction or expulsion. Having associated the plight of American Negroes with the institution of slavery, Tocqueville expressed his astonishment at conditions in the North. "The prejudice of race," he wrote, "appears to be stronger in the states that have abolished slavery than in those where it still exists; and nowhere is it so intolerant as in those states where servitude has never been known." Where statutes made no racial distinctions, Tocqueville found that custom and popular prejudices exerted a decisive influence. Although Negroes and whites could legally intermarry in most northern states, public opinion would not permit it. Where Negroes possessed the right to vote, they often faced vigorous resistance at the polls. They might seek redress in the courts, but only whites served as judges; although they were legally entitled to sit on juries, the public would not allow it. Segregation confronted them in public places, including churches and cemeteries. "Thus the Negro is free," Tocqueville concluded, "but he can share neither the rights, nor the pleasures, nor the labor, nor the afflictions, nor the tomb of him whose equal he has been declared to be; and he cannot meet him upon fair terms in life or in death."

In the absence of any pertinent federal statutes, the future of the Negro was left to the states and to the dominant race. As a result, in some states Negroes obtained rights and privileges which in other states they found to be illegal or impossible to exercise. The Negroes' numerical strength, the geographic position of the state, political and economic factors, and public opinion combined to fix their status. This was not a static position, however, but one subject to constant change and fluctuation, ranging from the acquisition of full citizenship in Massachusetts to political disfranchisement in Pennsylvania and from quasi-freedom in New York to attempted expulsion in Ohio.

Nearly every northern state considered, and many adopted, measures to prohibit or restrict the further immigration of Negroes. Those people favoring such legislation included self-styled friends of the Negro, as well as avowed racial bigots. In either case, the professed aim of immigration restriction was to settle the problem of racial relations by expelling the Negro or at least by preventing any sizable increase of his numerical strength.

Basing their arguments largely on the alleged mental and physical superiority of the dominant race, restrictionists warned of the dangers inherent in any attempt to integrate the Negro into the political and social community, for "the natural tendency has been proven by experience, not to be elevation of the degraded, but the deterioration, the lowering, of the better class, towards the standard of the inferior class." Moreover, did not the Bible itself demonstrate conclusively that God had marked and condemned the Negro to servility and social leprosy? "The same power that has given him a black skin, with less weight or volume of brain," an Indiana senator argued, "has given us a white skin, with greater volume of brain and intellect; and that we can never live together upon an equality is as certain as that no two antagonistic principles can exist together at the same time."

Under these circumstances, restrictionists argued that exclusion would be both natural and politic. Indeed, several proclaimed their support for such a move as a natural consequence of their long friendship with the Negro. Separation of the two races would be mutually beneficial. The real enemies of the Negro were those who desired his continued presence in a country which would never afford him adequate opportunities for advancement. Robert Dale

Owen, Indiana politician and reformer, advanced this argument to defend restrictive legislation. A proposed bar on Negroes in his state would, he hoped, advance the cause of humanity, not repression. What would be the alternative to exclusion? Would not Negroes "remain, as now, a race legally and socially excommunicated, as the Helots of Sparta—as the Pariahs of India—disfranchised outcasts; a separate and degraded caste, to whom no honorable career is open; hopeless menials; the hewers of wood and drawers of water of those among whom they are tolerated, not received?" Could there be any decent person, Owen asked, who desired "the continuance among us of a race to whom we are not willing to accord the most common protection against outrage and death?"

• • •

In several of the newly admitted states, whites threatened drastic action if legislative protection were not forthcoming. The people of southern Illinois, a native warned, "would take the matter into their own hands, and commence a war of extermination." An Indianan told a state constitutional convention that "it would be better to kill them off at once, if there is no other way to get rid of them." After all, he added, "we know how the Puritans did with the Indians, who were infinitely more magnanimous and less impudent than the colored race." In southern Ohio, an aroused populace forcibly thwarted an attempt to settle the 518 emancipated slaves of Virginia's John Randolph. Defending that action, an Ohio congressman warned that "if the test must come and they must resort to force to effect their object, the banks of the Ohio . . . would be lined with men with muskets on their shoulders to keep off the emancipated slaves."

The nature of restrictionist legislation varied from state to state. Several states required from incoming Negroes certificates proving their freedom and attesting to their citizenship in another state. Connecticut forbade, without the approval of civil authorities, the establishment of any educational institution for the instruction of non-resident Negroes. Most of the new states, particularly those carved out of the Northwest Territory, either explicitly barred Negroes or permitted them to enter only after they had produced certified proof of their freedom and had posted a bond, ranging from $500 to $1,000, guaranteeing their good behavior. If enforced, this requirement alone would have amounted to practical exclusion. Violators were subject to expulsion and fine, the non-payment of which could result in their being whipped, hired out, or, under the Illinois statute of 1853, advertised and sold at public auction. Residents, white or Negro, who employed such persons or encouraged them to remain in the state were subject to heavy fines.

Three states—Illinois, Indiana, and Oregon— incorporated anti-immigration provisions into their constitutions.

• • •

Racial discrimination extended from the polls to the courtroom. No state questioned a Negro's right to legal protection and a redress of injuries, but some added significant qualifications. Five states — Illinois, Ohio, Indiana, Iowa, and California — prohibited Negro testimony in cases where a white man was a party, and Oregon forbade Negroes to hold real estate, make contracts, or maintain lawsuits. Under these circumstances, an Oregonian protested, the colored man "is cast upon the world with no defense; his life, liberty, his property, his all, are dependent on the caprice, the passion, and the inveterate prejudices of not only the community at large but of every felon who may happen to cover an inhuman heart with a white face." But this, nevertheless, was the Negro's judicial plight in a large part of the North and West.

Although rigidly enforced, restrictions on Negro testimony were subject to varying court interpretations. When a lower Indiana court, for example, rejected such testimony in a case involving a Negro charged with the attempted murder of a white man, the state supreme court ordered the witness be admitted, since the state was not "contemplated as a person of any particular color." The California Supreme Court, on the other hand, ruled that in a criminal action against a white man, a Negro, even if he were the injured party, could not testify.

Where courts refused to admit Negro testimony, legal protection obviously had its limits. A white man could assault, rob, or even murder a Negro in the midst of a number of Negro witnesses and escape prosecution unless another white man had been present and had agreed to testify. Such laws scarcely secured a Negro's life and property; indeed, a prominent Cincinnati lawyer told Alexis de Tocqueville that it often resulted in "the most revolting injustices." After dismissing a case because Negro testimony had been admitted, an Ohio judge angrily protested from the bench that in all of his judicial experience he could not recall a single instance where the law had served the purposes of justice. "The white man may now plunder the Negro," he declared, "he may abuse his person; he may take his life. He may do this in open daylight . . . and he must go acquitted, unless . . . there . . . be some white man present." In 1849, after many years of agitation,

Ohio finally abrogated the ban on Negro testimony, but in the southern portion of the state, where the Negro population was heaviest, observers admitted that the repealed law would still be practically enforced.

In most of the North, custom and prejudice, in the absence of any appropriate statute, combined to exclude Negroes from jury service. Only in Massachusetts, where the Negro advanced more rapidly toward equal rights than in any other state, were Negroes admitted as jurors prior to the Civil War. As late as 1855, a Boston Negro leader had protested the absence of colored jurors and had called upon his people to agitate relentlessly for equal judicial rights. Five years later, two Negroes were named as jurymen in Worcester, and they were called "the first of such instances" in the state's history.

The absence of Negro jurors, judges, and witnesses, when added to the general economic degradation of the colored people, largely explains the disproportionate number of Negroes in northern jails, prisons, and penitentiaries. Contemporary statistical studies demonstrated convincingly that Negroes made up a startling percentage of convicted offenders. One such study, published in 1826, revealed that Massachusetts Negroes comprised one seventy-fourth of the population but contributed one-sixth of the state's prisoners; New York Negroes constituted one thirty-fifth of the population but contributed one-fourth of the state's convicts; and Pennsylvania Negroes made up one thirty-fourth of the population but supplied one-third of the prisoners. "Already are our prisons and poor houses crowded with the blacks," a Pennsylvania state senate committee reported in 1836. "The disparity of crime between the whites and the blacks, which is at present so distressing to every friend of humanity and virtue, and so burdensome to the community, will become absolutely intolerable in a few years: and the danger to be apprehended is, that if not removed, they will be exterminated." While northern legislatures and governors expressed alarm over the situation, southern observers smugly concluded that this was simply an inevitable product of emancipation.

Statistics, however, ignored the two-sided nature of northern justice. In some states or cities, authorities arrested Negroes for various minor offenses, such as vagrancy, while ignoring similar infractions committed by whites; Negroes often found it difficult to obtain competent legal counsel and witnesses on their behalf; judges sometimes sentenced Negroes for longer terms than whites although both were convicted of the same crime; and Negroes found it much more difficult to secure pardons than whites or to pay fines imposed on them.

Had racial prejudice not permeated both bench and jury, it would have been remarkable. "It is hardly possible," a New Yorker told the 1846 constitutional convention, "that persons in their condition (Negroes) should have an impartial trial. Hated, trodden down, and despised, they had not the means to procure counsel to defend themselves against false and malicious charges, and false witnesses; and too often, an accusation against them was equivalent to conviction." After inspecting several northern prisons, speaking with their colored inmates, and surveying the general condition of the Negro in the North, English traveler Edward Abdy concluded that when a crime was committed, public opinion almost invariably turned upon the Negro. Moreover, he added, "want of work, ignorance, and the difficulty of finding unprejudiced witnesses and juries . . . have led too many of this unfortunate race to the prisons and penitentiaries of the country."

Improvement did not come easily. When Worcester admitted Negroes to the jury box, for example, some northerners viewed it as a frightening spectacle and a dangerous precedent. "Republicanism . . . in Massachusetts," an irate Indiana congressman warned, "would allow a white man to be accused of crime by a negro; to be arrested on the affidavit of a negro, by a negro officer; to be prosecuted by a negro lawyer; testified against by a negro witness; tried before a negro judge; convicted before a negro jury; and executed by a negro executioner; and either one of these negroes might become the husband of his widow or his daughter!" Although this statement exaggerated the consequences, it correctly reflected the improved legal position of Massachusetts Negroes. However, this was not the general northern pattern. By 1860, most Negroes still found severe limitations placed upon the protection of their life, liberty, and property.

While statutes and customs circumscribed the Negro's political and judicial rights, extralegal codes—enforced by public opinion—relegated him to a position of social inferiority and divided northern society into "Brahmins and Pariahs." In virtually every phase of existence, Negroes found themselves systematically separated from whites. They were either excluded from railway cars, omnibuses, stage-coaches, and steamboats or assigned to special "Jim Crow" sections; they sat, when permitted, in secluded and remote corners of theaters and lecture halls; they could not enter most hotels, restaurants, and resorts, except as servants; they prayed in "Negro pews" in the white churches, and if partaking of the sacrament of the Lord's Supper, they waited until the whites had been served the bread and wine. Moreover, they were often educated in segregated schools, punished in segregated prisons, nursed in segregated hospitals, and buried in segregated cemeteries. Thus, one observer concluded, racial prejudice "haunts its victim wherever he goes,—in the hospitals where humanity suffers,—in the churches where it kneels to God,—in the prisons where it expiates its offences,—in the graveyards where it sleeps the last sleep."

To most northerners, segregation constituted not a departure from democratic principles, as certain foreign critics alleged, but simply the working out of natural laws, the inevitable consequence of the racial inferiority of the Negro. God and Nature had condemned the blacks to perpetual subordination. Within the context of ante bellum northern thought and "science," this was not an absurd or hypocritical position. Integration, it was believed, would result in a disastrous mixing of the races. "We were taught by our mothers," a New York congressman explained, "to avoid all communications with them" so that "the theorists and utopians never would be able to bring about an amalgamation."

The education of northern youths—at home and in school—helped to perpetuate popular racial prejudices and stereotypes and to confirm the Negro in his caste position. In 1837, for example, a Boston Negro minister discussed the origins of racial attitudes in the younger generation. As children, whites were warned to behave or "the old nigger will carry you off," and they were reprimanded as being "worse than a little *nigger*." Later, parents encouraged their children to improve themselves, lest they "be poor or ignorant as a *nigger*" or "have no more credit than a *nigger*." Finally, teachers frequently punished their students by sending them to the "nigger-seat" or by threatening to put them in a Negro class. Such training, the Negro minister concluded, had been "most disastrous upon the mind of the community; having been instructed from youth to look upon a black man in no other light than a slave." Under such circumstances, white adults could hardly be expected to afford Negroes equal political and social rights.

Northerners drew the Negro stereotype in the image of his political, economic, and social degradation and constantly reminded him of his inferiority. Newpapers and public places prominently displayed cartoons and posters depicting his alleged physical deformities and poking fun at his manners and customs. The minstrel shows, a popular form of entertainment in the ante bellum North, helped to fix a public impression of the clownish, childish, carefree, and irresponsible Negro and prompted one Negro newspaper to label these black-face imitators as "the filthy scum of white society, who have stolen from us a complexion denied to them by nature, in which to make money, and pander to the corrupt taste of their fellow-citizens." Nevertheless, the minstrel shows, newspapers, and magazines combined to produce a Negro stereotype that hardly induced northerners to accord this clownish race equal political and social rights. As late as 1860, a group of New York Negroes, in an appeal for equal suffrage, complained bitterly that every facet of northern opinion had been turned against them. "What American artist has not caricatured us?" they asked. "What wit has not laughed at us in our wretchedness? has not ridiculed and condemned us? Few, few, very few."

In addition to persistent public reminders of their physical and mental inferiority, Negroes frequently complained that they had to endure "abusive epithets" and harassment when walking through white areas or shopping in white stores. In passing a group of white men, "ten chances to one" there would be a "sneer or snigger, with characteristic accompanying remarks." Children often tormented them in the streets and hurled insulting language and objects at them.

• • •

Anti-Negro sentiment did not confine itself to popular ridicule and petty harassment. It frequently took the forms of mob action and violence, especially in the large centers of Negro population. In 1829, Cincinnati mobs helped to convince more than half of the Negro inhabitants of that city that flight was preferable to violence and enforcement of the "Black Codes." Twelve years later, a mob descended on the Negro section and prompted its inhabitants to seek protection from city officials. Agreeing to disarm, Negro men found themselves placed in the city jail in order to avoid further violence. The mob then turned on their women and children. "Think, for one moment," the Cincinnati *Gazette* reported, "of a band calling themselves men, disarming, carrying away and securing in prison, the male negroes, promising security and protection to their women and children—and while they were confidently reposing in that security, returning with hellish shouts, to attack these helpless and unprotected persons!"

Sporadic outbreaks, preludes to the disastrous Draft Riots of 1863, occurred in New York City, but violence flared even more frequently in Philadelphia. Between 1832 and 1849, Philadelphia mobs set off five major anti-Negro riots. In July, 1834, a white mob stormed through the Negro section, clubbed and stoned its victims, destroyed homes, churches, and meeting halls, forced hundreds to flee the city, and left many others homeless. In assessing the causes of the riot, a citizens' committee cited the frequent

hiring of Negroes during periods of depression and white unemployment and the tendency of Negroes to protect, and even forcibly rescue, their brethren when the latter were arrested as fugitive slaves. To prevent further violence, the committee called upon influential Negroes to impress upon their people "the necessity, as well as the propriety, of behaving themselves inoffensively and with civility at all times and upon all occasions; taking care, as they pass along the streets, or assemble together, not to be obtrusive."

• • •

In explaining the need for a segregated society, whites usually referred to the economic degradation of the northern Negro and his inability to rise above the menial employments. However, those Negroes who managed to accumulate property and advance their economic position generally achieved a greater respectability only among their own people and found no escape from the scorn and ridicule of white society. "The worst are treated with contempt," an English observer noted, "while the better portion are spoken of with a degree of bitterness, that indicates a disposition to be more angry with their virtues than their vices." Indeed, economic improvement might incur even greater hostility and suspicion. Northern whites had come to accept irresponsibility, ignorance, and submissiveness as peculiar Negro characteristics, as natural products of the Negroes' racial inferiority. Consequently, those who rose above depravity failed to fit the stereotype and somehow seemed abnormal, even menacing. The "drunken, idle, ignorant, and vicious" Negro, Frederick Douglass explained, was the proper butt of the white man's humor; he was termed "a good-natured fellow" and was always the first to be asked to hold the horse or shine the boots of the white man. As long as he catered to white wishes and pride, as long as "he consents to play the buffoon for their support," he would be tolerated. But if he rejected this servile position, educated himself, and improved his economic position, he aroused white prejudice and jealousy for attempting to leave his "place" in society.

Editor's Note:

The United States Commission on Civil Rights, 1965, conducted an investigation into the practices of racial discrimination in voting in Mississippi. "Voting in Mississippi: A

Case Study" is excerpted from this report and traces the historical development of voting by black people in Mississippi. The Fifteenth Amendment, ratified in 1870, declared that the right to vote shall not be denied on account of race, color, or previous condition of servitude. Nonetheless, Mississippi and other southern states used all of the means at their disposal, including murder, to obviate this law. The Mississippi Convention of 1890 met to write a constitution with the express purpose, candidly stated by the delegates, to secure white supremacy. In 1867, there were 60,167 registered black voters compared with 46,636 white registered voters; in 1892, the figure had dropped to 8615 registered black voters although the black population had almost doubled during this period. Economic intimidation, fraud, violence, and legislative devices such as poll taxes, literacy tests, and disfranchising crimes were utilized to prevent black people from voting. The Civil Rights Commission presents evidence of personal threats, intimidation, violent reprisals, and seventy-five years of laws enacted and enforced on local citizens who attempt to vote. Mrs. Fannie Lou Hamer, one of the motivating forces in the formation of the Mississippi Freedom Party has successfully challenged this system and should be counted as one of the heroines in the struggle for justice.

VOTING IN MISSISSIPPI: A CASE STUDY

U. S. CIVIL RIGHTS COMMISSION

Reconstruction

Negroes first began to register and vote in Mississippi under the military government established at the conclusion of the (Civil) War. Following the passage of the Reconstruction Act of 1867, an election was held to select delegates to a constitutional convention. Negroes were permitted to register and vote freely in this election and they participated in large numbers. The Black and Tan Convention (as it was known), which assembled in 1868, numbered 16 Negroes among its 100 members. It drew up a constitution eliminating most qualifications for voting and extending the franchise to Negroes on the same basis as whites. This constitution was ratified in 1869. For the first time Negroes were permitted by State law to vote, and, in fact, comprised a majority of the electorate.

The peak of Negro political participation was reached between 1870 and 1873. In 1870 there were five Negro State senators, and the representatives from Adams, Washington, Warren, and the other river counties were all Negroes. The legislature met in January and promptly ratified both the 14th and 15th amendments to the United States Constitution, thus clearing the way for readmission to the Union. It also chose United States Senators, one of whom,

Hiram R. Revels, became the first Negro to sit in the Senate. In February 1870 Mississippi was readmitted by Act of Congress upon the condition that the constitution of the State "shall never be so amended or changed as to deprive any citizen or class of citizens of the United States of the right to vote who are entitled to vote by the constitution herein recognized . . . ."

In 1871 the first elections of local officials were held under the new constitution. Some Negroes were chosen as county officers in these elections, and their number was increased after the local elections of 1873.

1875–1890

During this period, white opposition to Negro political activity began to organize. Its principal weapons were economic intimidation and violence. In the election of 1875 local Democratic political clubs announced that no Negro who voted for a Republican could hope for any form of employment the following year. Checkers were stationed at the polls, and groups of armed men intercepted Negroes on their way to register. Negro political leaders were threatened that continued activity would result in death. As a result of these tactics, Negro voting diminished throughout the State and the Democrats returned to power.

The election of 1875 resulted in the defeat of the Radical government in Mississippi. In the words of a Congressional investigating committee in 1876, the new political leaders "secured power by fraud and force, and, if left to themselves, they will by fraud and force retain it."

The period between 1876 and 1890 was marked by enactment of the first of modern laws to discourage Negro voting. The Election Law of 1876 placed registration of voters in the hands of local registration officers appointed by the Governor. A prospective voter was required to give detailed information about his residence, including the election district, township, and ward of the town in which he lived and worked. Any error or confusion in his response was used as a basis for rejection. Despite this, Negroes continued to comprise a majority of the electorate. But after 1876 they were allowed to vote and hold office only under the direction and control of the white minority.

During these years white dominance was maintained by fraud and violence. Corruption became so pervasive that demands were raised to substitute a legalized disfranchisement of the Negro. In the words of one prominent white Mississippian:

Sir, it is no secret that there has not been a full

vote and a fair count in Mississippi since 1875—that we have been preserving the ascendancy of the white people by revolutionary methods. In plain words, we have been stuffing ballot boxes, committing perjury and here and there in the State carrying the elections by fraud and violence until the whole machinery for elections was about to rot down.

The convention of 1890

Early in 1890 the Mississippi legislature called for a convention to prepare a new constitution. The State of Mississippi, whose population at that time was almost 58 percent Negro, elected 134 delegates: 133 white men and 1 Negro. When the convention met in August 1890, its purpose, candidly stated by the delegates, was to secure white supremacy . . . .

The first device chosen was a $2 poll tax . . . .

Although poll tax receipts were designated for educational purposes, it is clear that the primary purpose of the tax was to restrict the franchise. According to one writer, it was adopted because

the leaders of the black counties were eventually able to persuade the convention that educational and property qualifications, with the addition of a poll tax, would be the best means of eliminating the negro vote.

As a delegate observed: "The very idea of a poll qualification is tantamount to the State of Mississippi, saying to the Negro: 'We will give you two dollars not to vote.'"

• • •

In 1934 the poll tax requirement was extended to primary elections. It is currently required both for State primary and general elections in Mississippi.

As the second major instrument of disfranchisement, the convention adopted a "literacy" test for registration. The test adopted required an applicant for registration either to read a section of the constitution *or* to understand the same when read to him *or* to give a reasonable interpretation thereof. The reading clause would, one delegate noted, take advantage of the fact that "in Mississippi at least 10 percent of the white, and 60 percent of the colored population can neither read nor write." The understanding and interpretation clauses were, according to proponents, "designed to furnish a loophole to qualify illiterate whites. . . ."

No standards were provided to control the registrar's choice of constitutional section. In fact, at least one delegate commented that the registrar could determine who would qualify by choosing hard or easy sections of the constitution.

The constitution of 1890 adopted by the convention was never submitted to or ratified by the people of Mississippi. The Judiciary Committee of the convention determined that such ratification was not required for lawful adoption.

The new constitutional provisions had quick and lasting effect. While in 1867 almost 70 percent of the Negro voting age population was registered, by 1892, two years after the adoption of the new constitution, less than 6 percent of the Negro voting age population was registered. In 1946 United States Senator Theodore Bilbo summed up the role of section 244:

The poll tax won't keep 'em from voting. What keeps 'em from voting is section 244 of the Constitution of 1890 that Senator George wrote. It says that a man to register must be able to read and explain the Constitution or explain the Constitution when read to him. . . . And then Senator George wrote a Constitution that damn few white men and no niggers at all can explain. . . .

Section 244 remained unchanged until the early 1950s. . . .

The legislature met next in 1954, during a period of heightened racial feeling following the Supreme Court's school desegregation decision. It again adopted a resolution to amend section 244 similar to the one rejected in 1952. This time the resolution also required the applicant to demonstrate "a reasonable understanding of the duties and obligations of citizenship under a constitutional form of government." Exempted from its requirements were all persons registered before January 1, 1954, *i.e.*, about one-twentieth of the eligible Negroes and roughly two-thirds of the adult white population. . . .

Other provisions of the constitution of 1890 furthered Negro disfranchisement. Various disabilities to voting were imposed which were thought to reflect the racial characteristics of Negroes. The requirement of long residency, two years in the State and one year in the election district, was aimed at the supposed "disposition of young Negroes . . . to change their homes and precincts every year." The disfranchising crimes were those to which Negroes were thought to be particularly prone: burglary, theft, arson, and obtaining money or goods under false pretenses. The more serious felonies of murder, rape, or assault were not included. . . .

• • •

246

Intimidation, reprisal, and fear

In all but a few Mississippi counties the number of Negroes registered to vote is so low that registration and voting are acts rendering the individual Negro conspicuous. In such counties the Commission found that fear of economic or physical reprisal influenced the individual Negro in determining whether to attempt to register or to vote. According to one Negro leader testifying before the Commission, Negroes "are afraid of physical violence, economic reprisals, losing jobs, or not getting jobs" as a result of such attempts. The Commission's purpose in exploring this subject was to evaluate the extent to which such fears have inhibited Negro registration and voting.

Interference by public officials

Incidents of violence at registration or polling places appear to affect seriously the willingness of Negroes to attempt to register or vote. Reprisal after attempted registration may produce a similar result. The Commission investigated allegations that such incidents had occurred in Humphreys, Tallahatchie, and Jefferson Counties.

In Humphreys County two elderly Negro women testified at the hearing that G.H. Hood, registrar of the county, abused them verbally when they attempted to register. Mrs. Mary Oliver Welsh, a woman in her 70's, described her conversation with the registrar:

> Mrs. Welsh. Well, when I went to register, the registrar asked me what did I come down there for. I told him "to register."
>
> He said, "register? For what?"
>
> I told him, "to vote."
>
> He said, "vote? For what?"
>
> And I told him I didn't know what I was coming to vote for.
>
> He hollered at me and scared me so, I told him I don't know what I came to vote for. I was just going to vote.

Both Mrs. Welsh and Mrs. Daisy Griffin, her companion, rely upon government surplus commodities, such as flour, meal, and rice, for some of their food. Before going to the courthouse they had expressed concern to civil rights workers in Belzoni that an attempt to register would cost them their commodities. They both testified that when they attempted to register Mr. Hood warned them about commodities. In the words of Mrs. Welsh, "Well, he told me I was going to get in trouble, and he wasn't going to give me no commodities. That's what he said." Mrs. Griffin corroborated this testimony.

When asked if she had passed the test, Mrs. Welsh replied, "Well, I didn't go back there. I didn't go back. After I went there and he scared me so bad, I didn't go back to see was I passed or no."

Other Negro witnesses testified that this registrar had referred to commodities, questioned them about their motives in seeking to vote, or harassed them by tapping on the table with a pencil while they completed their forms. In his testimony, Mr. Hood denied he had made the statements attributed to him.

The Commission also investigated the conduct of the sheriff of Humphreys County towards Negroes who attempted to register. Negro witnesses testified that their pictures had been taken as they left the registration office. The sheriff admitted he and his deputies had taken such pictures and submitted six prints of Negroes in response to the Commission's subpoena. He had not taken pictures of white applicants. He justified the photography by claiming that he wanted to show how peaceful Humphreys County had been in spite of the adverse publicity which the county and the State had received. Also, he said: "I wanted them for my own use. I take a lot of pictures." When asked whether he considered the effect which taking these photographs outside the registrar's office might have on Negro applicants. Sheriff Purvis replied, "I didn't consider it; no."

In two cases the sheriff's office arrested Negroes shortly after they had attempted to register. In the first case, Mrs. Mary Thomas of Belzoni, a grocery store owner, applied for registration in September 1964. As she was leaving the registration office, someone snapped her picture. Fifteen minutes after arriving home she was arrested by a deputy sheriff, pursuant to a warrant issued that day. The charge against her was selling beer without a State license. She was taken to jail and bond was set at $1,000. The following week she pleaded guilty and was fined $365.71; in addition, county officials suspended her permit to sell beer for one year.

The cost of the missing license was $15. Mrs. Thomas had been selling beer for eight years without such a license prior to attempting to register. During this time and at the time of her arrest, she possessed a current Federal Tax Stamp, as well as State and municipal beer permits. Sheriff Purvis testified he did not know at the time Mrs. Thomas was arrested that she had applied for registration. Several weeks earlier he had sent out notices to some 40 persons that licenses were required. According to him, all except Mrs. Thomas paid the tax or stopped selling beer. He further testified that once, years ago, he had arrested a white man for selling beer without a license in connection with a prosecution for selling whiskey in violation of the prohibition law.

The second case involved Mrs. Arlene Hunter of Belzoni, who attempted to register on January 4, 1965. Pursuant to law, her name was published in the *Belzoni Banner*, a local newspaper, on the seventh of January. The next day she was arrested at her home by a deputy sheriff on a charge of passing a bad check in the amount of $5.15. It is a practice in some rural communities to secure a sale on credit by requiring the purchaser to sign a check for the amount of the credit even though the merchant knows his customer has no bank account. The storekeeper may then initiate criminal proceedings against the customer for passing a bad check in the event the bill is not paid. It appears that the check signed by Mrs. Hunter was of this character, since it was made out by the store owner and drawn on a bank at which Mrs. Hunter had never had an account.

Mrs. Hunter testified concerning her arrest, as follows:

> Mrs. Hunter. On January the 8th I was at home making bed; the deputy sheriff came to my house and he asked me was I Alene Hunter; I told him yes.
>
> He said, "Well, Alene, I came after you."
>
> I said, "What for?"
>
> He said, "Well, I didn't exactly come after you," he said, "but I have a warrant to pick you up for $5.15." He said, "You owe it." I said, "Yes." I said, "I owe $5.15 to the store." He said, "Do you have it?"
>
> I said I had the $5. But he said, "It's more now; it's $12.15."
>
> I said, "Well, I don't have the $12."
>
> "Well," he said, "you have to go with me."

• • •

> Mr. Taylor. Where did he take you?
>
> Mrs. Hunter. To the jail. And when I got inside the jail he sit at a desk, so he wrote something down on the book and he said, "Alene," he said, "when I turn this key on you it will be $14.50. Do you know it?"
>
> I said, "I'm going by what you say." So he put me in jail.

Mrs. Hunter was released 15 minutes after she had been locked up. The deputy sheriff advised her that her fine had been paid but refused to say by whom. She felt she knew why she had been arrested.

> Mr. Taylor. Why do you think you were arrested, Mrs. Hunter?
>
> Mrs. Hunter. Because I registered.

Intimidation and reprisal by registrars or local officials against Negroes who have attempted to register is not confined to Humphreys County. There is a history of such practices in various parts of the State. In addition to reports of such incidents received by the Commission some of these cases have been the subject of judicial inquiry. In Walthall County in 1961 a voter registration worker accompanying Negro applicants for registration was struck by the registrar with the butt of a gun. Later that day he was arrested and charged with breach of the peace. When the Federal Government intervened, the prosecution was dropped. In Rankin County in 1963 the sheriff, armed with a blackjack, and several deputy sheriffs assaulted and beat several Negroes waiting in the registrar's office. In Holmes County in 1963 two firebombs were thrown into the house of Hartman Turnbow, a local Negro farmer and a leader in the registration effort, a few weeks after he and others had attempted to register. Turnbow and four voter registration workers were arrested the next day on suspicion of arson. The grand jury returned a "no bill" on the arson charge, but indicted Turnbow and his wife for unlawful cohabitation. They pleaded guilty and paid the fine.

Private violence

In Tallahatchie County, the Commission investigated the effect of threats of violence by private citizens on the registration and voting process. Tallahatchie is an agricultural county at the eastern edge of the Delta with a population of 30,000, of which approximately 53 percent is Negro. The county is particularly significant because of the contrasting progress of registration in neighboring Panola County. In both counties the Department of Justice had been successful in simplifying the registration test.

On October 16, 1961, the Department of Justice brought an action against the Panola County registrar and a month later, a similar suit was instituted against the Tallahatchie registrar. At the time, there was one Negro registered in Panola County and none in Tallahatchie.

In May 1964 the District Court directed the Panola County registrar to cease using the constitutional interpretation test. The Court further directed him to register Negroes who demonstrated literacy by completing the preliminary questions concerning name, age, and residence, and by copying a brief section of the Mississippi constitution. Under the decree they were entitled to such help as they might need. A month later a Federal District Judge ordered the Tallahatchie County registrar to register all applicants who were able to complete the preliminary questions. Under this decree, applicants were not required to copy or interpret any constitutional section.

By the end of November 1964, about a thousand Negroes had succeeded in registering in Panola County while only 64 Negroes in Tallahatchie County had attempted to register. The Commission sought to determine the factors producing such a wide difference in Negro registration attempts under similar circumstances.

In August 1964, the first group of Negroes in Tallahatchie attempted to register under the new court-imposed system. They were accompanied by civil rights workers and Justice Department representatives. When they reached the county courthouse, 25 to 30 white spectators were standing outside with several county law officers. The Negroes were directed to stand on the lawn outside the courthouse and permitted to enter four at a time to register. Each applicant was photographed as he approached the registrar's office. While the second group of four was taking the test, those who had finished were directed to stand outside in the yard. A Negro witness, Mr. Jesse Brewer, described the scene:

> When we got back out there, there were about 65 gathered around there. A lot more white people drove up there in pickup trucks with gun racks on them. They had guns on them and one ranch wagon comes with three white men with guns and they told us, "you niggers get away from the courthouse. You don't have any business up here." They circled the courthouse about three or four times and when they registered all the people who were up there, the sheriff told us, we did what we came up there to do and to get out of town. . . .

As the Negroes drove away, they were followed by the ranch wagon and cursed by its occupants. The Justice Department attorneys who had accompanied Mr. Brewer left him at the entrance to the dead-end road leading to his home. Shortly thereafter, two pickup trucks drove up.

> Mr. Brewer. After they passed the house they stopped, parked, got out and turned around and came back and drove around slow, and between that time and night I reckon seven, eight cars came in, pickups, and all of them had these same gun racks in the back of them and the guns, and these two to three guns, in the back window of the truck where you could see.
> . . .All night after twelve o'clock they would come in. Sometime they would have the lights off, two or three at a time. . .so when they got up near the house they would flash

the lights on, go on by and cut them back off. That went on regularly for 3 weeks, I know.

●   ●   ●

Commissioner Hesburgh. Mr. Brewer, were you afraid when all of this was going on?

Mr. Brewer. Yes, sure was.

According to Mr. Brewer this experience was directly responsible for the failure of at least one group of Negroes to attempt to register.

Mr. Taylor. Is what happened to you known to other people in your community?

Mr. Brewer. Well, no sir. Well, they know I went down to register. I didn't tell them the bad part of it. I told them the good part because 35 or 40 had promised they would go the next day.

Mr. Taylor. You don't think the word got around about the cars around your house, the trucks around your house?

Mr. Brewer. That was the reason why they didn't go the next day because they seen all them cars and guns and everybody. They got scared and in fact they didn't go into the fields for about the next week. They stayed hid in the woods, everybody.

In Panola County there were few reported incidents of violence or intimidation accompanying Negro registration. Civil rights workers were able to operate effectively and the success of the registration drive was attributed by witnesses to their activites. A similar drive did not occur in Tallahatchie because the workers were reportedly "afraid to come to Tallahatchie and work" and because local Negroes were afraid to house them. With these incidents of violence and the absence of encouragement from the outside, few Negroes were willing to attempt to register in Tallahatchie County.

Fear of violence may not only deter registration but in rural counties may also prevent voting. Registration takes place at the county courthouse, while ballots were cast at polling places frequently located in isolated rural areas. The Commission heard testimony from several Negroes who were able to register but who were prevented from voting or afraid to vote.

One witness, Mr. James Rayburn, who had registered in 1963, attempted to vote in that year. He believed himself to be the only Negro registered to vote in his election district. As he approached the rural polling place at Dogwood Flats he was met by a white man who stopped him outside the building, "He asked me where I was going. I told him I was going to vote. The white man said, 'Well, you won't vote here,' and he begun to curse." The witness then entered the polling place. Inside another white man informed him that the election officer was absent.

> Mr. Rayburn. He...walked back to the door and said, "you go out there and ... wait out there under that tree." And I stood and looked at him and said, "Under the tree?" He said, "Yes, go out there and wait under the tree." And I walked off and the man that challenged me as I was going in, he challenged me again and this time he had a stick with a piece of iron in it.
>
> He asked me where did I live. I told him. Asked me my name. I told him. He said, "I'll make sure"—he cursed again—"that you won't vote no more. You vote now, you won't vote any more."
>
> I would have voted if they would have allowed me, regardless of what he said. But see, the man in there told me to go out and get under the tree, and I knew out under the tree wasn't no place to vote, and I didn't sit around because he might have been building up to most anything. You could see he had a knife or pistol or something and I had just nothing but my hand, and that's just Negro bone.

When asked what he was told would happen if he voted, Mr. Rayburn replied, "They would kill me." He left the polling place without voting and said he did not dare return to vote in November 1964.

> Vice Chairman Patterson. You said you didn't want to go alone to Dogwood Flats to vote. Would you go alone now?
>
> Mr. Rayburn. I would. I believe I would, but I would seek better protection, or some protection.
>
> Vice Chairman Patterson. Where would you go to get that protection?
>
> Mr. Rayburn. Possibly I [would] have to pull several different strings. I might not go directly to the law, but I might pull the strings with some fellows who would have influence over the law.
>
> Vice Chairman Patterson. A white man?
>
> Mr. Rayburn. Yes.

Another witness, Mrs. Adlena Hamlett, a retired school teacher, was one of the first Negroes to register in Tallahatchie. She had registered to vote in 1962. When her name was published in the newspaper pursuant to State law, she returned home to find a life-sized effigy of a woman hung above her mail box. Asked why she thought this was done, she testified, "to scare me." Although she did go to the county seat to register, she said that fear of violence made her unwilling to go to her polling place to vote in the elections which followed.

In Jefferson County, located in southwest Mississippi, the voting-age Negro population is approximately 3500—more than double that of the white. Yet only a single Negro is registered. The commission heard testimony of an attempt to register by two Negro families which resulted in a visit from the Ku Klux Klan. Mrs. Dorothy Mae Foster stated that she, her husband, brother-in-law, and sister-in-law took the registration test in September 1963. A few weeks later she and her sister-in-law were each visited by a party of five men who warned them to withdraw their names. They handed her a card.

Mrs. Foster replied, "Those names are signed in ink and they are there to stay." One of the men answered that someone would return. None of their group succeeded in passing the test and they were not visited again. Since that time, no Negroes are known to have attempted to register in Jefferson County.

The legacy of violence

Violence in reprisal for registration or voting has an immediate impact upon the willingness of Negroes to attempt to register or vote. A history of violence may have a similar impact even in the absence of recent incidents. In a county with a history of repeated episodes of brutality by law enforcement officers or where night riders have engaged in violence, Negroes may be expected to approach the registration process with great hesitation. Their apprehension is magnified when recent incidents of violence or reprisal in other areas in Mississippi or in neighboring states suggest that past practices in their country may be revived. The feeling of fear has become so ingrained that one witness described it as "an inherent pattern, ... [a] reluctance to come forward on all matters ... something that is handed down ... from one generation ... to another."

A history of violence appeared to be an important contributing factor preventing Negro political participation in Carroll County. This county lies in the hills at the eastern edge of the Delta. While Negroes make up roughly half the voting-age population of 5700, only five were registered to vote at the time of the hearing. Four had been registered in 1959 following the voiding of a murder conviction on the ground that Negroes had been systematically excluded from the jury rolls. Because Mississippi law at that time required jurors be drawn from among registered voters, the sheriff requested the four to register and the registrar assisted them.

One of the Negro farmers who had been registered in this way, Mr. Jake Cain, subsequently asked the former registrar who had helped him to register, whether he would be allowed to vote. He was told that there might be trouble and that he would see the sheriff. This Mr. Cain was unwilling to do:

> But I wanted him since he guided me in the registering. I wanted him to guide me through the voting. I wanted him to go like he did when he registered me, for some protection. But, he wouldn't go, didn't go. He told me to go alone.

He never attempted to vote. Asked why, Mr. Cain replied, "Well, we was raised kind of on the atmosphere that kept us under the fear of even asking, going up to vote."

The atmosphere of danger in Carroll County is rooted in a history of violence by its white community against local Negroes. The incidents, which are part of the county's folklore, began with a mass killing of Negroes attending a trial in the county courthouse in 1886. Mr. Cain, who is 78 years old, described in testimony how his father had been wounded and his uncle killed at the courthouse on that occasion:

> Mr. Cain. Well, my father was in that riot or mob or whatever they would call it because the white people said that it was a riot, but the older folks said it was a mob, I know my father was shot through and through. He was shot back under his left breast there and it came out under his shoulder blade there, the bullet hole; I mean the scar showed on his, just under his left shoulder blade, and his brother were killed on the steps of the courthouse at the same time. My father said he jumped from the upper stair, upper deck, down and ran until he ran to the corporate limits of the town, and thereby he fell, but he did recover, God knows it.

Continuing violence has reinforced the tradition. As William Eskridge, a former school teacher, described it:

> Now, mind, this continues; this didn't stop there. We had less violence, but it continued throughout the years. Whenever a colored person was killed, nothing done about it. Whenever a white man got ready to hit one over the head, he hit him over the head and asked him if he liked it, and he had to tell him that he did.

Both Mr. Eskridge and Mr. Cain agreed, however, that the situation in Carroll County was improving. Recent sheriffs had stopped violence by subordinate law enforcement officials and there was less fear in the Negro community. Encouraged by what seemed to be some change in attitude, Mr. Cain asked his grown daughter, the only one of his seven children remaining in Carroll County, to attempt to register.

> Mr. Cain. I spoke to my daughter there a few months ago, . . . it seems to have softened up some. I asked her if she would go and she said, "I about make up my mind but everytime I go to the courthouse something tells me not to go in." But this time she says when she went in to pay her tax, something told her to go in, so she went in and took the test, but how she came out I couldn't tell you.

Her fear in making an attempt to register was reflected in Miss Cain's testimony.

> Mr. Taylor. Miss Cain, did you attempt to register this time?
>
> Miss Cain. I did.
>
> Mr. Taylor. Have you ever gone to the courthouse before to try to register?

> • • •

> Miss Cain. Yes, I have, but that was my first time to attempt to register.
>
> Mr. Taylor. You had gone to the courthouse before but had not gone in to register?
>
> Miss Cain. I was afraid.
>
> Mr. Taylor. But, this time you decided to?
>
> Miss Cain. I decided.

> • • •

> Commissioner Rankin. Miss Cain, you have talked about registering; haven't you?
>
> Miss Cain. Yes, I have.
>
> Commissioner Rankin. And, it is fear that keeps them from trying to register? Is that correct?
>
> Miss Cain. That's correct.

> • • •

> Commissioner Rankin. Do you agree with your father that it's better to go one by one than for a group to go down?
>
> Miss Cain. Well, I agree maybe more than one by one, but I wouldn't—
>
> Commissioner Rankin. You would like to have had somebody with you; is that right?
>
> Miss Cain. Well, I wasn't alone because I had prayed, and I believed that Somebody was with me. That's why I had the courage that I had when I went there. . . .

> • • •

251

Findings

1. The State of Mississippi, for the purpose of preventing registration by Negroes, has enacted over the past 75 years a series of laws establishing a constitutional interpretation test, and other tests for registration, and has vested broad discretion in county registrars to administer these requirements. The stringency of these tests was increased at a time when most whites were already registered and few Negroes were registered.

2. Registration records indicate that county registrars in a large number of Mississippi counties have discriminated against Negroes in the administration of these tests primarily by (a) giving Negroes more difficult constitutional sections to interpret than whites; (b) disqualifying Negroes for insufficiencies in the completion of the application form or in the interpretation of the selected constitutional section when comparable or greater insufficiencies failed to disqualify white applicants; and (c) affording assistance to white applicants but not to Negroes.

3. The Mississippi poll tax was established and made a qualification for voting for the purpose of preventing the exercise of the franchise by Negroes. In some counties local officials have refused to accept payment of the poll tax from Negroes, or have encouraged white electors to pay such tax and have failed to encourage, or have discouraged, Negroes from doing so. The poll tax was adopted on the belief that Negroes as a class would find it more difficult to pay than whites as a class. In 1890, when the poll tax was adopted, this belief was justified and it remains so today. In light of actual economic conditions, the payment of a poll tax is a significantly heavier burden for most Negroes than it is for most whites.

4. Negro applicants for registration, Negroes seeking to vote, and civil rights workers have been harassed and intimidated by local officials in connection with registration and voting activities. On occasion such persons have suffered violence from private persons.

5. Negro applicants for registration, Negroes seeking to vote, and civil rights workers have, on occasion, suffered acts of economic intimidation and reprisal in connection with registration and voting, both from public officials and from private persons.

6. There is widespread fear in many Negro communities that an attempt to register or vote would result in economic or physical reprisals. Such fears have been increased by the provision of Mississippi law which require newspaper publication of the name and address of any applicant, and by the practice of requiring the applicant to return to the office of the registrar to determine whether he has passed the test. Fear of reprisal is a major factor inhibiting attempts by Negroes to register or vote. In counties where fear is great, Negroes will not attempt to register in significant numbers without assistance or encouragement.

7. Most Negro Mississippians now of voting age have been educated in segregated public schools which were and still are inadequate and greatly inferior to public schools provided for white children. Public education of Negroes has been so poor and so inferior to the education afforded whites that any test of skills taught in the public schools is inherently unfair as a prerequisite to voting.

8. Existing Federal remedies have not proved adequate to eliminate discrimination and to prevent reprisals for voting. Law suits against registrars have proved too slow and too cumbersome a device to remedy discrimination. Recent judicial approaches promise more speedy relief but are still inadequate in that the registration machinery will remain in the hands of State officials who have demonstrated an unwillingness to enforce Federal law. Law suits aimed at acts of reprisal have been filed in only a few cases and do not appear to have provided an effective remedy.

9. As a result of the foregoing, it is estimated that in Mississippi less than 7 percent of the Negro voting-age population but more than 70 percent of the white voting-age population are registered to vote. Mississippi has by far the lowest rate of Negro registration of any State in the South and has shown virtually no increase in such registration as the result of the enactment of Federal legislation designed to eliminate discrimination in voting.

Editor's Note:

The following testimony is that of John McFerren, a black citizen of Fayette County, Tennessee. The Volunteer Civil Rights Commission held hearings in Washington, D.C. in 1960. The statement presented here indicates the high price some citizens must pay if they presume to exercise their rights.

THE FIGHT FOR THE VOTE

(Testimony gathered by the
Southern Christian Leadership Conference)

Q. (Mr. Lawson) What is your name?
A. John McFerren. I was born and raised in Fayette County, in the State of Tennessee.

Q. What is the population there?

A. The population of that county is 20,000 Negroes.

Q. How many white people?

A. I do not know the number of whites.

On August 1, 1959, the members and myself went up to the courthouse to vote. First we went to the fire station. I pulled out my registration card and handed it to the registration lady and she picked up the card and looked at it and said—she called one of the other men over and said—he asked her—he said, "What are you going to do with these people?" He said, "Where do you live, the country or in town?" She said, "You go to the courthouse and vote."

When I got to the courthouse, me and my four other companions, I pulled out my registration card and handed it to the lady. She looked at the card and called over the man. She said to the man, she said, "If we turn all of these people down, we will get in trouble with the federal government."

Then I immediately turned and went out and called our legal counsel and our legal counsel advised us later we would bring a federal suit against the county. During the federal suit, the F.B.I. came out in the field and investigated me. When they investigated me, he brought back the report and gave the report to the sheriff. That put me on the hot dog stand.

Johnson was the F.B.I. man. He gave the report to the sheriff and immediately after then, my life was threatened.

(At this point, the witness was unable to continue.)

Q. We will give him a few minutes to relax and come back, if there is time.

(Witness temporarily excused.) . . .

Q. Will you pick up where you left off?

A. The F.B.I. notified the sheriff and the F.B.I. came out there while I was picking cotton. They told me to go to tell the sheriff everything I know, that that was the thing to do, and so that night, I received a threatening telephone call. From that day to this, my wife and family and myself were threatened. And this F.B.I. man who came out to investigate the rights to vote, he was a native of Fayette County. He knew my father and before him, my grandfather, and we went back and talked with our legal counsel and we wrote to Hoover here in Washington. They sent another investigator out. I was on the hot dog stand. That is where I was.

Now, the teachers in the county are scared to register. They are even scared to talk to me on the street. When they see me coming, they run the other way and many farmers are harmed, today, on account we want to come to be first-class citizens. They are making a move by the hundreds. They took the crop from the farm; would not sell it. They made them move because the even tried to raise it. When we go up to register, the landlord would walk up and down to see if any of his tenants were in line. When they go to register, the sheriff calls the names and calls the landlord, and the landlord would make him move that night.

Q. Have you tried to make a loan? Do you know of any people who tried to make a loan down there and could not make it?

A. No Negroes in the County of Fayette County have a G.I. loan for a farm. They are all local loans down there thrown on the Negro ten or fifteen years ago. You cannot get a local loan to buy a farm. Now there is a few local loans that charge 25 percent interest on the money, but where they put that interest on the money, they take it out before you get the money. If you borrow $200, he will take the interest out before you get the money and I have borrowed money in my lifetime. I know what he gives me.

Q. Those 25 percent interest charges are from private lenders?

A. They are from private lenders, but the banks, they charge us 12 percent interest. I had not borrowed no money from the bank in about two or three years, but I have some notes at home I can show you, that charge 12 percent interest. Here is the way they do that. If you go in there to borrow some money, he will take out the interest before you get your money. What have you got to show?

Q. Does the note read 12 percent?

A. They don't put no interest at all on the note.

Q. Any questions?

Mr. Camponeschi. What do they threaten to do?

A. They call my wife. I reported this to the F.B.I. headquarters. They call my wife over the telephone. They groan over the telephone like somebody died. And I have a two-and-a-half ton truck. I do public hauling on the side and they threaten my driver. They said they would push him off the road. And I, myself, was threatened in that way. "If you keep moving with that voting issue, you will come up with a necktie around your neck."

The teachers in our county are under a tremendous strain because they are between the other side and ourselves. Now, we have registered—I do not have the accurate number—but approximately between 1000 and 1300 registered, by standing at the door, counting. But this count is not accurate because I have no records of the books.

Q. Have you ever voted?

A. I never voted in my life.

253

Q. Have you been trying to vote all these years, ever since you have been 21?

A. I tried to vote this year—last year, pardon me. Last year.

Q. Tell us precisely what happened last year. Very briefly, what happened when you tried to vote?

A. Well, four of us went out there together to vote. When we went in to vote, to the fire station, when I pulled my card out the fire station lady, she called another man over, and said, the man said, "Where do you live. In the country or town?" I told him I lived in the country. He told me, "You have to go to the courthouse to vote." When I got to the courthouse, I pulled the card out and gave it to the registration lady and they called another gentleman over and asked him, "What are we going to do with these folks? There are too many of them coming here and trying to vote. We will get in trouble with the federal government." He said, "This is an all white, Democratic primary election." That is what he said.

Q. Thank you very much.

There is one final thing I think the audience would be interested in.

A. Now, you might know, because of this voting issue, my mother was run down with a two-and-a-half ton truck.

Q. What happened? Has there been any investigation of that?

A. In other words, my mother was up in the yard and this guy, this man, with the two-and-a-half ton truck, was riding eight or nine miles an hour. He hit me and went across to my mother's yard and ran over her. She has not come back, yet. She is going to get all right, yet.

Q. She is in the hospital?

A. She has been in there.

(Witness excused.)

Editor's Note:

Advocates of black nationalism have always been actively present and highly vocal in black communities. There have been differing emphases and receptivity, but in one form or another black nationalists have proselytized their programs and ideas persistently. One of the recurrent themes in the social history of the Afro-American has been the question of independence and sovereignty. Paul Cuffe, Marcus Garvey, W. E. B. DuBois, Malcolm X, Imamu Baraka (Leroi Jones), the Nation of Islam, and the Republic of New Africa

are some of the better-known names of those persons and groups who represent this point of view, covering the social, political, economic, and cultural spectrum. Black nationalism should be viewed as a natural response to the white nationalism that has pervaded the institutions and practices of American society. This brief selection by Robert Allen gives some perspective on the development and current status of black nationalism. The Nation of Islam is presented here also as one of the prototypes of black nationalism found in large urban areas.

BLACK NATIONALISM AND THE NATION OF ISLAM

ROBERT L. ALLEN

Black power as a variant form of black nationalism has roots that reach deep into the history and social fabric of black America. Like an unsatisfied need or a nagging conscience, black nationalism is an insistent motif that wends its way through black history, particularly of the last 150 years. One writer has called nationalism the rejected strain, implying that assimilationism—the desire to be fully incorporated into the surrounding white society—is the dominant, and the only significant, sentiment among black people.

A glance at history suggests that it would be more correct to say that nationalism, and overt separatism, are ever-present undercurrents in the collective black psyche which constantly interact with the assimilationist tendency and, in times of crises, rise to the surface to become major themes.

Both nationalism and assimilation spring from black people's wish to be an integral part of a jargon society. This, after all, is what is meant by saying that man is a social animal. Nationalism, however, is rooted in the Afro-American's experience of being forcibly excluded from and rejected by a society which is usually overtly, and always covertly, racist and exploitative. In periods of social crisis—that is, when repression and terror are rampant or hopes of progress have been dashed—the resulting suspicion that equal participation is impossible becomes a certainty. Nationalist leaders and intellectuals come to the fore and assert that not only is racial integration not possible, it is not even *desirable*. Such an eventuality, they contend, would destroy the group's distinctive culture and its sense of ethnic identity.

Thus in the decade prior to the Civil War, a period of increasing despair for blacks, emigration movements were in vogue. The Fugitive Slave Act was passed by Congress as part of the Compromise of 1850, and thousands of fugitive slaves were forced to flee to Canada if they were to secure their freedom. In 1854 the Kansas-Nebraska Act opened northern territory to slavery and, in the infamous Dred Scott decision of 1857, the U.S. Supreme Court sanctioned the notion that black people were not citizens. These were indeed grim years for the nearly 4½ million blacks then living in this country.

Many free blacks, such as Frederick Douglass, became active in the abolitionist movement, but others sought some other way out of an increasingly oppressive situation. Martin R. Delaney was one of the latter. In 1852 Delaney advocated that black people emigrate to the east coast of Africa to set up a nation of their own. "We are a nation within a nation," he argued, sounding a now familiar note, "as the Poles in Russia, the Hungarians in Austria; the Welsh, Irish, and Scotch in the British dominions." Delaney called for a convention of the best black intellects—"a true representation of the intelligence and wisdom of the colored freedmen"—to lay plans for his colonial expedition. A convention to thrash out the question of emigration was actually held in 1854. Three proposals were presented to this convention. In addition to Delaney's, there were proposals that blacks emigrate to Central America or to Haiti. Envoys were dispatched to these proposed areas of colonization to investigate conditions and sound out local governments.

The emigrationists were not without their critics. Many free blacks opposed the idea of emigration. Douglass, for example, expressed the fear that the emigration effort would encourage the best educated of the race to depart the country, leaving behind those least qualified to press forward with the emancipation struggle. But this was not the only reason that blacks were critical of colonization schemes.

One of the earliest colonization attempts was undertaken in 1815 by Paul Cuffee, a relatively wealthy New England black sailor. Cuffee arranged for a small group of black colonists to travel to Africa. This action is believed to have inspired the formation of the white-controlled American Colonization Society in 1816. By and large, however, blacks were hostile to the Society's colonization plans. Their opposition stemmed not so much from any lack of desire to separate from whites but rather because they strenuously objected to the racist reasoning whites used in justifying emigration. The Society, which counted a number of slaveholders among its founders, had as its express purpose the removal of free blacks to Africa on the grounds that they were a "dangerous and useless part of the community." This slur incensed most free blacks and turned them irreversibly against any thought of colonizing Africa. Only a few wanted so desperately to escape the

torture that was America that they would solicit aid even from racists. Abraham Camp, a free black from Illinois, wrote a letter in 1818 to the Society accepting its offer of aid in traveling to Africa, "or some other place." "We love this country and its liberties, if we could share an equal right in them," Camp wrote, "but our freedom is partial, and we have no hope that it will ever be otherwise here; therefore we had rather be gone. . . ."

The Civil War and its aftermath put an end to talk of emigration. The Emancipation Proclamation formally ended slavery, and black people were officially granted citizenship. Hopes were high among blacks that equality and the good life were just over the horizon. Blacks sought in every conceivable way to participate fully in the nation's life, to become just ordinary Americans. It truly seemed that Douglass's faith, the faith that white America could change and accommodate itself to blacks, was justified.

Black men were elected to serve in every southern legislature. South Carolina could even boast of a black majority in its legislative chambers. Some twenty blacks served in the U.S. House of Representatives, and the state of Mississippi sent two black senators to Washington. These were the years of Reconstruction, and even the Ku Klux Klan and its campaign of terrorism seemed for the moment insufficient to stem the rising tide of black hope.

But what the Klan and southern terrorists alone could not bring about, a tacit alliance of southern reactionaries with northern business interests and an uneasy northern white populace could indeed accomplish. Historian Lerone Bennett, Jr., has noted that

Throughout this period, Northern reporters and Northern opinion-makers were shrewdly and effectively cultivated by Southerners who dangled the bait of profit, telling Northern industrialists that nothing stood between them and maximum exploitation of the rich resources of the South except "Negro governments."

The northern industrialists, being businessmen, fell for the bait of promised profits and began clamoring for a "settlement" of the troubles which had developed in the South as a result of terrorist violence and the Depression of 1873. Meanwhile, nervous whites in the North, more concerned with maintaining domestic tranquillity than insuring justice for all, were nearly panicked into a stampede by the seemingly indecisive Hayes-Tilden presidential election of 1876 which brought with it the threat of a new civil war.

Hayes, a Republican, was bitterly opposed in the South, but it appeared that he had won a majority of the electoral votes. The southerners staged a filibuster, which disrupted the orderly counting of the electoral votes in the House of Representatives. An ominously threatening atmosphere developed as it become clear that inauguration day would come and pass without a President having been chosen. With pressure mounting from both industrialists and the general northern public, a "settlement" was reached in the form of the Hayes-Tilden Compromise of 1877. Hayes promised the white southerners "the right to control their own affairs in their own way." In return for an end to the filibuster, he also said he would withdraw the federal troops remaining in the South.

These federal troops have been practically the only thing standing between black people and their tormentors. True, there were some black militia units organized, but with the return of state power to the hands of white racists, these black men didn't stand much of a chance. The "settlement" was climaxed when the U.S. Supreme Court, in another infamous decision, declared the Civil Rights Act of 1875 unconstitutional. Southern states rewrote their constitutions to disenfranchise black people, and any blacks who still showed an interest in the ballot were terrorized and murdered by the Klan. Segregation replaced slavery as the accepted mode of black subjugation.

This was a bitter experience for blacks, who realized that as far as their supposed white friends were concerned, when self-interest conflicted with anti-slavery idealism, the latter proved dispensable.

Thousands of blacks were lynched in the South between 1880 and 1900. Hundreds of thousands of others soon began the great northward trek in a vain search for some nonexistent promised land. They were met by hatred and violence little different from what they had known in the South. There were anti-black riots in New York in 1900; in Springfield, Ohio, in 1904; in Greensburg, Indiana, in 1906; and another massive riot in Springfield in 1908.

• • •

Writing in *Look* magazine in the same month that he was killed, King once again articulated his basic philosophy and his continuing hope: "We have, through massive nonviolent action, an opportunity to avoid a national disaster and create a new spirit of class and racial harmony. . . . All of us are on trial in this troubled hour, but time still permits us to meet the future with a clear conscience." Time, however, ran out, and the verdict of guilty which history first passed on white America in 1619 was once again confirmed.

With the apparent failure of the integration movement in the middle 1960s, black nationalism

again became a visible force on the American scene. White journalists started quoting the same nationalist spokesmen whom they dismissed as madmen before. Malcolm X was still called a firebrand and an agitator, but the journalists realized now that he spoke for many black people. This was confirmed in 1966 when both SNCC and CORE openly embraced nationalism. The subsequent Black Power Conference in Newark and the revelation that the undeniably white Ford Foundation was financing CORE completely stilled any lingering doubts that black nationalism was nothing more than a fringe phenomenon. One could be for it or against it, but it was no longer possible to ignore nationalist sentiment.

If it is admitted that black nationalism is a serious component of black thinking, both in the past and present, the question naturally arises why this ideology is vigorously advocated only during certain times of social stress. Does black nationalism exist only at certain historical junctures, or is it always there like the subterranean stresses which precede an earthquake?

It is usual to ascribe nationalist feeling to black "frustration" and to imply that this is a pathological response. But to understand outbursts of nationalism fully, it is necessary to delve into the social fabric of Afro-American life. The foregoing historical sketch strongly suggests that nationalism is an ever-present but usually latent (or unarticulated) tendency, particularly among blacks who find themselves on the lower rungs of the socioeconomic ladder. The members of this class traditionally exhibit a sense of group solidarity because of the open hostility of the surrounding white society. This hostility stems from the fact that whites historically have viewed this class of blacks as "irresponsible Negroes," the spiritual descendants of the "field niggers" of slavery. Whites not only held these beliefs but they acted upon them, treating ordinary blacks as a thoroughly worthless and despicable lot.

In addition to its historical origins, this white hostility also grows out of one of the hard facts of American economic life—that there is insufficient productive space in the American economy for twenty million black people. This is one reason why white workers today are among the worst bigots and racists. They know that their jobs, and consequently their economic security, are directly threatened by integration efforts. On the other hand, black workers cannot help but become increasingly conscious of the fact that the American economy is structured to preclude their full participation.

Black unemployment, especially among youth, normally assumes disaster proportions. For example, in the years since 1954, a period of unprecedented prosperity for the United States, the rate of over-all black unemployment, according to U.S. Labor Department statistics, has consistently stayed well above 6 percent, a situation that would be termed a major recession if it occurred among whites. Furthermore, the jobs which blacks do hold usually offer substandard wages and great instability. Even in recent years the overwhelming majority of employed black males have held low-paying jobs in the unskilled and semiskilled categories. At the same time, again relying on government findings, Negro life in general in the hard-core city slums is getting no better, and, in many instances, is growing noticeably worse.

Not only is the economic situation of the masses of blacks grim, but the prospects are that it will not improve, rather it will continue to deteriorate. This is due partly to the unregulated impact of automation. Leonard Broom and Norval Glenn, in a careful study of this problem, wrote the following conclusion in 1965:

> Mechanization and automation in industry and consequent decreased demand for unskilled and semiskilled workers are tending to push Negroes farther down in the economic hierarchy, and prospects do not seem good for an offsetting increase in Negro education and skills during the next few years. At best, a majority of adult Negroes will be rather poorly educated for another four or five decades, and in the absence of an extensive and unprecedented job retraining program, they are going to fall farther behind other Americans in economic standing.

Since these words were written, various retraining schemes have been tried, not the "massive and unprecedented" program called for by these authors, but small-scale projects which have had commensurate results.

More recently a business writer corroborated the findings of Broom and Glenn:

> Negro gains in income, it is true, have been more rapid than whites' gains recently. However, the long-term trend has not been so favorable. In 1952, during the Korean-War boom, median family income for non-whites climbed to 57 percent of the white figure. After a couple of dips and rises, it was only three percentage points higher in 1966. Even this gain largely reflects the movement of Negroes out of the South, were income levels are generally low. Relative gains *within* the South, and within the rest of the U.S., have been negligible.
>
> The median figures, of course, lump together Negroes who are advancing economically with those who are not. The reality seems

to be that *some* Negroes, especially those in the middle and upper income brackets, are gaining rapidly on whites, while others, especially slum dwellers, are losing ground in relative terms.

Black workers and unemployed quite rightly conclude from these facts that there is no productive role for them in the structure of the American economy. In such a situation, as A. James Gregor argued in an insightful 1963 essay, a turn toward nationalism is a perfectly sane and rational response. "Negro nationalism is," Gregor concluded, "the spontaneous and half-articulated answer of the lower-class and petty-bourgeois Negro to *real* problems little appreciated by white liberals and half-understood by the 'new' Negro middle class. Negro radicalism seeks solution to problems which afflict the Negro masses as distinct from problems characteristically those of the semi-professional and white-collar Negro bourgeoisie."

If the general society which envelops a given ethnic group refuses to protect the economic security and human dignity of that group, then the only recourse is for the group in question to fall back upon its own resources. This is a logical conclusion. It is in the *application* of this conclusion that much confusion has arisen. What baffles many people, but is completely intelligible, as will be shown, is the tendency for this nationalism to withdraw into mystical, religious fantasies, escapist dreams of a massive emigration to Africa or utopian hopes that American capitalism will somehow see fit to grant black people a chunk of its territory.

Whites do not notice the substratum of nationalism among ordinary blacks until it is verbalized. This nationalism has always existed in the cultural life of black people, especially in their music, but most whites are unaware of it until it finds a conscious advocate.

•   •   •

The Muslims had been around since the early 1930s, but their membership had never climbed much above 10,000 in prewar years. In fact, by 1945, their ranks had dwindled to about one thousand in four temples. After the war, however, there was a steady growth both in the number of members and in the number of Muslim temples scattered in cities across the country. The NAACP and integrationism were boosted to national prominence in 1954 when the U.S. Supreme Court handed down its famous public school desegregation decision. Some people thought the struggle was close to reaching a successful conclusion. But this decision had little effect on the steady growth of the Muslim organization. In 1955 there were fifteen temples. This number rose to thirty temples in twenty-eight cities by March of 1959. With the insight gained by the passage of time, it is now clear that the Muslim appeal was not diminished by the 1954 decision because their base was fundamentally different from that of the NAACP and CORE. Both CORE and the NAACP were middle-class organizations which directed their attention to attacking the legal forms of segregation which were prevalent in the South. The Muslims were strongest among working-class blacks who resided in the urban areas of the North. Court decisions and southern freedom rides had little or no effect on the concrete economic status of these blacks.

It was in the summer of 1930 that a mysterious "prophet," W.D. Fard, appeared in Detroit peddling raincoats and silks, and dispensing strange teachings about Africa, the white man, the Christian Church, and Islam. Soon he organized the first Temple of Islam, and by 1934, when Fard mysteriously disappeared, the movement had grown to eight thousand members. It was then that Elijah Muhammad came into power. Muhammad was Minister of Islam under Fard. Born Elijah Poole in Georgia, his family migrated to Detroit where he joined the new movement and was given his "original" Islamic name. His "slave name," Poole, was then dropped.

Under Muhammad's guidance Fard was deified and indentified with Allah, and the Muslim movement grew into a dedicated, tightly disciplined bloc with a membership estimated in the early 1960s at between sixty-five thousand and one hundred thousand. Muhammad set himself up in a mansion in Chicago, where Temple No. 2, the Muslim headquarters, is located. The Muslims established a "University of Islam"; their temples are found in practically every major American city; and they are collectively engaged in far-flung business and real estate activities.

The Muslim ideology is compounded of a fantastic mythology coupled with elements of orthodox Islamic doctrine. The Muslims reject Christianity, which they regard as the "white man's religion," and instead have constructed their own version of Islam. Allah is seen as the "Supreme Black Man," and it is asserted that the first men were black men. C. Eric Lincoln, in his classic study of the Muslims, described their beliefs:

The "originality" of the Black Nation and the creation of the white race by Yakub, "a black scientist in rebellion against Allah"—this is the central myth of the Black Muslim Movement. It is the fundamental premise upon which rests the whole theory of black supremacy and white degradation. . . .
These devils [white men] were given six

thousand years to rule. The allotted span of their rule was ended in 1914, and their "years of grace" will last no longer than is necessary for the chosen of Allah to be resurrected from the mental death imposed upon them by the white man. This resurrection is the task of Muhammad himself, Messenger of Allah and Spiritual Leader of the Lost-Found Nation in the West.
With this resurrection the white slavemasters are to be destroyed in a catastrophic "Battle of Armageddon."

The Muslim program calls for racial separation and a complete economic withdrawal from white society; this is to culminate in the establishment of a separate black state. On the back page of each issue of *Muhammad Speaks*, the weekly Muslim newspaper, are detailed the Muslim demands.

We want our people in America whose parents or grandparents were descendants from slaves, to be allowed to establish a separate state or territory of their own—either on this continent or elsewhere. We believe that our former slave masters are obligated to provide such land and that the area must be fertile and minerally rich. We believe that our former slave masters are obligated to maintain and supply our needs in this separate territory for the next 20 to 25 years—until we are able to produce and supply our own needs.
Since we cannot get along with them in peace and equality, after giving them 400 years of our sweat and blood and receiving in return some of the worst treatment human beings have ever experienced, we believe our contributions to this land and the suffering forced upon us by white America, justifies our demand for complete separation in a state or territory of our own.

These obviously are long-term demands. In the interim the Muslims want equality of legal treatment, employment, and educational opportunities, although in the latter they want schools which are segregated by sex.

The Muslim organization grew in response to a perceived threat to the economic security of a certain class of black people. Black workers made significant occupational advances after 1940 in intermediate-level jobs such as operatives and kindred workers. But this category of workers was hard hit by technological unemployment due to automation. In 1960, for example, the unemployment rate in this category was 6.4 percent for males and 9.9 percent for females—a higher rate of unemployment than among any other category of workers except laborers. At the same time that some black workers were moving into this new category, the demand for unskilled and semi-skilled labor, categories in which blacks are traditionally overrepresented, was declining faster than black workers could be retrained for other lines of work. Economic self-sufficiency of the race as a whole, the Muslims proposed, followed a by now well-worn path, is the only solution to this problem. Racial integration is no answer, they contended, because it can't work.

The effectiveness of the Muslims was limited, however, by their religious mysticism, which alienated many blacks and obscured the question of how to change power relations in American and by the fact that their organization served in large part as simply an alternative route to middle-class status for some blacks, rather than actively attacking the problem of general black oppression.

Nonetheless, the nationalist position was measurably strengthened in the middle 1960s when it became obvious to many observers that the integrationist civil rights movement had reached its peak and was in decline, having only minimally affected the lives of ordinary black people. This failure compounded the crisis which was precipitated at the close of the war years.

Editor's Note:

> *What white Americans have never fully understood—but what the Negro can never forget—is that white society is deeply implicated in the ghetto. White institutions created it, white institutions maintain it, and white society condones it.*—Report of the National Advisory Commission on Civil Disorders

The Kerner Commission Report cites "white racism as being essentially responsible for the explosive mixture which has been accumulating in our cities since the end of World War II." Although these statements and findings were difficult for many white Americans to accept, a criticism that has been leveled against the Report, and a well-founded one, is its superficial treatment of racism. Blauner points out its reluctance to confront the colonial relationship between black people and the larger society, "emphasizes attitudes and feelings rather than the system of privilege and control." Knowles and Prewitt make a similar charge, "It is the immediate conditions giving rise to civil disorders which the Report stresses, *not the causes behind the conditions.*" And further, "the categories with which the commission operated screened out the responsibility of white institutions and

pushed the commission back to the familiar account of 'black pathology.' " Jewell Prestage in this analysis of "Black Politics and the Kerner Report" makes some assessment of political socialization from the point of view of black Americans. The alienation from the political system, as a whole, is explored together with "personal disaffection" and sense of futility which is becoming increasingly manifest in urban ghettoes. Or as the Commission puts it, "the nation is rapidly moving toward two increasingly separate Americas." One of the questions raised, with serious implications for white and black is: "Does exclusion from participation coupled with exclusion from benefits of 'the good life' of the system, not only remove the obligation to obey, but also give rise to the obligation to disobey or revolt?

BLACK POLITICS AND
THE KERNER REPORT

JEWEL L. PRESTAGE

Reactions to the report of the *National Advisory Commission on Civil Disorders* have been widespread and varied, both in terms of their sources and their content. This discussion is essentially an effort to relate the *Report* to some of the theories and research findings in three areas of political science; namely, political socialization, democratic theory, and black political strategy. Any value accruing from this effort will probably be the results of the questions raised rather than directions or answers given.

Political socialization

One of the comparatively new and rapidly developing fields of inquiry for political scientists is political socialization. Greenstein defines political socialization as ". . . all political learning formal and informal, deliberate and unplanned, at every stage of the life cycle, including not only explicitly political learning but also nominally nonpolitical learning which affects political behavior. . . ."

Because political socialization has been interpreted as involving "all political learning at every stage of the life cycle," the dimensions of research possibilities are indeterminable. It has been suggested that a full-blown characterization of political socialization would include classifications of: (1) who learns, (2) what is learned, (3) the agents of political socialization, (4) the circumstances of political socialization, and (5) the effects of political learning.

An understanding of the political socialization function is essential to the understanding and analysis of any political system, and the stability and continued existence of a political system depend, in no small measure, on the extent to which the citizenry internalizes political norms and attitudes supportive of the system. Political socialization, then, is induction into the political culture, the means by which an individual "comes to terms" with his political system. The *Report* would seem to suggest that "coming to terms" is an especially traumatic experience for black people in America.

Examined in the context of current findings of political socialization research, the *Report* gives rise to several crucial concerns. The nature of these concerns is implicit in the observations which follow.

First, the political world of American blacks is so radically different from the political world of American whites that it might well constitute a "subculture" within a dominant or major culture. Even though there has been a great volume of writing and research on political socialization, very little has been directed to political socialization of American blacks. The studies suggest that black people tend to relate rather differently to the political system and have a far greater sense of personal alienation and political futility than do similarly located whites. Ghetto residents, like other citizens, tend to formulate their attitudes toward the political system largely on the basis of their contact with the system. For example, ghetto blacks believe that police brutality and harrassment occur in their neighborhoods to a much greater extent than whites believe that violations occur in white areas. In Detroit, for example, 91 per cent of the rioters believed anger at police had something to do with causing the riots. It is not surprising that the policeman, primarily a symbol of law and order in white neighborhoods, is for ghetto people a symbol of injustice, inhumanity and of a society from which they are alien as well as alienated. Studies of white policemen assigned to ghetto areas indicate that black fears and reservations about the police may not be entirely imaginary. Bobby Richardson, writing about police brutality in New Orleans, states ". . . brutality, man, is a state of mind, not just a whipping with a billy, although plenty of the brothers get beat up on. They know that brutality is the way you are treated and the way a policeman will arrest one man and not another. And the way he will talk to you and treat you. Brutality is just an extension of prejudice, and it is easier to brutalize one man than it is another."

Similarly, blacks tend to be less trusting of their political systems (local and national) than do their white counterparts. Surveys done in Newark reveal that both "rioters" and "non-involved" blacks have a high distrust of local government with 44.2 per cent and 33.9 per cent, respectively, reporting they could "almost never" trust the Newark government to do what is right. In Detroit, 75 per cent of the rioters

and 58.7 per cent of the noninvolved felt that "anger with politicians had a "great deal" or "something" to do with causing riots.

Especially crucial for students of political socialization is the proportion of blacks, rioters and noninvolved, who indicated that the country was not worth fighting for in a major world war. In Detroit the percentages were 39.4 for rioters and 15.5 for the noninvolved, while the Newark survey revealed these sentiments on the part of 52.8 per cent of the rioters and 27.8 per cent of the noninvolved. These figures are striking, especially those related to the non-involved blacks, and would seem to indicate substantial disaffection among blacks. Similar results were ascertained in a recent study of black youth in Atlanta where 49 per cent took a negative stance on the proposition, "Black Americans should be proud to be fighting in Viet Nam."

Given the above data, it is interesting to note the Commission's contrasting finding that rioters were not seeking to change the American system, but merely to gain full participation in it. However, the deep disaffection from the system by blacks and the continued reluctance of the system to accept blacks as full participants might lead one to question the Commission's conclusion. Could it be that black rioters were attempting to change the system and to gain full participation simultaneously? Or, more directly, would not full participation by blacks in itself represent a fundamental change in the system? Such reservations regarding the goals of rioters receive some support from the recent report of Mayor Richard Daley's committee to study Chicago's riots of April, 1968. This committee reported a growing feeling among blacks that "the existing system must be toppled by violent means." This feeling was said to have its strongest expression among black teenagers, where there is "an alarming hatred for whites." Such feelings were found to be based on the attitude that "the entire existing political-economic-educational structure is anti-black."

Assuming the blacks of the ghetto have internalized the American dream of freedom, equality and justice, there is small wonder that "coming to terms" with the system has produced deep alienation, frustration and despair. Throughout the history of this country, blacks have, for the most part, been excluded from full benefits of this society. The fact that the rest of the country has experienced progressive affluence (flagrantly paraded before blacks through mass media) while blacks became poorer is a story much too familiar to belabor here. In the face of "the American dream" of equal opportunity and abundance, blacks have been forced to live "the American nightmare" of poverty, discrimination and deprivation. Despite some progress, American blacks continue to live in this "credibility gap" and part of the results are distrust, estrangement and violence.

Data from the Detroit survey indicate that all blacks included in the survey were not equally alienated and distrusting. Least alienated were the "counter-rioters," a major portion of whom (86.9 per cent) regarded the country as worth fighting for. Of this group, 88.9 per cent felt that getting what you want out of life is a matter of "ability" rather than "being in the right place" as compared to 76.9 per cent of the rioters and 76.1 per cent of the noninvolved. The typical counter-rioter was described as an active supporter of existing social institutions and considerably better educated and more affluent than either the rioter or the noninvolved. This would lead one to speculate that black attitudes or perceptions may be changed when "reality" changes.

Finally, the *Report* attributes responsibility for the present civil disorders to "white racism" in America, "the racial attitude and behavior of white Americans toward black Americans." The fact that a political system theoretically committed to democratic values finds itself embroiled in a major crisis resulting from undemocratic practices raises some fundamental questions regarding the real operative values of the system. How do white Americans reconcile theory and reality? What are the special problems which this situation suggests relative to political socialization of white Americans? Is resocialization of American whites a prerequisite for the fundamental policy changes recommended by the Commission? A number of scholars and writers, some black and some white, have long maintained that the race problem in America is essentially a white problem, created and perpetuated by whites. If the problem is to be solved it must be solved by whites. As Myrdal stated many years ago, "all our attempts to reach scientific explanations of why the Negroes are what they are and why they live as they do have regularly led to determinants on the white side of the race line."

Coming to grips with the fundamental cause of the riots, white racism, is more a task for American whites than for blacks. The process will no doubt necessitate an admission on the part of white Americans that the American dream remains a dream, that full democracy in America is yet to be realized. In short, it will entail alteration of the American political culture, a re-examination of basic values and possibly a rewriting of American history to revise the image of blacks in the minds of whites and blacks. More fundamentally, it will possibly require a restructuring of the socialization process for blacks and

whites if our commitments to democratic values are to be translated into actual practices. The question for which the *Report* provides no answer is "how can this be done?" It is in the delineation of the broad outlines of such a process that political science and other social science research can possibly make its most significant contribution.

Democratic theory

"Democracy is . . . characterized by the fact that power over significant authoritative decisions in a society is distributed among the population. The ordinary man is expected to take an active part in governmental affairs, to be aware of how decisions are made and to make his views known."

Any attempt to view the *Report* in the context of democratic theory would seem to raise an array of tantalizing questions, one of which is the relationship between *political obligation* and *consent.*

In a democracy the basis of political obligation is consent. Such consent implies a high level of citizen participation in the political process or at least the unrestricted right of the interested citizen to participate. Consequently, democratic political systems have traditionally institutionalized certain structures and practices that allow for the orderly and periodic involvement of citizens in decision making. A brief examination of the record tends to substantiate the Commission's contention that throughout the course of American history, black men have been essentially "subjects" rather than "participants" in the political process.

Black men arrived in America in 1619 and began what was to become a 244-year legacy of chattel slavery. Slaves were, by definition, nonparticipants in the political process. The lot of free Negroes was not markedly different from that of slaves. The end of the Civil War, the Emancipation Proclamation, and ratification of the Fourteenth and Fifteenth Amendments heralded the period of Reconstruction and relatively widespread participation in politics by black people. A return to white control and patterns of excluding Negroes from southern politics followed the Compromise of 1877 and withdrawal of federal troops from the South. Southern states revised their constitutions to deny the franchise to Negroes and as the Negro entered the twentieth century, his political future looked dismal and bleak. Since 1900, blacks have staged an uphill battle in quest of full participation in the body politic. Most significant among legal victories for blacks have been the outlawing of white primaries in 1944, the passage of Civil Rights acts in 1957, 1960, and 1964, the Anti-Poll Tax Amendment in 1963 and finally the Federal Voting Rights Act of 1965.

Perhaps the most reliable source of information on current black registration and voting in the South is the Voter Education Project of the Southern Regional Council. According to its director, Vernon Jordan, the 1965 Voting Rights Act has had a marked impact on voter registration among southern Negroes. He states that significant gains have come in Alabama, Louisiana, Georgia, South Carolina, Virginia, and Mississippi. In Mississippi, Negro registration jumped from 8 per cent to nearly 60 per cent in just two-and-a-half years.

The most recent figures on voter registration supplied by the Voter Education Project are presented in Table 1.

Also noteworthy is the election of over 200 blacks to public office in the South since the Voting Rights Act was passed. There are presently 50 blacks holding local, parish, and state offices in Louisiana, all elected since 1965.

These accelerated advances in black registration and election are indeed impressive, but they do not eradicate the voting problem. With the exception of Texas, black registration percentages are still below white percentages in all the states included in the Voter Education Project survey, and in many areas blacks still experience substantial difficulties in gaining the franchise. Also, the number of blacks holding statewide positions in government and political parties is in no way proportionate to the number of blacks in the population.

Wilson observes, "that the political participation of the Negro in the North is significantly higher than in the South but even so is lower than that of most other Northern population groups." It ought to be pointed out that low participation in the North cannot be attributed to the type of legal restrictions historically operative in the South. Social science surveys have indicated that persons with low socioeconomic status tend to vote less than persons of higher socioeconomic status. In addition, Negroes in the urban North are more geographically mobile than whites and are less likely to be able to satisfy residence requirements for voting. Nonpartisan elections, candidates running at-large and weak party organization also contribute to low turnout among low income voters. And it could well be that "the extent to which an individual feels effective as part of the institutionalized process may well determine the degree to which he participates in those processes. In sum, the individual's perception of his personal effectiveness should be supportive to the values he places on participation." Thus, while there are no legal deterrents to Negro voting in the North, the cultural deterrents (income, education, occupation) are attributable to the system. That is, the prevailing social, economic and educational arrangements operate in a manner that relegates Negroes to this status, and as long as Negroes face these artificial barriers it is reasonable to assume that their level of political participation will not change.

The extent of constraints on black participation, North and South, would seem to suggest an

Table 1

VOTER REGISTRATION IN THE SOUTH, WINTER-SPRING, 1968

	White Registered	Per Cent White VAP[a] Registered	Negro Registered	Per Cent Negro VAP[a] Registered
Alabama	1,119,000	82.7	271,000	56.3
Arkansas	616,000	72.4	121,000	62.8
Florida	2,194,000	83.8	293,000	62.3
Georgia	1,450,000	80.6	334,000	54.5
Louisiana	1,122,000	87.0	301,000	58.5
Mississippi	655,000	88.9	264,000	62.5
North Carolina	1,555,000	77.5	293,000	53.2
South Carolina	567,000	63.6	183,000	49.3
Tennessee	1,434,000	80.6	225,000	71.7
Texas	3,532,000	72.3	540,000	83.1
Virginia	1,200,000	63.9	247,000	56.6
Totals	15,454,000	76.9	3,072,000	61.2

Source: Voter Education Project, *News*, 2 (June, 1968).
[a]VAP = Voter-Age Population

absence of consent by blacks and thus possible relief from obligations traditionally incumbent upon citizens in a democracy. Of interest in this connection is a recent re-examination of the principles of obligation and consent and related problems rendered by Pitkin.

Pitkin, in a highly provocative treatise, holds that obligation depends not on any actual act of consenting, past or present, but on the character of the government. If it is just government, doing what a government should, then you must obey it. If it is unjust, then you have no such obligation. Or, your obligation depends not on whether you have consented but on whether the government is such that you ought to consent to it. Are its actions consistent with the type of government men in a hypothetical state of nature would have consented to establish and obey? Pitkin's study would suggest that any assessment of the riots and the rioters would of necessity involve grappling with these kinds of concerns.

The propensity among blacks to disobey certain basic canons of the political system has produced strains in the system which threaten to destroy its very foundation. Could this propensity derive fundamentally from the unwillingness of the system to incorporate blacks as full partners in the political process? Cook has projected that "on the empirical level, a tradition of exclusion from participation in the political system breeds disrespect for, and disloyalty to, that system." "Men rarely question the legitimacy of an established order when all is going well; the problem of political obligation is urgent when the state is sick. . . ."

Does exclusion from participation, coupled with exclusion from benefits of "the good life" of the system, not only remove the obligation to obey, but also give rise to the obligation to disobey or revolt? These queries are relevant, but they are also difficult in as much as they solicit precise guidance in specific and varied kinds of situations. Pitkin underscores the inadequacy of classical democratic theory as well as her own theory on consent by noting that both provide insufficient cues for determining what authority to resist and under what conditions. In the same way, both provide only imperfect guidelines for assessing and evaluating the consistency between civil disorder of the magnitude of riots and the obligation of citizens to obey the authority of society invested with the duty of enforcing the law.

Black political strategy

Scoble suggests that Negro leadership and politics represent a quest for effective political power. Negro politics can be best understood if viewed as pursuit of power and influence over authoritative policy decisions. On the other hand, Wilson, in a recent article on the subject, writes, "Because of the structure of American politics as well as the nature of the Negro community, Negro politics will accomplish only limited objectives. This does not mean that Negroes will be content with those accomplishments or resigned to that political style. If Negroes do not make radical gains, radical sentiments may grow." The crucial problem of the black man in the American political arena seems to revolve around the magnitude of the needs of the black people, (as set forth in the *Report* and elsewhere) in relationship to the limited potential of politics as a vehicle for ministering to those needs. More succinctly put, it now seems incumbent upon black men to decide if politics, in the traditional sense, is now more of an irrelevancy rather than an imperative in the search for solutions to their problems. If politics is relevant, then what types of strategies will best serve the needs of the black community, North and South? If irrelevant, what are the alternatives?

Questions of strategy are significant and there are those who feel that his aspect of the black protest movement has not received sufficient attention from leaders in that movement. In fact, the alleged absence of a programmatic element in radical politics in America today, especially the black protest movement, provoked Lasch to state, "the very gravity of the crisis makes it all the more imperative that radicals try to formulate at least a provisional theory which will serve them as a guide to tactics in the immediate future as well as to long-range questions of strategy." Along the same general lines, Crozier points out that America is now committed to the omnipotence of reason and the black protest movements are out of step with that development. Very pointedly, he reflects that "it is no longer possible to make good through mere numbers, through the vote or through manual labor, but only through the ability to play the game of modern calculation. And in that area the Negro is still fundamentally disadvantaged. The more rational the society becomes, the more he loses his foothold." Could it be that traditional politics characterize the black subculture while a more rational-calculating variety of politics has long been the pattern in the dominant political culture?

The literature of the discipline and popular periodicals are replete with suggestions of appropriate strategies and/or programs for solving the race problem. Some of the more popularly suggested and researched strategies include black-liberal white coalitions, black-conservative white coalitions, fluctuating or *ad hoc* coalitions, separate black political parties, Black Power, ghetto power. No examination of this proliferation of literature can be made in this limited commentary. Nor will any full-blown theory or strategy be offered. However, it does seem reasonable to submit that any strategy designed to redefine the status of black people in America must of necessity be devised with certain considerations.

First, political strategy for blacks must take into account the difficulties inherent in being a numerical minority. Minority strategy must be highly flexibly based, to a large degree, on the fluctuating attitudes and actions of the white majority in any given setting. It must also be directed toward overcoming traditional constraints on the exertion of effective power by Negroes endemic to the black community itself. Second, any therapeutic strategy must acknowledge the reality that blacks in the ghetto already constitute a "separate society," and must address itself seriously to black charges of control by "alien, outside" agents. Indigenous control of the ghetto and similar demands cannot be summarily dismissed as, for example, "old wine in new bottles." Third, given the general apathy and insensitivity of whites toward problems of blacks, it seems reasonable to suggest that any meaningful gains for blacks will come as a result of *demands*, supported by evidence of black willingness to cause great inconvenience to the community at large if these legitimate demands are ignored. Fourth, it might be that the Commission placed too much emphasis on the material aspects of the black man's problem (and the material aspects are indeed important) and did not devote enough attention to such psychological needs as dignity, self-respect and identity and to the relationship between the latter and any corrective actions, political or otherwise. Taking these psychological dimensions into account will probably necessitate innovations in and restatements of traditional concepts and theories regarding democracy, civil disobedience, protest, and other forms of political activity. New tactics, new rhetoric and new sources of leadership will most probably emerge and must be accommodated by the system. Fifth, and in a similar view, it would seem that black strategy and black strategists ought not be constrained to political alternatives if these alternatives prove to be mostly dysfunctional for blacks, and there is a growing opinion which holds that they may well be. Finally, the magnitude of the problems faced by blacks is such that the correctives must be radical. If radical programs are not adopted, the Kerner Report may be more a prelude to, rather than a summation of, the worst race riots in the history of this nation, for there seems to be little reason to believe that black rioters will be satisfied with anything less than radical corrective action.

Editor's Note:

John Conyers, Jr., Representative of the First Congressional District, Detroit, Michigan, since 1965 and member of the Congressional Black Caucus, presents here a cogent argument for the active participation of blacks in politics. One of the primary aims is "to maximize and unify the political power of twenty-four million blacks." Conyers delineates several important points for consideration: the issue of white racism vs. this nation's survival; the possibility of an imminent police state; the increasing clamor for suppression of unpopular ideas; the augmentation of police force with military force; the conscription of young black men for Vietnam; and other concerns that can be dealt with by the polity. He stresses the need for politics from the black point of view, with black people acting as a force for change. In the years since this article was written, the political scene has witnessed several major events: the Congressional Black Caucus has expanded to include representatives from across the country; Shirley Chisholm, an erudite black woman, has actively sought nomination for President of the United States; and a black national convention, hosting 8,000 blacks of differing backgrounds and viewpoints, met in Gary, Indiana, to plan strategy and programs for the most viable use of the potential power that lies in the hands of black voters.

POLITICS AND THE BLACK REVOLUTION

JOHN CONYERS, JR.

Nowhere are prejudices more mistaken for truth, passion for reason, and invective for documentation than in politics.—John Mason Brown

There are those who insist that it is time for black people to "give up on politics." I disagree. How can we give up on our one access to government—a government that controls the destiny of us all? Government makes, interprets and enforces the laws that set the limits of our lives. It determines the extent to which we will be educated, the kinds of jobs we may have, where we may live, the kind of health care we may receive. It selects which of us shall fight and, if necessary, die, in its name. It even defines our personal freedoms and dictates in large measure the quality of life that each of us, every single American, shall have.

Politics is important—much too important for black people to "give up" on the political process through which, today, with the heightening of black awareness and the stirring of long dormant black voter power, black people can gain control of large cities, can exert strong influence on state governments, can pressure Capitol Hill and force quite a bit of listening at the White House.

Within the last few months the political process has placed hundreds of blacks in office all over the

U.S.–especially in the South. The towns of Grand Coteau, La., Fayette, Miss., and Chapel Hill, N.C., now have black mayors. There are growing numbers of city councilmen, judges and sheriffs. Three new black U.S. congressmen are now in Washington and more will join them soon, I'm sure.

The one thing that characterizes almost all these new black officials is that their allegiance is to the black people who elected them, and not, as in the past, to white political manipulators, Northern or Southern variety, who have always been present behind-the-scene. Quite frankly, if a "brother" wants to get elected these days, he'd better be "in good" with the "brothers" instead of with a white political boss or a white-dominated political machine. A recent development which reflects this new reality was the formation of the National Committee of Inquiry, a group of politically aware blacks from all parts of the nation who came together last year to examine the platforms and voting records of the 1968 presidential candidates. The NCI tore apart and discussed these platforms and records in an effort to evaluate each candidate's relevance to the needs and goals of 25 million black Americans. While the NCI is national in scope, similar "inquiry" groups are forming in black communities in several cities. Candidates–black ones as well as white ones–are going to have to come up with some mighty good answers to the questions that aware blacks will be asking from now on. This new questioning, the new demands, are beginning to add up, I believe, to first steps in the development of a new and relevant political ideology that will effect significant change in the status of blacks everywhere. We have the bright young black men and women to develop the ideology and we have the growing power to effect the change. For the doubtful, I might remind that Sen. Eugene McCarthy showed that it doesn't take an army to make a major impact on the system. His one-man effort didn't capture the White House, but it forced its very powerful former occupant to pack up and move out. A similar challenge was seen in the courageous struggle of the black hospital workers in Charleston, S. C. A relatively few people confronted a system that had denied them union recognition, decent wages and non-discriminatory working conditions. Under the able leadership of local activists and the Rev. Ralph David Abernathy of the Southern Christian Leadership Conference, those few people rocked Charleston, the State of South Carolina, and, actually, the entire South, to their foundations in this first major black challenge to the traditional Southern slave wage system.

All this would be called "revolutionary" by growing numbers of blacks. And there is, indeed, a certain revolutionary thrust in the rejection by blacks of systems that have bred the oppressive second-class status in which we have been for such a long time. But "revolution" is a word, warned Malcolm X, that ought not be used lightly. If one is not talking about a bloody struggle for land and the establishment of a new political system, Malcolm said, then it would perhaps be wiser to use another word. A *revolution*, we ought to remember, grows out of a successful *rebellion*. Thus, perhaps "rebellion" is the better word, especially as it relates to blacks and politics. We are not in the midst of a *revolution*–in politics or in anything else. Black Americans by the millions are angry because they are aware of the republic's shortcomings. But the majority of blacks have few fundamental objections to the Constitution and to the form of government we have. (It is interesting to note that, when the chips are down, many who style themselves "revolutionaries" turn unfailingly to the Constitution in defense of their right to participate in "revolution.") What blacks are after–and most Americans know this–is a change in habit, in the old ways that government–and thus politics and politicians–have circumscribed black lives. That's what the rebellion is all about, no matter how those who control the country opportunistically fan fears among whites with rumors that blacks are on the verge of invading and shooting up and burning down the comfortable lily-white suburbs.

The power structure would not permit, nor could it afford to permit, even revolutionary talk that could be described as "incendiary" if it were taking all the rhetoric seriously. It seems someone–perhaps white America–is "running down a game" on us, making us believe that we're making revolution so that a real revolution won't occur. (So far, only such people as Malcolm X, Eldridge Cleaver, Rap Brown and Fred "Ahmed" Evans, and such organizations as the Black Panthers and the W.E.B. DuBois Clubs have been considered "revolutionary" enough to be systematically harassed or prosecuted or raided by the FBI.)

But let us make no mistake. Beneath the thin veneer of this supposedly highly civilized nation, there exists a potential for violence without historical precedent. The presence of heavily-armed white vigilantes in combination with the most devastating military arsenal ever assembled by one government makes it more than reasonable to conclude that there is only the most remote possibility that a black revolution could ever take place in this country. In fairness it should be pointed out that a white revolution has no more prospect for success than a black one.

This does not in any way preclude the increase

of violence that is likely to flow from a nearly inexhaustible combination of black-white confrontations which have yet to occur. Thus it appears to be clear that any temporary or sustained urban eruptions—not to mention guerilla activity—would immediately precipitate a violent over-reaction on the part of a nervous government and many of its citizens as well. The application of the military theory of "overkill" would probably then see its first domestic application. The increasingly repressive tendencies in the government, which apparently have not reached their final magnitude, have reached the point that Americans of any color who dare to promote radical change are faced with electronic surveillance and police harassment, as well as easy susceptibility to harassment through continued prosecution in the courts.

Now that we know who we are and have restored our image, studied ancient African cultures existing when Europeans were still in caves and embraced the beauty of blackness, we are able to share this knowledge, keeping in mind that a full appreciation of it will not come easily. For a number of years and in many different ways we tried to teach the white man what we already know: that America's racism, not our reaction to it, is the real threat to the nation's survival. It did not take the last five years of urban insurrections to dramatize to black people why this struggle will increase in intensity until it is resolved one way or another. We did not need the Kerner Commission report to tell us what the score is and has been for us. These were educational aids for white people. But have they learned?

Lyndon Johnson ignored the Kerner Report, though he requested it. Richard Nixon disagreed with its conclusions.

But if white Americans are slow learners, must we be, too? There is much information around us that is useful, if only we keep our eyes and ears open. Is it incidental that each day brings new evidence that we are moving in the direction of a police state? How could the increasing clamor for the suppression of unpopular ideas go unnoticed, or the routine manner in which urban police forces are being augmented with military force?

Until recently, few would have believed that the late Dr. Martin Luther King, Jr., whose advocacy of non-violence won him world-wide acclaim, would have been considered so dangerous to the security of his country that he would have been subjected to continuous electronic surveillance by government officials over a period of years.

There is a distinct possibility that repression and the curbing of freedoms could worsen. Need we be reminded of the infamous McCarran Act and the concentration camps (by whatever name) it authorized 19 years ago? Provisions of that act could be carried out at any time.

For some considerable period of time the government has been operating under several crippling disabilities: a coalition of conservative and reactionary elements which included both Democrats and Republicans and which effectively fought off progress and reform of any kind; a wide range of corporate interests that exert powerful pressures upon the government in the pursuit of their own self-interest; a two-party political system that makes the likelihood of presenting the electorate with genuine differences on the vital issues of the day increasingly unlikely; and an electorate that receives little real assistance in understanding the fallacies that undergird white racism, how 50 million Americans could be raised out of poverty, or the menace of the military-industrial complex domestically and internationally.

In the Congress—the most reactionary branch of the government—the evidence of these disabilities is manifest daily. In no other place does the result of the close cooperation between the conservative forces in both the Democratic and Republican parties produce more negative results, blocking vitally needed domestic legislation defending massive Pentagon plans for all kinds of costly military hardware, enthusiastically promoting law-and-order-type legislation and sending more non-military aid to Vietnam than to the more than 43 independent African nations combined. These forces ignore racial and urban crises, the mounting number of hard-core unemployables and push aside any realistic programs that might provide quantity low-cost housing on an integrated basis.

The Congress of the United States has conscripted our young men to kill and to be killed in a disastrous war 10,000 miles from our shores. It has taxed the citizens exorbitantly and squandered the resources of America in unconscionable waste. It frequently gives the impression of making great progress when, in fact, the opposite is true, for it has turned its back on the poor and oppressed in America and the rest of the world. It has supported oppressive dictatorships, thus denying the rights of people all over the world to food and freedom. It has caused this nation, which was once a source of hope to the oppressed, to become the object of fear and hatred.

As long as the American public applauds politicians who proclaim the virtues of anti-Communist super-patriotism, there is little hope for bringing about the profound changes we need. It is easy to be a tough defender of law-and-order when toughness means coercing the weak and rewarding the strong. The war in Vietnam, the anti-ballistic missile and other mammoth weapons systems on the Pentagon's shopping list are symptoms of a national belief that order can be obtained through force, and that cooperation can be compelled with threats. It is the same society that has met its internal crises of poverty and race by training 400,000 National Guardsmen and police in local riot control. It is time we recognized that those who struggle to feed the hungry and bring justice to blacks and other oppressed minorities are more the defenders of our real national security than are the military planners. The ultimate security of our country is in the welfare of its people, its human resources.

Meanwhile, the rich get richer and the poor get children. In 1953, 1.6 per cent of the adult population owned 32 per cent of all privately-owned wealth, including 82 per cent of all corporate stock. Subsequent studies 10 years later showed that the trend toward concentration was even more pronounced.

We must exert our influence, too, on the related issues that do not look black but which profoundly affect black people; such things, for example, as our vast expenditures in Vietnam and in space. We can help to force a realignment of our national priorities.

It is all very well, for instance, to have legislation that bars discrimination in the sale and rental of housing. But our housing problem goes beyond segregation. There is not enough decent housing in the country for the people, black and white, who need it. We must not only address ourselves to the question of segregation, which is a black problem, but also the question of supply, which is not exclusively a black problem.

Unemployment looks like a black problem because there are more black people out of work, proportionately, than there are white people out of work. But to concentrate on equalizing the joblessness is meaningless. There is something critically wrong with a system that needs a growing scrap heap of unemployed human beings to maintain its stability. This must be corrected.

Then too, we have to develop the knack for stepping back from time to time to reassess what we have to do. Now imagine, if you will, the beneficial impact we blacks could have on this country, if we had 12 senators and 55 congressmen—our minimum fair share—rather than the present count of one senator and nine representatives. Imagine the impact of having at least one fourth of the Southern congressional delegations chosen by black people. There could be no more effective way of breaking up the bi-partisan conservative coalition that has blocked so much progressive legislation. Whenever I witness

congressmen, both Southern and Northern, voting against basic social legislation, I remember Lorraine Hansberry's admonition about white inhumanity toward whites. Black congressmen would unquestionably support measures that would, in effect, benefit disadvantaged whites as well as blacks.

I am talking about politics for *our* point of view—from the *black* point of view. Our own intelligence about the oppressiveness of the kind of society which would like to forget us along with other historical "mistakes" should give black people a unique force in effecting change in America. An infusion of blacks into the political arena might provide the moral force of "soul" which America either lost or never had. No longer will we be content to stand on the sidelines and rail against the powerful forces that shape our lives. Instead, we propose to enter the political arena and wrest for ourselves a share of that decision-making power.

I think it is possible to get some of the necessary things done through politics. The South has been hell for black people primarily because we have been forcibly denied the opportunity for political involvement. With the help of such vital legislation as the Voting Rights Act, the vital importance of which we should understand even if the Nixon Administration doesn't (or maybe it does?), we can force a political realignment that may one day put the South in the vanguard of progressive politics. And we may be able to devise a means of governing the urban sprawl in which most of us live.

We know that the reason we are able to move a wounded Marine from a jungle in Vietnam to the finest medical care in minutes, yet cannot do the same for a child on the Mississippi Delta or in an urban ghetto is very much bound up in the image of America. Being the greatest power in the world carries not only quite enormous political and economic implications but racial ones as well.

Incredibly enough, it is only in this century that those in power felt obligated to even talk about solving the kinds of problems under discussion. The real difference that may be discerned between our plight and that of our grandfathers is that in this generation there is being developed the power to transform talk into action. But to make that transformation effective is another way of stating the challenge which presents itself to us. Frederick Douglass captured for all time the essential meaning of this concept when he wrote: "If there is no struggle, there is no progress. Those who profess to favor freedom, and yet deprecate agitation, are men who want crops without plowing up the ground. They want the rain without thunder and lightning. They want the ocean without the awful roar of its many waters. This struggle may be a moral one; or it may be a physical one; or it may be both moral and physical; but it must be a struggle. Power concedes nothing without a demand. . . ."

Adding to that magnificent statement is the observation that struggle without understanding or purpose may be meaningless or even dangerous. Certainly it will solve nothing. In the imperfections of our prosecution of this struggle it is clear that there have been instances of rushing in "to plow up the ground" without the real knowledge of how much ground should be plowed or what seeds planted.

For the first time in its development, black America is shaking off the myth of inferiority, becoming proud of its blackness, beginning to learn of its great past. This self-knowledge is the basis of all knowledge and so in a sense we are just beginning to learn. We are finding out who we are, our image is clearing and our perception is becoming more critical. Thus the economic and political realities with which we are presently confronted begin to come into sharp perspective.

But to achieve anything at all, we will have to pool our resources, our knowledge and our political skills. We will have to learn that it is possible to get ourselves together and still be free to make those coalitions that forward our mutual goals. This is what Julian Bond is talking about when he says that we must align ourselves with anyone who will help—but with this new distinction: *we will lead.*

When I speak of black people becoming politically involved, I mean a very great deal more than just registering, voting and running for office. The ancient Romans were registering and voting when their civilization went down the drain. It is already being argued that our much-vaunted civilization may be headed toward that same drain hole. Certainly there is no holy writ which says America must last forever simply because it is America.

The present situation requires all of the imagination and boldness that we can summon. We need to ask a very fundamental question of ourselves: What kind of country do we want the United States to be?

Now that black America has finally ended its preoccupation with what Congresswoman Shirley Chisholm calls "look-how-far-we've-comeism," we are free to move ourselves and the country forward. It may be the supreme irony of history that the ethnic group that has been most abused by this country may turn out to be the country's salvation. I'd like to see us give it a try.

Some see the black American's choice as between withdrawing from this "hopeless" government or overthrowing the entire system. I see our choice as between political involvement or political apathy. America is the black man's battleground. It is here where it will be decided whether or not we will make America what it says it is. For me, at least, the choice is clear.

PART IV:

PERSPECTIVES TOWARD
A NON-RACIST SOCIETY

THE WHITE HOUSE

CLAUDE McKAY

Your door is shut against my tightened face,
And I am sharp as steel with discontent;
But I possess the courage and the grace
To bear my anger proudly and unbent.
The pavement slabs burn loose beneath my feet,
A chafing savage, down the decent street;
And passion rends my vitals as I pass,
Where boldly shines your shuttered door of glass.
Oh, I must search for wisdom every hour,
Deep in my wrathful bosom sore and raw,
And find in it the superhuman power
To hold me to the letter of your law!

*. . . I tremble for my country when I re-
flect that God is just: that his justice
cannot sleep forever.* —Jefferson

These sentiments are echoed in the reflections of
James Baldwin on an America that has yet to examine the
cataclysmic forces unleashed by a heritage of fear, hatred,
violence, alienation, and nihilism. In posing the question,
How can the American Negro past be used, Baldwin has
perceptively focused on what may well be the Achilles heel
of one of the great powers of the world. The question needs
to be answered by all concerned forthrightly, honestly, and
intelligently. To do less is to underestimate the role of the
past as a fulcrum for the future. Baldwin proposes that white
Americans reexamine everything they believe in and evaluate
the political reality of placing a negative value on people of
color.

THE PAST FOR A FUTURE

JAMES BALDWIN

. . . I submit then, that the racial tensions that
menace Americans today have little to do with real
antipathy—on the contrary, indeed—and are involved
only symbolically with color. These tensions are
rooted in the very same depths as those from which
love springs, or murder. The white man's unadmitted
—and apparently, to him, unspeakable—private fears
and longings are projected onto the Negro. The only
way he can be released from the Negro's tyrannical
power over him is to consent, in effect, to become
black himself, to become a part of that suffering and
dancing country that he now watches wistfully from
the heights of his lonely power and, armed with
spiritual traveller's checks, visits surreptitiously after
dark. How can one respect, let alone adopt, the values
of a people who do not, on any level whatever, live
the way they say they do, or the way they say they
should? I cannot accept the proposition that the
four-hundred-year travail of the American Negro
should result merely in his attainment of the present
level of the American civilization. I am far from
convinced that being released from the African witch
doctor was worthwhile if I am now—in order to
support the moral contradictions and the spiritual
aridity of my life—expected to become dependent on
the American psychiatrist. It is a bargain I refuse. The
only thing white people have that black people need,
or should want, is power—and no one holds power
forever. White people cannot, in the generality, be
taken as models of how to live. Rather, the white man
is himself in sore need of new standards, which will
release him from his confusion and place him once
again in fruitful communion with the depths of his

own being. And I repeat: The price of the liberation
of the white people is the liberation of the blacks
—the total liberation, in the cities, in the towns,
before the law, and in the mind. Why, for example—
especially knowing the family as I do—I should *want*
to marry your sister is a great mystery to me. But
your sister and I have every right to marry if we wish
to, and no one has the right to stop us. If she cannot
raise me to her level, perhaps I can raise her to mine.

In short, we, the black and the white, deeply
need each other here if we are really to become a
nation—if we are really, that is, to achieve our
identity, our maturity, as men and women. To create
one nation has proved to be a hideously difficult task;
there is certainly no need now to create two, one
black and one white. But white men with far more
political power than that possessed by the Nation of
Islam movement have been advocating exactly this, in
effect, for generations. If this sentiment is honored
when it falls from the lips of Senator Byrd, then there
is no reason it should not be honored when it falls
from the lips of Malcolm X. And any Congressional
committee wishing to investigate the latter must also
be willing to investigate the former. They are expressing exactly the same sentiments and represent
exactly the same danger. There is absolutely no
reason to suppose that white people are better
equipped to frame the laws by which I am to be
governed than I am. It is entirely unacceptable that I
should have no voice in the political affairs of my
own country, for I am not a ward of America; I am
one of the first Americans to arrive on these shores.

This past, the Negro's past, of rope, fire,
torture, castration, infanticide, rape; death and humiliation; fear by day and night, fear as deep as the
marrow of the bone; doubt that he was worthy of
life, since everyone around him denied it; sorrow for
his women, for his kinfolk, for his children, who
needed his protection, and whom he could not
protect; rage, hatred, and murder, hatred for white
men so deep that it often turned against him and his
own, and made all love, all trust, all joy impossible
—this past, this endless struggle to achieve and reveal
and confirm a human identity, human authority, yet
contains, for all its horror, something very beautiful.
I do not mean to be sentimental about suffering—
enough is certainly as good as a feast—but people who
cannot suffer can never grow up, can never discover
who they are. That man who is forced each day to
snatch his manhood, his identity, out of the fire of
human cruelty that rages to destroy it knows, if he
survives his effort, and even if he does not survive it,
something about himself and human life that no
school on earth—and, indeed, no church—can teach.
He achieves his own authority, and that is unshak-

able. This is because, in order to save his life, he is forced to look beneath appearances, to take nothing for granted, to hear the meaning behind the words. If one is continually surviving the worst that life can bring, one eventually ceases to be controlled by a fear of what life can bring; whatever it brings must be borne. And at this level of experience one's bitterness begins to be palatable, and hatred becomes too heavy a sack to carry. The apprehension of life here so briefly and inadequately sketched has been the experience of generations of Negroes, and it helps to explain how they have endured and how they have been able to produce children of kindergarten age who can walk through mobs to get to school. It demands great force and great cunning continually to assault the mighty and indifferent fortress of white supremacy, as Negroes in this country have done so long. It demands great spiritual resilience not to hate the hater whose foot is on your neck, and an even greater miracle of perception and charity not to teach your child to hate. The Negro boys and girls who are facing mobs today come out of a long line of improbable aristocrats—the only genuine aristocrats this country has produced. I say "this country" because their frame of reference was totally American. They were hewing out of the mountain of white supremacy the stone of their individuality. I have great respect for that unsung army of black men and women who trudged down back lanes and entered back doors, saying "Yes, sir" and "No, Ma'am" in order to acquire a new roof for the schoolhouse, new books, a new chemistry lab, more beds for the dormitories, more dormitories. They did not like saying "Yes, sir" and "No, Ma'am," but the country was in no hurry to educate Negroes, these black men and women knew that the job had to be done, and they put their pride in their pockets in order to do it. It is very hard to believe that they were in any way inferior to the white men and women who opened those back doors. It is very hard to believe that those men and women, raising their children, eating their greens, crying their curses, weeping their tears, singing their songs, making their love, as the sun rose, as the sun set, were in any way inferior to the white men and women who crept over to share these splendors after the sun went down. But we must avoid the European error; we must not suppose that, because the situation, the ways, the perceptions of black people so radically differed from those of whites, they were racially superior. I am proud of these people not because of their color but because of their intelligence and their spiritual force and their beauty. The country should be proud of them, too, but, alas, not many people in this country even know of their existence. And the reason for this ignorance is that a knowledge of the role these people played—and play—in American life would reveal more about America to Americans than Americans wish to know.

The American Negro has the great advantage of having never believed that collection of myths to which white Americans cling: that their ancestors were all freedom-loving heroes, that they were born in the greatest country the world has ever seen, or that Americans are invincible in battle and wise in peace, that Americans have always dealt honorably with Mexicans and Indians and all other neighbors or inferiors, that American men are the world's most direct and virile, that American women are pure. Negroes know far more about white Americans than that; it can almost be said, in fact, that they know about white Americans what parents—or, anyway, mothers—know about their children, and that they very often regard white Americans that way. And perhaps this attitude, held in spite of what they know and have endured, helps to explain why Negroes, onthe whole, and until lately, have allowed themselves to feel so little hatred. The tendency has really been, insofar as this was possible, to dismiss white people as the slightly mad victims of their own brainwashing. One watched the lives they led. One could not be fooled about that; one watched the things they did and the excuses that they gave themselves, and if a white man was really in trouble, deep trouble, it was to the Negro's door that he came. And one felt that if one had had that white man's worldly advantages, one would never have become as bewildered and as joyless and as thoughtlessly cruel as he. The Negro came to the white man for a roof or for five dollars or for a letter to the judge; the white man came to the Negro for love. But he was not often able to give what he came seeking. The price was too high; he had too much to lose. And the Negro knew this, too. When one knows this about a man, it is impossible for one to hate him, but unless he becomes a man—becomes equal—it is also impossible for one to love him. Ultimately, one tends to avoid him, for the universal characteristic of children is to assume that they have a monopoly on trouble, and therefore a monopoly on *you*. (Ask any Negro what he knows about the white people with whom he works. And then ask the white people with whom he works what they know about *him*.)

How can the American Negro past be used? It is entirely possible that this dishonored past will rise up soon to smite all of us. There are some wars, for example (if anyone the globe is still mad enough to go to war) that the American Negro will not support, however many of his people may be coerced—and there is a limit to the number of people any government can put in prison, and a rigid limit indeed to the practicality of such a course. A bill is coming in that I fear America is not prepared to pay. "The problem of the twentieth century," wrote W.E.B. DuBois around sixty years ago, "is the problem of the color line." A fearful and delicate problem, which compromises, when it does not corrupt, all the American efforts to build a better world—here, there, or anywhere. It is for this reason that everything white Americans think they believe in must now be reexamined. What one would not like to see again is the consolidation of peoples on the basis of their color. But as long as we in the West place on color the value that we do, we make it impossible for the great unwashed to consolidate themselves according to any other principle. Color is not a human or a personal reality; it is a political reality. But this is a distinction so extremely hard to make that the West has not been able to make it yet. And at the center of this dreadful storm, this vast confusion, stand the black people of this nation, who must now share the fate of a nation that has never accepted them, to which they were brought in chains. Well, if this is so, one has no choice but to do all in one's power to change that fate, and at no matter what risk—eviction, imprisonment, torture, death. For the sake of one's children, in order to minimize the bill that *they* must pay, one must be careful not to take refuge in any delusion—and the value placed on the color of the skin is always and everywhere and forever a delusion. I know that what I am asking is impossible. But in our time, as in every time, the impossible is the least that one can demand—and one is, after all, emboldened by the spectacle of human history in general, and American Negro history in particular, for it testifies to nothing less than the perpetual achievement of the impossible.

When I was very young, and was dealing with my buddies in those wine- and urine-stained hallways, something in me wondered, *What will happen to all that beauty?* For black people, though I am aware that some of us, black and white, do not know it yet, are very beautiful. And when I sat at Elijah's table and watched the baby, the women, and the men, and we talked about God's—or Allah's—vengeance, I wondered, when that vengeance was achieved, *What will happen to all that beauty then?* I could also see that the intransigence and ignorance of the white world might make that vengeance inevitable—a vengeance that does not really depend on, and cannot really be executed by, any person or organization, and that cannot be prevented by any police force or army: historical vengeance, a cosmic vengeance, based on the law that we recognize when we say, "Whatever goes up must come down." And here we are, at the center of the arc, trapped in the gaudiest, most

valuable, and most improbable water wheel the world has ever seen. Everything now, we must assume, is in our hands; we have no right to assume otherwise. If we—and now I mean the relatively conscious whites and the relatively conscious blacks, who must, like lovers, insist on, or create, the consciousness of the others—do not falter in our duty now, we may be able, handful that we are, to end the racial nightmare, and achieve our country, and change the history of the world. If we do not now dare everything, the fulfillment of that prophecy, recreated from the Bible in song by a slave, is upon us: *God gave Noah the rainbow sign, No more water, the fire next time!*

Editor's Note:

Technological advances requiring discrete training and skills have made the question of equality of opportunity between the races an anachronism. In a cybernetic society even racists can afford to speak and act benignly, since an equal chance excludes all but the technocrats. The poor, unemployed, untrained masses of black people have no skills to offer the machine. Thus, the question again becomes one of justice. Interestingly enough, black voices in the past have often cried for justice. But now the answer is a crucial one. The posture of this country on the matter of justice may well provide the epitaph in the history of a nation torn asunder because it preached but could not practice justice.

EQUALITY OR JUSTICE?

SIDNEY WILLHELM

To insist that "the highest and continuing priority should be assigned to the goal of national unity through the method. . .of equality of opportunity" assures a Negro equality but without employment and, therefore, nostalgia for an opportunity to work, to attain improved education, housing, income, and more meaningful social identity through separation from whites; the demands for improvement through separation of the races grow more plentiful as Negroes are "muzzled" through equality. "The Negro who is told that the 'desegregation' of a bus terminal in Georgia somehow represents 'progress,'" LeRoi Jones bluntly states, "is definitely being lied to."

As White America calls for equality to accord with its latest technological development, Black America demands *justice* to accord with Negro aspirations. White offers of equality for submergence

274

are now being met by blacks insisting upon justice for the emergence of a viable race.

The change from equality to justice as a more typical contemporary stance is everywhere apparent. Martin Luther King, in a late work, stressed not equality but justice. He once advocated nonviolent strategies to reach levels on par with whites, but at the end of his life he sought justice: "Giving our ultimate allegiance to the empire of justice, we must be that colony of dissenters seeking to imbue our nation with the ideals of a higher and nobler order." James Farmer pledged, as the leader, a "CORE maintaining vigilance and demanding justice," a shift which, he acknowledged, requires "new techniques and emphases."

Throughout history the radical Negro has advocated justice above all else. In the most radical Negro pronouncement ever to be uttered, David Walker appealed, during 1829-1830, for justice:

> I ask every man who has a heart, and is blessed with the privilege of believing—Is not God a God of justice to *all* his creatures? Do you say he is? Then if he gives peace and tranquillity to tyrants, and permits them to keep our fathers, our mothers, ourselves and our children in eternal ignorance and wretchedness, to support them and their families, would he be to us a God of *justice?* I ask, O ye *Christians!!!* who hold us and our children in the most abject ignorance and degradation, that ever a people were afflicted with since the world began—I say, if God gives you peace and tranquillity, and suffers you thus to go on afflicting us and our children, who have never given you the least provocation—would he be to us a God of justice?

During the Civil War one of the most radical blacks, Frederick Douglass, relentlessly demanded justice:

> Let the American people, who have thus far only kept the colored race staggering between partial philanthropy and cruel force, be induced to try what virtue there is in *justice.* First, pure, and then peaceable—first *just*, then generous.—The sum of the black man's misfortunes and calamities are just here: He is everywhere treated as an exception to all the general rules which should operate in the relations of other men. He is literally scourged beyond the beneficient range of *truth and justice.*—With all the purifying and liberalizing power of the Christian religion, teaching, as it does, meekness, gentleness, brotherly kindness, those who profess it have not yet even approached the position of treating the black man as an *equal man and a brother.* The few who

have thus far risen to this requirement, both of reason and religion, are stigmatized as fanatics and enthusiasts.

There was no doubt in Douglass' mind that justice —not equality—must be the first consideration of an emancipated Negro:

> What shall be done with the Negro if emancipated? Deal *justly* with him. He is a human being, capable of judging between good and evil, right and wrong, liberty and slavery, and is as much a subject of law as any other man; therefore, deal *justly* with him.

In the dismal twenties, the one voice resounding in behalf of the Negro masses, Marcus Garvey, proclaimed in the preamble to the Universal Negro Improvement Association, "Let justice be done to all mankind, realizing that if the strong oppresses the weak, confusion and discontent will ever mark the path of man. . . ."

The demand for justice identifies the more radical posture among Negroes of recent times. Robert F. Williams, a Negro removed by the national office as head of a local NAACP chapter in Monroe, North Carolina, for his advocacy of self-defense through violent means to counter violence from whites, explained his stance within the framework of justice: ". . . a campaign of self-defense and survival must be based on the righteous cause of *justice.* It must not be anti-white but anti-oppression and *injustice.*"

The nationalistic separatist movement exemplified by the Black Muslims emphasizes justice. In one of his speeches delivered in mid-1964, Elijah Muhammad, leader of the Muslims in America, placed his call for justice before his bid for equality, saying, "We want justice. Equal justice under the law. We want justice applied equally to all, regardless of creed or class or color."

The formulation of wrongs as injustices of the majority against the black minority provided the basis for Malcolm X's belief in racial separation. When he was a follower of the Black Muslim faith under Elijah Muhammad, Malcom X reasoned that ". . .because we don't have any hope or confidence or faith in the American white man's ability to bring about a change in the *injustices* that exist, instead of asking or seeking to integrate into the American society we want to face the facts of the problem the way they are, and separate ourselves."

When rebellion burst forth in July 1967 a militant Negro group in Detroit, the Inner City Organizing Committee, invoked injustice, not inequality, in sending the following telegram to the U.S. Attorney General, the Michigan Attorney General, and the president of the Michigan State Bar:

The fundamental cause of the black rebellion in Detroit as elsewhere is the injustice which is being practiced against black people. Further injustice in the courts will only increase the alienation of black people and make continued violence inevitable. Increasingly to black people justice is more important than law and order and must be guaranteed by all agencies of government if a society in which black men and white men can live together is to be possible.

The establishment of justice to supplant equality means an entirely new perspective. Individuals advancing the Negro cause along the pathway of justice must not only establish closer affinity with radical black leaders such as David Walker, Frederick Douglass, Robert F. Williams, Marcus Garvey, and Malcolm X but also with the advocacy of revolution rather than reform. While the dispute focusing upon the role of violence in the struggle to win a just rather than an equal cause rages among Negroes, the black leader nonetheless shifts from the role of a mere critic to a radical figure—from an advocate of reform to a proponent of revolution—in seizing upon demands for justice. Where he once contemplated the possibility of parity with whites by amending America to accommodate the Negro, he must now proclaim an inevitable necessity for altering the very fabric of White America; where he once sought acceptance as an equal, he must now overturn all America to win his sense of justice; where he could be content with integration, he must now express contempt; instead of being the subject of change, he must be the instigator of change.

As White America implements economic repudiation of Negroes, Black America responds in kind, insisting upon a *new* America. There is something wrong *with* the system itself, not something *within* the system. The entire system is so corrupt in so many ways that it cannot be cured but rather must be discarded. Negroes are "a people who have been oppressed by the system," exhorts Stokely Carmichael, "who have tried, unsuccessfully, to coexist peacefully within this system for 400 years. We have no other alternative but to take arms and fight for our total liberation and for a total revolution in the United States." He goes on to inform his audience, "We want you to know that ours is not a struggle for peace, for law and order. Ours is a struggle for *justice*, equality and the redistribution of wealth within the U.S. . . ." The bid for justice heading the list of grievances induces the call for revolution resting, according to Carmichael, upon violence; a peaceful upheaval cannot cast aside what must be replaced to bring the Negro into his own being.

Martin Luther King eventually advanced a revolutionary call to bring forth a just order for all mankind. "A true revolution of values," he asserted, "will soon cause us to question the fairness and justice of many of our past and present policies. We are called to play the Good Samaritan on life's roadside; but that will be only an initial act. One day the whole Jericho Road must be transformed so that men and women will not be beaten and robbed as they make their journey through life." He appealed to America as "the richest and most powerful nation in the world," to "lead the way in this revolution of values." The revolt, a revamping of basic values, must come however through nonviolent social change. While sharing the revolutionary ideology of Carmichael, King abhorred embracing violent tactics to institute a new social order; he encouraged radical change for today, just as he favored reform for the accomplishment of equality yesterday, to attain justice through peaceful confrontation of the opposition.

Observers other than Negroes demonstrate the affinity between justice and revolution; a number of white writers call for a revolution in setting forth justice to settle the racial issue. A ". . .new order must be based on justice—and we must understand that justice is neither an abstraction, nor a sentiment, nor a relationship, but an *act*," Charles Silberman argues. "When the Prophets of old spoke of justice, their injunction was not to *be* just but to *do* justice; it is the act that counts." And to see that justice is done, Silberman affirms, "nothing less than a radical reconstruction of American society is required if the Negro is to be able to take his rightful place in American life. And the reconstruction," he continues, "must begin not just in Oxford, Mississippi, or Birmingham, Alabama, but in New York, Philadelphia, Chicago, and other great cities of the North as well."

There is a growing disenchantment among Negroes with the values of White America, a questioning of the merit to join. The Negro perceives the collapse of American civilization in failing to deliver justice to all. It was once thought possible to achieve "economic rights, economic freedom, economic citizenship, and public power" by "the enlargement and broadening of the base of civil rights to involve the basic freedoms." Such notions fail to meet compelling needs, since there could be considerable civil rights achievements without economic opportunity in light of the economics of automation. Consequently, Farmer, adhering to thoughts of justice, maintains that CORE "must inject Negro activity into the political life of the community. It must teach Negroes to act upon America in America in the presence of Americans. It must begin the great task of redefining nationalism and redefining integration, so that we can incorporate proud black men and self-assertive black communities as legitimate partners in a *new* America." And King portrayed a bleak possibility of a faltering America, clearly stating the imperative for recovery:

> Arnold Toynbee has said that some twenty-six civilizations have risen upon the face of the earth. Almost all of them have descended into the junk heaps of destruction. The decline and fall of these civilizations, according to Toynbee, was not caused by external invasions but by internal decay. *They failed to respond creatively to the challenges impinging upon them.* If Western civilization does not now respond constructively to the challenge to banish racism, some future historian will have to say that a great civilization died because it lacked the soul and commitment to make *justice a reality for all men.*

How can the Negro's shift from the banner of equality to justice and his outcries for a new America rising out of the ashes of racism through a creative black effort be explained?

As we have seen, the Negro reached new heights of prosperity, although somewhat erratic at times, during and through the Second World War and to the end of the Korean War. But in spite of improved economic circumstances, the Negro continued to feel the restraints of being colored in White America. To be sure, the Negro fully appreciated white animosity for all the centuries of his existence upon American soil, yet the ten years following the Second World War etched upon his memory more fully the failure of whites to extend the privilege to qualified Negroes. With economic success more apparent than at any other time, the Negro insisted more than ever on equality. Being in a better economic position, the Negro reasoned he needed only the opportunity to be equal to whites regardless of color to take full advantage of America's blessings. The demands for integration spread from the lips of millions, black and white alike, working with the assumption that the dismantling of racial barriers blocking the avenues of success would initiate another era of opportunity. As one legal restraint faded after another in the courts of law, as one civil rights bill after another passed from the halls of Congress to the White House, and as one Negro after another registered upon the voting rolls for the first time, Negroes sensed the assurance of acceptance into mainstream America.

But then came the late fifties and early sixties. Suddenly the Negro grew aware of his deterioration relative to whites. Finding himself among the unemployed in numbers unequal to whites, he learned that any rights bestowed might as well remain denied unless they can be fully practiced. Still, his yearning to be received by White America caused him to voice renewed appeals for equality in spite of new economic conditions; he remained convinced that civil rights assured economic rights. The words of Ralph Bunche in the early sixties express the view of most Negroes in this state of mind:

> I do not doubt that my wants and feelings are fairly representative of those of most of my race. I want to be a man on the same basis and level as any white citizen—I want to be as free as the whitest citizen. I want to exercise, and in full, the same rights as the white American. I want to be eligible for employment exclusively on the basis of my skills and employability, and for housing solely on my capacity to pay. I want to have the same privileges, the same treatment in public places as every other person. But this should not be read by anyone to mean that I want to be white; or that I am "pushy," seeking to go where I am not wanted. Far from it. I am as proud of my origin, ancestors, and race as anyone could be. Indeed, I resent nothing more than a racial slur or stigma. I want to go and to do only where and what all Americans are entitled to go and to do.

It would not be until the mid-1960s that Negroes seriously reflected upon their *own* values as expressed by Ralph Bunche. And upon reflection they detected a White America fulfilling *their* demands—"employment exclusively on the basis of . . . skills and employability." Indeed! As whites extended more of the equality Negroes sought, the more certain the colored would fall behind. In being treated more like whites, Negroes became less like whites by the terms administered under equality.

The Negro then became conscious of his economic as well as his racial plight. The spread of automation spread havoc within the black communities throughout the nation, and the appearance of mechanization for the production of crops posed the loss of jobs for Negroes on southern farms. To be equal would invite total oblivion; to attack only racism while neglecting the economic motives of White America offered little hope for Negro salvation. The elimination of racism could not be achieved while the Negro's economic status deteriorated. Thus, to meet both racist and economic issues, the Negro activist now promotes a drastic reformulation of race relations and the economic order. He undertakes the task to define what it means to be a human being made superfluous not only on the basis of race but also economics.

Editor's Note:
    A thought-provoking proposal is presented here that suggests a "Negro Bill of Rights" modeled after the G.I. Bill. This Bill of Rights is based on a quantifiable debt accrued from the subsidization of white affluence by black impoverishment.

WHAT WHITES OWE BLACKS

RICHARD AMERICA

Herbert Gans wrote an illuminating article last spring in the *New York Times Magazine*, in which he raised the welfare issue in a relatively new way. He expressed the view that "ultimately an end to the welfare problem requires either remaking the economy so that it produces full employment at a living wage, or altering public beliefs about welfare so that the government will provide the unneeded and underpaid with a decent income."

Altering public beliefs requires that new information and analysis be made broadly available. Gans touched on the nub of the problem when he asked, "Who is, and who should be, subsidized by the government, either directly or through tax exemptions?" Later he noted, "We are still paying for the effects of slavery, and if things go on the way they are, our descendants may not get all the bills for polarization until the twenty-second century."

An emerging subject of interest—in think tanks, university economics departments, and soon in the mass media and public debate—is the thesis that not only are the effects of slavery still being felt, but the benefits from slavery and from discrimination are still being enjoyed by parts of the population. These sectors of the public, the "haves," do not acknowledge this fact; probably they do not recognize it. But such recognition is crucial for proper policy formulation. Research leading to a broad understanding of how slavery and discrimination economically benefit the upper-income, white, tax-paying population and corporations is essential.

This research is technically possible now, as it has not been previously. It only remains for the National Science Foundation, large private foundations such as Ford, Rockefeller, or Mellon, and congressional committees—such as Senator Mondale's Subcommittee on Evaluation and Planning of Social Programs, or Representative Bollings's Subcommittee on Urban Affairs—to fund the research and to publicize the findings. Several sets of research projects should go forward simultaneously on the subject so that a range of findings can be presented and the differing assumptions and calculating techniques examined.

Let us look again at Gans: "If the excluded and underpaid, who are citizens and taxpayers like everyone else, and actually pay a higher proportion of their income in taxes than anyone else, had to be incorporated into the economy as full members, they would reduce the affluence of the majority. Consequently, if the poor indirectly subsidize the affluent by being discriminated against, the affluent ought to subsidize the poor in return by income in lieu of work."

This is in substantial contrast to Richard Nixon's, and most corporate leaders' current views on work and income. What Gans says, in effect, is that there is a debt. It is a debt from the affluent, largely white, upper-income groups to the poor and especially, if we look at the economic history of slavery and discrimination, to the black poor.

"Opponents of this position," Gans wrote, "will argue that before we resort to paying without requiring work, the poor ought to be forced to take the jobs they are now reluctant to take, whatever the wage; in a similar vein, whites who came up the hard way have insisted that the black poor ought to make it the same way instead of going on welfare."

Gans then noted that this argument ignores the fact that "the blacks came up in harder ways than anyone else, having worked as slaves for no pay whatever." The fact that the benefits of slavery and post-slavery discrimination are now beginning to be noted in the respectable media is a tremendously important sign. Without that recognition of the basic problem—involuntary income transfer, the historical black subsidization of whites—there is little chance that we will develop appropriate domestic policies on race and urban problems. Poverty is largely a condition caused by historical income transfers.

Amatai Etzioni wrote in *TransAction*, September, 1970, "The majority of Middle America now feels that Negroes already have the same or better opportunity than white Americans in getting jobs, education, housing and other advantages." Etzioni pointed out that the majority—tax-paying, white Americans—tend to resist domestic programs that seem to favor one group. They are much more likely to support programs that are believed to benefit everyone, the only exceptions being programs aimed explicitly at a group that a majority considers deserving of charity—such as the needy, hungry, or aged.

He characterized two motives operating—the politics of guilt and the politics of self-interest: "The first allows support for a group other than your own; the second requires that only your own group's interests merit priority. The politics of guilt are effective only as long as the amounts involved are not very large, times are prosperous, and the recipients are or seem to be grateful; their gratitude is the major payoff to the donor groups whose guilt is to be relieved."

Importantly, Etzioni noted that "in recent years, the majority has come to think of blacks as ungrateful." The concept of quantifiable social debt will allow us to get beyond notions of gratitude—of the deserving and undeserving poor.

Turning to the legislation of the nineteen-sixties, Etzioni said, "The liberals often proceeded as if it would suffice to motivate the public to support civil rights and antipoverty legislation on the basis of altruism and guilt (the first kind of motive), and that the political payoff would be limited to relief from a bad conscience; however, this relief does not carry programs very far even for those liberals who do have a bad conscience—many conservatives do not feel a special obligation to the poor or the minorities."

What are we speaking of in the case of the debt concept? Guilt or self-interest? I believe that it falls somewhere in between. Most upper-middle and upper-income whites—including corporate leaders—do not feel guilty about the effects of slavery and discrimination. Most are not yet even conscious of any benefits flowing to them. Likewise, they are not yet really aware of the continuation of economic discrimination as being in any sense in their self-interest. If anything, they would be motivated to deal with the debt concept and to support redistributive programs on the basis that once a debt is established, and the concept gains legitimacy, they would prefer to be consistent with American virtues, among which is the reasonably prompt and full payment of legitimate and agreed-upon debts.

It is on that basis, I believe, that a coherent policy dealing with family assistance, job creation, revenue sharing, and the general rebuilding of the urban scene can be based. But at the moment we are witnessing a contrary phenomenon.

The *Atlantic Monthly*, in an editorial of March, 1971, said: "What is becoming clear in the President's proposals is a rather definitive politics of class. Not only is much of the Great Society (i.e., help for the poor) to be dismantled, but the upper classes are to be relieved of some of their relative share of the tax burden. This could be done partly through lifting the requirements that state and local governments put up some of the money for federal programs. The Administration is also working up a proposal for a value-added tax (i.e., a national sales tax)."

The *Atlantic* column reported on Joseph Alsop, who had said that the President wants "to finance reasonable reductions in the present corporate and personal income taxes" and to allow reductions in property and other state and local taxes. This would result in a redistribution of the tax burden from the upper to the lower classes, and possibly a net reduction in taxing and spending for the public sector. Key aspects of the Administration's new economic policy dramatically bear out this forecast."

How much information and analysis would be required to persuade the majority of those white Americans earning more than, say ten thousand dollars a year, and their business leaders and legislative representatives that there is really any such thing as a debt owed to the poor, and specifically to the nonwhite poor? I would guess a great deal, and that the debate would have to extend over many months. It is timely that it is beginning now with a Presidential campaign just ahead. But the solution to our dilemmas requires nothing less than such persuasion.

Listen to the words of Theodore Gilman, writing to the editor of the black weekly newspaper, the New York *Amsterdam News* (February 14, 1970):

It seems to me that the key reason for the gap between the races is the just about total failure of generations of whites to confront the 'Great Atrocity,' i.e., slavery. . . .

The blindness with which most whites view slavery is not unlike the drunkard who suffers a blackout; he vaguely realizes that something awful happened during his binge but, rather conveniently, he can't quite put his finger on it. . . .

Most whites respond to questions about slavery with a mixture of anger and ignorance. It is also interesting to note that many blacks in confrontation with whites fail to reveal their true passions, their deeply rooted hatred of the white man because of slavery.

As a white myself, I feel this is true because to put the matter out in the open. . . would weaken its usefulness as, one might say, a secret weapon to be aimed at benighted whites. If I am accurate here then we have the sad spectacle of self-defeating game-playing on both sides.

Is there any way to bring white Americans to a fully conscious acceptance of its past and present complicity in one of the world's most heinous events? Does white America have the guts, the stamina, the honesty to cope with the truth? I don't know but I shall continue to try to find out.

The spirit of continuing to try to find out is essential. It motivates the increasing interest in research into the economics of race, and particularly into the economic benefits that continue to flow from past slavery and current discrimination into today's generations of upper-income white voters and taxpayers, personal and corporate.

Suppose such research is accomplished, the results made public, and the sums found to be very large, in the hundreds of billions of dollars. What can be done about it?

One remedy was proposed by the Schickle Environmental Development Company of Ithaca, New York, in a rather remarkable and largely unnnoticed full-page advertisement in the *New York Times* of November 17, 1967: *"AN OPEN LETTER TO CONGRESS, PRESIDENT JOHNSON, AND THE PEOPLE OF THE UNITED STATES."* Schickle proposed a National Act of Restitution:

It is now over two hundred years since the Negroes of the United States were brought here in slavery, and while it is over one hundred years since the abolition of slavery, its brand still exists in the minds of both blacks and whites. . . .

Despite the temptation for whites to disclaim any responsibility for what happened in the past, we do not believe that there exists a responsible American who does not feel guilt about the situation. The truth is that 'the sins of the fathers are visited upon the sons,' and that, like it or not, we must cope with the situation left us by our ancestors, or prepare to be guilty of handing down to our children the fruits of our indifference. . . .

We propose a national act of restitution to the Negro, which would last for twenty-one years and cut across an entire generation. It would be a Negro Bill of Rights patterned after the G.I. Bill of Rights. . . .

The G.I. Bill . . . was a nation's way of making up for the disruption to their lives that the war had caused. Who can calculate the benefits to individuals, families, and to the nation from that act of national generosity and foresight?

The Negro Bill of Rights would be our attempt, however inadequate, to make up for a hundred years of educational and economic deprivation, and unequal treatment.

This corporation suggested that such a bill would include a right to free education; free medical and dental care; and very low-interest, long-term, high-ratio loans for the purchase of homes and business enterprises: "The benefits of this program would be his [the Negro's] by right. It would make him an important economic power. . . . In addition to being a payment on a moral debt to the Negro, the program would be an economic, social, and political benefit to the nation."

The Schickle proposal spoke of a debt accumulated over only a hundred years of deprivation, and here we are speaking of three hundred and fifty-two years. Likewise, it talked about a moral debt. Perhaps it is ultimately a moral debt, but it is also a quantifiable debt. It is researchable, and statistical techniques will enable us to gauge roughly the magnitude of the debt in 1971 dollars. It is moral to pay debts once established and agreed upon, and in that sense it is a moral debt. But the crucial point here is that we can, using the latest social, scientific, and statistical techniques, measure the subsidy from blacks to whites (and perhaps generally from the have-nots to the haves), to compute the income that has been involuntarily transferred upward.

There would of course be a great deal of initial resistance to the concept and to the implications—fiscal and spiritual—of such research and such debate. But it is reasonable to suppose that once the research is completed and the results made public and fully debated, the idea, if it has scientific merit, will rather quickly gain fairly wide acceptance, including acceptance among business leaders. Its policy implications can then be made tangible in the form of redistributive programs which would be based largely on the orderly taxing power of government at all levels.

What we would have is a new rationale for a domestic Marshall Plan, an idea that has been frequently offered and that is most commonly associated with the late director of the National Urban League, Whitney Young.

The domestic Marshall Plan estimated that comprehensive solutions to health, education, welfare, housing, and related urban problems would cost in the range of two hundred billion dollars over a period of ten years. What may become clear is that, in a very real sense, that money, and possibly much more, is owned by white, upper-income groups and corporations to black lower-income groups. This is a bitter pill, no question. Like many such pills, taking it may be the best, indeed the only, way to health. And it should greatly help to settle the question of relative social responsibilities of business and government.

THE LEGAL, SOCIAL, AND IDEOLOGICAL FORCES THAT INFLUENCED THE DEVELOPMENT OF THE BLACK COMMUNITY

CARLENE YOUNG

Whom they have injured they also hate.— Seneca.

The great American ideals of life, liberty, the pusuit of happiness, and the dignity of the individual are excellent starting points from which to assess the plight of the black American. From their inception these ideals have been exclusive and selective in applicability. The Constitutional Convention of 1787 was concerned with slavery only insofar as it determined how long the importation of slaves should continue and whether slaves were merely property or human beings as well. The result was the infamous "three-fifths compromise," whereby a slave, for purposes of representation and taxation, was considered three-fifths free and two-fifths chattel property. The "self-evident truth" that all men are created equal was a sentiment expressed by a majority of men who were themselves slaveholders. How these conflicting postures are to be reconciled is the key to understanding American democracy, and for this reason, the black experience may well serve as the catalyst for the confrontation between democratic ideals and racist realities.

The combinations of forces that resulted in the African slave trade, the institution of slavery in the United States, the subsequent emancipation and subordination of blacks and the attitudes and ideologies that provided the foundation and support for these endeavors were all essential components in the creation of what we now know as the black American. Very seldom have Americans left to chance those things that are conducive to their benefit and interests. This has never been demonstrated more clearly than in the case of the black man, whose role and function in the society has been explicitly legislated, reinforced, and maintained. The point at which it became economically desirable to dehumanize the African was the point at which the legal, religious, political, and social forces moved to ensure this condition.

Slavery: similarities and contrasts

Slavery, in and of itself, cannot be considered uniquely aimed at blacks, particularly in view of the fact that slavery has been one of the universals in human society. Slavery existed in the most noted ancient civilizations—Egypt, Babylonia, Greece, and Rome, among others. In fact, the experience of slavery in the ancient world was so common that Plato ventured to suggest that "Every man has many slaves among his ancestors," while Cicero's famous advice to Atticus was "Do not obtain your slaves from Britain, because they are so stupid and so utterly incapable of being taught that they are not fit to form part of the household of Athens."[1] As C. W. Greenidge points out, "Slavery arises from wars and conquest, and could even be said to represent an advance upon a more primitive practice. For at first man simply killed his victims, and sometimes ate them. Only when he adopted a settled way of life did he find it more useful to spare their lives and enslave them, thus freeing himself from the burden of regular work."[2] Today, some authorities maintain that slavery still exists in isolated parts of the world.

The Code of Hammurabi, established in the golden age of Babylonia, around 1750 B.C., took the universal practice of enslavement of war captives for granted and made provisions for the ransom of state officials and the remarriage of women whose husbands were taken prisoners. In addition to captives, slaves came from the ranks of defaulting debtors, unemployed men and women who sold themselves voluntarily, and minors who were either sold outright by their parents or who were forced into a position in which only slavery could save their lives. There were no slave merchants or trade *per se*. The same merchant who dealt in wheat, cattle, real estate, etc., also dealt in slaves. The slave could be adopted into the family, manumitted, or could buy his freedom. Slavery was considered a misfortune that could befall any man. This new status was not irrevocable. To the ancients, "The slave is a man and suffers from the same pains, and delights in the same joys, that all men do.... The distinction between slavery and freedom is a product of accident and misfortune, and the free man might have been a slave."[3] The equality of human nature was the underlying premise in all of the societies that found themselves with slaves, even black slaves. Frank Tannenbaum, noting the differences between slavery in Spanish America and colonial America, points out:[4]

The master had, in fact, no greater moral status than the slave, and spiritually the slave might be a better man than his master. *Las Siete Partidas* was framed within this Christian doctrine, and the slave had a body of law, protective of him as a human being which was already there when the Negro arrived and had been elaborated long before he came upon the scene. And when he did come, the Spaniard may not have known him as a Negro, but the Spanish law and mores knew him as a slave and made him the beneficiary of the ancient legal heritage.

Slaves could marry even against the will of their masters, and once married they could not be sold apart, except under conditions permitting them to live as man and wife. They were encouraged to earn their freedom. They could hire themselves out and keep part of their wages. Parents having ten children could claim freedom. Slaves could appeal to the courts, serve as witnesses, and purchase their freedom in installments. The most significant difference between the two systems lay in the fact that:[5]

The element of human personality was not lost in the transition to slavery from Africa to the Spanish or Portuguese dominions. He remained a person even while he was a slave. He lost his freedom, but he retained his right to become free again and, with that privilege, the essential elements in moral worth that make freedom a possibility.

Another crucial distinction pointed out by Tannenbaum:[6]

He was never considered a mere chattel, never defined as unanimated property, and never under the law treated as such. His master never enjoyed the powers of life and death over his body, even though abuses existed and cruelties were performed. Even if justice proved to be blind, the blindness was not incurable. The Negro slave under this system had both a judicial and a moral personality even while he was in bondage.

Taking into consideration the many variations and differences among peoples and without losing sight of instances of cruelty and inhumane treatment afforded slaves on the whole, no other country can equal in systematic perniciousness the form that slavery took in the United States. Neither economic exploitation, fear or large numbers of slaves and revolts, nor conditions produced by slavery itself can satisfactorily explain a dehumanization based on a race fixation unequalled in the annals of history. Never before in the history of the world had slavery been a condition predicated solely on race. Although economic opportunism rather than racial prejudice dictated the beginnings of Negro slavery in North America, by the end of the seventeenth century and thereafter, only Negroes were slaves. Benjamin Quarles tells us:[7]

The increased needs for slaves in colonial America came at a time when slavery had become synonymous with Negro. Whites were never slaves; a master might try to lengthen the term of his white servant for life. The increased need for slaves also came at a time when Negro

servitude had become Negro slavery. Not completed until the latter half of the seventeenth century, slavery was a gradual development, one halting step followed by another. The legal conversion of a Negro into a chattel may be traced in Virginia, where the statutes and court decisions on slavery were more numerous than in any other colony.

Maryland has the distinction of having declared in 1663 that "all negroes or other slaves within the province, and all negroes and other slaves to be hereafter imported into the province, shall serve *durante vita.*"[8] Stanley Elkins explains the development as "the most implacable race-consciousness yet observed in virtually any society. It was evolved in the Southern mind, one might say, as a simple syllogism, the precision of whose terms paralleled the precision of the system itself. All slaves are black; slaves are degraded and contemptible; therefore all blacks are degraded and contemptible and should be kept in a state of slavery."[9] That the black, as a species, was thus contemptible seemed to follow by observation. Elkins further clarifies:[10]

. . . The very thought of such a creature existing outside the pale of their so aptly devised system filled the most reasonable of Southerners with fear and loathing. Quite apart from the demands of the system itself, this may account for many of the subsidiary social taboos—the increasing severity of the laws against manumission, the horror of miscegenation, the depressed condition of the Free Negro, and his peculiar place in Southern society: all signs of how difficult it was to conceive a non-slave colored class. Nothing in their experiences had prepared them for it; such a class was unnatural, logically awry, a blemish on the body politic, an anomaly for which there was no intellectual category.

African ancestry

The ancestors of the Afro-American came from various regions but were primarily of West African descent. The Gold Coast, Senegal, Congo, Niger Delta, and Guinea Coast were the points of origin for the vast majority. Their history and background present a striking contrast with the image created by the advocates of slavery. The Dahomey, Yoruba, Ashanti, Ibo, Bambara, Fanti, and Mandingo are some of the peoples who populated these areas and are still a part of present-day Africa. The early kingdoms were products of an iron-using superiority. "Everywhere in the ancient world iron proved a revolutionary equipment that enabled men to build new and more complex societies."[11] Another historian states, "Iron and steel enterprises, foundries, artistry, and skill in the treatment of gold and jewelry impressed early European visitors."[12]

Although these communities were essentially agricultural, they "manifest a considerable degree of specialization, from which are derived the arrangements for the exchange of goods. . . . Mutual self-help is found not only in agricultural work, but in the craft guilds, characteristically organized on the basis of kinship."[13] Ironworkers, weavers, wood carvers, traders, potters, basketmakers, bronze casters, blacksmiths, and goldsmiths were some of the specialized crafts. The Ashanti, known for their silk and cotton cloth designs (*Kente* cloth) "are also famous for the metal gold weights they cast from bronze, accurate to the fraction of an ounce and fashioned in a wide range of representative and geometric figures."[14]

Dahomey had a plantation system very much similar to the ones found later in the American colonies. Division of labor was the rule rather than the exception in these societies. Royal courts related the various social systems and insured orderly process. "One outstanding fact about the old states of Africa, well understood in earlier times but afterwards forgotten, is that they were seldom or never conquered from outside the continent. They remained inviolate."[15] Dahomey was not captured by the French until 1894. The Ashanti met the British in battle seven times and defeated them at least four of those times. Kumasi, the capital of the Ashanti kingdom, was taken over only in 1901.

History and historians

R.S. Rattray, Melville Herskovits, C.K. Meek, W.R. Bascom, J.S. Harris, T. Edward Bowdich, and Joseph Greenberg are just a few of the writers whose works have been almost entirely neglected, although they conducted scientific field studies, were excellent observers, and maintained objectivity in spite of the period in which they lived. On the other hand, Jerome Dowd, Joseph Tillinghast, and W.D. Weatherford have had the greatest influence on concepts dealing with the "Negro" African heritage, their emphasis on superstition and savagery giving much unwarranted support to racial stereotypes. Since the latter three writers all went to the same sources for their African materials and often referred to the works of each other, and since not one of them had any firsthand contact with any of the peoples about whom they wrote, "their substantial agreement in describing and, what is more significant, in evaluating the civilizations is not surprising. The unanimity of their findings is important for the

support is as afforded the concepts of an aboriginal cultural endowment of the Negro presented by any one of them."[16] "According to Tillinghast, African Negroes were 'savages,' subject to the 'unfathomable . . . mysterious force' of heredity."[17] A significant figure in American history is their pupil, Ulrich B. Phillips. "Phillips' interpretation of African life has had a profound effect upon students of American Negro slavery, but it depends on the now discredited work of Joseph Tillinghast and Jerome Dowd."[18] Their colleagues have repudiated many of their claims. Tillinghast, Dowd, and others upon whose works Phillips draws have applied untenable methods, made dubious assumptions, and produced work that anthropologists today consider of little or no value. Phillips' major work, *American Negro Slavery* (1918), noted for its scope, depth, and original sources, was a scholastic triumph. It had for its basic assumption the innate and inherited racial inferiority of Negroes. Phillips, the son of a Georgia merchant, was "reared in an atmosphere of reverence for the values and standards of the old planter class."[19] Travelers' accounts and legal codes were of little importance to him; his primary source was plantation records, which emphasized the geniality and cheerfulness of the slave-master relationship and the contentment and childlikeness of the faithful black. "On the whole the plantations were the best schools yet invented for the mass training of that sort of inert and backward people which the bulk of the American Negroes represented."[20] The twentieth century had been waiting for one of its own to legitimatize the racial inferiority treatise.

Transformation begins

The metamorphosis—the change from African to slave to Negro—took place gradually but implacably. Africans brought to this country as slaves were soon divested of as much of their heritage as systematic dehumanization could accomplish. Some remnants of the old life style did remain and helped shape the form that the Black Experience took in the United States. As successive shiploads of slaves reached these shores, however, they found themselves increasingly adapting to the accommodations Africans were forced to make as chattels, to what became the established "Negro" behavior. The newly purchased slave had to be broken in; he had to become habituated to plantation life—slavery—in a strange, different land. This involved separation from all those who knew and cared for him, placement under special overseers, acclimatization, learning to understand and speak a new language, learning to eat new food, mastering unfamiliar work assignments, rejecting suicide, and accepting alienation and degradation. Slave life was expendable and mortality was high. It was considered cheaper to buy than to breed; that is, economics and practicality deemed it better to work every bit of strength out of a slave and then replace him instead of attempting to maintain his good health. An "act about the casual killing of slaves" in Virginia provided that if any slave resisted his master and under the extremity of punishment chanced to die, his death was not to be considered a felony and the master was to be acquitted. This law was repeated with minor variations throughout the slave states. Frederick Douglass, recalling the terror and atrocities of slave life, repeats a common saying in Maryland, " 'It was worth but half a cent to kill a nigger, and a half a cent to bury him,' and the facts of my experience go far to justify the practical truth of this strange proverb."[21]

Slave codes

The treatment of slaves and laws regulating slavery were left entirely to the colonies. "Although English common law before 1620 did not recognize human slavery, neither did it prohibit. The American colonists, then, were free to develop their own law; this was made easier by their distance from the mother country and a judicial ruling that the colonies, since they were the king's plantations, did not come under the English common law."[22] Slavery had not existed in England itself since the Norman conquest in 1066, and judges had ruled in 1569 "that England was too pure an air for slaves to breathe in."[23] As a result, each colony determined who was a slave and exactly how this slave was to be treated. "As a rule, a slave code was an accurate reflection of the fears and apprehensions of the colony, the extent to which the white settlers thought it necessary to go to keep the slaves from getting out of hand—staging a revolt, disturbing the peace, or running away. Hence the more numerous the blacks, the more strict the slave codes."[24] The mere hint of a rebellion or slave unrest brought about stringent measures. "After the Vesey uprising in 1822 South Carolina enacted a law requiring the imprisonment of all Negro seamen during the stay of their vessel in port."[25]

Slave codes were the measures adopted by every slave state to ensure the proper relationship between slave and master. There were some minor variations, but the focal points were essentially the same, covering every aspect of life for the chattel property. "The regulatory statutes were frankly repressive and the whites made no apologies for them. They represented merely the reduction to legal phraseology of the philosophy of the South with regard to the institution of slavery."[26] Slaves were not to be taught to read or write, employed in setting type in printing offices, or given books or pamphlets. The beating of drums or blowing of horns were also forbidden. A slave could not enter into contracts, marry, or offer testimony against a white man. He could not visit homes of whites or free blacks. Assembly without a white person present was unlawful. Slaves could not practice medicine, or raise cotton, swine, horses, mules, or cattle. They could not leave the plantation without a pass, which had to be shown to any white man who asked to see it. The striking of a white person, even in self-defense was forbidden. The working day was limited to fifteen hours. Slaves could not hire themselves out or own property. No slave could possess arms and ammunition. Further, "neither baptism nor a white father gave him the status of a free man. Some Negroes were already free, but all others thereafter arriving in the colonies—an ever increasing number—were doomed to lifelong slavery, they and their children."[27]

Slave patrols were a primary responsibility for enforcement of Black Codes. These "pader ollers" were hated and feared by slave and freedman; they were the particular nemesis of fleeing fugitives and their means of transportation, the "underground railroad." Punishment was swift and brutal:[28]

> Violations of the state and local codes were misdemeanors or felonies subject to punishment by justices, sheriffs, police, and constabulary. Whipping was the most common form of public punishment for less than capital offenses. By mid-nineteenth century branding and mutilation had declined ... slave felons still had their ears cropped. Mississippi and Alabama continued to enforce the penalty of 'burning in the hand' for felonies not capitally punished. But most slave offenders were simply tied up in the jail or at a whipping post and flogged.

The slave family was viewed as an impediment to the fluidity of the selling and breeding process. Advertisements from the newspapers of this era clearly indicate there was no regard for the family, no questions of the right of the owner to sell his slaves separately. The double standard had become an integral part of the society and was clearly evident in the statutes:[29]

> State criminal codes dealt more severely with slaves and free Negroes than with whites. They made certain acts felonies when committed by whites; and assigned heavier penalties to Negroes than whites convicted of the same offense. In Louisiana a slave who struck his master, a member of the master's family, or the overseer, 'so as to cause a contusion or shedding

of blood' was to suffer death—as was a slave on a third conviction for striking a white.

This transformation from African to Negro also involved adaptation and internalization of patterns of role behavior conducive to acceptance of racial inferiority and subjugation. The means used to assure this stigma of color were neither haphazard nor accidental. On the contrary, historical evidence paints a portrait of legal and extra-legal contrivances, the institutionalization of practices and ideologies warranting the derogation of black people:[30]

A wise master did not take seriously the belief that Negroes were natural born slaves. He knew better. He knew that Negroes freshly imported from Africa had to be broken into bondage; that each succeeding generation had to be carefully trained. This was no easy task, for the bondsman rarely submitted willingly. Moreover, he rarely submitted completely. Slave masters wrote discourses on the proper approaches and most effective means of creating the ideal slave. Five major steps can be identified.[31] The first step was to establish and maintain absolute and strict discipline. Slaves were expected to obey instantly and at all times and never to question the orders of the master, no matter what the circumstances. The second step was to implant in the slave the inexpungeable consciousness of his own personal and racial inferiority. Black skin was made to seem the emblem of degradation. The third step was to awe the slave with a sense of the master's enormous power, which was contrasted with the slave's total powerlessness. The fourth step was to induce the slave to identify his well-being with the success of his master's enterprises. The final step was to extinguish all vestiges of independence and initiative and to persuade the slave that he was wholly dependent on his master for every material need. Douglass comments on the seeming adoption of this role:[32]

> Slaveholders ever underrate the intelligence with which they have to grapple. . . . Ignorance is a high virtue in a human chattel; and as the master studies to keep the slave ignorant, the slave is cunning enough to make the master think he succeeds. The slave fully appreciates the saying, "where ignorance is bliss, 'tis folly to be wise."

Urban slaves

Not all slaves lived on plantations or farms. In 1850, there were 400,000 bondsmen living in cities. Large numbers of them possessed some skill, including those of engineers, coopers, carpenters, blacksmiths, brickmakers, stone masons, mechanics, shoe-makers, weavers, millers, and landscapers.[33] According to the Charleston census of 1848, there were more slave carpenters than there were free Negroes and whites, and there were slave tailors, barbers, cabinet makers, painters, plasterers, seamstresses, and the like.[34] They worked in textile mills and iron and lead mines and as stokers, lumberjacks, bakers, cotton press operators, dock laborers, stevedores, and clerks in stores. Almost every railroad in the ante-bellum South was built at least in part by bondsmen; in Georgia they constructed more than a thousand miles of roadbed.[35]

Many white artisans and laborers were violently opposed to the training of slaves and protested having to compete with them for jobs. By 1890 skilled Negro workers had been eliminated as competition for whites.

Religious factors

Religion played a major role in the particularistic developments of slavery in the Americas—the Catholic church dominating in Latin America and Protestant Christianity in North America. Tannenbaum in *Slave and Citizen* lists five popes, dating from Pius II, on October 7, 1462 to Gregory XVI, on December 3, 1839, who condemned the slave trade:[36]

> Without interfering with the institution of slavery where the domestic law accepted it, the church early condemned the slave trade and prohibited Catholics from taking part in it. The prohibition was not effective, though it in some measure may have influenced the Spaniards to a rather limited participation in the trade as such.

Another dimension added to the condemnation of the trade itself was the church's insistence that slave and master were equal in the sight of God. The master had an obligation to protect the spiritual integrity of the slave, and the slave had a right to be baptized and considered a member of the Christian community; in fact, the Catholic church insisted that masters bring their slaves to church to learn the doctrine and participate in the communion.[37] Preserving the sanctity and stability of marriage for all subjects, slave or free, was also one of the clergy's prime concerns. In these societies there was a general favoring of manumission. Once the Negro was free, he became an active functioning member of the community limited only by his own skills and abilities. Many of them became the great artists, musicians, sculptors and craftsmen in the society. The British and American settlements were almost exactly opposite in all respects. The English church felt that the privileges of Christianity should be denied the slaves, particularly as it might give them some claim to freedom. Some of the Protestant sects, however, like the Southern Baptists and Methodists, exhibited considerable antislavery sentiment. Yet Christianity provided one of the major rationales for slavery itself. According to U. B. Phillips, "They were heathens who by transportation to some Christian land might attain eternal bliss at the mere price of lifetime labor."[38] This position posed a dilemma for masters of slaves who were baptized and in cases where baptism might be interpreted as protection against enslavement. Soon, however, the legal machinery moved to remedy the situation. Virginia authorities in 1667 held that "Baptism does not alter the condition of a person as to his bondage or freedom; that divers masters freed from this doubt, may more carefully endeavor the propagation of christianity." Maryland in 1671 ruled, "Any Christianized slave is at all times hereafter to remain in servitude and bondage for all intention and purposes as he was and subject before becoming Christian or receiving of the sacraments of baptism." The Hamitic myth or curse of Canaan was regarded as the reason for the "all wise Creator's" dictum that the African (Ethiopian) be a servant of servants to his brethren."[39]

The church was an ardent ally of the slaveowner, arguing that the propagation of Christianity would tend to make slaves meek and submissive, rather than the reverse:[40]

Through religious instruction the bondsmen learned that slavery had divine sanction, that insolence was as much an offense against God as against the temporal master. They received the Biblical command that servants should obey their masters and they heard of the punishments awaiting the disobedient slave in the hereafter.... The master class understood, of course, that only a carefully censored version of Christianity could have this desired effect. Inappropriate Biblical passages had to be deleted; sermons that might be proper for freemen were not necessarily proper for slaves.

A Methodist missionary related a slave's confession that the Gospel had saved more rice for the master than all the locks and keys on the plantation. Religion played a major part, both positive and negative, in the life of the slave. For many it meant acquiescence and submission, but for others it provided the spark of hope needed to resist moral degradation, to escape and search for freedom, or to rebel and fight. Sojourner Truth, Harriet Tubman, Frederick Douglass, Gabriel Prosser, Denmark Vesey, and Nat Turner are but a few of the outstanding bondsmen who utilized religion as a force harnessed on behalf of their needs and goals. There were thousands more.

Owners and the owned

The aristocracy of the South was successful in creating the illusion of *noblesse oblige* with regards to slavery and the life of the plantation owner:[41]

Fully three-fourths of the white people of the South had neither slaves nor an immediate economic interest in the maintenance of slavery or the plantation system. And yet, the institution came to dominate the political and economic thinking of the entire South and to shape its social pattern.

The census of 1860 records 12,302,000 people in the slave states. Total U. S. population was 31,443,321. Total Negro population was 4,441,830. Almost 4,861,170 were white, 3,953,760 were slaves and 448,070 were free. In the South there were 384,884 slaveowners:[42]

If membership in the planter class required the ownership of at least twenty slaves, the "typical" slaveholder of 1860 certainly did not belong to it. For 88 percent of the owners held less than that number, 72 percent held less than ten and almost 50 percent held less than five.... The planter aristocracy was limited to some ten thousand families who lived off the labor of gangs of more than fifty slaves. The extremely wealthy families who owned more than a hundred slaves numbered less than three thousand, a tiny fraction of the southern plantation.

The profits and conveniences of the slaveowner —the predilection of a leisure class for the social graces, together with the "gentleman's code of honor"—were all part of the facade that hid a festering, reprehensible social and psychological system.

The planter's wealth and power depended on his reluctant laborers:[43]

The slaveholder commanded the products of another's labor, but by the same process was forced into dependence upon this other. This simultaneous dependence and independence contributed to that peculiar combination of the admirable and the frightening in the slaveholder's nature: his strength, graciousness, and gentility; his impulsiveness, violence, and unsteadiness. The sense of independence and the habit of command developed his poise, grace, and dignity, but the less obvious sense of dependence on a despised other made him violently intolerant of anyone and anything threatening to expose the full nature of his relationship to his slave.

Douglass, describing the Lloyd's plantation on which he was a slave, puts it this way:[44]

Viewed from his own table and not from the field, the colonel was a model of generous hospitality. . . .Who could say that the servants of Col. Lloyd were not well clad and cared for, after witnessing one of his magnificent entertainments. . . .Master and slave seem alike in their glory here. Can it all be seeming? . . .The poor slave, on his hard pine plank, but scantily covered with his thin blanket, sleeps more soundly than the feverish voluptuary who reclines upon his feather bed and downy pillow. Food, to the indolent lounger, is poison, not sustenance. Lurking beneath all their dishes, are invisible spirits of evil, ready to feed the self-deluded gourmandizers with aches, pains, fierce temper, uncontrolled passions, dyspepsia, rheumatism, lumbago and gout; and of these the Lloyds got their full share. To the pampered love of ease, there is no resting place.

Slaves were well aware that their labor benefited only the master. One critic of the productivity of slaves remarked,[45] "Half the population of the South is employed in seeing that the other half do their work, and they who do work, accomplish half what they might do under a better system." The "nigger hoe" and other tools were manufactured for their special use since the regular tools were destroyed almost as quickly as they received them. Virginia, where it was first introduced, fixed the hoe's weight at four pounds. Georgia and the Carolinas also adopted them. They were at least one-third heavier and stronger than those of northerners. Resistence took many forms, both covert and overt. Arson became a favorite method of retaliation:[46]

States made arson a capital crime; towns and cities kept mobilized in fear of it. . . .Unestimated millions of dollars went up in flames, and the setting of fires was so common that the American Fire Insurance Company of Philadelphia in 1820, had to decline making insurance in any of the slave states.

Raymond and Alice Bauer record, in "Day-to-Day Resistance to Slavery," observers' comments on this phenomena:[47]

A well-informed capitalist and slave-holder remarked: "In working niggers, we always calculate that they will not labor at all except to avoid punishment, and they will never do more than just enough to save themselves from being punished, and no amount of punishment will prevent their working carelessly or indifferent-

ly. It always seems on the plantations as if they took pains to break all the tools and spoil all the cattle that they possibly can, even when they know they'll be directly punished for it."

The same writers quote another source to the same end:[48]

The overseer rode among them, on a horse, carrying in his hand a raw-hide whip, constantly directing and encouraging them; but, as my companion and I, both, several times noticed, as often as he visited one line of the operations, the hands at the other end would discontinue their labor, until he turned to ride toward them again.

Court records belie the fact of the contented slave. Records of slaves killing masters, infanticide, self-destruction, destruction of property, runaways, and revolts tell the story. Yet there were many slaves who did not resist and succumbed to the malaise of inferiority and submission in will and behavior:[49]

Trained from the cradle up, to think and feel that their masters are superior, and invested with a sort of sacredness, there are few who can outgrow or rise above the control which that sentiment exercises.

Richmond required Negroes and mulattoes to step aside when whites passed by. Charleston slaves could not swear, smoke, walk with a cane, assemble at military parades, or make joyful demonstrations.[50] There was a proper way to walk—a gait not too proud in bearing, slumped shoulders, and bent head and lowered eyes when speaking to whites. The proper attitude was of utmost importance. It was to be apparent at all times that submissiveness was incorporated into the personality. A cheerful, happy-go-lucky demeanor was prized:[51]

Slaves are generally expected to sing as well as to work. A silent slave is not liked by master or overseers. "Make a noise, make a noise" and "bear a hand" are the words usually addressed to the slaves when there is silence amongst them.

Free blacks

There were always free blacks to contend with; some had established themselves as men of property before the introduction of slavery. In answering a question of a Dr. Morse of Liverpool, Madison wrote that free Negroes were "generally idle and depraved; appearing to retain the bad qualities of the slaves, with whom they continue to associate, without acquiring any of the good ones of the whites, from whom they continue separated by prejudices against their color, and other peculiarities."[52]

Table I gives the numbers of free and enslaved black people for the years 1790–1860.

TABLE I

Year	Slaves	Free
1790	697,897	59,466
1800	893,602	108,435
1810	1,191,362	186,466
1820	1,538,022	233,634
1830	2,009,043	319,599
1840	2,487,355	386,293
1850	3,204,313	434,495
1860	3,953,760	488,070

There were attempts to restrict and direct the lives of free blacks almost as stringent as the controls developed for slaves:[53]

Several states required registration, such as Virginia, Tennessee, Georgia, and Mississippi ....Florida, Georgia, and several other states compelled free Negroes to have white guardians. All Southern states required them to have passes; and if one was caught without a certificate of freedom, he was presumed to be a slave.

In several of the states they were given the opportunity to choose their master and reenslave themselves. Their freedom was precarious, and the community citizens did not accept them. Interestingly enough, free blacks and slaves "worked like brothers, each giving the other the benefit of any temporary advantage that it possessed."[54] Many freedmen owned slaves; loved ones and family members were often purchased. Other freedmen were large landholders, highly educated, and activists in the Abolition movement.

In 1845 Chancellor Harper, of the Supreme Court of South Carolina, made plain the reason for this discrimination against the free person of color:[55]

A free African population is a curse to any country...and the evil is exactly proportional to the number of such population. This race, however conducive they may be in a state of slavery...in a state of freedom and in the midst of a civilized community, are a dead weight to the progress of improvement. With few exceptions they become drones...governed mainly by the instincts of animal nature, they make no provisions for the morrow....They become pilferers and marauders, and corrupters of the slaves....

Although they were disfranchised in a majority of the states, they were still required to pay taxes. In 1840 only Massachusetts, New Hampshire, Vermont, and Maine permitted free blacks to vote. In the North, the upper and lower classes shared a common dislike for the freedman. To the wealthier members of society, it seemed that he served only to swell the relief rolls and increase the crime rate. To the laboring man, it seemed that he served mainly to force down wages. Massachusetts had already gone as far as it legally could when in 1800 it ordered the expulsion of 240 blacks who were not citizens of the state. "Ohio, meanwhile, attempted to prevent the immigration of others. In 1807, it forbade any black from entering the state without first posting bond guaranteeing good behavior. This was as near as Ohio could come to outright prohibition."[56]

Black codes

Black codes were enacted immediately after the Civil War and were aimed at restoring the antebellum relations between the races. They were models of the restrictive measures resorted to in the face of threatened equality. The harshest codes were found in Louisiana, Mississippi, and South Carolina. The South Carolina apprentice law, for example, stated,[57] "A child over the age of two years, born of colored parents, may be bound by the father...or mother as an apprentice...a male until...twenty-one years, and a female until...eighteen." Louisiana required all black people to register during the first ten days of January. They had to make contracts for the ensuing year or the year following expiration of the present contract. The Black Codes forbade assembly, voting, and serving on juries. Mississippi prohibited freedmen from owning or renting land outside of incorporated towns. Marriage now became a legal right, but statutes such as vagrancy laws could be interpreted to jail practically anyone whose behavior was disliked.[58]

The colored man was free in name only in many cases. The apprentice, vagrancy, and other provisions of these statutes forced the Negro into situations where he would be under the uncontrolled supervision of his former master or other white men who were ready and willing to exploit his labor.

The Black Codes were eventually abolished during the Reconstruction, but vestiges remain in contemporary vagrancy laws, lien laws, debt peonage, and convict-lease systems. It was not until March 1972 that the U. S. Supreme Court ruled vagrancy laws unconstitutional.

The ruthless determination of the whites is illustrated by the campaign plan of the South Carolina Democratic Party before the election of 1876. Article 12 of the plan stated, "Every Democrat must feel honor-bound to control the vote of at least one Negro, by intimidation, purchase, keeping him away or as each individual may determine, he may best accomplish it."[59] Article 16 stated, "Never threaten a man individually. If he deserves to be threatened, the necessities of the times require that he should die. A dead Radical is harmless—a threatened Radical or one driven off by threats from the scene of his operations is often troublesome, sometimes dangerous." This was also the era which spawned the Ku Klux Klan, the Knights of the White Camellia, the White Brotherhood, and similar secret organizations across the South. Their use of whippings, castrations, burnings, murder, and other forms of violence and intimidation against the black man and his supporters was aimed at the maintenance of white supremacy. Lynchings reached their peak at this time. The NAACP published a study, *Thirty Years of Lynching in the United States, 1889-1918*, and led the fight for an antilynch bill. According to another study, between 1889 and 1899, 1875 lynchings were reported.[60] Only one-fourth of these grew out of rape or accusations of rape. Serving as a witness in court, insisting on eating in a white restaurant, trying to "act like a white man," acting as a strikebreaker discussing a lynching, making boastful remarks, slapping a white boy, insisting on voting, throwing stones, uttering allegedly disrespectful remarks against President Wilson, being a member of Labor's Non-Partisan League, giving poor entertainment to whites, seeming too prosperous, riding on a train with white passengers, and not turning out of the road for automobile driven by white persons were some of the many reasons given for lynching.[61]

Jim Crow laws

A complete refinement of the previous legislative endeavors was to be found in the Jim Crow laws. These segregation codes[62]

> . . .lent the sanction of law to a racial ostracism that extended to churches and schools, to housing and jobs, to eating and drinking. Whether by law or by custom that ostracism extended to virtually all forms of public transportation, to sports and recreations, to hospitals, orphanages, prisons, and asylums, and ultimately to funeral homes, morgues, and cemeteries.

Neither were libraries, courts, juries, or churches exempt. These supposedly "separate but equal" provisions in the law solidified the caste lines for all blacks. Jim Crow legislation was financially and economically profitable only because it fostered discriminatory practices and facilitated the provision of inferior accommodations. Had the agencies of society been required to honor the "separate but equal" constitutionality, the cost would have been prohibitive. The legal system has been a tool, particularly in the South, manipulated by the white community to place privileges and power in the hands of the white populace and at the same time exploit, intimidate, and subjugate the black community. Myrdal reminds us that "illegal practices have also the sanction of tradition behind them. The pattern of illegality was firmly entrenched in Southern politics and public morals." He goes on to observe:[63]

> It is the custom in the South to permit whites to resort to violence and threats of violence against the life, personal security, property and freedom of movement of Negroes. There is a wide variety of behavior ranging from a mild admonition to murder, which the white man may exercise to control Negroes.

*   *   *

But quite apart from laws, and even against the law, there exists a pattern of violence against Negroes in the South upheld by the relative absence of fear of legal reprisal. Any white man can strike or beat a Negro, steal or destroy his property, cheat him in a transaction and even take his life, without much fear of legal reprisal.

*   *   *

> White people are accustomed—individually and in groups—to take the law into their own hands and to expect the police and the courts to countenance this and sometimes lend their active cooperation.

This lack of justice or impartiality on the part of the law and its agents was not lost upon the black community. The same laws that denied him schooling and free association with those who chose to associate with him, that denied him the right to hear testimony against a white, to enter into any contract, even marriage, or to serve on a jury, and that denied him suffrage (yet demanded that he pay taxes) all stemmed from the same body politic that today exhorts its citizenry to respect and obey the law. Again, to quote Myrdal:[64]

> They [black people] will not feel confidence in, and loyalty toward, a legal order which is entirely out of their control and which they sense to be inequitable and merely part of the system of caste suppression. Solidarity then develops easily in the Negro group, solidarity

against the law and the police. The arrested Negro often acquires the prestige of a victim, a martyr, or a hero, even when he is simply a criminal. It becomes part of race pride in the protective Negro community not to give up a fellow Negro who is hunted by the police.

Laws that have been passed to ensure civil rights have never been enforced with the consistency and vigor expended by those who would exclude the black American from the rights of citizenry. The freedom that the Emancipation Proclamation and the Fifteenth Amendment brought to black people was a prototype of the legalistic guarantees that were never to be honored. Over a century has passed with a plethora of laws enacted, sometimes to restrict and sometimes to foster a citizenship that is an accepted fact for those of the white race but still a goal for those of African ancestry.

Social Relations

Ideological commitment to white supremacy pervaded every aspect of life in the South. The primacy of the Anglo-Saxon was too vital a concern to be left to chance. Vigilantes, lynch mobs, the Klan, and various other agents of the citizenry enforced the mores of a nation committed to white superiority and black inferiority. Racial etiquette prescribed the acceptable social intercourse to be tolerated within mixed communities. The black person's place was fixed as a menial, servile, eager-to-please, in short, a "shiftless, irresponsible darky." The merest detail was attended to. He was never to be addressed by titles of respect, such as "Mr.," "Mrs.," or "Miss." On entering a white home they were expected to use the back door, and, "When driving their own cars they were expected to maintain their roles as Negroes and in all cases to give whites the right-of-way."[65] America's favorite greeting—the handshake—was included in the taboo.[66] "The white man may offer to shake hands with the Negro, but the Negro may not offer his hand to the white man." Although there were no laws to support this etiquette, the police and the courts considered racial etiquette an extension of the law, and[67]

> The courts recognize disturbance of the peace as having almost unlimited scope. The main sanctions are those of individual or group opinion and violence. Deprived of police and court protection, and usually dependent economically on white opinion, the Negro cannot take the risk of violating the etiquette.

This adherence to racial etiquette was essentially a southern phenomenon. Northern patterns took a different form, that of "institutionalizing and rendering impersonal a limited number of types of segregation."[68] There was much segregation of public facilities and private commercial establishments. Actually many stores, hotels, and other establishments refused service without excuse unless someone asked the police or the courts to take action Occasionally businesses displayed "Whites Only" signs. Indirect devices were also used to discourage black persons from seeking service, e.g., by telling him there was no food left in the restaurant or room in the hotel or motel, by giving him dirty or inedible food, by charging him outrageous prices, by insulting him verbally, and by hundreds of other ways of keeping facilities from him without violating the letter of the law. These tactics extended to residential segregation, refusal of credit or business loans, slow, inefficient deliveries to business men, and managerial refusals of services. Even today, there are many places in the North where black people know or are made to know that they are not welcome and are refused service on some pretext or are served discourteously.

A recent writer placed the entire matter of social relations in its proper perspective when he stated:[69]

> The most frequent complaint on the part of the Negroes is not about the restriction of social relations by etiquette but the restriction of economic privileges. This is prompted by direct and indirect refusals of white men to work with Negroes, and by objections to being served by them as clerks or as employees of public-utility companies. Latent race sentiment frequently appears among white and Negro workers in competition for jobs and is employed as a measure to fend off such competition. In this respect the white worker has an advantage, because he can use the issue of race to support him in group and individual competition.

Ideological commitments

The purveyors of the doctrines of white supremacy were representative of the best-educated, most articulate, and most highly positioned persons in this society. The fact of the matter was that there were so many historians, psychologists, anthropologists, geneticists, biologists, sociologists, and politicians giving voice to racist sentiments that the average citizen could not be heard. The period when their ideas seemed to coalesce, 1877-1918, has been referred to by the historian Logan as "the Nadir"; perhaps from the opposite point of view it might be called "the Zenith."

It would be fallacy to limit racism to the confines of the United States:[70]

Racist thinking in the Anglo-Saxon world, in Germany, and to a lesser extent in other European countries was in the ascendancy in the 1830's and 1840's; throughout the second half of the century it retained the status of firmly established, respectable orthodoxy, and it received the accolade of science, both natural and social, in the United States, Canada, Britain, Australia, Germany, and to some degree in the Low Countries and France.

Count Joseph Arthur de Gobineau (1816-82) can be credited with popularizing the Aryan myth. In his *Inequality of Human Races* (1853-55; English translation, 1915), he introduced the concept that racial composition was the determining factor in superior civilizations. For him, the highest type of civilization was the English. Houston Stuart Chamberlain (1855-1927), son-in-law of Richard Wagner, took these ideas to Germany, added anti-Semitism, and transferred the superior racial role to all German people. His *Foundations of the Nineteenth Century* (1899; English translation, 1910) foreshadowed Nazi doctrines. The influence of these two men was reflected, in turn, in a number of writings by Americans; however, it was most evident in *The Passing of the Great Race* (1916) by Madison Grant (1865-1937). The Exclusion Movement and the Quota Act were responses to his warnings about maintaining the continued dominance of Nordics, Teutonics, and Anglo-Saxons, "as opposed to allowing immigrants from southern and eastern Europe."[71] Henry Baxter Adams of Johns Hopkins and John Burgess of Columbia adapted the "Teutonic Germ Theory" to the university. Theodore Roosevelt, one of Burgess's students, came close to his ideal of a future ruler of the country. In a personal letter to the novelist Owen Wister, Roosevelt said, "Now as to the Negroes, I entirely agree with you that as a race and in the mass they are altogether inferior to whites."[72] And in 1895 he affirmed, "A perfectly stupid race can never rise to a very high plane; the Negro, for instance, has been kept down as much as by lack of intellectual development as anything else."[73] William Howard Taft, claiming to be free from the slightest "race prejudice or feeling," told a group of black college students in North Carolina in 1909 that they would be wise to emigrate:[74] "Your race is adapted to be a race of farmers, first, last and for all times." Woodrow Wilson, who had campaigned for the support of Negroes, proceeded in his administration to remove Negroes from responsible positions in federal civil service employment and to segregate eating and toilet facilities. D. W. Griffith, a talented craftsman and film director, had been a student of Wilson's at Johns Hopkins University. Griffith, the son of a Confederate soldier, had an affinity for the "lost cause" and gave a private showing of *Birth of a Nation* for the President and members of the Cabinet and on the following night for the Supreme Court and members of Congress. The story was based on the virulent racism of Thomas Dixon's *The Clansman.* President Wilson and Chief Justice Edward White, a former Klansman, approved and endorsed the film. Pierre Van den Berghe points out some of the distinguishing characteristics of this kind of racism:[75]

> Apart from its geographical spread, no other brand of racism has developed such a flourishing mythology and ideology. In folklore as well as in literature and science, racism became a deeply ingrained component of the Western Weltanschauung. Western racism had its poets like Kipling, its philosophers like Gobineau and Chamberlain, its statesman like Hitler, Theodore Roosevelt, and Verwoerd; this is a record not even remotely approached in either scope or complexity by any other cultural tradition.

The names of Bilbo, Talmadge, Beveridge, Eastland, and Vardaman have become synonomous with racism and the racial epithet, but they do not exhaust the list. *The Betrayal of the Negro* by Rayford W. Logan documents the culmination of these attitudes as they were expressed by leading magazines, newspapers, artists, writers, sociologists, and politicians.

This period also saw the beginning of the eugenics movement:[76]

> The eugenicists were primarily interested in attempting to prove that geniuses tend to come from superior human stock and that feeble-mindedness, criminality, and pauperism are also strongly influenced by hereditary factors. The movement began in England where its leader was Francis Galton.

Galton believed, "The average intellectual standard of the negro race is some two grades below our own."[77] Even contemporary scholars are not exempt from the contamination. It should be kept foremost in one's thinking that it has never been demonstrated that the educated are any less prejudiced or discrimination-minded. On many issues they show as much prejudice as the less educated, and on some issues they show more. Henry Steele Commager and Samuel Eliot Morison, outstanding historians, in *Growth of the American Republic* (1950 ed.), still begin the section on slavery with "As for Sambo, whose wrongs moved the abolitionists to wrath and tears, there is some reason to believe that he suffered less than any other class from its 'peculiar institution.'"[78]

In addition to the ideological factors,

investigations have demonstrated that "whites, both North and South, derive occupational and income gains from the prevailing race structure."[79] In the words of one investigator:[80]

> The findings of this study lend credence to the view that discrimination and its supporting prejudice persist mainly because majority (dominant group) people gain from them. One should not go so far as to attribute the perpetuation of discrimination entirely to its functions to the majority, nor should the many known and possible dysfunctions of discrimination to the majority be overlooked. However, one should also avoid viewing discrimination as merely a self-perpetuating carry-over from a past era. . . .

Oliver Cromwell Cox, a foremost Marxist, in *Caste, Class, and Race* maintains that racial discrimination is a direct outcome of economic exploitation and the benefits of status gains, sexual gains, and political gains that accrue from these vested interests.[81] A racist society is an expensive endeavor, both economically and psychologically. The loss of manpower, creativity, and social contributions can never be adequately measured. The toll extracted in terms of illnesses, psychoses, neuroses, maladapted personalities, and deadening of humanistic values in white and black society alike will never be fully known. William Alexander Perry, a white southerner, who lived through "the Nadir" summed up the effects upon whites,[82] "To live habitually as a superior among inferiors, be the inferiority intellectual or economic, is a temptation and a hubris, inevitably deteriorating." Chester Pierce, a psychiatrist, explains:[83]

> For it is from feelings of superiority that one group of people proceeds to brutalize, degrade, abuse, and humiliate another group of individuals. The superiority feelings and the accompanying contemptuous condescension toward a target group are so rampant in our society that is virtually impossible for any negotiation between blacks and whites to take place without the auspices of such offensive tactics.

Dr. Pierce also describes racism in the United States as a public health illness:[84]

> It is a mental disease because it is delusional. . . .a false belief, born of morbidity, refractory to change when contrary evidence is presented concerning the innate inferiority of any person with dark skin color. Thus everyone in this country is inculcated with a barrage of sanctions which permit and encourage any

white to have attitudes and behavior indicative of superiority over any black.

Perhaps the words of Douglass are more ominous for having been spoken such a long time ago:[85]

> Where justice is denied, where poverty is enforced, where ignorance prevails, and where any one class is made to feel that society is an organized conspiracy to oppress, rob, and degrade. . .neither persons nor property will be safe. . . .Hungry men will eat. Desperate men will commit crime. Outraged men will seek revenge.

Conclusion

Black Americans left the South for the same reasons immigrants left Europe and farmers moved to the cities. They were seeking a better life—the opportunity to earn a living and provide for their families. The black Americans came to the cities when there was no longer a market for agricultural and unskilled workers. The Europeans came at a time when these were viable means of mobility. Machines had displaced the masses of blacks in the South, but seemingly opportunity beckoned in the cities. The migration to the central cities began with higher rates of segregation for blacks than has ever been the case for any foreign-born whites or even the more visible Puerto Rican. The white immigrant was able to flee his ghetto, if his earnings allowed and he chose to do so. The black migrant has never had these alternatives. Even when he could afford improved housing, racial restrictive covenants and other social taboos condemned him to the fringes of the ghetto. Realtors, brokers, bankers, credit institutions, contractors, builders, and licensing agencies have played a significant role in maintaining these enclosures. Forced to live apart from the mainstream of American life, the ghetto has evolved a life of its own, developing value systems, institutions, and services geared directly to its needs:[86]

> The spatial isolation of Negroes from whites created Negro "communities". . . .[This isolation] also increased consciousness of their separate subordinate position, for no whites were available to them as neighbors, schoolmates, or friends, but were present only in such roles as school teachers, policemen, and social workers, flat janitors, and real-estate agents, merchants and bill collectors. . . .

Afro-Americans, whose numbers fill the urban ghettos to overflowing, whose birthright accrues from over two hundred years of labor without compensation, and who have participated in every war fought by the United States, have watched with interest and increasing anger as former enemies in war, refugees from oppression, and just average nationals from foreign lands have become naturalized American citizens with all the rights and privileges that have been denied the black man. Well-intentioned whites who attempt to ameliorate and temporize the racism by referring to the "progress" of the black man and the need for patience refuse to see these practices for what they are and are disconcerted when black people cannot exult with happiness and joy because several blacks are "allowed" to move into a decent neighborhood, or receive a management-level position that they no doubt honestly earned and well deserved, while the masses of black people are not extended the rights of citizenship.

There are those who maintain that the black American is no different from his white counterpart except in color. Often this is the shield that hides those whites who would do nothing and see nothing because expediency dictates perpetuation of the *status quo*. Liberalism, objectivity, and naïveté are the disguises they use. Their overtly racialist counterparts see and act in the proclaimed interest of white dominance. They use no disguises. The results, from both, are the same. They create the reality, the stark, brutal reality of being black in white America. The black American *is* different, but that difference has come from the struggle for survival, not from some inherent, inferior genetic trait.

Black people have worked in white homes, and nursed and reared white children. They have seen and heard the ruling class at its best and at its worst. They have plowed and sowed the fields of plantation owners, tenant farmers, and others, but seldom have harvested their own. They have observed white people at work and at play. They have sometimes shared their pleasures and sorrows, but always in their place and respectfully at a distance. In other words, they have always been in but never a part of the white world.

Perhaps the explanation lies in the following analysis:[87]

The United States and South Africa have been described as "Herrenvolk" democracies, that is, democratic for the master race but tyrannical for the subordinate group....The scope of applicability of the egalitarian ideals was restricted to "the people"—the whites.

Vast numbers of the white majority disavow any association with the ideals of slavery or its residual effects. They maintain a posture of innocence and nonresponsibility for the deeds and guilt of their ancestors. Perhaps that is as it should be. And yet, they actively support and maintain a system that derives its benefits from the institutions and patterns of race relations based on the subordination of its black citizenry. Assumptions of guilt are irrelevant and unnecessary in a community where the *rights of one* are of as much significance and concern as the *rights of all*. However, there is the matter of being able to *face up to* and then *deal with* the racism that permeates American society.

Slavery institutionalized an ideology of white superiority and black inferiority. It evolved role patterns to substantiate these ideas and rigidified these concepts. The North as well as the South incorporated these ideas and patterns into all aspects of community life. An equivalent marshaling of forces in the political, social, economic, and educational spheres of life to counteract these practices has never occurred. It would stand to reason that if such extensive measures were necessary for the inculcation of negative stereotypes and beliefs about a people—beliefs that can become realities on any given day, in any given ghetto—then equally extensive measures should be brought to bear on their eradication.

The Black Experience has been shaped in a crucible of violence, hatred, and brutality. It begins with a people torn from their homes and loved ones, enslaved in a hate-filled environment, and forced to function as beasts of burden and as outlets for the frustrations and perversities of their masters. Slaves were freed with no resources and left to the mercy of former owners and of poor whites, now economic competitors. The North did not welcome or want them, and proceeded to institute measures that made this apparent. These measures, both social and legal, assured the formation and continuance of the ghetto. The list is long: restrictive covenants, exclusion from skilled trades and training, inferior schools and teachers, unequal pay for equal work, exorbitant prices for consumer goods, substandard debilitated housing, and the despised ranking of an inferior are but a few of the factors that created and maintain the ghetto. Add to them the pathologies of disease, crime, poverty, and suppressed rage and the picture even grows more somber. Yet against these dark shadows are displayed all those intangible elements that have sustained the Afro-American during his travail in this land:[88]

One must always remember that the Negro started after the Civil War with nothing at all; he had neither education, nor property, nor position, nor the psychological readiness for achievement and personal growth. To have gone so far and to have accomplished so much...is a very great accomplishment indeed. To have done it against the prejudice, denial, and opposition with which his path has been strewn bespeaks both spiritual resilience and purposefulness. The record in the face of the same kind of handicaps has probably never been equaled before.

Put another way, "How did this minority, with no rights or power, unloose its shackles and come slowly but surely to the perimeter of American democracy, only steps away from the inner ring?"[89] This is a question that all Americans—black and white—should ponder when assessing the Black Experience in its totality. And it is a question that each black American especially should ask and answer, and in the answer find the pride and strength to go on.

NOTES

1. Lerone Bennett, *Before the Mayflower* (Chicago: Johnson Publishing Co., 1962), p. 33.

2. C. W. Greenidge, *Slavery* (New York: The Macmillan Co., 1958), p. 15.

3. Frank Tannenbaum, *Slave and Citizen* (New York: Vintage Books, 1946), p. 46.

4. Ibid., p. 48.

5. Ibid., p. 97.

6. Ibid., p. 98.

7. Benjamin Quarles, *The Negro in the Making of America* (New York: The Macmillan Co., 1964), pp. 34-35.

8. Bradford Chambers, *Chronicles of Black Protest* (New York: The New American Library, Inc., 1969), p. 36.

9. Stanley Elkins, *Slavery* (New York: Grosset & Dunlap, 1963), p. 61.

10. Ibid., pp. 61-62.

11. Basil Davidson, *The Lost Cities of Africa* (Boston: Little, Brown and Company, 1959), p. 81.

12. W. E. Abraham, *The Mind of Africa* (Chicago: The University of Chicago Press, 1962), p. 49.

13. Melville Herskovits, *The Myth of the Negro Past* (Boston: Beacon Press, 1958), p. 62.

14. Ibid., p. 76.

15. Basil Davidson, *The African Slave Trade* (Boston: Little, Brown and Company, 1961), p. 8.

16. Herskovits, op. cit., p. 54.

17. Eugene Genovese, *The Political Economy of Slavery* (New York: Random House, 1961), p. 72.

18. Ibid.

19. Elkins, op. cit., p. 10.

20. Ulrich B. Phillips, *Life and Labor in the Old South* (Boston: Little Brown and Company, 1929), p. 514.

21. Frederick Douglass, *My Bondage and My Freedom* (reprint ed., New York: Dover Publications, Inc., 1969), p. 127.

22. Eli Ginzberg and Alfred Eichner, *The Troublesome Presence* (New York: The New American Library, Inc., 1966), p. 27.

23. Helen Catterall, *Judicial Cases Concerning American Slavery and the Negro* vol. 1, (Washington, D. C.: The Carnegie Institute, 1929), p. 9.

24. Quarles, op. cit., p. 40.

25. John H. Franklin, *From Slavery to Freedom* (New York: Vintage Books, 1969), p. 188.

26. Ibid.

27. Ginzberg and Eichner, op. cit., p. 28.

28. Kenneth Stampp, *The Peculiar Institution* (New York: Vintage Books, 1965), pp. 209-210.

29. Ibid., pp. 210-211.

30. Ibid., p. 144.

31. Ibid., pp. 144-147.

32. Douglass, op. cit., p. 81.

33. Stampp, op. cit., p. 59.

34. Franklin, op. cit., p. 196.

35. Stampp, op. cit., p. 62.

36. Tannenbaum, op. cit., p. 62.

37. Ibid., p. 63.

38. Phillips, op. cit., p. 2.

39. Stampp, op. cit., pp. 158-159.

40. Ibid., p. 158.

41. Franklin, op. cit., p. 186.

42. Stampp, op. cit., p. 31.

43. Genovese, op. cit., p. 33.

44. Douglass, op. cit., p. 111.

45. Raymond Bauer and Alice Bauer, "Day-to-Day Resistance to Slavery," *Journal of Negro History*, 27 (October 1942), p. 389.

46. Sanders Redding, *They Came in Chains*, (New York: J. B. Lippincott, 1969), p. 86.

47. Bauer and Bauer, op. cit., p. 390.

48. Ibid., p. 391.

49. Douglass, op. cit., p. 251.

50. Stampp, op. cit., p. 209.

51. Douglass, op. cit., p. 97.

52. Peter Bergman and Mort Bergman, *The Chronological History of the Negro in America* (New York: Harper and Row, 1969), p. 121.

53. Franklin, op. cit., p. 218.

54. Benjamin Brawley, *A Social History of the American Negro* (New York: The Macmillan Co., 1970), p. 33.

55. Redding, op. cit., p. 88.

56. Ginzberg and Eichner, op. cit., p. 77.

57. Charles Mangum, *The Legal Status of the Negro* (Chapel Hill, N. C.: The University of North Carolina Press, 1940), p. 25.

58. Ibid., p. 27.

59. Chambers, op. cit., p. 127.

60. Arthur Raper, *The Tragedy of Lynching* (Chapel Hill, N.C.: The University of North Carolina Press, 1933), p. 10.

61. Ibid., pp. 16-19.

62. C. Vann Woodward, *The Strange Career of Jim Crow* (New York: Oxford University Press, 1966), p. 7.

63. Gunnar Myrdal, *The American Dilemma* (New York: Harper & Row, 1944), pp. 558, 559, 560.

64. Ibid., p. 525.

65. Charles Johnson, *Backgrounds to Patterns of Negro Segregation* (New York: Thomas Y. Crowell Co., 1970), p. 125.

66. Myrdal, op. cit., p. 613.

67. Ibid., p. 618.

68. Ibid., p. 615.

69. Johnson, op. cit., p. 155.

70. Pierre Van den Berghe, *Race and Racism* (New York: John Wiley & Sons, 1967), p. 16.

71. Thomas Gossett, *Race: The History of an Idea* (New York: Schocken Books, 1965), p. 354.

72. Barry N. Schwartz and Robert Disch, *White Racism* (New York: Dell Publishing Co., 1970), p. 72.

73. Rayford W. Logan, *The Betrayal of the Negro* (New York: The Macmillan Co., 1969), p. 270.

74. Schwartz and Disch, op. cit., p. 42.

75. Van den Berghe, op. cit., p. 13.

76. Gossett, op. cit., p. 155.

77. Ibid., p. 156.

78. Henry Steele Commager and Samuel Eliot Morison, *Growth of the American Republic* (New York: Oxford University Press, 1950), p. 554.

79. James W. Vander Zanden, *American Minority Relations* (New York: Ronald Press, 1963), p. 106.

80. Norval D. Glenn, "Occupational Benefits to Whites from the Subordination of Negroes," *American Sociological Review*, 28 (1963), p. 447.

81. Oliver Cromwell Cox, *Caste, Class and Race* (Garden City, N. Y.: Doubleday & Co., 1948), pp. 528-538.

82. Redding, op. cit., p. 202.

83. Chester Pierce, "Offensive Mechanisms," in *The Black 1970's* ed. Floyd Barbour, (Boston: Porter Sargent, 1970), p. 265.

84. Ibid., p. 266.

85. Douglass, op. cit., p. 97.

86. St. Clair Drake, "The Social and Economic Status of the Negro in the United States," in *The American Negro* Talcott Parsons and Kenneth B. Clark, (Boston: Beacon Press, 1967), p. 97.

87. Van den Berghe, op. cit., p. 18.

88. Tannenbaum, op. cit., p. 113.

89. Ginzberg and Eichner, op. cit., p. 15.

Editor's Note:

Various organizations and spokesmen have emerged from the black community proposing goals and programs to alleviate conditions under which the majority of Afro-Americans have had to function. Each of these approaches has validity and meaning for those who are found among their constituency. Except for subordination based on color, there are as many differences among black people in terms of viewpoints, personality types, understandings, and life experiences as found in any people subject to the complexities of life in highly urbanized societies; thus, there is a decided need for multiple approaches and points of view. St. Clair Drake, drawing on his vast experiential background and knowledge, provides an analysis of some of these proposed alternatives, noting the implications and the significance of them for race relations in the future.

"TCB"—TAKING CARE OF BUSINESS

ST. CLAIR DRAKE

*"TCB"—Taking Care of Business** *

After widespread violent outbursts of anger following Dr. King's assassination, black communities settled down to taking care of business on the local level. With two martyred charismatic leaders in their graves—Malcolm and Martin—other types of leaders became dominant. The first few years of the 1970's are likely to be devoted to consolidating the gains of the previous two stormy decades rather than to dramatic mass movements. Black theoreticians in 1970 were insisting that the integration versus separation dichotomy poses a spurious issue that could seriously divide the black community, and were forming united fronts that included Black Muslims as well as NAACP leaders in pursuit of limited local goals. To them, the issue is liberation. Maximizing the high black power potential in the South and rehabilitating northern ghettos assume priority. A mood of optimism prevails within the ranks of virtually all black southerners and among the 70 percent of northern ghetto dwellers who are above the poverty line. There is wide consensus as to what is necessary if conditions are to continue to get better, as most Afro-Americans seem convinced they inevitably will. Certain goals are clear:**

1. Achievement of parity with whites in occupation and income
2. Access to adequate housing within or outside black neighborhoods, to reduce the high proportion of blacks now living in poverty areas
3. Closing of the educational gap, as measured by median years of schooling for both sexes and the proportion of youths completing high school, four years of college, and graduate schooling
4. Drastic reduction of differentials in morbidity and mortality rates
5. Strengthening of the entire black institutional structure—family, church, schools, voluntary associations, and businesses

6. Maximization of the present black power potential, both economic and political
7. Improvement of the reputation of the ethnic group

These are interlinked objectives that feed back on each other.

Seen from the black perspective, the primary task in the struggle for liberation during the decade 1970–1980 is to move as far as possible toward achieving group parity with white fellow citizens in median income and proportion of men and women employed and firmly established above the poverty line. Attainment of this goal involves getting at least a proportionate share (11 to 12 percent) of jobs within the major occupational categories, at the same pay as whites, or concentrating upon movement into selected well-remunerated fields. With money in their pockets, Afro-Americans can take care of other kinds of business themselves. Achievement of this goal depends upon two interrelated processes: (1) utilizing economic and political pressure to force access to jobs and training for jobs where the opportunity is now denied, and (2) overcoming handicaps imposed by inadequate formal schooling—including improving predominantly black educational institutions at all levels, taking advantage of opportunities provided in integrated schools, and inspiring, motivating, and retooling those who have been crippled by inferior schooling or the direct or indirect impact of a racist society upon their lives. Most black Americans assume that these tasks can be carried out within the system, but only as the system is drastically reformed in the process.

• • •

By any means necessary?

The integration-separation antithesis does not reflect the contemporary American reality or the probable direction of movement, nor does the violence-nonviolence dichotomy. Except for Dr. King, a minority of his most devoted followers, and some of the members of CORE, few black Americans in the Civil Rights movement had a religious or ethical commitment to absolute nonviolence. (Although Garrison and Thoreau held such views, there is no record of any prominent black abolitionist who did. Most of them preferred to trust the "lightning of His terrible swift sword," and John Brown and Nat Turner, as well as the black men in blue, were cherished as the instruments of liberation.) It is a tribute to King's personal qualities that he was able to keep young militants of SNCC within the framework

---

*Stokely Carmichael devotes a chapter to this concept (or slogan) in Carmichael and Hamilton, *Black Power.*
**A 1969 Gallup poll reported that 3 out of 5 black Americans felt that their jobs and their children's opportunities had improved since 1964. Over 50 percent had secured better housing. Two-thirds expected things to be "still better" during the next five years. Only 22 percent were "satisfied," and nearly 60 percent thought the pace of change was too slow.

of the nonviolent movement from 1960 until he was assassinated, for they accepted the method only as a tactic, not as an ethical principle. It is not surprising, therefore, that they later proclaimed the principle "Any Means Necessary," which most Afro-Americans have always really believed in; tempered of course by the caveat that the means have some chance of getting results without bringing down disaster upon them.

Dr. King insisted that those in his movement not destroy property nor become participants in fights, the throwing of objects, or the use of firearms, but he did *not* refuse to accept governmental armed force to protect his nonviolent demonstrators or to coerce his opponents. Nor did he denounce the Deacons of Defense, though he stated his own personal aversion to their protecting him. With him it seemed to be a matter of how "legitimate" the violence was.

The street people of the northern ghettos seemed to take the position that nonviolence so defined might be a proper and adequate technique for the South, but not for them—if it included a ban on destruction of property. They showed how they felt during the "hot summers" of 1964, 1965, and 1967, as well as in their reaction to King's death.

King's method did achieve its objective in the South: desegregation. The wholesale destruction of property and the looting in the North achieved something, too. It made the nation face up to the facts of ghetto life. By 1969, however, the northern masses themselves seemed to have decided, at least temporarily, that it was to their advantage to "cool it." Meanwhile, some black militants had begun to experiment with other violent forms of attack such as sniping and bombing.

It would be hazardous to speculate about possible patterns of violence in the future. One can only say with assurance that there is no evident widespread revulsion in black communities against those who are alleged to be developing guerrilla warfare tactics, and there is a firm belief that both violence and nonviolence have been factors in bringing about favorable changes during the 1960s. This attitude must be taken into account.

A 1970 Harris poll reported that 77 percent of the black respondents in the sample felt that continous pressure must be kept up to complete the work of black liberation in America, but 58 percent felt that the ultimate victory could be won without violence. (Age made little difference in the responses.) Yet 40 percent of those interviewed in 1969 felt that riots had helped more than they had hurt, and an even larger proportion seemed to feel they were inevitable, 2 out of 3 respondents saying they

"expected more riots in the future." The overwhelming majority, however, stated that they did not expect to participate themselves.

In view of the recent shift in patterns of violence away from mass outbursts toward incipient urban guerrilla warfare, it is significant that over two-thirds of the black respondents in 1970 agreed with the statement "Panthers give me a sense of pride." Only one-fourth, however, said they agreed with Black Panther ideology. It is unlikely that many of these respondents were familiar with the details of the neo-Marxian analysis that Panther para-intellectuals are developing, a view that assigns the vanguard role in the American socialist revolution to the black *Lumpenproletariat*—the chronically unemployed, the criminals and ex-criminals, the street gangs and the juvenile delinquents—after they have become politicized. Those whom Marx rejected the Panthers say they will organize. It is precisely their success in giving a sense of social concern to some of the people in this stratum that appeals to their black middle-class admirers, who also vicariously identify with the Panthers for their boldness and reckless courage. But insofar as the middle classes are even vaguely aware of the full implications of the Panther critique of the social order they must oppose the ideology. The Panthers assail black capitalists as being as reprehensible as white capitalists, and black preachers and politicians are defined as corrupt misleaders. Pride in the Panthers will likely evaporate quickly should they ever decide to bring pressure to bear upon established black community leaders and their organizations.

Admiration of the Panthers is also related to the automatic acceptance by black Americans of the legitimacy of the peculiarly American pattern of inducing social change. A certain amount of violence is viewed as a normal reaction to oppression, and liberals use it, or the probable outbreak of it, to shake the conservatives and the indifferent out of their smugness or complacency so that they will sanction reforms within the system. The Panthers may think of their violence as leading toward revolution, but others see them only as a minority necessary to scare "Whitey." Such a view always takes into account the possibility of backlash and assesses the point at which violence may become counterproductive. There was widespread discussion within black communities during the late 1960s and throughout 1970 over the possibility of repressive measures being taken toward such groups as the Panthers and the Revolutionary Action Movement (RAM), but even moderate leaders had a tendency to oppose attempts to wipe out such groups by police violence or suspected legal frame-ups. This tolerance could, of course, disappear.

Alternatives and perspectives

The Black Panthers visualize a future socialist America in which racism will no longer exist, a society to be brought into being by a violent revolution in which black people, Mexican-Americans, Amerindians, Puerto Ricans, and the white poor will participate. The Panthers comprise one small segment of the country's alienated youth, most of whom are not committed to violent revolution, but many of whom feel that radical social change will only come after a period of right-wing repression that, from their perspective, has already begun. During the late 1960s and the early 1970s white liberals were fearful that the excesses of the youth subculture and the violence of some left-wing groups would inevitably bring on such repression. They, unlike many of their black counterparts, also felt that if the government ever became convinced that Afro-Americans were serious when they spoke of "Any Means Necessary," the danger from the Right would increase. Negroes were prepared to risk it; whites weren't. White liberals urged the revival of the labor-liberal coalition, allied with disadvantaged minorities, to stop what they visualized as a drift toward facism.

These fears were not the fantasies of political paranoids, for the emphasis of the Nixon-Agnew-Mitchell administration upon "law and order," its strategy of building a coalition upon those elements that constitute what they call Middle America—involving a "southern strategy" that ignores the wishes of the black electorate—does have fascist potential. There is also an element of self-fulfilling prophecy in the behavior of militant activists, for if they escalate urban guerrilla warfare, they invite repressive legislation and provide a legitimate excuse for the right wing to take actions that have ends other than the mere restoration of "law and order": the muzzling of criticism of imperialistic plundering at home and abroad; the enforcement of cultural conformity; and the preservation of entrenched power and privilege throughout the social system.

The process of disengagement from the War in Vietnam will test the strength of democratic institutions in the United States. If it involves widespread unemployment due to an unwillingness on the part of the federal government to plan carefully for peacetime reconversion and full employment; if federal aid to states and cities for welfare needs is not increased; if black ex-soldiers are subjected to employment discrimination and other forms of humiliation, then vigorous and violent expressions of discontent are likely. If such violence escalates and assumes political

implications, it is not inconceivable that the federal government will resort to measures so extreme as to warrant the designation "fascist."

However, it is very unlikely that a consolidation of right-wing power (by what President Eisenhower once called the military-industrial complex) at the national level or in northern and western states would be explicitly anti-Negro. Even in the South, expressions of racism would be muted by the new codes of speech and conduct that became institutionalized during the 1960s, though more overt racism would be expressed there than in the North. In all regions, however, it is highly probable that an attempt would be made to make sure that all blacks (and members of other minorities) do not gravitate to the liberal left end of the political spectrum.

It is likely that at the nation's capital and in northern states the power structure of a repressive right-wing government would install a token representation of conservative blacks in some high-level posts in army units, police forces, administrative cadres, and the judiciary. Attention had been given, by 1970, to strategies for incorporating some blacks into the milieu and mystique of Middle America. For instance, it is significant that when Daniel Patrick Moynihan made his widely publicized statement advocating "benign neglect," it was embedded in a position paper that emphasized the point that enough black Americans had now reached a middle socio-economic level to build a new black-white coalition that would isolate black extremists. The Nixon administration's emphasis upon black capitalism was explicitly defined as an attempt to create a stratum that would have a stake in the system. The defense of "no-knock laws" and similar legislation is put in terms of protection for blacks, who suffer more from criminal depredations than do whites.

Most black leaders would probably oppose a repressive right-wing national government, but there are likely to be some who would feel that their own best interests would be served by it. The leaders of the black middle class in the North are in the position to make some profitable trade-offs with the Right. The tiny stratum that has become integrated into the upper levels of politics and business (and even into some suburban neighborhoods) can maintain its status and privileges by a clear, open repudiation of radicalism in all its forms and by its high visibility lend this country legitimacy and credibility in the eyes of the world. These Afro-Americans would be invaluable showpieces for a nation that cannot ignore its international relations, however right-wing it might be. That segment of the black middle class populating the inner cities in metropolitan areas such as Newark, Washington, Cleveland, and Chicago, among others, would be in a position to win merit and economic rewards for cooperating in the rounding up and detention of black militants whose pressure they would be feeling and resenting. Facing the fact that black capitalism will always be dependent on white industrial and commercial institutions, black businessmen could bargain for a larger "cut" through more franchises, deposits in local banks, and partnerships in ghetto enterprises. Ghetto politicians, in alliance with the police, could guarantee a good investment climate and function as agents of indirect rule, as tribal chiefs did in British colonies in Africa. Prosperous churches and voluntary associations within ghettos, as well as modest guaranteed family incomes, could create a level of personal satisfaction that would take the pressure off white suburbia. Black community control in middle-class hands would have its payoff to both blacks and whites, but would require rigid control of "militants" and "criminals." Black police and judges, instead of white officials, might be used to do the job, however, thus relieving white consciences.

Many black militants are convinced that they would be "ripped off first" during a period of severe repression, and that a policy of genocide would then be carried out against the entire black population, except for a few collaborators. They see nothing improbable in the bizarre, disastrous end depicted in the King Alfred extermination plan in John A. Williams' novel *The Man Who Cried I Am.* But to believe, as they do, that the ghettos will be cordoned off and masses of black men and women herded into vans en route to gas chambers in the deserts, or that mass executions will take place in southern forests, swamps, and bayous, is to assume that what white Americans find easy to do in Southeast Asia they could also bring themselves to do upon their own soil, and that they could get away with it. But even when race riots and lynchings were frequent, genocide was never the goal.* The need for black labor, the basic American value structure, and the web of interpersonal ties between black and white people are likely to prevent such wholesale slaughter in the future, even to provide a scapegoat during some

national disaster. Genocide has become a convenient propaganda term, too loosely used, for very real evils that fall far short of the precise meaning of the term—persecution of the Black Panthers, the attack on the Jackson State College dormitory in 1970 by Mississippi state police, or indiscriminate shooting during ghetto rebellions. A roundup of the militant black minority is entirely possible, but this would not be genocide. The deliberate extermination of over twenty million black Americans is inconceivable.

Concern with the possibility of a right-wing drift was voiced by major television newscasters during the acrimonious election campaign of 1970. Over a year before such Establishment spokesmen used the term publicly, the Black Panthers had convened an "antifascist" conference, and members of both the old and new Left had begun to revive memories of the 1930's by supporting this Panther initiative. The present generation of concerned black college students will have to make the decision whether they wish to join such a coalition or to develop initiatives of their own, looking toward a coalition with the new breed of liberal—though not radical—white students as a means of preventing a victory for the Right. Students will not decide the issue, although they may play a crucial role during elections when liberal leaders are trying to mobilize support, in organizing progressive blocs within the two major political parties, or in forming new political parties.

It is not inconceivable that black individuals and black institutions will actually play a vanguard role in some future antifascist united front, not the role that the Black Panthers hope they will play in a future revolution. The willingness of whites to follow black leadership in a liberal coalition has been shown in the cases of Julian Bond and Charles Evers in the South and Ron Dellums in northern California. Arnold Schuchter, in suggesting an alternative to James Forman's concept of a black-led Marxist revolution, has outlined a bold plan for carrying out a program of reparations that he prefers to call redress. It includes suggestions for "Building New Communities in Negative Urban Space," "Transfer of

---

*From the end of the Civil War until the outbreak of World War II, however, there was the hope and expectation in some circles that disease and constitutional debility would eliminate the black population. Thus, one prominent statistician, writing about thirty years after the end of the Civil War, expressed a prevalent point of view:

The Negro is subject to a higher mortality rate at all ages, but especially so at the early age periods. . . . The natural increase in the colored population will be less from decade to decade and in the end a decrease must

take place. It is sufficient to know that in the struggle for race supremacy the black race is not holding its own; and this fact once recognized, all danger from a possible numerical superiority of the race vanishes. (F. L. Hoffman, quoted in S. J. Holmes, *The Negro's Struggle for Survival* [Berkeley: University of California Press, 1937], pp. 15-16.)

In 1930, Dr. Raymond Pearl, a biologist, spoke of an "absolutely definite. . . final extinction." (Raymond Pearl, quoted in Holmes, *The Negro's Struggle for Survival*, p. 16.)

Slum Ownership," "Breaking White Union Barriers," and "Redress [of] Financing Mechanisms." Central to the preparation of the public for such innovations is his concept of "Centers of National Reform." As he visualizes them, they would involve the building of a coalition of black and white students, with blacks as leaders. He states the main purposes of the centers as follows:

(1) to prepare conversion plans and guidelines, operating in effect as "think tanks" for a reparations program in a peace economy; (2) to watch government policies and operations that support militarization at the expense of conversion to a peace economy; (3) to educate blacks and whites in changing the dominant institutions of our society in accordance with the goals of redress, with a special focus on universities; (4) to prepare plans for new cities and towns as well as for the renewal of existing urban communities, with an initial focus on opportunities in the South; (5) to play a key role in political mobilization and education in the South aimed at accelerating black acquisition of political power; (6) to attract the largest possible number of scientists, engineers and technicians displaced by a contracting war economy to teach in black colleges, to assist in preparing realistic conversion plans, new communities and the renewal of cities; (7) in general, to upgrade dramatically the cultural and educational opportunities of black colleges, in part for the purpose. of attracting talented white students committed to the goals of redress; (8) to educate clergy from all religious denominations so that they can return to their churches as missionaries for the goals of redress; and (9) to provide a setting in which whites and blacks from diverse backgrounds, from the Black Panthers to Wall Streeters, can exchange ideas on national conversion policies and the innumerable problems involved in making American society livable for blacks and whites.

In 1970, models for future action like Schuchter's had a very limited appeal to black Americans, for they were inclined neither to cast themselves in the role of trying to help America to save itself, nor to accept the degree of white leadership implied. They were concerned with what Vincent Harding, director of the Institute of the Black World, calls a Black Agenda, with taking care of business for themselves. Yet, the most broadly based movement in existence in 1970, the Southern Christian Leadership Conference, and the most highly publicized one, the Panthers, were both, however dissimilar they were in other respects, committed to

the ultimate realization of the Dream as King dreamed it. And both held out an invitation to poor whites to join in the struggle for the goal, though very few accepted it. In fact, nearly all Afro-Americans, except for the most extreme black nationalists, have accepted the necessity of coalition formation after black groups are sure they have "defined themselves for themselves" and have "got themselves together." The determination of with precisely whom coalitions are formed involves a matter of principle, but the decision to form coalitions is primarily a matter of timing. Being a numerical minority dictates the need for coalition politics. It does not necessarily imply acceptance of a Messianic vanguard role.

The working out of cooperative relations with white groups, on terms defined by blacks, was already becoming a trend in the early 1970s. However, structuring satisfactory relationships with any white Americans, after decades of insult and subordination to most of them, is a complex process. Sharpening boundaries is crucial for increasing group solidarity, but if pushed to a point that makes coalition politics impossible, it becomes self-defeating. It is also difficult to draw the line between the personal and the political, as current controversies over the acceptability of interracial marriage, dating, and even friendship indicate. The danger of psychological cooptation is ever present, and some of the revulsion against school desegregation and the frequent demands for a measure of separatism on predominantly white college campuses are rooted in this fear. Since the cults of Africa and soul have been made salable commodities by the opinion makers of the press, film, radio, television, and the record industry, and since black Americans now function in a diversity of new occupational roles and work settings, old derogatory stereotypes are rapidly disappearing, thus preparing white Americans for a new black modus vivendi. For the first time, black Americans may be able to decide how much integration they desire. One of the ongoing processes during the 1970s will be the evolution of new patterns of interracial behavior consistent with a pluralism that preserves group identity without destroying freedom of association and collaboration across ethnic lines.

The demand for black solidarity will continue as long as racism manifests itself in American society. There is increasing empirical evidence, however, to indicate that impermeable boundaries between blacks and whites cannot be maintained except within cults and sects with which only a small portion of the black population is ever likely to be affiliated. Both the economic system and the political system impose a high degree of integration in work situations, in occupational and professional associations, in conferences and public meetings connected with coalition politics, and in social and quasi-social extensions of these contacts. The line may hold in the more intimate relations of family, recreational associations, and religious congregations, but it will continuously be broken in economic and political situations, as it has been forcibly broken in transportation and public accommodations and in educational institutions at all levels in both the North and the South. It is likely, however, that the black caucus pattern will become the institutionalized expression of a group *presence* and will be considered normal in so-called integrated situations.

The internal structure of black communities underwent profound changes between 1950 and 1970 due to a dramatic rise in educational level, access to a wider range of occupations, and the growth of black consciousness. Whether viewed in terms of social class or of life style, the choices facing individuals became more complicated. The conflict between wanting to get ahead as an individual and a sense of obligation to the black community has posed problems for ambitious and fortunate individuals. One social process among Afro-Americans that began in the 1950s will certainly continue on into the 1970s: the black population will remain split into a majority group above the poverty line and a smaller group that exhibits a poverty dependency syndrome. The black middle class has always been concerned about the fate of the black lower class, even when it showed its fear of that stratum by dissociating itself from it (as all upwardly mobile Americans have done with respect to lower strata whose life styles differ from theirs). The most effective way the professional classes can pay their dues is not by artificial and strained attempts to relate socially, but by the use of their power and influence as leaders in coalition with whites to mobilize public pressure: for a guaranteed annual income that will be no less than the annual median; for a comprehensive plan of free medical care; for low-cost housing and experimental cooperatives fitted to the needs of black communities. There was much talk of community development during the 1960s, but it often boiled down to planning for black capitalism as a panacea. In the long run that road is more likely to lead to the same kind of action against the black middle class that was visited upon "Whitey" in the ghettos during the 1960s.

The process of social differentiation has thrown up a small stratum of almost completely integrated Afro-Americans and will continue to do so. This is one of the results of tokenism at the top levels of industrial, commercial, and governmental bureaucracies. This group will have to be written off as black

leaders, though they do bring prestige to the Afro-American ethnic group and function as pioneers on new frontiers. Many of them are in roles where their first concern must be for general interests rather than black interests (though these are not necessarily antithetical).

The elections in the fall of 1970 suggest that an increasing number of black individuals will be finding themselves in such a position. In California, a distinguished black educator was elected Secretary of Public Instruction in a state administration headed by a conservative governor. He, like Senator Brooke of Massachusetts, finds himself responsible to a broad interracial electorate and not primarily responsible to the black community. Another black candidate barely missed appointment as Secretary of State. A militant black leader won a congressional seat through the energetic work of white liberals and radicals as well as black supporters. These electoral victories may portend a future situation in which the white public will respond to black leadership as it has to Jewish leadership in the past—that is, choose an individual in whom they have confidence despite their prejudiced attitudes toward the ethnic group from which he comes, but remain disinclined to have any intimate social relationships with him or members of his ethnic group. This trend toward election of black leaders responsible to integrated constituencies may imply a need to develop a parallel group of equally competent leaders whose primary concern would be for the welfare of the black community, and a need to strengthen the black institutional structure, which can support them as adequately as the broader structure does the "integrated" Negroes.

Integrated blacks are always suspected of being bought off or coopted, or of having sold out. Among them are a few executives of large corporations, professionals and administrators in the educational system, judges, ambassadors, foreign service career officers, mayors of northern cities, and denominational representatives of "white" churches. There has been a widening of the area of interracial social participation through the friendship groups and voluntary associations associated with these occupations. Black professionals find new opportunities to take up residence outside ghettos in areas deemed appropriate for persons of their status, and some families do not pass up the chance to live in such a setting. Ironically, the expansion of this segment of the black upper class is taking place during a period when pressure from within the black community against integration is stronger than it has ever been. It is unlikely, however, that this attitude will deter many black Americans who have the chance to accept the rewards of that limited integration from doing so. What it is doing,

301

and will continue to do, however, is to pressure those who have moved into these circles to give some attention to paying dues—finding ways to relate to the basic institutions of black communities. Most will respond positively, since except for the tiny minority who can pass for white, they are well aware that when the chips are down in this society, they are still black.

The interracial dynamics of the future will continue to be what they have been in the past, an ongoing process of restructuring *social* relationships between individuals and groups defined as white and black. For over two hundred years, the basic cleavage was between white masters and black slaves, but by the end of that long time span there were 500,000 free Negroes in interaction with about 4,000,000 slaves and various classes of whites other than the slaveholders. The second phase of the black experience extended over the eighty-five years between 1865 and 1950 during which relations between blacks and whites in the South were organized by a caste system while in the North a system of institutional racism became a firmly entrenched feature of an ethnic class system. For the past two decades the system of race relations has been undergoing rapid and profound transformation. By the end of the 1960s the caste system in the South had been broken and institutional racism in the North was under persistent attack. New values and new social structures are in the making in both the North and the South. These basic changes were initiated by Afro-Americans themselves, who had determined to tolerate caste and institutional racism no longer and were willing to suffer and sacrifice in order to destroy the old order. The 1970s will be characterized by an intensified process of restructuring race relations.

The future grows out of a present that has been shaped by the past. The fate of black Americans during the 1970s will involve the development of trends that were very evident in the 1950s and 1960s as well as the unfolding of events whose seeds have already been sown but whose results are only barely discernible. A stream of technological innovations continuously generates changes in social relations and values as well as in the economic system. Changes in fertility, birth, and death rates have long-term repercussions on relations between ethnic groups and races.*These basic factors affecting

relations between black and white Americans are reflected in the evanescent rhetoric of militants, right and left, but, amidst the flux and flow, great dreams remain as constants in the historic process, never being realized, but pulling mankind onward. The voices that evoke images associated with the dreams, inspiring men and leading them onward, pass away—but the dreams never die. Martin Luther King's dream was one of these. It will be an integral part of the American future.

Editor's Note:

A conceptual framework is proposed that offers an alternative to the either/or black/white situation that is the basis for much of the racial conflict which afflicts this country. Vernon J. Dixon calls this approach "diunital"—literally, "something apart and united at the same time." The author raises some salient points about difficulties that arise when people attempt to function from positions of total exclusion or total inclusion.

THE DIUNITAL APPROACH TO BLACK-WHITE RELATIONS

VERNON J. DIXON

Introduction

How, indeed, do we liberate ourselves from racial polarization in American society? A viable answer cannot wait. The urgency of the situation has led the National Advisory Commission on Civil Disorders to warn that "within two decades the [Black-White] division could be so deep that it would be almost impossible to unite."

---

while white fertility rose by 88 percent. . . . The great increase in nonwhite birth rates represents an astonishing reversal and occurred, interestingly enough, even while the Negro was becoming rapidly urbanized and metropolitanized. . . . The phenomenal increase in nonwhite fertility is a result of the striking rise in nonwhite urban fertility, largely because of the decrease in childlessness brought about by improved health, including reduction in venereal and debilitating diseases. . . . The nonwhite rate of population growth in 1960, if sustained, would double the Negro population in a little over thirty years. In contrast, the continuation of the 1960 white rate would require over fifty years before doubling the population. (Philip M. Hauser, "Demographic Factors in the Integration of the Negro," *Daedalus* 94, no. 4 [Fall 1965]: 848.)

---

*The demographers' predictions referred to in the previous note were not realized, of course, and a population expert indicates why and projects a trend:
Between 1940 and 1960, the birth rates of both whites and nonwhites rose with the postwar baby boom. Nonwhite fertility increased by 90 percent . . .

Recently, Princeton University experienced this separation of races in microcosm. The university formed a committee of Black and White members from the university community. The charge of our committee was (1) to study the relationship between the apartheid policy of South Africa and the university's present investments in American firms doing business with that country, and (2) to recommend an investment policy that would lessen apartheid.

When the moment arrived to decide which policy to recommend, the committee split. The White members chose to recommend continued investment and then stated that they understood how we as Black people could not agree to their policy.

We Blacks responded that their decision was very rational, given their particular approach to evaluating evidence—an approach in which we had been trained for many years. Therefore, we could detail the assumptions that they had used in assessing the evidence, how these had influenced their theory of the effects of investment on apartheid, and, in turn, how all this had led to their recommendation of continued investment.

We then asked these Whites, who ostensibly "could understand our decision," to explain in the same fashion how our "Black" approach could rationally lead to it. They could not, for they simply did not know. This was the crisis; the subsequent rallies, sit-ins, occupations of buildings, and other campus confrontations were its aftermath. It was now clear to us Blacks why two separate racial groups had formed.

The Whites used a different conceptual framework than we Blacks. A conceptual framework or paradigm is a particular way of forming ideas, a particular way of ordering experience, a particular way of knowing. Their framework was either/or. According to this approach, everything falls into one category or another, but cannot belong to more than one category at the same time.

*   *   *

Uncritical acceptance of the either/or approach is so widespread and pervasive that only recently has its role in formulating American foreign policy, for example, been perceived and recognized.

In race relations, *Black* falls into the category of *nonWhite*, and *White* falls into the category of *nonBlack*; therefore the either/or habit of mind easily allows one to conceive of Black and White as mutually exclusive opposites. Then only Black is relevant, or only White is relevant. Take your choice; you can't have both.

In a similar either/or fashion, the White committee members had acknowledged only *their* analytical process. In their minds, they had reached their decision in a rational and objective manner; therefore they interpreted our Black decision as irrational and nonobjective. They could not understand our analytical process. Recognizing only their White experience, they could not give any validity, any authenticity, to our radically different Black experience. Their underlying either/or approach had sealed them in Whiteness.

In contrast, we Blacks were sealed in Blackness and Whiteness. To us, both were relevant. Our conceptual framework was what I term "diunital."* According to this approach, something is both this element and now this element at the same time and in the same aspect. Something is simultaneously apart and united, divided and undivided. We were at once both Black and not Black. We were this contradiction harmoniously, without inherent antagonism. Therefore, we could acknowledge positively the objectivity of the Whites' analytical process, the rationality of their decision, and the authenticity of their White experience. Diunitally speaking, a similar proposition was simultaneously valid for us Blacks. In other words, our approach to the evidence was one, yet two.

*   *   *

The Either/Or Approach in Black Americans. (The American environment produces in all Black Americans a conflict involving ethnic and national identities. It results from the following situation.

White Americans embody commonality through their national or American identity and they embody uniqueness through their ethnic identity or White culture. But, most important, these two identities are the same; American culture *is* White culture. Furthermore, these Whites, on the conceptual level, do not acknowledge the authenticity, validity, or value of Black culture. As a consequence, either/or Whites have a sense of one society, a sense of one membership, a single consciousness.

In contrast, the ethnic and American identities of Afro-Americans are *not* the same. Black culture is radically different from White American culture. It develops such African-oriented attributes as com-

---

*I constructed the neologism *diunital* in the following manner: Webster tells us that *di* means "akin to two" or "apart." Unital, the adjectival form of the word *unit*, means a "single thing that constitutes an undivided whole." Diunital, therefore, is literally something apart and united at the same time.

munal or collective interests, the superiority of feelings or emotions, and figurative language. Therefore, Black Americans have a sense of "twoness," a sense of dual membership, a double consciousness.

Yet they fully and positively accept this duality. Their American identity and their Black ethnic identity are genuine and valuable. They are authentic members of both societies. As W. E. B. DuBois said: "He [the Black man] would not Africanize America, for America has too much to teach the world and Africa. He would not bleach his Negro soul in a flood of White Americanism, for he knows that his Negro blood has a message for the world." Consequently, the embodiment of two radically different cultures in and of itself is not the conflict.

As the action of a pair of scissors, the conflict results from the simultaneous cutting of two blades. From my experience, duality is only one blade. The other is the feeling of not having this twoness, of suspension between two societies, of being neither full-fledged Americans nor full-fledged Blacks. This feeling results from interacting with either/or Whites, because one aspect of defining yourself is the way in which others define you.

Recall that White Americans relate to Black people using a theory of White cultural assimilation. In this context, Whites offer to Black people membership in their group. This is tantamount to Whites recognizing the American or national identity of Black people, because to these Whites national and White ethnic identity are one and the same. However, they withhold their recognition until Blacks achieve the impossible task of expunging their Black cultural identity. Thus, Whites do not treat Black Americans as people having a genuine national or American identity. Furthermore, these Whites can see no authentic value in a Black ethnic identity, because only Whiteness is valid. Thus, Whites do not treat Blacks as a genuine group with its own culture.

Therefore, Black people, to White Americans, are quite rationally neither full-fledged Americans nor a full-fledged Black group with a Black culture. Because Blacks use this White mirror, it is no surprise that Afro-Americans likewise perceive themselves not as people having a sense of twoness, but as suspended between two societies and two memberships.

Accordingly, the real conflict, most likely occurring subconsciously in Black people, is that on one hand, they have a sense of embodying two racially different identities, one White American, one African-oriented (Black); on the other, they have a sense of not embodying these same two identities.

• • •

The diunital approach in Black and White Americans

Americans who adopt this approach start from the conceptual position that acknowledges Blackness and Whiteness as authentic, valid, and valuable. Their conceptual world of Black and White is identical to the actual world. No longer must they reconcile these two worlds by assimilating or destroying cultural differences.

According to the diunital approach, Black and White Americans desire to perpetuate the existence and development of both ethnic cultures. One way to achieve this perpetual though changing union of opposite cultures is through what I call the "theory of cultural diunity." The national culture, rather than being synonymous with Whiteness, now becomes a union of opposite or different cultures.

Because each cultural group has its special norms, such as languages, religion, kinship forms, or aesthetics, this defines such economic, political, educational, or recreational institutions that distinguish members of a given racial group from adjacent groups.

Each group may have its own institutions or the two groups may share participation in the same institutions. Regardless of the resulting structure, cultural diunity means that these institutions are exclusive and inclusive in character. They allow for the cultural expression of Blackness and Whiteness.

In an America structured by Whiteness, institutions associated with a collective-oriented Black culture, for example, communally owned property, receive affirmative support, not marginal toleration or suppression. Blacks are not a pluralistic minority group, which according to Louis Wirth, "is one which seeks toleration for its differences on the part of the dominant group." This toleration of differences does not depend upon the size of any group nor is it normative, i.e., something that ought to be. Rather, it is inherent in the diunital approach that underlies cultural diunity. In other words, if people think diunitally, then it follows that they not only tolerate cultural differences but actively encourage them.

• • •

American Blacks rather than Whites are more deeply attuned to a diunital existence for two reasons. First, we live in a dual existence. We are American citizens, yet we are not. American institutions are ours, yet they are not. We have one identity that is two identities. This experience of living two lives in one results from the inability of American

304

Whites to accept Blacks as Blacks. Thus we tend toward thinking diunitally as a reaction to our exclusion by Whites from the status of full-fledged Americans.

Secondly, we may embody a predisposition to diunity that arises from our African identity. Janheinz Jahn points out that the union of opposites characterizes traditional thinking throughout Africa, for African philosophy as such. Jahn states that

This systematic unity of views and attitudes that often appear irreconcilable in European terms has indeed been observed by European scholars, but has led to serious misunderstandings. Since it could not be accommodated to European systems of thought, the African way of thinking was considered non-logical. Levy-Bruhl called the attitude of the primitives "pre-logical," a term by which he meant to characterize *a kind of thought which does not refrain from inner self-contradiction, a kind of thought in consequence of which "objects, beings, phenomena can be, in a fashion unintelligible to us, both themselves and at the same time something other than themselves."* At the end of his life Levy-Bruhl renounced his theory of "prelogicism" and thus furnished a rare example of scholarly integrity.

Euro-Americans, in turn, are less conscious of their dual existence in a union of opposites. They are more attuned to a sense of oneness, a sense of unitary existence. They perceive the American identity as their identity. American institutions are their institutions. Furthermore, these institutions, such as private property, are put forth as universally valid for all Americans. They give no valid recognition to that which they are not (Black), in order not to destroy that which they are (White). Consequently, Whites appropriate Black expressions, music, dances, etc., as if they had invented them. In their eyes, there is one authentic existence—White.

Yet Whites do act diunitally. They, as Blacks, focus not only on the words when reading a letter, but also focus at the same time on the nonword; they both read "between the lines." If they theoretically stated this action in which a union of opposites occurs, then they have formulated the diunital approach.

Some White American youths are currently taking the first steps toward thinking diunitally. They are questioning the validity of accepting only what is in America. They are seeking what is not, in drugs, communes, socialism, or Eastern religions. However, the danger is affirmation through negation. Instead of preserving what is valuable in American Whiteness, they may seek to completely reject it to accept its opposite. In this way, they only affirm their Whiteness by negating it absolutely.

Blacks, in turn, must consciously and vigorously strive to maintain their dual cultural existence. Our danger is succumbing to an either/or approach to achieve Black liberation. This approach is clearly part of us, because of our prolonged and pervasive exposure to Western rationalism. Our strength is our dual existence. Our weakness appears in the Western either/or split between the Black revolutionary nationalists and the revolutionary Black cultural nationalists.

Acceptance of the diunital approach, moreover, strengthens our Blackness rather than dilutes it. We no longer must repress all of our White Western heritage. Instead, we can use its valuable aspects, for instance its tools of analysis, to explicate and develop further our Blackness. This book is one such example.

More specifically, I felt it most important to generalize how I have interpreted my Euro-American and Black experience. In this period of increasing social polarization and conflict I hope that the diunital approach may suggest to other people a way in which they too can be pro-Black without being anti-White and be pro-White without being anti-Black. This means an alternate America in which people mutually acknowledge the authenticity, validity, and value of Black and White cultures.

305

EPILOGUE:

THE BLACK EXPERIENCE—
A SUMMING UP

"IT'S GREAT TO BE A PROBLEM"

J.D. WORK

It's great to be a problem,
A problem just like me;
To have the world inquiring
And asking what you be.
You must be this,
You can't be that,
Examined through and through;
So different from all other men,
The world is studying you.

My grandfather cursed my father,
For Noah cursed Ham, you know;
Therefore, my father's children,
The rocky road must go.
We can't turn here,
We can't turn there,
Because the world's in doubt,
What we would do,
Where we would go,
What we would be about.

I'm sullen if I speak not,
I'm insolent if I speak;
Must curb my aspirations,
I must be lowly, meek.
I can't eat here,
I can't sleep there,
Must "Jim-Crow" on full fare;
The world can't know
What I would do
If I were treated square.

It's great to be a problem,
A problem just like me;
To have the world inquiring
And asking what you be.

307

Editor's Note:

One of the renowned scholars of this century shares with us some of his perceptions and assessments of the Black Experience. St.Clair Drake, researcher and lecturer *par excellence*, draws on his expertise in anthropology and sociology as well as insights gained from personal relationships with some of the greatest minds and leaders produced by the black community. Professor Drake places the Black Experience in an historical perspective that is worldwide. While so doing, he also provides a frame of reference for a synthesis of the forces and circumstances that played significant roles in the particularistic development of Afro-American society.

THE BLACK EXPERIENCE IN BLACK HISTORICAL PERSPECTIVE

ST.CLAIR DRAKE

Part One: Before and After the Birth of Racism

If Europeans had not discovered the "New World" near the end of the fifteenth century and then decided to enslave millions of Africans to develop its resources, and to hold their descendants in slavery, the "Black Experience"—as such—would, in all probability, never have become a subject for discussion. Before the fifteenth century, there was, of course, a "Black Experience" in the sense of history connected with people we now call "black" or "Negro." But nobody involved in making that history or viewing it conceptualized what was happening in racial terms, as *"Black* Experience." It was only the determination of Europeans to make the concept of "blackness" synonymous with slavery that gave the term "black" its *social* salience. It was only this insistence upon using anatomical traits to define the status of human beings as inferior that fixed attention upon skin color as a crucial social determinant. After the expansion of Europe overseas, race became what sociologist Raymond Mack refers to as "invariably relevant." Before then, other things about men were much more relevant than their anatomical traits or assumed genetic potential—a person's religion, the customs of his people, the extent to which his way of life was considered "civilized," his degree of willingness to accept change, etc. Ethnocentric aesthetic appraisals of hair and skin color are present in many cultures in mate selection, but the idea that such traits could, or should, affect a person's position in the economic or political order, or fix his or her total social position, is a peculiarly modern European conception—and a pernicious one.

White racism had, as one inevitable response, what might be called "protective racial solidarity," the most intellectualized expression of which is in the concept of *negritude* as elaborated by the poets Leopold Senghor and Aimé Cesaire. Once white men had defined being "black" or "Negro" as something of supreme import in the lives of sub-Saharan Africans and their descendants, black intellectuals would have been irresponsible as well as foolish not to have exploited these definitions—however silly they were—for all they were worth. The role of leaders is always to use ideas and words for the welfare of their people. For instance, if a Pleistocene African skull showed prognathism and a wide nasal aperture, archaeologists (nearly all of whom were white) called it "Negro," although they had not one iota of knowledge about what kind of flesh or hair may have once enveloped the bones. If it had no prognathism, but possessed a straight, oval face and narrow nasal structure they called it "Caucasian"—"*Hamitic* Caucasian"—not knowing whether, when alive, the person was white or brown or black. Most of the Africans actually in existence who had these kinds of measurements were brown-skinned and had wavy or kinky hair. When anthropologists insisted upon calling both these fossils and these people "Caucasian," black scholars usually laughed with derision. Why? Because these very same archaeologists called such people who lived in the U.S.A. "Negroes," as did custom and the law books. Most black scholars were not disposed to let white scholars have their genetic cake and eat it too in order to defend white supremacy. As Dr. W.E.B. DuBois used to say, "If a light Hamitic-looking person lived in Georgia they'd call him a Negro and put him in a Jim Crow car. Why is the very same type classified as white, Caucasoid, and Hamitic, when he appears as a king on a throne in an Egyptian painting?" Black scholars would, no doubt, have preferred to deal with problems of mankind as *human* problems, but Western science insisted upon defining them in terms of "race." They, therefore, have reacted in the same terms. There is a black historical perspective as well as a white one, and it is equally valid as a frame of reference for research.

Many contemporary black scholars insist upon viewing "The Black Experience" as one unified whole extending through at least 10,000 years of recent time with its roots down deep in Egypt and surrounding areas, but ultimately covering the entire globe. (After all, Matt Henson was with Peary at the North Pole, and Corliss Lamont presents a picture of a black collective farmer in Soviet Georgia.) To foreshorten or truncate this experience is to rob it of its deepest significance for a generation of young blacks who are trying to "define themselves for themselves" and to "get themselves together." For them, Dr. James Harris' discoveries of African maharajahs who once sat upon Indian thrones is a facet of the Black Experience as significant as that favorite of American white historians, slavery in the American South. This is not the first generation to throw its net wide for data to integrate into a reconstruction of the Black Experience. As soon as Afro-Americans in colonial North America had discovered the fact that the Bible mentioned Egypt and Ethiopia, their leaders used every reference to develop a prepolitical ideology, "Ethiopianism," which invested those they claimed as their ancestors with dignity and sometimes with heroism. They rested their own deep faith in ultimate liberation from slavery upon a prophecy in the Psalms: "Princes shall come out of Egypt, Ethiopia shall soon stretch out her hands unto God." (Ps. 68:31.) Edward Wilmot Blyden and W.E.B. DuBois secularized this "ethiopianist" tradition, but it remains strong in black church circles.

A comprehensive Black perspective inevitably asks, "When and where did 'Negroes' first appear upon this planet?" This is a matter that has kept myth makers busy for centuries—each African tribe having its own origin myth and Mr. Muhammed having given the Black Muslims a comprehensive origin story to replace the ones found in Genesis. The question is also still a matter for lively but inconclusive discussion among archaeologists. About all they can agree upon is the application of the term "Negro" to some skeletal remains dated at about 10,000 years ago that have been found scattered across the southern Sahara Desert at isolated spots from near the Atlantic Ocean to the Nile River. These bone fragments have measurements and a "look" that leads experts to the conclusion that the people whose skeletons they are, resembled the people who now inhabit West Africa. How long before this 10,000-year-old time-horizon such people were in existence and whether or not they also lived elsewhere is unknown. No fossils have yet cropped up to provide possible answers, but consideration of other kinds of evidence has brought some specialists to the point of suggesting that "Negroes" once inhabited the entire area now covered by the Sahara Desert and its scattered oases. This was when it was well-watered, green, and grassy, and these ancient blacks were fishermen and herders. Back behind them would stretch a million years of African prehistory in which the ancestors of the "Negroes" as well as those of Pygmies, Hottentots, Bushmen, and even Hamites—in fact the ancestors of all mankind—diverged from some common generalized African ancestor. It is taken for granted by these scholars that "Negroes," like the other physical types, came into being over this tremendous time span as a result of the combined processes of spatial isolation, mutation, natural selection, and social selection. But just when the emergence of Negroes took place, or where, no one hazards a guess. (The old theory that they came into Africa from Asia has been generally discarded, however.)

By the time the great food-producing revolution—domestication of cereal grains, cattle, and small animals—occurred in the Middle East around seven or eight thousand years ago, Negroid people in the central African area, it is now thought, may have already domesticated some tropical plants. There is rather general agreement, too, that as the Sahara dried out "Negroes" drifted into the savannah land south of the desert and ultimately began to cultivate it across its entire expanse, later building cities and kingdoms and empires within it.

Thus, the history of the blacks is an integral part of the dawn of civilization at a time when their close kinsmen—Bushmen, Hottentots, Pygmies, and, perhaps, now extinct "others"—hunted in the forests and steppes of most of the continent, and their more distant relatives led a similar way of life in Europe and Asia.

When prehistory became transformed into history with the invention of writing, around 3000 B.C., Egyptian and Mesopotamian writers, who began the written record, never referred to human beings in terms of their color but rather in ethnic and geographical terms. For instance, there is one kingdom in Mesopotamia that many black scholars claim as "black"—Elam. No cuneiform tablets say so. Its "blackness" has to be inferred from portraits on pottery. The Egyptians who lived near the mouth of the Nile at the dawn of history were obviously aware of the wide range of physical differences. They painted themselves reddish-brown with bodies and features somewhat like those of present-day Yemenite Arabs. The people living farther south up the Nile were depicted as what Europeans later came to call "Negroes" but whom the ancient Egyptians simply called "Nehesi" or "people of the South." The great Chicago Egyptologist, Henri Frankfort, has written, "The talented and industrious were not frustrated by a rigid class distinction or by a colour bar. A Nubian frankly calling himself Panehsi 'the Nubian,' or 'negro' might be found in the highest places. . . ."* Nehesi and northern Egyptians ultimately mixed their genes to such an extent that Dr. DuBois was quite accurate in referring to Egypt as a "mulatto nation" in his book *Black Folks Then and*

---

*Henri Frankfort, *The Birth of Civilization in the Near East*, a Doubleday Anchor Book, 1956, p. 107.

Now. But when Europeans first saw the Sphinx, the negroidness of its features startled and surprised them. They were even more surprised, as well as embarassed to find the statuette of Queen Tyi, the mother of Egypt's great reforming Pharoah, Ikhnaton, looking like an Afro-American woman in a Mississippi cotton field. One glance at the statue of Ikhnaton's daughter who married King Tutankhamen (now in the Metropolitan Museum of Art) leaves no room for any kind of doubt as to whether or not the XVIIth Dynasty was "touched with the tarbrush." Egypt, "Land of the Two Kingdoms," continuously pushed southward into the Negro heartland beyond the third cataract of the Nile, into the area that the ancients refer to interchangeably as Nubia, Kush or Ethiopia. The XXVth Dynasty of Egypt is generally known as the Ethiopian Dynasty, for by this time Kush had got itself together, thrown off Egyptian rule, and moved northward to conquer its conquerer. (Josephus tells an interesting story in his *Antiquities of the Jews* of how Pharoah's daughter sent Moses on an expedition against the Ethiopians. He ended up marrying the Kushite king's daughter!) The Ethiopian pharoahs, leading combined Egyptian and Ethiopian forces, offered assistance to Syria and Phoenicia as well as Judah in their resistance to the fierce Assyria, which defeated them. The Ethiopians withdrew far up the Nile to Meroë and there, with this great iron-smelting center as their base, spent the next few centuries in conquest and settlement throughout central and southern Africa. By this time an urban center near what is now Timbuctoo was also beginning to grow up, and from it, eventually, would spring the empires of Ghana, Mali, and Songhay. Nobody was surprised at power because it was black.

Herodotus, sometimes referred to as "The Father of History," wrote a passage that has often been a stumbling block for people with fixed ideas about the place of black people in world history. He said:

> There can be no doubt that the Colchians are an Egyptian race....I made inquiries....My own conjecture was founded first on the fact that they are black skinned and have wooly hair....*

The fact of the matter is that those whom the Greeks called Ethiops ("Those with the burnt faces") were highly esteemed by them as people of intelligence and character. Nubian archers were in great demand in the armies of Middle Eastern and Mediterranean empires, and such a distinguished individual as Sappho, the poetess, found no embarrassment in referring to herself in a poem as black. Professor Frank Snowden, of Howard University, has recently put this whole matter in its proper perspective in *Negroes in Ancient Greece and Rome.*

The experiences of Ethiopians, Egyptians, and other African people were not interpreted as experiences determined by the color of the skin. People were thought of as either civilized or barbarian, and some peoples in each category were black and some nonblack. As individuals, Egyptians and Ethiopians traded and fought, fornicated with and married, Babylonians, Assyrians, Jews, Greeks, Romans, and the myriad other ethnic groups of the ancient world. As organized entities, black kingdoms made and broke alliances as equals in a system of competing states.

When Christianity emerged within this polychrome and polyglot ancient world, it proclaimed a new principle: "There is neither Greek nor barbarian, Jew nor Gentile, bond nor free, for we are all one in Christ Jesus." Paul did not need to mention color, for color was not a barrier! An Africa-based branch of the Christian church, the Coptic, emerged early. Nobody considered it unusual that its visibly black monks, bishops, and archbishops from Ethiopia functioned as equals with other orthodox functionaries throughout the Byzantine, Arabic, and Ottoman Empires. Church fathers such as Origen and St. Augustine lived out their lives in North Africa, but we have no way of knowing whether they were what men today call "blacks" and "Negroes" any more than we have of knowing whether Cleopatra and Hannibal were. North African writers did not consider their color important enough to mention.

When the Islamic invaders from Arabia broke across North Africa bringing a new religion, the Berbers, who were already there, adopted it and began to push south across the desert as well as northward into Europe. They began to trade, convert, conquer, and dominate. Some Arabs struck straight across Africa into what is now northern Nigeria, and all of these invaders of Black Africa from 900 A.D. onward did react with color-consciousness. The whole area stretching across Africa between the desert and the forest was given the name Bilad-as-Sudan or "land of the Blacks." There is no denying the fact that the cultures of the people in this area were considered inferior. They were "pagans," people without the Book. Paganism was equated with being black, just as being a Christian infidel was equated with being white. Both groups were people to be converted and transformed into Muslims. When they became Muslims, they were no longer counted as "inferiors." This was cultural imperialism not racism; color-

---

*Quoted in Francis R.B. Godolphin, *The Greek Historians*, New York, Random House, 1942, pp. 130-131.

consciousness without caste. Even before the Arabs began to spread, one of the greatest heroes among them was the warrior-poet, Antarah Ibn Shaddad al-Absi, whose father was a prominent Arab and whose mother was a slave. He was always referred to as Antat the Black, descriptively and with pride, not pejoratively. The Ethiopians were always highly respected, for they had befriended Mohammed—even though they were considered both black and Christian.

When the New World was discovered, the great 800-year-old struggle between the Muslims and the Christians was just drawing to a close, and Spain and Portugal were pushing out the last of the brown and black men who had ruled over them for centuries. The most immediately relevant question still, however, was not "Is he black or white?" but "Is he Muslim, Christian, Jew, pagan, or infidel?" When Africans were bought or captured for export to the New World, the operation was legitimated by the argument that they were lawful prey or that they were being done a favor by rescuing them from heathendom. It was well into the nineteenth century before the argument was used that they were sub-human biological inferiors. Some scholars today are emphasizing what is certainly a fact—that color-prejudice against blacks was present in Britain during the sixteenth century even though this may not have been so in Portugal and Spain. The fate of West Indians and Afro-Americans was of course affected by this fact, but these feelings of prejudice were almost irrelevant, for there was constant free and easy association as equals across race lines among the British lower class, a fact attested to in Kenneth Little's *Negroes in Britain* as well as by the savage legislation required to curb marriage and interracial fornication in Britain's New World colonies. The crucial fact was that the necessities of a slave system transformed mild social prejudices into rigid racist ideologies. A system of slavery based upon race emerged for the first time in human history, to be replaced later in some places by color-caste.

Up to 1500, the "Black Experience" differed very little from the "Red Indian Experience." On three continents where these groups had lived for millenia, some had become agricultural or pastoral and had moved on to develop what anthropologist A.L. Kroeber called cultural climaxes: around Mexico City with the Aztecs in North America; the Andean highlands in South America with the Inca; the Nile Valley, the big bend of the Niger and the Niger Delta, that is, among Egyptians, Mande and Yoruba in Africa. Around these centers of civilization and incipient civilization swirled groups who remained hunters and gatherers or herdsmen. The Black Experi-

ence was also little different from the white experience. Europe had remained "tribal" until nearly A.D. 1000—its Franks and Gauls, Norsemen and Britons, Helvetians and Picts being similar to Pygmies, Zulus, or Ashantis. Under the impact of Roman conquest, urbanization had begun a millenium before, and a few civilized centers arose. The church had converted and educated, writing vernacular down in Roman block letters. Kingdoms and empires arose and fought for supremacy, then struck outward toward the Near East in the Crusades. Then, between 1300 and 1500, Europeans borrowed some important artifacts and ideas from the Mediterranean world and Asia—Arabic numerals, gunpowder, the compass, algebra, and cartography. They integrated these with what they had and began the great expansion.

The African slave trade followed and introduced a tragic and traumatic element into the contact situation. Differences that formerly had been defined in terms of ethnicity now became defined in terms of color and race. The Black Experience from now on was "different," and the black psyche has never recovered from this epic disaster that began with the Great Dispersal some 500 years ago. The Europeans and their New World descendants became infected with a sickness from which they have not yet been able to recover—color fetishism, obsession with pigmentation, race dementia. In self-protection, colored people had to become preoccupied with color, too.

The Black Diaspora carried over 10,000,000 Africans into exile before the Atlantic slave trade finally ended in the 1880s. It resulted in a nostalgic yearning for the ancestral homeland on the part of many of the exiles, but eagerness to forget and to be assimilated and amalgamated on the part of others. From the beginning of the Great Dispersal, whether Africans were placed under the dominance of Englishmen, Frenchmen, Dutchmen, Danes, or Spaniards; whether they were on plantations or in mines and cities; as they became dispersed from Nova Scotia to the Argentine and from the Atlantic to the Pacific, during half a millenium they insisted upon trying to define situations for themselves however much their oppressors tried to force definitions upon them. From the Black perspective they always asked and tried to answer questions such as these in every local setting where they found themselves:

1. How can we maintain or develop institutions conducive to group solidarity?

2. How can this group solidarity be used for protection against cruelty and degradation and to secure freedom from enslavement?

3. How can individuals preserve a sense of personal worth and dignity and gain a

311

maximum of self-expression without betraying group interests?

In some places the "group" was one thing; in other places, another. Here it was an ethnic fragment—some Ibos or Congos or Coromantees trying to maintain their customs and their solidarity; there, for the moment it might be an entire plantation incensed and preparing to revolt. Or it might be a band of escapees establishing a Maroon community in the hills or the backlands, or again, a group of "Free Negroes" existing side-by-side with enslaved relatives and acquaintances.

The whites who monopolized economic and political control in New World situations allowed a basic cleavage to emerge everywhere between a small privileged segment of free persons of color often related "by blood" to the masters and the rest of those of African descent whom they contemptuously referred to as "les noirs," "the blacks." Those so denigrated tended to define their own identity by insisting that they were *Africans*. They retained as much of their African culture as they could to form the basis of that morale that was necessary for their survival. This we can say, but the comparative sociology of the Black Experience is yet to be developed. It would be premature to generalize much about the Black Experience as a whole over the 500 year time-span of the Diaspora. Before doing that, we need considerably more basic work on local situations. For some regions, however, there is a wealth of data, among them the United States, but the data needs reviewing and reworking from a *black* historical perspective. Most of it has been gathered and organized within other frames of reference.

Part Two: Patterns of Response to American Racism

In the sub-Sahara heartland of the Black World, the overwhelming majority of the people are black. The consciousness of every individual is molded and shaped by this fact. Feasible goals of political action have been crystal clear—attainment of national sovereignty. The same situation prevails on a smaller scale in most of the West Indian islands. But there are other situations that pose quite different problems as, for instance, Trinidad and Guiana, where half the population is of East Indian origin. Throughout the New World Diaspora there are situations where Africans have been, or are, a numerical minority. The United States is one such situation, but this fact alone would not give it that uniqueness that makes the Black Experience there a very special case within the Black World as a whole. The circumstances that have made it so are these:

1. When the first permanent settlement of blacks was made in 1619, slavery had already been in existence in other parts of the New World for over 100 years. Thus, there were models for social action that both whites and blacks adopted from the Caribbean. Until slavery was abolished in the United States, both blacks and whites were always looking over their shoulders toward the West Indies. Since Emancipation, the West Indies and Afro-America have influenced each other profoundly, but population, affluence, and access to education and skills have always given North American blacks an advantage.

2. By the middle of the nineteenth century, over 3,000,000 Africans and peoples of African descent were living within the same political entity, the United States, but within two very different culture areas—the North and the South, uneasily bound together. Almost 500,000 Afro-Americans were free Negroes by 1860. The others were living in a wide variety of situations in terms of numbers and degree of control to which they were subject.

3. The abolition of slavery came as one aspect of a fratricidal civil war, in which blacks played a crucial part, but which left them in a "scapegoat" role within the poverty-stricken southern region that emerged defeated in 1865.

4. The process of social differentiation accelerated after Emancipation and produced a highly segregated but also highly class-stratified segment of the Black World in the United States.

5. During the century since their emancipation, Afro-Americans have been involved in a process of dispersal throughout the country that has resulted in scattered, black communities—enclaved, surrounded, "sealed-off," and looked down upon by a white population that outnumbers them nine to one. Demographically and ecologically the Brazilian situation is similar, but culturally very different. There was no Civil War to free the slaves, and the Latin Catholic ethos resulted in high status for mixed bloods with none of the "uptightness" and furtiveness about miscegenation that the WASP culture of the United States dictated.

The problem facing Afro-Americans since Emancipation has been how to relate to that massive

312

white majority that surrounds and almost suffocates them; that separates and subordinates, but continuously exploits them. The Black Muslims have elaborated one response: to define all whites as "Devils"—both dangerous and contaminating, to be avoided as much as possible. The majority of Afro-Americans, however, have always espoused a strategy that Carmichael and Hamilton made explicit in their book, *Black Power*, namely, judicious coalition formation made from a position of strength based upon Afro-American group solidarity. As a numerical minority, the ultimate political goals cannot be what they are in Africa or the West Indies.

From 1619 up to the outbreak of the Revolutionary War there were intermittent unsuccessful slave revolts, but there was also the steady growth of a small, free Negro population that, whether in the North or the South, was characterized by an attempt to develop styles of life of small independent farmers and stable artisans. This acceptance of European values and rules-of-the-game by Africans and their descendants was exemplified during the first fifty years of colonial life by the famous court case involving one Anthony Johnson, who became a planter and eventually went into the Virginia courts to force a white planter to return one of his indentured servants who had run away. On the eve of the Revolution, in the Border States and in the North, a literate free Negro group was highly visible and included within its ranks Jupiter Hammond and Phyllis Wheatley, writers of poetry; Benjamin Banneker, surveyor and almanac maker; and Prince Hall and Paul Cuffee, merchants. When the upper classes did not frustrate them, these free Negroes conceived of themselves as group leaders and viewed the Revolutionary War as *their* war as well as a white men's war. Phyllis Wheatley's famous poem to George Washington exemplifies this attitude. There is also much evidence to indicate that at more humble levels there was a tendency for blacks to interact as equals with their white counterparts.

Many blacks—perhaps most—visualized the Revolution as affecting them, for, after all, the Preamble to the Declaration of Independence contains the words, "We hold these truths to be self-evident, that all men are created equal. . . ." A lot of blacks took those words very seriously. They began to exhibit what became one form of recurrent social action, what might be called "Proving Patriotism." The first blood shed on Boston Commons, that of Crispus Attucks, was the harbinger of black volunteers throughout New York and New England. And these blacks expected a change in status for their people as a reward.

The period between the proclamation of the Declaration of Independence in 1775 and the founding of the American Colonization Society in 1817 was characterized by a rising curb of optimism among blacks until the turn of the century, followed by a downswing of increasing disillusionment. The optimism was stimulated by the wiping out of slavery in the northern states as one outcome of the Revolutionary War, and the open verbalization against slavery by leaders such as Thomas Jefferson, George Washington, and Benjamin Franklin. The Great Awakening in religious circles was accompanied by the rapid growth of the Baptist and Methodist denominations, which not only opposed slavery but, also, in many places, integrated Negroes into local congregations upon a basis of complete equality. But equally encouraging was the success of the great insurrection in Haiti that brought a new nation into being in 1804 and seems to have been a factor in stimulating some mainland revolts including that of Gabriel Prosser in Virginia. These violent episodes became the first cases in a recurrent pattern, the exploitation of acts of violence by moderate black leaders and their white allies. A famous speech is on record by Prince Hall, founder of first black Masonic Lodge, who warned that the United States was likely to have its own Santo Domingo if it did not free its slaves, and Thomas Jefferson said virtually the same thing to the Virginia legislature.

Yet, there was an ominous, disquieting note in whatever Jefferson said about black people. He denounced slavery but he also said that he wasn't convinced that black people had equal capacities with whites for learning. He was for emancipation but felt that all ex-slaves should be deported. It was not surprising that he threw his support behind those who, in 1817, organized an American Colonization Society to transport ex-slaves to Africa. It was they who founded the settlement that became Liberia, and a U.S. naval vessel carried the first batch of Afro-Americans over to Africa. Some blacks had always been in favor of *voluntary* emigration to Africa, and one prominent leader, Paul Cuffee, had actually taken a group of "returnees" to Sierra Leone in a vessel he owned, sailed by an all-black crew. But this was something entirely different from the Doctrine of Providential Design taught by white colonizationists who claimed to see God's benevolent hand in slavery bringing Africans from darkness to light so they could return and redeem their motherland. A few blacks believed this too (including the poetess Phyllis Wheatley), but most of the free Negro leaders, including the great orator, Frederick Douglass, declared themselves to be anti-colonizationists.

Most free Negro institutions had borne the name "African." Now free Negro leaders organized

Colored Men's Conventions and stressed the stake their sweat, tears, and blood had given them in America's soil. They formed a coalition with that wing of the white anti-slavery movement that shared the same basic ideology, namely, that free Negroes should supply leadership to the slave in a nonviolent struggle including use of the Underground Railroad and political action by northern whites. This became the coalition that eventually ended slavery as the nonviolence was complemented by the heroic acts of those who followed Denmark Vesey, Nat Turner, and John Brown. The whole process shaped up into the Civil War, in which blacks fought for their freedom alongside whites.

The Civil War came at the end of a thirty-year period of increasing polarization between northern abolitionists and southern die-hard defenders of slavery. The anti-slavery movement was characterized by all of the dilemmas and contradictions that have plagued the coalitions of liberals and blacks in the U.S. ever since. The preponderance of economic and political power was in the hands of the white allies, and the black leaders had to fight against their paternalism and their insistence upon "calling the shots." For instance, when Frederick Douglass started a newspaper, William Lloyd Garrison was indignant. Why, he wondered, wasn't *his* newspaper, *The Liberator*, enough? Douglass answered manfully and masterfully in his first editorial:

It is neither a reflection on the fidelity, nor a disparagement of the ability of our friends and fellow laborers, to assert what "common sense affirms and only folly denies," that the man who has suffered the wrong is the man to demand redress, that the man struck is the man to cry out....It is evident that we must be our own representatives and advocates—not exclusively, but peculiarly—not distinct from, but in connection with our white friends.

Blacks found themselves forced to work closely with people who spoke of them as did the Illinois anti-slavery editor who wrote:

I am resolutely opposed to the equalizing of the races, and it no more necessarily follows that we should fellowship with Negroes because our policy strikes off their shackles, than it would to take felons to our embraces because we might remonstrate against cruelty to them in our penitentiaries.

This attitude came through strongly among Union soldiers in the South. There were also the little tragedies that arose among those who went "all the way," as when personal affection interfered with "the cause." Nervousness over sexual affairs between blacks and whites within the ranks, was always

present, and involved even Representative Thaddeus Stevens, leader of the Radical Republicans during and after the Civil War.

The coalition carried over into the post-Civil War period, but now the Radical Reconstruction group in Congress prevailed. It decided that blacks must be enfranchised and that Federal military power must be used to enforce and protect them. They passed the Civil Rights Bill of March 1866 over President Johnson's veto. The Fourteenth Amendment was passed by the middle of 1866 and the required number of states had ratified it by the middle of 1868. The Fifteenth Amendment was in force by March of 1870 and an Enforcement Act was in being a year later. The rise of the Ku Klux Klan was the southern response, and this necessitated legislation against it in 1871. A full-scale Civil Rights Act was passed in 1875. Meanwhile, the Freedman's Bureau was laying the foundations for a system of black schools and colleges. From 1865 through 1876, a complex but effective apparatus for effecting social change was at work. The radical wing of the Republican party took care of business in Washington, and a part of that business was securing the vote for the ex-slaves in the South. Some northern whites went South to live and work as soldiers, politicians, teachers, and "Carpetbaggers" and they cooperated with a white southern minority ("Scalawags") and the voting blacks to write new state constitutions and to institute social reforms. Federal bayonets were always in reserve, close at hand.

When solid middle-class southern leadership groups began to demand Home Rule, egging the Klan on to give them leverage, the big-money backers of the Republican Party in the North opted for cooperation with them in order to assure a better investment climate. The "Hayes-Tilden Compromise" of 1877 led to withdrawal of Federal troops. The distinguished southern historian at Yale, C. Vann Woodward, has stated his considered judgment in the *Strange Career of Jim Crow* that it was this withdrawal of northern radical pressure that pulled the rug from under those southerners of diverse class levels who were prepared to oppose racism and caste as the basis for a new southern society. Northern white liberals were becoming tired of "the Negro problem"—not the last time this would happen.

The thirty years between the Hayes-Tilden Compromise in 1877 and the beginning of the great northward migration of blacks in 1916 institutionalized a rigid system of racial segregation and discrimination in the South backed up by massive intimidation and violence as well as by debt-peonage. Racial prejudice was rife in the more fluid northern situation. The key to the persistence of a caste-system in the South was disfranchisement—making sure that blacks had no political power. The two great symbolic acts that gave legitimacy to this system were Booker T. Washington's famous "Atlanta Compromise" speech in 1895, where he advised that in all matters purely social blacks and whites should remain as separate as the five fingers on the hand and that blacks should stay out of politics. In an appeal to the industrialists he asked that they incorporate Negroes into the new industries of the South in preference to using aliens who were prone to organize labor unions and strike. To Negroes he preached one constant sermon: "Get education. Get money. Be thrifty, clean, and well behaved; all else will come later." The other symbolic act was the Supreme Court's ruling in *Plessy* vs *Ferguson* in 1896, ruling that "separate" if "equal" would meet all requirements of the Fourteenth Amendment. Booker T. Washington had founded Tuskegee in 1881, offering agricultural and industrial education and character building. By the turn of the century, Booker T. Washington could write his ticket for financial support from Andrew Carnegie, Julius Rosenwald, and much of the new railroad money. The rise of what DuBois called the "Tuskegee Machine" can be fully understood only if it is seen against the background of "trade-offs"—deliberate or incidental—as well as specific coalitions. The basic "trade-off" was the implicit agreement on the part of northern capital not to touch the southerners' basic labor pool as they industrialized the North, but to scour Europe for labor. They also gave *carte blanche*, through an indulgent Republican government, to southerners to use any means necessary to maintain a docile labor supply and to keep it from running off to homestead in the West or emigrating to Africa. The use of European labor in a rapidly industrializing North had, by 1877, led to a situation in which, while the government was withdrawing some troops from the South, it was hurling others at labor to break some very serious strikes, particularly in railroading. Labor troubles in the North were endemic throughout the 1880s and 1890s. Very few blacks were admitted into the labor movement, and even fewer were active with the Socialist Labor Party, founded in 1877, and the Social Democratic Party, founded in 1899. Yet one of the leading black intellectuals, T. Thomas Fortune, wrote a book in 1888 calling for solidarity of blacks and whites in an overthrow of landlordism and capitalism. Then in 1891, a spectre seemed to have come alive when the Peoples Party was founded in Cincinnati and ran a presidential candidate who polled a million votes against Cleveland. At the grassroots level this Populist movement included white organizations such as the Southern Farmers' Alliance and the Colored Farmers' Alliance and Cooperative Union. As Professor Otey M. Scruggs has phrased it:

> Despite continued intimidation and violence, the black electorate remained a political factor in the South after 1877. White Populist leaders knew they must have the black vote or at least be able to neutralize it. They also hoped that recognition of a common economic interest would overcome antagonism toward color, and so they appealed for black-white political unity and moved to bring the black man into the Party....Not since Reconstruction had the ruling party clique of politicians, landowners, merchants, lawyers, and editors faced such a threat to their hegemony. Mixing concession, force, corruption, and strident appeals to racism, they proceeded to put it down.

The savage sell-outs by former Populist friends is an oft-told story with assessment of blame for the collapse of the coalition still being made.

Booker T. Washington was sure of the outcome before the alliance was ever made, but he miscued, too. The new capitalists made their peace with upward mobile poor-whites and let them institute caste relations in industry. The employers did not rescue blacks from the cotton fields. Washington was still convinced, however, that Negro welfare depended on close ties with wealthy whites.

It was inevitable that young college-trained northern blacks would question Booker T. Washington's philosophy and his power. In 1905, the Niagara Movement emerged with Monroe Trotter and W.E.B. DuBois, both New England born and bred, in the lead. The movement stood for total and absolute equality and the refranchisement of the Negro in the South. Leading white philanthropists tried to make peace between them and Dr. Washington. This was impossible. Then in 1908 a lynching in Springfield, Illinois—near the Lincoln shrine—shook up the children and grandchildren of the Abolitionists, who joined with a few socialists to persuade the young Niagara Movement blacks to cooperate in organizing the *interracial* National Association for the Advancement of Colored People (NAACP). Not all the blacks were willing to do so, but some did, among them W.E.B. DuBois, whose magazine, *Crisis*, became the recognized spokesman of the more militant segment of the black bourgeoisie. Using propaganda, education, lobbying, and legal action, the NAACP moved to attack every vestige of segregation and discrimination in American life. It is significant that from its inception until today it has always had a white president and a mixed board, although the Executive Secretary has always been black. Malcolm X was, later, to attack it on that score.

Booker T. Washington died in 1915, on the eve of a mass movement that ran counter to his basic doctrine of "Let down your bucket where you are" enunciated in 1895. An expanding war economy with a shutoff of European immigration led northern industrialists to begin the recruiting of black labor in the South. Between 1916 and 1921 over a million Negroes moved from the cotton fields to urban areas, and most of them went to northern and midwestern cities. The stage was now set for totally new forms of action. To use modern terminology, the situation had a high "Black Power Potential." The growth of large Black Belts made possible the organization of political and economic power on a massive scale. All "race leaders"—in church, business, associations, politics, and con games—were quick to recognize that potential.

A charismatic leader arose between 1917 and 1925, whose own mass movement collapsed, but who gave a stimulus to every local leader, movement, or organization that was trying to maximize Black Power. This was Marcus Garvey from Jamaica who challenged all "integrationist" philosophies with his ringing slogans such as "One God! One Aim! One Destiny!" or "Black is Beautiful." His Universal Negro Improvement Association (UNIA) defined the United States as the white man's country and called upon black Americans to support the idea of "Africa for the Africans—at Home and Abroad." The UNIA established the Black Star Line to knit together the scattered fragments of the Black World in communication and trade. Although Africa was the spiritual home of the people of the Diaspora and would become the actual home for many returnees, masses of blacks would continue to live in exile—what Garvey called "the beloved and scattered millions" living as Malcolm X later said "in the belly of the beast." Like Booker T. Washington, Garvey advised the black masses to leave white men's politics to whites and repudiated social equality and miscegenation. But the UNIA could not avoid relationships with whites, and where Booker T. Washington sought allies among the top industrialists, Garvey sought them among the Ku Klux Klan! With a commitment to separation of the races, the two organizations had a basis for some forms of cooperation. The NAACP denounced Garvey for attempting such a *modus vivendi* with the Klan. When Garvey was sentenced to a Federal prison in 1925, he instructed his followers to support a Republican presidential candidate in the hope that his sentence would be commuted. It was.

A less extreme form of black solidarity remained popular after Garvey's deportation in 1927—the development of black segments of big city political machines and the mobilization of purchasing power to wring concessions from whites doing business in Black Belts. In 1928, the black electorate in Chicago sent the first black man to Congress since Reconstruction days. In Washington, Chicago, and Harlem, "buying power campaigns" forced local businesses to employ black sales people. A philosophy and technique for living in, and with, America was shaping up in all-black communities: demand complete and total integration into the economic system at all levels; organize as a group to wield political power, both for personal gain and in the fight for racial advancement; strengthen black institutional life—churches, associations, and families; make no claim for social integration or amalgamation. This point of view has remained dominant.

Garvey had fought a two-front battle against forces he defined as enemies of black solidarity. The NAACP he saw as the main enemy—"integrationist" and enlisting the allegiance of the highly educated leaders among black Americans. W.E.B. DuBois became the personal embodiment of all that Garvey despised. The newly organized Communist Party was also seen as a formidable foe, emphasizing as it did working-class solidarity over racial solidarity. Here was "integration" at another class level threatening black cohesiveness. The interplay between the Garvey movement and the Communist movement stimulated the latter to a definition of the black situation in the South as a "national" question. It was ironic that the very capable editor of Garvey's newspaper *The Negro World* was T. Thomas Fortune who, in his youth, had called for unity of blacks and poor whites in the South years before the Populist Party did so.

The stock market crash in 1929 tipped the scales somewhat in favor of Garvey's left-wing opponents. The Communists with their two slogans, "Black and White Unite" and "Self-Determination for the Black Belt," and a capacity for organizing the unemployed and dramatizing matters such as the Scottsboro Case, won enough of a following among intellectuals and the black professional classes to make possible the organization of such united front groups as the National Negro Congress and the Southern Negro Youth Congress in which Communists played a key role. They, along with other Marxists, in cooperation with the staunch Republican labor leader, John Lewis, brought the CIO into being. Blacks helped to organize it and profited greatly from it. It could be argued that the coalition of black leaders with the "left" between 1931 and 1941 gave the greatest payoff to Afro-Americans of any cooperative relations with whites since the days of the Abolition Movement. Research and evaluation based upon a black perspective may lead to a very different conclusion from a conventional white scholar's perspective. Indeed, the hypothesis might be advanced that the Communist movement in the South in the 1930s was a key factor in preparing the way for the success of the Civil Rights Movement of the 1950s.

Paradoxically, however, from a black perspective, cooperation with the Communist Party began to have diminishing returns at the very point when the Party's value to the United States was at its height. From the day that the Soviet Union was attacked in 1941, the Communist Party became the leading patriotic party in order to marshal aid for "the Soviet Motherland." This was the very moment when black Americans were anxious to embarrass the country as much as they could, short of mutiny and treason, in order to force changes in treatment of black citizens. Blacks began to see the Communist Party as a "go slow" influence in *their* fight. During the war, too, they became increasingly conscious of the fact that Communists, like all white allies since Abolition days, felt that they knew better what was good for Negroes than they knew for themselves. So, except for certain very prominent figures like Paul Robeson and W.E.B. DuBois and some convinced Marxists, Afro-Americans "cooled" on the Communists during World War II.

It was no accident that the big dramatic move in the black liberation struggle of the World War II period, the threatened march on Washington, was not planned by the Communists. Its leader was A. Philip Randolph who had recently resigned from the presidency of the National Negro Congress with a blast at the Communists. Yet, Randolph was himself a "leftist," a socialist, an "integrationist." The liberal-left-labor coalition supporting the Democratic Party, was still the focus of black political allegiance and the fulcrum of their action in both the North and South. There was an eclecticism in membership that meant that blacks often belonged to the NAACP, and integrated trade union, a Marxist party or a front organization, and a half dozen black organizations all at the same time with no sense of strain.

World War II transformed the consciousness of all Americans—both black and white—in the area of race relations. The war was fought as a crusade against Fascist racism, and black organizations insisted that the victory must be a "Double V"—victory over Fascism abroad and at home. Many white people also took the crusade very seriously—particularly Jewish organizations and national committees of Protestant and Catholic denominations. The implications for the home front were clear, and these organizations began to propagandize for the elimination of racism at home. Some black leaders felt these white leaders had a tendency to "take over" in the field of race relations rather than to cooperate with existing black organizations.

It was Douglass vs Garrison all over again, the recurrent theme of class solidarity vs racial solidarity. A new variable entered the picture during the war years. A small nonviolent action group using Gandhi-like tactics against restaurants in the North that discriminated, pacifist and interracial, CORE (Committee on Racial Equality) won covert support and financing from many respectable middle-class blacks who approved of what it was doing though they would not participate. Simultaneously, the NAACP was able to attract members for the first time from the black lower-middle class, especially from among those who belonged to CIO unions. That organization now had to face a demand for mass action to complement its court action. Unwilling to change its image or tactics, the NAACP lost the chance to organize the masses of youth. But perhaps it could have not done so had it tried. On the whole, the war years created a climate of opinion in which a series of Supreme Court decisions was possible after the war that presaged a "Civil Rights Revolution." Here the NAACP was very effective.

In 1948, the Supreme Court ruled that restrictive covenants were unenforceable in the courts. In the 1920s the NAACP had won rulings against *laws* segregating Negroes residentially. Now a breach had been made in the rings of covenants around black communities. The case was significant because it represented a joint effort of the NAACP and Jewish organizations in fighting the case of a woman who was denied the right to live in the same house with her Gentile husband. This was only one of many post-war victories, some chipping away at segregation, on public carriers, others trying to force southern states to provide the equality in segregated education that Plessy vs Ferguson required if they refused to desegregate. Then in 1954, the NAACP won the "big one." The Supreme Court ruled that forced segregation in public schools was unconstitutional. While these legal victories were being won, the Army, the Roman Catholic Church, and a number of other agencies, including some businesses in which a top-level bureaucracy could make a decision stick, were "desegregating" and removing some discriminatory barriers. The southern black lower-middle class picked the issue upon which it was prepared to fight and go to jail in 1955 with the Montgomery Bus Boycott. Southern youth picked their issue in 1960—lunch-counter desegregation. A new epoch in the Black Experience had begun.

The period from 1955 to 1965 might be referred to as "The Desegregation Decade." The caste system in the South was dismantled by a nonviolent

317

Civil Rights Revolution in which blacks with a few white allies were the front-line shock troops, sitting-in, lying down, freedom-riding, registering voters, and being beaten and imprisoned. Financial support came from the liberal-labor-black alliance in the North, which also provided favorable press, TV, and radio coverage. An occasional crucial assist came from the Democratic regime in Washington with its eye on the crucial blocs of black voters in northern ghettos. The massive March on Washington in the summer of 1963 was the peak of this upsurge and Martin Luther King became its key symbol, and later its martyr.

By 1965, the northern white lower-middle class was complaining about what it perceived as an alliance between upper-class whites and the minorities to force colored ethnics into their neighborhoods and schools and into jobs they had reserved for themselves. A so-called "backlash" was beginning to surface. Meanwhile, the less affluent ghettoized northern blacks saw no gains for them in the highly publicized victories being won down south. The Black Muslims proposed a program of disciplined separatism. The street crowds of 1964-1968 repeatedly demonstrated their contempt for the philosophy of nonviolence and the dogmas about the sanctity of private property. The Voter Registration Act began to put political clout in southern black hands for the first time since the post-Reconstruction process of disfranchisement. At this critical juncture, the leaders of SNCC (Student Nonviolent Coordinating Committee) threw forth a new slogan, "Black Power." To the street mobs that had gone into action in 1964 in Harlem, Rochester, and Philadelphia; in 1965 in Watts; in Chicago, in 1966; and all over the country during the summer of 1967, the exercise of "Black Power" meant direct, violent action against a demeaning, constricting, physical and social environment. What the slogan meant to the man who was believed to have coined it is clearly revealed in the subtitle to the book that Carmichael and Hamilton wrote in 1967, *Black Power: The Politics of Liberation in America.*

The first two steps toward liberation as taught by the spiritual ancestors of the Black Power movement, Marcus Garvey and Malcolm X, were stated in slogans popularized by Stokely Carmichael and his followers: "Define Yourself for Yourself!" and "Get Yourselves Together." In achieving these goals the young black militants in CORE and SNCC felt it necessary to eliminate white members from their organizations and to define a relationship with them which said, in effect, "You work against racism among whites; we will organize our people to take care of *black* business." The youngsters of the New Left who had their first initiation into social action

through the Civil Rights Movement now organized SDS (Students for Democratic Action) and began to emphasize the anti-Vietnam-War Crusade. Many of the black leaders left the South just as the prospects for voter registration emerged and tried unsuccessfully to supply leadership to the volatile northern urban ghetto masses—their first attempts to work out the implications of "Black Power."

The American "Establishment" did not define "Black Power" as subversive. Instead, an attempt was made to "co-opt" the leadership in support of conventional politics and the existing economic system. The first large Black Power conference, meeting in Newark in 1967, was financed by a group of major industrialists. "Black Capitalism" became something deemed worthy of support. Emphasis upon ghetto development was not at all inconsistent with attempts to keep blacks out of the suburbs. Also, as whites fled to the suburbs to live they needed reliable allies to take care of their interests in the core cities that blacks were inheriting. The philosophy of Booker T. Washington, including his brand of alliances, reappeared in twentieth-century dress, sometimes dashiki-clad but with white foundation money, national church funds, and governmental handouts backing up small business ventures occasionally organized even by predatory street gangs! Experiments in community control of schools were given Ford Foundation support in New York. Even so ardent a Black Nationalist as Imamu Ameer Baraka (LeRoi Jones) began to play coalition politics in Newark when the chance to elect a black mayor was imminent. Significant electoral victories throughout the South during the early 1970s suggested the possibility of consolidating pockets of Black Power at the local level that would work out their relations with whites to achieve shared power at the state and national levels. New patterns of pluralism were in the making.

Black solidarity increased dramatically throughout the 1960s and the gains accruing from it were obvious. It is, therefore, highly significant that both the most powerful mass movement among black Americans and the most highly publicized militant group constantly stated their preference for a nonracial strategy of struggle based upon class rather than race, and for a nonracial society. Whites, not blacks, reject that vision. They leave no choice but for blacks to emphasize their blackness. Despite Martin Luther King's assassination in 1968, the Southern Christian Leadership Conference (SCLC) remained the only organization that could mobilize masses of black people of both sexes and all ages for demonstrations, support of the streets for trade unionists during strikes, or economic boycott. And the SCLC remained committed to the two causes that Dr. King was espousing vigorously when he died—opposition to the war in Southeast Asia and mobilization of all the poor to struggle for a better life "within the system." Organizing black and white labor together in the South was one of SCLC's dreams, and here and there it achieved a striking success. "Integrationist" in philosophy and "populist" in its politics, the SCLC drew much of its support from liberal white church circles. The rift in the ranks that led to the Rev. Jesse Jackson being relieved of his Operation Breadbasket duties was not because of any basic ideological disagreements, despite differences in leadership styles. The name of his new organization expressed the essential nonracial goals Jesse Jackson has in mind: PUSH (People United to Save Humanity). This is a recurrent theme in the Christo-African New World Experience—"Black Messianism."

The Black Panthers started out as militant Black Nationalists, and Bobby Seale has told the story in *Seize the Time* of how a shift took place toward the view that the black *Lumpenproletariat* had a historic mission to be the vanguard of the socialist revolution in America. Huey Newton eventually developed his own brand of post-Marxist thinking, elaborating the theory of "Intercommunalism." Under the stress of persecution, as well as prosecution, of Panthers, and as serious splits developed between their leaders, the organization had, by 1972, settled for a moderate ghetto "survival" program. It still favored, however, a close coalition between the organizations of blacks, reds, browns, and yellows, and some groups of whites—the poor and the student activists particularly. The organizers of the defense of Angela Davis have carried on the older tradition of a close alliance with the Communist Party, U.S.A.

There are echoes of what might be called "Black Messianism"—an essentially nonracial view—even in the preamble to the National Black Political Agenda that was the basic working document at the National Black Political Convention, March 11, 1962. For instance:

> It is the challenge to consolidate and organize our own Black role as the vanguard in the struggle for a new society. . . .If we are serious, the Black Politics of Gary must accept major responsibility for creating both the atmosphere and the program for fundamental far-reaching change in America. Such responsibility is ours because it is our people who are most deeply hurt and ravaged by the present systems of society. . . . The Agenda we now press for in Gary is not only for the future of Black humanity, but is probably the only way the rest of America can save itself from the harvest of its criminal past. . . .

Despite the rhetoric of the Black Muslims and the Republic of New Africa, when most Afro-Americans say "It is nation-building time" they are not referring to some large separate spatial entity here or in Africa. They mean simply the unity of all black Afro-Americans wherever they live. The nonterritorial nation becomes, like a territorial nation, a unified group composed of all kinds of opposites—a functional unity—that includes Panthers and Muslims, the NAACP and the Republic of New Africa, all class levels, all ideologies. Their survival and progress as blacks demands "protective solidarity." Each group develops alliances and coalitions with those whites with whom, for the moment, such action seems wise. The goal is most frequently expressed in a slogan: *"Not integration or separation, but black liberation."* The shape of the future is open.

319

Acknowledgments

Thanks are due the following for permission to use material indicated (listed according to order of appearance in the book):

Alfred A. Knopf, Inc.: for "Harlem" from *The Panther and the Lash* by Langston Hughes, © Alfred A. Knopf, Inc.; used by permission. Holloway House Publishing Company: for *Pimp: The Story of My Life* by Robert Beck ("Iceberg Slim"),© Holloway House Publishing Company; used by permission. Pathfinder Press, Inc.: for "Testament" by Clarence Harris from Etheridge Knight (ed.) *Black Voices from Prison* © 1970 by Pathfinder Press, Inc.; used by permission. Edward B. Marks Music Corporation: for "Lift Every Voice and Sing" by James Weldon Johnson, © Edward B. Marks Music Corporation; used by permission. Coward, McCann, and Geoghegan: for *Go Up for Glory* by Bill Russell as told to William McSweeny, © 1966 by William Felton Russell and William Francis McSweeny; used by permission. Twayne Publishers, Inc.: for "Outcast" from *Selected Poems of Claude McKay,* © 1953 by Bookman Associates; used by permission. Doubleday & Company: for "Time Chart of African History," "The Empire of Ghana," "Mansa Musa," "How People Lived," "Production, Trade, and Money," "Cities," "The Stratification of Society," and "Resistance to the Slave Trade" from *A History of West Africa* by Basil Davidson, © 1965 by Longman's Green & Co., Ltd.; © 1966 by Basil Davidson; reprinted by permission of Doubleday & Company, Inc. Thomas Hodgkin: for "Kingdoms of the Western Sudan" by Thomas Hodgkin, from Roland Oliver (ed.) *The Dawn of African History* (New York: Oxford University Press, 1968), article © 1968 by Thomas Hodgkin; reprinted by permission. Adu Boahen: for "The Rise of the Akan" by Adu Boahen from Roland Oliver (ed.) *The Middle Age of African History* (New York: Oxford University Press, 1967), article © 1967 by Adu Boahen; reprinted by permission. Alan Ryder: for "The Rise of the Benin Kingdom" by Alan Ryder from Roland Oliver (ed.) *The Middle Age of African History* (New York: Oxford University Press, 1967), article © by Alan Ryder; reprinted by permission. Doubleday & Company, Inc.: for "African Families" and "Slavery and the Slave Trade" from *Africa and Africans* by Paul Bohannan, © 1964 by Paul Bohannan; reprinted by permission of Doubleday & Company, Inc. Sterling A. Brown: for "Southern Cop" by Sterling

322

Index